ETHNIC GROUPS OF INSULAR SOUTHEAST ASIA

VOLUME 1: INDONESIA, ANDAMAN ISLANDS, AND MADAGASCAR

FRANK M. LEBAR, Editor and Compiler

Contributing Authors:

GEORGE N. APPELL

J. B. AVE

R. H. BARNES

JAMES J. FOX

FRIEDRICH W. FUNKE

HILDRED GEERTZ

DAVID HICKS

M. A. JASPAN

KOENTJARANINGRAT

RUTH KRULFELD

E. K. M. MASINAMBAW

MONI NAG

RODNEY NEEDHAM

C. H. M. NOOY-PALM

H. G. SCHULTE NORDHOLT

ROGER D. PERANIO

D. J. PRENTICE

CLIFFORD SATHER

NANCY TANNER

HUMAN RELATIONS AREA FILES PRESS

New Haven

Compilation and publication of this volume has
been financed in part by grants GS1763 and
N3409 from the National Science Foundation.

Library of Congress Catalog Card Number: 72-90940

International Standard Book Number: 087536-403-9

Copyright © 1972 by the Human Relations Area Files, Incorporated

All rights reserved

Printed in the United States of America

DEDICATION

To Raymond Kennedy

1906-1950

PREFACE

This is the first of a two-volume survey of the peoples and cultures of insular Southeast Asia. The present volume covers Indonesia, the Andaman and Nicobar Islands, and the Malagasy-speaking peoples of Madagascar; Volume Two includes the Philippine Islands and the aboriginal tribes of Taiwan. Together with *Ethnic Groups of Mainland Southeast Asia,* by Frank M. LeBar, Gerald C. Hickey, and John K. Musgrave (HRAF Press, 1964), these volumes provide a series of descriptive ethnographic summaries, with accompanying bibliographies, synonymies, terminological indexes, and ethnolinguistic maps, covering the whole of what might be termed greater Southeast Asia, including the culturally-related regions of southern China and Assam. Summary formats and technical apparatus remain the same in all three volumes, the intent being a corpus of systematically arranged data, providing insofar as possible comparable descriptive categories and terminology for the entire area. For the original conception of the project and a discussion of earlier problems of ethnic group identification and classification with respect to the mainland, the reader is referred to the preface in LeBar et al. (1964). The identification of ethnic groups and the ordering of ethnic entries in the present volume follow closely the approach adopted by Raymond Kennedy in his various surveys of Indonesian peoples and cultures, i.e. a combination of geographic, linguistic, and cultural criteria. Thus the tribe, nation, or category subsumed under any one ethnic entry generally occupies a specifiable territory or habitat; the people do (or did) feel themselves to be one people or somehow historically related, and they did until the twentieth century, at least, have certain cultural and linguistic traits in common which served to set them off from neighboring groups. These criteria are purposely qualified as to tense, since much of the ethnographic literature dates from the turn of the century or earlier and thus ethnic entries, unless based on modern fieldwork, do not necessarily reflect recent change. A survey of this kind, focusing on the traditional culture, does have the advantage of complete coverage of an entire area according to a single format —thus providing a body of systematically arranged data for comparative use as well as a base from which to project studies of recent change. Considerable reliance has been placed on linguistic classification, since it is felt that demonstrated genetic relationships among languages remain the best indicators of present or past cultural ties among the speakers of those languages. The indigenous languages of Indonesia and Madagascar belong, with a few exceptions, to a single language family—Malayo-Polynesian. Extensive use has been made of the more or less standard classification of Indonesian languages by Esser (1938) and the recent lexicostatistical classification of MP languages by Dyen (1965). In most cases where it is given, Dyen's placement of a particular language or language group in his overall classificatory scheme has been noted; the scheme itself has not, however, been adopted as a basis for the ordering of ethnic entries, since it is felt that the lexicostatistical data alone, without testing or verification against other types of linguistic evidence, do not warrant their use in this way at present.

Technical notes. In general, groups are called by the name used most frequently in the literature, e.g. Iban rather than Sea Dayak. Each cultural summary is prefaced by a list of synonyms for the name of the group, wherever such are reported. Only generic synonyms are listed. All names, including variant spellings, names of local or restricted usage, subgroup names, etc. are included in an index at the back of the book, where each is keyed to the relevant group name as it appears in the table of contents. Pluralization of names in general follows popular usage as reflected in the literature. The summaries are, with some exceptions, written in the present tense. In each case, however, the reader should consult the historical section and also refer to the publication dates included in the documentation, in order to form his own judgment of the contemporaneousness of the data. A special effort has been made to document each summary section, and often each paragraph. References pertaining to an immediately preceding sentence or paragraph are enclosed in parentheses; those encompassing an entire section or several sentences or paragraphs are enclosed in brackets. The sources used for a particular entry are listed alphabetically by author in the bibliography section at the end of the entry, as well as in complete form in the master bibliography at the back of the book. Diacritical marks indicative of an author's transcription of native words have in general been omitted; the reader wishing to do so can easily find the relevant reference in the bibliography and proceed from there to consult a particular author's phonetic system. Anthropological terms for kin groups and descent rules have generally been reported as the original author uses them; where reference is made to Murdock's terminology, the reader should consult his *Social Structure* (New York, 1949). The authors of individual contributions are indicated in the table of contents, opposite the names of groups on which they have written summaries. Unless otherwise specified, all remaining entries and introductory materials have been compiled by the editor. Ethnolinguistic sketch maps for each of the major geographical divisions (e.g. Madagascar, Indonesia), as well as for individual islands (e.g. Sumatra, Celebes) will be found at the back of the book. In some cases, contributing authors submitted more data than could conveniently be included within the present volume, necessitating editorial abridgment. In cases where significant amounts of ethnographic data have been thus omitted, the Human Relations Area Files will make available to interested readers copies of the original manuscripts by future listing in its *Hraflex Books* series, a low-cost publishing program designed for descriptive ethnographic materials.

Acknowledgments. In compiling a work of this kind, particular problems are posed by a region such as Indonesia, due to the outdated nature of much of the literature and the fact that the bulk of it is in Dutch, a language unfamiliar to most English speakers. A special effort was made, therefore, to enlist the aid of scholars in Holland, Indonesia, and elsewhere in the initial stages of this project. A grant from the Wenner Gren Foundation for Anthropological Research made possible a trip to Holland in 1966, and special thanks are due the Foundation and also to Professor P. E. de Josselin de Jong and his colleagues at the University of Leiden for help in the initial planning and implementation of the project. Through the good offices of Professor de Josselin de Jong, it was possible for one of his students, Drs. A. C. M. Peeters, to serve during 1968-69 as a research assistant to the project, compiling notes in English based on research in the Dutch literature at both Leiden and The Hague. Thanks are also due Professor Koentjaraningrat and his colleagues at the University of Indonesia for helpful advice and the preparation of a number of ethnographic summaries. In all, nineteen scholars with recent fieldwork experience agreed to contribute summary statements on particular ethnic groups. In addition, many of these individuals gave freely of their advice on a variety of problems, and their help is hereby gratefully acknowledged. Other scholars who have aided the preparation of this book include L. Onvlee, with reference to Sumba and the Sumbanese; Drs. B. Westerkamp, of the Royal Tropical Institute, with reference to West Irian; Alfred B. Hudson, Tom Harrisson, and George N. Appell, with reference to the classification of Bornean groups. B. Westerkamp, D. Hicks, and J. B. Avé aided in the preparation of ethnolinguistic maps of West Irian, Timor, and Southern Kalimantan, respectively. Special thanks are due also to Peter J. Wilson, of Otago University, who provided information on Malagasy groups and generously agreed to prepare draft manuscripts for much of the Celebes section from data supplied by the editor. Members of the Human Relations Area Files staff, including Elizabeth Swift, Judith Tulchin, Lorna Bissell, Deborah Hugo, Penny Wait, Robert O. Lagacé, George Bedell, Phyllis Munson, and Hesung Chun Koh, aided at various times in the preparation, editing, and publication of the book. Particular thanks go to two colleagues at HRAF, Timothy J. O'Leary, who helped with bibliographic problems and also prepared a draft summary of Atjehnese, and Frank W. Moore, for his unfailing help in administrative problems and his cartographic skill in preparing the ethnolinguistic sketch maps. Grateful acknowledgment is due also to the National Science Foundation, for its generous aid in support of both research and publication costs.

TABLE OF CONTENTS

PREFACE

PART I. MADAGASCAR

PART II. ANDAMAN-NICOBAR

PART III. INDONESIA

PART I. MADAGASCAR

IT IS VERY LIKELY that by the beginning of the Christian era, Malayo-Polynesian-speaking Indonesians were making coastwise voyages as far north as China and as far west as the east coast of Africa. The effect of these early Indonesian contacts on the cultural history of Africa has yet to be assessed, but it may turn out to be considerable (cf. Murdock 1959). The most conclusive evidence of Indonesian penetration occurs on the large island of Madagascar, some 250 miles off Africa's southeast coast, specifically with respect to the physical appearance, languages, and cultures of the indigenous peoples of that island, collectively known as Malagasy. Problems of ethnic origins on Madagascar are, however, complex; the modern population of over five million is a composite of racial and cultural strains, with Negroid (African) predominating on the west coast and Mongoloid (Indonesian) in the interior plateau, with, in addition, a wide scattering of Caucasian (Arab) blood. The indigenous languages (collectively termed Malagasy) are, however, basically similar and of undoubted Malayo-Polynesian type, seemingly most closely related to Maanyan, a language of southern coastal Borneo (Dahl 1951, Dyen 1965). The problem is not, in fact, the authenticity of an Indonesian component in the ethnic makeup of Madagascar, but rather one of correctly identifying the African component and accounting for its presence there. Alfred Grandidier, dean of French *Malgachisants*, generally negated the possibility of an African contribution to the evolution of Malagasy culture, particularly with respect to the development of complex political institutions. Kent (1970) refutes this view: consideration of the archaeological, linguistic, and ethnological evidence leads him to postulate an initial movement of Indonesians into coastal and interior East Africa and the formation there of a hybrid Afro-Indonesian culture, which was largely obliterated on the mainland by the later expansion of Bantu peoples, but which, beginning about 600-700 A.D., was carried to Madagascar and survived there. This hybrid Afro-Malagasy migration brought rice agriculture, megaliths, terracing, stone-walled villages, village chiefdoms, ancestral cults, and ritual slaughter of cattle (Kent 1970: 263). The antecedents of the African components of this culture seem in Kent's view to point to the lake regions of central Africa and Rhodesia and, peripherally, to Zimbabwe. Kent's conclusion, that the "traditional past of Madagascar makes absolutely no sense without Africa," seems in fundamental agreement with that reached by Murdock (1959), who also postulated an initial sojourn of Indonesians on the East African littoral and the introduction from there into Madagascar of a hybrid culture—the most important African components of which, in Murdock's view, were certain political institutions associated with paramount chieftainship. Precolonial Madagascar was dominated politically by the expansionist Merina kings, who established hegemony in the interior plateau regions as early as the sixteenth century. The island became a French colony in 1896 and continued so until 1958, when it proclaimed itself an autonomous republic. Roughly one third of the population today is Christian.

BIBLIOGRAPHY. Dahl 1951; Dyen 1965; Kent 1970; Murdock 1959.

MALAGASY

ORIENTATION. Anthropologists conventionally distinguish some 20 different ethnic groups or tribal complexes among the Malagasy-speaking peoples of Madagascar. These were grouped by Linton (1928) into three culture areas, actually ecological zones [population figures from Kent (1970) added]: *East Coast,* including the Betsimisaraka (915,000), Anteifasy (40,000), and Anteimoro (212,000); *Plateau,* including the Betsileo (736,000), Merina or Hova (1,570,000), and Sihanaka (135,000); *West Coast,* including the Sakalava (360,000), Mahafaly (91,000), Antandroy (326,000), and Bara (228,000). The Tanala (237,000), Bezanozano or Tankay (44,000), Tsimihety (429,000), Antankarana (42,000), and Antanosy (149,000) were seen as intermediate between the three areas. Physical and cultural differences correlate roughly with this threefold division, most noticeably with respect to basic economy: east coast tribes rely chiefly on swidden rice; plateau tribes on terraced, irrigated rice; and west coast peoples chiefly on herding and fishing (Murdock 1959). Although Linton in his 1928 article emphasized cultural variety, Southall (1971) wonders whether the many Malagasy "tribes" in reality represent regional groupings of an essentially similar cultural base that have undergone differing ecological adaptations and degrees of alien admixture.

SETTLEMENT PATTERN AND HOUSING. Generally compact, fortified villages, with extensive use of palisades, stone walls, and tunnel entrances. Domestic architecture varies considerably, ranging from simple bamboo and reed construction to mud walls and mortised wood plank design. In general, houses are rectangular with steeply-pitched, gabled roofs, at the ends of which may be carved representations of bullock horns. Houses raised above the ground on posts occur principally in the eastern part of the island; elsewhere they may be set directly on the ground or, in some instances, built on raised stone or earth platforms. Longhouses of the typical Bornean type appear to be absent. [Sibree 1880; Linton 1928; Murdock 1959.]

ECONOMY. Agriculture is universally practiced, but is of varying economic importance. Maize and/or rice are the staple crops, the latter grown on elaborately constructed, irrigated terraces by the plateau Merina. Other crops include taro, sweet potato, millet, and manioc. According to Murdock (1959), the Malaysian agricultural complex (rice, taro, bananas, arrowroot) ranks first in importance, although African cultigens are also present. Cattle are everywhere a symbol of wealth; they are used for animal sacrifice —as are chickens—and milk is consumed as food on the west coast. Pigs, although present, do not appear to be of either economic or ritual importance. Indigenous industries include the making of bark cloth and pottery and weaving on a fixed horizontal loom. Ironworking, employing the Malaysian double-piston bellows, is present among most groups, but the degree of technical expertise varies. Outrigger canoes are used by some coastal peoples. [Linton 1928; Murdock 1959.]

KINSHIP. Southall (1971), after reviewing the data on kinship and social structure, finds an essentially cognatic orientation throughout Madagascar, i.e. optative descent line affiliation, which may for certain purposes emphasize the male line. Southall's findings refute the oft-repeated contention of widespread unilineality (patrilineal clans and lineages) and, with respect to social structure, point to Malaysia rather than to Africa. Murdock, accepting the common interpretation of patriliny, explains it as "what one would expect in a Bornean [Indonesian] bilateral society that was subjected to patrilocal influences through Arab and Cushitic [African] contacts and that had to adapt to the increasing importance of cattle" (Murdock 1959: 220). Kinship terminologies are mostly of the generational (Hawaiian) type.

SOCIOPOLITICAL ORGANIZATION. Malagasy societies are generally stratified into three (often endogamous) classes: hereditary nobles, free commoners, and slaves. Political organization is everywhere developed beyond the village level, with widespread occurrence of petty states ruled by despotic paramount chiefs. Beginning in the sixteenth century, the interior plateau Merina achieved a conquest state, together with the concept of divine kingship and elaborate court ritual—a development attributed by Grandidier and Grandidier (1908-28) to Javanese conquest. Petty warfare among the various Malagasy states was endemic, chiefly for cattle and slaves. Both cannibalism and headhunting seem to have been absent altogether. [Murdock 1959; Sibree 1880; Linton 1928.]

RELIGION. The indigenous Malagasy possessed an ancestor-oriented religion, featuring elaborate mortuary rites and including secondary burial in stone vaults or caves. Among the Hova (Merina), the erection of stone memorial tombs by persons of consequence entailed the assembling of a large work force and the expenditure of much wealth in the form of cattle sacrifice. Among other groups, death memorials took the form of elaborately carved wooden posts or stone menhirs. The skulls of sacrificed cattle were in some areas displayed on posts. The custom of ritually collecting the body fluids from a decomposing corpse, also widespread in Malaysia, was practiced among some groups. [Sibree 1880; Linton 1928.]

BIBLIOGRAPHY. Deschamps 1936; Dubois 1938; Grandidier and Grandidier 1908-28; Kent 1970; Linton 1928; Murdock 1959; Sibree 1880; Southall 1971; Wilson 1971.

PART II. ANDAMAN-NICOBAR

THE ORIGINS of the indigenous tribes of the Andaman and Nicobar islands are unknown. Geographically, the islands constitute a more or less continuous chain lying some 400 miles off the western coast of peninsular Southeast Asia. Reasoning from geography alone, it might be supposed that the inhabitants would demonstrate a common racial and cultural identity; such in fact is not the case, and it seems obvious that the islands have been subjected to differing influences in the not too remote past. The native Andamanese are Negritos, speaking a language as yet unclassified within any known language phylum; racially and culturally they appear to be related to remnant Negrito groups now living in Malaya and the Philippines. The peoples of the Nicobars, on the other hand, are of Mongoloid physical type, similar racially and in some respects culturally to the inhabitants of Mentawei and Enggano off the western coast of Sumatra. However, they speak a Mon-Khmer (Austroasiatic) language, whereas the languages of Sumatra are Austronesian and thus genetically unrelated insofar as is known. Unfortunately, much of the available data on the Andamanese and Nicobarese peoples is unfocused and of relatively little scientific value; the Andamanese, now virtually extinct as a physical or cultural entity, have been studied by few investigators conversant with the native language. Thus many questions raised by the complex ethnic makeup of these islanders—crucial to an unraveling of the culture history of Southeast Asia—remain largely unanswered. It is probably the case, however, that the entire island chain was originally inhabited by an archaic (possibly prelithic) people or peoples. The Andamanese prior to Western contact are reported to have been without stone tools, salt, or domesticated animals and ignorant of the art of making fire. These early inhabitants were presumably part of a Negritolike or archaic Australoid stratum once widespread throughout the area. If this population was indeed present on the Nicobars, it has been displaced or absorbed by a later influx of alien racial, cultural, and linguistic influences. (Whether this influx was in the form of an in-migration of a people or peoples from the direction of Sumatra [as some have supposed] is unknown at present.) Despite their enigmatical origins and their relatively remote island location, there is little doubt that the peoples of the Andamans and Nicobars are racially, linguistically, and culturally part of the world of Southeast Asia, and they have accordingly been included in the present survey of the insular portion of that world.

ANDAMANESE*

Synonym. *Mincopie*

ORIENTATION. **Identification.** The term Andamanese refers to the indigenous tribal population of the Andaman Islands in the Bay of Bengal. The name might have been derived from either (1) Andamanain (used by Marco Polo)—an Arabic dual signifying two islands (great and little)—or (2) Handumans (used by Hindus settled in Sumatra and Java)—the islands of the Handumans mentioned in the Hindu epic *Ramayana* (Portman 1899: 15). The Andamanese tribes described in the classical monograph of Radcliffe-Brown (1922) and in the writings of Man (1882-83), Portman (1899) and others are by now almost extinct.

*The author, Moni Nag, is Associate Professor, Department of Anthropology, Columbia University. He acknowledges with thanks the financial assistance of the Southern Asian Institute of Columbia University in writing this entry.

But three tribes, namely the Onge, Jarawa, and North-Sentinelese still survive, although perhaps in dwindling numbers, and can be classed among the most primitive peoples living in the contemporary world. Radcliffe-Brown (1922) arrived at two broad groupings based on linguistic and cultural distributions at the time of his fieldwork, 1906-08, viz. the Great Andaman group and the Little Andaman group. The former consisted in Radcliffe-Brown's time of the following tribes: Northern group (Aka-Cari, Aka-Kora, Aka-Bo, Aka-Jeru); Southern group (Aka-Kede, Aka-Kol, Oko-Juwoi, A-Pucikwar, Akar-Bale, Aka-Bea). The Little Andaman group included Onge, North-Sentinelese, and Jarawa. The Jarawa occupy at present a portion of the Great Andaman. The Andamanese as a whole are sometimes referred to in the older literature as Mincopie. Among the Andamanese themselves, the coastal groups are known as Aryoto and those living in the forest as Eremtaga (Man 1882-83: 102). The Andamanese are characterized by very short stature, black skin, peppercorn hair, and steatopygia (Cipriani 1966: 16). There are some physical and cultural similarities with the Semang of the Malay Peninsula and the Aeta of the Philippines. It is supposed that the Andamanese are descendants of a Negrito racial stock, which perhaps occupied a wide area in Southeast Asia and Oceania in prehistoric times (Radcliffe-Brown 1922: 407; Cipriani 1955: lxvi). **Location.** A chain of 204 islands between 10°30′ and 13°30′ N. and between 90°0′ and 92°33′ E. The Little Andaman are located about 40 miles south of the Great Andaman. **Geography.** The islands of the Andaman chain appear as a series of hills covered with dense tropical forests. Fish and mollusks abound on offshore reefs and in tidal creeks. Pigs and civet cats are found in large numbers. Many species of birds are seen, but snakes and lizards are limited. **Linguistic affiliation.** The Andamanese languages are customarily classed together as one family, as yet unrelated to any known phylum. Speakers of Andamanese are in fact often cited as the only living examples of a pygmy people who speak their own language, i.e. who have not borrowed the languages of neighboring groups (Voegelin and Voegelin 1966: 10). Greenberg, in an unpublished memorandum cited by Murdock (1964: 123), postulates an Indo-Pacific phylum to include Andamanese together with certain non-Austronesian languages. There are two main dialect divisions: (1) Onge, Jarawa, and possibly North-Sentinelese and (2) tribes of Great Andaman (Radcliffe-Brown 1922: 11-12). **Demography.** Severe depopulation has occurred among the tribes of Great Andaman, whose number decreased from about 4,500 in 1858 to 19 in 1961. Colonization began in 1789, and at present intrusive groups (chiefly from mainland India) far outnumber the native Andamanese. In 1961 the total population was 63,548, of which only an estimated 698 were indigenous. **History.** According to

Radcliffe-Brown (1922: 5), the Andamanese arrived from Burma either by land in late Tertiary times or later, by sea. Cipriani (1966: 139-41) thinks that they came from Sumatra via the Nicobars. Significant colonization occurred only in 1858, when the British government in India founded a penal settlement at Port Blair. Since Indian independence in 1947, various plans have been initiated for the economic development of the islands. **Cultural relations.** The Jarawa and North-Sentinelese are still hostile to outsiders. The Onge have been in slight contact with Indian mainlanders for the last few decades, but this seems to have had little effect as yet except to make them habituated to smoking. The Great Andamanese have been in contact with Indian convicts and others since the latter half of the nineteenth century. By 1908, the process of depopulation that followed first contact had already altered their social organization (Radcliffe-Brown 1922: 19).

SETTLEMENT PATTERN AND HOUSING. **Settlement pattern.** Seminomadic people living in bands. Encampments, rarely inhabited by more than 50-80 persons, consist of several huts. Coastal tribes select sites that are good for fishing and turtling. Huts are usually faced inward, leaving an oval-shaped inner space for dancing. There are separate huts for unmarried men and boys. The large beehive type of communal hut, representing almost the whole encampment, with all huts drawn together and roofs meeting in the center, is characteristic of the Onge of Little Andaman rather than the Great Andamanese. [Man 1882-83: 107-08; Radcliffe-Brown 1922: 29-35; Nigam 1962a: 46-47.] **Housing.** Thatched lean-to huts among the Great Andamanese. The beehive huts of the Onge are capable of accommodating up to 100 persons, being 50-60 feet in diameter and 20-30 feet in height (Cipriani 1966: 56-61; Radcliffe-Brown 1922: 35).

ECONOMY. **Agriculture.** Indigenous Andamanese culture is characterized by complete absence of agriculture, although recently the Onge have been introduced to plantation cultivation. [Cipriani 1966: 35.] **Fishing.** Coast dwellers obtain much food from the sea, using harpoons, bows and arrows, and nets. All groups poison or stupefy fish in pools. Resin torches are used for turtle fishing in the sea at night. [Radcliffe-Brown 1922: 36, 417-18; Nigam 1963: 150-54; Cipriani 1966: 116-24.] **Hunting.** During the rainy season, the people live in permanent encampments, the men going off each day to hunt, chiefly for wild pig. Hunting is done with bow and arrow, although spears have been used since the introduction of dogs. [Radcliffe-Brown 1922: 36-37, 417; Nigam 1963: 147-50.] **Gathering.** All Andamanese depend heavily on gathering. Wild foods are more plentiful in the cool season, and during this time the people leave the main encampment for up to three months. Items sought include citrus fruits, yams, pandanus, honey, larvae, and turtle eggs. [Radcliffe-Brown 1922: 36-39; Nigam 1963: 154-56; Cipriani 1966: 103-04.] **Domestic animals.** The only domesticated animal is the dog, introduced after colonization in the 1850s. [Radcliffe-Brown 1922: 417; Cipriani 1966: 21.] **Industrial arts.** Cooking pots, made only in certain parts of the islands, are hand-molded, sun-dried, and partially baked in fire. Coast dwellers make dugout canoes, with and without outrigger. Shell adze heads have only recently been replaced by iron. It is reported by all sources that until recently the Andamanese were ignorant of any method of making fire. [Portman 1899: 47-48; Radcliffe-Brown 1922: 447-91; Cipriani 1966: 65-66.] **Trade.** When forest dwellers meet coast dwellers, the former acquire shells, red paint, iron scraps, etc. in exchange for forest products (Radcliffe-Brown 1922: 42, 83). There is no external trade. **Property.** Hunting and gathering territories are owned by communities. Articles such as cooking pots or canoes, when not required by the owner, are regarded as public property by members of the same community. [Man 1882-83: 114, 340; Radcliffe-Brown 1922: 41; Nigam 1963: 154-56.]

KIN GROUPS. **Descent.** The rule of descent appears to be bilateral. **Kin groups.** It is not clear whether any kin group other than the nuclear family is present. Portman (n.d.: 23) and Bonington (1935: 175)—perhaps following Portman—refer to tribal divisions or "septs." Radcliffe-Brown (1922: 28) thinks that these are perhaps groups consisting of four or five local groups each who have friendly relations with one another. **Kin terminology.** A few selected terms used by the tribes of Great Andaman are:

	N. Great Andaman	S. Great Andaman	
	All four tribes (Radcliffe-Brown 1922: 54)	Akar - Bale (Radcliffe-Brown 1922: 56)	S. Great Andaman Aka-Bea (Man 1882-83: 421-22)
Fa	*mai*	*da (ab-atr)*	*maiola (dar-odinga)*
Mo	*mimi*	*in*	*canola*
ElBr	*otoatue*	*en-toaka-nga*	*en-toka-nga*
ElSi	*otoatue-cip*	*en-toaka-nga*	*en-toka-nga-pail*
YoBr	*arai-culute*	*ar-dotot*	*doatinga*
YoSi	*arai-culute-cip*	*ar-dotot*	*doatinga-pail*

MARRIAGE AND FAMILY. **Adolescence.** Scarification commences when a child is quite young and is repeated at intervals until the whole body has been scarified. The period of childhood of a girl is brought to a close by a ceremony on the occasion of her first menarche. She is secluded in a hut for three days, at the end of which she resumes her daily life in the camp but continues ritual bathing in the sea. She is given a new name and is so addressed until the birth

of her first child. From the time of this puberty rite, the girl enters a new condition termed *aka-op*, a period of ritual restrictions chiefly concerned with food. There is no physiological event so clearly marked when a boy enters the *aka-op* period. The total *aka-op* may last from one to several years, accompanied by intermittent ceremonies. It lasts longer for girls than for boys, normally until after a girl's marriage. [Radcliffe-Brown 1922: 91-106; Man 1882-83: 129-35.] **Mode.** Marriage among the northern Great Andaman tribes is arranged by older men and women, and exchange of gifts is a part of the marriage negotiations. Man (1882-83: 136) observed that among the southern Great Andaman tribes, parents and foster parents have the power of betrothing their children in infancy. **Form.** Monogamy (Man 1882-83: 135; Radcliffe-Brown 1922: 70). **Extension of incest taboos.** Radcliffe-Brown (1922: 71-72) observed that marriage was forbidden between near consanguineals but that marriage between cousins was not altogether forbidden. **Residence.** Both Man (1882-83: 137) and Radcliffe-Brown (1922: 29) imply that residence is ambilocal, but some of the latter's remarks (1922: 78-80) indicate a tendency toward virilocal residence. **Domestic unit.** Nuclear families are of great importance as social and economic units. Children are desired, and a marriage is not regarded as fully consummated until the birth of a child (Radcliffe-Brown 1922: 23, 70-71). **Inheritance.** Individual ownership exists in relation to trees, canoes, implements, and the like. **Divorce.** Rare (unknown after the birth of a first child). Desertion of a wife by a husband is considered a breach of tribal morality. [Man 1882-83: 135; Portman 1899: 39; Bonington 1935: 175.] **Secondary marriage.** Radcliffe-Brown found no instance of the levirate among the northern Great Andamanese. Man, referring to the tribes of southern Great Andaman, states that marriage between a widow (if not old) and her deceased husband's unmarried or widowed younger brother or cousin is almost obligatory. Man also reports that a childless widower is expected to marry the deceased wife's younger sister. [Man 1882-83: 136-39; Radcliffe-Brown 1922: 75.] **Adoption.** Common among all Andamanese. Man (1882-83: 124) observed that children above six or seven years rarely resided with their parents.

SOCIOPOLITICAL ORGANIZATION. **Political organization.** The Andamanese tribe, composed of independent and autonomous local groups, has a name of its own and is fundamentally a linguistic (dialect) division recognized by the natives themselves. Each local group, averaging 20-50 members, has its recognized hunting territory. Two or more neighboring groups may meet together and join in feasting and dancing, but such meetings may also be sources of long-standing feuds. According to Man (1882-83: 108), the head chief of a tribe has overall authority, but

Radcliffe-Brown (1922: 44-47) thinks that there is no organized chieftainship. Cipriani (1954: 72) states that among the Onge each community hut (housing the equivalent of a local group) has a headman, but that his authority, if any, never goes beyond the hut. **Social control and justice.** Justice is administered by the simple method of allowing the aggrieved party to take the law into his own hands. The injured person may seek vengeance if he dares. Man (1882-83: 110-12) adds that a man, or even a boy, may show his resentment by destroying his own property as well as that of his neighbors. **Warfare.** Feuds between local groups and between tribes may result in bloodshed. After one or two small raids, a peace is normally made, mainly through the negotiations of women. Head-hunting is unknown. Cannibalism, although imputed by early accounts, is not confirmed in the ethnographic literature. [Radcliffe-Brown 1922: 85-86; Man 1882-83: 112; Bonington 1935: 175.]

RELIGION. **Religious systems.** No conversions to any major world religion. Religion characterized chiefly by animism. **Supernaturals.** The Great Andamanese believe in: (1) spirits inhabiting the forest (*lau*) and the sea (*jurua*), and (2) spirits associated with phenomena of nature. The spirits of deceased persons are included in the first category (Radcliffe-Brown 1922: 136-40, 163). Man (1882-83: 152-58) and Portman (1899: 44) report belief in a spirit (Puluga), similiar to a supreme being. The Onge conceive the universe as a multilayered structure, with Little Andaman as its center. Each layer is the abode of a particular type of spirit (Ganguly 1961: 244-45). **Practitioners.** There is no clear line between those who possess supernatural power and those who do not. A person may acquire supernatural power by direct communication with the spirits, through dreams or during a state of unconsciousness (Radcliffe-Brown 1922: 48, 175-79). **Ceremonies.** Major religious ceremonies are those connected with initiation and death. On these and other occasions, much use is made of clay to decorate the body. Body painting and ritual dancing are important accompaniments to most ceremonies. **Illness and medicine.** Spirits are the cause of all sickness. Medicine men (*oko-jumu*) use substances or objects believed to have the power of keeping spirits at a distance, e.g. human bones and burned yellow ochre in paint form (Radcliffe-Brown 1922: 139, 178-83; Portman 1899: 39). **Soul, death, and afterlife.** When a person dies, his double or "soul" leaves the body and becomes a spirit. There is a belief that spirits of jungle and sea are actually spirits of dead persons, thus a deceased jungle dweller becomes a *lau*, which lives in the jungle, and a deceased coast dweller becomes a *jurua*, which lives in the sea. [Radcliffe-Brown 1922: 90-91, 166-75.] There are two modes of disposing of the dead among the Great Andamanese: (1) in a grave dug in the ground, and (2) upon a platform placed in a tree. The latter is considered more honorable. Any space a little distance from the camp may be used as a graveyard. The corpse, in a flexed, squatting posture, is wrapped in a sleeping mat and tied with a rope. The camp is deserted during mourning, the essentials of which include the use of clay on body and head. Mourning should last long enough for the flesh of the dead body to decay from the bones, after which the bones are dug up and washed. The skull and jaw bone are decorated with red paint and preserved. They may be worn around the neck by near relatives, and eventually they become community heirlooms. The limb bones are generally painted red and kept in the roof of the hut. There is a ceremony at the end of mourning characterized by dancing, singing, and weeping. [Radcliffe-Brown 1922: 106-14.] The Onge of Little Andaman bury their dead in inhabited huts. Personal objects of the deceased are buried secretly in the forest, where termites destroy them. Exhumation is still practiced. The long bones, painted red and white, are reburied in the hut. Jaw bones are carried around the neck by near relatives, but not the entire skull. [Cipriani 1954: 74; 1966: 76.]

BIBLIOGRAPHY. Bonington 1935; Cipriani 1954, 1955, 1966; Ganguly 1961; Man 1882-83; Murdock 1964; Nigam 1962a, 1963; Portman 1899, n.d.; Radcliffe-Brown 1922; Voegelin and Voegelin 1966.

NICOBARESE*

Synonyms. *Tarik, Pai, Paiyuh, Shompen, Shab Dawa*

ORIENTATION. **Identification.** The term "Nicobarese" refers in general to the people of the Nicobar Archipelago, including twelve inhabited and seven uninhabited islands. "Nicobar" seems to be a corrupt form of the South Indian term Nakkavaram (land of the naked), which appears in the Tanjore inscription of A.D. 1050. The name has been regularly used from the time of Marco Polo (Whitehead 1924: 25). The inhabitants of Car Nicobar speak of themselves as Tarik (man) while those of the central group of islands call themselves Pai or Paiyuh (man). [Datta-Majumder 1955: 1.] There are two main subgroups: (1) the coastal population of all the inhabited islands, commonly known as Nicobarese, and (2) the interior inhabitants of the largest island, Great Nicobar, known as Shompen. In the coastal Nicobarese dialect of Great Nicobar, *shom* means "native" or "people," and *pen* denotes the particular tribe designated. Sometimes the Shompen call themselves Shab Dawa. [Man 1886: 429, 432.] The Nicobarese and Shompen have no racial or cultural affiliation with their immediate neighbors, the Andamanese, although it was previously believed that the Shompen provided a missing link with the Semang of the Malay Peninsula (Man 1886: 429). There are obvious physical and cultural differences between the Nicobarese and the Shompen, but both seem to have migrated in the remote past from mainland Southeast Asia. The Shompen are considered by some to be an aboriginal stock, driven into the interior by later immigrants. It is supposed that they survived only in the Great Nicobar. There is evidence of Malay, Burmese, and Siamese mixture in the not-too-distant past, but the Shompen are known to have been exclusive for a long time. Ossuary practices and some other customs suggest affinity with Melanesian tribes and with islands off the west coast of Sumatra. The Shompen are medium-headed and generally light brownish in skin color; the Nicobarese are broad-headed and somewhat fairer. [Man 1886: 429-31; Man 1889: 367-72; Bonington 1935: 177-78; Nag 1967: 29-30.] **Location.** The Bay of Bengal, between 6°–10° N. and 92°42′–94°0′ E. The archipelago extends south-easterly for about 160 miles from the Car Nicobar in the north to the Great Nicobar in the south, the latter about 120 miles from the northern tip of Sumatra. **Geography.** Car Nicobar and Chowra are flat, while the central and southern islands are mountainous, with elevations up to 2,000 feet. The climate is warm, with an average annual rainfall at Car Nicobar of about 100 inches. Coconut trees are plentiful, as are casuarina, banyan, pandanus, areca palm, and mangrove. The fauna is limited to wild pigs, monkeys, pigeons, and a few reptiles. **Linguistic affiliation.** Greenberg (1953: 281) accepts Schmidt's (1906) suggestion that Nicobarese belongs to an Austroasiatic stock including other language groups such as Mon-Khmer and Munda. There are at least six clearly distinct dialects: Car Nicobar, Chowra, Teressa, Central, Southern, and Shompen (Whitehead 1924: 22-23). **Demography.** According to the 1961 Census of India (Sharma 1966: 15), of the 14,563 inhabitants of the Nicobar Islands, 13,903 are Nicobarese. The non-Nicobarese mostly belong to mainland India and are concentrated on Car Nicobar. Car Nicobar, with only 49.0 square miles, has a population of 9,879; while Great Nicobar, with 403.5 square miles, has a population of only 203 (Sharma 1964: 66). The Nicobarese are known to have increased in population during recent decades, but this may not be true for the Shompen. The estimated population of the latter was 300-400 in 1905 (Sharma 1966: 17), while the estimate made by the present author in 1966 was 150-200. **History.** The Nicobars lie along an ancient trade route between China and the west. They are mentioned by Ptolemy ca. 140 A.D., and they are spoken of as the "land of naked people" by the Buddhist monk I-Tsing in 672 A.D. Beginning in the sixteenth century, various European nations tried to colonize the islands. The British maintained control from 1869 until the Second World War. Since 1947, the Nicobars have been part of the Indian territory known as the Andaman and Nicobar Islands. **Cultural relations.** Nicobarese living in Car Nicobar, the administrative and trading center, have experienced maximum contact with outsiders. Although Christian missionary activities began in the early eighteenth century, they have had a substantial

*The author of this entry, Moni Nag, is Associate Professor, Department of Anthropology, Columbia University. He acknowledges with thanks the financial assistance of the Southern Asian Institute of Columbia University in writing this paper. The author emphasizes that he has used the term "Nicobarese" to refer generally to all the inhabitants of the Nicobar Islands except the Shompen. The available literature refers primarily to Car Nicobar, a small but heavily populated island. There is but scanty literature on the Shompen, and the author draws heavily on his own field investigation among them in 1966.

effect only since the end of the nineteenth century, and then only on Car Nicobar (Stevenson 1935: 190). It is possible to identify the influence of trading groups, such as the Burmese, Malays, Chinese, and Gujarati Muslims. Traces of temporary Hindu colonization about 900 years ago are also evident (Bonington 1935: 178; Gupta 1955: 51). The development programs of the present Indian administration are expected to have far-reaching effects.

SETTLEMENT PATTERN AND HOUSING. **Settlement pattern.** The Nicobarese live in permanent villages in coastal areas; the Shompen in semipermanent hamlets in the interior. According to the 1961 Census of India (Sharma 1964: 46), the average population of Car Nicobar villages was 617, while that of Little Nicobar villages was only 11. Car Nicobar village land is divided into four parts: *el-panam* land is in the coastal area, where big beehive houses are located, along with maternity and preburial huts. *Thuhet* is the homestead area. Beyond this lies the *tulong*, with coconut plantations extending inland to the forest. Areca palms and pandanus trees are found in the *tulong*, but more abundantly toward the inner region, called *tavat*, meaning "jungle" (Shyamchaudhury 1955: 6). Shompen hamlets are located inland and are often situated on the summits of hills (Man 1933: 174). **Housing.** Each kin group in a Nicobarese village has one large, round beehive-type house, erected on wooden piles, five to eight feet above ground level. Lesser houses are generally of gable type, built on rectangular bases supported on piles (Shyamchaudhury 1955: 9). Shompen houses are generally smaller and ruder than those of the Nicobarese, but are also raised on wooden piles. Beehive huts with roofs made from large sheets of bark occur in hamlets farthest from the coast (Man 1933: 181).

ECONOMY. **Agriculture.** The Nicobarese get over one half of their subsistence from horticulture, whereas the Shompen get less than half. Coconut and pandanus are the staple food crops, although extensive coconut plantations are rare in Shompen settlements. Other important crops are areca nuts, yams, and bananas. On Car Nicobar, pineapple, papaya, sugarcane, and pumpkins are grown in abundance (Whitehead 1924: 91). A few Shompen groups are reported to grow tobacco (Raja Ram 1960: 78). Neither Nicobarese nor Shompen make use of fertilizer or artificial irrigation. Large iron blades obtained through trade serve for harvesting of coconut and pandanus. **Fishing and hunting.** Next to horticulture, fishing is the most important means of livelihood for the Nicobarese, as hunting is for the Shompen. The former use spears for catching octopus and large fish in the sea, and fish left behind in pools when the tide goes out are sometimes poisoned with grated *kinyav* seeds mixed with ashes. The Shompen use spears for catching fish in streams. [Whitehead 1924: 98-100; Man 1933: 82.] Wild pigs are rarely hunted nowadays, but the Great Nicobarese still go out in the rainy season with spears and dogs. Some use crossbows for bringing down pigeons (Man 1933: 81). The Shompen are skilled in hunting wild pigs with the help of dogs. **Gathering.** The Nicobarese collect mollusks and turtle eggs along the seashore. The Shompen, who depend more on gathering, collect wild roots and fruits, including pandanus, as well as larvae and honey. **Domestic animals.** The Nicobarese eat pigs and fowls only on ceremonial occasions, when the sprinkling of sacrificial blood is considered auspicious. Both Nicobarese and Shompen are fond of dogs, used chiefly for hunting wild pigs. **Industrial arts.** Large clay pots are made on the island of Chowra, a craft tabooed on the other islands (Man 1933: 33). The Chowra people also have the monopoly of making large racing canoes. **Trade.** Pottery and canoes are traded internally through Chowra. Coconuts, areca nuts, and canes are sold to foreign traders in exchange for textiles, utensils, implements, rice, and other articles. **Property.** Important items of property are land, coconut and pandanus trees, canoes and huts. On Car Nicobar, village land is considered the property of the headman, who grants usufruct rights to families within his village (Bonington 1935: 182-83; Gupta 1955: 56).

KIN GROUPS. **Descent.** Field studies by Shyamchaudhury (1955) on Car Nicobar and by the present author on Great Nicobar indicate that descent is ambilineal, in the terminology suggested by Murdock (1960: 2). A person is usually affiliated with either parent's kin group at birth and has the choice of changing his/her affiliation to his/her spouse's kin group after marriage, but cannot retain affiliation with more than one kin group at a time. **Kin groups.** A functional kin group (*kinem*) was observed by Shyamchaudhury (1955: 9) on Car Nicobar and was designated by him as a "lineage." But it appears from his description and that of a similar group (*haidechiya*) observed by the present author on Great Nicobar that the term "ramage" as proposed by Murdock (1960: 11) is more appropriate. Among the Nicobarese, it is a localized and exogamous group with corporate activities. **Kin terminology.** The kinship terminology is of Hawaiian type. Terms of reference on Car Nicobar (obtained by correspondence from Shyamchaudhury) and on Great Nicobar (collected by the present author) are:

	Car Nicobar	Great Nicobar
Fa	*yong*	*doyit*
Mo	*yong*	*hend*
So	*kuon*	*koot*
Da	*kuon*	*ulaiye*
ElBr	*mem*	*hause*
YoBr	*kahem*	*taure*
ElSi	*mem*	*anon*
YoSi	*kahem*	*anon*

Male cousin (El)	*mem*	*hause*
Male cousin (Yo)	*kahem*	*taure*
Female cousin (El)	*mem*	*anon*
Female cousin (Yo)	*kahem*	*anon*
Uncles and aunts	*yong*	*uiye*
Nephews and nieces	*kuon*	*kohol*
Hu	*piho*	*kaot*
Wi	*piho*	*kat*

MARRIAGE AND FAMILY. **Adolescence.** When a girl attains puberty, she must remain secluded in one portion of the familial hut for some two weeks and must abstain from various foods during this period. A wooden board on which various scenes are painted (*hentakoi*) is prepared for the magical welfare of the girl, and she carries an auspicious stick with her whenever she goes out of the hut. A concluding feast announces that the girl is ready for marriage, and thereafter she is free to begin having affairs with eligible boys. **Mode.** Marriage is arranged usually by the partners themselves, but the consent of the parents is considered necessary. There is no dowry, but bride service and bride-price may be said to exist in a minimal sense. There is usually a feast after a couple live together for some time as husband and wife. Among the Shompen, early betrothal of the girl and marriage by capture seem to be prevalent. [Man 1933: 124-25; Bonington 1935: 180-82; Stevenson 1935: 188.] **Form.** Monogamy, with some sororal and nonsororal polygyny among the Shompen. **Extension of incest taboos.** Marriage and sex ideally prohibited among members of a Nicobarese ramage, especially among those known to be related consanguineally. Cousin marriage is rare. **Residence.** Murdock's (1967: 156, 198) designation of Nicobarese marital residence as uxorilocal, with virilocal as a numerically significant deviation, seems appropriate. Choice of residence, however, depends considerably on the economic condition of each spouse. Marital residence among the Shompen seems similar to that of the Nicobarese. **Domestic unit.** Among the Nicobarese the extended family located in a single household is not uncommon, but there is a tendency among married couples to move to a separate household as early as possible. Shompen bands consisting of a few related nuclear or polygynous families share some activities, but among them the family is relatively more independent. **Inheritance.** Land, trees, and canoes are generally owned by the ramage, and members of both sexes are entitled to rights of usage. In the central islands, land is held on an individual basis and is inherited in equal shares by all surviving children (Gupta 1955: 56). Individual property is mostly destroyed or buried when a person dies. **Divorce.** Divorce freely permitted and common. Man found many Nicobarese who had had two or more partners before age 30. Children are usually apportioned between the husband and wife. [Man 1933: 50, 125; Whitehead 1924: 222; Bonington 1935: 182.] **Secondary marriage.** The widowed and divorced among the Nicobarese are free to remarry, but it is decorous for a widow to wait two or three years (Man 1933: 126). No evidence of levirate or sororate. Among the Shompen, both levirate and sororate are present, but it is not clear whether these are prescriptive, preferred, or circumstantial. **Adoption.** On a very limited scale among the Nicobarese (Man 1933: 121).

SOCIOPOLITICAL ORGANIZATION. **Political organization.** The head of the oldest and traditionally most important ramage (*ma-ku-kinem*) is usually the headman (*ma-panam*) of a Nicobarese village. Every ramage (*kinem*) within a village organizes its own social and economic affairs, but issues that concern the entire village or more than one ramage are dealt with by an assembly of elders. **Social stratification.** No classes or age-grades among the Nicobarese. On Great Nicobar, the Shompen are regarded by Coastal Nicobarese as belonging to a lower class. No evidence of slavery. **Social control and justice.** On Car Nicobar, offenses are dealt with by the village council (Shyamchaudhury 1955: 11). In a case of adultery, a fine or corporal punishment is imposed. When an individual wishes to avenge a wrong done to him, he may occasionally inflict some loss or injury upon himself, rather than on the real offender (Man 1933: 47; Whitehead 1924: 223). The institution of "devil-murder" was prevalent among the Nicobarese until recently (Bonington 1935: 181-82). **Warfare.** No headhunting or cannibalism. Man (1886: 432) mentions constant feuds between Coastal Nicobarese and Shompen and also among the Shompen groups themselves. Hostile Shompen still make looting raids on the Coastal Nicobarese.

RELIGION. **Religious systems.** According to the 1961 Census of India (Sharma 1964: 358), 71 percent of the population is Christian and some 20 percent "other religion" (exclusive of Hinduism, Islam, and Buddhism). Christian Nicobarese are almost entirely confined to Car Nicobar (Datta-Majumder 1955: 1-3; Whitehead 1924: 127). **Supernaturals.** Spirits of dead ancestors are distinguished from evil spirits. Paintings on wood and carved wooden figures are made to scare away the latter. A person possessed by evil spirits may cause harm to others, and it may be necessary to murder him, hence the institution of "devil-murder." The Car Nicobarese believe in a High God, Teo, creator of the sun, moon, sky, and earth, who is worshiped once a year at a thanksgiving festival. The sun, moon, and stars are benevolent to human beings, and prayers are offered to them. [Man 1933: 159-63; Stevenson 1935: 187; Datta-Majumder 1955: 1-3.] **Practitioners.** Shamans, *menluana*, can cure disease and can identify an offender and make him confess his guilt. Both sexes can become shaman. The position, which is highly respected, is not hereditary; a *menluana* usually has a few apprentices in training.

The Shompen of Great Nicobar have also institutionalized the status of shaman, a fact ascribed to the influence of the Coastal Nicobarese. [Man 1933: 47-48, 158; Bonington 1935: 180-85; Stevenson 1935: 190.] **Ceremonies.** In the central Nicobars no less than ten feasts of a memorial character are held in honor of deceased persons. Ossuary feasts, lasting several months, are celebrated only when a community is able to provide the necessary materials. An essential element is the digging up of the bones of all recently deceased persons, washing them, and burying them again to the accompaniment of animal sacrifice. Large feasts are accompanied by continuous singing, dancing, and drinking of palm toddy. Sprinkling the bare body with warm blood from sacrificed pigs and fowls is common. **Soul, death, and afterlife.** The spirits of the dead are classified into three types: (1) *iwi-ka*, the good spirits of good ancestors (2) *iwi-pot*, the evil spirits of wicked ancestors and of people murdered or murderers and evildoers, and (3) *iwi-mekuya*, the spirits of recently departed relatives; these may be gratified by libations and offerings and the destruction of all their movable property. After the memorial feasts for a person, his spirit is believed to go to Henakla, a region to the east resembling the present world. [Man 1933: 158-61; Whitehead 1924: 184-85.] On Car Nicobar, the corpse is carried to a preburial hut and thereafter buried in the village graveyard facing the beach. Portable property is destroyed and deposited near the grave. Mourners are required to take vows, the termination of which coincides with the successive memorial feasts in honor of the deceased. The shaman functions in the burial ceremony and in the subsequent memorial feasts. [Man 1933: 130-38; Whitehead 1924: 184-95.] On Chowra and Teressa islands, dead bodies are not buried (Whitehead 1924: 196). They are wrapped in cloth and leaves and put into one half of a canoe, which is placed on posts about six feet above the ground in a thick grove or on the beach. The bodies may decompose or fall to the ground, in which case they are devoured by pigs. Every three or four years, bones are collected and deposited ceremonially in a communal ossuary. Elements of ancestor worship can be found in Teressa and Bompoka, where the skull of a revered personage is preserved and placed on a life-size wooden body in a sitting posture (Bonington 1935: 185). The remaining bones of the deceased are placed inside the hollow wooden body. The bones of ordinary persons are preserved in small hollowed logs. Among the Shompen, corpses are buried in a sitting posture with the hands lashed together near the mouth, in which a bit of pandanus pulp is placed. The body is not subsequently disinterred as among the Nicobarese. A year later, a large feast, lasting some six to eight days, is held, accompanied by dancing. The camp is immediately deserted and never occupied again. It is, however, revisited for the collection of ripe fruits. [Bonington 1935: 180.]

BIBLIOGRAPHY. Bonington 1935; Datta-Majumder 1955; Greenberg 1953; Gupta 1955; Man 1886, 1889, 1933; Murdock 1960, 1967; Nag 1967; Raja Ram 1960; Schmidt 1906; Sharma 1964, 1966; Shyamchaudhury 1955; Stevenson 1935; Whitehead 1924.

PART III. INDONESIA

INDONESIA, the world's largest island complex, extends along the equator for over 3,000 miles. Many of the thousands of islands are small and uninhabited, and others are only sparsely populated. Some two thirds of Indonesia's more than 100 million inhabitants live on Java and nearby Madura; the remainder of the country—the "Outer Islands"—has an average population density of only 19 per square kilometer (Pelzer 1963). The archipelago is customarily considered in terms of a three-fold geographical division: the Greater Sundas, including the large islands of Sumatra (Sumatera), Java (Djawa), Borneo (Kalimantan), and Celebes (Sulawesi); the Lesser Sundas (Nusa Tenggara), including Bali, Lombok, Sumbawa, Sumba, Flores, Solor, Alor, and Timor; and the Moluccas (Maluku), including Halmahera, Ceram, and numerous small islands east of Timor. Former Dutch New Guinea (now West Irian) has since 1963 been part of the Republic of Indonesia, and its coasts and off-lying islands have for centuries been colonized by ethnic Indonesians. Coastal Irian must therefore be included in a survey of Indonesian peoples and cultures, although the majority of the inhabitants are of Papuan or Melanesian stock and thus outside the scope of the present study. • Indonesia, when viewed from the standpoint of culture history, is clearly a part of greater Southeast Asia. Traditional views of the prehistory of this entire region are currently being reworked by W. Solheim (1969), K. C. Chang (1969), and others. As new data accumulate it is increasingly evident that Southeast Asia must be seen as an area of fundamental cultural innovations—as a nuclear area rather than a mere cul-de-sac receiving influences from the outside. There is now clear evidence that island Southeast Asia, including Indonesia, participated in these early developments and that it was part of the Southeast Asian cultural world at least by the fifth millennium B.C. (Harrisson 1958b; Fox 1967; Solheim 1969). The recorded history of Indonesia is intimately involved with the process of Hinduization that enveloped the mainland beginning as early as the fifth century A.D. and culminated, in the islands, in the powerful fifteenth-century empire of Madjapahit. Later Islamization centered on Sumatra and Java, from which centers it spread to become the dominant religion throughout the archipelago. The Dutch and Portuguese, attracted initially by the profits of the Moluccan spice trade, were in the area as early as the sixteenth century, and by 1650 the East India Company had gained a virtual trade monopoly. In 1816 the Dutch East Indies became a colonial possession of Holland and continued so until the Japanese occupation in 1941. Independence from Holland was won finally in 1949, the date of the founding of the independent Republic of Indonesia. • Diversity of historical influences, together with isolation on often remote islands or in interior mountain valleys, have produced a complex mosaic of self-conscious ethnic groups and categories. M. A. Jaspan arrived at a provisional total of 366 ethnic groups in Indonesia inclusive of Malaysian Borneo and West New Guinea (Jaspan 1959). Raymond Kennedy, in various publications, customarily classified the peoples of Indonesia into some 60 or 70 clusters for descriptive presentation. The present survey attempts to accomplish this task within the framework of 90 specific ethnic entries. The order of entries is by and large by island, starting in the west with Sumatra, although islands have been grouped under a single geographic heading where ethnolinguistic similarities or known historical associations warrant such treatment. The peoples of Indonesia have been classified in a variety of ways, e.g. by physical type (Kleiweg de Zwaan

1925; Kennedy 1937), traditional law or "adat" areas (van Vollenhoven 1918-33), language (Esser 1938; Berzina and Bruk 1963; Dyen 1965) and sociocultural or technoeconomic types (H. Geertz 1963; Avé 1970). Any classification can be useful for the purpose for which it is intended; for the purpose of descriptive presentation the present volume follows closely the approach adopted by Kennedy (1935, 1943, 1962), i.e. a combination of geographic, linguistic, and cultural criteria. A further discussion of these criteria in ethnic unit identification and classification procedures can be found in the preface.

BIBLIOGRAPHY. Avé 1970; Berzina and Bruk 1963; Chang 1969; Dyen 1965; Esser 1938; Fox 1967; H. Geertz 1963; Harrisson 1958b; Jaspan 1959; Kennedy 1935, 1937, 1943, 1962; Kleiweg de Zwaan 1925; Pelzer 1963; Solheim 1969; van Vollenhoven 1918-33.

SCATTERED GROUPS

SEA NOMADS

Seminomadic boat people (Orang Laut or Moken) are found near river mouths, in marshy coastal areas, and on offshore islands all along the west coast of the Malay Peninsula as far north as Burma. Both Kennedy (1935: 308-20) and Sopher (1965) assume the existence of an original stock (probably related to the "aboriginal Malays" or Jakun peoples of southern Malaya) in the vicinity of the Malacca Strait, with subsequent migrations throughout much of insular Southeast Asia. Sopher (1965: 345) supposes that these outward migrations were historically related to those of Islamic Malays, coincident with the sixteenth-century expansion of the China trade and the international spice trade. Later, during the nineteenth century, Sea Nomads gained a notorious reputation as participants in the piratical activities of Straits and Borneo Malays as well as Buginese. The Sea Nomads appear to have been originally of Proto-Malay stock, probably with a strong Veddoid component (Kennedy 1935), although subsequent intermarriage with alien peoples has resulted in widely varying physical characteristics. Nowadays the boat peoples all speak dialects of Malay or related Malayo-Polynesian languages, e.g. Buginese. They are distributed throughout much of Indonesia, including: (1) the Sumatran east coast and Riau-Lingga Archipelago, where they are known generally as Orang Laut or by local terms, such as Mantong, Barok, Sekah, Rayat, or Kuala (2) the coastal estuaries and offshore islands of northern and eastern Borneo and Celebes, where they are generally called Bajau or Badjaw (3) the Moluccan islands, particularly Batjan and Obi, and also along the northern coasts of Flores, Sumbawa, and Adonara. [The Bajau Laut of Borneo are related linguistically to Samal-speaking peoples scattered throughout the Sulu Archipelago and beyond to southern Mindanao; they are therefore included in Volume 2, along with other Philippine groups bordering the Sulu Sea.] As might be expected, population statistics are highly unreliable. Sopher (1965: 174) estimates a total in the midnineteenth century of some 20,000, including the Orang Laut of Malaya. Since that time, however, their numbers have undoubtedly declined, in part because of an increasing tendency to adopt a sedentary existence on land, a process whereby their ethnic identity as boat people is lost as they become assimilated within established coastal populations. It is likely that the number of true boat nomads is relatively small at present and that the few remaining groups still oriented to this way of life will soon disappear as distinct ethnic entities.

BIBLIOGRAPHY. Hagen 1908b; Kähler 1960; Kennedy 1935; Nimmo 1968; Sopher 1965 [bibliography, pp. 389-403]; van Verschuer 1883.

COASTAL MALAYS

The greatest concentration of Malay speakers is in the area of the Malay Peninsula (West Malaysia) and along the neighboring coast of eastern Sumatra, including the intermediate islands of the Riau-Lingga Archipelago. They are sometimes referred to as Riau Malays, although their identification with historic coastal principalities throughout Indonesia and north into the Sulu Sea, together with their characteristic association with maritime pursuits, may make the term "coastal Malays" more appropriate. Locally, these people are most often known by the name of a former coastal principality with which they identify historically, e.g. on Borneo the Brunei, Sarawak, Sambas, or Kutei Malays; on Sumatra, the Djambi, Siak, or Benkulen Malays. Kennedy (1935: 145) estimated the number of coastal Malays in the whole of the Indonesian Archipelago at between four and five million. Malays were very early involved in the European spice trade and in the subsequent spread throughout Indonesia of the Malay language as a lingua franca. They were likewise most closely identified with the propagation of Islam that accompanied the founding of coastal principalities as far east as Ternate and Batjan. A Pasisir (Malay, "coastal") culture—an amalgam of Malay, Javanese, Macassarese, Arabic, and Indian elements—arose in these trading centers and was subsequently diffused throughout the archipelago; nowadays it is characteristic of most of Indonesia's coastal and urban population centers (H. Geertz 1963). Aside from its strong Islamic content and a generalized orientation to marketing activities, this Pasisir culture type is difficult to characterize in specific terms. Economic pursuits are likely to be highly variable, and social relationships are seldom structured in terms of well-defined categories of kinsmen. This generalized diffuseness pertains also to the physical components of these coastal populations, the result of a long process of "Malayanization" of indigenous peoples—of *masok melayu* ("becoming Malay"), i.e. adopting the Malay language and the Muhammedan religion. The term "Para-Malay" has been suggested for groups in Sarawak currently undergoing this assimilation process (Leach 1950). Thus the problem of specifying, in either physical or cultural terms, what is or is not "Malay" can be a complex one. On linguistic grounds, too, the situation is complicated by the existence of inland or mountain peoples who may lack some or all of the classic characteristics of Malay culture, but who speak dialects closely related to those of the Riau or coastal Malays, e.g. the Minangkabau of Sumatra and the Iban of Sarawak (cf. Dyen 1965; Cense and Uhlenbeck 1958). On Borneo, non-Muslim speakers of Iban and certain other "Malayic Dayak" languages are supposed by Hudson (1970) to represent a category similar to the "aboriginal Malays" of Malaya—people whose ancestors arrived on Borneo prior to the spread of Islam in Southeast Asia. The Minangkabau are supposed by Kennedy (1935: 143) to have originally been one people with the Malays of Malaya and eastern Sumatra, with centuries of relative isolation in the western Sumatran highlands producing the distinctive Minangkabau culture type.

BIBLIOGRAPHY. Cense and Uhlenbeck 1958; Dyen 1965; H. Geertz 1963; Gullick 1958; Harrisson 1970; Hudson 1970; Kennedy 1935, 1955d; Leach 1950; Wilken 1893: 352-89.

CHINESE

Overseas Chinese in the Indonesian Archipelago (including Malaysian Borneo) number close to three million, and as such constitute by far the largest and most important alien category within the population. They are found throughout the Archipelago, chiefly in port cities and towns, with the largest concentrations occurring in Java, eastern Sumatra and western Borneo. In Malaysian Borneo (Sarawak and Sabah), the proportion of Chinese to the total population is significantly larger than in the Republic of Indonesia. Chinese merchants have been in Indonesia for centuries, but wholesale immigration commenced only in the latter half of the nineteenth century, as part of the Dutch colonial policy of recruiting alien labor for plantations and mines. These early immigrants were single males, chiefly Hokkien and Hakka speakers from Fukien and Kwangtung provinces in South China. The Dutch also encouraged expansion of the Chinese into middle-level commercial and financial sectors, but it was not until the twentieth century that Chinese women were permitted to emigrate to Indonesia in significant numbers. These historical factors, in particular the extensive intermarriage of Chinese males with indigenous females in the early years, complicate the modern definition of "Chinese," e.g. for census purposes. There are persons of Chinese ancestry who nevertheless speak and behave as Indonesians, while others retain the Chinese surname and dialect and to all intents live as Chinese. The position of any one community on this assimilation continuum is likely to be a function of the recency of recruitment into it of China-born females. The older communities, e.g. those on Java, are made up largely of locally-born individuals of only part Chinese ancestry. These *peranakan* Chinese are relatively more assimilated (de-Sinicized) and tend to identify their future with that of Indonesia. By contrast, communities of *totok* Chinese, largely persons born in China or of recent Chinese ancestry, tend to be less assimilated to Indonesian ways and more China-oriented. The two categories differ in their life styles and value systems (Skinner 1963). Since Independence, the status of the overseas Chinese has been uncertain. Government policies have been largely restrictive and repressive, and anti-Chinese sentiments, exacerbated by the favored position of the Chinese under the Dutch, have flared into open violence, e.g. in connection with the anti-communist riots of 1965. Many Chinese now residing in Indonesia are without clearly defined citizenship status, a problem which continues to vex the new nations of Southeast Asia with large communities of overseas Chinese.

BIBLIOGRAPHY. Fortier 1964; Leigh 1964; Ryan 1961; Skinner 1963 [see annotated bibliography, pp. 494-98]; T'ien Ju-k'ang 1953; Williams 1960; Willmott 1960, 1961.

SUMATRA

THE DIVERSITY of existing cultures on Sumatra and its outlying islands is remarkable even for Indonesia. The reasons are many, but certainly the facts of geography and their implications for historic contacts and internal development need to be considered. Sumatra's northern tip faces India and the west, while much of the island's eastern littoral borders the Strait of Malacca, a natural gateway to Java and the China Sea. Trade, mediated initially by Indian merchants, favored the development of coastal Hinduized city states, culminating in the tenth-century kingdom of Srivijaya on the site of modern Palembang (cf. Coedès 1968; Wheatley 1964). With these developments came Buddhism, court Brahmanism, and new religious, political, and legal concepts which were to transform the indigenous coastal chieftaincies but which also found their way by degrees into the tribal societies of the interior highlands. Later on, Arab, Portuguese, and Dutch influences—in particular Islam and Christianity—added diverse new elements to the cultural mix. Geography contributed also to regional isolation, itself an important factor in the evolution of cultural diversity. The narrow western littoral rises steeply to the rugged Barisan Range, where a series of lakes set in fertile volcanic plateaus—from Toba in the north to Ranau in the south—favored the development of a chain of distinctive highland cultures. Here intensive agriculture, coupled with fishing, supported sizable indigenous populations which were viable enough, culturally speaking, to resist wholesale conversion to ideas emanating from the lowlands. The outlying islands of Nias, Mentawei, and Enggano, by virtue of their remote location, also resisted cultural absorption until modern times. Thus autochthonous cultures on Sumatra have until recent times survived and proliferated, enriched by what they borrowed from Hindu and Islamic coastal culture but in each case absorbing and reshaping according to an indigenous idiom—and without in the process losing their ethnic identity. There are, however, evident underlying similarities amidst this diversity—in particular among the non-Malay peoples with respect to descent systems, marriage patterns, and political arrangements. According to some, these similarities reflect fundamental patterns, e.g. the idea of phratry dualism, common to a wide area and perhaps part of an early proto-Malay (Indonesian) stratum (cf. de Josselin de Jong 1951). According to others, they are more likely a reflection of the widespread diffusion of elements of Hindu culture. The comparative ethnology of Sumatra and adjacent regions has as yet no final answers to such questions. Kennedy (1935), on the basis mainly of similarities in language and culture, was able to group the peoples of Sumatra into ten major categories: Atjehnese, Gayo-Alas, Batak, Minangkabau, Riau Malay, Redjang-Lampong, Kubu, Nias, Mentawei, and Enggano. His classification, which more or less parallels that adopted by the Dutch census (*Volkstelling 1930*), by the linguist Esser (1938), and by the ethnologist Loeb (1935), has been followed in general in the present compilation, with the major exception of his Redjang-Lampong category. Here recent field data, unavailable to Kennedy, have been drawn upon by two contributing authors to make possible a finer classification of peoples in the Pasemah-Redjang highlands versus the Abung and other peoples in the Lampung districts. Kennedy's Riau Malays—the Palembang, Djambi, Benkuelen, and other Malays of Sumatra's old coastal Malay states—are treated elsewhere in this volume under the more general heading of Coastal Malays.

BIBLIOGRAPHY. Coedès 1968; Esser 1938; de Josselin de Jong 1951; Kennedy 1935; Loeb 1935; *Volkstelling 1930*; Wheatley 1964.

ATJEHNESE

Synonyms. *Achehnese, Achinese, Atchinese*

ORIENTATION. **Identification.** The Atjehnese are the native inhabitants of the modern Indonesian province of Atjeh, in northernmost Sumatra. They have been divided by some into hill people (*ureueng tunong*) and lowland people (*ureueng baroh*) on the basis of physical type and minor cultural differences. Racially, they are a product of many centuries of interbreeding of indigenes with Bataks, Hindus, Dravidians, Javanese, Arabs, Chinese, and Niasan slaves. No good anthropometric data exist, but observers agree that there is considerable physical divergence between the inland population, of a fairly homogeneous proto-Malay type, and the coastal Atjehnese, who are physically quite heterogeneous, although relatively slim, tall, and almost Caucasoid in appearance. [Kennedy 1935.] **Location.** The entire northern end of Sumatra. The Atjehnese divide the country into four regions, including Atjeh proper (Great Atjeh) at the extreme northern tip. Settlement follows the coastline, penetrating inland where rivers permit. The central region is largely waste mountain land and unpopulated, except around the few fertile valleys and plateaus, where there are coffee plantations and settlements of the Gayo peoples (Siegel 1969: 14). **Linguistic affiliation.** The Voegelins, following Dyen, classify Achinese as a group of the Malay subfamily of the Indonesian branch of Austronesian. Notable are the many evidences of similarity to the Cham languages of Indochina. [Voegelin and Voegelin 1964: 59, 66; 1965: 4.] **Demography.** The province of Atjeh in 1969 had a population of about 2,000,000, 90 percent of which was ethnically Atjehnese (Siegel 1969: 6). **History.** Chinese sources dating from as early as 500 A.D. contain references to the kingdom of Poli in North Sumatra, within the present bounds of Atjeh, which apparently was ruled by Buddhists of Indian extraction. In the middle of the fourteenth century, Ibn Batuta found at Pasè a flourishing Islamic state, which had evidently been in existence for some time before his arrival. By the beginning of the sixteenth century, the center of power had moved to the valley of the Atjeh River, and from 1507 until the beginning of the twentieth century a long line of sultans existed here, whose domain at some periods extended over most of Sumatra, but whose actual power was quite limited outside the confines of Great Atjeh. The last of the sultans, Tuanku Muhamat Dawot, surrendered to the Dutch in 1903, after a war of more than 30 years. However, unrest continued, and the Dutch kept a military government in the area until 1918. The Dutch did not return to Atjeh after World War II, and from 1945 until the transfer of sovereignty to Indonesia in 1949, Atjeh was ruled chiefly by Daud Beureueh, the leader of the Islamic modernist movement. For various reasons Atjeh was in rebellion from 1953 until 1961, when it became a province of Indonesia. Because of its geographical position, Ajteh has been heavily engaged in foreign trade for more than a thousand years, particularly with Malaya across the Strait of Malacca, and ultimately with China and India. [Kennedy 1935; Siegel 1969.]

SETTLEMENT PATTERN AND HOUSING. **Settlement pattern.** The village usually lies in the middle of a rice field complex, the houses hidden from view by foliage. On the north coast, in the vicinity of Pidië, villages may consist of clusters of houses owned by sisters and aunts (mother's sisters). The size of this cluster depends on the size of the family and the availability of land (Siegel 1966: 48). Each village has one or more communal houses (*meunasah*), large pile-raised structures open on all sides, which are used for prayer, as sleeping places for young men, as guesthouses for strangers, as schools, and for public ceremonies. Each house in the village is said to be associated with a *meunasah* (Siegel 1969: 141). Loeb (1935: 221) notes that on the north coast it is the *meunasah* and its associated houses that make up the smallest territorial unit. Depending on the size of the population, a village may contain a mosque, or a mosque may be associated with neighboring villages, but lie outside them (Snouck Hurgronje 1906: 1, 34-35; Loeb 1935: 222). **Housing.** According to Kennedy (1935: 26), houses may be multifamily dwellings, with annexes added to the original houses or built separately within the same compound. However, in Pidië every married woman owns her own house (Siegel 1969: 141). Houses are raised on piles about six feet above the ground, with walls of planks or bamboo and thatched roofs of sago or nipa-palm leaves. The ground plan is rectangular, the roof a two-slope gable type, with the gable ends oriented east and west. Chiefs and wealthy people have larger and more costly houses with room for daughters, while poorer people generally erect an annex for married daughters. [Kennedy 1935: 26-27; Loeb 1935: 220; Snouck Hurgronje 1906: 1, 34-41.]

ECONOMY. The Atjehnese are essentially agriculturalists. Hunting is unimportant as a food source, but fishing is an important occupation along the coast and in the rivers. Herding of cattle and buffalo is carried on as a subsidiary occupation to rice growing. **Agriculture.** Rice is the main crop and forms the chief article of diet. Both wet- and dry-rice culture are carried on, the former predominating in the lowlands, the latter in the hills. Wet-rice fields are laid out in swampy areas, the water being retained in the fields after rains by dams and dikes of heaped-up earth; only in the Pidië valley is irrigation from streams used to any extent. Plowing is done with the aid of cattle or water buffalo. Rice, sugarcane, maize, tobacco, rubber, pepper, ground nuts, areca nuts, and coconuts are the main crops, with coffee becoming popular in the eastern highlands around Lake Tawar. It was largely due to the great pepper demand of the seventeenth and eighteenth centuries that the east and west coasts were thoroughly settled. [Siegel 1969; Kennedy 1935; Snouck Hurgronje 1906: 1, 260, 273.] **Hunting and fishing.** Fishing with casting-nets, seines, lines, and traps. Along the north coast, the beach is sectioned among guilds of professionals (*pawang*), each guild with its own chief. Each *pawang* has his own boat and crew, all sharing in the proceeds. [Snouck Hurgronje 1906: *1*, 280; Kennedy 1935: 25.] **Industrial arts.** Metal work is well known, and the weapons made by the Atjehnese are especially fine. Gold and silver work is carried on extensively. Cotton and silk fabrics of high quality are woven by the women, who formerly also made a good, unglazed pottery. Boat building was important through the nineteenth century. **Trade.** "The extent of trade and Atjehnese reliance on it for the needs of everyday life is striking" (Siegel 1966: 7). The most heavily trafficked markets are those at the mouths of navigable rivers, since the latter are the principal means of access to the interior. The more important villages have markets consisting of an open space or short road flanked by rows of shops under a single roof. The *uleebalang* formerly derived much of their income from the control of these markets. **Property.** Snouck Hurgronje (1906: *1*, 285) notes that rights to all that the primary jungle contains arise only through clearing; the right to a cleared plantation is lost as soon as all traces of the clearing have disappeared. Rice fields and gardens always belong to one particular village. The associated land includes *umong* (padi fields) and *padang* (noncultivated land). *Umongs* become personal property, but gardens in the *padang* do not.

KIN GROUPS. Descent in the coastal lowlands is reckoned bilaterally. There is (or was) a sib organization, about which there has been much controversy. In the coastal regions the sibs are probably no longer functioning, but in the more backward upland districts they were still in force in 1935, although rapidly losing significance (Kennedy 1935: 36). The sibs are called *kawoms*. Membership was reckoned patrilineally, common descent being traced from a male ancestor. There were four great sibs, one of which may once have been composed of four sibs which united. In places where the sib system still functioned, intermarriage was not allowed between members of this latter sib and the other three, leading to something resembling a moiety or caste system. The sibs functioned mainly in matters of blood revenge and responsibility for fines. Kennedy (1935: 37) notes that Snouck Hurgronje believed they represented a very ancient form of Atjehnese organization, basically patrilineal, and that the bilateral system with matrilineal preference existing in the lowlands was a product of later development. While the Atjehnese Hawaiian-type kin terminology does not distinguish between relatives traced through the mother and those traced through the father, they do have terms for these two groups. Paternal relatives are termed *wali*, maternal relatives *karong*. Since residence is generally uxorilocal, and

since a large percentage of men marry into villages other than the one into which they were born, the two groups are locally distinct (Siegel 1969: 138). The main characteristic of the kin terms, aside from the perfectly symmetrical bilateral reckoning, is the sharp distinction between older and younger relatives on the same generation levels (Kennedy 1935: 39). Snouck Hurgronje (1893: *1*, 504-06) lists kin terms for Great Atjeh.

MARRIAGE AND FAMILY. **Mode.** Islamic marriage rules are followed, except where they conflict with adat. The groom and the bride's representative meet usually in the *meunasah* in the presence of witnesses, and the groom delivers the bride-price (*jinamèe*) to bind the contract. Adat marriage takes place in the bride's home, the ceremony including a large number of formal observances, processions, feasting, and magical practices such as exorcising evil spirits. The "common meal" of the bride and groom seems to be the focal point of the ceremony. [Kennedy 1935: 34.] **Form.** In return for the bride-price, the bride's parents support her and her children, including the provision of a house, for a certain number of years according to the amount of the bride-price paid—either to the birth of the first child or for three to four years. Polygamy is not a general practice except among the upper classes and the rich. **Marriage rules.** In accordance with Muhammadan law, marriage is forbidden with relatives in the direct ascending or descending line, as well as with collateral kinsmen to the third degree of relationship. There are, however, many cases of first cousins marrying, but this is considered very unlucky, especially if they are parallel cousins. **Residence.** In Great Atjeh, residence is uxorilocal. After marriage the bride remains in the house of her family or in another nearby which is built for her by her parents, her husband coming to live with her there. The husband always considers his mother's family's village his real home. Villages are not exogamic, and the chiefs encourage intravillage mating. When the latter occurs, the house of his mother's family is the husband's home; however, he sleeps in the village *meunasah* on nights when he is not staying with his wife. In Pasè, on the northeast coast, the decision as to whether residence will be uxorilocal or virilocal depends on the financial situation. If the girl's father happens to be rich, he will probably transfer some of his land to the couple and build a house for them. In Tamiang, the husband goes to live with his wife if she is an heiress, or if no bride-price is paid. He may transfer his residence if within seven days after marriage he accepts a refund of one half the bride-price from his father-in-law. In Pidië, a large percentage of the male heads of families are away for extended periods, trading or growing coffee, coming home generally for Ramadan. [Kennedy 1935: 32-33; Siegel 1969: 141.] **Household.** The nature of the domestic unit seems to depend on the wealth of the parents involved. In Pidië, if the wife's parents are wealthy enough, they build a separate house for the daughter and her children (Siegel 1969: 51-52). Where the parents are poor, the wife generally remains in the same house with her parents, with the husband visiting—a situation resembling the extended family. **Inheritance.** Children inherit from both parents, the daughters usually receiving the house, the sons the rice fields. Inheritance follows Islamic law, with two shares going to males for each one share going to females, modified by the practice of giving women houses at the time of marriage. The result is to give the bulk of village land resources to the men. However, regardless of the ownership of the land, control is generally in the hands of the women, since the men are so often away. [Snouck Hurgronje 1906: *1*, 434-39; Siegel 1969: 139-40, 145-46.] **Divorce.** Although Snouck Hurgronje believes that divorce is less frequent in Atjeh than in other parts of Indonesia, Siegel (1969: 174) states that in Pidië 50 percent of the marriages end in divorce. Jacobs (1894) also reported divorce very frequent, some women being married 10 to 15 times. According to Kennedy (1935: 35), if a wife dies during the period she is being supported by her parents, her husband either receives a refund of half the bride-price or is given a sister or near relative of his deceased wife as a substitute. On the other hand, the widow of a man is almost always taken over by one of her deceased husband's male relatives (Snouck Hurgronje 1906: *1*, 364).

SOCIOPOLITICAL ORGANIZATION. **Political organization.** Political organization is based on a series of territorial divisions, the smallest being the village. There is a village chief (*keuchi*) as well as a religious chief, *teungku*, the latter an administrator of Islamic law. The *keuchi* has charge of all matters relating to family law, rice culture, housing, and meat distribution at village feasts. A council of elders, composed of mature male villagers, meets with the *keuchi* and the *teungku*. The latter two offices are elective, but tend to be hereditary in the male line. Above the village is the district, *mukim*, composed of several villages, all the men of which worship in a common mosque. The chief officer of the *mukim* is the chief priest (*imeum*), in practice an administrative position, although theoretically a religious office only. Above the *mukim* was a larger district ruled by the *uleebalang*, whose office was hereditary in the male line. These districts were composed of several villages and/or *mukim*, and were quite autonomous. According to Siegel (1969), the rights of the *uleebalang* were concerned primarily with trade. Their revenues derived from control of markets rather than the administration of justice, and they actually had little contact with the villagers whom they supposedly ruled. The *uleebalang* were retained by the Dutch as administrative officers; most of them were slain in the 1945-46 rebellion. In Great Atjeh, there were three major confederations called the three *sagi*, or corners, of Atjeh, also called the XXII Mukims, the XXV Mukims, and the XXVI Mukims, after the number of *mukim* in each. At the head of each confederation was an elected *panglima sagi*. Formerly these confederations functioned mainly in war and in support of the sultanate. The sultan, whose power was nebulous outside the region of the three *sagi*, lived in Kota Radja, the chief port on the northern tip of Sumatra, until dispossessed by the Dutch. The office was normally hereditary in the direct male line. In recent times there have been few privileges inherent in the sultanate, and the running of the country has been in the hands of the *uleebalang*. **Social differentiation.** Nineteenth-century Atjehnese society appears to have been stratified in terms of royalty, nobility, peasantry, and a mobile religious group, plus slaves. As Siegel (1969: 11) states: "Atjeh was not a society bifurcated into Islamic and customary elements, but one divided into four groups—*uleebalang*, *ulama* [religious scholars], peasants, and the sultan and his group—each of which had its own view of the nature of Islam and adat." The chiefs, the peasants, and the sultan were all born to their state, while the *ulama* status was achieved by men leaving village and kin relationships for the different relationships achieved by uniting as Muslims in the religious schools. Only the *ulama* and the peasants or equivalent groups are now left, and the division may actually be between wealthy and not wealthy, although there is little information on this. Foreigners were, and perhaps still are, treated as a special category to be taken advantage of. **Social control.** Snouck Hurgronje called Atjeh a "land of polyarchy and misrule." Adat and the Islamic religious law (*hukom*) supposedly ruled side by side, but adat played by far the greater role in practice. There was no formal judicial system. The village chiefs and the *imeum* of the *mukim* were essentially arbitrators and could hand down few final decisions. The *kawom*, where they existed, took care of disputes concerning bodily injuries, hurt, or manslaughter. The *uleebalang* theoretically acted as final judges in important matters, although litigants rarely took cases before them because of the high costs involved. Ordeals and oaths had some part in the administration of justice, the most common ordeal being the gradual tightening of a cord around the thigh of the suspect. **Warfare.** The state of Atjeh waged war periodically on neighboring states during the sixteenth through eighteenth centuries. A sort of guerrilla warfare was waged, mainly under the direction of the *ulama*, during the great Atjeh war of 1873-1903 against the Dutch. There is record of slaving expeditions, particularly to the island of Nias.

RELIGION. Of Islam's "five pillars of faith," the Atjehnese is zealous in his adherence to three: the *haj*, or pilgrimage to Mecca; the *zakat* (*pitrah*), tax or tithe; and the *puasa*, or fast in the month of Ramadan (Kennedy 1935: 41). According to Kennedy, the saying of ritual prayers is much neglected, although Siegel (1969: 104) disagrees. The confession of faith is adhered to properly so far as reading the Koran and learning the laws are concerned, but heretical, pantheistic mysticism is widespread (Snouck Hurgronje 1906: 2, 281-83). Kennedy also notes that the graves of famous mystics are the objects of pilgrimages from all over Atjeh. Indigenous beliefs and superstitions persist in a weakened form. Exorcistic practices, e.g. "cooling" the individuals involved, are part of most ceremonies. Magical practices are employed in agriculture and other activities, and interpretation of dreams and omens is widespread. Sickness is attributed to the influence of evil spirits and is generally cured by magical means. A form of shamanism seems confined to females. Funeral practices are generally Muhammadan. The body is washed and wrapped in a shroud, a ritual service held, and burial takes place. A notable institution is the *bhom*, or family burial place. Children are taken to the burial ground of their father's family for interment. [Kennedy 1935.]

BIBLIOGRAPHY. Drewes and Voorhoeve 1958; Snouck Hurgronje 1893, 1906; Jacobs 1894; Kennedy 1935; Kreemer 1922-23; Loeb 1935; Siegel 1966, 1969; Voegelin and Voegelin 1964, 1965; Veth 1873.

GAYO

Synonym. *Gajo*

ORIENTATION. The Gayo highlands of northern interior Sumatra lie within the modern province of Atjeh, bounded on the north, east, and west by coastal Atjehnese and on the south by Batak highlanders. Under the Dutch, the Gayolands were divided into the administrative districts of Tamiang, Takingeun, Serbudjadi, Gajo Loeos, and Alas. The indigenous population, numbering in 1930 some 50,000 and located chiefly in the lake plains and river valleys around and southeast of Lake Tawar, is generally referred to under the term Gayo (Gajo). The Alas are a minority group in the Alas Valley of the southern Gayolands. Kennedy (1935: 44ff.) regarded the Gayo-Alas peoples as representative of an early proto-Malay stratum, closely related to Batak. Linguistically, Gayo appears close to Batak (Dyen 1965), and Voorhoeve, in fact, regards Alas as a northern dialect of Batak (Voorhoeve 1955: 13). Until the twentieth century, the Gayolands remained isolated from contact with Westerners, although their independent village states had earlier been conquered by coastal Atjeh and rendered vassals of the Atjeh sultans. Borrowings from Atjehnese are evident in the language, marriage customs, housing, and other aspects of the culture. Information on Gayo culture stems mainly from the reports of early Dutch administrators (cf. Kreemer 1922-23; Palmer van den Broek 1936; Beets 1933; Snouck Hurgronje 1903); however, the culture of these isolated highlanders has yet to be studied at first hand by a trained investigator familiar with the language. The reports by Kennedy (1935) and Loeb (1935) are both secondary compilations.

SETTLEMENT PATTERN AND HOUSING. Generally similar to Batak. Rectangular, raised, multi-family houses, *umah*, containing up to 60 persons, with men's and women's galleries front and back and sleeping quarters, *bileq*, in the center. Houses may be arranged close together within fortified villages or in a more scattered, hamletlike pattern. Villages frequently house members of several patrilineal kin groups, segregated in separate wards, each with its own combination men's house-community pavilion, *meresah*. [Kennedy 1935; Loeb 1935.]

ECONOMY. Irrigated rice is grown in valley bottoms, while upland swiddens are planted to tobacco, maize, and various tuberous crops. Herding of cattle, buffalo, goats, and sheep is important. Technology and material culture generally similar to Batak, with evident borrowings from Atjehnese. [Kennedy 1935.]

SOCIAL ORGANIZATION. At the basis of the social order are localized segments of exogamous patrilineal sibs, *blah*; these also served as the basic indigenous political units. The sibs within a district are typically classed genealogically into a three-fold phratrylike division, with exogamy prescribed at the phratry level. It is not known whether this arrangement reflects an earlier pattern of circulating connubium; information on preferred or prescribed marriage partners, if any, is lacking. Marriage is almost entirely according to Islamic rules and preferences. [Kennedy 1935; Loeb 1935.]

RELIGION. The Gayo peoples are professed Muslims, conversion dating back to their seventeenth-century subjugation by the sultans of Atjeh. They continue, however, to believe in local spirits, transmigration of souls, the efficacy of omens, and similar remnants of an earlier animism. [Kennedy 1935.]

BIBLIOGRAPHY. Beets 1933; Dyen 1965; Kennedy 1935; Kreemer 1922-23; Loeb 1935; Palmer van den Broek 1936; Snouck Hurgronje 1903; Voorhoeve 1955.

BATAK

Synonyms. *Batta, Battak*

ORIENTATION. **Location and identification.** The Bataklands of interior north-central Sumatra occupy a high rolling plateau, surrounded by mountain peaks and centering on Lake Toba at approximately 2°30′ N. by 99° E. There are cultural, linguistic, and physical evidences of early Hindu contact, and in the past century there has been widespread conversion to Christianity. But despite these influences and the fact that they are surrounded by Islamic peoples—Atjehnese and Gayo to the north, Minangkabau to the south, Coastal Malays to the east—the Batak retained until recently a way of life characterized by Kennedy as the paradigm for all ancient proto-Malay cultures of the Indonesian Archipelago. In part, this may be explained by the factor of isolation, in turn related to an apparently well-earned reputation for ferocity and cannibalism (cf. Marsden 1966). • The Toba, in the area around Lake Toba in North Tapanuli, are the largest of several named Batak subgroups. Others include Angkola, Karo, Mandailing, Pakpak (Dairi), and Simalungun (Timur). All, according to Keuning (1958) and Kennedy (1935), speak what is essentially one language and share in an essentially similar culture pattern. All regard the Toba territory as the original Batak homeland. Consciousness of subgroup differences has been exacerbated by the creation of artificial administrative boundaries under the Dutch as well as by differential conversion to Christianity and Islam; as a result, the Toba, with the largest Christian population, find themselves opposed to other Batak on a variety of political, economic, and educational issues (cf. Keuning 1958; Cunningham 1958; Liddle 1967). Many Batak, principally Christianized Toba, have in recent decades migrated to East Sumatra, where those in urban centers hold positions as teachers, officials, clerks, and the like. In the period 1950-56 the number of such migrants amounted to some 250,000 (Cunningham 1958: vii). **Linguistic affiliation.** Dyen (1965) classes the Batak languages together as a subfamily within his West Indonesian Cluster of Malayo-Polynesian, thus related to Malay and Minangkabau but not closely coordinate; the closest immediate affinities seem to be with Gayo. Dialect differences, corresponding to named subgroups, are minimized by Keuning (1958: 2), although Voorhoeve (1955: 9) evidently regards them as more fundamental. There is an indigenous, Indian-derived script, either incised on bamboo or written on bark leaves bound in book form. Esoteric idioms are spoken at times by specialized status categories such as priests and female mourners (Kennedy 1935: 65-66). **Demography.** Bataks numbered slightly over 1,000,000 in 1930 (*Volkstelling 1930, 4:* 105). A 1961 estimate puts the figure at just over 2,000,000; the Toba Batak account for upward of one half of this total (Berzina and Bruk 1963). **History.** Kennedy viewed Batak culture as an amalgam of Indian elements superimposed on an old Proto-Malay foundation; although evidences of early Hindu contact are evident, its nature and extent are unknown. According to tradition, all Batak are descendants of Si Radja Batak, a hero-ancestor of supernatural parentage born on a holy mountain adjacent to Lake Toba. Through him the Batak received their sacred adat. His sons founded the first two *marga* (patrilineal sibs), from which are descended, by subsequent dispersal and subdivision, the present *marga* throughout the Bataklands. A long period of relative isolation was terminated in the nineteenth century, first by the spread of Islam from Minangkabau north to the Mandailing Bataks, and later, beginning about 1860, by the rapid spread of Protestant Christianity through the efforts of the Rheinische Mission. Western education, furthered by missionaries and by the Dutch colonial government, gained ground rapidly, particularly among the Toba. Colonies of these people are today located throughout Indonesia, and the Toba intelligentsia is well represented among the governing and professional elite of Djakarta. The traditional life persists most strongly among the Karo, in the hills north and west of Lake Toba, although even urbanized Toba in Medan attempt to follow the Batak adat and maintain lineage ties with their home villages in the highlands (Bruner 1961).

SETTLEMENT PATTERN AND HOUSING. **Settlement pattern.** Large villages occur only among the Karo and Mandailing. The Toba village, *huta*, consists of a main street bordered by from six to ten closely spaced, multifamily houses, the whole formerly surrounded with a palisade or earth rampart containing a tunnel-like entrance. Additional structures include rice barns and an open-sided communal hall, *sopo* or *bale*, which serves as council hall, trophy room, and sleeping place for boys and unmarried men. *Huta* appear formerly to have consisted of members of a single localized patrilineal kin group; nowadays a number of *huta* may be joined together into larger confederations containing members of several kin groups related by affinal or blood ties. **Housing.** Toba houses are raised on piles with access through a trapdoor in the floor. Roofs are high and saddle shaped and project for a considerable distance front and rear. Plank walls, gable ends, and main posts carry decorative carving, including carved buffalo horns. Mats and curtains serve to mark off the interior into sleeping quarters for married couples. [Kennedy 1935; Keuning 1958; H. Geertz 1963.]

ECONOMY. Primarily agricultural, with rice the chief crop. The fertile valleys around Lake Toba are the chief areas of irrigated wet-rice culture. Swidden rice, sweet potatoes, yams, and maize are important food crops in more infertile areas. Tobacco, sugarcane, fruits, and vegetables are also grown. Herding of water buffalo, cattle, and horses is an increasingly important economic pursuit in areas unsuited to agriculture. Fishing is confined mainly to Lake Toba. The traditional diet consisted of rice mixed with vegetables, dried fish, and spices; meat (pork, beef, buffalo, chicken, dog) was consumed only on ceremonial occasions. **Industries.** The traditional technology (highly skilled and artistically sophisticated) includes metalworking, wood carving, canoe making, weaving, tie-dyeing, and work in bone, shell, and bark. Batak subgroups are distinguished by differences in dress and personal ornamentation—the latter including massive silver earrings, shell armbands, and copper wire neck and arm rings. These crafts and customs are disappearing, however, as is the old habit of tooth filing and blackening. Tattooing is alleged to have been practiced formerly. Among the Karo, ironworking was accompanied by religious taboos and precautions. [Kennedy 1935.] **Trade.** Weekly markets are held in the chief towns of districts. Salt, dried fish, iron, and copper are imported from the coasts in exchange for forest products, horses, and vegetables. [Kennedy 1935.] **Property.** Descendants of the founders of a district, i.e. the *marga radja*, retain the right of eminent domain over village lands. Jurisdiction of this right is exercised by the village chief or an elder member of the *marga radja*. Individual families enjoy usufruct rights to such land; it can be patrilineally inherited within a family but never totally alienated by sale or gift. [Kennedy 1935: 86; Cunningham 1958: 20-21.]

KIN GROUPS. **Descent.** Patrilineal. **Descent groups.** A unilineal segmentary descent system, in which the term *marga* is used for nonlocalized maximal lineages (sibs) as well as for localized minimal lineages. The membership of a sib formerly inhabited a district (*marga*), consisting of a single village or village complex with surrounding lands, and functioned as a corporate, exogamous adat group. These latter characteristics nowadays pertain more often to the lineage than to the sib, although males continue to take as a surname the name of their sib. In each district, one sib is considered the "ruling sib," or *marga radja*, i.e. descendants of the founding ancestors. The Toba recognize two great *marga* complexes, Sumba and Lontung, which may reflect a former moietylike division of society with respect to marriage regulations and ritual observances. [Kennedy 1935; Keuning 1958; Loeb 1935; Cunningham 1958; Vergouwen 1964.] **Kinship terminology.** The following Toba terms of reference are taken from Cunningham (1958: 170); affinal terms are explored thoroughly in Fischer (1966). The cousin terminology is bifurcate merging in Murdock's typology:

GrFa	*ompung doli*	FaElBrSo	*ankang*
GrMo	*ompung boru*	FaYoBrSo	*anggi*
Fa	*amang*	FaBrDa	*ito*
Mo	*inang*	FaSiSo	*lae*
FaElBr	*amang tua*	FaSiDa	*ito*
FaYoBr	*amang uda*	MoBrSo	*lae*
FaSi	*namboru*	MoBrDa	*pariban*
MoElSi	*inang tua*	MoElSiSo	*ankang*
MoYoSi	*inang uda*	MoYoSiSo	*anggi*
MoBr	*tulang*	MoSiDa	*ito*
ElBr	*ankang*		
YoBr	*anggi*		
Si	*ito*		

MARRIAGE AND FAMILY. **Mode.** Premarital chastity is not highly valued. Mandailing Batak girls sleep in special houses presided over by older women, where formalized visiting by boys includes dancing and poetry contests between the sexes. Infant betrothal is marked by an exchange of gifts, and the wedding ceremony, presided over by the village chief, by payment of a bride-price (formerly rice or cattle). The amount of a girl's bride-price depends on that of her mother (Kennedy 1935). **Form.** Polygyny occurs rarely among commoners, but is more frequent among chiefly lineages. **Marriage rules.** The sib is theoretically exogamous, although actual exogamy may nowadays be restricted to lineages. Preferred marriage is with the MoBrDa, an important element in Batak adat being a system of asymmetrical connubium in which lineages are related as "bride-givers" (Toba, *hula-hula*) or "bride-takers" (Toba, *boru*). This relationship between any two lineages is maintained by frequent exchange of gifts and food—symbolic of a dualistic world view expressed both in ritual and social structure (cf. Vergouwen 1964). At marriage a man acquires, by virtue of this relationship, fixed consanguineal and affinal ties which give him full civil status within the adat community; prior to marriage a Batak is said to "have no adat" (Kennedy 1935: 83). **Residence.** Normally patrilocal, although temporary bride service in the home of the girl's father occurs in cases where the full bride-price cannot be met. *Ambil anak* marriage occurs rarely (Kennedy 1935). **Domestic unit.** The basic domestic unit is the nuclear family living either in a single family dwelling or, in the case of traditional adat houses, in multifamily dwellings. Among the Karo these average from four to eight families per dwelling. [Singarimbun 1967; Kennedy 1935.] **Inheritance.** Patrilineal, with preference to eldest and youngest sons. **Divorce and secondary marriage.** Divorce was apparently difficult and statistically rare in former times. The death of a spouse normally results in either the levirate or sororate pattern of secondary marriage (Kennedy 1935: 90-91).

SOCIOPOLITICAL ORGANIZATION. **Political organization.** Traditionally the village chief, *radja huta*, was a member of the "ruling sib" (*marga radja*) of the district. He was assisted by two functionaries, one a member of his own kin group (usually a brother) the other a member of the kin group standing in the relation of "bride-givers" to his own group. A village council met in the village *sopo* in the presence of assembled villagers. Confederations of villages occurred among the Karo; and the Simalungun were at one time governed by chiefly families who ruled large territorial units or districts in despotic fashion. Thus the Batak had developed some measure of supra-village government in pre-Dutch times, and Loeb (1935: 43) has characterized them as "well on the way to the construction of petty states." These developments were, however, sporadic; in general the indigenous political system has been integrated at the village or village complex level and has been democratic rather than despotic or aristocratic. Leadership has always been more a matter of individual ability than of inherited status (Keuning 1958: 8). ● Under the Dutch, villages were combined into administrative kampongs, and appointed officials tended in time to usurp the powers of the old adat chiefs. Higher level administrative units, e.g. *negeri*, tended to combine under one authority numbers of the old kin-based territorial units, with the result that appointment to higher level chieftainships was a continual source of trouble for Dutch administrators (Keuning 1958: 16ff.). As part of the Republic of Indonesia, the Bataklands fall within the province of North Sumatra with its administrative capital in Medan, the majority of Bataks being within the two districts (*kabupaten*) of North and South Tapanuli. **Social differentiation.** Marked class differences have been in evidence only among the Simalungun and Mandailing—the two regions in which early Hindu influence seems to have been strongest. In these areas, chiefs (radjas) were able to gain wealth by cattle trading and purchase of slaves as field hands (Loeb 1935: 38-39). In these and some other parts of the Bataklands, only chiefs were entitled to own slaves or engage in polygyny. Thus there was in some districts what amounted to a chiefly aristocracy; in addition, chiefly status could everywhere be claimed by those who could demonstrate membership in a *marga radja*. However, chiefly status was nowhere rigidly hereditary, and leadership was attained by demonstrated ability—not ascribed by birth. Slavery (chiefly of war captives and debtors) was formerly widespread, although the status and treatment of slaves varied among the different Batak subgroups, being most repressive among the Simalungun. [Kennedy 1935; Loeb 1935.] **Social control.** According to Keuning (1958: 8), the Toba are a proud people and prone to litigation. Prior to the introduction of law courts by the Dutch, justice was administered by a panel of chiefs sitting in the village *sopo*. Oratorical skill in the presentation of evidence and the administrating of oaths and ordeals were important features of the traditional system. The supreme insult and the most degrading of all punishments was reserved for major violations of the adat, e.g. incest: those judged guilty of such crimes were condemned to be eaten by their fellow villagers. Lesser crimes were punished by fines or banishment. [Kennedy 1935.] **Warfare.** Among the Toba, disputes over land formerly led to bloody feuds; these most often took the form of brief skirmishes and guerrilla raids on fortified villages, although occasionally they were settled by duels between champions representing opposing forces. Captives were enslaved or eaten. Cannibalism, most prevalent among the Pakpak, was restricted to war captives or those judged guilty of major violations of the adat. Generally, only token bits of flesh were eaten. The heads and hands of war captives were on occasion preserved as trophies. Weapons consisted chiefly of spears, knives, swords, shields, and muskets; the bow, the sling, and the blowgun were used, but only for hunting birds. Villages were elaborately fortified with earthen ramparts, traps, pitfalls, and the like. [Kennedy 1935.]

RELIGION. Christianity has made great inroads, in particular among the Toba, and Islam has penetrated the southern portions of the Bataklands. Nevertheless indigenous religious beliefs persist, chiefly among the Karo. The summary of the traditional religion that follows is taken principally from Kennedy (1935), who in turn made use of the publications of Winkler (1925), Joustra (1926), Tideman (1922), Vergouwen (1933), Warneck (1909), and Ypes (1932). **Supernaturals.** A pantheon of higher deities, of obvious Hindu origin, is supported by an elaborate cosmology and mythology. These aspects, however, play a relatively minor role in everyday life; more important are the spirits of departed ancestors, *begu*, the propitiation of which forms the basis of a developed ancestor cult. The *begu* of wealthy or powerful individuals attain revered and exalted status in the spirit world by virtue of sacrificial ceremonies performed by living descendants. As such, they are eminently helpful to the living in combating a host of lesser ghosts and spirits, most of which are malevolent in nature. **Practitioners.** Male priests, *datu*, are specialists in occult knowledge, which they gain through a rigorous apprenticeship. They prepare talismans and protective devices, including carved human figures; are experts at divination, using a Hindu-derived zodiac and magical tables; and are skilled in sorcery through the use of natural poisons (Loeb 1935). To contact spirits of the dead, priests employ female mediums, *sibaso*, who, through dancing, inhaling incense, and beating drums and gongs, induce a trance state and spirit possession. These shamanistic practices, employed in cases of illness, are aided by the priest, who chants in a special language to induce the spirit to enter the body of the medium. **Ceremonies.** Primarily animal sacrifices, including the sacrifice of a sacred breed of horses. The most important rites, for the ancestral spirits, are on ordinary occasions performed by a housefather for members of his household. Larger ceremonies, honoring especially revered ancestors of high status, are carried out by priests on behalf of large genealogical units. Public ceremonies at times of crises are conducted by priests and chiefs within the framework of the *bius*, a territorial-political entity not necessarily equivalent to a single genealogical unit (Vergouwen 1964). **Soul, death, and afterlife.** The Batak believe that *tondi* is the vital force or "soul-stuff" in all persons and also in rice and iron. *Tondi* has a life and will of its own; it can leave its host body temporarily or permanently, in which latter case death ensues. Much effort of a religious nature is expended in keeping one's *tondi* in a contented state, since temporal wealth and power are associated with quantity and quality of *tondi*. At death one's *tondi* departs to dwell in another organism, while what is left of the deceased's essential being becomes a *begu*, or spirit. Unless raised to exalted status by the efforts of living descendants, *begu* remain envious of man and potentially dangerous; they must be dealt with magically lest they harm the living by capturing or enticing away *tondi*. Cremation occurs among some Karo and Pakpak groups; the body, encased in an elaborate coffin, is left on a platform for upward of a year, after which the entire structure is burned. The charred remains of cremated persons are periodically collected in small jars, placed on miniature boats, and floated down river. Such rites are expensive and limited to the wealthy. The bodies of influential or wealthy persons among other Batak subgroups are customarily kept in a boat-shaped coffin above ground for a year or more, during which time the body fluids are allowed to drain off through a hole in the coffin. The bones may be treated to repeated secondary burial rites, and, among some groups, the skulls are preserved in baskets attached to high poles. The bodies of commoners are most often wrapped in mats and buried in the ground. The Batak conception of an afterlife is somewhat vague, but consists in general of a life much like that enjoyed by the deceased on earth.

BIBLIOGRAPHY. Berzina and Bruk 1963; Bruner 1961; Cunningham 1958; Dyen 1965; Fischer 1966; H. Geertz 1963; Joustra 1926; Kennedy 1935; Keuning 1953-54, 1958; Korn 1953; Liddle 1967; Loeb 1935; Marsden 1966; Singarimbun 1967; Tideman 1922; Tobing 1963; Vergouwen 1933, 1964; *Volkstelling 1930*; Voorhoeve 1955; Warneck 1909; Winkler 1925; Ypes 1932.

MINANGKABAU*

Synonyms. *Menangkabau, Urang Padang, Urang Awak*

ORIENTATION. **Identification and location.** The Minangkabau (rarely, Menangkabau) are matrilineal Muslims whose traditional homeland is the highlands of west-central Sumatra, but who are also found scattered throughout the Indonesian Archipelago and Malaysia. They are often called Urang Padang (Padang people, after their provincial capital). Those living outside their own area frequently refer to themselves as Urang Awak (our people). Three inland districts of West Sumatra—Tanah Data, Agam, and Limo Pulueh Koto—are frequently referred to as their original homeland, from which they spread outward to all of what is now West Sumatra, parts of the Sumatran provinces of Riau, Djambi (including Kerintji), South Sumatra, and Atjeh, and to the Malay Peninsula, particularly Negri Sembilan. The process of temporary or permanent migration (called *marantau*) still continues, and today small Minangkabau communities are found in towns and cities throughout Sumatra and on islands to the east and west. In the rest of Indonesia, they are found in the larger cities, especially Djakarta. **Linguistic affiliation.** Malayo-Polynesian, one of an extremely closely related group of Malay languages in parts of Sumatra, the Malay Peninsula, and on islands east of Sumatra. Numerous dialects provide material for linguistic jokes, thus reinforcing regional and village identities. A specialized, rather poetic speech style is used in ceremonies, while a standard version of Minangkabau, influenced by the national language, is developing. [Kähler 1965; Tanner 1966.] **Demography.** The population of West Sumatra is almost two and one half million. At least 85 percent is rural and is almost entirely ethnically Minangkabau. Other Sumatran provinces with more than 5,000 inhabitants giving place of birth as West Sumatra—thus for the most part ethnically Minangkabau—are as follows: Riau, 35,000; Djambi, 16,000; North Sumatra, 16,000; South Sumatra, 10,000. [McNicoll 1968.] The Minangkabau population of Djakarta, the capital of Indonesia (population approximately 3,000,000), has been estimated at about 2 percent of the total, or 60,000 in 1961. [Castles 1967; McNicoll 1968; Milone 1966.] **History.** Myths and quasi-historical legends provide most of what is

---

*The author of this entry, Nancy Tanner, studied anthropology at the University of California, Berkeley, and at the University of Chicago. She did fieldwork among the Minangkabau from 1963 to 1966, and is currently an Assistant Professor of Anthropology, University of California, Santa Cruz. The interpretation of contemporary Minangkabau social structure presented here is based primarily on the author's own fieldwork. A somewhat different interpretation of traditional Minangkabau culture, based on an analysis of historical sources, is contained in de Josselin de Jong (1951).

known about the precolonial Minangkabau state (cf. Abdullah 1970). Archeological remains have been dated as early as the twelfth century, and inscriptions of the mid-fourteenth century link the area with the court of Madjapahit in Java (Schnitger 1937). Portuguese records indicate a lively trade with Malacca in the sixteenth century, and Minangkabau were bringing pepper to both east and west coast ports as early as the beginning of the seventeenth century (Cortesão 1944; Marsden 1811; Schnitger 1937). Atjehnese suzerainty in the early seventeenth century led to increased Islamic influence, culminating in the "Padri War" of 1803-37, a confrontation between Islamic leadership and traditional adat rule. The result was the entry of the Dutch into the highlands in support of adat leaders. The Dutch reorganized the government and set up schools. Dutch forts in time became towns, and many Minangkabau came to live urban lives. The twentieth century saw the growth of the Islamic modernist movement, which supported secular education and provided the basis for the growth of Islamic political parties. Many Minangkabau were active in the Indonesian revolution (1945-49), and an important segment of the leadership of the modern Republic of Indonesia is ethnically Minangkabau.

SETTLEMENT PATTERN AND HOUSING. Rural Minangkabau settlements vary from tiny hamlets, often consisting of the houses of one matrilineage, to villages (*nagari*) of one to three thousand, consisting of a number of house clusters (each the locale of a matrilineage) and also including public facilities, such as a mosque, a *surau* ("prayerhouse," where youngsters learn to recite the Koran and where unmarried men may sleep), and a traditional adat council house. Villages may be subdivided into hamlets; clusters of villages are also found. The traditional Minangkabau house, called *rumah gadang* (big house), is famous for its curved peaked roof (reminiscent of the curved horns of the "winning water buffalo" of mythology and of the Minangkabau woman's ceremonial headdress). It is rectangular in shape; about one half of the house is a long common room, which in addition to daily use as "living and dining room" is used for ceremonies and kin meetings. The remainder is divided into bedrooms, most of which are set aside for the daughters of the household and their husbands. The house is very much the province of the women.

ECONOMY. **Agriculture.** Wet-rice *sawah* agriculture, together with dry-plot *parak* market gardening, dominate the central highland region of Minangkabau, an area of relatively dense population and rich volcanic soils; while a swidden-market garden pattern is characteristic of the outlying Minangkabau and adjacent *rantau* (emigré) regions. In the first pattern, after the rice is harvested the rice stubble is burned, the land is hoed or plowed, and dry crops such as peanuts,

potatoes, corn, tomatoes, cabbage, or chili peppers are planted. Only after the dry crop is harvested is the land once more irrigated, fertilized with ashes, and planted with rice seedlings. Rice is thought of as primarily a subsistence crop, while the dry-field crops are thought of as cash crops. Although the volcanic highland soil is fertile, agriculture alone is no longer sufficient to meet the needs of the increased population. Highland villages, where agricultural prospects no longer seem particularly promising in comparison with other opportunities, produce many emigrants. Rather than attempting more labor-intensive cultivation, the Minangkabau often prefer *marantau*. Swidden agriculture involves clearing a jungle plot ("slash-and-burn"), planting it with annuals (such as dry rice, corn, cassava, pumpkins), then letting the land lie fallow for a number of years, and finally planting it with perennials such as rubber, cloves, cinnamon, pepper, coffee, coconut trees, sugar palm trees, or fruit trees. The tropical forest is thus gradually transformed into a producer of market and export commodities. The traditional Southeast Asian swidden subsistence cycle, in which remote forest peoples grow subsistence crops and are but slightly integrated into a market economy, is hardly characteristic of the Minangkabau. **Domestic animals.** Chickens, ducks, cattle, water buffalo, dogs, horses, and goats are domesticated. All but dogs and horses are used for meat, and water buffalo are also milked. (The thickened milk is eaten like yogurt.) **Hunting, fishing, and gathering.** Only wild pigs are regularly hunted, and these for sport; the meat is given to the dogs who aid in the hunt. Fishing is important, not only for coastal groups and those Minangkabau living on the shores of the inland lakes but also for those who fish in their own fishponds. Gathering of forest products is uncommon among the Minangkabau. **Home industries and trade.** Marked differentiation in skills and trade is accompanied by a well-developed market system. Villages are known for their specialized products. One village is known for its sugarcane, a neighboring village for schoolteachers and woven reed purses, another for imitation gold jewelry, and its neighbor for selling this jewelry. Each town has one or two main market days, and traders make weekly cycles. Trade goods are brought into West Sumatra from Djakarta via Padang or from the east coast of Sumatra and on into the highlands. Much of this trade is financed by Chinese businessmen, but the Minangkabau are also directly involved. The Minangkabau entrepreneur is often a middleman, linking the productivity of the land and of handicrafts to internal and external markets. This role is supported by the Minangkabau valuation of success through *marantau*. **Property.** The two major property classes are *harato pantjarian*, or earned (personal) property, and *harato pusako*, or ancestral (lineage) property. Most *harato pusako* is ancestral land, use rights to which are generally divided among the senior women of a lineage. Land pawning (*gadai*) is common. Houses are generally the property of minor lineages or of individual women. *Harato pantjarian*, individually earned property, is usually movable property—trade goods, gold coins, clothing, etc. It may also be an interest in a water buffalo, taxi, or bus or a share in a business.

KIN GROUPS. **Descent.** The Minangkabau are matrilineal: membership in named descent groups called *suku* is through the mother, and the titles of *suku* headmen pass from mother's brother to sister's son (this may be a classificatory relationship, but it is usually a genealogical one). In the coastal regions once ruled by Atjeh, the matrilineal descent system coexists with a ranked title system, in which titles are inherited by sons from their fathers. **Kin groups.** Each cluster of houses in a village is the locale of one matrilineage. If the lineage was one of the first to settle the village, it may have ownership rights over more of the land than other more recently arrived lineages. Such an "early settler" lineage will also own at least one type of traditional title. The bearer is the titular head of the lineage and its ceremonial representative. Latecomers to the village attach (*malakok*) themselves to one of the village's original lineages (preferably one with the same generic *suku* name as their own) and come under the leadership of the headman to whose lineage they have attached themselves, but their descendants—except in special circumstances—cannot succeed to his title. The "kinship" units of Minangkabau villages thus include stratified quasi-sibs, whose component lineages are not genealogically related, as well as genealogical kin groups such as lineages and major lineages. The stratification of lineages within a quasi-sib can be minimal, with the lineage of later arrivals having lands of their own and (if their lineage becomes large and prominent) perhaps eventually being given the right to have their own hereditary title; conversely, it may be quite extreme, involving many traditional work obligations, distinct lower status, and marriage restrictions. In some cases very low status lineages are descendants of slaves (although slavery was abolished in the mid-nineteenth century). Lineage segmentation is common: if it occurs within the village, land rights are divided and titles duplicated or added. Village major lineages may result from this sort of segmentation, which contrasts with the type of "agglutination" described for quasi-sibs. Major lineages have no corporate entity, but should a lineage or minor lineage die out (*punah*), distant lineal kin may attempt to establish that the property used by the *punah* lineage is "high" ancestral property ("major lineage property"), thereby establishing their rights to the property. In the past it was also common for lineage segments to migrate to other areas, in some cases becoming the founding lineages of settlements that eventually evolved into new villages. In other cases they moved to already settled areas that still possessed uncleared land. Such "splinter" lineages (*balahan*) remember their origins and, for several generations, often maintain ceremonial ties to their original lineages. Later, a sense of relationship with certain lineages in other villages may still exist, but the knowledge of which lineage and which village was the original one is often lost. Thus, genealogical sibs scattered over a wide area are also found in Minangkabau. **Kin terminology.** There is a strong generational emphasis, but terms are more widely extended within the matrilineage than for affinal kin. In general, kin terms and titles are used for both address and reference (and teknonomy is used referentially) for people "above" oneself in age or generation; names or nicknames are used for those who are younger except in explanatory references. This means that "kin" terms, as used for address, are not limited to genealogical kin. There is regional variation in terms; more variants are recorded for mother than for other terms. There are a number of referential terms which may be added to the basic classificatory terms to clarify degree of relationship: own, not classificatory, *kandueng, kontan*; step, *tirih*; distant, *djaueh*.

MARRIAGE AND FAMILY. **Mode.** In the highlands, most expenses of the marriage ceremony are borne by the bride's family, which also normally initiates marriage negotiations. In the coastal areas, there is a formal groom-price, *uang djemputan*, negotiated between the kin of bride and groom. Traditionally the amount of the groom-price varied with the man's title rank. **Form.** Marriage may be monogamous or polygynous (up to four concurrent wives are allowed according to Islam, but men today rarely have more than two wives at a time). A man with more than one wife commutes between the homes of his wives, or he may have one wife in the village and another in the *rantau*. Divorce and remarriage are common for both men and women. **Preferences and prohibitions.** The genealogical matrilineage is exogamous, as is a quasi-sib with the same headman. People with the same generic *suku* name, but with no known genealogical relationship and different headmen, may marry; in some areas this was not allowed in the past, however. Cross-cousin marriage was probably preferential in the past and is still practiced to some extent today. Value is placed on village endogamy, and a majority of marriages are within the village. **Residence.** Matrilocal in the village, with the husband residing with his wife's matrilineally extended family. The husband who lives in the village may still spend considerable time at his mother's house helping with agricultural work. If he is a craftsman, he often keeps his workbench and tools there. A man gradually moves his possessions to his wife's house if he feels the marriage is a stable one, and gradually moves them out again if the marriage seems to be breaking down. When the couple has a daughter, they begin to think of building a house of their own and usually do so if they can afford it. This house, though it may be built by the husband, belongs to the wife and her children and, on divorce, the husband must leave. In the towns, residence tends to be neolocal. **Domestic unit.** Village households are usually composed of matrilineally extended families. Urban households are more likely to be composed of a bilaterally extended family, plus unrelated members. **Divorce.** Separation and divorce are common; prior to the introduction of Islam, they may not have been differentiated. Today, however, a man may simply leave his wife and marry someone else, but a woman must either obtain a written divorce statement from her husband or be divorced in court before she may remarry. Extramarital relationships are rare. **Secondary marriage.** The first marriage is the socially relevant marriage, and the one that is most likely to be arranged by older kin. Should a man's wife die—particularly if they have been married for some time and have children—a common practice is for him to *ganti lapiek* (lit. change sleeping mats), i.e. to marry another woman of the matrilineage, usually his wife's younger sister or sister's daughter. **Adoption.** Apparently not very common traditionally, although procedures for it existed. **Inheritance.** In general, *harato pusako*, ancestral property, is considered uninheritable, since it belongs to a corporate group, the matrilineage, which persists through time. Use rights to the main forms of ancestral property—land and houses—generally are divided among the senior women of a matrilineage and pass from mother to daughter. As lineage segments grow in size and generation depth, property disputes may occur, sometimes leading to formal division of lineage property and duplication of hereditary titles. Disputes rarely occur over the inheritance of a woman's personal property, which is normally divided among her daughters. But a man's property is another matter. His matrilineal kin may claim that lineage resources financed his beginning in business and that his earned property is, therefore, not really his individual property, but that his minor lineage also has rights to it. His wife or wives may claim that it was jointly earned property, *harato suarang*, not individually earned property and that according to a traditional saying she or they have rights to at least one half of it. To avoid such potential disputes, a man often keeps little property in his own name. In addition, formal gifts or sale of property to the person a man wants to inherit it are common.

SOCIOPOLITICAL ORGANIZATION. **Political organization.** The first period we know anything about is characterized by a patterned opposition between "democratic" and "aristocratic" adat, Bodi-Tjaniago and Koto-Piliang. The former incorporates a very old

Minangkabau political ideology, one favorable to local government through the deliberation of unranked or minimally ranked *panghulu* (kin headmen) in village councils, village autonomy within a loose confederation of villages and no royal superstructure, as well as a personal ethic of achievement in the characteristic style of the Minangkabau, that is, by *marantau* (traveling, emigrating, going abroad). The latter adat, on the other hand, represents the imported Indic tradition of a court state and an aristocratic ideal of social order, in which both leaders and followers are hierarchically ordered and social position is largely a function of birth. It is with the latter ideology that the institutions of the Minangkabau state were more closely associated. This state is said to have had three radjas, each with his own village headquarters. Below these were a series of leaders, initially four, called *basa ampek balai*. Within the villages of Lareh Koto-Piliang, the *panghulu* were ordered hierarchically. This is expressed symbolically even today by the different levels in the village *balai* (meeting hall), where village leaders are seated according to their rank. A radja could pardon and give protection to those expelled from their villages and in this way maintain a personal following. In the villages of Lareh Bodi-Tjaniago, the *panghulu* were said to "stand equally high, to sit equally low." ● The political organization described above can be roughly dated as extending from the time of Aditiavarman in the midfourteenth century until the Parang Hitam-Putieh or "Padri War" (ca. 1803-37). The period as a whole may be characterized in terms of several conflict themes, including an implicit opposition between matrilineal and patrilineal principles of inheritance. But it must be clearly understood that this "patrilineal principle" has nowhere in Minangkabau been elaborated into a patrilineal lineage system (the aristocracy was an endogamous class—which at its highest levels linked village to village through intermarriage—and strictly speaking it was neither patrilineal or matrilineal). The Islamic revolution of the early nineteenth century (the "Padri War") eroded the authority of the traditional state and exterminated the ruling families. The Dutch instituted a supravillage administration and imposed obligatory coffee cultivation and other types of forced labor, resulting in repeated anti-Dutch uprisings (Radjab 1964). The modern province of West Sumatra is organized into districts, *kebupaten*; subdistricts, *ketjamatan*; and villages, *kenagarian*, with provincial, district, and village level "parliaments." The old village adat councils still meet occasionally, mainly to adjudicate disputes. **Social stratification.** Minimal at the village level. Differences of wealth exist, but do not necessarily correlate with status as determined by kinship position, Islamic learning, or secular education. There is a tendency for the *urang aseli* (early settlers) of a village to intermarry; it is they who have a relative monopoly of traditional titles, and often they own more land than *urang datang*, newcomers. However, wealth or education is often thought to be more important in choosing a husband for a girl than is traditional status, and it is not only the *urang aseli* who are highly educated or rich—often to the contrary. Slavery did exist at one time, and those who are known to be descendants of slave families may be avoided as marriage partners. **Social control and dispute settlement.** Teasing, advising, gossip, and withholding neighborly help or friendly interaction are the most frequently used modes of social control. A person who has committed an offense may also be fined or required to hold a ceremony in which community members eat together; if the matter is very serious, he or she may be disowned by his or her kin group and exiled from the community. Disputes over land are common. **Warfare.** When speaking of the distant past, the Minangkabau sometimes refer to *parang batu*, lit. "stone wars." In those days villages were often surrounded by hedges or groves of a type of bamboo having sharp protrusions. Usually there were also forested areas around villages where guards could hide themselves and waylay hostile intruders. A common contemporary tactic—one which probably has a long history—is called *hilang malam*, lit. "lost at night"; it usually consists of abduction and murder. In most cases, nothing further is heard of the victim. There is no record of either headhunting or cannibalism among the Minangkabau.

RELIGION AND MAGIC. **Religious systems.** The Minangkabau are an Islamic people. Islam probably came to Minangkabau both from the east (via trade with Malacca) and from the west coast (Atjehnese influence). The early twentieth century saw the birth of the Islamic modernist movement in Minangkabau. Muhammadijah, a modernist Islamic social organization which started in Java, found widespread popularity in West Sumatra. After Independence, much of the Minangkabau leadership of Muhammadijah became active in Masjumi, a modernist Islamic political party of national importance. **Supernaturals.** Today, in addition to belief in the one god of Islam—Allah, or Tuhan—many Minangkabau have some belief in a host of indigenous spirits capable of conferring mystical power on humans; they may be associated with sacred places (*tampek-tampek nan sati*)—usually relatively remote mountain, hill, or jungle areas. Some spiritual beings operate more or less independently, such as the *urang djadi-djadian*, who can become tigers; the *tjindaku*, human-appearing monsters, sex unspecified, who eat people and of whom children are especially terrified; the *djindai* who look like beautiful women with long, flowing hair and who laugh in an eerie manner; and ghosts, *hantu*, who haunt cemeteries. The *palasik*, women who make little children sickly and weak, are born with their power and have no conscious control over it (although people believe that there are ways of pacifying *palasik* so that they will not harm a child). Some objects appear to have inherent supernatural power—e.g. the stones that men use in rings. Other materials, particularly hair or fingernail parings of a person who is to be placed under some spell, and items such as tiger claws or skin from the back of a tiger's neck, are used as ingredients for black magic charms. Crystallized elephant sperm is an especially powerful ingredient for use in love magic. A wide range of herbs and foods are used for medicinal purposes. **Practitioners.** The famous *tuangku*, the Islamic teachers to whom young men came from all over Minangkabau, are no more, and the *angku kali*, or *kadhi*, is no longer a judge; rather his main function is to perform marriage ceremonies. The role of *hadji*, one who has made the pilgrimage to Mecca, persists. The roles concerned with Islamic ceremonies appear to have remained relatively constant. Practitioners of magic may include highly respected members of society and leaders (particularly traditional Islamic teacher-mystics and penghulu), almost always male, who have a type of supernatural knowledge or power that is actually used for the practitioner's own benefit: he protects himself from magical harm, he performs magical feats such as disappearing and reappearing immediately in a distant place, and he shows that his magical powers are superior to those of others (as by making a speaker forget his speech at a ceremony). It is said that a prominent person needs to *baisi paruik seketek* (literally, to have a little something in his stomach, that is, to know a little magic). Paid general practitioners include the *dukun* (medicine men, sorcerers), who may be either men or women. *Dukun* may have other social roles, including those of penghulu or Islamic teacher-mystic. Their primary function is to *maubek*, to medicate. Many *dukun* are experts in finding lost or stolen objects, and they may practice various types of love magic and mild forms of black magic such as *ramuan* (small magical bundles placed in or near someone's house in order to bring them bad luck or make them sick). They also remedy the effects of these types of magic. A third group consists of *tukang siie*, i.e. *dukun* experts in black magic (*ilimu siie*) and, more extreme, *ilimu kasa* (also experts in black magic, but more dangerous and clearly anti-Islamic; literally, rough or violent knowledge). Those who possess *ilimu kasa* use their skills not only to earn money but also to strengthen their own positions. One who knows *ilimu kasa* is reputedly impervious to bullets or knife wounds; he is a dangerous, irreligious man, strong in his knowledge of black magic. Each type of practitioner may have access to aid from supernatural beings—from Allah and/or from the pantheon of indigenous spirits. A *dukun* is sometimes possessed by his own familiar spirit. **Ceremonies.** There are two major ceremonies of the Islamic year,

Hari Raja (Idulfitri), at the end of the fasting month (Bulan Puaso), and Hari Raja Hadji, about a month later, as well as several life cycle ceremonies. Sunat, or circumcision, occasions very little ritual for most boys and almost none for girls; formerly, the boys' ceremony was more elaborate. Although most of the Minangkabau wedding ceremony is based on adat, there is a small quiet preliminary Islamic ceremony in which the groom presents the *mas kawin* (or *mahar*), a nominal payment, and repeats the marriage vows after the *angku kali*. The rituals surrounding birth and early childhood are adat ceremonies and are usually quite small, but the funeral rituals are almost totally prescribed by Islam. In addition to yearly and life cycle ceremonies, people may have ceremonial meals, *mandoa* (lit. to pray), to celebrate good luck or the settlement of a dispute. There are also small agricultural ceremonies concerning the rice crop, such as the prayers said by a man before the women begin to winnow the grain or before his circling of the rice field with incense prior to the harvest. **Illness and medicine.** Two frequently mentioned "causes" of illness are magic and poison. The most typical indication of poisoning is a long, wasting illness, usually resulting in death. Like many magical potions, poison is hidden in food and is said usually to have been procured from a *dukun*. Magic is a broad-spectrum therapeutic: it is used to cure sicknesses for which doctors have no medicines, to enact hostilities which people are reluctant or afraid to express directly, and to serve as psychological support, mystical protection, and supernatural ammunition in a world which encourages achievement but which is nonetheless hostile to the powerful and successful. There are *dukun* who specialize in massage and who correct muscular disorders and organ displacement. Many *dukun* are knowledgeable in herbal medicines; they may utilize foods such as citrus fruits, bananas, eggs, or green coconuts. Formerly there were many female *dukun* who were midwives. Now, however, for the most part they have given up their practices in favor of the younger, hospital-trained *bidan* (nurses specializing in midwifery). Trained *bidan*, male nurses, doctors, clinics, and hospitals have been widely accepted among the Minangkabau. **Soul, death, and afterlife.** The Minangkabau have an indigenous concept of soul, *angok* (soul or breath). Like other Muslims, they also believe in Heaven, or *sarugo*, and in *nirako*, or Hell. In addition to the usual Islamic beliefs concerning *sarugo*, the Minangkabau have their own distinctive beliefs, e.g. that "Heaven is below the sole of mother's foot" and that a person cannot go to Heaven if he mistreats his mother. Hell is thought of in the usual Islamic ways. The funeral begins with the washing and wrapping of the corpse. After the deceased has been wrapped in white cloth, the *angku imam* prays; in the more traditional areas, this prayer (*mandoa*) follows eating and is accompanied by incense. The corpse is placed in front of the house, facing west, and there are further ritual prayers by the men. The group then carries the corpse to the graveyard (some of the men—kin and friends—will have prepared the grave earlier). The corpse is placed in the grave with its head to the north, feet to the south, right shoulder to the ground and facing west toward Mecca. The burial is followed by a *pasambahan*, ritual speech, urging the workers to return to the home of the family of the deceased for a meal. In some areas, money may also be distributed to the people (especially children) who attend the funeral.

BIBLIOGRAPHY. Abdullah 1970; Bachtiar 1967; Castles 1967; Cortesão 1944; Dobby 1950; Gould 1956; Hamka 1963; Johns 1958; de Josselin de Jong 1951; Junus 1964, 1966; Kähler 1965; Kemal 1964; Marsden 1811; McNicoll 1968; Mitchell 1969; Milone 1966; Naim 1968; Nasroen 1957; Radjab 1964, 1969; Schnitger 1937; Schrieke 1955, 1960; Tanner 1966, 1969. [For bibliographies of older Dutch sources, see Joustra 1924, 1936; Kennedy 1962.]

REDJANG COMPLEX

THE HISTORIC HABITAT of the autochthonous peoples of South Sumatra, whom Kennedy (1935) classed together in a "Redjang-Lampong Group," appears to have been the fertile highland valleys and plateaus of the Barisan Range. There is a long history, however, of contact with lowland Hindu and Malay states and of movement into surrounding coastal and plains areas, resulting in varying degrees of acculturation to the Hindu-Javanese tradition. Physically, the Redjang peoples appear to be the product of Javanese, Malay, and Minangkabau additions to a formerly predominant Batak-like stock. This blending of peoples and cultures—Javanese, Djambi Malay, Redjang, Kerintji, Minangkabau—has resulted in a complex mosaic of ethnic names and identities, although Kennedy, on the basis of what he interpreted as a common culture pattern, felt justified in treating the entire South Sumatran highlands as a single culture area. The region is remarkable for the number and variety of megalithic remains reminiscent of those on Nias and in the Batak highlands; and on the basis of these and other similarities, Heine-Geldern (1935) posited the spread throughout the area of early megalithic and bronze age cultures from the mainland. Although government in the

Redjang-Lampung districts is now virtually entirely territorial in nature, the whole region was formerly organized on the basis of genealogical units tracing descent in the male line—essentially similar to Batak kin-based groupings. The situation in Redjang country has been obscured, however, by the recent transition from patriliny to matriliny (Jaspan 1964b). Although there would appear to be some justification for Kennedy's "Redjang-Lampong Group," final judgment is rendered difficult by the unevenness of the data presently available, in particular the paucity of adequate linguistic analyses. The present volume therefore treats Redjang and Lampung as separate categories, restricting the discussion of Lampung peoples primarily to the Abung, the best-known of indigenous groups in that area.

BIBLIOGRAPHY. Heine-Geldern 1935; Jaspan 1964b; Kennedy 1935.

KERINTJI*

Synonyms. *Koerintji, Kurintji, Korintji, Korinchi, Corinchee, Korinci, Corinchi, Corinchia*

ORIENTATION. **Identification.** A culturally homogeneous and closely-knit ethnic group, sometimes mistakenly considered a Minangkabau subgroup (cf. Lekkerkerker 1916: 22; *Volkstelling 1930, 4:* 15; Mansoer Jasin et al. 1954). Despite close economic ties with the Minangkabau, their language shows distinct differences (Voorhoeve 1955: 17-18); nor is their system of matrilineal descent reckoning and inheritance identical to that of the Minangkabau (van Aken 1915; Morison 1936). **Location.** The westernmost division of Djambi Province, bordering the northern part of Bencoolen (Bengkulu) Province to the south and the province of West Sumatra to the west and northwest. The heartland of Kerintji country is the fertile, high altitude "Kerintji Basin," surrounding Lake Kerintji at an elevation of 2,200 feet. **Linguistic affiliation.** While Esser and other linguists classified Kerintji as a Minangkabau dialect, Voorhoeve considers this judgment to be mistaken (1955: 18). The Kerintji sound system corresponds in a number of respects with Redjang as spoken in Lebong. The

Kerintji, moreover, have an indigenous Indic-type script akin to that of Redjang and Pasemah (Westenenk 1922). **Demography.** According to the 1930 census, the number of Kerintji was 76,547.

SETTLEMENT PATTERN AND HOUSING. Traditional Kerintji houses (*umah*) may be classed in the genre of Southeast Asian longhouses, but are probably unique in that they do not have any public or communal gallery or passageway linking the adjoining family apartments (*bile*). As is the case with the Minangkabau, the central rooms belong to the oldest living matrilineal inheritrix.

ECONOMY. The earliest European visitors to the Kerintji highlands were impressed by the irrigated rice fields and by the industry and relative prosperity of the people (Marsden 1783: 286). Marsden also remarked upon the large number of horses. Large tea estates were developed by Dutch companies on the mountain slopes. Lacustrine fishing, using simple craft and methods, is practiced on Lake Kerintji.

KIN GROUPS. All kin groups are based on ties of matrilineal descent. The smallest unit is a *sapiyau*, "one stomach," consisting of a mother and her children. Two or more *sapiyau* descended from the same grandmother form a *sapintu*, "one door," sometimes called a *pintu tumpu*. Two or more *sapintu* descended from the same great-grandmother form a matrilineage (*kalbu* or *kalebau*), and two or more *kalbu* constitute a matriclan (*pehau'* or *p'haut*, "womb"). A *luhoh* constitutes a wider matrix of clans descended from the same matrilineal ancestor. Several related *luhoh* make up a *dusun*, of which four or more constitute a *mendapo*, which is the largest constituent sociopolitical entity in Kerintji (Morison 1936).

MARRIAGE AND FAMILY. There is only one form of marriage, in which the husband (*ohang semendau*) becomes attached to, though never part of, his wife's natal family and household. No bride-price is paid. A married man is, however, the de jure head of his sister's household. Daughters are preferred to sons. When there are no daughters in a family, it was formerly the custom to arrange the marriage of one of the sons by bringing a wife into the household for him (*semendau suhau'*). If this was not done, it was feared that the lineage would die out. With this exception, marriage residence was and is always matriuxorilocal. Although a title of rank is transmitted from a mother's brother to his sister's son, property in land and houses is transmitted from a mother to her daughters. This is lineage property, i.e. belonging to the *luhoh* by whom it is managed. The actual managers are the mature maternal uncles (*nine-mama*) of the lineage's heiresses. The domestic unit consists of a

---

*The author of this and other entries grouped under "Redjang Complex" is M. A. Jaspan, Professor of South-East Asian Sociology and Director, Centre for South-East Asian Studies, University of Hull. His fieldwork among the peoples of South Sumatra extended over a period of 18 months in 1961-63, principally among the Redjang of the Lebong and Lais-Bencoolen areas.

married woman and her children. Her husband lives partly with her and his children, partly at his own lineal longhouse.

SOCIOPOLITICAL ORGANIZATION. **Political organization.** Before Dutch rule the Kerintji lived under a system of noncentralized, genealogically derived shires (*mendapo*), each territorially localized. The older term for a shire was *helai kain*, "a length of cloth." Kerintji then consisted of four *mendapo*. The political integration of matriclans and territorial shires resulted in a system designated "Kerintji of the Four Chiefs and Eight Lengths of Cloth." Each of the four original clanlands was ruled by a *depati*, assisted by three officials. The majority of Kerintji live in what is now the Kerintji regency of Djambi Province. **Social stratification.** Considerable importance is still attached to inherited chiefly status, and men of high social standing invariably have a title of rank. Slave origin is attributed to certain families, and these tend often not to possess "high property" such as inherited wet-rice fields. Most people are reckoned to be commoners. **Religion.** Little is known of the pre-Islamic religion, other than that it included elements of ancestor worship, animism, and Indic pantheism.

BIBLIOGRAPHY. Lekkerkerker 1916; Marsden 1783; Mansoer Jasin et al. 1954; Morison 1936; van Aken 1915; *Volkstelling 1930;* Voorhoeve 1955; Westenenk 1922.

BATIN

Synonyms. *Orang Batin, Bathin, Orang Bathin*

ORIENTATION. **Identification and location.** Essentially a lowland riverine people, inhabiting the Tembesi River drainage east of the Kerintji highlands. Some of their swiddens reach higher into the Barisan foothills. The main markets are at Sarolangun, Muara Tembesi, Muaru Tebo, and Muara Bungo. There is no general agreement regarding the Batin, either as an identifiable ethnic group (cf. Wellan 1932: 115) or as a Malay subculture subject to strong Minangkabau influence. Minangkabau, Kerintji, Javanese, and Malay elements are all present. Wellan (1932: 115) suggests that the population of the mid-Tembesi River area derives from the intermingling of an autochthonous Kubu population with Kerintji immigrants. During a brief field tour in 1963, it appeared to the author that the Batin now have a distinctive group consciousness, distinguishing themselves from their Kerintji, Minangkabau, Djambi, Rawas, and Kubu neighbors. **Demography.** District officials in Bangko and Sarolangun estimated the total Batin population (including the penghulu) at about 70,000 in 1963. **History and cultural relations.** The Batin now regard themselves as the original inhabitants of Djambi,

before it became subject to a Malay sultanate in Djambi town. They claim to have been divided into twelve original tribal sections (*batin* or *suku*), each with a chief who bore the title of *pangeran* or *temenggung*. The twelve chiefs formed a council called the *pangeran ratu* (Mansoer Jasin et al. 1954: 1017-20). After the establishment of the sultanate, all land not then under cultivation by Batin was declared crown land (*tanah radja*). The remaining land, cultivated under a system of communal usufructory tenure by the indigenous Batin people, was thereafter called "Batin lands" (*tanah batin*) (Mansoer Jasin et al. 1954: 1023-24). The spread of Islam, the introduction of rubber cultivation, and the extension of Djambi authority are all factors that have tended to reinforce Malay as the language of trade, administration, and education and to enhance among the Batin sentiments of a "Djambi Malay" identity and allegiance.

BIBLIOGRAPHY. Mansoer Jasin et al. 1954; Wellan 1932.

MUKO-MUKO

Synonyms. *Moco-Moco, Moko-Moko, Mokko-Mokko, Moeko-Moeko*

ORIENTATION. **Identification and location.** A mixed population of Minangkabau, Kerintji, Pekal, and Bencoolenese Malays, mainly in the Muko-Muko district of the North Bencoolen regency, from about 2° to 2°50′ S., including the shire (*marga*) of XIV Kota. Much of the area is uninhabited mountain forest. **Demography.** About 15,000 in 1930 (*Volkstelling 1930, 4*: 138). **History and cultural relations.** Muko-Muko has always been regarded by the Minangkabau as part of their *rantau* (outer lands), subject to the minor sultans of Indrapura to the north. Muko-Muko sometimes elevated its own local chiefs (*pangeran*) to the status of sultan, challenging Indrapura's overlordship. It also claimed a degree of suzerainty over the coastal people extending south to Anak Sungei (Marsden 1783: 286-87). When Indrapura was incorporated by the Dutch into the province of West Sumatra, Muko-Muko became the northernmost district of the Bencoolen Residency.

BIBLIOGRAPHY. Marsden 1783; *Volkstelling 1930.*

PEKAL

Synonyms. *Anak Soongey, Anak Sungei, Orang Cattown, Orang Ketaun, Orang Seblat, Orang Ipuh, Mekëa*

ORIENTATION. **Identification and location.** A mixed community of Minangkabau, Kerintji, and Redjang origin. The Pekal inhabit the coast from the northern side of the Urei estuary south of the Ketaun, to approximately the mouth of the Bantal River, south of Muko-Muko; from this coast their territory extends to the foothills of the Barisan Range. The Minangkabau regard Pekal as an outlier of their southern *rantau*. The Redjang, on the other hand, regard this people, whom they call Mekëa, as an outlying subject community of their Four Pillar Federation. The English East India Company (Bastin 1965) described the Pekal as Anak Sungei, a coastal sultanate whose capital was at or near Muko-Muko (Marsden 1783: 286-87). Marsden described the government of Anak Sungei as "Malay," but the majority of its inhabitants he called the "original *dusun* people." **Linguistic affiliation.** The language may best be described as "south-coast Minangkabau," as spoken in Muko-Muko, though modified by Redjang vocabulary, idiom, and occasional nasalization. **Demography.** According to the 1930 census, the total population of the three Pekal shires was 13,524.

BIBLIOGRAPHY. Bastin 1965; Marsden 1783.

REDJANG

Synonyms. *Rejang, Djang, Tun Djang, Redjang Empat Petulai*

ORIENTATION. **Identification and location.** The people call themselves Keme Tun Djang, "We the People of Djang," after an eponymous ancestor. The four sons of Djang, regarded as princely bhikkus (*bikau*) founded the four Redjang patriclans, resulting in a politicosocial confederation known as Djang Pat Petulai ("Redjang Four Brothers") or Djang Tiang Pat ("Redjang Four Pillars") (Marsden 1783: 178; Hoessein 1932: 1-5; Jaspan 1964a: chaps. 1 and 3). Each of the four Petulai is regarded as the founding ancestor of one of the four major patriclans who together constitute the Bang Mego Pat ("Four Clan Doors"), commonly referred to as the "Four Pillar Clans." Although the founding ancestors of their Four Pillar Clans are believed to be descendants of the Javanese royal house of Madjapahit, the Redjang regard themselves, in contrast to their Malay, Lembak, Pekal, Bengkulu, and Minangkabau neighbors, as the original and autochthonous inhabitants of South Sumatra. Marsden (1783: 37) adopted the Redjang as a standard of description for the indigenous highland people of Sumatra not yet entirely subject to Malay influence. There are five main groups and two subgroups: (1) Djang Lebong or Djang Bele Tebo, inhabitants of the fertile upland Lebong district of the Redjang-Lebong regency in Bengkulu (Bencoolen) Province. These are considered the original or true Redjang, the direct descendants of the four founding ancestors. They themselves regard all other Redjang territories

as "the end of the smoke-trail" (*mar udjung aseup*). (2) Djang Musai, the Redjang of the fertile upper Musi Valley in the Redjang district of the Redjang-Lebong regency. (3) Djang Lai, the Redjang of the Lais (Laye), Bintunan, Air Padang, Palik, Perbo, and Kerkap shires (*marga*) on the Indian Ocean coast from Ketaun to Kerkap and inland to the foothills of the Barisan Mountain Range. (4) Djang Bekulau, the Redjang of Bencoolen, mainly in the *marga* of Selupu Lama, Djurukalang, Bermani Sungei Hitam, and Proatin XII. (5) Djang Abeus or Djang Aweus, the Redjang of Rawas, who live on the relatively inaccessible upper reaches of the Rawas tributary of the Musi River, in the Musi-Rawas (Mura) regency. The two subgroups are Bang Hadji and Semitul, probably Redjangized communities of Lembak and Minangkabau origin, in the low foothills northwest of Bengkulu. Much of Redjang territory consists of mountain peaks and ridges of the Barisan Range, largely covered with tropical rain forest. **Language.** Regarded by Voorhoeve (1955) as an independent language, closely related to Malay. **Demography.** On the basis of administrative statistics and sample checks carried out in 1961-63, Jaspan (1964a: 42) estimated a total of 180,000 Redjang. **History and cultural relations.** According to Redjang tradition, Lebong was inhabited by Redjang at an early date, when the chiefs of the country, which was then called Renah Sakalawi, bore the title *adjai*. The *adjai* period was characterized by constant feuding and by intervillage or inter*marga* raiding of women and cattle. Eventually the *adjai* were replaced by four immigrant chiefs from the Madjapahit kingdom in Java. Their coming has been placed in the twelfth or thirteenth century by Hoessein (1932: 3), but in the fourteenth or fifteenth by Jaspan. The four, each with a substantial following, established themselves in Lebong as a confederation of territorially localized patriclans. The first or oldest village of each clan is still its most sacred shrine and place of pilgrimage. In time, the clan populations expanded, and new settlements were established outside Lebong, but the original pattern of patriclan territorial localization continued. In contrast to the highlands, which remained independent of Malay intrusion and European control until the early 1860s, the Lais and Bencoolen coastal area and hinterland foothills became subject to Minangkabau, Atjehnese, and Bantam (Java) influence from about the fourteenth century onward, and became converted to Islam and subject to Malayanization in varying degrees. Since 1950, Redjang have increasingly entered the mainstream of provincial and national life. Simultaneously there has been a growth of ethnic consciousness and incipient movements for the preservation of the Redjang language, traditional script (*ka-ga-nga*), and customary law.

SETTLEMENT PATTERN AND HOUSING. **Settlement pattern.** Each of the four main patriclans has its own original territory in Lebong; the bifurcating subclans likewise have their own territories in the other "smoke-trail" regions. Each subclan territory, which now coincides with a government-recognized *marga*, comprises between 8 and 32 villages located largely on the banks of rivers or nearby eminences. Each village (*sadeui*) traces descent linkage with every other village of the same subclan and patriclan, although such links are now increasingly notional. Within each village there are four patrilineages (*dju'-eui* or *sukau*); in the past, each inhabited a discrete ward within the village. Each patrilineage formerly had its own territorial domain within which members planted hill rice in shifting swiddens. Each patrilineage has one or more hamlets (*talang*) in its domain, providing a residential base for its relatively isolated swidden farmers. Until recent times, such hamlets gradually developed into independent villages. Village populations vary from about 15 to 900 hearthholds, the largest villages, in intensively irrigated parts of Lebong, having populations in excess of 4,000 persons. In the past, most villages were surrounded with earthworks and stockades. A so-called village Long Hall, *baleui*, serves for ceremonial dancing and feasting. **Housing.** Traditional Redjang houses are built with intricately carved horizontal beams, octagonally shaped piles, and ornamented, colored panels in traditional designs. The veranda or the front room is the place for receiving guests and male suitors. In stem family households, where a daughter is married uxorilocally and residential partition has not yet occurred, the in-marrying son-in-law (*semendo* or *ano' stamang*) must keep to this part of the house—he is not expected to have free access to the quarters of his wife's sisters, who have separate cubicles.

ECONOMY. Regardless of occupation, every adult Redjang retains his or her rice field. Until the 1860s, farming was mainly extensive and was based on the cyclic clearing of swiddens. It is now more dependent on irrigation of one type or another, with supplementary swiddening. Dry rice is preferred from both the culinary and ritual viewpoints. Job's tears (*Coix lachryma-Jobi*), which was regarded as an alternative staple in ancient times, is sown around rice swiddens and along the sides of inner paths within the field. A small quantity of millet is also grown. Animal husbandry, fishing, hunting, and gathering still play their parts in the economic life, varying in importance according to the nature of the terrain, altitude, forest cover, and rivers.

KIN GROUPS. **Descent.** Until the 1930s, descent was reckoned patrilineally, except in circumstances where a man had no sons and a uxorilocal inmarriage (*semendo*) enabled the patrilineage to continue through a uterine link. Because the four original clan founders are said to have been brothers, the sons or descend-

ants of Djang, all Redjang belong to one "umbrella" genealogy. Since the worldwide depression of 1929-32, and the stigmatization of bride-price marriage as profane in Islamic law, descent has changed from patriliny to matriliny, and lineal succession from male primogeniture to female ultimogeniture (Jaspan 1964b). Among a minority of urbanized, Malayanized Redjang, the rule of descent is claimed to be ambilineal (*semendo radjo-radjo*), though marriage residence tends to be uxorilocal or uxorifocal even when notionally neolocal. **Kin groups.** The four founding ancestors each established a patriclan (Bang Mego Pat—"the Four Clan Doors") territorially localized in the original Redjang heartland in Lebong and the western Musi highlands. The "Four Clan Doors" later split into subclans, which extended the area of settlement to the eastern Musi and across the Barisan Mountains to the Lais and Bengkulu coastal regions. The original pattern of territorial localization was generally adhered to in the new subclan settlements. Each subclan was ruled by a hereditary chieftain designated *pangeran*, *radjo*, or *pesirea*. While a subclan consists of about 10 to 30 villages in the heartland, there are as few as 4 or 5 villages in the smaller *mergo*, such as Perbo, in the lowlands. In theory, each village is a major patrilineage of the subclan. Within the village there are usually four, but sometimes three or five patrilineages (*sukau* or *dju'eui*). Each patrilineage is represented in village government and ritual by its hereditary "elder" (*tuai dju'eui*). Although descent is now reckoned uterinely, the former lineage and clan groups still persist, and there has thus far been no change in their nomenclature. **Kin terminology.** This is predominantly lineal, but there are variations between the terms used in the former patrilineal system and in the present matrilineal dispensation. The variations are most marked with respect to classificatory terms used by male speakers and female speakers for agnatic and uterine kinsmen in the patrilineal system; they do not occur where the transition to matriliny has taken place more than four generations ago. Other principles are distinctive terms to mark elder or younger siblingship and sibling affines and special terminology for aunts and uncles and their spouses. The principal consanguineal kin terms in the Lebong highlands are:

Relationship	Patrilineal term	Matrilineal term
FaFa	*nini*	*nini*
FaMo	*sebeui*	*sebeui*
MoFa	*nini kenepun*	*nini*
MoMo	*sebeui kenepun*	*sebeui*
Fa	*bapo'*	*bapo'*
Mo	*indo'*	*indo'*
FaElBr	*uwo, mama* or *nguaneui bapo'*	*uwo, wa dan*
FaYoBr	*penguai bapo'* or *mamang*	*pa'tji*
FaElSi	*klaweui bapo'*	*uwo*

32

MoElBr	*mama* or *nguaneui indo'*	*mama* or *uwo*
MoYoBr	*pengu'ai indo'* or *mamang*	*tamang* or *uwo*
MoElSi	*klaweui indo'*	*uwo* or *bibi*
MoYoSi	*mineun*	*bibi*
ElBr	*kako* or *nguaneui tuai*	*kako*
YoBr	*asua* or *nguaneui uai*	*asua* or *adi*
ElSi	*kako* or *klaweui tuai*	*kako*
YoSi	*asua* or *klaweui uai*	*asua* or *adi*
FaBrSo	*nguaneui* or *spasua danea umea*	*ngesano'*
FaBrDa	*klaweui* or *spasua danea umea*	*ngesano'*
FaSiDa	*ngesano'*	*ngesano'*
MoBrSo, MoBrDa, MoSiSo, MoSiDa	*ngesano'*	*spasua danea umea*
So, Da	*ano'*	*ano'*
BrSo, BrDa	*ano' spasua,* or *ano' nguaneui*	*tu'*
SiSo, SiDa	*ano' klaweui*	*tu'*
SoSo, SoDa	*kepau*	*tjutjung*
DaSo, DaDa	*kepau ano' bleui*	*tjutjung*

MARRIAGE AND FAMILY. Preliminaries.

Elaborate rules of courtship include an exchange of stylized verses (*berdjung* or *sambea*) between boys and girls sitting at opposite ends of the Long Hall during *kedjai* dance-feasts. Boys and girls also exchange messages, formerly inscribed with the point of a kris on bamboo strips or cylinders (Jaspan 1964a). **Mode.** There are two principal forms of marriage contract: the first, which predominated until the 1930s, necessitated the payment of substantial bridewealth (*beleket*); the second, known as *semendo,* required a smaller bride-price, for which bride service could be substituted. Where bride-price had been paid, the offspring of the marriage were affiliated to their father's lineage and clan; otherwise they were affiliated to their mother's lineage and clan, though a subsequent payment of the bride-price could ensure the legal and ritual transfer of the children to their father's lineage (Jaspan 1964b: 270). **Form.** In Redjang adat law, monogamous marriage is preferred, but in *beleket* marriage there was prescriptive leviratic marriage between a widow and her deceased husband's younger brother and, conversely, sororal marriage between a man and his deceased wife's younger sister or classificatory sister. Polygyny occurred among clan and subclan chiefs. **Extension of incest taboos.** Originally sexual relations and marriage were prohibited between members of the same clan. This was later modified to members of the same subclan, and later still to descendants of the same great-grandparent. Since the transition to matriliny, the extension of incest taboos has become considerably relaxed, and intravillage marriage is not uncommon (though not between descendants of the same grandparent). **Residence.** Whenever bride-price is paid, marriage residence is prescriptively virilocal; in *semendo* marriage, residence is prescriptively uxorilocal. Urbanization and increasing pressure of population in irrigated farming areas is tending to reduce the period of uxorilocal marriage to one or two years, followed by neolocal residence. **Domestic unit.** In the past it was unusual for the domestic stem family to consist of more than one married child. When a second child married, the parents might assist in building a smaller house near their own. Often, however, a newly married couple would spend the first few years of their married life at a swidden farm or in an outlying farm hamlet (*talang*). **Inheritance.** Lineal property (house and farmland) was almost always inherited by the eldest son until the 1930s. Since the 1950s, it has usually been inherited by the youngest daughter. Joint (movable) property is shared equally among the remaining children. Rice fields may not be sold without the permission of the lineal segment concerned, and even then a magico-ritual sanction of provoking the wrath of the lineage ancestors acts as a further deterrent.

SOCIOPOLITICAL ORGANIZATION. Political organization.

The village community (*kutai nateut*) is a recognized political, juridical, and ritual concept. Each household (*umea*) is represented by its head (*tuai umea*), who is always the oldest married man in the household. The village community is further divided into four major patrilineages, the hereditarily senior member of each being its "elder" (*tuai dju'eui*). The four patrilineage elders, together with one other "village elder" (*tuai kutai*) constitute a kind of executive committee of the village community. This is the domain of traditional government. The modern administration, however, recognizes only a village headman, elected by all adult males. The chief of the shire (*pesirea mergo*) is likewise now elected by popular adult male suffrage, as are a number of shire councillors (*wakea madjelis mergo*). In traditional Redjang society, the chiefs of the several patriclans formed a supreme council of justice and war, the Four Pillars Council or the Four Brothers Council. This Council ceased to meet after the Redjang were conquered by the Dutch. At the suprashire level, there is now an elected assembly for the regency, as elsewhere in Indonesia. **Social stratification.** There were four strata in preconquest Redjang society: (1) clan and subclan chiefs, enjoying hereditary titles, heirlooms, and privileges, including the right to public labor to cultivate the "royal" rice fields and to a foreleg of any venison yielded by hunting in the shire (2) village headmen, former headmen, and sometimes counselors, who enjoyed such entitlements as a higher bride-price for their daughters and a percentage of taxes collected and of legal fees levied in dispensing justice at the village tribunal (3) ordinary "free" villagers, enjoying neither honorific titles nor bound to serve other men as serfs or slaves, and (4) slaves (*budo'*), usually of non-Redjang origin who were captured in wars and raids, and debtor slaves (*mengiring*), who were mainly Redjang. This status differentiation continues to form the backbone of present-day stratification. **Social control and justice.** The most powerful instrument of social control is belief in the power of ancestral spirits, guardians of traditional moral standards and values. The formal legal system operates through a tribunal of village elders presided over by the headman, whom the government recognizes as the sole person entitled to impose sentences or collect fines. **Warfare.** Before Dutch conquest, villages were fortified and guarded. Raiding parties (*tenabeun*) for women and livestock were frequent and usually resulted in retaliatory feuds. A principle of lineal accountability made it necessary for the clan of a murderer to pay blood or "resurrection" money.

RELIGION. The highland Redjang formerly practiced a syncretic religion based principally on reverence for their ancestors, fear of animistic spirits, and a belief in Hindu deities and sometimes in a great or divine god. Beginning in the 1860s, all Redjang have now been converted to Islam. **Practitioners.** Before Islam, the *dukuen* served the multiple roles of priest, diviner, doctor, druggist, ritual specialist, chronicler, and bard. He still carries out many of these functions, though some are shared with Muslim priests, medical aides, and village clerks. **Ceremonies.** Public religious ceremonies include the great annual holy day feasts of Idul Fitri, at the termination of the Puaso fast month, and Bilai Adjai, the day of the Prophet's Pilgrimage, when thanksgiving buffalo or goats are slaughtered. Ceremonies based on the "old religion" are also held, when vows are redeemed by liberating a pair of doves from a cage or by holding a ritual feast at which the *dukuen* propitiates ancestors or deities. Major ceremonies require the participation of representatives of all four original patriclans. For weddings, there is a traditional *kedjai* feast, accompanied by dancing between virginal boys and girls in the Long Hall. The greatest Redjang ceremony, the *mdundang*, held traditionally in five-, seven-, or nine-year cycles, celebrates the ritual remarriage of the male and female principles in padi, to ensure its renewed potency and fertility (Jaspan 1964b). **Death and funerary practices.** A candle is lit beside the corpse, and a vigil is kept by close kinsmen until the corpse is placed in a wooden coffin and buried. Traditional graves were of the recessed shelf type. A Muslim priest intones prayers at the graveside, and prayers for the dead are recited after sundown for one week after the burial (Jaspan 1968: 487-91).

BIBLIOGRAPHY. Hoessein 1932; Jaspan 1964a, 1964b, 1968; Marsden 1783; Voorhoeve 1955.

LEMBAK

Synonyms. *Lumba, Lemba, Lembah, Lembaq, Sindang, Orang Sindang, Sindang Merdeka, Lembak Sindang Merdeka*

ORIENTATION. **Identification.** The Highland Lembak regard themselves as the pure or original Lembak, from whom the Lowland Lembak (Lembak Pesisir, Lembak Bengkulu, Lembak Sungei Hitam, Soongy Etam) originated before their migration to the Bengkulu coastlands and their intermarriage with Serawai and Bengkulu Malays. While the Redjang, their neighbors to the west and south, regard them as a Malayanized Redjang subgroup—as do some writers such as Hazairin (1936)—they regard themselves as neither Redjang nor Malay, but an independent ethnic group (*suku*). **Location.** The Padang Ulak Tanding subdistrict of the Redjang-Lebong regency, Bengkulu Province. The terrain consists mainly of the eastern foothills of the Barisan Range, together with gently undulating lowlands through which flow tributaries of the Rawas and Musi rivers. **Linguistic affiliation.** Lembak is probably a "Middle-Malay" dialect, according to the classification of Helfrich, Brandes, and Esser, later adopted by Voorhoeve (1955). However, it is heavily influenced by Redjang. The Lembak have a *ka-ga-nga* script, identical to that of the Redjang. **Demography.** Approximately 29,000 in 1961. **History and cultural relations.** Prior to the extension of Dutch suzerainty, Lembak was regarded by the Redjang Four Pillar Confederation and the Sultanate of Palembang as a semi-independent buffer state, Sindang Merdeka (Free Marches), which paid occasional homage to both. Culturally they are more closely related to the Redjang, Ampat Lawang, and Pasemah than to the Rupit, Rawas, and other Malay subcultures of the Musi.

BIBLIOGRAPHY. Hazairin 1936; Voorhoeve 1955.

PASEMAH

Synonyms. *Besemah, Pasoemah, Pasumah, Passummah*

ORIENTATION. **Identification and location.** In a broad sense, Pasemah is a congeries of ethnolinguistically kindred groups, including: Ampat Lawang (Lintang), Gumai, Kikim, Kisam, Lematang, Mekakau, Pasemah Lebar, Semendo, and Serawai. Strictly speaking, the term Pasemah relates only to the people of the Pasemah Lebar highland plateau in the central Bukit Barisan highlands. The Pasemah and their ethnic cognates are all believed to have descended from Atung Bungsu, who in turn is believed to be a descendant of an unspecified Madjapahit king in Java. The correct name of the people, Besemah, is derived from the term *semah*, a prized river fish of the region. **Linguistic affiliation.** The languages of the Pasemah congeries were designated "Middle Malay" by Brandes in 1884. This term has never been used by the Pasemah and their neighbors, and is no longer acceptable to most students of South Sumatran linguistics. Dyen (1965) classifies Besemah as a Malay dialect within the Malayan subfamily of West Indonesian. There is a Pasemah script of Indic derivation, which closely resembles Redjang. **Demography.** There were some 82,430 Pasemah enumerated in the 1930 census (*Volkstelling 1930*, 4: 173, 221). **History and cultural relations.** The Pasemah Lebar plateau contains some of the most important megalithic statuary in Southeast Asia (van der Hoop 1932; Schüller 1936). Megalithic sites are still used as shrines by modern Pasemah, for propitiating ancestors and redeeming vows. The Pasemah were nominally subject to the control of the Sultans of Palembang in the seventeenth and eighteenth centuries (Marsden 1783: 182), although they seldom paid homage and relations between them and the lowland Malay sultanate appear to have been mediated by the buffer "free" (*mardiko*) clans or subclans. Pasemah Lebar was annexed by the Dutch in 1864-66, and incorporated into the Palembang Residency (Lekkerkerker 1916: 18). Islam gradually pervaded the area, until all Pasemah had become Muslims by about 1910. Since 1950, Pasemah have taken an increasingly active part in the government of the South Sumatra Province (Manurung et al. 1954).

SETTLEMENT PATTERN. Villages (*dusun*) were traditionally small, each having a number of outlier hamlets (*talang*). Communal houses (*bale*) for strangers and guests, reported in the early literature, had all disappeared by 1961 and had been replaced by mosques or chapels (*surau*).

ECONOMY. Extensive irrigated padi fields, producing sufficient rice both for domestic consumption and for export. Catch crops include beans, cucumbers, and maize. Tobacco, tea, and coffee are grown on a modest scale, and European vegetables are exported to Palembang.

KIN GROUPS. The Pasemah had a patrilineal system of descent reckoning and a kinship organization similar in all major respects to that of the Redjang (Marsden 1783: 226-27; Hoven 1927; Jaspan 1964b).

MARRIAGE AND FAMILY. There were two forms of marriage, each resulting in a distinctive type of family. In the past the predominant form, *belaki* ("with man"), necessitated the payment of bridewealth (*kule*) to the bride's parents. Its consequence was virilocal marriage residence, the affiliation of the wife to her husband's clan and lineage, and likewise of their children. If the husband pays no bride-price and lives uxorilocally, however, this is *tambi anak* or *ambil anak*. In this form of marriage the husband has no jural rights to his wife's property or estate, though he is often its manager.

SOCIOPOLITICAL ORGANIZATION. **Political organization.** As among the Redjang, there was and is no centralized political system. Marsden referred to an executive of four independent *pangeran*, representing the four founder clans. In local government,

before Dutch conquest, there was an inferior *pangeran* or village headman in almost every village, chosen by its inhabitants and confirmed by the superior *pangeran*. **Warfare.** In preconquest times, the Pasemah warred with the Malays in the lowlands, with the Redjang and Ampat Lawang, and with their kindred Serawai. Fighting between the Pasemah and their cognates, and on occasion between Pasemah clans or subclans, was almost endemic because of the customary law of retaliation; when peace was agreed upon a balance was struck and the side that had taken a surplus of heads was required to pay *bangun* or blood money.

RELIGION. **Indigenous religion.** Islam has been the predominant religion since about the third quarter of the nineteenth century. Prior to Islam, there was a syncretic Buddhist-Hindu-ancestor cult. Archeological research and the large anthropomorphic megaliths provide evidence of a still earlier though as yet not adequately described religion (van der Hoop 1932; Schüller 1936). The syncretic pre-Islamic belief system survives to a greater or lesser extent, both in public ceremonies at which shamans (*dukun*), headmen, or chiefs officiate and in hearthhold rites. At times of national stress there are great public ceremonies at which a buffalo is slaughtered and the ancestors are called upon to bestow blessings and stave off ill fortune. The most important vow redemption shrines are located on Mount Dempo and at certain riverine megaliths.

BIBLIOGRAPHY. Brandes 1884; Dyen 1965; Hoven 1927; Jaspan 1964b; Lekkerkerker 1916; Manurung et al. 1954; Marsden 1783; Schüller 1936; van der Hoop 1932; *Volkstelling 1930*.

ABUNG *

Synonyms. *Lampong, Lamponger*

ORIENTATION. **Identification and location.** The modern Indonesian residency of Lampung comprises that part of southern Sumatra bounded on the north by the river Tulang Bawang and by Lake Ranau, on the west by the Indian Ocean, on the south by the Sunda Straits, and on the east by the Java Sea. The name "Lamponger," in common use formerly for all the inhabitants of this area, in fact comprises several ethnic categories with different cultural histories. Abung is a generic term for a people now widespread in central and eastern Lampung. The Abung tribes have a common historical tradition of having come from the mountains to the west, where they had, prior

---

*The author of this entry, F. W. Funke, is Professor of Ethnology in the University of Cologne. His fieldwork among the Abung was carried out in 1953, mostly in the Selagai-Nunjai district and in the region of the river, Tulang Bawang.

to the fifteenth century, what by all accounts was a megalithic culture akin to that of the Niasans and Batak. Their culture today appears to be a syncretism of these earlier indigenous traits with later coastal Malay (Islamic) culture introduced from eastern Sumatra and Java. The Paminggir are descendants of Malays who emigrated from Minangkabau in western Sumatra in the thirteenth century. The present dispersed settlements of the Pubian (Pabean) represent the former population of the eastern lowlands, who for centuries have been obliged to withdraw before the encroaching Abung and Paminggir. Nowadays they live in a small territory in central Lampung. A series of transmigration schemes, started by the Dutch in 1905, has resulted in large numbers of eastern Javanese being settled in the Lampung plains. At present they are living on clearings in the forest, where they carry on hoe cultivation. Earlier, in the sixteenth and seventeenth centuries, Javanese from Bantam (western Java) emigrated to the east coast of Lampung, where they are nowadays called Orang Maringgai. For centuries the highlands left by the Abung remained uninhabited; recently they have been occupied by groups of Rabang- and Ogan-Malays from eastern Sumatra. [van Royen 1930; Funke 1955.] **Linguistic affiliation.** The Abung speak a dialect which differs little from Riau Malay. The indigenous script (a phonetic transcription, like that of the Batak) is remembered by only a few old people. The Paminggir, Pubian, and Maringgai speak Malay. **Demography.** In 1955 the total number of all the inhabitants of Lampung was about 600,000, including some 220,000 Abung, 100,000 Javanese transmigrants, and approximately 250,000 Paminggir and Pubian. [Funke 1958-61.] **History and cultural relations.** According to the annals of the coastal Malays and to their own genealogical traditions, the Abung prior to the fifteenth century occupied the west-central highlands of Lampung, which they called "Sekala Berak." Here they practiced a religious system characterized by sacrifice, headhunting, and a megalithic cult. Relics of these rites in the form of megaliths are found today in the highlands near former Abung settlements (van der Hoop 1932; Funke 1958-61: *vol. 1*). According to early Malayan annals, the Abung were driven from the highlands during the period between 1450 and 1780, as a consequence of their headhunting raids on the lowland Malays of Kroë and Semangka. About 1450, under the leadership of Minak Paduka Begeduh (who is still a culture hero to modern Abung), the first clans emigrated over the eastern passes into the lowlands. Here they first encountered the Pubians, and during the ensuing century gained ground as far as the east coast. Under the leadership of the Nunjai clan, who traced their descent directly to the hero Minak Paduka, nine tribes founded the confederation Abung Sewu Mego. Those clans from the Lake Ranau area settled in the region of the Tulang

Bawang, where they formed the confederations Mego Pak ("Four Tribes") and Buwei Lima ("Five Genealogical Tribes"). About 1550, Bantam (western Java) extended sovereignty over southern Sumatra, paying a high price for pepper and conferring honorary titles on Abungs as a reward for increased production. The result, over several centuries, has been a complicated system of titles incorporated into the indigenous system of social differentiation. Headhunting, human sacrifice, and megalithic initiation rites were interdicted by the Dutch, but continued into the nineteenth century. Initiation (the *papadon* rite) is still practiced today, with dancing in place of headhunting and with buffalo instead of human sacrifice. The Javanese, and later the Dutch, tried in vain to change Abung political structure (the genealogical *buwei* system) by the introduction of administrative *marga*. Definitive changes seem finally to be occurring under the influence of Indonesian nationalism. [Funke 1958-61: *vol. 1*.]

SETTLEMENT PATTERN AND HOUSING. **Settlement pattern.** The Abung village is the permanent settlement of a genealogical adat community (*tiuh*), in which each clan has its permanent house. However, these clan houses are inhabited by only a few, nearly always old, people; while working adults and children live in seasonal settlements, *umbulan,* most of the time. A village generally maintains several *umbulan;* these continue for several years, i.e. until all suitable virgin forest in the vicinity has been used up, and the individual houses, *umbul,* that make up the *umbulan* are old and no longer habitable. Then a new *umbulan* is established at a distance, although *umbulans* and swiddens must be within the territory of the genealogical *buwei*. A village contains up to 3,000 individuals, with as many as 120 clan houses. In every village there is a festival house, *rumah sesat,* in which, with the participation of the whole *tiuh* or *buwei* community, the initiation rites of the *papadon* feast are held. **Housing.** The ancient Abung house built on piles has the form of a rectangle, with saddle roof and open veranda. The walls are of wooden slabs and the roof covered with alang grass. The most highly developed form is the large *penjimbang* house (the house of the clan), which may have a base of more than 15 by 30 meters. [Funke 1958-61: *vol. 2;* van Royen 1930.]

ECONOMY. **Agriculture.** Within interior Lampung, the Orang Paminggir, the Orang Pubian, the Javanese transmigrants, and especially the Abung cultivate dry rice on clearings made by burning (ladang). Usually, after one harvest of rice the best ladangs are planted to pepper, *ladar*. A *kebun ladar* remains productive for 20-25 years. For centuries this kind of pepper cultivation has provided a cash crop among the Abung—and it is pepper that provides the economic base for the *papadon* feasts, which are celebrated at great expense. [Funke 1958-61: *vol. 2.*] **Fishing and hunting.** Fishing is of most importance in the territory of the Mego Pak Abung—the swampy areas on the Tulang Bawang, where dry-rice cultivation is scarcely possible. At the beginning of the monsoon rains and the annual flooding, the Mego Pak Abung move from their permanent villages into *umbuls*, from where they do not return until the end of the fishing season. Hunting is of little importance. **Domestic animals.** Include water buffalo, a few zebu cattle, the small Lampung cow, goats, poultry, and ducks. **Trade.** Confined to the sale of cultivated pepper and wild jungle products. Traders come from the coast each year to buy these products on a fixed contract basis. Articles of consumption are purchased from shops in the towns. **Property.** Within the territory of a tribe, any member may clear virgin land. Cultivated ladangs, pepper gardens, kampong houses, and *umbulans* are the property of the clans; rules of ownership are laid down in the adat. The tribal or village council, the members of which are the chiefs of the clans, arbitrates property disputes.

KIN GROUPS. The fundamental kin group is the exogamous patrilineal clan, *suku*, whose head is the *penjimbang*—a position hereditary in the male line. He administers the clan property (exclusive of land, which is owned by the tribe), decides the form and regularity of agricultural activities, and arbitrates marriage and bride-price contracts. Normally there are about ten *suku* within a village community. Marriage is generally patrilocal. If a married son has a large family, he may establish a household of his own, which is, however, subordinate to the *penjimbang*. Splitting off of new clans is rare, partly because the population is not increasing and partly because such an event necessitates the celebration of all the *papadon* rites—the responsibility for which, including the accumulation of the necessary wealth, falls mainly on the primary clan. The members of a clan were formerly localized within a village clan house. [Funke 1958-61: *vol. 2.*]

MARRIAGE. Prior to the marriage contract, Abung adat theoretically forbids any contact between the sexes which is not sanctioned by definite rules. This is accomplished in Abung villages by the institution of *mandjau* feasts, held several times each year. On these occasions the village's marriageable girls and young men, festively adorned, assemble in the festival house, *rumah sesat*, under the control of the *penjimbangs* (clan heads) of the village. They form two long rows, according to sex, and seated on the floor facing one another. After the eldest *penjimbang* has warned against infraction of the adat rules, the *mandjau* is opened. The young men and girls sing one another ciphered love songs, *pantun*, scarcely intelligible to the uninitiated. Late in the evening these verses are written on paper in Malayan script and thrown into the lap of the young girl or man of his or her choice. Formerly they were written in the ancient script of the Abung. Late at night the *mandjau* draws to a close, and at this time future marriage partners may become more intimate. Later, a young man will ask his father to negotiate concerning the bride-price, *djudjur*. The father usually requests his *penjimbang* (clan head) to do this for him. The bride-price is determined by the rank of the girl's family, e.g. for a girl of the lowest social class (*penjimbang suku*) it is 600 rupees and four water buffalo. The buffalo are killed ritually on the day of the marriage as a substitute for the human sacrifices performed formerly. ● The mode of marriage varies according to local adat. Elopement, especially common among the Mego Pak tribes, does not negate payment of the *djudjur*. Marriage among the highest *papadon* class necessitates payment by the bridegroom's father of rice, coconuts, and money to the clan of the bride. On the day of the wedding the bridegroom is carried about the village in a wooden cart of honor (*rato*), for which he must pay a high fee to the village community and in addition furnish a sacrificial buffalo. During the ceremonial ride he is obliged to give a present to each of the village *penjimbang*. This is followed by an enactment of the ancient war dance, *tari tigel*, in the village festival house, during which the bridegroom acts out the various phases of the headhunt, formerly the precondition to a marriage. The levirate is sanctioned by adat in some areas. Polygyny is allowed, but is in fact found only among the very wealthy. Exogamy is a feature of the Abung clans, but not of the genealogical tribe, *buwei*. Incest prohibitions encompass brothers and sisters and extend laterally to all degrees of cousin relationship. Divorce is theoretically impossible according to the adat; if a wife leaves her husband he must pay a fine to the village adat council. Residence after marriage is always patrilocal. [Funke 1958-61: *vol. 2.*]

SOCIOPOLITICAL ORGANIZATION. **Political organization.** The Dutch sought in vain to replace the traditional genealogical organization with an administrative one; under the Indonesian government traditional genealogical units have taken on modern administrative functions. The village community is divided into *suku administratif* (administrative wards or *sukus*), under chiefs, *kepala suku*, who are in fact always *penjimbangs*, i.e. chiefs of the old genealogical *sukus*. Nearly 20 households, i.e. genealogical *sukus*, belong to a modern administrative *suku*. The chief of the genealogical adat community is the head of the village (*kepala kampong*), and nowadays he appoints the *kepala sukus*. The former community adat council, *proatin tiuh*, assists the head of the village. According to custom, all the genealogical clan chiefs belong to this council. The next higher administrative unit is the *marga*. These modern units bear the same

names and are of the same size and extent as the ancient genealogical tribe, *buwei* (*buei*). The chief (*passirah*) of the *marga* is chosen by all the members of the *marga* for a period of four years. He is assisted by a council, *proatin marga*. The chief and the council are the local representatives of the national government, responsible for all territorial affairs and the collection of taxes. A subdistrict chief, *wedana*, is the lowest government official and has under him the *passirah* of his subdistrict. The residency of Lampung is divided into three districts, *kebupaten*, each under a district chief, *bupatih*. The North Lampung District is in large part identical with the territory of the Orang Abung. [Funke 1958-61: *vol. 2.*]
Social differentiation. The Abung have a system of initiation and social advancement which differentiates them from neighboring Indonesian-Islamic groups. Every Abung clan belongs to one of three *papadon* grades: (1) *papadon suku* (2) *papadon tiuh,* or (3) *papadon marga* (*buwei*). This grade is what determines an individual's obligations with regard to the community; the highest grade entails the greatest obligation. Although every Abung belongs to one of the three *papadon* grades at birth, the male members of a clan may pass through two different initiation ceremonies. In early life a boy bears his childhood name, but just before contracting marriage he ascends (mounts) the *rato* (ceremonial wooden cart) and drops his childhood name—taking, in addition to the title "*pangeran,*" a new name. Either soon thereafter, i.e. still in conjunction with the marriage, or at the birth of a first child or the marriage of a first child, he may ascend the *papadon*, dropping the title *pangeran* and his old name, and adopting through this ceremony the title *sutan* and his final name. Whether or not a man can accomplish both ceremonies depends on the wealth at his command (in particular the success of his pepper gardens), since the *papadon* rite is much more costly than the initial *rato* ceremony. Formerly headhunting was the precondition for these initiation rites, the pinnacle of which was the enthronement of the candidate on a dolmen of stone (*papadon batu*). At the present time the headhunting aspect has been replaced by the ancient war dance, *tari tigel*, together with a communitywide feast and buffalo sacrifice.
Slavery. The Abung formerly had slaves, whom they bought from Buginese seafarers. Slaves were sacrificed on special occasions such as the *papadon* feast or the building of a house. Slavery was abolished in the nineteenth century; nowadays wealthy Abung clans have Javanese farmhands, dependent on the clan chiefs. **Social control and justice.** The ancient Abung adat covers matters of property ownership, hereditary rights, and lesser crimes. Formerly those in positions of servitude, i.e. slaves, had few legal rights. At the present time, Javanese labor is considered outside the adat law. [Funke 1958-61: *vol. 2;* van Royen 1928; Hissink 1904; Neumann n.d.]

RELIGION. The religious ideas of the Abung are the result of centuries of influence of Javanese high culture and of Islam on a people who were formerly swidden farming headhunters with megalithic practices. Nowadays everyone in the Lampung districts is theoretically Muslim.

BIBLIOGRAPHY. Funke 1953, 1955, 1958-61; Hissink 1904; Neumann n.d.; van Royen 1928, 1930; van der Hoop 1932.

SIMALUR-BANYAK

Synonyms. *Orang Maruwi, Simaloerezen, Banjakkers*

ORIENTATION. The Simalur (Simulue, Simaloer) and Banyak (Banjak) islands, off the northwestern coast of Sumatra (2°45′ N. by 96° E.), form the northernmost group in an island chain that includes Nias, Mentawei, and Enggano. According to tradition, the islands were settled from Nias, and one of the languages spoken on Simalur, viz. Sikhulé, is evidently related to Nias (Voorhoeve 1955; Esser 1938). Any evidence of a Nias culture type was, however, obliterated under the impact first of trade and slaving relations with Atjeh and later of Islam introduced from Minangkabau (Kähler n.d., 1952). The modern population, numbering some 20,000, is a mixture of Malay, Atjehnese, Minangkabau, and indigenous elements with a culture of generally Coastal Malay type. Buffalo raising for export to Atjeh, along with wet-rice agriculture introduced from Minangkabau, form the basis of the economy.

BIBLIOGRAPHY. Esser 1938; Kähler 1952, n.d.; Voorhoeve 1955.

NIASANS

Synonyms. *Niasser, Ono Niha, Niha*

ORIENTATION. **Identification.** Niasans (in Dutch publications, Niassers) call themselves *ono niha*, "children of the people" (Suzuki 1959: 139 n. 1). Kennedy, after surveying the anthropometric data of Kleiweg de Zwaan (1913-15), concluded that the population is mixed, possibly representing the addition of Mongoloid deutero-Malay to a basic stock of Veddoid and proto-Malay (Kennedy 1935: 231). Suzuki (1959: iv) tends to discount the cultural distinction, made by Schröder and others, between North, Central, and South Nias. The monumental use of stone and wood, the complexity of social and religious forms, the presence of feasts of merit, and the importance of headhunting and human sacrifice within the aboriginal culture (largely as described by Schröder for South Nias) have long caught the imagination of ethnological theorists, with consequent suggestions of cultural similarities and connections with (among others) the Batak of Sumatra, Naga of Assam, Ngadju Dayak of Borneo, and the aborigines of Formosa (Kennedy 1935; Heine-Geldern 1928; Suzuki 1959; Schnitger 1964). **Location and geography.** A single large island 70 miles off the western coast of Sumatra, between 0°30′ and 1°30′ N. and 97° and 98° E. The Batu Archipelago, about 50 miles southeast, is midway between Nias and Mentawei. Mostly rolling hills and mountains, covered with tropical forest. **Linguistic affiliation.** Dyen thinks that Mentawei and Nias will both be shown eventually to be closely related to the Malayo-Polynesian languages of western Indonesia. The southern Nias dialect is spoken also by Batu Islanders. [Dyen 1965: 56; Voorhoeve 1955: 25-27.] **Demography.** According to Suzuki (1959: iii), the indigenous population at present numbers approximately 200,000, including some 18,000 Niasans resident in the Batu Archipelago. **History.** Traditional history mentions six legendary ancestors, some descended from the upperworld of the gods. Recorded history dates from the beginning of the nineteenth century, stimulated by Dutch military expeditions and German missionary activity. Complete control by the Dutch was effected around 1914. Native Christian revival movements started in 1917 and have continued intermittently since then, greatly increasing the pace of acculturation. [Suzuki 1958; Müller 1931; Schröder 1917: Pt. III; Schneider 1941.]

SETTLEMENT PATTERN AND HOUSING. **Settlement pattern.** Villages, *banuwa*, on South Nias may contain some thousands of inhabitants; elsewhere they generally average a few hundred people each. The village ground plan is rectangular, with a central square containing a small temple. Houses are arranged along two opposite sides of the rectangle, at one end of which is the village chief's house. Villages are generally built on naturally fortified sites or are fortified with stone walls. Stone is used extensively, e.g. for paved streets, bathing pools, staircases, benches, upright pillars, and horizontal slabs erected as memorials to the dead. According to Suzuki, the village layout is symbolic of a mythological view of the cosmos and of the Niasan socioreligious system that expresses this view. [Schröder 1917: 256-323; Suzuki 1959: chap. 4; Kennedy 1935: 235.] **Housing.** The houses, *omo*, of the chiefly aristocracy of South Nias are imposing structures, rectangular in shape and raised on a substructure of wooden beams and stones. Massive wooden posts support a high, steeply-pitched gable roof which overhangs the walls, creating a hooded effect. Decorations include carved and colored panels and moldings. The interior may be divided into a communal room, a sleeping area for unmarried men and boys, and rooms for married couples. On North Nias, houses are less imposing, more varied in type, and with a predominant oval shape. The house, like the village, is a symbolic representation of the cosmos as recounted in Niasan myth and legend. [Schröder 1917: 324-97; Suzuki 1959: chap. 5; Kennedy 1935: 234-35.]

ECONOMY. Mainly agriculture and pig raising, with hunting and fishing of secondary importance. The chief food crops are yams, rice, maize, and taro. Some wet rice is grown in swamps; in South Nias, dry-rice fields form large agricultural complexes, tilled under the guidance of the chiefly aristocracy. Pigs, domestic and wild, are the preferred ceremonial food and also a source of wealth and prestige. The most honored crafts are goldsmithing, carpentry, and copper working. Gold ornaments are in South Nias associated with the chiefly aristocracy. Exports include copra, pigs, rubber, and (in the past) slaves. Dried pig flesh served formerly as a standard of value in exchange transactions. [Schröder 1917; Kennedy 1935; Suzuki 1958.]

KIN GROUPS. **Descent.** Patrilineal (Schröder 1917: 420). **Kin groups.** Information on kin groups is unclear. Kennedy (1935: 244-46), using data primarily from Schröder, describes a system of patrilineal sibs, which he supposes has developed through the spreading out of formerly localized exogamous genealogical units in a manner analogous to that among the Batak. Nowadays a district or village may contain members of several sibs (segregated, in villages, into wards, *gana*); those who trace descent from the original settlers, however, claim superior status and the right to the paramount chieftaincy of both villages and districts. The latter appear to be in the nature of territorial-genealogical federations, which function as adat areas (cf. Samson 1936; Suzuki 1958: 47).

MARRIAGE AND FAMILY. **Mode.** Premarital sexual relations strictly forbidden. Infant betrothal formerly customary. In North Nias, the prospective couple must avoid one another; whereas in the south, a boy may perform bride service in the house of his future bride (Schröder 1917: 261). Marriage entails a complicated exchange of feasts and gifts, the most important of which is the *bowo*, or bride-price. The amount of the latter is dependent on the rank of the bride (Schröder 1917: 335) and consists mainly of pigs and gold. **Form.** Polygyny is permitted and is often the consequence of a man marrying the wives (with the exception of his biological mother) of his deceased father (Schröder 1917: 418, 425). **Extension of incest taboos.** Ideally, marriage within the clan (Kennedy's sib) is prohibited (Schröder 1917: 418). There is a fixed connubial relationship between groups, and throughout Nias the ideal marriage is with the mother's brother's daughter (Schröder 1917: 261). Suzuki (1959: 95-97) suggests the former existence of a circulating system of marriage with a phratry-dualism. **Residence.** Ultimately patrilocal, in the family house of the groom (Schröder 1917: 263).

Domestic unit. The patrilocal extended family (Suzuki 1959: 65). **Inheritance.** Sons receive the bulk of the inheritance, including real property, with the first-born having first claim (Schröder 1917: 424-25, 264). **Divorce and secondary marriage.** Divorce may be initiated by either husband or wife. The woman's family can demand a separation if her husband is slow paying the bride-price installments. The levirate occurs frequently, but is not everywhere prescribed. **Adoption.** If a man has no sons, he may adopt the son of one of his brothers. An adopted boy acquires the rights and obligations of an own son (Schröder 1917: 1072).

SOCIOPOLITICAL ORGANIZATION. **Political organization.** The traditional political unit is the village, with authority vested in a village chief, *siulu* or *salawa* (cf. Kennedy 1935: 245). The village is often a single genealogical unit (Samson 1936: 444) except in South Nias, where larger villages are divided into wards, each inhabited by a separate patrilineal kin group. In the larger villages, a paramount chief and lesser chiefs (positions patrilineally inherited within aristocratic lineages) are assisted by a council of commoner elders. Federations of clans and villages, *mado* and *ori*, sometimes translated as districts, predated Dutch colonial rule. They appear to have been based on a combination of territorial and genealogical ties (cf. Samson 1936), and were attributed by Loeb (1935: 141) to Hindu influence. They regulated such matters as boundary disputes, standards of weights and measures, amounts of bride-price, and the like. Marsden, reporting conditions in the late eighteenth century, mentions that the island was divided into 50 districts, each under a chief or radja, who were constantly at war with one another (Marsden 1966: 475). Under the modern government of Indonesia, the regency of Nias is divided into 12 administrative districts. **Social differentiation.** There are three classes, almost castelike in their rigidity (Suzuki 1959: 34; Schröder 1917: 887-912), viz. aristocrat-chiefs (sometimes called nobles), commoners, and slaves. Aristocrats (*siulu* in South Nias, *salawa* elsewhere—terms which have come to mean chief) differ from commoners not only by virtue of birth but also in appearance (dress, ornaments) and "morally" (Suzuki 1959: 34-37). According to Schröder (1917: 341), the relationship between aristocrats and commoners is largely one between creditors and debtors; aristocratic farmers and pig-raisers loan money and goods to commoners, thus making them permanent debtors. This situation is furthered by the institution of *owasa* (Suzuki 1959: 40-42) whereby commoners and aristocrats are obliged to give a series of feasts before they can acquire full rank and title. Suzuki (1959: chap. 8) makes a striking comparison between these "feasts of merit" and the potlatch of the Northwest Coast Indians. The *owasa* feasts involve the accumulation

and display of wealth—primarily in the form of gold and pigs—human sacrifice, and the erection of a stone memorial bench or slab. The latter may be of massive proportions, with the degree of prestige gained dependent on the amount of labor and expenditure of wealth involved in transporting and setting it up (cf. Schnitger 1964: 145-64). Both Schnitger and Suzuki call attention to the belief that the *owasa* of aristocrats are of benefit to the entire community—in terms of Niasan cosmology and the symbolic association of aristocrats with the upperworld, fertility, and community well-being. Slaves become so through capture or indebtedness; many in South Nias spend their lives in the fields or the homes of chiefly aristocratic families as symbols of rank and prestige. **Warfare.** Interdistrict feuding was endemic prior to Dutch rule, the most frequent causes being blood revenge and the desire for slaves and heads. The latter were required in connection with the building of a new village or temple, the secondary burial rites for an aristocrat-chief, during the making of gold ornaments, and (in Central Nias) as a preliminary to marriage. The main weapons of warfare were spears, swords, and shields. Warriors wore vests of buffalo hide or crocodile skin and helmets of metal, leather, or plaited rattan, sometimes decorated with "horns" of filigreed gold or copper. [Schröder 1917: 433; Kennedy 1935: 242.]

RELIGION. Many Niasans are nominally Christian, the result of missionary effort dating back to the 1850s. However, Christianity has in recent decades become confused with a rash of messianic-nativistic movements (Müller 1931). Islam has made headway only among the people along the coast, particularly near the harbor city of Gunung Sitoli. The indigenous religion has been described by some as a combination of animism and ancestor worship (cf. Schröder 1917; Chatelin 1881); while Suzuki (1959) presents an interpretation of Niasan religion and society based on the concept of an integrative, totemic, cosmological system, derived from a study of the mythological, artistic, ceremonial, and socioeconomic aspects of the culture. **Supernaturals.** The religion is highly complex and shows Hindu influence (Suzuki 1959). The creation triad includes the three high gods: Lowalangi, Lature Dano, and Silewe Nazarata. The spirits of ancestors—especially the culture heroes Hia, Daeli, and Hulu—as well as wood and forest spirits and spirits of the sky and water are all important. The belief system includes elements such as the cosmic tree, the magic river, and the cosmos divided into nine layers. [Schröder 1917: 447-554; Suzuki 1959.] **Practitioners.** Both men and women may be priests, *ere*, representatives of the divine totality, Silewe Nazarata. The person destined to become an *ere* may disappear, i.e. be carried off by spirits; on his return he is instructed by experienced *ere* in the performance of ritual chants, the use of cocks in sacrifices, the making of images, and techniques of curing sickness. Ritual prostitution and transvestism appear to be absent or of relatively little importance, although there is little information on this subject (Suzuki 1959: 52). No use is made of a secret language. Priests and priestesses are intimately associated with the village temple, *bale*, where the sacred images (*adu*), the sacred weights for measuring gold and pigs, and the skulls of heads taken for ceremonial occasions are housed. Temples were formerly larger than they are now and served as council halls where questions of adat were discussed and disputes adjudicated. The *kataruna*, mostly women and girls, specialize in trance behavior, during which they manifest oracular and curative powers. [Suzuki 1959: 48-55.] **Ceremonies.** Ceremonies occur throughout the life of the individual, e.g. at birth, naming, teeth filing and blackening, circumcision, and marriage. Individuals are required to sponsor successive feasts of merit which validate rank and title, the culminating one being the *boro n'adu* ceremony, held every seven or fourteen years, and featuring the destruction by priests of totemic symbols at the spot where the legendary ancestors descended from the upperworld. Most ceremonies include ritual chanting by priests, animal sacrifice, dancing, and mock battles. In daily life, offerings are made to the *adu*, wooden ancestor images. [Kleiweg de Zwaan 1913-15: *1*, 137-55; Suzuki 1959: chaps. 6-9; Chatelin 1881: 134-68; Schröder 1917.] **Soul, death, and afterlife.** According to Schröder (1917: 544ff.), Niasans distinguish between the material body, *boto*, the life-giving breath, *noso*, and the *lumolumo*, a sort of second ego or "soul." Following death, the body disintegrates, the *noso* returns to the high god, Lowalangi, and the *lumolumo* becomes a ghost. In South and Central Nias the corpse is usually placed in a coffin (*owo*, meaning boat) on a wooden platform; whereas in North Nias the bones are placed in a separate container after the body has decomposed. The bodies of slaves are simply thrown into the forest. The funerals of chiefly aristocrats may require the making of a wooden image, *adu*, and the transference into it of the ghost of the deceased. For this purpose a spider, believed to be the dead man's *lumolumo*, is brought from the grave and applied to the image. Secondary burial rites may include the cleaning of bones and (in some cases) placing the skull within a stone slab or within a small pyramid of stones. This was formerly the occasion for the sacrifice of a slave and for headhunting. [Schröder 1917; Suzuki 1959; Kennedy 1935.]

BIBLIOGRAPHY. Chatelin 1881; Dyen 1965; Heine-Geldern 1928; Kennedy 1935; Kleiweg de Zwaan 1913-15; Loeb 1935; Marsden 1966; Müller 1931; Samson 1936; Schneider 1941; Schnitger 1964; Schröder 1917; Suzuki 1958, 1959; Voorhoeve 1955.

MENTAWEIANS*

Synonyms. *Orang Mantawei, Mentaweier, Poggy-Islanders*

ORIENTATION. **Identification.** The Mentaweians can be divided into (1) the inhabitants of the Pagai Archipelago—the Sakalagan, or "people of the village" (2) the inhabitants of the island of Sipora, the Sakalelegan or Sakobau, and (3) the people of the island of Siberut. The Sakalagan and the Sakalelegan can be considered as one group, differing in certain respects from the inhabitants of Siberut. The Mentaweians are of Mongoloid stock, with some Veddoid and even Caucasoid characteristics (van Beukering 1947). **Location and geography.** The Mentawei Islands (Siberut, Sipora, North and South Pagai) lie some 70 miles off the west coast of Sumatra between 0°15' and 3°20' S. and 98°35' and 100°30' E. Nias lies some 125 miles to the northwest and Enggano approximately 170 miles to the southeast. The topography is more or less flat, the coastlines marshy with only occasional beaches. Dense tropical vegetation covers the islands for the most part. **Linguistic affiliation.** The Mentaweian languages have received relatively little serious study (Adriani 1928; Voorhoeve 1955). Although their position within Austronesian is at present obscure, Dyen (1965: 56) feels that a close relationship with the languages of Western Indonesia can ultimately be demonstrated. There is no evidence of an autochthonous writing system. **Demography.** The population of Sipora in 1966 amounted to 4,616; that of the Pagai Islands was 7,523. The total population, including Siberut, is estimated at about 20,000 (Nooy-Palm 1968: 161). **History and cultural relations.** According to Sakalagan tradition, the people came from Siberut. From Siberut they moved to Sipora, and from there to the Pagai Islands. Some believe that the word Mentawei originates from Ama Tawe, the name of a culture hero-ancestor who is supposed to have resided on Nias. Early accounts of Mentaweian culture emphasize its archaic characteristics, i.e. the lack of betel and of such traits as pottery making, rice agriculture, weaving, and metal working (cf. Crisp 1799; Marsden 1966). There is no evidence of stonework, and megalithic monuments are absent. Contact with outsiders remains negligible, limited to a few government officials, Batak and Chinese shopkeepers, Minangkabau copra merchants, and German missionaries. The latter arrived in 1901, but large-scale conversion to Christianity has occurred only since the 1950s. At present over 90 percent of the Pagai-

---

*Dr. C. H. M. Nooy-Palm, the author of this entry, is a member of the Anthropology Department, Royal Tropical Institute, Amsterdam. Her data are based in part on fieldwork in 1966 on the Pagai Islands and Sipora. The author cautions that Siberut, the other major island in the Mentawei chain, is not included in the present summary.

Sipora population is nominally Christian. As a result of these and other acculturative influences, the indigenous socioreligious structure is largely nonfunctional, although informants can still describe the traditional culture in considerable detail.

SETTLEMENT PATTERN AND HOUSING. A village, *laggai,* is normally located near a riverbank at some distance from the coast. Village populations range from 100 to 500, with an average on Pagai of 140 (Nooy-Palm 1968: 171). A village may consist of one or more wards or "barrios" (Nooy-Palm 1968: 172), each occupied by members of one or more patrilineal clans. The center of each ward (or of the village, if there is only one ward) is the *uma sabeu,* the Big House. In addition, a ward may have several *lalep* houses and *rusuk* huts, the former possessing kitchens and family altars. The *uma sabeu,* a raised longhouselike structure, is the social and religious center of the ward. New members are periodically initiated into the "*uma* community" (Nooy-Palm 1968), a genealogical and ritual group composed of ritually adult *ukkui* families who occupy rooms within the *uma sabeu* or separate *lalep* houses. The *uma* served formerly as a sleeping place for men and adolescent boys, and was the center of hunting magic and ritual; here were kept the skulls of slain animals and (probably in former times) of human enemies. Ritual attributes included metal gongs, wooden signal drums, sacred posts, a dancing floor, and a ritual field or garden. The *uma* and its surrounding houses, i.e. the "*uma* community," seems formerly to have consisted of the members of a single patrilineal clan—a situation still said to be the case on Siberut (Nooy-Palm 1968: 193). The *uma* (and the social and religious institutions associated with it) has largely disappeared with the widespread conversion to Christianity in recent decades.

ECONOMY. Agriculture is important for the food supply, as is fishing. Hunting, as well as deep sea fishing, both done by men, formerly held strong religious connotations. **Agriculture.** The principal food crop is taro, *gette* (*Colocasia esculenta* L.), which can be eaten the year around. Wet taro, more important than the dry variety, is grown on permanent fields subject to riverine flooding or to inundation by rain. The cultivation of taro is done by women, who also care for other tubers: *bio* (Indonesian *bia, Alocasia macrorrhiza*?) and *liaket* or yam (*Dioscorea alata* L.), formerly an important ceremonial food. Nowadays there are permanent rice fields on the Pagai Islands and on Sipora, laid out at the initiative of missionaries and the government. Every household has its own orchard. Although sugarcane is grown, no sugar is made. **Fishing and hunting.** Gathering of mollusks and capture of small fish and shrimps is done by women. Men fish with bow and arrow or fishing line. Ceremonial fishing expeditions to cap-

ture dugong and turtle with harpoon or net belong to the past. Monkeys and deer were once hunted with bows and arrows and dogs. **Domestic animals.** Pigs, chickens, and dogs. The cat is a recent introduction. There are no draft animals. The meat of pigs and chickens was formerly consumed on ceremonial occasions. **Food.** Taro is the staple. In the eastern part of South Pagai, sago is eaten; elsewhere it is used as fodder for pigs and chickens. Supplementary foods include yams, bananas, sugarcane, and durian. Very little that is edible is overlooked. The chewing of betel is unknown, but small cigars are popular. **Trade.** Coconuts are a cash crop on Pagai and Sipora, although the coconut was unimportant aboriginally (Nooy-Palm 1968: 168). Imports include iron for knives, iron cooking pots, fishhooks, tobacco, textiles, mosquito nets, and (until World War II) beads.

KIN GROUPS. **Descent.** The Mentaweians are patrilineal; there is no suggestion of former matrilineal descent (cf. Loeb 1928; Kruyt 1923b; Wallace 1951). **Kin groups.** The population of the Pagai Islands and Sipora is divided into 25 exogamous, patrilineal clans called *muntogat* (Nooy-Palm 1968: 200-01). The *muntogat* has no head or chief; each is divided into smaller units, groups of households which form part of an *uma.* Most have a story about their origin from a particular ancestor. Although ancestors as individuals are not worshipped, as a group they are very important. **Kinship terminology.** The main terms of reference are as follows (Nooy-Palm 1968: 202-03):

Fa	*ukkui*
Mo	*ina*
FaBr	*badja*
MoBr	*kamaman*
FaSi	*kameinan*
MoSi	*kalabai*

The aunt terminology is bifurcate collateral. The cousin terminology is Iroquois, as demonstrated by the following terms of reference, male ego speaking:

FaBrSo	*patogat ama*
FaBrDa	*patogat ama*
FaSiSo	*taluba*
FaSiDa	*taluba*
MoBrSo	*taluba*
MoBrDa	*taluba*
MoSiSo	*patogat ina*
MoSiDa	*patogat ina*
ElSib	*kebbu, maniu* (m.s., w.s.)
YoSib	*bagi, maniu* (m.s., w.s.)

There is no obvious explanation for the Iroquois cousin terminology, although the important economic role of the women with respect to taro gardens may be a factor.

MARRIAGE AND FAMILY. **Mode.** Premarital sex is generally tolerated. Characteristic of the Pagai Islands and Sipora, but nonexistent on Siberut, is the *mandi* stage, during which the young couple sleep together in a *rusuk* hut but do not eat together. Each remains economically part of his or her parents' household. Children born during this period belong to the mother's clan. At the age of about 35, the *mandi* husband becomes an *ukkui*, an event marked by an initiation ceremony; thereafter children born to ·the couple belong to the clan of the father. Concomitantly, the wife becomes a *sinanalalep* and the family moves into a *lalep* house with an ancestral altar and its own kitchen. Thereafter the family takes its meals in the *lalep*. A bride-price was paid formerly on the Pagai Islands and on Sipora, but this custom had fallen into disuse by 1920 (Kruyt 1923b, 1924). Although the status of *ukkui* has more prestige than that of *mandi*, the latter entails definite obligations, e.g. in case of divorce. The presence of *mandi* on the Pagai Islands and Sipora may point to the important economic significance of children in the household; the *silainge* (adolescent boys) and the *mandi* young men did the heavy work like making copra, the sale of which has been of greater economic importance on the Pagai Islands and Sipora than on Siberut. Adulthood (in the social sense) is reached when one becomes an *ukkui*, concerned mainly with ritual tasks and obligated to refrain from heavy labor. With widespread conversion to Christianity in recent decades, the *mandi* system has become a thing of the past. **Form.** Monogamy, both formerly and at present. **Extension of incest taboos.** The clans, *muntogat*, are exogamous. A man is forbidden to marry either his FaBrDa or his FaSiDa. He is likewise prohibited from marrying anyone in his mother's *muntogat*. In general, persons descended from the same great-grandparents are not permitted to marry, because "the ancestors dislike such marriages." **Residence.** A man is allowed to choose his partner in his own *uma* or village, provided the incest rules relating to clan membership are observed. A *mandi* husband or wife belongs to the household of his or her parents. **Domestic unit.** The household of the ritually mature family, the *ukkui* husband and his *sinanalalep* wife, is of the independent nuclear type and may include a *mandi* son or a *mandi* daughter with her children. Adolescent boys may not sleep at home; their sleeping quarters are in the *uma sabeu*. Males of *mandi* and *ukkui* status likewise sleep in the *uma* during *punen* periods, when sexual intercourse is prohibited. **Inheritance.** Traditionally, taro fields pass from a mother to her daughters; coconut and banana plantations from a father to his sons. At present, however, all fields (including rice fields) are shared equally by all the children. **Divorce and secondary marriage.** Relatively easy and common, although a fine is supposed to be paid. A man may marry his deceased wife's sister, although this is not compulsory (Nooy-Palm 1968: 209). Marriage between a widow and her deceased husband's brother is common.

SOCIOPOLITICAL STRUCTURE. **Traditional struc-**ture. The principal territorial unit was the village, inhabited by persons belonging to several different clans. A distinction was made between descendants of the founders of the village (*bakkat laggai*) and newcomers, *toi*. The head of the family that claimed direct descent from the village founders (i.e. the "owners of the land") functioned as a kind of village chief (Nooy-Palm 1968: 171). Religious affairs concerned with the *uma sabeu* were taken care of by a functionary entitled *rimata*, i.e. the head of the *uma* community, assisted by the *sikaute lulak* and the *sikamuriat*—all three subject to numerous activity and food taboos. The *sikerei*, medicine man, was also sometimes the *rimata*. **Social stratification.** The division into age-grades is important (for an extended age-nomenclature, see Nooy-Palm 1968: 215): (1) *silainge*, adolescent boys (2) *siokko*, adolescent girls (3) *mandi*, a young man who sleeps in a *rusuk* hut without ancestral altar or kitchen; a young woman who sleeps in the *rusuk* hut shared by her *mandi* partner, but who economically belongs to her father's household (4) *ukkui* (*simanteu*), a man living with his wife and children in a *lalep* house with kitchen and altar, and (5) *sinanalalep* (*simaiso*), a woman living in a *lalep*. **Social control.** Carried out by the community as a whole, mainly through accusations of witchcraft. **Warfare.** Rare; in cases of disagreement or quarrels, one moves to another village or founds a new *uma*. Headhunting was practiced formerly, but only Siberut was notorious in this respect.

RELIGION. **Supernaturals.** Named deities include: Teteu (Teteu Djodjo Lalep), the Grandfather (who shakes the houses), i.e. the spirit who causes earthquakes; Batukerabau, the male spirit responsible for the welfare of the *uma* community, whose abode is in or near the post, *batukerabau*, at the entrance to the *rimata's* room [Batukerabau is represented by sacred elements (a bead or beads), which constitute his *"punen,"* known only to the *rimata*]; Ina-n-oinan, the Mother of the River or Mother of the Water (water has a "cooling" effect which can cure illness and may be associated with fertility). There are in addition a host of forest spirits, water spirits, and sky spirits (cf. Loeb 1929a, 1929b). Forest spirits are the guardians of hunted animals; sea animals important in fishing are guarded by the sea spirits. Ancestral spirits are important because they are close to human beings. Attention is paid to the flight or call of birds, regarded as omens. Roots, leaves, and flowers may avert evil influences or have a "cooling" effect, and can serve as mediators between men and the invisible world. Tattooing, according to modern informants, had no religious significance. However, according to Hinlopen and Severijn the transition from *rusuk* marriage to "sacral" marriage took place at about age 40, when all the tattoo designs had been applied (Hinlopen and Severijn 1855, cited in Nooy-Palm 1968: 217). Also, successful headhunters received a special tattoo mark. **Practitioners.** The *ukkui* (house fathers) perform ceremonies concerning the individual households. The *rimata* carries out ancestral sacrifices and rituals concerning the entire *uma* community. When a hunting party sets out, the *rimata* remains in the *uma,* moving as little as possible to facilitate the hunt, i.e. representing the hunted animal. The party is led by the *sikaute lulak,* the ritual assistant to the *rimata.* The *sikerei,* a medicine man or shaman, may go into trance in order to cure illness, interpret omens, forecast the future, or exorcise evil spirits (Loeb 1929c). Both sexes may be *sikerei.* **Ceremonies.** The word *punen* may denote a secret of magic or religious significance or a feast of sacred character, during which people abstain from work and often also from sexual intercourse (Börger 1932a, 1932b). The most important *punen* is the *punen puenegetat,* held in conjunction with the building of a new *uma sabeu.* During this ritual feast, new *uma* members are initiated. Participation is not restricted to members of the new *uma,* but may include also those of other *uma* in the same village or even those of other villages, since the feast is held so infrequently. Divination is practiced by examining the entrails of sacrificed and/or captured animals. **Illness.** May be caused by malevolent spirits, soul loss, or by witches (male or female). Witches are hung or banished from the village. **Soul, death, and afterlife.** Every plant and animal has a soul. *Simagere* are the souls of living people and animals, *ketsat* the souls of the dead. The souls of animals pursued in the hunt are lured into the *uma sabeu* by a ceremony during which the spirits of the forest are invited to let these animals pass into the realm of men. This may be facilitated by construction of an *orat simagere,* a ladder by which the animal souls enter the world of men and become visible. The dead are buried in a cemetery at some distance downstream from the village. The corpse is carried on a bier by unmarried young men (*silainge*) and girls (*siokko*), part of the journey being by dugout canoe. A distinction is made between those who have undergone the *punen puenegetat* and those who have not, with members of the two categories being buried in separate cemeteries. The souls of the dead go to Laggai Sabeu (the Large Village), situated overseas to the west.

BIBLIOGRAPHY. Adriani 1928; Börger 1932a, 1932b; Crisp 1799; Dyen 1965; Hinlopen and Severijn 1855; Kruyt 1923b, 1924; Loeb 1928, 1929a, 1929b, 1929c; Marsden 1966; Nooy-Palm 1968; van Beukering 1947; Voorhoeve 1955; Wallace 1951.

ENGGANESE

Synonym. *Etaka*

ORIENTATION. **Identification.** The island of Enggano is supposed to have been named by sixteenth-century Spanish and Portuguese navigators, although by Indonesian traders it has long been called Pulau Telandjang. The indigenous inhabitants reject such designations and refer to themselves as *etaka* ("human beings"). The origins of the Engganese are obscure, and the indigenous culture, now virtually extinct, is known only from the casual accounts of early visitors (summarized by Keuning 1955). Judging from these accounts, the people possessed an archaic technology and appear to have had relatively little contact with the outside world. Diseases introduced by traders, beginning in the midnineteenth century, virtually decimated the indigenous population; today the few remaining Engganese are largely of mixed blood, Christianized, and living in towns along the coast. Kennedy describes the indigenous physical type as a mixture of Proto-Malay and Veddoid and cites ten Kate's reference to the striking similarity in physical type to that of the Nicobarese (ten Kate 1894b: 211, cited in Kennedy 1935: 290). **Location and geography.** Enggano and four smaller islets lie approximately 80 miles off Sumatra's west coast and some 170 miles south of Mentawei. The main island, 20 miles long, is largely low, rolling, hill country covered by secondary jungle growth. Nowadays the population is mainly concentrated on narrow plains near the sea. [Helfrich 1888; Suzuki 1958.] **Linguistic affiliation.** In vocabulary and structure, Enggano strongly deviates from other languages of Sumatra. Dyen, on the basis of lexicostatistical evidence, classed Enggano as a member of his Austronesian Linkage, but was unable to group it with any other West Indonesian language (Dyen 1965). Voorhoeve (1955) assumes that the language showed considerable dialect differentiation in former times. **Demography.** By all accounts the Engganese suffered a catastrophic decline in population beginning in the midnineteenth century—from an estimated 6,400 in 1866 to some 400 in 1961. At present, Javanese, Malays, and Chinese far outnumber Engganese. [Jaspan 1964c; Suzuki 1958.] **History and cultural relations.** Early contact of Engganese with Europeans was sporadic, beginning with a Dutch landing in 1596. At the time of first contact, the Engganese reportedly lacked weaving, rice, and metal working and were relatively isolated from surrounding peoples (Keuning 1955: 182). During the nineteenth century, Indonesian traders, many of whom settled on Enggano, appointed Engganese as intermediaries in the coconut trade, resulting in new forms of wealth and increased social differentiation among the Engganese. Islam, introduced by Muslim traders, initially had little effect; on the other hand, the Rhenish Missionary Society, beginning in 1902, has had considerable success in converting Engganese to Christianity. In 1961, the government of Indonesia designated Enggano as a rehabilitation center for youthful Javanese offenders, and as of 1963 some 2,600 had been transferred to Enggano (Jaspan 1964c).

SETTLEMENT PATTERN AND HOUSING. **Settlement pattern.** Originally fortified villages or hamlet clusters, containing unwalled council houses raised on piles. Villages were formerly situated in the hilly interior, but in the nineteenth century commercial possibilities lured the population to the shore. At present, the Engganese live in three villages along the northeast coast. [Jaspan 1964c; Kennedy 1935: 293.] **Housing.** Houses were originally circular in shape (beehive), about ten feet in diameter, and raised on piles about 15 feet above the ground. The entrance to each house was an elliptical hole in the wall, just large enough for a man to crawl through. Nowadays, houses are of the common Malay type.

ECONOMY. **Agriculture.** Originally cultivators of tuberous plants, such as taro and cassava, on swiddens. Nowadays swidden agriculture has been largely abandoned, and the people depend primarily on the exchange of copra for rice. [Helfrich 1888: 282-83; Jaspan 1964c: 111.] **Fishing and hunting.** Fishing is important and was formerly done with nets and spears, the hook and line reportedly being unknown. Wild pigs are hunted with nets and dogs, and birds caught with nets or snared with lime. **Domestic animals.** Domestic pigs are well cared for and eaten only at feasts. There were reportedly no dogs or chickens on Enggano originally; along with cattle, they have been imported within recent centuries. [Keuning 1955: 200; Suzuki 1958.] **Industrial arts.** The Engganese are skilled wood workers and carvers, as witness their elaborately carved women's headdresses, surmounted by crouching human and animal figures. Weaving was formerly unknown, and clothing was made from barkcloth or banana fibers. Pottery making and metallurgy, although present, are poorly developed and may not be indigenous. Double-outrigger canoes are used for fishing along the shore. [Kennedy 1935.] **Property.** The nuclear family possesses its own house, implements, and fields. Waste land is village-owned. According to Jaspan (1964c: 112), most property, including all immovable property, is nowadays legally vested in the wife.

KINSHIP. Older sources describe the Engganese as being divided into four (also five, six, or eight) exogamous, matrilineal nonlocalized "clans." Jaspan (1964c) found vestiges of this system on present-day Enggano, with at least three clans present in each village. His informants failed, however, to confirm Keuning's (1955: 191) supposition of an earlier moiety system. Clans function with respect to marriage regulations, inheritance rules, and mutual aid. There appear also to have been genealogical units (possibly associated with territorial divisions of some kind)

that regulated use of land, water, and fishing rights (Suzuki 1958; Kennedy 1935).

MARRIAGE. A bride-price of weapons and ornaments seems formerly to have been the rule. Nowadays a wedding feast is held in the bride's home, with the groom and his kinsmen contributing to the cost. Most marriages are monogamous, and the household normally consists of a single nuclear family. There is a preference, persisting to the present, for marriage with the MoBrDa. Residence immediately following marriage is almost everywhere uxorilocal, but following the birth of the first child the couple thereafter reside neolocally. [Jaspan 1964c; Kennedy 1935.]

SOCIOPOLITICAL ORGANIZATION. Indigenous political organization does not appear to have existed above the village (or possibly clan-barrio) level. According to Jaspan (1964c: 111), an elder acts as head of the clan, *kapa'ehida.* Transgressors of adat were formerly required to pay a heavy fine in ancient, highly valued beads; nowadays the fine, paid to the clan head in cases of violation of incest rules, consists partly of cash. Enggano is at present a subdistrict within the North Bencoolen Regency; each indigenous village has an elected headman and an adat elder. [Ancona 1935; Helfrich 1888: 288-89; Jaspan 1964c; Kennedy 1935.] **Warfare.** Intervillage feuding and warfare was endemic in former times. Heads were apparently taken on occasion, but there is little information as to their ritual significance, if any. Women apparently on occasion fought alongside the men. [Oudemans 1889; Kennedy 1935.]

RELIGION. Information concerning the indigenous religion is scanty and of doubtful reliability. Most Engganese have converted to Christianity, introduced in 1902 by the Rhenish Mission, aided by Toba Batak evangelists. Since World War II, there has been a tendency among the Christian Engganese to convert to Islam. The traditional religion contained elements of spirit propitiation, including that of ancestral spirits. A major annual festival, reminiscent of the *boro n'adu* ceremony of Nias, featured a coming together of the total population, the presence of "priests," and the division of the participants into two groups engaged in a ritual tug-of-war. Death was marked by an extended mourning period and the imposition of rigorous taboos on social intercourse. A deceased's family, and on occasion an entire village, were under certain circumstances required to change residence. The dead were wrapped in barkcloth and buried in the ground outside the village. [Jaspan 1964c; Suzuki 1958; Helfrich 1888: 280-82; Modigliani 1894: 187-205.]

BIBLIOGRAPHY. Ancona 1935; Dyen 1965; Indonesia 1954; Helfrich 1888; Jaspan 1964c; Kähler 1942-45; Kennedy 1935; Keuning 1955; Modigliani 1894; Oudemans 1889; Suzuki 1958; ten Kate 1894b; Voorhoeve 1955.

KUBU

Synonym. *Koeboe*

ORIENTATION. **Location and identification.** Scattered throughout Sumatra's swampy east coast lowlands and extending westward into the foothills of the Barisan Range are remnant groups of forest dwellers, some of whom still practice a primitive nomadic or seminomadic form of hunting and gathering economy. The term Kubu (possibly from *ngubu*, "elusive") is used by Palembang and Djambi Malays to refer in a generic sense to these peoples. Like such Malay terms elsewhere—Sakai, Benua, Utan—the term Kubu is a pejorative one, having the general connotation of "backwoodsman" or "primitive." As such it is resented by the peoples so designated, who refer to themselves by local names or as Orang Darat ("people of the land") or by the name of the dominant ethnic group with which they wish to be identified (e.g. Orang Mandailing, Orang Djambi). Named populations of Kubu include Mamak (Mamaq, Mamma), along the Kuantan, Gangsal, and Retih rivers, supposed by some to be the autochthones of the ancient kingdom of Indragiri; Sakai (also Batin—not to be confused with the Batin of the Tambesi drainage farther south in Djambi and noted elsewhere in this volume under Redjang), Akit (Aket, Akik), Talang, and Tapung—all in Siak, along the banks of the Siak, Kampar, Mandau, and Rokan rivers; and Orang Utan and Orang Rawas, at the mouth of the Siak and adjacent coastal swamplands. Farther inland, in the foothills and lower ranges of the Barisan Mountains, are the Lubu (Loeboe) and Ulu (Oeloe) of the Mandailing and Padang Lawas regions of the Bataklands; and farther south, the Rawas, Duwablas, and Mountain Kubus. Off Sumatra's east coast, in the wooded interiors of Banka, Billiton, and the Riau-Lingga Islands, remnant forest nomads are known by the Malay generic, Benua, or more locally as Orang Darat, Orang Lom, Orang Mapor, or Orang Kepor. ● Following Kennedy (1935), the term Kubu has been adopted as a generic designation for all these peoples. According to Kennedy, they represent an ancient primitive stratum of basic Veddoid physical type, once more widespread throughout the Malaysian Archipelago but since obliterated or physically assimilated into later Malay populations. Nowadays this ancient stratum is represented by scattered remnant groups which include, in addition to those found on Sumatra and the Riau-Lingga Islands, the so-called Jakun and Sakai (Senoi) tribes of the Malay Peninsula. Practically everywhere these groups are being physically and culturally absorbed into the dominant settled populations with which they are in closest contact. Those on Sumatra's east coast, for example, are for the most part living in squalid conditions as marginal members of poorer rural Malay villages and practicing an indifferent kind of settled agriculture. As a further example, the Lubu in the central Barisan mountain region near Panjabungan in Great Mandailing (Bataklands) are despised by the Batak, who suspect them of witchcraft; the Lubu, on the other hand, do their best to pass as Muslim Mandailing Bataks and call themselves Orang Mandailing (Maasland 1940; Helbig 1933: 366-69). Prolonged linguistic, cultural, and, to a considerable extent physical, assimilation to Coastal Malays, Minangkabau, Batak, Kerintji, and Bankanese renders attempts to reconstruct the "original" language or culture of these forest nomads virtually fruitless. [Kennedy 1935; Loeb 1935; Hagen 1908a; van Dongen 1910; Indonesia 1954.] **Linguistic affiliation.** At present the various peoples herein termed Kubu speak the language or dialect of the dominant group with which they are most closely associated, e.g. Riau or Djambi Malay, Minangkabau, or Mandailing Batak. Alleged unintelligibility, from the point of view of Malay speakers, is due to peculiarities in sound system or intonation, according to Voorhoeve (1955: 19). The statement by the same author that the Kubu do not possess a language of their own implies the loss of an original language—a frequent assumption, together with the implication, on the part of some writers, that the lost language must have been unrelated to Malay or possibly even non-Austronesian. An alternative possibility is suggested by Hudson's recent grouping under the rubric "Malayic Dayak" of the languages of certain non-Muslim tribes of southwestern Borneo, with the suggestion that the speakers of these languages, together with the Iban, "represent a group similar to the so-called 'aboriginal Malays' of the Malay Peninsula, whose ancestors migrated to Western Borneo from Sumatra or Malaya prior to the advent of Islam in Southeast Asia" (Hudson 1970). Under this hypothesis, the Kubu-type languages would be members of Hudson's proposed "Malayic" category, a "general term to refer to the various descendants of proto-Malayic, such as Malay, Iban, Selako [Land Dayak], and Minangkabau, wherever they occur" (Hudson 1970: 3). **Demography.** Reliable population figures for scattered groups of forest nomads are notoriously difficult to obtain, while the case of the Kubu peoples is rendered more difficult by the process of assimilation—of Kubu "passing" as Djambi Malays or Mandailing Bataks—and the consequent imprecise usage of census categories. In 1935, Kennedy estimated a total for the peoples he termed Kubu of possibly 25,000, but ethnic assimilation and mortality due to worsening living conditions have undoubtedly reduced this number considerably. Estimates of subgroup populations include: Lubu, 2,500, and Ulu, 4,000 (Maasland 1940: 1341); Sakai, 3,000 (Moszkowski 1909: 91); Akit, 300 (Kennedy 1935); and Mamak, 2,000 (Obdeyn 1929: 357).

SETTLEMENT PATTERN AND HOUSING. Most Kubu have become settled agriculturists and are now living in rural Malay villages, where they construct crude Malay-type huts. By all reports they were formerly nomadic or seminomadic, camping for a few days or a week at a time in bamboo and leaf shelters built on low, raised platforms. Some groups, such as the Sakai, build multifamily Malay-style dwellings in villages hidden deep in the jungle; such villages are moved every few years. [Kennedy 1935; Hagen 1908a: 93-104.]

ECONOMY. Most Kubu groups rely on hunting, fishing, and gathering, combined with the growing of yams, maize, rice, plantain, and sugarcane in ill-kept fields. The few remaining nomadic groups plant maize and tubers in partially cleared sites, moving off on a round of hunting and gathering activities and returning to harvest the crop when it matures. Elephant, wild pig, and monkey are hunted with nets, poison, blowguns, and spears. Among nomadic groups, the only domestic animals are the cat and dog. Indigenous industries consist chiefly of the making of bark cloth, mats, and baskets. Weaving is absent, and metal working sporadic and crude—presumably learned from Malays. Pottery making is absent except on Banka and Billiton. Kennedy believes that body mutilations such as tooth filing and supercision, found nowadays among some Kubu peoples, have been adopted from neighboring groups such as Batak and Kerintji. The Kubu economy has always relied on trade with settled villagers—in particular the exchange of forest products for necessities such as metal and salt. [Kennedy 1935; Loeb 1935; van Dongen 1910: chap. 4; Hagen 1908a: 104-17.]

SOCIOPOLITICAL ORGANIZATION. Under nomadic conditions the Kubu move in bands or "hordes" of families related by blood or affinal ties; the oldest man, if physically fit, acts as leader. Settled Kubu tend to be absorbed into the economic and political spheres of coastal Malay sultans and to adopt the customs of dominant Djambi, Riau, or Palembang Malays. In addition many Kubu have attached themselves to villages of Minangkabau, Kerintji, and Redjang immigrants into the eastern lowlands. As a result, some Kubu are organized into *suku* or subtribes, each with a chief and subchiefs bearing titles of Hindu (Sanskrit) derivation. The Talang, Sakai, Mamak, and Akit possess a matrilineal sib structure similar to Minangkabau (Obdeyn 1929; Schneider 1958; Moszkowski 1908; Tideman 1935); and the Lubu have adopted the Mandailing Batak pattern of separate sleeping quarters for girls, exogamous *margas*, MoBrDa marriage, and bride-price (Helbig 1933: 174-78; Kreemer 1910: 311-12).

RELIGION. Settled Kubu for the most part claim to be Muslims, thus asserting their identification with Coastal Malays. Shamans practice curing rites, in which dancing, drum beating, and chanting in an archaic language lead to spirit possession (van Dongen 1910: 240-46). Bird omenology is carried out in connection with hunting activities. The Lubu have the idea of a great protector or original ancestor, although there appears to be relatively little development among Kubus of ancestor cults or secondary burial rites. The more primitive nomadic groups seldom bury the dead; rather, the corpse may be abandoned or cremated within the hut where death occurred or, occasionally, on a specially constructed scaffolding. Alternative methods include binding the body in a knee-to-chest position before placement within a hollow tree. Settled groups bury the corpse, wrapped in cloth, in an earth grave, the surface of which may be marked with a small hutlike structure, with poles decorated with streamers, or with earthen mounds. [Kennedy 1935; van Dongen 1910: chap. 9; Keereweer 1940.]

BIBLIOGRAPHY. van Dongen 1910; Hagen 1908a; Helbig 1933; Hudson 1970; Indonesia 1954; Keereweer 1940; Kennedy 1935; Kreemer 1910; Loeb 1935; Maasland 1940; Moszkowski 1908, 1909; Obdeyn 1929; Schneider 1958; Tideman 1935; Voorhoeve 1955.

JAVA

JAVA AND THE JAVANESE have played an important role in the ethnohistory of the Indonesian Archipelago. Java was a center of development of the early Hinduized states of the region, represented at its peak by the fifteenth-century kingdom of Madjapahit. Through the conquests of Madjapahit, Hindu-Javanese high culture penetrated much of what is now modern Indonesia. Although the acculturative impact of this penetration has been most pervasive in coastal areas, it has not been without its effect on interior upland peoples. In short, the cultural amalgam of modern Indonesia cannot be understood without reference to the historical impact of Indian civilization—in particular its manifestation in the form of early Hindu-Javanese high culture. Although the inhabitants of Java are customarily referred to in a collective sense as Javanese, there is an awareness of some degree of physical and cultural differentiation within the indigenous population; thus it is customary to distinguish the Javanese proper, who constitute by far the bulk of the population, from other major categories, such as Sundanese and Madurese, and from relatively minor groups such as Tenggarese and Badui. The differences that mark off these ethnic categories appear to be the result primarily of differing degrees of exposure to alien cultural influences, principally that of early Hindu civilization. The Sundanese and Madurese were apparently less subject to Hinduization than were the peoples of central and eastern Java—those who now constitute the Javanese proper—although later Islamization contributed a cultural inventory common to all three. The distinctiveness of the Tenggarese and Badui seems to lie primarily in their history of resistance to Islam.

JAVANESE*

Synonyms. *Orang Djawa, Wong Djawa, Tijang Djawi*

ORIENTATION. **Identification.** The Javanese call themselves Wong Djawa or Tijang Djawi. Orang Djawa is the Indonesian term. According to philologists, the word *djawa* was originally the Prakrit form of the Sanskrit word *yawa*, meaning "barley." It appears in ancient Javanese royal inscriptions as early as A.D. 732; in Javanese literary works as early as the eleventh century, it refers to the Javanese as constituting a nation. **Location.** The area of the Javanese includes all of the eastern and central portions of the island of Java. There are also Javanese colonies in other parts of Indonesia, some dating back more than a century (e.g. Tondano and Pineleng in North Celebes). **Linguistic affiliation.** Javanese belongs to the West Indonesian branch of the Hesperonesian subfamily of the Malayo-Polynesian family (Dyen 1965). The language has a long literary history that goes back to the eleventh century. Modern Javanese is characterized by an elaborate system of nine styles of speech, which incorporate obligatory distinctions in regard to differences in status, rank, relative age, and the degree of acquaintance between addresser and addressee. In addition, there exist in Javanese about 300 alternative references called *krama inggil*, which are obligatory in reference to possessions, body

parts, actions and qualities of the addressee and to those of a third person who is higher or older than the speaker. The current process of change from a traditional agrarian and feudalistic society to a modern, industrial, and democratic state, will no doubt simplify these systems of Javanese speech levels (cf. Soepomo Poedjosoedarmo 1968). **Demography.** The island of Java accounts for more than two thirds of the total population of Indonesia, having commenced its phenomenal growth in the first half of the nineteenth century. In the census of 1931, Java had more than 41.7 million inhabitants, about 27 million of whom were Javanese. In the census of 1961, which failed to record ethnicity, the figure for Central and East Java alone is more than 42 million, but since Java is now populated by large numbers of immigrants and since many Javanese have migrated to places all over Indonesia, it is impossible to estimate the current number of ethnic Javanese. [See Indonesia 1960; Hawkins 1967; McNicoll 1968.] **History.** Like the Sundanese, the Javanese had wet-rice agriculture and a state organization prior to Hinduization. These early states later made use of Indian Brahmans to advise them on a type of government ritual which supported a hierarchical state organization under a sacred king. One of these petty kings, Sanjaya of Mataram, managed to achieve supremacy over parts of Central Java during the early eighth century. An East Javanese state flourished under King Airlangga during the first half of the eleventh century, with its capital near the present town of Kadiri, and port towns on the Gulf of Surabaja became flourishing centers of trade with other parts of Indonesia and with the Malay Peninsula. In the thirteenth century, the capital was moved again, to Singosari. The ruler, Kertanegara, set out to establish his influence over other parts of Indonesia and the mainland, and even felt strong enough to defy the envoys of Kublai Khan. His son-in-law, Vijaya, founded a new kingdom, Madjapahit, which achieved the greatest expansion of any of the early Javanese empires, extending from the mainland of Southeast Asia to the west coast of New Guinea. Both Shivaism and Mahayana Buddhism were recognized by the State. A *kraton* (palace) style of life with a distinctive grandeur flourished, contrasting strongly with the life of the wet-rice peasants in the villages. International trade was dominated by foreign merchants, Indian Muslims and probably a few Chinese, living in separate quarters in port towns. As the power of Madjapahit declined throughout the fifteenth century, the important trade routes from the spice islands in the Moluccas came under the control of Indian Muslims (and at a later date Malay Muslims). As a result, the Javanese port-town aristocracies adopted Islam; a *santri* (Muslim-oriented) way of life developed within these *pasisir* or coastal areas. Subsequently, Islam penetrated the interior of Java, either through activities of Muslim missionaries or through

---

*The author of this entry, Koentjaraningrat, is Professor of Anthropology in the University of Indonesia.

political confrontation of Muslim *pasisir* states with Madjapahit's declining power. During the sixteenth century, the kingdom of Mataram arose in Central Java. Its ruler, Sultan Agung, was concerned by the expanding power of the Dutch East India Company in its attempts to monopolize the Indonesian spice trade. His attempts to attack the base of Dutch power in Batavia (present-day Djakarta) failed. After Sultan Agung's death in 1645, large parts of Mataram's territory passed into the hands of the Dutch East India Company and subsequently, in 1799, into those of the Dutch colonial government. ● The removal of the Dutch by the Japanese during World War II opened many administrative and technical positions to Indonesians in general and to Javanese in particular. Between the moment of Japan's surrender and the landing of the allied forces, the Indonesians proclaimed their independence on August 17, 1945. The Dutch returned under cover of the allied forces; but with guerrilla warfare that lasted for almost four years, mainly in the Javanese rural regions of Central and East Java, the young Indonesian Republic succeeded in safeguarding her independence. The Dutch gave in, and the formal transfer of sovereignty which occurred in The Hague on December 27, 1949, made Indonesia a fully independent state.

SETTLEMENT PATTERN AND HOUSING. **Settlement pattern.** Villages range from 300 to over 3,000 inhabitants. Mountain and hill villages often consist of clusters of spatially distinct hamlets set in luxuriant groves of vegetation, with cultivated fields in between; while lowland villages tend to form nucleated settlements comprising rows of houses along a road, with occasional clustering. Landholdings are generally small and extremely fragmented. **Housing.** The average house in a Javanese village is a small, rectangular, thatched-roof structure built directly on the ground. The inside of the house is divided into small compartments by movable bamboo panels. Floors are earthen. The Javanese distinguish several house styles, determined by the shape of the roof, one of which is restricted to families who consider themselves descendants of the original inhabitants and therefore the village's "upper class." Most villages also contain houses reflecting urban influence, with brick walls and tiled roofs. Houses of high ranking administrative officers and members of the nobility are usually fronted by a large, open pavilion used for gatherings or celebrations.

ECONOMY. The subsistence economy depends mainly on irrigated, wet-rice agriculture; livestock production is unimportant, except in villages near main highways. Coastal villages in East Java depend more heavily on fishing. **Agriculture.** For most of Central and East Java, rice is the principal item of diet. In arid or densely populated areas such as the mountainous west or the limestone hills of the south, the peasant population has shifted to manioc. Peasants in densely populated areas may acquire land by renting, pledging, or sharecropping; the majority, however, are landless agricultural laborers. The supply and control of water is the key factor in wet-rice growing, and many farmers still practice traditional methods of augury for delicate timing of flooding, sowing, and transplanting. Fields are worked with a plow pulled by bullocks or water buffalo—or by men, in densely populated areas. After plowing, the field is harrowed with a drag, also pulled by bullocks, buffalo, or men. The crop is harvested by women, who cut the stalks by hand with a small, hoe-shaped knife. The grain is threshed in hollowed out wooden logs. The rice harvest is followed by a variety of dry-season crops such as vegetables, soya beans, peanuts, yams, chilies, and sometimes tobacco and sugarcane. **Domestic animals.** Domestic animals include chickens, ducks, cattle, sheep, and water buffalo. **Food and stimulants.** The main dish of a Javanese peasant meal consists of steamed or cooked rice with dried salted fish, vegetables, soy-bean cake and curd as side dishes, while chilied sauces further enliven the meal. Alcoholic beverages include rice wine and palm wine (*arak*). Tobacco is consumed in the form of homemade cigarettes. Betel chewing, practiced by the older generation of women, is gradually disappearing. **Industrial arts.** Small-scale cottage industries in Central Java, e.g. silverwork, batik, hand-weaving, and the making of native cigarettes, absorb a high degree of labor input per unit of raw material. Capital, distribution, and marketing problems have prevented the rapid expansion of small-scale industry. **Trade.** Local markets integrating four to five villages are found throughout rural Java. The majority of retailers are women (Dewey 1963). **Land tenure.** Earlier land tenure surveys revealed that in rural Central and East Java, individual property rights were less strongly developed than in West Java, and that the right of disposal of the land by the community continued to be strong during the nineteenth century. Even today, communal land is reserved for schools, roads, cemeteries, and for support of the village headman and his staff. In former days, village heads had to recruit corvée labor for the king, the princes, or for the Dutch colonial government. For this they had to rely on a group of villagers (*kuli*), who constituted the productive and labor force of the village. As compensation, village communities allotted to the *kuli* plots of communal land for usufruct during their periods of service. In parts of Java, *kuli* became a hereditary status, descending together with the plot of communal land to a son of the previous occupant. Many Javanese villages have in addition tracts of communal land allotted to the population for usufruct on a rotating basis.

KIN GROUPS. **Descent.** The Javanese reckon descent bilaterally. **Kinship terminology.** The following is an abbreviated list of kin terms in their *ngoko* forms from Koentjaraningrat (1956: 78-80; 1961: 108-09):

FaFa, MoFa, FaMo, MoMo	*mbah*
Fa	*bapaq*
Mo	*ibu*
So, Da	*anaq*
FaElBr, FaElSi, MoElBr, MoElSi, FaElBrWi, FaElSiHu, MoElBrWi, MoElSiHu	*uwa*
FaYoSi, MoYoSi, FaYoBrWi, MoYoBrWi	*bibiq*
FaYoBr, MoYoBr, FaYoSiHu, MoYoSiHu	*paman*
ElBr	*kakang*
ElSi	*mbaqju*
YoBr, YoSi	*adiq*
SoDa, SoSo, DaDa, DaSo	*putu*

Javanese kinship terminology reflects the social importance of the nuclear family. The criterion of sex is ignored in the terms for children. Sibling terminology reflects relative age, but only elder siblings are differentiated terminologically by sex. Cousin terminology conforms to the Eskimo pattern, while the degree of collaterality is differentiated by separate terms up to the third cousins. The terms for the parents' siblings extend matri- and patrilaterally, differentiating relative age in relation to the parents and differentiating sex in relation to the parents' elder siblings. Classificatory terms for grandparents and grandchildren extend collaterally. **Kin groups.** In general, the range of kinship affiliation is limited primarily by memory, acquaintance, and needs, rather than by structure, custom, or common residence, and therefore differs from individual to individual. Javanese peasants show little interest in relatives beyond the second ascending generation and the first degree of collaterality. The interest in second cousins is only a consequence of the existence of a marriage taboo. The Javanese *prijaji* (the class of government officials and members of the civil service) are much concerned with genealogies which can indicate kinship relations with princely families at the courts in Central Java, although this interest has lessened since World War II and the lowered prestige of the nobility. ● The nuclear family (*kulawarga*) is the basic kin group in the life of every Javanese. Outside the nuclear family, the Javanese recognize the *golongan*, an occasional bilateral kin group, whose members are mainly co-resident in one village, and who contribute to or participate in life cycle ceremonies. The *golongan* closely resembles the usual concept of the kindred. In many rural areas of Java, however, especially in those where Islam did not strongly influence the world view of the people, the peasants make a clear distinction between the *golongan* and the *alur waris*, an unambiguous, optional, ancestor-oriented, ambilineal kin group, which shares the obligation of caring for its ancestors' graves. The members of the *alur waris* who

reside in the village are practically the same as those of the *golongan*. However, it also has members outside the village, i.e. former villagers who have emigrated (cf. Koentjaraningrat 1968). **Extension of incest taboos.** Unions between members of the nuclear family and between second cousins are prohibited—the latter sanctioned by supernatural punishment. This taboo, though apparently unknown among the higher classes, is very strong among peasants and in rural families. Although theoretically prohibited, disapproved marriages can nevertheless be arranged by the performance of preventive rituals. Unions of this type include: (1) those between consanguineal relatives where the groom belongs to a younger generation than the bride (2) those between paternal parallel cousins (3) sororate unions and in general any marriage with a relative of a deceased spouse. Marriage is permitted between "adopted" children in a nuclear family and between maternal parallel cousins. In general, the Javanese do not have the notion of approved or preferred marriages. In several areas, to be sure, unions with a cross-cousin are regarded with positive favor, but in other regions cross-cousin marriages are simply a frequent form of permitted marriage.

MARRIAGE AND FAMILY. **Mode.** Although in rural communities and among orthodox families of the nobility marriages are still arranged by the parents, Javanese youth in general do their own courting and make their own choice of a mate—but with parental approval. The wedding, which is the most important and elaborate ceremony in the entire life cycle, includes the following elements: (1) the presentation of the bridal gift to the bride's parents by the groom's paternal and maternal relatives (2) the gathering party of the bride's kindred at her house, on the evening before the wedding (3) the conclusion of the marriage contract by a Muslim religious official, and (4) the ceremonial meeting of the bride and groom. **Form.** Polygyny is rare in Javanese society, except among the lower levels of the urban population and the more orthodox high ranking *prijaji* and nobility. **Residence.** There is no fixed rule of residence determining where a married couple should live. The ideal is an independent household, but in villages of South-Central Java there is a definite pattern of initial uxorilocality. Permanent residence in many such cases is uxorilocal, although the couple may live virilocally if the husband has prospects of inheriting a larger amount of land from his own parents. In urban *prijaji* families, neolocal residence is the norm. In families of high ranking *prijaji* and of the nobility who live in large extended family houses, utrolocality seems to be the pattern. Because of the acute housing shortage in the larger cities, urban couples tend to reside after marriage in the home of either the bride's or the groom's family—depending upon convenience—and hence in utrolocal residence. **Domestic unit.** A household (*somah*) in rural communities and among the average urban *prijaji* is usually a monogamous, nuclear family, although retired parents, grandparents, nephews and nieces, and a young couple residing initially in uxorilocal residence may be added. Among the high ranking *prijaji* and the nobility, the household is often a polygynous, utrolocal, extended family. A Javanese household is never a stable unit, however, and its composition is subject to continual change. In most of Java, the average per household is between five and six; for the town of Modjokuto, in East Java, for instance, it is 5.27 (H. Geertz 1961: 32). **Divorce.** In regard to separation and divorce, Javanese of all classes follow the rules laid down by Muslim law. Divorce may be granted upon request of the husband without the consent of the wife. Infants who require maternal care always follow the mother. Each spouse retains the property which he or she brought into marriage, but the property they acquired together is divided two thirds to the husband and one third to the wife. The incidence of divorce appears to be quite high, especially in rural areas but also among the lower levels of the urban population. **Inheritance.** Each dwelling with its surrounding garden land is regarded as an inseparable complex. In rural areas, when the parents are at retiring age, a married daughter or married granddaughter is chosen to reside permanently in the house with her husband and children, being charged with the obligation of caring for the aging couple. Her husband assumes the responsibilities of head of the household, and automatically inherits the house and garden of his wife's father or grandfather, when the old man dies. Cultivable land, fruit trees, and domestic animals are inherited in equal shares by children of both sexes. Heirlooms, consisting of sacred weapons and other small or valued objects, are given to one of the sons, usually the eldest.

SOCIOPOLITICAL ORGANIZATION. **Traditional structure.** Traditional Javanese social organization seems to have adopted the terminology and outward symbols of an early Indian caste system. Groups of peasant villages in defined areas were ruled by a landed nobility or gentry who represented the king at the central court, while some areas were allotted by the king to his relatives as appanage. The so-called free villages, always situated near sites of royal tombs and state temples, had the obligation of caring for those structures. For compensation, the king declared them *desa merdikan* and granted them freedom from taxation. Sea trade was mainly in the hands of Chinese, Gujaratis, Tamils, and Malays, concentrated in coastal and port towns. Authority in the port towns was vested in the harbor prince, with his armed force and administrative apparatus. The nobility lived in court towns in the interior, inhabited by courtiers,

court literati, craftsmen, and a prestigeful priestly caste. They surrounded the ancient Javanese kings, sustaining their power by an elaborate system of rituals and symbols, which included Brahmanistic as well as indigenous Indonesian elements (Berg 1938). These were based on the principle of the cosmic role of the divine king, who was considered to be the magical center of the kingdom and the universe (Heine-Geldern 1942; Moertono 1968). During the Islamic period, the main picture of Javanese social structure seems not to have changed substantially, except that the priestly caste ceased to exist. With the establishment of the Dutch colonial system subsequent to 1755, two other social classes emerged, viz., the nonpeasant laborers in the towns and the white-collar workers and civil servants, called *prijaji*. Within this latter category, Western education and the command of Dutch became the most potent means for upward mobility. An important subgroup of the *prijaji* consisted of those who had received advanced academic training. In the colonial period up to 1940 there were only three schools of university level, the first graduates of which came into Javanese society in the period before World War I. Many of these *prijaji* became active in nationalistic movements before World War II (Van Niel 1960). In several areas of North-Central and East Java and at the principality court towns, Javanese merchants succeeded in establishing themselves in those sectors of the economy not yet occupied by the Chinese, i.e. small-scale cottage industries. They have tended to form a separate social class, the *wong sudagar*, who usually live in a separate quarter, called *kauman*. **Contemporary structure.** Since World War II and Independence several basic changes have occurred, although peasants still form the main part of the population (84.7 percent, according to the 1961 census). There is a growing category of landless agricultural laborers, many of whom have migrated to the cities, and the large urban proletariat is becoming an urgent problem. Extension of educational facilities and shifts in the bureaucratic structure have contributed to the drive for upward mobility on all levels (Van Niel 1960; Palmier 1960). Many peasants have become *prijaji* through education and occupational advancement in government service, and today the *prijaji* class is more open and more differentiated than formerly. Young people from the merchant class have also entered the civil service and the professional occupations, while people from other than the traditional commercial class have entered business. A strong modern commercial class, however, has not yet developed in Javanese society. The nobility in the court centers of Jogjakarta and Surakarta in Central Java has today lost most of its traditional prestige and its significance as the chief repository of Javanese values. **Warfare.** The traditional history of Java is characterized by recurrent wars. The Dutch preferred to recruit soldiers for colonial forces from among the

Ambonese or Menadonese. On the other hand, the Japanese drew heavily upon the Javanese for combat units to fight in Burma, New Guinea, and Melanesia. During the Indonesian armed revolution (1945-49), fought mainly on the island of Java, the Javanese experienced almost four years of guerrilla warfare against Dutch troops. Since Independence, Javanese army units have participated in combat against domestic rebels such as the extremist Muslim Darul Islam bands in West Java, the separatist movement of South Moluccas, the PRRI in West Sumatra, and the Permesta in the North Celebes.

RELIGION. **Major religions.** The majority of Javanese are Muslims. According to a 1950 estimate, 400,000 are Catholics (Minderop and Vriens 1950), and about 105,000 Protestants (Boland 1950). Javanese distinguish two categories of Muslim, based upon the degree of participation in Islam, i.e. the *wong abangan* and the *wong putihan* (or *santri*), the latter being those who rigorously observe Islamic principles. The two can be regarded as distinct subcultures with contrasting world views, values, and orientations within the Javanese culture as a whole (C. Geertz 1960b). **Belief system and supernaturals.** Almost every Javanese male peasant, as well as every *prijaji*, has at least once in his life pronounced the Muslim confession of faith, i.e. at his circumcision ceremony. The average *abangan*, however, does not comprehend the formula, and many do not respect the taboo on eating pork, the daily performance of *salat*, or the fast during the month of Ramadan. Despite the limited religious knowledge of the average *wong abangan*, he believes intensely in Allah. The peasant *wong abangan* also believes in the rice goddess Dewi Sri (the Javanese version of Shri, Vishnu's wife in Hindu mythology), and in Batara Kala, the god of time and death (the Javanese equivalent of Shiva in Hinduism). More important in everyday life are numerous benevolent as well as malevolent spirits which inhabit wells, crossroads, banyan trees, etc. Impersonal magical power (*kesaktian*) exists in amulets and in heirlooms, especially the Javanese dagger or *keris*; in parts of the human body (nails, hair); and in sacred music instruments (especially drums). It is extensively utilized in magic, curing, and sorcery, which center around the role of the *dukun* (the specialist in magical practices, curer, or sorcerer). The *prijaji* and higher levels of Javanese society who adhere to the *abangan* world view have put great value on mysticism, meditation (*sumedi*), and extreme forms of religious asceticism (*tapa*). There also exist in *prijaji* society various movements, organizations, and sects, which seek mystical enlightenment for their members under the leadership of a teacher (*guru*). The *santri* are much concerned with Islamic doctrine, and look down upon *abangan* beliefs. *Santri* are present among all social levels, but they predominate among the commercial classes. Most *santri* perform the *salat* five times a day, attend the communal *salat* every Friday at noon, and fast during the month of Pasa (Ramadan). One of their major objectives in life is to make the pilgrimage to Mecca at least once, and they observe the taboo on eating pork. **Ceremonies.** The central ritual in Javanese *abangan* religion is the *slametan*. This ritual involves a communal sacred meal, either very simple or very elaborate, depending on the importance of the occasion (C. Geertz 1960b: 11-15), and has the function of promoting *slamet* (emotional calm). Household *slametan* rituals are performed at various points in the individual life cycle (e.g. at the seventh month of pregnancy, at childbirth, at the falling off of the umbilical cord, at the first contact of the child with the earth, at circumcision, at the presentation of the bride-price, at the wedding, at burial, at mortuary rites, and at ceremonies on the seventh, fortieth, one hundredth, and one thousandth days after death). *Slametan* are likewise associated with the Muslim ceremonial calendar, with agricultural rites and with rites furthering the social integration of the village (*bersih desa*). **Magic and sorcery.** Magic and sorcery are important at all social levels, although a range of specific variants exist in which the dominance of folk magic among the peasants shifts to an emphasis on more refined and elaborate practices of magico-mysticism among the *prijaji* and higher social levels of the *abangan* Javanese. Magic and sorcery center around the role of specialists in magical practices called *dukun*. There are specialists on agricultural rituals and fertility rites (*dukun wiwit*); specialists in preventing natural misfortunes (*dukun siwer*); mediums (*dukun prewangan*); wedding specialists (*dukun penganten* or *dukun paes*); circumcisors (*dukun tjalak*); masseurs (*dukun pidjet*); specialists who cure by inserting needles under the skin (*dukun susuk*); curers who rely on spells (*dukun djapa*); curers who are specialists on herbs and native medicines (*dukun djampi*); midwives (*dukun baji*); sorcerers (*dukun sihir*); and specialists in numerical divination (*dukun petungan*). Curers and diviners remain an important part of Javanese culture, not only in rural but also in urban communities and among the *wong abangan* as well as the *santri*. Even those who go to medical doctors make use of the services of the *dukun*, often for particular kinds of persistent illnesses and psychosomatic complaints. [C. Geertz 1960b: 86-111.]

BIBLIOGRAPHY. Bachtiar Rifai 1958; Berg 1938; Boland 1950; Dewey 1962, 1963; Djojodigoeno and Tirtawinata 1940; Dyen 1965; C. Geertz 1956a, 1956b, 1957, 1960a, 1960b, 1965; H. Geertz 1961, 1963; Guritno 1958; Hawkins 1967; Heine-Geldern 1942; Indonesia 1960; Jay 1963; Koentjaraningrat 1956, 1961, 1968; McNicoll 1968; Minderop and Vriens 1950; Moertono 1968; Palmier 1960; Salim et al. 1959;

Selosoemardjan 1962; Soedjito Sosrodihardjo 1957, 1959; Soepomo 1931; Soepomo Poedjosoedarmo 1968; Van Niel 1960; Widjojo Nitisastro 1959.

MADURESE*

Synonyms. *Orang Madura, Wong Medura, Tijang Medura*

ORIENTATION. **Identification and location.** The Madurese inhabit the arid and infertile island of Madura off the eastern coast of Java. There are, however, even more Madurese on the northern coast of the eastern extension of Java and on the Kangean Islands, east of Madura. The culture is basically similar to that of the East Javanese, although the languages are mutually unintelligible. **Demography.** According to the 1930 census, there were close to 2,000,000 Madurese on Madura, with an additional 2,500,000 on the northern coast of the eastern extension of Java, i.e. the regencies of Panarukan and Bondowoso (88 percent Madurese), the regencies of Probolinggo (72 percent Madurese) and Djember (61 percent Madurese), and in several other East Javanese areas, where the population is less than 50 percent Madurese. **Linguistic affiliation.** Madurese is closely related to Javanese, but the two languages are mutually unintelligible. Many Madurese, however, are bilingual. There are two dialects, that of Pamekasan, spoken mainly on the western part of the island, and Sumenep, which is spoken on the eastern part. There is an indigenous written literature in Javanese script, which is much influenced by Javanese literature of the Islamic period, although typical Madurese stories do exist (Sosrodanoekoesoemo 1927). The language has been extensively studied by Dutch linguists (Kiliaan 1897, 1898, 1904-05). **History and cultural relations.** The earliest history consists mainly of legends recounting the origin of various localities and villages (Pa' Kamar 1926: 231-35). During the fourteenth century, Madura appears to have been part of the Javanese empire of Madjapahit, becoming independent subsequent to the decline of that empire. However, the Madurese lacked a well-developed state organization of their own until the arrival of Islam at the beginning of the sixteenth century. Subsequently Madura became part of the Javanese empire of Mataram. Uprisings against Javanese domination occurred, of which the Trunodjojo revolt (1672-80) was the most extensive. Under the Dutch, Madura was divided into two principalities, each under an indigenous princely family. In 1882, the Dutch abolished the princedoms and imposed direct administration.

---

*The author of this entry, Koentjaraningrat, is Professor of Anthropology in the University of Indonesia.

SETTLEMENT. Madurese villages are clustered settlements surrounded by agricultural land, seemingly lacking any patterned arrangement.

ECONOMY. **Animal husbandry.** Animal husbandry is much more important on arid Madura than on fertile Java. The Madurese keep mainly cattle, but also sheep, goats, and chickens. Cattle are exported to Java. Bull racing and bull fighting are favorite folk sports (Overbeck 1926; Munnik 1926). The water buffalo is unimportant. **Fisheries.** Coastal fishing is a major means of subsistence, and the Madurese go for miles into the Strait of Madura with their double outrigger canoes to catch fish with large nets. They also use a variety of hooks and traps (Wongsosewojo 1926a). **Food and stimulants.** The main dish consists of rice mixed with ground corn. Side dishes include dried salted fish and dried meat and vegetables, spiced with chilied sauces. Water or tea is taken with meals; extensive consumption of rice wine (*tuwak*) was prohibited under the Dutch. **Industrial arts.** The Madurese know the art of batik, but their products are less refined than those of Java. Special effort is devoted to the decoration and carving of the equipment for bull racing. **Land tenure.** A survey by the Dutch in 1868 reported strongly developed individual rights of ownership. However, even today there is in most villages communal land reserved for public purposes, and also plots of land for support of the village headman and his staff.

KINSHIP SYSTEM. **Descent.** The Madurese reckon descent bilaterally. **Kin groups.** The nuclear family, the only important kinship unit in Madurese peasant society, constitutes a household. It is a man's obligation, however, to house his aging and retired parents-in-law. Among upper-level Madurese, the Javanese style of life prevails, with the existence of occasional kindred activities at weddings or family gatherings.

MARRIAGE. **Mode.** The parents of the boy request the girl's hand by offering food and presents (fabrics, batik, and jewelry among the well-to-do). An important and essential part of the bride-price is cattle. A rural wedding ceremony involves the services of a Muslim religious official, and the ceremonial meeting of the bride and groom is marked by a string-cutting ceremony. **Form.** Polygyny is rare. **Residence.** Although the ideal is an independent neolocal household after marriage, many young couples stay at the wife's parents' house for the initial period of married life. One of the daughters, moreover, remains permanently, with the obligation to care for the parents in their old age. **Divorce.** Divorce appears to be less frequent than among the Javanese or Sundanese. Property accumulated during the marriage is divided according to agreement.

SOCIOPOLITICAL ORGANIZATION. Historically, Madura has been a vassal principality or part of a Javanese kingdom, until the Dutch established direct administration in 1882. Consequently, the Madurese nobility has disappeared or has been reduced to the status of impoverished government officials. Regional heads formerly imitated the Javanese *prijaji* style of life.

RELIGION. Most Madurese are at least nominally Muslims. The conceptual distinction between *abangan* and *santri* does not exist; the Central Javanese *abangan* religion, with its many magico-mystical influences from Hinduism and Buddhism, never developed to a large extent on Madura. Madurese civil servants, who have tended to adopt the Javanese style of life, have usually preferred the *santri* world view. Despite the fact that missionary activity started early in the present century, only a small proportion of Madurese are Christians. **Ceremonies.** Similar to *slametan* among the Javanese and *hadjat* among the Sundanese; communal sacred meals called *kenduri* are also ceremonially important. **Magic and sorcery.** Magic and sorcery are essential parts of Madurese religion, especially as a consequence of bull racing and bull fighting, where participants make extensive use of magical practices to outdo their rivals.

BIBLIOGRAPHY. Kiliaan 1897, 1898, 1904-05; Munnik 1926; Overbeck 1926; Pa' Kamar 1926; Prajudi Atmosoedirdjo 1952; Sosrodanoekoesoemo 1927; van Gennep 1921; Wirjo Asmoro 1926; Wongsosewojo 1926a, 1926b.

SUNDANESE*

Synonyms. *Orang Sunda, Urang Sunda, Urang Prijangan*

ORIENTATION. **Identification.** The Sundanese call themselves Urang Sunda. Orang Sunda is the Indonesian term. The word Prijangan refers to the central area of West Java, the Prijangan Highlands, thus Orang Prijangan means "people of the Prijangan Highlands." **Location.** The area of the Sundanese includes all the western part of the island of Java as far eastward as the line demarcated by the Tjitanduj and Tjidjulang rivers to the south, and the town of Indramaju to the north. There are, however, many Sundanese speakers elsewhere on Java. The population of extreme northwestern Java speak a dialect of Javanese called Banten-Javanese. Many of them are, however, bilingual, speaking Banten-Javanese as well as Sundanese. South of Rangkasbitung is an isolated

---

*The author of this entry, Koentjaraningrat, is Professor of Anthropology in the University of Indonesia.

area with an archaic population who call themselves Urang Kanekes or Urang Badui. Their language is an ancient form of Sundanese. **Linguistic affiliation.** Sundanese, like Javanese, belongs to the West Indonesian branch of the Hesperonesian subfamily of the Malayo-Polynesian family (Dyen 1965). A comparative lexico-statistical analysis of several languages of this West Indonesian branch reveals a close affiliation of Sundanese with Malay (Harimurti Kridoleksono 1964). Although many Sundanese believe that there once existed a separate Sundanese script (Sungkawa 1957), the oldest manuscripts were in fact written in Javanese or Arabic. Modern Sundanese sacred literature emerged in the early twenties of this century, and today many Sundanese authors are actively writing poetry and prose in their own language (Rosidi 1966). **Demography.** The census of 1930 recorded over 8 million Sundanese. The 1961 figure for West Java (minus Djakarta), an area of about 46,300 square kilometers, is over the 17 million mark, giving a density of 380 per square kilometer. **History and cultural relations.** The Sundanese, at least in the coastal areas, must have known wet-rice agriculture and a state organization prior to Hinduization. By the fourth century, a Sundanese state had assumed an Indianized form, probably by inviting Indian Brahmans to advise on the organization of government ritual (Heine-Geldern 1942). During the sixteenth century, Banten (Bantam) was a power in the western part of the archipelago, its capital a commercial center which reached its peak in the middle of the seventeenth century (cf. Djajadiningrat 1913). During the latter half of the seventeenth century, however, Banten was weakened rapidly by internal quarrels over succession, and by 1684 the Dutch were able to destroy its commercial position. No information is available on the indigenous history of the Sundanese heartland, except in legends about kingdoms such as Galuh and Padjadjaran, and epical stories about the legendary king Siliwangi (Sutaarga 1966). During the Dutch colonial period, the Prijangan Highlands became an important center of forced coffee cultivation. In 1880, Banten was the scene of a vigorous peasant rebellion, the focus of which was the rejection of foreign domination and the nativistic idea of restoring the old order, i.e. the old Banten Kingdom, with an Islamic Holy War led by rural religious leaders, or *kjais* (Sartono Kartodirdjo 1966).

SETTLEMENT PATTERN AND HOUSING. **Settlement pattern.** A superimposed administrative structure has to a large extent changed the traditional settlement pattern of the Prijangan Highlands. The average Sundanese village is at present much larger than the average Javanese village, with a range from 1,000 to over 7,000 inhabitants. Most villages consist of clusters of separated and dispersed settlements, with cultivated fields between. Land holdings are small, fragmented, and scattered. **Housing.** Traditional Sundanese architecture has disappeared. Sundanese houses do, however, contrast strikingly with those of the Javanese in that most of them are built on piles, with stone bases.

ECONOMY. The Sundanese were for a long time associated with the Dutch colonial estate economy of the Prijangan Highlands. These estates occupied almost 10 percent of the total arable land of West Java. The peasant economy is mainly based on wet-rice agriculture, while the Sundanese of the southwestern areas of West Java still practice slash-and-burn agriculture. **Agriculture.** Techniques of wet-rice cultivation are similar to those of Central and East Java, including traditional methods of augury, carried out under the direction of an augur, or *tjandoli*. In between the rice crops, as many as three in one year, vegetables, soya beans, peanuts, yams, chilies, and onions are cultivated. **Domestic animals.** Animal husbandry is unimportant. The bullock is the most important draft animal, while the water buffalo is used for the plow. **Food and stimulants.** Although basically similar to a Javanese rice meal, the Sundanese cuisine is not complete without a salad of raw vegetables with a wide variety of chilied sauces. Goldfish dishes are a particular Sundanese delicacy. Fermented rice and fermented cassava are consumed as snacks. The Sundanese follow Islamic principles seriously and do not drink alcoholic beverages. Among the older generation, tobacco is consumed in the form of home-made cigarettes wrapped in dried young palm leaves. Tobacco and betel chewing, practiced by the older generation of women, has almost disappeared. **Land tenure.** An 1868 Dutch land tenure survey revealed that at that period individual property rights were already strongly developed in the Prijangan Highlands. Yet even today, most Sundanese villages have communal land reserved for common benefit. Land is likewise reserved for villagers who are original members of the community and who have served the community well, and for village administrators who, as in Central and East Java, receive no salaries from the government, but are supported in part by the usufruct of land allotted to them during their period of service.

KIN GROUPS. **Descent.** The Sundanese reckon descent bilaterally. **Kinship terminology.** The following is an abbreviated list of kin terms.

FaFa, MoFa, FaMo, MoMo	*embah*
Fa	*bapa, rama, kolot*
Mo	*indung, ema, kolot*
So, Da	*anaq*
FaElBr, FaElSi, MoElBr, MoElSi, FaElBrWi, FaElSiHu, MoElBrWi, MoElSiHu	*ua*
FaYoSi, MoYoSi, FaYoBrWi, MoYoBrWi	*embi*
FaYoBr, MoYoBr, FaYoSiHu, MoYoSiHu	*emang, paman*
ElBr	*angkang*
ElSi	*entèh*
YoBr, YoSi	*adi*
SoDa, SoSo, DaDa, DaSo	*intju*

Sundanese kinship terminology is similar to that of the Javanese. **Kin groups.** Peasants seldom reckon relationships beyond the second ascending generation and the first degree of collaterality. Only upper-class families have been interested in tracing genealogies to prove relationship with mythical figures or ancient Sundanese kings. The nuclear family (*kulawarga*) is the basic kin group in the life of every Sundanese. Only toward members of his *kulawarga* does he have major obligations, and only from them can he expect maximal attention and care. Outside the nuclear family, the Sundanese recognize the *golongan*, an occasional bilateral kin group. In village communities, the members of the *golongan* are mainly coresident and contribute to or participate in life cycle ceremonies, of which circumcisions and weddings are the most important. The *golongan* thus resembles the usual concept of the kindred. Especially at higher social levels, the Sundanese also recognize an ancestor-oriented ambilineal kin group, symbolized by an ancestor's grave that must be visited on particular occasions and by specific taboos. This kin group is often called a *bondorojot* (Wilcox Palmer 1967: 314). Members of the *golongan* are included in the membership of the *bondorojot*.

MARRIAGE AND FAMILY. **Mode.** Sundanese youth in general do their own courting and make their own choice of a mate, subject to parental approval. Both rural and urban weddings include a series of ceremonies, of which three are the most important: (1) the presentation of the bridal gift (*pamawakeun*) to the bride's parents by the groom's relatives (2) the conclusion of the marriage contract by a Muslim religious official, and (3) the ceremonial meeting of the bride and groom, which, especially among the upper classes, involves an elaborate "door opening" ceremony (opening the front door of the girl's house). **Form.** Polygyny is rare among the peasant Sundanese, but more frequent among the lower levels of the urban population and the more orthodox high ranking families. **Residence.** The ideal is an independent neolocal household after marriage; in practice, however, young couples stay for a considerable time at either parental household. Shifts in residence also occur frequently. **Domestic unit.** The household usually consists of members of one nuclear family, but frequently includes other relatives (members of the *golongan*), boarders, or servants. It is an unstable unit, its composition constantly changing as married children or other relatives come and go. **Divorce.** Property accumulated jointly during marriage is divided by mutual agreement. There is no definite rule determining which of the divorced parents the children should follow, but infants who require maternal care always follow the mother. **Inheritance.** The personal property of a deceased spouse is divided equally among the surviving spouse and the children; in case of death of the surviving spouse, the personal property of the latter, property acquired during marriage, and cultivable land are divided equally among the children of both sexes. The house, the furniture, and the garden surrounding the house remain an undivided unit, inherited by one of the children who remains at home to care for the aged parents.

SOCIOPOLITICAL ORGANIZATION. **Contemporary structure.** Little is known about the traditional structure of Sundanese society. With the establishment of the Dutch colonial system, social classes emerged within the administrative towns of West Java earlier than in Central and East Java. These included the nonpeasant laborers in the towns as well as indigenous white-collar workers and civil servants in the colonial government. Administrative personnel (*pamong pradja*) became the core of this gentry and enjoyed the highest prestige in Sundanese society. Within the category of white-collar workers, Western education and the command of Dutch became a potent means for upward mobility.

RELIGION. **Major religions.** The majority of the Sundanese are Muslims. The Javanese distinction between *abangan* and *santri* is unknown. **Belief system and supernaturals.** In addition to his belief in Allah, the peasant also believes in the important role of the rice goddess Nji Pohatji Sangjang Sri (Hidding 1929). Like the Javanese, the Sundanese know about Hindu deities who play a role in Sundanese mythology, and the wooden puppet folk plays (*wajang golek*). Spirits, in general called *lelembutan*, play a role only in ceremonies along the individual life cycle. Of these, circumcision (*ngislamkeun* or *njunatan*) is considered the most important and is celebrated with an elaborate feast (cf. Hidding 1929: 62-68). The boy is then considered to have officially become a Muslim (*ngislamkeun* means "to make Muslim"). Village life is often dominated by religious teachers or *kijaji*. Some have a wide reputation and many followers throughout large parts of the Prijangan Highlands, and thus form power centers which have to be taken into consideration by the government and the administration. **Ceremonies.** The *hadjat*, like the *slametan*, is a communal sacred meal, performed within the household and attended by the nearest neighbors. It accompanies religious ceremonies performed along the individual life cycle and at mortuary rites and rituals on the seventh, fortieth, one hundredth, and one thousandth

days after death. In the villages, *hadjat* meals in connection with agricultural fertility rites are also customary. **Mysticism and magic.** Magic and sorcery form an important sector of Sundanese religion at all social levels. Magic mainly centers about curing, divination, and numerology (*petangan*). The Sundanese gentry has not developed a refined and elaborated system of magico-mysticism such as has emerged in Javanese *prijaji* culture. There are, however, Islamic-based mystical movements, usually centering about rural Islamic religious schools (*pesantren*). Members of these movements seek to experience the religious ecstasy of a mystical unity with God (*titeuleum*). **Practitioners.** The Sundanese of the Prijangan Highlands usually distinguish four categories of practitioners: (1) *tukang ngubaran*, usually women curers who specialize in herbs and native medicine (2) *tukang njampe*, specialists in producing protective amulets and fetishes and in love magic (3) *tukang katitihan*, also usually women who are mediums, and (4) *tukang palintangan*, numerologists, diviners, and fortune tellers. **Soul, death, and afterlife.** The Sundanese believe in a life substance, the soul (*njawa*), and in the existence of a spiritual double of the human body (*suksma*). At death the *njawa*, released from the body, unites with the now autonomous *suksma* and becomes a spirit (*lelembutan*). During the initial 40 days after death, the *lelembutan* roams about the graveyard, often returning to the house where it has lived as a human being. It then enters the world of the dead (*alam kubur*), remaining there until Judgment Day. Popular Sundanese folk beliefs include the idea that people who have died in disgrace become roaming malevolent spirits (*ririwa, dedemit*).

BIBLIOGRAPHY. Adiwidjaja 1954; Djajadiningrat 1913; Dyen 1965; Geise 1952; Harimurti Kridoleksono 1964; Heine-Geldern 1942; Hidding 1929, 1935; Moestapa 1946; Rosidi 1966; Sartono Kartodirdjo 1966; Sungkawa 1957; Sutaarga 1966; Wilcox Palmer 1967.

TENGGERESE*

Synonyms. *Orang Tengger, Wong Tengger*

ORIENTATION. **Identification and location.** The Tenggerese inhabit the slopes of a large volcanic crater high in the Tengger Mountains of East Java. They speak a rather archaic dialect of Javanese and are considered refugees from the ancient Hindu-Javanese kingdom of Madjapahit who retreated to the mountains at the fall of Madjapahit in the early six-

---

*The author of this entry, Koentjaraningrat, is Professor of Anthropology in the University of Indonesia.

teenth century. Others believe that the Tenggerese occupied their present location much earlier even than the Madjapahit period. **Demography.** According to a description of 1897, there were at that period over 6,500 Tenggerese living in 28 villages. According to the 1930 census, the population had increased to almost 16,000; a recent study of one of the largest villages, Wonokerta, reported a village population of 4,083 and a rapid rate of increase of almost 4 percent a year (Soebijakto 1965).

ECONOMY. Maize agriculture on dry permanent fields (*tegalan*) or on swiddens with slash-and-burn techniques (*ladang*). For more than a century and a half the Tenggerese have grown vegetables and potatoes as cash crops. **Land tenure.** According to a survey in one of the largest Tenggerese villages, based on a village register dated 1939, the average size of landholding is about one hectare per household. Land is inherited bilaterally, and male as well as female descendants get an equal share. The average size of landholdings must be considerably smaller and more scattered today because of the rapid population increase, especially since World War II. The number of landless peasants has increased greatly, and migration to the cities and coastal areas has been going on for more than a decade.

KIN GROUPS. **Descent.** The Tenggerese reckon descent bilaterally.

MARRIAGE AND FAMILY. **Mode.** Tenggerese youth do their own courting, although parental consent is required. The marriage ceremony, where the groom formally meets the bride, takes place in the bride's house. A priest (*wong sepuh*) blesses the couple. The groom's family does not present a bride-price. **Form.** Polygyny is rare. **Residence.** There is no fixed rule of residence determining where a married couple should live. The ideal is to set up an independent household, but many cases of uxorilocality as well as virilocality occur. **Domestic unit.** Households (*somah*) on the average consist of between seven and ten members. In addition to children, many households include additional relatives of the family, usually nephews and nieces, or younger brothers, sisters, or cousins. A recent survey in one of the largest villages revealed that one third of the households consists of extended families, including a senior couple with their married daughters, married sons, or married daughters and sons. **Divorce.** In contrast to other places in Java, divorce seems to be a rare phenomenon in Tenggerese communities. **Inheritance.** Land is inherited bilaterally, male as well as female descendants getting an equal share.

SOCIOPOLITICAL ORGANIZATION. A Tenggerese village is usually a cluster of hamlets, with a headman, *petinggi*, elected for life by the adult citizens of the village, male as well as female. He is assisted by village functionaries and controls the headmen of the various hamlets (*kamitua*).

RELIGION. Although they have been exposed to the outside world for more than a century, and although, unlike the Badui, they have no system of taboos that resists influence from the outside world, the Tenggerese have managed to maintain their original religious concepts and practices. They have not adopted Islam or Christianity, and only recently have Indonesian missionaries attempted to spread Buddhism. The indigenous belief system is mainly oriented toward ancestor spirits and deities of nature. Deities have the Hindu names Hyang Batara Guru, Hyang Batara Wisnu, and Hyang Batara Siwa, and are considered manifestations of a supreme being called Sang Hyang Tunggal. Spirits and deities are represented by puppets made from plants and flowers. Sacred places for worship and ritual (*pundèn*) are the tops of three sacred hills, while each house has its private house shrine, called a *sanggar*. In addition, house poles, large banyan trees, crossroads, wells, etc. are supposed to be dwelling places of spirits. Rituals are carried out by a priest called *dukun* (or *kamifawa*), assisted by men called *legèn*. Ritual equipment consists of pots, plates, and bells. In addition to household rituals, there exist large ceremonies, in which many people and families participate. In the *entas-entas* ceremony, the spirits of deceased relatives are released from their ties with this world in order to enter Heaven. Because of the large expense involved, people may wait many years after the death of a relative before the ceremony can be held, sharing expenses with other families who hold their rituals at the same time. The *entas-entas* ceremony does not involve exhumation of the bones of the deceased in order to be burned; the release of the spirit is carried out symbolically. The *kesada* is a large communal offering ceremony to the god of the mountains, Sunan Perniti. The offerings are thrown into the Tengger volcanic crater. Not only Tenggerese participate in this ceremony but also many people from other parts of Java who come to the sacred crater as pilgrims.

BIBLIOGRAPHY. Jasper 1928; Nieuwenhuis 1948; Postma 1961; Soebijakto 1965; Wibisono 1956.

BADUI*

Synonyms. *Badoei, Baduj, Bedoej, Kanekes, Orang Badui, Urang Kanekes, Urang Rawajan, Urang Parahiang*

ORIENTATION. **Identification and location.** The Indonesian name for this isolated group of people in

---

*The author of this entry, Koentjaraningrat, is Professor of Anthropology in the University of Indonesia.

extreme western Java is Orang Badui (Sundanese: Urang Badui). The people call themselves Urang Kanekes (Kanekes being the name of their sacred territory) or Urang Rawajan (Rawajan being the term for their inner villages), or Urang Parahiang (Parahiang being a name for a mythological kingdom inhabited by spirits). The area of the Badui includes the rough northern slopes of the Kendeng Mountains in South Banten (Bantam), south of the district town Lebak. They live in 35 villages, 3 of which are situated within a sacred area (*taneuh kadjeroan*), absolutely taboo to outsiders. **Linguistic affiliation.** The Badui speak an archaic dialect of Sundanese. They consider the art of writing taboo and resist Sundanese, Arabic, as well as Latin script. Inscribed flat bamboo sticks, used nowadays in magical ceremonies, contain remnants of what was apparently an ancient indigenous script. **Demography.** In 1928, there were 1,521 Badui. According to reports of the same year, they had small families, with an average of 1.5 children (van Tricht 1928: 78-79). **History.** There has been much speculation about the origin of the Badui. The most popular theory considers them refugees from the ancient Sundanese kingdom of Padjadjaran, who fled to the mountainous jungles of South Banten when the capital of Padjadjaran was destroyed by Muslim Bantamese in 1579. Their religion does not, however, show the degree of Hindu influence that one would expect if the Badui are indeed descendants of refugees from the strongly Hinduized state of Padjadjaran.

SETTLEMENT PATTERN AND HOUSING. Of 35 Badui villages, 3 are situated in an innermost sacred area (*taneuh kadjeroan*), 25 in an intermediate sacred area (*taneuh kanekes*), and 7 in an outer area, interspersed among non-Badui villages of Muslim Bantamese or Sundanese. Each of the 3 superior villages in *taneuh kadjeroan* controls several villages in the *taneuh kanekes* and in the outer area, and each has a particular village in the outer area, where individuals in its territory, or in the *taneuh kanekes* villages under its control, can be exiled when they have violated the law. Badui villages are nucleated settlements of 10 to 20 small nuclear family houses set in luxuriant groves of vegetation, surrounded by cultivated fields. The outer villages show a more dispersed settlement pattern, alternating with cultivated fields.

ECONOMY. The nuclear Badui practice slash-and-burn agriculture on swiddens (*huma*) which are occupied for two to three years, while those living in the outer area cultivate rice on irrigated fields (*serang*). Livestock production is unimportant. Fish are taken in streams and rivers, and deer, small animals, and birds are hunted with bow and arrow. **Food, stimulants, and beverages.** The main dish consists of cooked rice, with vegetables and meat as side dishes. Coconut is an important ingredient, and chilied sauces further enliven the meal. The main alcoholic beverage is palm wine (*waju*). Betel chewing with sirih leaves (*Piper betle L.*) is widely practiced.

KIN GROUPS. **Descent.** The Badui reckon descent bilaterally.

MARRIAGE AND FAMILY. Marriages within the two sacred territories are arranged by parents. A father selects a bride for his son, but the mother of the boy is the one who must request the girl's hand. The period of engagement lasts for several months to more than a year, during which time the young people are secluded from one another and subject to strict regulations. The wedding ceremony is quite simple. The father presents the groom to the head (*pu'un*) of one of the three superior villages, depending upon the circumstances of the marriage. This head then presents the groom to the bride's father, who takes him home for a ceremonial meeting with the bride. A ritual meal concludes the wedding party. **Form.** Marriage is strictly monogamous. **Residence.** The rule is to set up an independent household after marriage. **Domestic unit.** The nuclear family, with an average of 1.5 children (in 1928). **Divorce.** According to an early source, divorce is rare (van Tricht 1928: 79).

SOCIOPOLITICAL ORGANIZATION. The three villages in the most sacred inner region are inhabited by families who consider themselves descendants of the gods. According to the sacred mythology, the headmen, *pu'un*, of the three villages are direct descendants of three of the seven sons of the supreme god Batara Patandjala. The inhabitants of the sacred villages are called *kedjeroan*. Those families who inhabit the intermediate area, the *kanekes*, belong to a lower class of commoners called *panamping*. Some villages in the *kanekes* area, however, contain noble families or *kedjeroan*. The *kanekes* settlements have no headmen. The outer villages, or *dangka*, are inhabited by both noble families and commoners (*kedjeroan* and *panamping*). Each has a headman called a *djaro-dangka*, who is assisted by two or three *kaumdangka*. The *dangka* villages are divided into three groups, each group being subordinate to one of the three sacred *kedjeroan* villages. The heads of the *dangka* villages, however, control the inhabitants of the *kanekes* area. They do not control particular settlements, but rather each controls a number of families who live scattered in a number of settlements. Consequently, each *kanekes* settlement is inhabited by families who are subordinate to several *djaro-dangka* in the outer villages. Important decisions regarding the whole of the Badui community are made by a council consisting of the three *pu'un*, their assistants, the *djaro-dangka*, a number of older men, *baresan*,

58

usually from the three most sacred villages, and seven family heads, also selected from the most sacred villages. The three *pu'un* preside over the council by turns (van Tricht 1928: 71-78).

RELIGION. The Badui have managed to resist both Islam and Christianity. Little is known about their indigenous religious system and life. They seem to have an elaborate mythology with spirits and deities, many of whom have Hindu names. They also seem to believe in magical power, magical practices, and divination. For these practices, they make extensive use of bamboo tablets (*kolendjer*), engraved with a script which can only be read by the *pu'un*, the priests (*tangkesan*), and a few older people. The religion seems to impose a puritan existence, with numerous food taboos—especially the meat of most large animals—color taboos, etc. A great number of the religious rituals have to do with harvest celebrations.

BIBLIOGRAPHY. Geise 1952; Jacobs and Meijer 1891; Pleyte 1909, 1912; van Tricht 1928.

BAWEAN ISLANDERS*

Synonyms. *Orang Babian, Orang Boyan, Orang Bawean*

ORIENTATION. **Identification and location.** The inhabitants of Bawean Island, northwest of Madura, call themselves Orang Babian. They were originally Madurese, who migrated to the island where they have mixed with other migrants from South Celebes (Buginese, Macassarese), from Bandjarmasin (South Borneo Malays), and Javanese. Although their language is only a dialect of Madurese, the Baweanese do not consider themselves as Madurese. A large number live in Singapore. **Demography.** Bawean had over 14,000 inhabitants in 1813; 145 years later, in 1958, the population had increased almost three times to 48,000 (Vredenbregt 1964). **History and cultural relations.** The first Madurese migrants must have arrived on the island in the middle of the fourteenth century. There is no record of an indigenous population. In 1743, the island came under the rule of Tjakraningrat IV, the principal of Madura. The Dutch built a small fortress on the island in 1784, but did not establish a permanent administration until 1872 (Jasper 1906).

ECONOMY. The principal means of subsistence are agriculture and fishing. **Agriculture.** Agriculture (mainly rice) is practiced on irrigated fields and on dry fields without irrigation. Slash-and-burn agriculture also exists on the forested hills in the interior. **Food.** The main dish consists of steamed or cooked rice, supplemented by fish. Fish boiled, salted, and preserved in earthenware jars is exported to Java. **Industrial arts.** An important local industry is the plaiting of pandanus mats, formerly exported to Java. **Trade.** The Baweanese are noted as traders. Both sexes travel regularly to Java or East Sumatra to sell mats and fish. The interest in traveling (*merantau*) and the tendency to leave home have been explained as a consequence of Bawean child-rearing patterns (Vredenbregt 1964: 120-22).

KIN GROUPS. **Descent.** The Baweanese reckon descent bilaterally. **Kin groups.** As among the Madurese and Javanese, the range of kinship affiliation is limited primarily by memory, acquaintance, and needs, rather than by custom, structure, or common residence. The only kin group in Bawean society is the nuclear family. **Residence patterns.** The general rule of residence determining where a newly married couple should live is uxorilocal (Vredenbregt 1964: 120-21). **Domestic unit.** The Baweanese household is a dynamic unit. Because of the fact that the parents are frequently away from home on business trips to Java or Singapore, Bawean children are often left to the care of grandparents, relatives, or neighbors. Boys are brought up mainly outside the household environment. From the sixth year, they attend a Muslim school, returning home only for meals; at night they sleep in the mosque or in a house of prayer (*surau*).

SOCIOPOLITICAL ORGANIZATION. **Contemporary administrative structure.** Bawean Island is a district of the regency of Surabaja. It is administered by a district officer, assisted by two subdistrict officers (*tjamat*). Villages (*kelurahan*) are made up of clusters of hamlets (*kampong*). Village heads are elected by the villagers. All other administrative officers from the subdistrict heads upward are appointed by the central government.

RELIGION. Most Baweanese are Muslims, of the *santri* worldview. Many have the desire to make the pilgrimage to Mecca at least once in their lives. According to Vredenbregt (1964: 117), the pilgrimage to Mecca broke the island's isolation and may have had a stimulating effect.

BIBLIOGRAPHY. Atmadja and Uijfferbroek 1891; Jasper 1906; Lekkerkerker 1935; Siegel 1901; Verloop 1905; Vredenbregt 1964.

---

*The author of this entry, Koentjaraningrat, is Professor of Anthropology in the University of Indonesia.

BALI - LOMBOK - SUMBAWA

UNDER THE TERM Bali-Sasak, Esser (1938) grouped together the languages of Bali (Balinese), Lombok (Sasak), and western Sumbawa (Semawa). The pervasive spread of ancient Hindu-Javanese high culture, and later that of Islam, together with the political impact of neighboring Goa in the southern Celebes have, however, largely obliterated any indigenous linguistic or cultural features once common to this area. As a matter of convenience of presentation, the present volume has grouped the peoples of eastern Sumbawa—the Bimanese, Dompu, and Donggo—with those of western Sumbawa. On linguistic grounds and to some extent historically, however, they are perhaps more properly included within Esser's Bima-Sumba group, comprising not only eastern Sumbawa and Sumba but also the peoples of western Flores—Manggarai, Ngadanese, Endenese—and the inhabitants of Savu Island, midway between Sumba and Timor. From the point of view of physical characteristics, language, and culture, this entire area appears transitional between eastern and western Indonesia; one might hazard a guess that the area was once characterized by the type of sociopolitical structure typical of much of eastern Indonesia, a situation later complicated by the rise to power of the Malay states of Java and South Celebes (modern Sulawesi). The distribution of physical types and language relationships within the area appear to reflect the flow of cultural-historical forces and movements of peoples that would agree with this hypothesis.

BIBLIOGRAPHY. Esser 1938.

BALINESE*

ORIENTATION. **Identification and location.** The Balinese are the major population on the island of Bali, which lies just east of Java, latitude 8°, longitude 115°. There are small numbers of persons, mostly traders, from other ethnic groups in Indonesia: Javanese, Sasak, Bugis, and Sumatrans, and a group of *peranakan* Chinese. The Balinese are culturally homogeneous, although some of the literature gives the erroneous impression that one subgroup, the Bali-Aga, are culturally distinct. **Geography.** Bali is mountainous in the center, where there is a cluster of active volcanoes. Short, rapid streams are the source of extensive irrigation of rice paddies. Flora and fauna are similar to those on Java, but there are no large wild animals. The climate is tropical, with a dry season from May to November. [Dobby 1950; Robequain 1954.] **Linguistic affiliation.** Balinese is a Malayo-Polynesian language, genetically nearer to the languages of eastern Indonesia than it is to Javanese. Until the twentieth century, Balinese was written only in Javanese script, although today there are also many publications in Roman letters. **Demography.** In 1961, the population was 1,783,000, with a density of 321 per square kilometer (Pelzer 1963). **History and cultural relations.** Balinese history, for the most part unrecorded, can be tentatively reconstructed. An ancient substratum of generalized "early Indonesian" or "Polynesian" culture (Goris and Dronkers n.d.; Swellengrebel 1960) has been heavily overlaid by several waves of cultural influences, first directly from India from the eighth century to the eleventh, then from Hinduized Java from the eleventh to the fifteenth. After the Islamization of Java in the fifteenth century, a significant number of Javanese priests, princes and scholars migrated to Bali, forming at first an influential elite which soon lost its distinct Javanese identity. Bali never became Muslim and was more or less isolated from that time until the twentieth century. [Covarrubias 1956; Swellengrebel 1960.] Balinese religion and traditional political conceptions derive from Hinduism, but have been considerably altered over the centuries; the ritualistic and dramatic aspects of Hinduism are more prominent than the philosophical and mystical. There are status distinctions which bear the names of the Hindu varna system, but important elements in the Hindu caste system as found today in India are absent on Bali. Dutch administration, imposed around the turn of the century, discouraged Western commercial agriculture and Christian missionary activity. With the establishment of the Indonesian Republic in 1950, there has been increasing political participation, popular education, and the development of tourism. However, the material technology, local social organization, reli-

*The author of this entry, Hildred Geertz, is currently Visiting Lecturer in Anthropology, Princeton University. She has done extensive fieldwork on both Java and Bali.

gious and aesthetic activities, and cultural values remain much in their traditional form. [Franken 1960; C. Geertz 1963b; Holt 1967; Last 1955; Swellengrebel 1960.]

SETTLEMENT PATTERN AND HOUSING. **Settlement pattern.** Settlements vary in size, small ones containing a hundred or so inhabitants, large ones reaching several thousands. They are tightly clustered, usually set on higher ridges between streams, with rice fields and coconut groves around them. At a central crossing of each settlement are set the main local public buildings—usually an important temple or two, a large wall-less pavilion where village councils meet and dance performances are held, a roofed cockfighting ring, a slit drum for signaling public announcements, and a coffee shop. If there is a prominent gentry family resident there, its courtyard and temple may be located near the settlement center. A number of other temples—familial, cultic, or other—are found elsewhere in the settlement. A graveyard with its associated temple is usually, but not necessarily, located just outside the village. [Covarrubias 1956; C. Geertz 1959, 1963b, 1964b; Goris 1960a; Korn 1960.] **Housing.** The typical residence is a high-walled, rectangular courtyard or a cluster of courtyards connected by narrow doors. Within the courtyard are a number of small structures, for the most part wall-less, raised pavilions, with stone platforms, wooden posts, and peaked thatched or tiled roofs. One or two of these may have closed, windowless, masonry-walled rooms, but the others have removable hanging bamboo shades for occasional privacy. Furniture is minimal: mats for sitting, a high sleeping platform, and in some houses a simple wooden table and chairs. A ground-level hut serves for cooking, and there may be a raised, peaked-roof storage shed for rice. [Covarrubias 1956.]

ECONOMY. The cultivation of wet rice dominates the economy. There is some herding, but with the absence of extensive forests, little hunting or gathering of forest products. Fishing is of some importance in coastal villages. **Agriculture.** The main crop is rice, but in poorer and dryer portions of the island, maize and cassava are important crops. Commercialization of agriculture has been and remains very limited. In the late nineteenth century, small mountain tobacco plantations were introduced by Chinese merchants under the protection of the indigenous kings, and some of these still exist. There were no Dutch plantations on Bali. [Dobby 1950; Robequain 1954.] **Industrial arts.** Certain crafts are the specialty of particular villages: the making of simple earthenware pottery; the forging of simple iron tools, such as plows, and of bronze musical instruments; silver and gold work; painting and wooden sculptures, mainly for export; the carving of temple decorations; and the making of

drums and of elaborate masks and costumes. The artisans who make the more complex and difficult products are of high status, although not necessarily of high title. Some crafts were traditionally the province of particular localized title groups and of family stems within these groups, but in more recent years this monopoly has broken down (Geertz and Geertz 1964). Lesser crafts (tailoring, carpentry, brickmaking) are carried on by scattered workmen. Weaving and batik work were formerly quite widespread, but have now been nearly eclipsed by the import of cheap Javanese and Japanese cloth. [Covarrubias 1956.] **Trade.** Small village markets function for a few hours every morning; larger permanent markets are open daily but reach a peak every fifth day. There is also a large weekly cattle market. This market network is very ancient. In the past, the finest luxury craft products were not sold in the market but were made on commission for the princes and gentry, who therefore had special patron relationships with certain craft-specialized villages. Today this function in regard to sponsoring the crafts has been taken over by private and government firms, which funnel the craft products into the tourist and export markets. Aside from these artistic objects, the only export of any importance is livestock. [C. Geertz 1963b; Robequain 1954.] **Organization of labor.** Work may be organized by teams, an important institution in this regard being the *seka* groups, formed around particular temples, common ownership of land, or certain crafts. *Seka* groups may undertake agricultural tasks, notably harvesting, irrigation labor, roof thatching, and the like. Individual agricultural labor may be organized in complexly varying sharecropping arrangements made according to different tasks or different contributions of livestock and seed, and the payment correspondingly is in differing fractions of the harvest. Much of the work may be done by the landowner himself and his family, or he may hire wage labor by the day for certain tasks. [C. Geertz 1964b; Grader 1960; Korn 1936.] **Property.** Property of any sort may be owned by individuals or by corporate *seka* groups. Houseland is often owned by the village group as a whole, the *krama bandjar*. The walls and the structures within them are the responsibility of the resident family, but if the family is expelled from the village for committing a crime, or if the family dies out, the land and its buildings become the property of the village again. In normal situations, houseland is inherited by one or several of the sons of the household head. The village group retains the right to admit immigrants into the village, to expel unwanted citizens, or to distribute excess land to newly formed households. The village group normally owns other real estate in the settlement—several temples, the cockfight shed, and the market square, for instance. It may also own several plots of rice land or dry coconut palm gardens, which are cared for by sharecroppers. ● Individual or group ownership of plots of rice land entails certain responsibilities. The layout of rice land is in terms of the branching of the irrigation network, and each set of owners for a block of commonly watered plots of land is organized into a *seka* called a *subak*. The members of a *subak* have common responsibilities for the upkeep of the physical network and for the rather heavy ritual expenses and duties. These responsibilities go with ownership and use of the rice plot. In the past, certain rice plots also had specific tax burdens on them to particular lords in the vicinity. Regardless of ownership, whether individual or corporate, the land can be sold, rented or pawned. [C. Geertz 1964b; Grader 1960; Korn 1936.]

KIN GROUPS AND DESCENT. Descent is patrilineal, residence is virilocal, and marriage is preferentially endogamous to kin group, title group, and village. Gentry families keep long genealogies, often written down, which establish their claim to noble birth and specify the precise ranking of their kin group, particularly vis-à-vis the local princely line. In each generation, those who are closest to the reigning prince—his brothers, cousins, and near collaterals—are highest in rank, and in succeeding generations the relationships between their various descendants are similarly ranked. The result is a group of related gentry kin groups internally differentiated and ranked into a core descent line of high rank, together with various collateral lines of subtly differing rankings. Usually, among a group of gentry brothers, first place and hereditary office fall to the oldest son. Half siblings by the same father are ranked according to the status of their mothers, and their descendant kin groups carry the same relative ranking. Commoners do not preserve genealogies, and descent is in fact patrifiliative rather than patrilineal. In many commoner groups the youngest son, rather than the oldest, steps into the father's position, particularly in regard to ritual duties at the family temple. For gentry and commoners alike, the important cultural concept uniting a kin group—regardless of what size—is not the notion of a descent line stemming from a personalized ancestral figure, but rather the idea of a single and impersonal ultimate genetic source, an ancestral origin point symbolized sometimes by a deity, but most often simply by a geographical spot on which a certain temple stands. ● The group of family members who live within one houseyard may be thought of as a kinship group, for it is more than simply a domestic unit. It is also a worshiping group, with its specific houseyard temple. Anywhere from one to about ten nuclear families may make up this extended family grouping, but most of these component groups maintain separate hearths and separate property. Usually a houseyard consists of the nuclear families of a man

and several of his sons. Internal subdivision of a houseyard group is marked by the shift to a separate houseyard temple by a portion of its members. While the houseyard group is largely a domestic unit, there are larger corporate kin groups which are not domestic in function, but are instead, political, economic, and ceremonial. Most important of all, these larger kin groups (called *dadia* by commoners) act to establish and maintain the social rank of the members—for commoners within the village community, for gentry within the region. A *dadia* is an association of couples (usually man and wife) for the immediate purpose of support and worship at a large temple. It is the presence of this *dadia* temple that distinguishes a corporate kin group in Bali from an unincorporated, simple network of related families. In some villages, up to 80 percent of the population is organized into *dadia*, while in others the proportion is reversed. Where commoner *dadia* exist they are highly organized, with elected leadership, treasuries, property in land and temples, and with strong corporate identities. They may have as many as a hundred adult members. A few commoner kin groups have regional organizations connecting numerous localized *dadia*, but this is not the usual pattern. In nineteenth-century Bali, the gentry *dadia* were the units in the supralocal political system, and today these gentry *dadia*, while deprived of their political functions, have branches throughout the island. Family visits, endogamous marriages, adoption of kinsmen, and yearly worship at the original *dadia* temple serve to keep these sprawling gentry kin groups together. [Belo 1936; Geertz and Geertz 1964; C. Geertz 1959, 1964b.] **Kin terminology.** The terminology is Hawaiian. The terms are used referentially only, almost never vocatively. Kinsmen are addressed as others address them, by personal name (if a child), birth-order name, status title, or by teknonymy (Belo 1936; C. Geertz 1966; Korn 1936):

Reference Terms (Consanguineal)

Mo, MoSi, FaSi, FaBrWi, MoBrWi	*mèmèn (ibu, bijang)*
Fa, FaBr, MoBr, MoSiHu, FaSiHu	*nanang (bapan, adjin)*
OBr, PaSibSo older than Ego, PaPaSibChDa older than Ego	*belin*
OSi, PaSibDa older than Ego, PaPaSibChDa older than Ego	*mbok (mok)*
YSib PaSibCh younger than Ego, PaPaSibChCh younger than Ego	*adin*
Ch	*pianak*
SibCh, FaSibChCh, PaPaSibChCh	*keponakan*
FaMo, MoMo, ChCh, FaMoSi, MoMoSi, FaFaSi, MoFaSi, FaSibChCh, PaPaSibChChCh	*tjutun (dadong, miyang, mbah)*
FaFa, FaFaBr, MoFa, MoFaBr, FaMoBr, MoMoBr	*kaki (pekak, kiyang)*
PaPaPa, ChChCh	*kumpi*
PaPaPaPa, ChChChCh	*kelab*

Affinal Kin Terms

Sp	kurenan
SpFa	nanang matua
SpMo	mèmèn matua
ChSp	mantun
HuWi, SiHu, WiSib	ipah
ChSpPa	wareng

Cousins can be distinguished from own siblings by the use of several terms: *misan*, PaSibCh; *mindon*, PaPaSibChCh. A distinction can also be made between patrilateral parallel cousins: *misan kapurusa*, FaBrCh, and all the other cousins, *misan ulian luh*, FaSiCh, MoSibCh.

MARRIAGE AND FAMILY. Marriage rules.

Marriages are prohibited among members of the nuclear family. Marriages between aunt and nephew, even classificatory aunt and nephew, are frowned on, while those between uncle and niece are not. The preferred marriage is that with one's parallel patricousin, one's father's brother's daughter; if one cannot or will not marry this woman, then he should marry a member of his *dadia*, and if not a *dadia* member then at least, for commoners, a member of the village, and for gentry, a member of the same general title group. Exogamous marriages do take place, but then they are either a matter of protracted negotiations (for the gentry) or of elopement (real or sham) and kidnapping (for the commoners). **Mode.** Acceptance of the woman into the domestic unit, the houseyard, is marked by a simple temple ceremony, the *masakapan*, in which the woman is presented to her husband's ancestors, and accepted by them into his kin group. Her relationship with the temple of her father's family is then severed. There are no other rituals required nor payments of bride-price. [There is some reference to bride-price in the literature (e.g. Korn 1936: 486-88), but this is in fact a fine paid by the husband in the case of some kin group exogamous marriages, either to the paramount prince or via the prince to the offended father of the girl.] **Form.** Monogamy is the usual form of marriage, although polygyny is permitted. Divorce is marked merely by separation and public announcement; it is not uncommon. **Residence.** Residence after marriage is virilocal, and usually in the houseyard of the man's parents, for at least the first few years of marriage. The couple usually remains in that houseyard or in an adjacent one. **Inheritance.** One son only fully succeeds the father as head of the houseyard, guardian of the houseyard temple, and sometimes to his membership in the hamlet council, *krama bandjar*. For commoners the usual custom is ultimogeniture, for gentry it is primogeniture. The remainder of the father's property, especially his land, is divided equally among all sons. Daughters do not inherit, although they may be given gifts of land. **Adoption.** If a man has no children he may adopt an heir by public announcement in the village and a ritual in the houseyard temple. If he has no son, but has a daughter, he may adopt his son-in-law, making him his full legal heir, the young man then relinquishing all claims on his paternal inheritance. This is the so-called "borrowed man" pattern. [Korn 1936.]

SOCIOPOLITICAL ORGANIZATION. Local level.

Villages are not closed, multifunctional, corporate territorially defined groupings, as is the case in some peasant societies. Even though settlements are tightly clustered and densely populated, institutional structures for governing, worship, and agricultural activities often pertain to slightly differently bounded units, or may not be territorially defined at all. The inhabitants of any given settlement are usually grouped into several types of crosscutting social units for several different purposes, and the memberships in these units are not completely coordinate. The situation is highly structured and very complex: a series of major principles of organization are combined in different ways in different localities, with differing weights, resulting in considerable variation in "village structure" and conceptual difficulty in identifying "the" fundamental "village." C. Geertz (1959) has analyzed these differing principles of social affiliation, all based on the notion of the *seka*-group, into seven "planes of social organization": (1) shared obligation to work at a given temple (2) common residence, e.g. the *krama bandjar* or hamlet council (whose members are adult couples), which concerns itself with matters of local government and justice (3) ownership of rice land within a single watershed, i.e. the *subak* group (4) commonality of ascribed social status, i.e. the title system and the groupings it entails (5) consanguineal and affinal kinship ties (6) common membership in one or another voluntary organization, e.g. housebuilding, dancing, or drama associations (7) common legal subordination to a single government official, e.g. the government-appointed village head, *perbekel*. **Political organization above the local level.** Bali in the nineteenth century was governed by princes (*radja*) and lesser lords. Boundaries between principalities were set not so much by territory as by the allegiance of the inhabitants and their leaders. Continual political maneuvering occasionally erupted into assassination and war among these petty states. Each kingdom was, itself, a highly unstable pyramid of authority, built up of dyadic ties of allegiance between heads of gentry *dadias* on the basis of a cultural ideology of hereditary rank and spiritual power. Commoners were "owned" by the various lesser lords as well as directly by the paramount prince in each region, and they could be "bestowed" on others as gifts or seized from them as a result of military conquest. These ties of "ownership" of commoners were of various types, all highly specific and clearly stated. Some commoners paid only taxes to a lord, some were obliged to contribute goods and services for massive ceremonial festivals, while others worked for the lord as retainers or sharecroppers. Each individual commoner typically had several different types of relationships to several different lords, and most villages had a number of different lords "owning" various of their inhabitants. However, the governing of the village community itself was not the prerogative of the gentry, nor did the lords have much of importance to do with the irrigation societies. They served only as courts of last appeal for commoner disputes that could not be settled through their own councils. The main functions of the lords and princes, from the point of view of the village communities, were symbolic and ritualistic in that the ceremonies that the lords held periodically directly involved all the local population. When the Dutch entered South Bali (1906-08) they replaced this complex political system with a simple territorial one, with the villages headed by appointed head men (perbekel) at the base, above them larger districts headed by appointive gentry officials (punggawa), and above them seven regional units, with the traditional radja as administrative chief, through whom the Dutch colonial officials ruled indirectly. This territorial administration continues today under the Republic, and members of the former gentry ruling class are prominent in the upper levels of the government. [C. Geertz 1963b, 1967; Korn 1936.] **Social stratification.** A crucial institution for the understanding of Balinese society is the title system, or system of ascribed rank as indicated from the title inherited patrilineally. Commoners as well as gentry have titles, but while gentry are almost always addressed by title, commoners rarely are. Gentry titles are minutely graded; commoner titles are also graded, but there are ambiguities and contradictory elements in their actual application. Deferential behavior is of great importance, particularly in the areas of seating arrangements, posture, and speech. Marriage is sharply regulated by the title system, with preference for endogamy within the title group and a prohibition against a woman's marrying a man of lower title than her father. Wealth is not necessarily a function of title. Occupations are not specified by title, and there are few restrictions on commensality between holders of different titles. The traditional supravillage political roles were filled in accordance with the title system, to a certain extent. That is, inheritance of a title could make a man eligible for certain political or religious roles, such as "king" or "priest," but attainment of the role depended on training and social acceptance. Stratification by wealth is not very great. Income is largely based on landownership, and while some royal houses, taken as a single property owner, have extensive holdings, these are actually the individual possessions of a number of members of the family, no one of whom is very wealthy. In any case,

the resources of a royal house are always depleted by the large numbers of indigent relatives and retainers it supports and by the expenses of the great ceremonial festivals. Within commoner communities, the same social brakes on individual accumulation of property apply. [C. Geertz 1963b, 1964b, 1966, 1967.] **Social control and justice.** Village charters (awig-awig desa adat) usually list a series of prohibitions and regulations on individual behavior, covering most sorts of criminal acts. Violations of these charters, and civil disputes, are brought to the attention of the hamlet council (krama bandjar), which adjudicates and levies fines and other punishments, the most severe being ostracism from the village. Disputes which cannot be settled by the village and most capital crimes were in the past taken to a local lord for judgment; today there is a system of government courts for this function. [H. Geertz 1959; Korn 1936, 1960.]

RELIGION. Balinese refer to their religion as agama Hindu-Bali or as agama tirta, "the religion of water," referring to the holy water which, blessed by the Brahmana priest (pedanda), is used for consecration in most important rituals. The pedanda, a member of the Brahmana title group, trained to understand the traditional ritual doctrines and to perform complex, precise prayers, has an important role in all ceremonies that concern the royal realm, for instance at the high temples in the mountains at the sources of the rivers. Most Balinese have a personal, inherited tie to a particular pedanda, from whom they receive the holy water for their private ceremonies, the rites of passage; each pedanda has such clients scattered over wide regions. [Hooykaas 1964, 1966; Swellengrebel 1960.] There are three or more temples in each settlement, each one concerned with a different social and cultural function, such as fertility, kinship, title group, death, and so on. Temple ritual and temple membership mark out the significant social activities and groupings of the society from political to agricultural. The membership of a temple (ranging from a few to several hundred people) is a permanent organized group, which as a corporate entity owns the temple, carries out its rituals, and is responsible for its maintenance. Its non-Brahmana priest (pemanku) is chosen from among its members, either by hereditary succession, popular election, or divine intercession via trance. The temples do not represent different sects. The deities worshiped may often be nameless, referred to usually as "the god of such-and-such temple." Every temple of whatever size has numerous calendrical festivals, including an important annual one (every 210 days if it is on the Javanese-Balinese permutational calendar; every 356 days if it is on the lunar-solar calendar) (Goris 1960b). These rituals consist of preparation and presentation of complexly-made offerings of flowers and foods, orchestral playing, dance performances and prayers by officiating priests, and the sprinkling of holy water. A trance during a ceremony on the part of any of the participants is common. [Bateson 1937; Belo 1953, 1960; Goris 1960a; Franken 1960; Hooykaas-van Leeuwen Boomkamp 1961.] An important complex of religious activity is the Witch-and-Dragon (Rangda and Barong) dance-drama, which is associated with the death temple and with the local community of the *desa adat*. [Bateson and Mead 1942; Belo 1960, 1970.] The important rites of passage are the following: (1) the third or fourth month of first pregnancy (2) the 42nd day after birth (3) the third month after birth (4) the 210th day after birth (5) the first menstruation, and (6) teeth filing, usually some time in adolescence. **Illness and medicine.** Illness is considered to have been caused by a supernatural being—a god or one of the lesser "followers" of the gods—or by the action of a witch (*leyak*), a human being who can change form, like a werewolf. Medical practice consists of divining or having a séance with a medium, and involves various ritual cures. Practitioners are known as *balian* or *sadeg*, and are of two types: those trained through the memorization of remedies and those "seized" through personal illness and trance with the magical power. [Belo 1960; Covarrubias 1956.] **Death.** The ceremonies after a death are as follows: (1) washing and burial of the body on the day of the death; (2) cremation some months or more usually, years afterwards. A cremation is a very expensive and lengthy affair, and often numerous people are cremated together with some very wealthy or highborn person such as a prince or a priest. [Bateson and Mead 1942; Covarrubias 1956; Swellengrebel 1960.]

BIBLIOGRAPHY. Bateson 1937; Bateson and Mead 1942; Belo 1936, 1953, 1960, 1970; Covarrubias 1956; Dobby 1950; Franken 1960; C. Geertz 1959, 1963b, 1964b, 1966, 1967; H. Geertz 1959, 1963; Geertz and Geertz 1964; Goris 1960a, 1960b; Goris and Dronkers n.d.; Grader 1960; Holt 1967; Hooykaas 1964, 1966; Hooykaas-van Leeuwen Boomkamp 1961; Korn 1936, 1960; Last 1955; Pelzer 1963; Robequain 1954; Swellengrebel 1960.

SASAK *

ORIENTATION. **Identification and location.** The Sasak are the major ethnic group on Lombok. Concentrations of Balinese and Sumbawanese occur in the western and eastern sectors, respectively. Bodhas, said to be the aboriginal population of Lombok, live in

---

°The author of this section, Ruth Krulfeld, is at present Assistant Professor of Anthropology at George Washington University. She has done fieldwork in Singapore, Jamaica, and Central America, and her present contribution is based on research in five Sasak villages of Lombok in 1960-62.

relatively isolated villages along the west coast. They appear somewhat distinctive culturally, but are undergoing rapid change. Other components of the population include so-called Arabs—largely descendants of Arab merchants and Sasak women, Buginese fishermen in villages along the coast, and Chinese, presently concentrated in the port of Ampenan. Javanese, Timorese, Sumatrans, and Rotinese, mostly in government, military, or police service, live in Mataram, the administrative center for both Lombok and Sumbawa. The Sasak classify themselves as Waktu Lima or Waktu Telu, categories based on cultural rather than racial or linguistic distinctions. They are a Malayo-Polynesian people, physically and culturally related to peoples on the nearby islands of Java, Bali, and Sumbawa. Waktu Telu Sasak tend to be located in the more remote villages of the south and the mountain villages of the northwest, north, and east of the island. The more numerous Waktu Lima are found in the central plains and in areas around roads and markets. **Geography.** Lombok, located east of Bali and west of Sumbawa, has a land area of 4,700 square kilometers. Mountains occur in the north and south, separated by a central plain. The south and east tend to be arid zones, while the plains get some rain during the dry season from April to October. Lombok is geographically transitional between the islands to its west, which have greater precipitation, and Sumbawa, which is drier. **Linguistic affiliation.** Sasak is a Malayo-Polynesian language closely related to Javanese and Balinese, with three caste-related language levels of high, middle, and low. Borrowed Sanskrit words occur in the high language, and Arabic loans are especially noticeable in Waktu Lima villages. There are a number of dialects (cf. Teeuw 1958). While romanized script has largely replaced Kawi script, lontar palm leaf books are still inscribed and chanted in Kawi. **Demography.** The 1954 population of the island was 1,105,195, with an overall density of 235 per square kilometer. Of this figure 60,000 were Balinese and 6,164 were recorded as "aliens." **History and cultural relations.** Myths recorded in lontar palm leaf books mention early religious contact with Sumatra as well as relations with Madjapahit (Goris 1936: 196; Bousquet 1939; Vogelesang 1922: 260-306). During the seventeenth century, Lombok apparently came under weak political control of Sumbawa and Macassar, and the former apparently ruled Lombok for a time (Cool 1897: 171-72; deGraaf 1941: 360). By the eighteenth century, the Balinese had become rulers of Lombok, defeating the Sasak kingdom of Selaparang and ruling until 1895, when the Dutch conquered the island (Cool 1897). During the Dutch colonial period, Waktu Telu and Waktu Lima became noticeable as different and antagonistic cultural groups. Since Indonesian nationalism this cultural differentiation has continued. Waktu Lima look upon Waktu Telu Sasak as pagan backwoodsmen, while

Waktu Telu look upon Waktu Lima as people who have given up their cultural birthright. The proselytizing Waktu Lima are hopeful of acculturating their more strongly adat-based compatriots, and many villages which had been Waktu Telu, especially those located close to major roads and market places, have become completely Waktu Lima. Sasak relations with Balinese have remained somewhat strained since the days of Balinese political dominance. This seems to be especially true of Waktu Lima-Balinese relations.

SETTLEMENT PATTERN AND HOUSING. **Settlement pattern.** Each of the approximately 176 villages on Lombok is classified as either Waktu Lima or Waktu Telu. The latter, more isolated and traditional in outlook, have populations of under a thousand, while Waktu Lima communities may reach several thousand or more. Only a small number of the villages on Lombok are Waktu Telu. Each village is a discernible unit, containing a mosque and frequently a school, and surrounded by rice fields. The village pattern is roughly a grid, which in larger settlements is marked off into several neighborhoods, or *gubug*. Aristocrats sometimes reside in a separate compound within the village. Roofed platforms for entertaining guests and raised, thatched, rice storehouses are especially characteristic of Waktu Telu villages. Incipient offshoot villages, *dasan*, occur. **Housing.** Waktu Telu houses are windowless, one-roomed, rectangular structures, with packed earth floors and walls of earth and bamboo. An opening between the thatched roof and wall top allows smoke to escape. Waktu Lima houses are more heterogeneous in style. Cooking may be done within the house or in small outside cooking sheds. Before the harvest, lean-to shelters are built in the fields farthest from the village to guard the crop against marauding animals.

ECONOMY. Lombok is primarily agrarian. Livestock tending and hunting and gathering are of minor importance. **Agriculture.** The staple crop is rice, grown in irrigated and terraced fields, *bangket aiq*. Only one rainy season crop is grown, but the fields are used during the dry season for vegetables and cash crops. Waktu Telu also have *lendang*, or dry-field cultivation, in which rainfall rice is grown in addition to vegetables for home consumption. The third category of land is *kebon*, orchard, in which coffee, coconuts, fruit trees, bamboo, sugarcane, and pandanus are planted. *Lendang* fields are concentrated in northern hill villages; swidden cultivation does not occur in the plains. Dry fields are fallowed for about four years after a year of use, and fertilizers are not used. Irrigation is handled by *subak* organizations associated with watersheds. A villager belongs to the *subak* whose water source irrigates his fields, and hence *subak* cross-cut village boundaries. Metal-bladed, wooden plows are drawn by water buffalo or

cattle. Hoes and long-handled sickles are also used. **Fishing and hunting.** The Sasak are not a seafaring people, and much of the fish eaten is obtained through trade. Small fry are caught in the canals and rivers by fish drives and traps. Hunting provides little more than variety in the diet during the dry season. **Gathering.** Fruit, honey, wild vegetable leaves, and bamboo shoots are collected for food. Bamboo, rattan, pandanus, and elephant grass are used in building, roofing, and weaving. **Domestic animals.** Dogs serve as scavengers and are occasionally trained for hunting. Water buffalo, the preferred meat for feasts, are used for plowing in the south, while cattle predominate as draft animals in the north. Horses are used as beasts of burden and to draw carriages. The Sasak also have chickens, ducks, and goats, and they keep a few cats and birds as pets. Cocks are especially bred and trained for fighting in some villages. **Industrial arts.** In Waktu Telu villages, all girls learn to weave cloth and sleeping mats, while most men make baskets, nets, traps, hide containers, tools, houses, carved and painted house posts, doors, and the wooden horses used as ceremonial mounts during life crisis rituals. Some women become expert weavers of the holy cloths made at each birth and of other ritual cloths. Waktu Lima tend toward greater individual and village craft specialization. **Trade.** Only Waktu Lima villages have formal marketplaces. Trade in isolated villages is facilitated by itinerant traders, usually landless Waktu Lima, since traditional villagers look with disfavor upon trade as a means of livelihood. **Property.** Jewelry is usually jointly held by those family members of the same sex residing in the household. Like the kris or dagger of the men, jewelry becomes *pustaka* or special inherited property. Land ownership is limited to men in some villages, but may be inherited by both sexes in others, according to the codified ratio of one share for the woman to every three shares inherited by her brother. While houses are privately owned, the land on which they stand is usually considered village property. Agricultural land may be owned by title, individually or jointly; it may be pledged as security on a loan with its use and yield as interest, or it may be sharecropped.

KIN GROUPS. **Descent.** Descent is bilateral, with a patrilineal emphasis. Most rights and duties occur with members of the *wirang kadang*, consisting of father, father's father, father's brother, father's brother's sons, one's own brothers and their children. Descent is patrilineal among the aristocracy, and succession to office tends to be patrilineal. **Kin groups.** The patrilineal kin group, *wirang kadang*, is named, while the matrilineage has no such named groups. This patrilineal kin group is responsible to its membership for donations of goods and labor for ceremonies and for providing bridewealth. Mother's kin are designated by the general term, *langan nina* or "woman's path," corresponding to the male kin group, *langan mama*. Because of a tendency to village endogamy most inhabitants of a village are related. **Kin terminology.** The term for consanguineal relatives is *kuni*, while that for affinal relatives is *tiri*.

GtGrPa	*balo*
GrFa, GrMo	*papuq*
Mo	*inaq*
Fa	*amaq*
other wives of Fa	*inaq tiri*
aunt (FaSi, MoSi)	*inaq saiq*
uncle (FaBr, MoBr)	*amaq saiq*
all siblings	*semeton*
elder siblings	*kakaq*
younger siblings	*adiq*
cousins (children of parent's siblings, first, second, and third cousins)	if child of parent's sibling —*pisaq*; if child of parent's *pisaq*, then *sempu (sekali, dua kali, telu kali)* These relatives are addressed as *kakaq* or *adiq* depending upon the relative age of the linking kinsman to that of ego's parent, i.e. the child of father's elder brother or sister is called *kakaq* regardless of the relative age of this kinsman to ego.
Ch	*anak*
GrCh	*papuq*
GtGrCh	*balo*

Primary kin terms of the appropriate generation are used in addressing more distant relatives as well as to show solidarity or respect toward nonrelatives.

MARRIAGE AND FAMILY. **Mode.** Marriages, regulated by caste rules, are of two major types, with mock bride capture, *tjuri*, the more common. The second form, *meminangan*, consists of a formal proposal of marriage by the man and his *wirang kadang* to the family of the bride. Bride payments are set by adat according to caste, and consist largely of ritual money and cash. Bride service is extremely rare at present. Ceremonies following the wedding are more complex for the aristocracy than for commoners and for Waktu Telu than for Waktu Lima. **Form.** The predominant pattern is serial monogamy; limited polygyny occurs infrequently among the Waktu Lima Sasak. **Extension of incest taboos.** Marriage with any cousin, *pisaq* or *sempu*, cross or parallel, is preferred, and is often prescribed for members of the higher aristocracy. Marriages between generations are prohibited. **Residence.** Residence is generally neolocal or ambilocal, although it tends to be patrilocal among the aristocracy. **Domestic unit.** Usually a nuclear family, including occasionally a widowed parent, divorced child, or an adopted person. Among court-centered aristocracy, the patrilineally-related extended family residing in the same compound is common and continues after the death of the parents. In cases of polygynous marriages, separate residences for second wives and their children are established. **Inheritance.** Adat land and buildings are inherited by males, while jewelry and household furnishings are passed down in the female line. In traditional inheritance, the rights of the members of the *wirang* are stressed. The most important inherited property is *pustaka*, ritual inheritance consisting of land, houses, special holy cloths, kris or daggers, and special jewelry. Such property is considered to be permeated with sacred power, and it has ritual use. Waktu Lima and some Waktu Telu in the last few decades follow Islamic inheritance law. **Divorce.** Divorce is frequent in both Waktu Telu and Waktu Lima villages. On the average a Sasak, male or female, is married about three times during a lifetime. While women say they have no real option to initiate divorce legally, they usually are able to find a way to make their husbands request a divorce if they wish to end the marriage. Children in Waktu Telu villages remain with either parent, or else go to either set of grandparents, while in Waktu Lima villages they tend to remain with the father and his relatives. **Secondary marriage.** Marriage to a brother of the deceased husband or to a sister of a deceased wife occurs, but is not common. **Adoption.** *Peras* adoption, preferably of a male patrilineal relative, is legal and binding, the adopted person giving up rights and obligations with regard to his biological family. Such adoptions occur in traditional villages in the absence of sons to inherit the irrigated fields and official positions, although they are infrequent. *Akon* adoption is common. *Akon* children live with the adopting family and are entitled to the necessary life crisis ceremonies; but unlike *peras* children, they have no legal rights to inherit from the adopting family.

SOCIOPOLITICAL ORGANIZATION. **Political organization.** Each village has its own village headman, *kepala desa*, nowadays an elected office. He is aided by neighborhood heads or *kaliang*, the irrigation official, *pekasih aiq*, the *penghulu* or chief religious official, a village clerk, and a village guard and messenger service. These officials, as well as other elders who are knowledgeable about adat but hold no titled office, compose the *kerama desa*, or village adat authorities. The actual decision-making powers of the village headmen vary. **Social stratification.** There are three major castes associated with an elaborate social etiquette. The *bangsawan*, or aristocracy, is composed of subcastes according to sex and production of offspring. Caste titles preface the individual's name. Membership in the commoner caste (*dengan*, "people") is indicated by use of different caste titles for males without offspring, for those who have fathered children, for women who have not yet borne children, and for those who have. In some villages all castes are present, some have only one of the aristocratic castes in addition to commoners, while others have only commoners and no aristocrats. Prior to the Dutch colonial period, there was a caste of slaves and serfs and their descendants. Caste membership is maintained through prescriptive marriage rules in which hypergamy operates. In some villages, members of certain aristocratic lineages of rulers live in separate compounds. Wealth is not limited to the aristocracy, who in many places tend to shun trade and who may even be poor. Waktu Telu villagers all own small amounts of land and approximately equal quantities of other goods, and there are few differences in wealth in such villages. **Social control and justice.** The *kerama desa*, composed of village officials and elders, decides problem cases according to village adat. This is replaced by codified law in Waktu Lima villages and on the district level. Traditional sentences include ostracism and shaming lectures given publicly by elders.

RELIGION. **Religious system.** Although the entire Sasak population is nominally Muslim, Waktu Lima are more Islamized than Waktu Telu. The former are proselytizing, and religious membership is individually achieved; whereas among the latter membership is through descent from a given set of ancestors and village residence. Waktu Telu religion is concerned largely with ancestor and local spirit beliefs and a network of ritual feasts based upon village adat (which tends to drop out of use in Waktu Lima villages, where it is replaced by *agama* [or Islam] and codified law). The traditional Waktu Telu concept of taboo, *maliq*, the breach of which is believed punishable by supernatural intervention during the lifetime of the individual, is replaced in Waktu Lima villages by the concept of *haram*, or sin, believed punishable in the afterlife. **Supernaturals.** Traditional supernatural beings include village founders, past rulers, ancestral spirits, and anthropomorphized beings of forest, mountains, and water called *samar* and *bakeq*. All of these, as well as spiritual doubles of people, *jinn* or *djim*, may cause disease, death, or disappearance. There is also belief in witches, *selaq*; in supernatural power located in ritual inheritance property; in the spirit of rice and the supernatural powers thought to reside in rice; and in supernatural powers, such as invulnerability, believed to be obtained through inheritance, purchase, or study. While belief in ancestral spirits, holy places, and ritual inheritance is considered pagan in Islamized Waktu Lima villages, other supernatural beings such as the *bakeq* and *djim* are feared, and there is a belief in sorcery. **Practitioners.** *Penghulu* and *kiyayi* are male Islamic experts who conduct marriage and funeral ceremonies, including washing and preparing the corpse. In Waktu Telu villages they are in the position of village priests who perform prayers and fast at the beginning of Ramadan on behalf of the entire village population. *Pemangku*

(male or female) who act as spirit mediums and guardians of traditional holy spots are present only in Waktu Telu villages. **Ceremonies.** Traditional Sasak ceremonies are divided into two classes: *gawe urip*, or life rituals, and *gawe bedina*, or death and mourning rituals. In Waktu Telu villages, ceremonies for naming, first haircutting, tooth-filing, circumcision, ear-piercing (for girls), and marriage usually take place in September, after the harvest and before the rainy season work on farms commences. Holy cloths are ritually woven at the birth of each individual (see Brink 1923; Damste 1923). Death ceremonies occur on the day of the death, with five to eight mourning ceremonies conducted at special intervals after death. Curing ceremonies are conducted at graveyards and holy spots. Fertility ceremonies are conducted for cattle and crops, and special rituals take place for every stage of agricultural work in the irrigated fields. There are also ceremonies for repairing the ancestral graves, as well as special village ceremonies in northeastern Lombok on Alip, the eighth year of the Muslim cycle (see van Baal 1941). Much of the yield beyond that needed for daily living is allocated for these ritual feasts. Waktu Lima villages have discontinued most of the above rituals with the exception of some which are more Islamized, i.e. those for marriage, circumcision, and death. **Illness and medicine.** Illness is thought to be caused by spirit possession, *ketemuq*; black magic, *seher*; breach of taboo, such as dishonoring ritual inheritance or not performing required rituals; and sometimes from disease, usually designated as *panas* (fever). Curing specialists are either *belian* (midwives, sorcerers, or medicine men) or *pemangku* (intermediaries relating villagers to the spirits of special holy places). Curing practices commonly include the spitting of masticated betel nut on the affected area with the proper chants, *djampi*; countersorcery; washing in or drinking the water obtained from washing inherited ritual objects; offerings to spirits at special holy places with a promise for a feast if the cure should be effected; the making of special medicines from fruits and leaves; and, more rarely, trance, with dancing on hot coals. In cases of epidemic, a village ceremony is conducted by *pemangku* to exorcise the disease. **Soul, death, and afterlife.** Waktu Telu believe that ancestral spirits affect the living, and rituals are performed at graves as part of a continuing interaction between living and dead villagers. Waktu Lima believe in the Islamic afterlife, with a heaven and hell, depending upon the individual's performance during his lifetime (Krulfeld 1966). Among both groups, the corpse is washed by a *kiyayi* and shrouded in white cloth. Burial takes place within one or two days. There is a procession to the graveyard, to which the Waktu Telu take food and other goods on special offering trays. A stylized pounding of rice producing a special rhythm notifies other villagers of the death and elicits their contribution of rice and labor for the funeral. The grave is usually dug to a depth of four to six feet; graves are reused after ten years, and old bones are unearthed and reburied. A platform of bamboo slats on which the body is placed is made within the grave, and the grave is covered with earth. Waktu Telu graves have rows of stones supporting the earthen mound and two stones on top of the mound, in addition to the common head and foot stones used by the Waktu Lima. For the Waktu Telu, a special feast is held at the grave, and the grave is visited before all important ceremonies by kinsmen who notify the ancestral spirit of the ceremony.

BIBLIOGRAPHY. van Baal 1941; Bousquet 1939; van den Brink 1923; Cool 1897; Damste 1923; Goris 1936; deGraaf 1941; Krulfeld 1966; Nieuwenhuyzen 1932; Teeuw 1958; Vogelesang 1922.

SUMBAWANESE-BIMANESE-DOMPU *

Synonyms. *Tau Semawa, Doü Bima, Doü Dompu*

ORIENTATION. **Identification and location.** The name Sumbawa originally designated only the western part of the island—the former Sultanate of Sumbawa —with the eastern part being known as Bima. The inhabitants of West Sumbawa, known as Sumbawanese or Tau Semawa, are culturally quite homogeneous, although there are some dialect differences. East Sumbawa evidences greater ethnic diversity, including lowland populations inhabiting the seats of former independent principalities, e.g. Bimanese (Doü Bima), Dompu, and Sanggar, as well as the hill-dwelling Doü Donggo (lit. "mountain people") and Doü Kolo, the latter now largely assimilated to lowland culture. The indigenous population is a mixture of Proto- and Deutero-Malay elements, related to the Sasak of Lombok; the presence on the north coast of recent immigrants from southern Sulawesi, Kalimantan, and Java adds to the racial and cultural diversity. In general, however, the Bimanese are darker skinned than the peoples of western Sumbawa. Sumbawa lies between 116°44′ and 119°13′ E. and 8°5′ and 9°6′ S. and is part of the volcanic mountain chain extending eastward from Java to Alor and Wetar. The population is settled mainly on the northern coastal plains, the plain of Dompu, and the hill valleys of Bima. **Geography.** Despite a long coastline, indented by deep bays, the population is not oriented to the

sea, and most villages lie 5 km. or more from the coast. Much of the island is covered by park landscape, with large tracts of open country dotted with small clusters of trees and shrubs—the result in part of swidden agriculture. Permanently irrigated rice lands occur mainly along the rivers on the northern coast and in river valleys in the central uplands. The climate is tropical, with little daily variation in temperature. There is a marked division of the year into wet (west monsoon) and dry (east monsoon) seasons. Flora and fauna are predominately Asian in type. **Linguistic affiliation.** The languages of Sumbawa are all Malayo-Polynesian, but there is a marked division between Sumbawan (Semawa), which is closely related to the Sasak language of East Lombok, and Biman, which is related to Savunese and shows some affinity with Manggarai. The Donggo and Sanggar people speak languages closely related to Biman, and the Doü Dompu speak Biman. **Demography.** The total population in 1930 stood at 314,000; whereas by 1951 it had increased to approximately 400,000. Of the 1930 population, 114,000 were resident in West Sumbawa, 177,000 in Bima, and 22,000 in Dompu. **History and cultural relations.** Local tradition credits Bima with a total of 52 princes, the tenth of whom, Maharaja Sang Bima, is said to have founded the realms of Dompu and Bima, which eventually extended their power over Sumba, Manggarai, and Timor. The names of early rulers testify to Hindu influence, and the Javanese epic of 1365, *Nagarakertagama*, mentions four places in Sumbawa as dependencies of the realm of Majapahit. The greatest influence on Sumbawan culture stems, however, from Macassar (Goa), beginning with the subjugation of Bima by Goa in 1616. The thirty-eighth ruler of Bima was converted to Islam in about 1640. First Dutch contact occurred in 1605, and the Dutch conquest of Macassar in 1667 marked the liberation of Bima from Goa and the conclusion of a contract with the V.O.C. (Dutch East India Company). Contact and intermarriage between Biman and Macassarese ruling families continued under Dutch hegemony; effective Dutch rule began only in 1905. Under the Dutch policy of indirect rule, native rulers continued in office. Since 1950, they have been integrated into the administration of the Republic of Indonesia as government officials.

SETTLEMENT PATTERN AND HOUSING. A village is often surrounded by its constituent hamlets, and in the mountains the population lives on the swidden complexes for part of the year, returning to the home village after harvesting. West Sumbawan houses are very fine, closely resembling those of the Macassarese and Buginese. Such houses consist of four to six rooms, with partitions that are easily moved so that an extra room may be added when a married daughter comes to live with her parents. Houses in the interior of West Sumbawa are of the same type,

---

*H. G. Schulte Nordholt, the author of this and the following entry on the Donggo, is Professor of Anthropology in the Institute of Social Science, Free University, Amsterdam. He resided on Sumbawa in 1937-38 as an official of the Dutch Colonial Government and has drawn on this experience, plus the available literature. He emphasizes that his description pertains primarily to the period of the 1930s.

though smaller, and more like those in Bima and Dompu. This is partly because marriages here are neolocal from the beginning.

ECONOMY. **Agriculture.** Mainly on fixed farm complexes, consisting of three types: (a) *sawah*, or wet-rice fields (b) dry-rice fields, and (c) garden plots with perennial crops surrounding the villages. Formerly there was sufficient room for swidden cultivation in the lowlands, but now it is moving to the mountains. After the ground has been cultivated for five years, a fallow period of eight to ten years is needed. Following the arrival of the Dutch, there was a marked expansion of the area under wet-rice cultivation. Secondary crops, grown chiefly for export, include onions, beans, and some tobacco and coffee. Fruits and vegetables are grown in the gardens around the villages. The implements used are the plow and the harrow, as in the islands to the west of Sumbawa. **Fishing and hunting.** Fishing is relatively unimportant, although the people do have fish ponds, which are also used for extracting salt during the dry season. Fishing is mainly a concern of Buginese, Wadjo, and Salajar immigrants. Since they are all Muslims—except for the Donggo—the inhabitants of Sumbawa do not hunt the wild boar, of which there are large numbers. Deer hunting is popular, however. **Gathering.** Sumbawa is rich in forest products and was formerly renowned for its *sapan* wood (*Calsalpina sappan*), on which the V.O.C. had a monopoly. At present the people gather large quantities of oleaginous nuts, such as candlenuts (*Aleurites moluccana*), as well as rattan and beeswax. **Domestic animals.** Bima has been known for its small but sturdy horses ever since the fourteenth century, when it was already exporting these to Java. In the 1920s, the island was an important horse-breeding area, with twice as many horses per square kilometer as the famous horse-breeding island of Sumba. The buffalo is of even greater importance, West Sumbawa being one of the major buffalo areas of the archipelago. Cattle ownership is important, with some people owning hundreds of head. **Trade.** Horses, buffalo, hides, onions, and beans are exported. Exports increased enormously after 1905, mostly as a result of regular interisland K.P.M. (Dutch Steamship Company) service (which, however, drove out Macassarese and Buginese *perahu* shipping to a considerable extent). Trade is focused on Surabaya and Macassar. **Markets and trading.** There are very few large indigenous markets. The cattle trade, and especially horse dealing, is monopolized by Arabs; while Chinese are chiefly engaged in buying export crops and importing and distributing trade articles. The Chinese are scattered among the district capitals, but are concentrated especially in Sumbawa Besar, the principal town of the sultanate. Arabs also operate as moneylenders. **Property.** Wet-rice fields, gardens with perennial crops, permanent dry-rice fields, and houses are owned individually. Swidden fields are laid out in the communal territory of the village, each cultivator tilling his own plot. Movable goods held in individual ownership include clothing, jewelry, and silver coins. A man's widow and his children, including his daughters, share his inheritance equally among them.

KINSHIP. Descent is decidedly bilateral in Sumbawa, Bima, and Dompu. The circle of kindred can be distinguished into different subcircles. The center is formed by the nuclear family. Then follows the circle of the parents' brothers and sisters and their children, or first cousins, i.e. all those who descend from the same four grandparents. This is followed by the circle of descendants of the same (eight) great-grandparents, and hence the second cousins as far as members of the same generation are concerned. This in turn is followed by the circle of descendants of the great-great-grandparents, of which the members of the same generation are the third cousins. This is virtually as far as the kinship horizons extend. Thus every person has a different circle of kindred, and only siblings share exactly the same relatives. Furthermore, in an isolated village community of 60-100 families (of which there are many in the mountains), a large number of people descend from the same great-great-grandparents, or in other words are each other's third cousins. Even so, a village is not in practice coterminous with a local, consciously recognized, bilateral kinship group. The Bimanese kinship terminology is as follows:

Fa	*ama*
Mo	*ina*
FaBr	*ori*
Term with which wife addresses husband (*ndai* = to serve as, in order to, i.e. to make a father)	*ama ndai*
Term by which husband addresses wife	*ina ndai*
Husband	*rahi*
Wife	*wei*
Br-in-law (WiBr)	*hera*
MoSi, lit. "little mother"	*ina-toi*
Child	*ana doïi*
Br	*ama niya*
Si	*ama ntjara*
GrFa	*ompu*
GrMo	*wai*
Ancestors (of either sex)	*waro*

MARRIAGE. **Mode.** A young man wishing to propose marriage will send an eloquent woman (*penati*), either with or without his parents, to the house of the young woman, and she will make the proposal in highly figurative language. Bridewealth (*pebeli*, Bim. *tjoi waä*) is higher in Sumbawa than in Bima and Dompu, but otherwise is entirely dependent on the status of the bride. The marriage is solemnized in accordance with Muslim law, after the adat ceremonies have taken place. The latter include ritual bathing of the bridal couple. **Residence.** In Bima and Dompu the marriage is immediately neolocal; in Sumbawa the young couple go to live with the bride's parents at first, and the husband has to render bride services for a considerable period; but this is only temporarily so, especially in the mountains. **Divorce.** Divorce is common, probably partly as a result of child marriages or of the practice of parents promising each other's children in marriage to one another. This is most frequent among the higher classes. **Form.** Polygyny is quite common, especially in higher circles. Men of noble families often have concubines in addition to the four wives allowed by Muslim law. In the villages, monogamous marriage is the rule. **Extension of incest taboos.** Sexual intercourse between members of the nuclear family is definitely regarded as incest. There is a further taboo on marriage between a boy and a girl who have grown up in the same house, even though they are in no way related; nonetheless it does occur, especially among the higher classes. There is also a taboo, according to Muslim law, on marriage between "milk siblings." Generational difference is extremely important, and is emphasized by the practice of teknonymy. In general, marriage between cousins—both parallel and cross—is preferred. According to a survey by Goethals (1967: 48) 26, 30, and 25 percent of the population of a village in the hills outside Sumbawa Besar were married to first, second, and third cousins respectively, and only 19 percent were married to unrelated persons. Of the 22 cases of first-cousin marriage, 13 were parallel cousin and 9 cross-cousin unions. This demonstrates the decidedly bilateral nature of kinship relations and the strong tendency toward intermarriage in the more isolated villages. The same pattern prevails in wet-rice areas, possibly even reinforced by the consideration that the wet-rice fields will remain in the family as a result of first- and second-cousin marriages. **Domestic unit.** The dominant pattern of the nuclear family does not exclude the occasional or temporary residence of other relatives within the household.

SOCIOPOLITICAL ORGANIZATION. Political organization.

At the local level, the most important sociopolitical unit is the village, in each case characterized by the presence of a mosque. Towns are further divided into wards, each under a head of its own. Many of these are constituted by communities of other ethnic groups, such as, for example, the large Kampong Bugis near Sumbawa Besar. A striking feature is the dualism between *hukum* and adat, between the hierarchy of the representatives of the *hukum* (Muslim religious law) and those of the adat, which after the disappearance of the tribal religion became focused principally on secular administrative affairs. A village cluster is headed by a *kepala gabun-gan* (Indon. *gabung* = cluster; *gabungan* = federation, union). In Bima and Dompu, he is called *gelara* (Donggo-*gelaran*, Mac.-*gallarrang*, cf. Jav. *gelar*). Under him are the *wakil kepala* (deputy heads) of the villages or residential communities, with at their side —in modern times—a Deputy Assistant to the Village Union. Each residential community has of old had a *mandur* (foreman) to see to the execution of orders. In addition there is a *malar*, or one who looks after the *lar* (land, the radical of *gelaran*). He is the custodian of the land and was originally responsible for the agricultural ritual and the distribution of land. Parallel with this administrative hierarchy is that of Islam. The Muslim religious head at the village level is the *lebè* (Indon. *lebai*), or head of the mosque, who is responsible for all the ceremonies, the religious anniversaries of the Muslim calendar, and for the rites of the agricultural cycle. He has at his side a *penghulu* (who in other parts of Indonesia is the head of the mosque). Junior members of the religious hierarchy are the *ketip* and the *marbat*. The former is responsible for mosque services and the recitation of the *chotbah* (sermon). The *marbat* is in charge of the building and the administration. **The sultanate.** Sumbawa's history is old, going back to the Hindu-Javanese period as far as Bima and Dompu are concerned. In Bima, the old name for which is Mbodjo, there were formerly three districts with *ntjuhi* at their head. *Ntjuhi* at present is the name for the ritual leader of the Doù Donggo. In the traditional structure, these *ntjuhi* were the heads of nuclear areas around Bima. Later there was also a prince (*ruma sengadji*; *ruma* = lord, *sengadji* = prince), who formed the center, in the town of Bima, of four districts—which should perhaps be regarded as a kind of federation. This situation still prevailed in 1891. And although it had disappeared in 1917, the prince still had his function bestowed on him by a *ntjuhi*, a *bumi* (an adat ritual leader), and a *gelara* upon his accession to the throne in that year. Within this traditional organization, the ruler was the ritual center. His title was also Dewa Sang Hien or Lord of the Spirits, and he retained this ritual character throughout the Muslim period. Like the Sultan of Sumbawa, he remained the religious head, even though he concerned himself more and more with practical administration after the introduction of colonial rule. The ruler is immobile, and he was formerly forbidden to leave his palace. The central administration is formed by the ruler as immobile center with at his side an executive authority, the Ruma Bitjara, who is the head of the *hadat*, or council of the realm, consisting of 13 *toreli*, 13 *djeneli*, and 13 *bumi*. The dignitaries of the realm, who belong to the nobility, have the Bumi-luma Rasa-nai as head in the east, and the Bumi-luma Mbelo in the west (*bumi*, soil; *rasa-nai*, large village; *luma* occurs in many titles). The first rulers were spirits and thus associated with heaven. The first rulers of Dompu and

Bima were born of a marriage of a ruler with a *naga*, however, symbolizing a union between heaven and earth. Among the nobility there appears a similar association of the dignitaries of the realm with the earth; they are even subordinate to the Lords of the Earth. But these in turn are subject to the dual monarchy of the Ruma Sengadji, the ritual prince, and his Ruma Bitjara. Similarly, each *djeneli* has a *bumi* at his side. The latter is in charge of ritual, and offers sacrifices when there is a threat of drought or famine. People still resort to *bumi* instead of Muslim religious leaders in times of difficulty. Couvreur (1917: 12) compares the structure of Bima to that of Sumba, which has close linguistic affinities. In Sumba there is a similar dualism of the Maramba, the head of the community, and the Mangu Tanangu, the custodian of the land and representative of the indigenous segment of the community. Possibly we are dealing here with a superimposed Macassarese structure, but in view of the old Bimanese tradition, which goes back to the Hindu-Javanese period, it is more probable that these structures are autochthonous. Following the introduction of colonial rule, a contract was concluded with the sultan as though he were absolute ruler, and he took advantage of the opportunity to become such. Subsequently the semi-autonomous parts of the realm became districts of the sultanate, and this is at present still so. **Social stratification.** Probably as a result of Macassarese influence, there is a rigid distinction into classes in Bima, Dompu, and Sumbawa. In Bima there are both upper and lower nobility, a class of commoners, and slaves. The common people are divided into a large number of *dari*. Elbert, following Jasper (1908: 106-08), mentions 26. A *dari* is, as Goethals (1960) aptly calls it, a "task group." These groups are sometimes also compared to guilds. The first four have a military task, the fifth a religious one, entirely in accordance with the general Indonesian pattern. The sixth supplies the servants of the two *bumi*. The seventh to the twelfth supply the different craftsmen. The thirteenth consists of artillerists, and the fourteenth to twenty-fifth are made up of the different trades and people who render certain services. The last are the *dari mardeka*, or those manumitted on the strength of certain merits. The death penalty can never be imposed on them. All *dari* are in the service of the court in a wide sense of the word and each has a representative with the ruler. These are called *anangguru*, and are the "mothers" of the people, while the *gelara* are the "fathers." The word *dari*, meaning "string," refers to a population group, the originally local groups connected with the palace for carrying out particular tasks. In Sumbawa there are five classes. First there is the nobility, which is distinguished into an upper nobility of the *datu* and a lower nobility. The second class is formed by the *tau djuran*. According to Ligtvoet (1876: 565), it was divided into five *ruwe*. The *tau djuran* lived

mainly in the capital, Sumbawa Besar, and hence also in the main towns of vassal states. The members of this class did not themselves own land, so that it is possible that they belonged to the group of palace retainers and were hence immigrants from Goa, who exercised a very strong influence on the court culture after 1600. This can hardly be true of the countless *dari* of Bima, however, or of all those engaged in tilling wet-rice fields. The third class is that of the *tau kamutar*, the ruler's subjects, divided into *ruwe* or lineages who render the ruler services. The fourth class is formed by foreigners. The fifth class consists of people called *tau merisi*, temporary slaves as a result of failure to pay debts. Genuine slaves, who can be sold, are also classed with these. They are often prisoners of war. There is a strong class consciousness in these communities. Normally people marry within their own class and task group. Where in Sumbawa a task group is designated by the same word as for genealogical group, this testifies to the preference for marriage inside the kinship group.

RELIGION. Except for the Doü Donggo, the whole of Sumbawa is Muslim. There has never been any Christian missionary activity in the island. Not all of Sumbawa was converted to Islam at the same time, however, South Sumbawa only having been Muslim for the past 60 to 70 years. For the rest, Sumbawa is even more orthodox than Bima, and is so to the same degree as South Sulawesi. This does not mean that the autochthonous religion has disappeared altogether. There are, for instance, many *sanro* (Bim. *sando*, Mac. *sonro*, Indon. *dukun*), or medicine men left.

BIBLIOGRAPHY. Arndt 1952; Bouman 1925; Couvreur 1917, 1924; Elbert 1912; Goethals 1959, 1960, 1961a, 1961b, 1967; Hederer and Lehmann 1950; Heine-Geldern 1947; Hoven 1930a, 1930b; Jasper 1908; Jonker 1893-96, 1904, 1934; Kuperus 1937a, 1937b, 1938, 1942a, 1942b; Lekkerkerker 1933; Ligtvoet 1876; *Militaire* 1930; van Naerssen 1938; Voorhoeve 1948; Zollinger 1850.

DONGGO *

Synonym. *Doü Donggo*

ORIENTATION. **Identification.** A numerically small population of swidden-farming, mountain people in the interior of East Sumbawa. The name, Doü Donggo, means literally "mountain people." They speak a Biman-related language, but are somewhat darker in skin color than the Bimanese.

SETTLEMENT PATTERN AND HOUSING. A total of six villages, with a population of 12,000 in 1930. Houses are crowded close together, and settlements

---

*Prepared by H. G. Schulte Nordholt.

are located high on mountain ridges and adjacent to steep cliffs. An open-sided structure in each village serves as a meeting and working place for both sexes. Houses are rectangular, raised on piles, with high, narrow-gabled roofs, which extend slightly below the level of the floor. In the space beneath are domestic animals as well as looms and spinning wheels. These houses are similar to the rice storage barns of the Bimanese and probably represent the original East Sumbawanese house form.

ECONOMY. Main reliance on swidden agriculture, with dry rice the staple crop. Wild boar are hunted with barbed lances, and birds are taken with blowpipes. Some coffee is sold for cash, and candlenuts have been a relatively important item of trade. The outstanding craft specialty is weaving.

KINSHIP. The Doü Donggo are organized into five exogamous patrilineal clans, each formerly inhabiting a separate village. Each agnatic descent group or patrilineage has its own burial place in its own territory. The leading clan, the London Doü Deke ("clan of the gecko men"), retains ritual leadership and supplies the hereditary priests, *ntsuhi*, for the entire tribe. In each village there is a girls' dormitory, in which the unmarried girls sleep and receive visitors. A marriage is arranged through an envoy of the boy's *london* (literally clan, but in practice patrilineage), who visits the girl's *london*. Bridewealth consists of buffalo, a caparisoned horse, and Chinese coins. Monogamy is the rule.

RELIGION. Unlike the remainder of the population on Sumbawa, the Doü Donggo are non-Muslims. The gods, *dewa*, include a supreme creator, Dewa Langi Lantu, who is honored at a major postharvest feast. On this occasion the souls of the deceased, *mbawa*, accompany the living to the sacred places in the mountains where the gods have their abode and where the ancestral spirits live in caves. The *ntsala*, or *kria dewa* (Bim., *karia*, "vagina"), is the sacred place, marked by a phallic stone, where the gods gather for sexual intercourse; here the Donggo priest offers sacrifices after first obtaining permission of the *gelaran* (custodian of the land).

BIBLIOGRAPHY. Arndt 1952.

FLORES - BANDA

THE PEOPLES INCLUDED in this section are essentially the inhabitants of islands bordering on the Banda and Flores seas, exclusive of southern Celebes. This is essentially the area of Dyen's (1965) Moluccan linkage—which in turn corresponds rather closely to the earlier Ambon-Timor group of the linguist, Esser (1938). It is, furthermore, essentially the area delineated by van Wouden in his *Sociale Structuurtypen in de Groote Oost* (1935), the term Flores-Banda as used in the present volume corresponding in large measure to the traditional Dutch usage of "Great East." Thus there is some basis on both linguistic and social structural grounds for a grouping of peoples in this fashion. The area as a whole is further characterized by the presence of the Papuan (Melanesian) physical type, although admittedly this criterion decreases in importance as one approaches its western limits; and Papuan types are found north of the area, on Halmahera. Any attempt to block out an ethnolinguistic region in this fashion runs into difficulty in the area of Sumba-Sumbawa-Flores. This is apparently a transitional zone, as was earlier recognized by the naturalist, A. R. Wallace, and by others who have attempted to draw lines dividing a "Malay" from an "Austro-Papuan" realm, e.g. H. J. T. Bijlmer. Here the distribution of languages, cultures, and physical types is such that a classification in terms of one criterion may make little sense in terms of another. On the island of Flores, for example, there is a marked break in physical type as between the extreme west and the rest of the island; whereas culturally and linguistically the break seems to come farther east on Flores, in the region of Sika. In the present volume, the ethnic entries for this transitional region are arranged simply island by island, e.g. the peoples of Flores, the peoples of Sumba-Savu, the peoples of Sumbawa. In so doing, the peoples of eastern Sumbawa —the Bimanese, Dompu, and Donggo—are included with those of western Sumbawa in the

Bali-Lombok-Sumbawa section; whereas on historical and linguistic grounds, at least, they might better go in the Flores-Banda section, within a subgroup that would include Sumbanese, Savunese, Manggarai, Ngada, and perhaps Endenese.

BIBLIOGRAPHY. Dyen 1965; Esser 1938.

SUMBA-SAVU

SUMBA (Humba, Zumba, formerly Sandalwood Island), one of the Lesser Sunda Islands, is situated south of Flores and midway between Sumbawa and Timor. The island may be regarded as a single cultural unit, although it is customary to distinguish between East and West Sumba, with Kodi in the extreme west considered separately. The population, numbering some 250,000 in 1960, is predominantly Proto-Malay in appearance, with a slight Melanesian influence (Keers 1948). Aliens include Savunese immigrants (approximately 10,-000, most of whom are Christian) and numerous colonies of Muslim Endenese. The Sumbanese speak dialects of a single language whose closest relationships are with Savu, Bima, and Manggarai (Esser's Bima-Sumba group). There are, however, sufficient linguistic differences to warrant a division into East Sumbanese (Kambera) and West Sumbanese (Waidjewa or Wewewa). These language differences correspond to some extent with cultural differences—at least to the extent that East Sumba constitutes a relatively homogeneous ethnolinguistic unit as compared with the rest of the island (Adams 1969: 4; Onvlee 1970). It is this area—East Sumba—that has received the most attention in the ethnographic literature (cf. Kana 1966, Adams 1969, Nooteboom 1940, Onvlee 1949). • Much of interior Sumba consists of extensive plateaus, with scattered, irregular hills, particularly in the western part of the island. The climate is hot and dry, especially in the east; soils are practically everywhere thin and nonvolcanic in origin. As a consequence, most of the population lives on the interior plateaus, where extensive grasslands support grazing and small-scale agriculture. Sacred myths that recount the traditional origin of Sumbanese clans from semidivine ancestors mention place names such as "Mecca" and "Djawa," but documented history begins only with the mention in fourteenth-century Javanese chronicles of Sumba as a dependency of Madjapahit. By the seventeenth century, Sumba was subordinate to Bima and famed for its sandalwood and horses. Somewhat later, the island fell under the influence of the powerful kingdom of Goa (Macassar) in the southern Celebes. In 1756, a contract was signed between the Dutch East India Company and a coalition of Sumbanese chiefs or "kings"; later, a Dutch civil officer was stationed on Sumba as a "political observer," but not until 1900 did Holland intervene actively in Sumbanese internal affairs. Under a policy of indirect rule through the appointment of native rulers as "radjas," the island was divided into two regencies, East and West Sumba, each composed of numerous "self-governing territories," a pattern maintained by the modern Republic of Indonesia except that districts are now administered by government officials. The former rulers—members of the Sumbanese nobility—have in many instances accepted positions within the civil service. • Relations with the island of Savu (Sawu), midway between Sumba and Timor, presumably predate the Dutch-sponsored migrations of Savunese to East Sumba during the nineteenth century; linguistic ties (noted by Esser) are paralleled by close cultural ties associated with a long history of intermarriage between royal families on the two islands (Onvlee 1970). The present volume therefore groups Savu together with Sumba within a Sumba-Savu section. It should be noted that the entry on Sumba is restricted to East Sumbanese in recognition of the fact that this portion of the island constitutes a relatively homogeneous area, both linguistically and culturally, and that the bulk of the ethnographic literature pertains to East Sumba and the Eastern Sumbanese.

BIBLIOGRAPHY. Adams 1969; Kana 1966; Keers 1948; Nooteboom 1940; Onvlee 1949, 1970; van Wouden 1956.

EASTERN SUMBANESE

Synonym. *Soembaneezen*

ORIENTATION. The inhabitants of East Sumba, numbering 95,000 in 1961, were formerly divided into some 50 independent domains or princedoms, for the most part at war with one another and acknowledging no central authority. Identification was largely with the princedom, and in particular with its fortified ceremonial center, the *paraing*. There is, however, a common language and elements of shared culture throughout East Sumba, due largely, according to Adams (1969), to the overlapping networks of exchange relationships which extend throughout the area.

SETTLEMENT PATTERN AND HOUSING. **Settlement pattern.** The inhabitants of a princedom occupy a fortified (walled) hilltop village, *paraing*, which is at the same time a ceremonial center. Within, large clan houses face a central square containing the stone slab tombs of important ancestors. For approximately one half of the year, the people live in small settlements of field houses located some distance away on the swiddens, returning to the *paraing* at the onset of the dry season. This pattern is breaking down in many areas, with a trend to nuclear family dwellings in small villages along river banks. These changes have not, however, noticeably affected older patterns of kin ties and ritual obligations. [Adams 1969; Onvlee 1970.] **Housing.** The traditional clan house, *uma kabihu*, is a large rectangular structure, raised on piles. The thatched roof slopes gently upward from all four sides, rising sharply toward the center to a characteristic high gable, supported on four massive center posts. A veranda extends along one side (the front) of the structure. The interior is sharply divided between masculine and feminine areas, with separate entrances for each sex. High up under the central gable is stored the *marapu* treasure—objects associated with the deified ancestral founders of the house group. Structural features and spatial layout within the house symbolize various aspects of Sumbanese cosmology and socioreligious structure (Adams 1969; Onvlee 1970). These houses, located in separate wards within a *paraing*, formerly housed the members of a patrilineal clan segment and served at the same time as a clan temple or ceremonial structure.

ECONOMY. Small-scale farming, supplemented by the raising of animals and exchange of goods, the latter associated with the ceremonial life and with patterns of social stratification and prestige. [Exchange as a system of reciprocity and redistribution is discussed in Adams (1969: chap. 3).] **Agriculture.** Rice (the highland staple) and maize are grown on swiddens, and there are in addition year-round gardens and tree crops. Ruling families have in recent years grown some irrigated rice along valley bottoms. Rice everywhere exceeds maize in ritual importance (Adams 1969: 178, note 4). **Domestic animals.** Large herds of wild horses are exploited as mounts and for export, although the export value of Bengal cattle, introduced in the 1920s, is increasing. Water buffalo

serve chiefly as ceremonial food and reserve wealth. **Industries.** Fine ikat textiles, woven from locally grown cotton by women of the northeast coast, are famous throughout Sumba and figure prominently in the ritual and social life of the people. **Trade and exchange.** Imports from Macassar, Bima, and Endeh include gongs, coins, gold jewelry, ivory, beads, and porcelain. Exports consist chiefly of horses, buffalo, and decorated textiles. Sales to foreign traders of Sumbanese horses and sandalwood formerly brought great wealth to native rulers and thus affected to a considerable extent local politics and interkingdom rivalries within East Sumba. An extensive intraisland exchange of goods (including regional craft products, imported goods, and crops such as rice) is part of a highly formalized system whereby labor, services, ceremonial food, and goods are exchanged among groups of relatives and friends. The system, with extensive social and ritual connotations, has as its primary stimulus the institution of asymmetric connubium, whereby marriages precipitate lengthy and complicated exchanges between affinal kinsmen. [Adams 1969; Kana 1966.]

MARRIAGE AND FAMILY. **Mode.** Puberty for boys is marked by circumcision [supercision?] and by tattooing and tooth-filing for girls (Kana 1966). Marriages are arranged by elders and, at least in the case of first marriages of aristocrats, are the subject of considerable prior negotiation. There is an exchange of goods, "masculine" in the case of the groom's family (gold, spears, slaves, horses) and "feminine" in the case of the bride's family (textiles, beads, pigs, ivory). **Marriage rules.** The preferred marriage is with a MoBrDa, either consanguineal or classificatory. This rule is followed most consistently among high rank families, but even in such cases the requirement may be met by a single exchange; thereafter daughters may be given to members of other, nonprescribed clans. In this fashion the affinal links of a clan can be extended geographically, an important consideration in terms of politics and prestige. Class endogamy is the ideal, but is actually maintained in only a single, preferred line. The clan (*kabihu*) is an exogamous unit, but marriage exchange occurs actually among the clan segments (*kabihu*) localized in the various villages. The exchange pattern is one of asymmetric connubium (Adams 1969: 16), wherein each *kabihu* is linked to a wife-giving *jera* and a wife-taking *laija*. The status of *jera* is always higher than that of *laija*. The linkage of *kabihu* in connubial exchange continues through time and imposes numerous economic/ritual obligations and expectations on successive generations of *kabihu* members. Needham's (1957) conclusion that this is a closed system (i.e. one of circulating connubium) is disputed by Kana's (1966) data (cited in Adams 1969: 177, note 15). **Form.** Polygyny is evidently permissible, at least among the aristocratic nobility. **Residential unit.** Under indigenous conditions the people evidently lived in large, pile-built, clan houses within the walled ceremonial center, *paraing*. These houses also served as clan temples. Nowadays houses occupied by nuclear families are becoming more common (Onvlee 1970). **Secondary marriage.** If a man dies before the bride-price is fully paid, his brother is obligated to complete the payments and automatically succeeds to his deceased brother's wife (Kana 1966).

KIN GROUPS. **Descent.** The East Sumbanese have a patrilineal segmentary lineage system, although the exact nature of the various units and their relation to such things as land ownership and territoriality is unclear. Part of the difficulty lies in the fact that structural patterns vary to some extent among the various princedoms. **Kin groups.** The term *kabihu* (*kabisu*) is commonly used to refer both to named patrilineal clans and to segments thereof. The former are more often nonlocalized; whereas the latter tend to be associated with a particular village or district. Within a clan, one lineage or "house" (*uma*) is designated the ranking lineage or "great house" in that it claims direct descent from an ancestral founder, *umbu*, who first obtained rights to settle and use the land in a given area. The more powerful *kabihu*, i.e. the ranking clans, in East Sumba are those who claim most direct descent from the original male siblings who first settled the island according to sacred legend. Some of these are of royal (*maramba*) rank. Clans, in turn, appear to be segments of larger, exogamous, nonlocalized, phratrylike divisions, in that all *kabihu* with a common name are considered to share descent from a single founder, whose deeds may be set in a mythical time (Adams 1969: 15). Thus in East Sumba, kin groups and territorial units do not always coincide; whereas according to Adams (1969: 15), in the Kodi district of West Sumba they do. **Kin terminology.** FaSiDa and MoBrDa are terminologically differentiated from siblings, parallel cousins, aunts and uncles, and nephews and nieces (Adams 1969: 177, note 14). Additional terminology is contained in Fischer (1957), Onvlee (1930: 346), and especially Kana (1966).

SOCIOPOLITICAL ORGANIZATION. **Territorial units.** Sacred legends associate the ancestor-founders of ranking lineages, *uma*, with specific localities in East Sumba, thus forming the nuclei of so-called princedoms, *tana*. Each *tana* has a fortified hilltop "capital" and a ceremonial center, *paraing*. Each clan within the princedom is represented by a large *uma* ("clan house," "*marapu* house") belonging to its ranking lineage or "great house." These clan houses, with associated stone slab tombs, face a village square, where buffalo sacrifices are carried out and where a dead tree, *antung*, is located, on the branches of which skulls were hung in former headhunting days

(Kana 1966). **Sacred authority.** Within a princedom, four royal (*maramba*) clans share the title of *kabihu mangu tana* ("those who possess the land"), and their priests (*ratu*) lead in agricultural rites. Lesser clans and clan segments share specific ritual duties and functions, formerly including warfare. **Secular authority.** Within a princedom, the status of ruler ("king," or "radja") is hereditary within a specified lineage of a royal clan, theoretically by primogeniture, although oratorical skills and leadership qualities occasionally favor the selection of a younger son or male relative. The ruler's authority rests on the purity of his descent from a legendary hero-founder of the district, together with the prestige and wealth of his clan. His *marapu* house within the *paraing* is considered the temple for the entire princedom; here is located the *marapu* treasure (gold, textiles, etc. associated with the hero-ancestors, *marapu*, who founded the district), of which he is the guardian. In his role as "father" (of both his own clan and the district or princedom) he participates in the arrangement and control of marriages; and he is empowered to deal with other princedoms and with foreign traders, including a levy on exports such as horses and cattle. As ruler, he is superior to, and central to, the four sacral leaders and is assisted by numerous titled functionaries. The ruler embodies the unity of the princedom—a religious/adat community linked, through the ruler, to a deified ancestor-founder and his temple. [Adams 1969.] **Modern administration.** The modern Republic of Indonesia does not recognize the autonomy of the former princedoms nor the traditional authority of native rulers. The princedoms are nowadays grouped within administrative districts, *ketjamatan*, and many former rulers have taken positions as advisors to the administration. **Social stratification.** The traditional culture recognized essentially two categories of people: *tau kabihu* ("humans") and *tau ata* ("slaves"), distinguished on the basis of kin group membership and thus access to land rights; the latter, war captives and violators of the adat, by definition had no *kabihu*. Within the *kabihu* category was a small elite aristocracy or "nobility" (*maramba*), those whose family lines were considered closest in direct descent to the founding ancestors; a few of these were ruling families, i.e. "royalty." Class distinctions, still recognized to a considerable extent, are hereditary, based on the status of both parents. Class endogamy, particularly for *maramba*, is the ideal, but is actually maintained in only a single, preferred line, i.e. a *maramba* man may take several wives, only one of whom may be of *maramba* descent. The result is a series of finer gradations within all three classes. The higher classes have greater access to land as well as sumptuary privileges of various kinds. The highest-ranking nobility thus acquire more wealth and can afford to maintain wet-rice fields, which further increases their wealth. Lower-class *kabihu* are generally poor and in what amounts to a client relationship to high-ranking patrons. Slaves may be relatively well off as household servants and artisans, or, at the bottom, they may serve as field hands and (formerly) human sacrifices. [Adams 1969.] **Wealth and prestige.** A major goal of family heads is the accumulation of wealth in such things as buffalo, horses, textiles, and jewelry, and the gaining of prestige by sponsorship of religious festivals at which the family displays its wealth and slaughters many buffalo. This may take the form of distinctly potlatchlike behavior, including the competitive destruction of valued goods while extolling, in songs and chants, the greatness of one's family line (Adams 1969: 25). The apogee of this wealth-prestige pattern occurs in connection with funeral rites. A major focus of Sumbanese culture is the manipulation of family estates, chiefly through marriage alliances, to achieve these goals. [Adams 1969, 1970.] **Warfare.** Armed conflict, chiefly over land and trading rights, was formerly endemic. Warrior clans were especially associated with the ritual and conduct of raiding and headhunting parties.

RELIGION. The social order is legitimized in lengthy, all-night recitations that tell of the creation of the world, of man's descent from the Upper World to a mythical mountain top, and of the origin and dispersal of the first clans, with details recalling the wanderings and travels of the ancestral founders—the deified culture heroes of the various princedoms. These recitations and songs comprise the sacred oral tradition (*li ndai*), the Sumbanese adat. Religion functions to maintain harmony between man and the spiritual world through maintenance and proper observance of the sacred adat. "The picture is of a people with divine origins who comprise a social order organized according to divine fiat and inherit a ritual of life determined by heavenly beings . . ." (Adams 1970: 90). **Supernaturals.** The generic term for the spiritual world and anything pertaining thereto is *marapu*. The ancestral spirits, some deified, are *marapu*, as is a Highest Being manifested in various attributes such as Creator, Mother Moon, but most essentially in the concept of Great Mother-Great Father, an aspect of the masculine-feminine dualism which is symbolized throughout the social structure and gift exchange system (Adams 1969: 42-43). There are in addition innumerable Lords and Protectors of fields, houses, wells, and the like. **Practitioners.** Clan priests (*ratu*), the descendants of deified clan ancestors, are of "royal" and lesser ranks. They officiate at clan ceremonies and at funerals of clan members. [Adams 1970.] **Ceremonies.** Communication with the spiritual world is primarily through blood sacrifice, food offerings, and invocations at *marapu* altars (racks, posts, stones) located in houses, villages, fields, and bush. Religious festivals are held on occasions such as hunting, house-building, marriage, and death, and are occasions for gift exchange between groups linked by affinal or other ties. Calendrical ceremonies include a New Year's festival at the beginning of the agricultural year, a "feast of first fruits" at harvest time, and village renewal festivals held every four or eight years. The ancestral spirits are invited to religious festivals, since these are regarded as occasions for reunion of the living with the dead. [Adams 1969, 1970.] **Death.** Funeral rites for deceased members of the nobility are prime occasions for the display and destruction of family wealth (principally buffalo and textiles) and for the gaining of social prestige. The rites may be extended over several years until sufficient capital can be accumulated for a second burial, accompanied by the slaughter of many buffalo, the sacrifice (formerly) of a slave, and the erection of a memorial tomb. The massive stone troughs and slabs for these sarcophagi must be dragged from quarry to hilltop village, a procedure requiring much expenditure of wealth, food, and labor. [Bühler (1949: 136) records a case in West Sumba of a stone tomb weighing 30 tons, which required the work of 40 men for 2 years to cut it and 1,000 men to drag it from quarry to village (cited in Adams 1969: 64).]

BIBLIOGRAPHY. Adams 1969, 1970; Bühler 1949; Bühler and Sutter 1951; Fischer 1957; Kana 1966; Needham 1957; Nooteboom 1940; Onvlee 1930, 1949, 1970; Roos 1872.

SAVUNESE*

Synonyms. *Dou Hawu, Sawunese*

ORIENTATION. **Identification.** The Savu islands consist of Savu (Rai Hawu), Raidjua (Rai Djuwa), and Dana (Rai Dana). The people refer to themselves as Dou Hawu. Dou is the term for man, and all Savunese regard themselves as "men of Hawu." Savu is divided into five traditional domains, recognized as administrative units by the national government of the Republic of Indonesia. Raidjua, traditionally a separate domain, forms a sixth administrative unit. **Location.** Midway between Sumba and Timor (121°10'-122°0' E. and 10°20'-10°50' S.). The largest island, Savu, covers an area of 697 sq. km. Savunese have migrated in large numbers to Sumba and in smaller numbers to Timor, and small colonies are also found on other islands in eastern Indonesia, particularly Flores. **Geography.** Except for some waringin and

---

* This account, written by James J. Fox, is based largely on published sources, but has been supplemented by information gathered from Savunese in 1965-66. The preliminary research, on which this summary is partially based, was supported by the National Institute of Mental Health and was conducted in Indonesia under the auspices of Lembaga Ilmu Pengatahuan Indonesia.

tamarind trees and large numbers of gebang, lontar, and coconut palms, the island is virtually without forest. Water is scarce and, in many areas, must be drawn from wells. A few natural springs feed small rivers near the coast, but these lead quickly to the sea. The island is elevated slightly on its southern half, though no elevation exceeds 250 meters. The east monsoon (April to October) is a period of dry wind and scorching heat; the west monsoon (November to March) brings irregular and inadequate rain. **Linguistic affiliation.** Savunese is most closely related to Ndaonese and to the languages of Sumba. While it shares a large number of cognates with Rotinese and other languages of the Timor-Ambon group, it is classified (Jonker 1915; Kern 1892) in the Sumba-Bima group of languages. There is some differentiation among dialects, but all are mutually intelligible. **Demography.** The 1930 census reported a population of 33,576, with an additional 6,000 Savunese on Sumba and Timor. **History.** Each domain has its local version of Savunese traditional history (cf. Teffer 1875: 207-27). There exists a legend about an early folk ancestor known as Madja-Pahi, sometimes regarded as a link with the fifteenth-century kingdom of that name on Java. The Portuguese were in contact with Savu before 1600 and made it an area of missionary activity. The Dutch, who signed a treaty with the island's rulers in 1756, recognized five domains, although these were later amalgamated under Seba, whose ruler became the Radja of Savu (Fox 1965: 200-05). With Independence, the former domains were given a *wilajah* status.

SETTLEMENT PATTERN AND HOUSING. **Settlement pattern.** Villages (*rae*) are discrete units, each surrounded by a stone wall; clans (*udu*) are localized, and each village is composed of members of a single clan and lineage (*kerogo*). The land around the village belongs to clan and lineage members (van de Wetering 1926: 490). Each village is organized around an "origin house" (*amu kepue*), in which the funeral ceremonies of deceased clan members are conducted. Lineage members who found a new village continue to recognize their village of origin (*rae kepue*) and often transport their dead to their original village for proper mortuary ceremonies. **Housing.** The house is a palm-leaved, three-level, single-family structure, with the floor raised on posts four or five feet above the ground. The space beneath is where women sit to weave during the day and where animals are penned at night. At floor level, the house is divided by a partition into a "male" half and a "female" half, each section having its own entrance. Cooking is done on the female side, and the loft where seed, cloth, and other valuables are stored is built above this side. Access to the loft is granted to the women of the house (van de Wetering 1926: 533-41; Fox 1965: 222-28).

ECONOMY. The Savunese are primarily dependent on the lontar palm (*Borassus flabellifer* Linn) for their subsistence and very survival. They tap their trees throughout the dry season, but concentrate their efforts in the months of August, September, and October, cooking the juice to a dark syrup. Some syrup is fermented to make beer, but, unlike the Rotinese, the Savunese do not distill their beer to gin. **Agriculture.** Animals are kept penned or corralled; hence fields are unfenced. Despite the scarcity of water, some irrigated rice is grown along the coast, where fields are worked to mud by driving buffalo through them. Crops grown on dry fields—any combination of which is probably more important than rice—include a species of sorghum (*terae Hawu*, claimed by the Savunese as their original grain food), millet, maize, various kinds of grams, tubers, and peanuts. **Fishing, hunting, and gathering.** There is little to hunt on Savu. Some commentators mention that women do offshore fishing and that men venture further to sea to fish. Gathering is confined to wild vegetables and to birds' nests from the caves of the south coast. **Domesticated animals.** The Savunese keep water buffalo, horses, sheep, goats, pigs, cats, dogs, and chickens. Cocks are raised for ritually important cockfighting. Savunese horses are renowned as among the finest, most spirited animals in eastern Indonesia. **Industrial arts.** The tying, dyeing, and weaving of native cloth, along with the plaiting of basketry, ropes and harnesses, are the major domestic arts. **Trade.** There are a few resident Chinese and Muslim traders in the town of Seba, which has what amounts to a small daily market. Other trade is confined to the exchange of animals and foodstuffs. Horses are the most prized export. **Property.** The major categories of property are land, animals, and trees. Household items, cloth, jewelry, *muti-salah* beads, and old weapons are additional forms of wealth.

KIN GROUPS. **Descent and kin groups.** The Savunese recognize a system of double (or bilineal) descent. According to van de Wetering (1926), every Savunese belongs to a localized "patrilineal" descent group and to one of two nonlocalized "matrilineal moieties." The term translated as "clan" is *udu* and refers to the stones that constitute the group's offering place. Clans are named after their founding male ancestors and are further divided into "lineages" (*kerogo*). The *kerogo* are exogamous; ritually they form the all-important mortuary groups that arrange the burial of their members. Membership in the *udu kerogo* is based upon the possession of an altering (symbolically male) descent name. Children for whom bridewealth has not been paid belong to the *udu* of their mother and receive a name accordingly. To judge from missionary reports, these children may constitute nearly half the population. While the *udu* for the Savunese is ideologically male in all its associations, ascription to it appears to be ambilineal rather than patrilineal. *Hubi* (literally "flower stalk") is the term for the matrilineal moieties. These are associated with the classes. *Hubi ae* (the greater *hubi*) is the noble moiety; *hubi iki* (the lesser *hubi*) the commoner moiety. *Hubi* membership is evident mainly at funerals, when women are obliged to wear differently colored identifying sarongs. **Kin terminology.** F. H. van de Wetering (1926: 493) records a complete terminology, with only slight confusion of specification and omission of alternative ritual terms for certain categories (Fox 1965: 215-21). Fa and FaBr are distinguished from MoBr; but Mo and MoSi are not distinguished from FaSi. Relative age is important in Ego's generation and in the first ascending and descending generations; opposite sex siblings and cousins are classified together. There is a special relationship, evidenced in the terminology, between MoBr and SiCh.

MARRIAGE AND FAMILY. **Mode.** Premarital sexual play is permitted the youth. Marriage is effected by the payment of bridewealth, which varies in accordance with the status of the parties concerned. Unions contracted without the payment of bridewealth are common, and the children of these unions (*ana manga keriwu*, "children of play") are reckoned as belonging to their mother's group. **Form.** Monogamy is strictly enjoined; polygyny is forbidden by native law. Concubines (for whom bridewealth is not exchanged) are permitted, though they may never enter the house of the legitimate wife. **Extension of incest taboos.** According to van de Wetering (1926: 494), marriage is permitted between the children of a brother and a sister, between the children of two brothers, and between the children of two sisters. Although any cousin is permitted as a marriage partner, the Savunese prefer a marriage between cross-cousins. Two brothers may marry two sisters, or two men may exchange sisters. There are, however, contrary statements to these of van de Wetering which indicate that parallel-cousin marriage is discouraged or forbidden. **Residence.** Following the marriage of a girl of the same *udu*, with or without bridewealth, residence is in the village of that *udu*. Following the marriage with bridewealth of a girl of another *udu*, the girl will reside in her husband's village; without bridewealth, the husband will reside in his wife's village. **Domestic unit.** The domestic unit is a nuclear family. One child, preferably a daughter, brings a spouse to reside in the family house. **Inheritance.** Sons and daughters have equal rights of inheritance from their father of both real and movable property. One daughter is given priority in the inheritance of the house, provided she marries within the *udu*. Daughters may also inherit all that their mother

brought at marriage, and sons have no right to this; hence at the death of a daughterless woman, her property returns to her family. A childless widow inherits all the property of her husband (van de Wetering 1926: 501). **Divorce, secondary marriage, and adoption.** Divorce is common; concubinage is permitted. There is no institution of levirate or sororate. There is no discussion of adoption in the literature.

SOCIOPOLITICAL ORGANIZATION. **Political organization and social stratification.** Until 1918, when the Dutch united the separate domains under a single radja, each domain was ruled by a "radja" (*dou ae*) and his complement, a "fettor" (*mone weto*), both of whom were assisted by a number of "village heads" (*temugu* or *temukung*). Although there is a recognized royal line in each domain, *dou ae* is for the Savunese a term applicable to the entire noble class and especially to householders of this class. The *dou mone aha* is the class of freemen or commoners from whose number, apparently according to *udu*, the "village heads" were chosen. There is also mention of a class of slaves (*dou enu*), which was officially freed in the nineteenth century. Other figures of importance include the *deo rai* ("God of the Earth") and his attendant, the *kiru lihu*; and the *pu lodo* ("Descendant of the Sun") and his attendant, the *dohe leo*. These figures claim ritual rights over the land, the right of judgment in certain cases, and the right to declare war, establish planting times, and initiate the harvest. All are involved with the ceremonies of Savu's calendrical cycle. **Social control, justice, and warfare.** Within a domain, law cases were settled by radja, fettor, and *temukung*, with the approval of the *pu lodo*, the traditional judge, in cases of customary law. From all indications, warfare was endemic among the domains throughout the eighteenth and nineteenth centuries, and feuds continue to this day. (Yet there is no mention of institutionalized "headhunting" with attendant rituals on Savu.) Every year as part of the ritual cycle following the end of lontar tapping, a ritual battle is staged to cool the earth (Donselaar 1872: 317-18).

RELIGION. **Religious systems.** In 1903 there were some 3,000 Christians on the island, though the trend was growing for Christian Savunese to emigrate to Sumba and Timor. It is possible today that a majority of Savunese regard themselves as Christians, although they apparently maintain important collective rituals associated with the indigenous religion. **Supernaturals.** The manifestations of the highest God are invoked by means of a formula of nine names. Donselaar (1872: 306-09) reports a belief in the dual gods: Pu Lodo Liru, God of the Above, and Pu Lodo Rai, God of Below. Under him, Pu Lodo Liru has Latia, God of Lightning and Thunder, and Uli Hia Hia Hejo, God of Wind and Rain. Under Pu Lodo Rai is Maukia, God of Strife. Misfortune and violent death are caused by Rue, the principle of evil. Ama Piga Laga is the psychopomp who conducts the souls of the dead to the west in his black ship. Much of the religious life is concerned with a variety of spirits, *wangu*. **Practitioners.** There are four categories of priest, and each is assigned a part in the ceremonial cycle. There is also a religious figure associated exclusively with the rituals for those who have died a violent, bad death. **Ceremonies.** The principal ceremonies of the life cycle are (1) those shortly after birth (2) name-giving (3) haircutting and native baptism (4) marriage (5) house-building, and (6) funerals. Circumcision for boys between 6 and 15 and tooth-filing for both sexes between 15 and 17 are performed without special ceremony. Considerable attention has been given to Savu's ceremonial calendar (Wijngaarden 1892; Cuisinier 1956; van de Wetering 1926: 551-60). The names of the months, their attendant ceremonies, and the insertion of the intercalary month vary among the domains. **Illness and medicine.** The *deo rai* category of priests is charged with maintaining the welfare of the domain. There are also male and female curers who are able to divine the cause of particular illnesses, prescribe offerings, and administer herbal medicines. Midwives (*beni deo*) are called to their vocation by dreams. Most illnesses are believed caused by the neglect of ancestors or by malevolent spirits. **Soul, death, and afterlife.** Mortuary ceremonies are complex. The soul is believed to remain near the corpse for some time after death and then to journey to a spirit land in the west, from which it may return to visit Savu. The corpse is washed, clothed, bound in a sitting position, and placed in the middle of the house. Burial occurs on the third, seventh, or ninth day, depending on the elaboration given the mourning ceremonies. These may be lengthy and may involve considerable expenditure of wealth and the feasting of many guests. The corpse is buried in a round grave facing west; food is carried to the grave for several days after burial. For those who have died a bad death, ceremonies are minimal. Secondary burial is not reported. [Van de Wetering 1926: 524-53; Donselaar 1872: 314-15; Niks 1888b: 88-89.]

BIBLIOGRAPHY. Cuisinier 1956; Donselaar 1872; Fox 1965; Heiligers 1920; Jonker 1915; ten Kate 1894a; Kern 1892; Letterboer 1902, 1904; van Lynden 1851; Niks 1888b, 1893; Riedel 1885a; Teffer 1875; van de Wetering 1926; Wijngaarden 1890a, 1890b, 1892, 1894, 1896. A comprehensive bibliography in Fox 1965: 269-73.

FLORES

Raymond Kennedy, after engaging in fieldwork in various parts of Flores in 1949-50, called it one of the most fascinating areas in all Indonesia, ethnologically speaking. The native cultures are, however, relatively little known aside from the publications, often in obscure journals, of missionaries such as Vatter, Vroklage, van Suchtelen, and Arndt. The topography, mountainous and volcanic in origin, has tended to isolate and differentiate the indigenous population, which is commonly characterized as comprising five major ethnolinguistic domains: Manggarai, Ngada, Sika, Endeh, and Larantuka. Modern ethnic designations and boundaries derive in part from the founding, in pre-Dutch times, of coastal states by Javanese, Bimanese, Goanese, and migrants from western Indonesia. Administrative boundaries imposed later by the Portuguese and Dutch tended to perpetuate these distinctions. The physical type shows marked Papuan and Melanesian admixture in the eastern and central portions of the island; the peoples of western Flores, on the other hand, are almost wholly Malay in appearance. Linguistically and culturally, there appears to be some basis for distinguishing a Manggarai-Ngada-Endeh cluster in central and western Flores, in contrast to a Sika-Larantuka cluster in the east. The former, characterized by a greater emphasis on territorial hierarchies associated with socially stratified classes, appears more closely related to the Bima-Sumba area to the south and west—possibly a reflection of former political domination by these states, as well as by Goa in southern Celebes. Sika and Larantuka appear ethnolinguistically closer to the Solor archipelago to the east, Larantuka at least being commonly included with Solor as a single linguistic and cultural area (cf. Arndt 1940; Vatter 1932: 8)—a distinction followed in the present volume (viz. Solor-Larantuka section, below). All cultures on Flores, however, show sufficient basic similarities to warrant the assumption of an originally common culture type with subsequent differentiation due to geographic isolation and the acculturative influence of neighboring states such as Bima and Goa.

BIBLIOGRAPHY. Arndt 1940; Vatter 1932.

MANGGARAI*

Synonym. *Ata Manggarai*

ORIENTATION. **Identification.** The Manggarai call themselves Ata Manggarai, or the people of Manggarai, with reference to the western part of the island of Flores. The physical type is that of Malayan Indonesians, with a minimum of Papuan features. Manggarai is mutually unintelligible with the languages of eastern Flores. Macassarese from South Celebes and Bimanese from East Sumbawa (Bima) have mixed with the Manggarai for more than a century. **Location.** The Manggarai area includes the western part of Flores, as far east as 120°61′ E., bordered by the Moke River to the south and Riung town to the north. **Geography.** Much of West Flores is mountainous, crossed by deep valleys where small rivers find their way to the south and the north. **Demography.** The 1930 census placed the population of the whole of Manggarai at 154,814. Kennedy (1955b: 385) quoted a total figure of 190,000, of which about half were said to be Christian. Recent figures collected by the local government give an estimated population of 251,000. **History and cultural relations.** The Manggarai seem to have developed a political organization beyond the village level prior to the early seventeenth century, when the Bimanese kingdom of East Sumbawa dominated various coastal areas in the northern and southern parts of West Flores. The early indigenous Manggarai principality had its center in today's Tjibal, at the center of West Flores. The major explosion of the Tambora volcano on East Sumbawa in 1815 greatly weakened Bima, and the Manggarai revolted. Supported initially by the Dutch, the Bimanese regained control over Manggarai in 1851; however, in 1907 the Dutch established their colonial administration in West Flores, and the Bimanese finally gave up control over Manggarai in 1929 (Bekkum 1946b). In 1917, Catholic missionaries began to survey the area, and missionary activity subsequently intensified.

SETTLEMENT PATTERN AND HOUSING. **Settlement pattern.** Villages (*béo*), especially the ancient ones, are usually situated on a mountain top or ridge. The settlement pattern is circular, with a central square and a large ceremonial house, or "drum house" (*mbaru gendang*). In the center stands a big banyan tree, surrounded by a pile of stones (*kota*). The whole settlement is usually enclosed by a fence of wooden logs or shrubs. Villages formerly contained from 5 to 20 dwellings, with an average population of from 200 to 500 people. On the swiddens are houses, *sekang*, occupied during busy periods in the agricultural cycle. Clusters of *sekang* may develop into more or less permanent new settlements, but these are not called *béo* until they have the full attributes of a separate community—the big banyan tree, the sacred drum or cult house, and the sacred pile of stones. **Housing.** The traditional dwelling is a large, circular structure, built on piles about one meter high. The central pillar sometimes rises more than six meters above the ground. There are no walls, and the high, thatched, conical roof rises straight up from the outer circumference of the floor to the central pillar. Through the middle of the house is a passage with four to five rooms on each side. Larger dwellings, capable of housing up to 200 people, existed formerly. Rectangular houses occupied by smaller virilocal extended families (*kilo*) or even nuclear families are a recent development. **Settlement and housing (addenda).** According to information obtained by Kennedy (1955b), a village formerly consisted of a single large, circular house, inhabited by the members of a totemic, exogamous, patrilineal clan. A high center post within the house was considered sacred; here sat the *tuan tanah* (or "lord of the land," sometimes *tu'a tenu*), a kind of clan priest, during communal village or clan ceremonies. Beginning in the early twentieth century, this pattern has gradually been altered by the construction of smaller houses. The main house within the village is still, however, that of the *tuan tanah*, and villages still tend to be inhabited by members of a single clan. In the middle of the village is a sacred tree surrounded by stones, the place of the village guardian spirits. Clan rites include buffalo sacrifices (with the animal tied to the tree) and the "feeding" of the stones with the blood of sacrificed animals. Kennedy mentions also the presence of circular fields, *lingko randang*, as a necessary aspect of pagan Manggarai villages.

ECONOMY. **Agriculture.** Mainly slash-and-burn cultivation of maize and rice on swiddens. The males of a number of extended families cooperate in cutting and burning; the swidden opened in this way is then divided according to previous agreement. Wet-rice cultivation on irrigated fields was introduced about 1920. **Domestic animals.** Buffalo are kept for prestige, for the bride-price, as a symbol of prosperity, or for ceremonial purposes. Horses serve as beasts of burden and for payment of bride-price. Chickens, and sometimes pigs, are eaten on specific occasions. **Food.** The staple is maize, in the form of roasted ears, maize cakes, or porridge, with meat or vegetables as side dishes. Rice is eaten only on special occasions. Rice wine, or *tuwak* (palm wine, according to Kennedy), is consumed in large quantities on ceremonial occasions. Betel chewing was popular a generation ago. **Land tenure.** Formerly the right of disposal over

---

* The author of this entry, Koentjaraningrat, is Professor and Head of the Department of Anthropology at the University of Indonesia. Supplementary information, added by the editor, is taken from Raymond Kennedy's field notes on his survey of Flores in 1949-50 (Kennedy 1955b).

pieces of arable land, forests, and fishing and hunting grounds was in the hands of particular lineages. Each lineage had a hereditary adat specialist on land, a *tuan tanah*, who was sometimes the lineage head himself, but more often from another branch of the family. In recent times, particular lineages have gained control over extensive territories and formed small principalities called *dalu*. However, the ruling lineage of a *dalu* may not interfere in the land rights of other lineages within the *dalu* territory. Therefore within each *dalu* there exist a number of subdivisions called *glarang*, large lineages with autonomous right of disposal over major portions of arable land. The ruling lineage only has the right of disposal over its own lineage land. Nowadays the *tuan tanah* allocates tracts of land to lineage members who have the right of usufruct; divides swiddens that are collectively opened by groups of villagers; directs fertility rites and ceremonies according to the agricultural calendar; and settles land disputes among lineage members. In addition to the land controlled by the *dalu* and *glarang* lineages, each territory includes smaller tracts autonomously controlled by lineages of commoners, located within or cutting across particular villages.

KINSHIP. **Descent.** The Manggarai reckon descent patrilineally. **Kin groups.** The people who occupy each large conical house constitute a minimal patrilineal lineage, or *wau*. Smaller houses are occupied by smaller virilocal extended families (*kilo*). Among the upper classes, there exists the notion of a larger kin group, a major patrilineal lineage of five to six generations in depth, called a *panga*. Since this term means "branch," these kin groups may originally have been branches of still larger kin groups. There exists another term, *uku*, which can mean "origin," as well as "bilateral relatives in general," but also "all patrilineal relatives." **Kinship terminology.** Most terms extend collaterally, and thus conform to the generation pattern. The terms for mother's brother and mother's brother's daughter form an exception. The following terms are from Coolhaas (1942):

Grandparent	*empo*
Fa, FaBr, MoSiHu	*ema*
Mo, MoSi, FaBrWi	*nde*
FaSi, MoBrWi	*inang*
MoBr, FaSiHu	*amang*
Si, FaBrDa, FaSiDa, MoSiDa	*weta*
ElBr, FaBrSo, MoSiSo	*kae*
YoBr	*ase*
FaSiSo, MoBrSo	*kesah*
MoBrDa, Wi	*wina*
FaSiSo, Hu	*rona*
Grandchild	*empo*

MARRIAGE AND FAMILY. **Mode.** Among orthodox, upper-class families, arranged marriages still exist, i.e. with the mother's brother's daughter (*tungku*-marriage). According to Kennedy (1955b), this is traditionally obligatory for an eldest son. Asymmetrical cross-cousin connubium is found among certain noble lineages. Among peasant families, youths usually make their own choices of mates. The large bride-price (*patjawina*) consists mainly of buffalo and horses, although a man who marries the preferred girl according to adat prescription, i.e. his mother's brother's daughter, does not seem to have the obligation to pay a large bride-price (Coolhaas 1942: 349-50). To avoid the bride-price, many couples elope, often with the consent of the girl's family. **Form.** Polygyny is not uncommon, but exists mainly among noble families. **Extension of incest taboos.** The preferred marriage is that with the mother's brother's daughter. Marriage with the father's sister's daughter, and also between maternal as well as paternal parallel cousins, is prohibited. **Residence.** The rule of residence determining where a married couple should live is virilocal. However, a man is supposed to live with his wife's family until the bride-price is paid, which may not be for several years (Kennedy 1955b: 107). **Secondary marriage.** According to Kennedy (1955b), the levirate is required (token bride-price). The sororate is allowed (full bride-price).

SOCIOPOLITICAL ORGANIZATION. Manggarai is today an administrative area (regency) within the Province of Eastern Nusa Tenggara. It consists of two subareas, Reo and Patta, traditional unities incorporating some 39 small principalities, *dalu*. Each *dalu* consists of a number of *glarang*, while social units subordinated to the *glarang* are the *béo*, traditional villages, and the *kampong*, new settlements. Each *dalu* is usually dominated by one lineage (*wau*), whose members consider themselves to be of noble origin. Certain of these noble lineages are related to each other through a system of asymmetrical cross-cousin connubium, and these are traditional allies; all other *dalu* areas are traditional enemies. *Glarang* are ruled by lineages which lack consanguinal ties with the ruling *dalu* lineages, although affinal ties through occasional intermarriage may exist. The prince of a *dalu* is usually called *kraeng* or *kraeng adak*. In addition to the *dalu* heads, there are other important functionaries, including a *tuan tanah* or adat specialist on land, who has authority over the land of the royal lineage but not over that of the *glarang* lineages. **Social stratification.** Traditional Manggarai culture recognizes three social classes: *kraeng*, *ata leke*, and slaves. The *kraeng* are members of dominant *dalu* and *glarang* lineages. The *ata leke* are the ordinary people—artisans, laborers, and peasants. Slaves were traditionally those captured in wars, people in debt, people expelled from their communities, or people of other ethnic groups traded by slave dealers. Slavery was officially abolished under the Dutch, but people are still conscious of the stigma of slave descent. There are subdivisions within the *kraeng* class based on relative seniority of the noble lineages or on the importance of the area which a particular lineage dominates. **Warfare.** Interclan warfare formerly endemic, but no evidence of headhunting or cannibalism. Weapons included spears, knives, and shields; neither blowguns nor bows are indigenous among the Manggarai. Warriors wore rattan helmets and war cloaks, both decorated with feathers. [Kennedy 1955b.]

RELIGION. Western Manggarai is largely Muslim, while the eastern *dalu*, e.g. Rodjong, are mainly Catholic. Central Manggarai, including the large, important *dalu*—e.g. Tjibal, Todo, and Pongkor—still adheres for the most part to the indigenous religion. **Belief system and supernaturals.** The most important spirits are those of deceased ancestors, *empo* or *andung*. Ancestral spirits inhabit the environs of the village and are called upon at life cycle ceremonies of lineage members. Nature spirits are called *ata pelesina* (those of the other side, or those of the supernatural world). Guardian spirits of the house and village are the *naga golo;* those who guard the land and the soil are the *naga tana;* those who guard the gardens, the swiddens, and the crops are the *ngara tana*, or *teno*. There are also earth spirits associated with the forest, rivers, streams, and water wells, collectively called *darat*. All these can be malevolent and the causes of sickness and calamity if not cared for by the proper ceremonies. The real malevolent spirits and ghosts, however, are the *djing* or *setan;* these exist in great variety in the ghost stories that the people love to tell. An important element in Manggarai indigenous religion is the belief in a Supreme Being called Mori Karaeng (more properly Moring Agunaran, according to Kennedy [1955b: 109]). Myths mention the way in which Mori Karaeng created the earth, man, the supernatural world, the animals (especially the cock), and the staple crops of maize and rice; while other stories tell of the way he created the wind, caused earthquakes, punished the moon with a lunar eclipse, and used lightning to punish the *djin*. A few stories portray him as helping man, but in many more stories he punishes those who violate the adat. [Verheijen 1951.] **Practitioners.** Indigenous ceremonial centers around a religious specialist called *ata mbeko*. The profession is not hereditary, and a person—male or female—becomes *mbeko* by assisting an established professional. These individuals perform household and communal ceremonies, cure disease, foretell the future, and provide people with magic liquids, amulets, and charms. They do not, apparently, function as shamans. **Ceremonies.** Household ceremonies are along the life cycle of the individual, which starts with the five-month pregnancy ritual (*djambat*) and ends with the release ceremony of a young married couple after a five-day stay at the bride's parental home (*wega nio* ritual). Communal rites include the initiation ceremony for a sacred drum house, fertility rites, and most rituals in relation to agriculture. At all major festivals the ancestral spirits are called in

to be present. Most communal ceremonies, and also mortuary rites, are accompanied by buffalo sacrifice. There is no indication of human sacrifice. Kennedy (1955b) adds information on a "cleansing of the *kampong*" ceremony, held in times of endemic illness and on the initiative of the *mbeko*. The latter may also decide that the village guardian spirits are no longer effective and that the village must be moved. A frequent accompaniment to major ceremonies, according to Kennedy, is a mock battle or formalized dance between teams of men dressed in traditional war costume and culminating in ritualized fighting with buffalo-thong whips. According to Kennedy, clan members return for major ceremonies to the "home village" containing the clan cult house (drum house) and the *tuan tanah besar*. Likewise, deceased clan members are taken back to the home village for burial. **Soul, death, and afterlife.** Funerary and mortuary practices are relatively elaborate. The deceased is inhumated in a sitting position with limbs drawn close to the body. Formerly the corpse was wrapped in a mat, but nowadays a coffin is used. Following death the soul (*ase-kae de weki*) remains in the vicinity of the house. Five days after burial a *kelas* ceremony is held and a buffalo sacrificed. Kennedy adds that formerly an elaborate postmortuary ceremony, including the sacrifice of many buffalo, was held for deceased *dalu*. After *kelas*, the soul becomes a spirit (*poti'*) and goes to the afterworld (*pelesina*), where Mori Karaeng resides. Ancestral spirits are close to Mori Karaeng and can thus act as his intermediaries with the living.

BIBLIOGRAPHY. Bekkum 1946a, 1946b; Coolhaas 1942; Heerkens 1930; Kennedy 1955b; Kuperus 1941; Meerburg 1891; Mennes 1931; Nooteboom 1939, 1950; Verheijen 1951.

NGADA*

Synonyms. *Badjavanese, Cata Bhai [Hata Bai], Cata Dua [Hata Dua], Cata Roka [Hata Roka], Nad'a, Ngad'a, Ngadanese, Ngadha, Rokanese, Rokka*

ORIENTATION. **Identification.** The name Ngada is drawn from that of their largest clan. The Dutch used it for an administrative district, which included, as well as the Ngada, the closely related but distinct Nage, Keo, and Riung. The Ngada are also referred to in the early Dutch literature as the Rokka, or Rokanese—a name deriving from the Roka (Inerie) volcano. Their neighbors refer to them by the name Hata Dua, "men of the mountains" (Arndt employs

---

* This entry on the Ngada has been compiled from the literature by R. H. Barnes, a candidate for the D.Phil. at the University of Oxford.

c for a voiced *h*), and the coastal Ngada use the same phrase to refer to the mountain Ngada. The Ngada are called Hata Roka by the Endenese and Hata Bai (from the Ngada word for "no," *bai*) by the Nage. [Arndt 1954: 4-5.] There is no indigenous word by which they designate themselves as a whole and separate group (Arndt 1933a: 1). Racially the Ngada have mixed Malay and Melanesian features. They have been characterized as Proto-Malay, and some researchers have claimed that they show Caucasian or Semitic elements. [Bader 1953: 125-30; Keers 1948: 59-66; Bijlmer 1929: 96, 189.] **Location.** The south coast of Flores around the Inerie volcano and inland on the high Badjava plateau, from about 120°48' to 121°05' E. and from about 8°40' to 8°55' S. The Ngada region borders that of the Riung in the north and the Nage to the east. It is separated from the Manggarai region to the west by the Moke River. [Arndt 1954: 3-4; Bader 1953: 1.] **Geography.** Three quarters of the population live in the highlands, which are covered mostly with reedlike (alang-alang) grass. The rainy season is from December to April, the period of the west monsoon. The dry season is from May to November. In the highest villages, the temperature may at this time drop to 0° C. Coconut, areca, koli, enau, and lontar palms, the tamarind, various sorts of bamboo, orange and lemon trees, bananas, breadfruit, and mangoes grow wild. The fauna include buffalo, horses, pigs, chickens, goats, dogs, cats, and monkeys. [Arndt 1954: 3-4, 482-89; 1963: 15, 21-22, 29, 110-11.] **Linguistic affiliation.** The Ngada speak a Malayo-Polynesian language within the Ambon-Timor group (Esser 1938). **Demography.** Arndt gives 35,000; Bader says around 40,000 (Arndt 1954: 4; Bader 1953: 1). **History and cultural relations.** Most Ngada clans traditionally believed themselves to have come from Java. Van Staveren estimates that they settled in the present region about 250 years ago. They were subdued by the Dutch in 1907, and missionaries began converting them to Christianity around 1920. [Bader 1953: 1 n.1, 23 n.49, 130-34; van Staveren 1916.]

SETTLEMENT PATTERN AND HOUSING. **Settlement pattern.** Two rows of closely spaced houses, facing across a square. Some villages have few houses, others as many as 50. Only small villages are inhabited by a single clan. In those which have more, the clans or clan segments may be assigned specific quarters. [Arndt 1954: 304-65.] Kennedy (1955b: 122ff.) mentions the existence in some villages of stone walls and stone pillars as well as ritual poles or posts associated with buffalo sacrifice. **Housing.** The wooden house, raised on piles, consists of the actual living quarters and the veranda, the former a single room with a straw-covered, gabled roof. [Arndt 1954: 176; 1963: 162-70.]

ECONOMY. The Ngada depend primarily upon agriculture, with some hunting, fishing, and gathering. Hunting was formerly of relatively greater importance as a source of food. **Agriculture.** Rice, maize, and millet are the principal crops. Other crops include beans, peanuts, gourds, cucumbers, melons, bananas, sugarcane, pineapples, spices, onions, various tuberous plants, tomatoes, betel, tobacco, and cotton. The Dutch introduced cassava and potatoes. Irrigation was introduced by the Dutch in 1920; otherwise, rice is grown in dry fields, where it is normally planted together with other crops. In the highlands, a field is planted for two years in a row and fallowed for one. Elsewhere, land may be worked seven or eight years in succession and fallowed for up to fifteen years. Digging sticks and field knives are among the few implements employed. [Arndt 1963: 30-32, 40, 43-46, 55-62; Kuperus 1941.] **Fishing and hunting.** Hunting is done either individually or in groups. Iron-pointed lances, short bamboo spears, long knives, bows and arrows, and (when hunting from horses) war-lances are employed. In the extreme east, monkeys and birds are hunted with blowpipes. Game is also trapped by use of snares, pitfalls, and nets. [Arndt 1954: 488; 1963: 115-25.] The people of Boba fish with hook and line in the open sea. Inland, fish are usually captured by hand methods in the small streams, although poison is also employed. [Arndt 1954: 490-91; 1963: 125-27.] **Gathering.** Gathering of food occurs usually only during periods of famine. Among such food sources are breadfruit, mangoes, yams, and the fruit of the lontar and tamarind trees. [Arndt 1954: 491; 1963: 110-11.] **Domestic animals.** Water buffalo, horses, pigs, chickens, goats, dogs, and cats. [Arndt 1954: 484-86; 1963: 64-93.] **Industrial arts.** Iron smithery is practiced in specific clans (as, formerly, was gold smithery). Other such skills, which are the exclusive province of certain clans or regions, include pot making and the dyeing of cloth. [Arndt 1954: 455-57; 1963: 127-56.] **Trade.** Highlanders have need of salt, lime, coconuts, betel, cotton, palm wine, and timber, all of which they obtain from coast dwellers in exchange for surplus crops. Formerly, Chinese, Buginese, and Goanese traders brought stones, gold, ivory, porcelain, and other products to be exchanged for slaves and crops. [Arndt 1954: 491-92; 1963: 175-85.] **Property.** Ngada territory is divided into regions with clearly determined borders. In each region, one clan controls the land, divided among its first-level segments (*cili* or *bhou*). The land held by each *cili* is similarly apportioned among its divisions (*sipo pali*), and thereafter is further subdivided among the component households. Land may be alienated so long as the transaction is between two households in a *sipo pali;* otherwise the permission of the head of this group has to be obtained. [Arndt 1954: 473-87.]

KIN GROUPS. **Descent and kin groups.** The Ngada are a cognatic society with a segmentary clan system. The largest of some one hundred clans (*socé*), the Vocé Ngada, has several thousand members. Each clan is composed of a group of people related to a common ancestral father or mother. Each is generally identified with a certain locality, marked by the original clan house inhabited by the head of the clan (the *culu vocé*)—a direct descendant of the ancestral father or mother—which is also a ritual center for the clan. In some of the larger clans, segments are distributed into other regions and may be found even among the Manggarai or the Nage. Large clans may be segmented into groups called *cili*, or *bhou*. These, likewise, are marked by a special house inhabited by the head of the segment and are composed of several extended families (*sipo pali*), descended from a common ancestral father or mother. Often a *cili* is newly formed or an existing one divided as a result of some misfortune which is taken as a sign that an ancestor believes himself to have been forgotten and wishes to be memorialized with a ritual pole and *cili* house. A *cili* may be divided into several *sipo pali*, each with a head who lives in an ancestral *sipo pali* house. Membership in a household, and consequently descent, residence, and the inheritance of property and one's name, depends entirely on whether one's father has paid the full bridewealth for his wife. If so, one is a member of his group; otherwise, one is a member of one's mother's group. [Arndt 1954: 176-213.] **Terminology.** Relationship is recognized both patrilaterally and matrilaterally. *Tuka mogo* signifies the closer relations descended from a common ancestral father, mother, or both. *Tuka yi* indicates the more distant ones, and *cura mogo* includes all possible relations, even the most remote. [Arndt 1954: 167-69; 1961.]

kadzo	Most distant ancestors
nusi	Great-grandparents and more distant ancestors
cebu	Grandparents
ciné cema	Mother and father, their brothers and sisters, and everyone else of the same generation related to a common ancestor; term of address for WiFa, WiMo, HuFa, HuMo
pamé	FaBr, MoBr (ref.)
piné	FaSi, MoSi (ref.)
tua	WiFa, WiMo, HuFa, HuMo (ref.)
kaé	ElBr, ElSi
kaé dela	Eldest brother or sister
cazi	YoBr, YoSi
cazi répo or *cazi kedhi*	Youngest brother or sister
cazi yé	Hu, Wi
doca	Br(m.s.), Si(w.s.)
veta	Si(m.s.)
nara	Br(w.s.)
tua cédza	Wife's male relatives
tua cipa	Husband's female relatives
cédza	WiBr (and all her male relatives of the same age), SiHu, DaHu
cipa	WiSi (and all her female relatives of the same age), BrWi
tua cana xaki	DaHu
tua cana faci	SoWi
cana	Child, niece, nephew, and everyone else of the same generation related to a common ancestor
cana doca	Children of a sibling of the same sex
cana veta	SiCh (m.s.)
cana nara	BrCh (w.s.)
vocé	All relations of the same age

MARRIAGE AND FAMILY. **Mode.** Bridewealth consists of money, buffalo, horses, jewelry, and slaves. When the full bridewealth is not paid, the husband lives in the home of his wife's relatives and works for them. In some regions the full bridewealth is never paid, and the husband always settles with the wife's family. Marriage by abduction is said to have existed formerly. [Bader 1953: 101-03; Arndt 1954: 42-46, 54-57.] **Form.** Monogamy is general, although polygyny is possible for those who can afford it. [Arndt 1954: 58-60.] **Marriage rules.** Marriage is prohibited between siblings and between relations or affines of different generations. Cousins may marry and are even encouraged to do so. In the districts of Wéré and Boba, one may not marry within the village. In these regions, a village contracts an alliance with another for the symmetrical exchange of women. The Ngada are strongly endogamous, to the point that they prefer to marry within the same *sipo pali*. [Arndt 1954: 18-19.] **Residence.** If bridewealth is paid, the couple live with the husband's relatives. If the full amount is not paid, they live with the wife's relatives. [Arndt 1954: 50-58; Bader 1953: 100-03.] **Domestic unit.** Although Ngada houses are small, several closely related families, numbering up to 20 individuals, may live in the same building. A household includes grandparents, parents, children, and the wives or husbands of children who have not settled with the spouse's relations. [Arndt 1954: 177.] **Inheritance.** The house and its associated land and granary belong to everyone living in the house. If the household decides to split into several, the property is divided among the different sections of the family. The house is inherited by the first married or oldest child remaining in the home. A woman living with her husband's group may be given a piece of land for her children, but this may never become the possession of her husband's relatives. [Arndt 1954: 480-82.] **Divorce.** Either a man or a woman may ask for a divorce. It seldom occurs when bridewealth has been paid, but is more frequent if this is not the case. [Arndt 1954: 69-72.] **Adoption.** Mostly among close relatives (Arndt 1954: 167).

SOCIOPOLITICAL ORGANIZATION. **Political organization.** The Dutch introduced the office of radja. Prior to this, the segmentary clan system and regional village confederations provided the political structure. The heads of clans and clan segments and other leaders are known as *mosa laki*. Among these are the clan and clan segment leaders who have authority over the land, the *mori tana*. It is the rule that political authority in a region is held by the leader of a different clan from that which contains the *mori tana*. [Arndt 1954: 425-34; Bader 1953: 97 n.20.] **Social stratification.** The Ngada in general are divided into three social classes, although as many as eight are reported in some regions. The highest is the *gaé mézé*, the second the *gaé kisa,* and the lowest the *cazi cana.* Formerly, every clan had representatives of these three levels. Membership is acquired by birth and is determined by the class of one's mother. Behavior between members of different classes is marked by a great number of rules and prohibitions. Formerly, the Ngada also possessed slaves. [Arndt 1954: 321-43, 466-69, 502-23; 1955.] **Social control and justice.** Cases are adjudicated by the clan leaders and elders. Several forms of ordeal are employed. [Arndt 1954: 500-43.] **Warfare.** Village confederacies often undertook warfare with neighboring villages, frequently in attempts to gain land. War also sometimes broke out between clans for a number of different reasons. Headhunting appears to have been absent. [Arndt 1954: 391-417.]

RELIGION. **Religious systems.** Roman Catholic missionaries have been working among the Ngada since 1920, and it may be assumed that a large portion of the population has been converted. **Supernaturals.** The High God (Déva) is Mori Mézé, associated with the heavens. His female complement is Nitu, associated with the earth. Numerous lesser beings are also designated by the term Déva, and in addition there are the *noca,* the gods of the clouds and mist; the *polo,* bad spirits; the *ngebu,* good spirits who protect the villages and the fields; and the spirits of the ancestors. **Practitioners.** Practitioners include the *mori tana,* who have responsibility over the land and represent spiritual authority; the *tora,* who can see the future; the *mali,* who are capable of curing illness; and the *teké ruu,* who have magical powers by which they can cause or cure illness. **Ceremonies.** The *reba* ceremony and a number of agricultural and hunting ceremonies occur annually. Occasional ceremonies include those at birth, circumcision, marriage, building a house, establishing a new clan segment, and contracting peace. The six-day *reba* ceremony is an occasion for marriages and associated activities such as exchange of bridewealth. The teeth of girls are filed and blackened at puberty, and boys are circumcised. [Arndt 1954: 95-163; Bader 1953.] **Soul, death, and afterlife.** Most frequently, Ngada say that a man has only one soul (*maé, macé*), which can leave the body even during life. After death, the soul returns to Nitu or Déva or to both, according to different opinions. Individuals killed in war, murdered, or poisoned are dressed in their war costumes and buried outside the village. After death the corpse must remain in the house for a full day before burial. Removal from the grave and reburial is not frequent. Mourning ceremonies may last from three days to three months. Formerly, a slave was buried, either actually or symbolically, with his dead master. [Arndt 1929-30, 1929-31, 1932a, 1936-37, 1954: 435-55, 1956, 1958, 1959a, 1959b, 1960a, 1960b; van Baal 1947; Bader 1953.]

BIBLIOGRAPHY. Arndt 1929-30, 1929-31, 1932a, 1933a, 1936-37, 1954, 1955, 1956, 1958, 1959a, 1959b, 1960a, 1960b, 1961, 1963; van Baal 1947; Bader 1953; Bijlmer 1929; Esser 1938; Keers 1948; Kennedy 1955b; Kuperus 1941; van Staveren 1916.

ENDENESE*

Synonyms. *Ende, Endeh*

ORIENTATION. **Location and identification.** Endeh comprises the southern portion of central Flores. The term has been used to mean the domain of the Radja of Endeh, and by extension the people within that domain, as well as their language. Although the Endenese are related culturally and linguistically to the peoples of neighboring domains, e.g. Ngadanese, Sikanese, and Lionese, there are differences in custom and speech that set these various peoples apart. The physical type is mixed, but with a sizable proportion of Papuan features (Kennedy 1935: 210). **Linguistic affiliation.** Esser (1938) appears to have included Endeh within his Bima-Sumba language group. Dyen (1965), on the other hand, classifies Endeh within his Moluccan linkage; its closest relationship seems to be with Sika, which in turn forms with Solor a Sikic subgroup. According to Needham (1968), there are two main dialects, *ata djao* and *ata akoe* (after the first-person singular pronoun in each case). A lontar script is remembered by a few older people. **Demography.** About 34,000 in 1930 (*Volkstelling 1930*, v. 5). **History and cultural relations.** Chiefly aristocratic families tell stories relating their ancestors through mythical exploits and magic events to the fifteenth-century Hindu-Javanese empire of Madjapahit (cf. van Suchtelen 1921). Catholic missionaries effectively penetrated the area beginning about 1920, and mission schools have been a major agent of acculturation. The Endenese are, however, by Kennedy's estimate a remarkably provincial people; much of the old adat continues despite the existence of a modern, literate administrative hierarchy and the fact that an estimated 50 percent of the people are Christian. The Endenese are chiefly in contact with the people of neighboring Lio, and a sizable proportion of Endenese clans are of Lio origin. Savunese and Chinese are present in the larger towns.

---

* Unless indicated otherwise, the data in this section have been taken from Kennedy (1955b).

SETTLEMENT PATTERN AND HOUSING. Settlement pattern.

Villages tend to be located near the coast, although most maintain ritual ties to former occupation sites in the hills, which are marked by the presence of sacred stones. A central plaza may contain an ancestral image or bone bundle house. A separate structure, *kuwu*, serves as a sleeping place for boys and unmarried men. Villages contain members of more than one clan, with some tendency to localization within named hamlet sections. Kennedy thinks that originally a village consisted of members of a single localized clan. **Housing.** Old style houses were large, with high, steeply pitched roofs. Houses nowadays are smaller and rectangular in shape, with grass thatch roofs extending downward in a hooded effect.

ECONOMY.

Subsistence based mainly on swidden agriculture, with maize the chief crop followed by rice, vegetables, and yams. Sago is absent. Irrigated rice was introduced about 1947. The meat of buffalo, pig, goat, and dog is consumed, but only in connection with ritual sacrifice. The Endenese also raise horses, but cattle are rare. Hunting with bow and arrow for monkeys and wild pigs is engaged in only occasionally. The chief industry is weaving of locally grown cotton on a horizontal backbar loom. Metal working is poorly developed or absent altogether. Customs such as teeth filing and blackening, betel chewing, and tattooing are rapidly disappearing. Trade is little developed beyond the village level. Traditional items of wealth include ivory tusks, gold pieces, and old beads—all carrying a semisacred connotation. The basic unit with respect to land and property ownership is the corporate patrilineage, with management of lineage estates inherited by eldest sons. Management of communal lands and agricultural ritual is in the hands of a *mosa laki mere*, who is theoretically "owner" of the land and thus a kind of *tuan tanah*, or "lord of the land."

KIN GROUPS. Descent.

Kennedy describes what he calls patrilineal clans, *pu'u* (Malay, *suku*), which he believes were formerly localized. These are divided into corporate patrilineages. Inheritance of property and of political status is patrilineal and by primogeniture, with those lineages tracing descent through eldest sons being of highest rank. Although the clan thus appears to be ideologically male, ascription to it would seem to be ambilineal (or possibly "utrolateral") rather than patrilineal, in that children of women for whom the bride-price has not been paid belong to the *suku* of the mother. **Kin groups.** Clans, *pu'u*, are theoretically exogamous. In the district (Dutch, *gemeente*) studied by Kennedy, one clan ranked first, its position supported by a legend of descent from the eldest of four brothers—founding ancestors who migrated from Java. Four other clans ranked as "original" clans, while clans of lesser rank consisted of those who had "moved in," e.g. Lionese.

Similarly, within the village, one clan held first rank as the "original" clan. Each clan owns a "clan house," *rumah berhala*, a kind of temple or ancestral image house, where the bones of noted clan ancestors are kept and where periodic ancestral rites are held. Associated with the *rumah berhala* are stone cist graves and an offering stone or post, *tuba musa*, used in the sacrifice of buffalo. Clans are named and have associated with them certain food taboos. **Kin terminology.** The following are Kennedy's terms (1955b: 236-37), as rearranged by Needham (1970):

GrPa	*ambu*
Fa	*baba*
Mo	*ine*
FaBr	*baba susu*
FaSi	*no'o*
MoBr, WiFa	*ada*
MoSi	*ine susu*
Br(ms), FaBrSo(ms), MoSiSo(ms), Si(ws), FaBrDa(ws), MoSiDa(ws)	*ari, ka'e*
Br(ws), FaBrSo(ws), MoSiSo(ws), MoBrSo(ws)	*nara*
Si(ms), FaBrDa(ms), MoSiDa(ms), FaSiDa(ms)	*veta*
MoBrDa(ms), Wi	*hai*
FaSiSo(ws), Hu	*aki*
FaSiSo(ms), MoBrSo(ms)	*edja*
FaSiDa(ws), MoBrDa(ws)	*ipa*

Kennedy noted the fact that cousin terms reflect a preference for MoBrDa marriage, and Needham feels justified, on the basis of this and other evidence, in characterizing the Endeh system as one of asymmetric prescriptive alliance (Needham 1970: 250).

MARRIAGE AND FAMILY. Mode.

Traditional marriage was a "clan affair," according to Kennedy. An exchange of gifts was necessary, conceptualized as "male things" from the groom's clan (ivory tusks, gold, animals) and "female things" from the bride's clan (cloth, mats, rice). Nowadays a bride-price is paid, chiefly in money and buffalo. **Form.** Sororal polygyny is practiced to some extent, despite attempts by Catholic missionaries to ban the practice. **Marriage rules.** Marriages were formerly arranged by parents. Clan exogamy, formerly strictly enforced, is beginning to break down. There is a preference for MoBrDa marriage, with marriage into one's father's clan forbidden. Kennedy was unable to demonstrate the presence of circulating connubium with the limited data at his disposal, although he suspected that such might have been the case in the past. Needham (1970: 257) evidently feels that the kin terminology, together with certain other diagnostic features (such as male-female exchange of gifts), argue strongly for an asymmetric system of alliances; the evidence, however, remains inconclusive. **Residence.** Ultimately patrilocal, although remains matrilocal until the bride-price is paid. **Domestic unit.** Larger houses may contain patrilocal extended families. Kennedy's sample of a single village averaged seven persons per household, with a range of from four to sixteen. **Inheritance.** Family-owned land is divided among sons. The eldest son inherits the house and stewardship of family ritual possessions. **Divorce and secondary marriage.** Divorce is rare or virtually nonexistent, both now and formerly. The levirate is common and expected; sororate marriages are frequent although not obligatory.

SOCIOPOLITICAL ORGANIZATION. **Political organization.** The state of Endeh was in the early 1950s divided into nine districts (Dutch, *gemeente*), each administered by a *kapitan*. Within these were *kampongs* or villages, each headed by a chief, *kepala kampong*. At the top, theoretically, was the Radja of Endeh. Paralleling this administrative-territorial hierarchy there was an adat-genealogical hierarchy consisting of chiefs drawn from aristocratic (*mosa laki*) lineages. Thus the village chief was assisted by four *mosa laki*, including the *mosa laki mere* (or *tuan tanah*, "lord of the land"), an arrangement repeated at the district level. Kennedy interpreted this as reflecting the imposition at some time in the past of territorial concepts on an essentially genealogical system of localized clans. It is probable, however, that indigenous Endenese society possessed something like ritual areas composed of persons related by common kinship ties, and that these were later transformed into administrative-territorial units which ultimately became the *gemeente* of the Dutch period. Within each district there is one highest-ranked or adat clan, with its clan house in an "original" or adat village. Members of this clan trace descent, through eldest sons, to the eldest of four original or founding brothers; and from this clan come high-ranking chiefs such as the *kapitan* and the *mosa laki mere* of the district. **Stratification.** Former stratification into slaves (obtained mainly through warfare), commoners, and aristocrats (*mosa laki*). Aristocratic lineages were ranked according to a system of patrilineal, primogenitural descent from founding ancestors. Aristocrats formerly wore symbols of rank consisting of gold ornaments—regarded as lineage heirloom property. Kennedy's informants ranked the radja no higher than, e.g., a high-ranking *mosa laki mere;* and Kennedy found no evidence of magical or supernatural powers associated with royalty or chiefly lineages in Endeh—in contrast with the situation in southern Celebes. **Warfare.** Enmity and jealousy among chiefly clans were formerly rife, and warfare was endemic. Disputes over land and acquisition of slaves were the main causes of warfare. Headhunting was associated in some degree with this pattern, but to what extent and for what reasons remain unclear.

RELIGION. Almost one half of the population has been converted to Christianity, with the result that the indigenous religion has lost much of its function as an integrative force in Endenese society. There is (or was) a pantheon of named deities, including the concept of a high god, Ngga'eh Dewa. Religious specialists include male and female priests, *bisa mari*, and medicinemen or curers, *dukun*. The *mosa laki mere* functions as ritual specialist during communal planting and harvest festivals. A clanwide ceremony is held when a new clan house is dedicated, on which occasion the *mosa laki mere* receives the lower jaws of sacrificed animals. Major rituals are carried out at death, particularly in the case of noted aristocrats. The body of a deceased aristocrat was formerly cocooned on a tree branch until it decomposed, after which the bones and skull were cleaned and placed within the clan house to the accompaniment of feasting and buffalo sacrifice. Nowadays bodies are simply buried in the ground or, in special cases, in stone tombs. Pagan burials continue to be made with the corpse in a knee-to-chest position.

BIBLIOGRAPHY. Dyen 1965; Esser 1938; Kennedy 1935, 1955b; Needham 1968, 1970; van Suchtelen 1921; *Volkstelling 1930*.

*SIKANESE**

Synonyms. *Ata Biang, Ata Sika, Ata Krowe, Sika*

ORIENTATION. **Identification.** The Sika, or Sikanese, are the people of east-central Flores, located between Lio and Larantuka. Specifically, Sika refers to a single village of the south coast, the seat of a Portuguese-Christian native ruler since the early seventeenth century. More generally, Sika has been applied to the domain under the rule of the Radja of Sika; to the territories claimed by the tributary mountain domains of Nita and Kangae (which were amalgamated with the domain of Sika in 1929); and, most generally, to all the lands claimed by these three domains, an area roughly equivalent to the former Dutch and present Indonesian administrative region of Maumere. The majority of Sikanese are concentrated in the western part of their territory. The dialect and customs of the eastern Sikanese appear sufficiently divergent to merit separate recognition. Another term, Krowe, or Ata Krowe (*ata*, "man"), has been used by natives and commentators alike to refer (a) to the people in the vicinity of Maumere (b) to pagans as opposed to Christians (*ata serani*), and (c) generally to the once non-Christian mountain peoples (*ata iwang*) from Nele to Tanah Ai, including all of the peoples under the rule of the Kangae. It is difficult to ascertain whether this term once referred to a separate ethnic group (cf. ten Kate 1894a; Le Roux, in *Volkstelling 1930: 5, 17*). The administrative adjustments, in this century, that made the

---

* This account, written by James J. Fox, is based mainly on published source material on Sika.

Sika territory coincident with the Maumere region provided official Sikanese control over a border area of Maumere with a large Lionese population. **Location.** The Sikanese occupy both the mountains and the coastal stretches of the Maumere region, a territory extending from the north to the south coast of east-central Flores and roughly from the river Nanga Napung in the east to the river Nanga Bloh in the west (approx. 122°02′ to 122°37′ E.; 8°30′ to 8°47′ S. **Geography.** A broken, eroded, and irregular terrain; a sharp contrast between coast and mountain; and erratic monsoons produce considerable climatic variation. Since the soil is porous and rivers are few, crops are dependent on irregular rainfall. A major problem for all of western Sika is the lack of sufficient, well-located, drinking water. **Linguistic affiliation.** Sikanese is related to Solorese; both have been classified within the Timor-Ambon group of languages (Jonker 1915: XII). **Demography.** The 1930 census reports a Sikanese population of well over 100,000, including nearly 20,000 Lionese. **History and cultural relations.** Native tradition attributes the foundation of the domain of Sika to the central figure of Don(g) Alésu, who is said to have journeyed to Malakka and returned to found his domain and to recognize the respective radjas of Nita and Kangae as his "left" and "right" hands (Wichmann 1891: 211; Arndt 1931: 107). Documents from 1613 list Sika as one of the (Portuguese) Christian states of the area (Rouffaer 1923-24: 212). Under the Dutch, the three native domains and their rulers were separately recognized until 1929, when Nita and Kangae were united with Sika to form a single domain under the Radja of Sika (van Dijk 1925-34). After independence, the Keradjaan Sika was given the status of an autonomous region (*daerah swapradja*) under the administrative supervision of the Radja of Sika, who was located in the town of Maumere (ten Dam 1950: 5).

SETTLEMENT PATTERN AND HOUSING. **Settlement pattern.** Mountain villages straddle strategic ridges or high points; others stretch along roads or parallel the coast. Houses are reportedly ranged in rows, with the village center (in non-Christian villages) marked by one or more large offering stones (*mahe*). An elaborately carved village house or structure (*woga*), containing ceremonial objects (gongs, drums, shields), is reserved exclusively for men and used as the place of male circumcision in most non-Christian villages (Arndt 1933b: 180-201). Arndt conjectures that formerly villages were divided into clan quarters or neighborhoods. Each clan within a village designates one house as its clan house. **Housing.** Houses are rectangular and raised on posts a meter or more above the ground. In western Sika, houses consist of two parts: a gallery (*tedang*) and an inner room (*une*), with further subdivisions within each part. Many houses are encircled, with their court-yards, by low stone walls. During periods of work in distant dry fields, makeshift huts are erected.

ECONOMY. Dependence on swidden agriculture. There are few herds, and only the coastal villages have the opportunity of offshore fishing. The traditional economy has been to some extent transformed by the Dutch-induced planting of the coconut palm and sale of copra. Main crops are rice, maize, and manioc, supplemented by millet, sorghum, and sweet potato. Domestic animals include dogs, cats, pigs, goats, ducks, chickens, and horses. Property rights are vested in land, trees, houses, horses, elephant tusks, gold, silver, cloth, and old armaments. The household is the main landowning unit, with residual rights over unclaimed land belonging to either the "lord of the earth" (*tanah puang*) or the radja.

KIN GROUPS. **Descent and kin groups.** In western Sika, descent is reportedly "patrilineal," in that a child belongs to his father's descent group after payment of bridewealth. The MoBr, however, maintains certain rights over his SiCh and must be paid a token sum at the birth of each child (Arndt 1933b: 46). In eastern Sika, descent is flexibly ambilineal; bridewealth is unimportant; and children apparently become associated with the descent group with whom their parents choose to reside. For western Sika, Arndt reports large, nonlocalized, nonexogamous, named descent groups (*ku'at* or *ku'at wungung*), each recognizing its own founding ancestor, possessing its own "history," and sharing a limited number of ritual prohibitions. These "clans" are not further divided into named segments. In eastern Sika, descent groups are referred to as *suku;* these are preferably endogamous and seem to be localized (Arndt 1933b). **Kin terminology.** There are three lists of kin terms for western Sika (Calon 1893: 190-91; Arndt 1933b: 57-58; Meye 1964). Fa and FaBr (*ama*) are distinguished from MoBr (*pulame* or *tiu*); Mo and MoSi (*ina*) are distinguished from FaSi (*aä*); cross cousins are distinguished from parallel cousins and according to the sex of the speaker; potential marriage partners (MoBrDa, FaSiSo), however, address each other as *ipar*. Kin and affine terms are coincident, and at the purely terminological level the system is strongly suggestive of prescriptive matrilateral cross-cousin marriage.

MARRIAGE AND FAMILY. **Mode.** In western Sika, marriage is effected by the payment of bridewealth, reckoned in horses, elephant tusks, and gold and silver coins; counterpresentations must be paid in pigs, cloth, and rice. **Form.** Most marriages are monogamous; although polygyny is permitted. **Extension of incest taboos.** Marriage is forbidden (1) between a parent and child; uncle and niece; aunt and nephew (2) between siblings (3) between the children of two brothers or the children of two sisters, and (4) between a boy and his FaSiDa (Arndt 1933b: 22-23). The desired marriage is between a boy and his MoBrDa. **Residence.** Throughout Sika, marriage is by preference village endogamous. In western Sika, a man may spend a year or more in the house of his wife or alternate residence between his parents' and wife's parents' house before establishing a residence of his own (Arndt 1933b: 45). **Domestic unit.** A household may include the elderly parents of either husband or wife and a recently married child with spouse. Ten Dam (1950: 24) and Arndt (1933b: 91) report royal houses with up to 50 persons, although the average in Nita is 10 per household. **Inheritance.** Property is divided among male siblings, but an elder brother may act on behalf of his other brothers to retain intact for another generation the household's dry fields (ten Dam 1950: 51-52). One child, with spouse, continues to reside with his or her parents and eventually inherits the house.

SOCIOPOLITICAL ORGANIZATION. **Political organization.** In the early 1950s, the Maumere region under the rule of the Radja of Sika consisted of 16 parishes, each headed by an officer with the title of *kapitan*. Each parish was divided into villages, each under a village headman (*kepala kampong*). The traditional political system included ritual titles such as *tanah puang*, "lord of the earth," with ritual rights over the land and authoritative knowledge in questions of adat (Arndt 1933b: 102-06; ten Dam 1950: 46). The *tanah puang* was regarded as a descendant of the founder of a village area, traditionally at enmity with the radja and his representatives. **Social stratification.** Sources indicate, for western Sika, a class of nobles, related to the Radja of Sika and the former Radjas of Nita and Kangae (*ata moang*); a class of freemen or commoners (*ata riwung*); and formerly a class of slaves, the result of debt or capture in war (*ata maha*). There is no class system reported for eastern Sika (Tanah Ai). **Social control, justice, and warfare.** Justice was dealt with by the radja, his representatives, the village headman and the village elders, including the *tanah puang*. Oaths and ordeals (*djadji*) were once part of the judicial process. Most western Sikanese villages waged limited warfare against the Lionese on their border. Enemy heads were generally hung at the village entrance on return from a raid; a coconut was then substituted for the head in the performance of village rituals (Arndt 1932b: 274-78).

RELIGION. Since the early seventeenth century, Catholicism has been associated with the rule of the radjas of Sika. As a result, native ceremonial life has been virtually replaced by Catholic ritual. **Supernaturals.** The traditional pantheon consisted of a number of coupled deities, e.g. Lero Wulang and Niang Tana, associated with the sun/moon and the surface of the earth respectively (Arndt 1932b). There exists also a belief in the spirits of the dead and a variety of female spirits or paired spirits whose female aspects are particularly dangerous to humans. **Ceremonies.** A major focus of the ancient ceremonial life was a male circumcision and initiation ritual, presided over by the *tanah puang;* boys were thereafter confined to the village men's house (Arndt 1932b: 278-85). **Illness and medicine.** There are two categories of curers: *ata rawing,* benign curers of either sex; and *ata busung,* predominantly male curers who can diagnose the cause of an illness, extract objects from the body, locate witches, and recall the soul (Arndt 1932b: 290-93). Most illnesses are believed caused by contact with sorcery stuff (*uru*), by witch's attack, or by the confrontation of the soul by a spirit. **Soul, death, and afterlife.** At death the corpse was traditionally wrapped with cloth or mats and buried in the ground. Coastal dwellers sometimes used coffins in the shape of boats. A bush, coconut, or jar was erected upon the grave. The soul journeyed either to Lero Wulang or to a seven-layered underworld, through whose stages it progressed by dying and being reborn again and by undergoing various ordeals (Arndt 1932b: 136-40).

BIBLIOGRAPHY. Arndt 1931, 1932b, 1933b; de Brabander 1949; Calon 1890-91, 1893, 1895; ten Dam 1950; van Dijk 1925-34; Engbers 1898; Ijsseldijk 1898; Jonker 1915; ten Kate 1894a; Meye 1964; Rouffaer 1923-24; Sevink 1914; *Volkstelling 1930*; Vosmaer 1862; Wichmann 1891.

LIONESE

Synonym. *Lio*

ORIENTATION. The majority of Lionese are found in the mountains of middle Flores, between Maumere (Sika) and Endeh. Kennedy regarded these people, who numbered slightly over 100,000 in 1930, as a "mountain branch of the Ende-Lio tribe, speaking the same dialect as the Ende coastal dwellers but with a different accent" (Kennedy 1955b: 21). The Lionese seem not to have formed a native state prior to Portuguese contact in the early seventeenth century. Paga, a village on the south coast, subsequently became a Christianized state with a court aristocracy, but the latter apparently never claimed control over any significant part of Lio territory (Fox 1970b). According to Kennedy, many of the mountain villages were in the early 1950s almost 100 percent Catholic.

BIBLIOGRAPHY. Fox 1970b; Kennedy 1955b.

SOLOR-LARANTUKA

THE POPULATION of the radjadom of Larantuka, in extreme eastern Flores, together with the inhabitants of the off-lying islands of Solor, Adonara, and Lomblen (the Solor Archipelago), are generally referred to as Solorese. Although the peoples of this area were never politically consolidated prior to the Dutch colonial period, they are nevertheless closely related with respect to cultural forms (cf. Arndt 1940; Vatter 1932) and language (e.g. their classification by Esser as a single linguistic group—Soloreesch—within his Ambon-Timor group). The area came under Portuguese control in the sixteenth century, and Portuguese Dominicans continued missionary work there until the beginning of the nineteenth century. Dutch Jesuits and Franciscans arrived during the period 1860-80, gradually focusing their activities in East Flores and particularly in Larantuka, which became an administrative center under the colonial regime. As a result of this long history of missionary effort, a considerable proportion of the Solorese-speaking population has converted to Christianity, resulting in fundamental changes in indigenous ideologies. Acculturation has occurred most noticeably in East Flores, although Kennedy, in a survey of the Larantuka area made in 1949-50, found ample evidence of indigenous beliefs beneath a veneer of Christianity. Kennedy's notes (1955b) present a fragmentary picture of the indigenous culture, but enough to indicate its considerable complexity with respect to structural and symbolic representations of cosmological beliefs and their embodiment in myth and ritual (much of this supporting the earlier findings of Vatter, Arndt, Beckering, and Ouwehand—including the interpretations of these data by van Wouden). Consciousness of ethnic identity in Larantuka is nowadays bound up with issues of Catholic versus Muslim and/or pagan, but there remain the older legends of descent from four brothers and the identification of these events with Ili Mandiri, the legendary mountain of the ancestors; and Larantuka clans are still ranked according to genealogical distance from an original or founding line. East Flores, like the rest of the Solorese-speaking area, is characterized by a moietylike division of the people into two mutually hostile parties—Demon and Padzi. Keers (1948) felt that the two categories could be shown to differ systematically according to physical type, and Arndt (1938) attributed their origin to a distinction between autochthonous and immigrant peoples. It is likely, however, that the basic pattern of opposition and ritual combat—widespread in Indonesia—is fundamentally ideological in origin, having to do with the expression in sociopolitical structure of dualistic concepts, in turn rooted in ancient and widely diffused cosmological beliefs of probable Hindu origin. This is the view of Downs, after reviewing the literature on ritual warfare and headhunting among Solorese, Toradja, and other groups in Indonesia, i.e. "two groups representing the two halves of the universe engaged in regular combat to produce human sacrifices for the securing of fertility and health" (Downs 1955: 55).

BIBLIOGRAPHY. Arndt 1938, 1940; Downs 1955; Keers 1948; Kennedy 1955b; Vatter 1932.

SOLORESE*

Synonyms. *Ata Kiwan, Holo, Solor, Solot*

ORIENTATION. **Identification.** Solor (or more commonly in native speech, "Holo") means "to be joined" or "to be united," and in older ritual texts it also means "man" (Arndt 1937: 3). The name, under the form "Solot" and later "Solor," came into European usage as a term for the whole Solorese linguistic area and its peoples in the sixteenth and seventeenth centuries. The whole population is irregularly divided into two opposed groups, the Demon and the Padzi (Paji). The division, supported by a mythological tradition, is of a common Indonesian type and is as much religious as military or political. It does not lead to concerted action or a sense of unity on the part of either group as a whole; fighting between the two groups is ceremonially motivated and is generally intermittent and local (Arndt 1938). The population shows mixed Malay and Melanesian physical features. In addition to the Solorese-speaking population, the islands are inhabited by a long-established Eurasian colony at Larantuka on Flores, as well as by coastal Muslims, Chinese traders, and several European missionaries. **Location.** From about 122°30′ to 123°40′ E. and from 8°10′ to 8°50′ S., including eastern Flores, Solor, Adonara, and Lomblen. The western border runs from the mouth of the Wai Ula on the south coast of Flores to a point opposite on the north coast, crossing meanwhile the plateau to the west of the Lobe Tobi volcano. To the west of this line are the Sikanese, who speak a

---

* The author, R. H. Barnes, is a candidate for the D.Phil. in anthropology at the University of Oxford. He has compiled this entry from the literature prior to undertaking fieldwork on Lomblen.

related but somewhat different language. Immediately to the east of the Solorese region are the islands of Pantar and Alor. **Geography.** Most of the people live on the slopes of the mountains, where they burn off the forest for agricultural purposes. Climate is influenced by the dry Australian land mass. Coconut, gebang, lontar, and areng palms are important economically. Other plants include bamboos, the waringin tree, and a lime tree. Alang-alang grass grows in the large, uninhabited plains. The fauna includes a species of small deer, wild pigs, buffalo, monkeys, dogs, goats, sheep, chickens, rats and mice, python, crocodiles, iguanas, numerous poisonous snakes, scorpions, large poisonous spiders, and poisonous centipedes. [Vatter 1932: 8-21.] **Linguistic affiliation.** Malayo-Polynesian, within the Ambon-Timor group (Esser 1938). Vatter (1932) postulates three main dialects: (1) West Solorese, bordering Sika (2) High Solorese, spoken on the rest of East Flores, Adonara, and Solor and in the Lewo Tolo and Lamalerap districts of Lomblen; and (3) East Solorese, spoken on the rest of Lomblen and perhaps in coastal enclaves on Pantar and Alor. Kedangese, spoken in the northeast of Lomblen, is the most aberrant dialect. [Esser 1938; Salzner 1960; Vatter 1932: 274-77.] **Demography.** In 1930 the population totaled about 131,000, of which there were some 33,000 on East Flores, 36,000 on Adonara, 15,000 on Solor, and 47,000 on Lomblen (Seegeler 1931; Symons 1935). **History.** Many clans believe themselves to have immigrated from Sina Djawa (a combination of the words for China and Java). Others have probably immigrated from Sika, Timor, and Seran (Ceram). Solor is mentioned as a dependency of Madjapahit in the *Nagarakertagama* (1365 A.D.). The Victoria, the only remaining ship of Magellan's expedition, sailed between Lomblen and Pantar in January 1522, the first European contact with the Archipelago. The Dutch gained control in 1859. **Cultural relations.** The Archipelago probably had contact with the other regions of Indonesia through traders from the early centuries of this millennium. Islam must have reached Solor quite early, for accounts of the sixteenth century report the presence of Muhammedans in coastal villages. Portuguese missionaries arrived in the sixteenth century, and long contact with Christianity has resulted in the conversion of a large portion of the population.

SETTLEMENT PATTERN AND HOUSING. **Settlement pattern.** Seegeler claims that the Solorese originally lacked villages and that each family and its slaves lived on its fields, where it built a house (Seegeler 1931: 55-56). Whether or not this is true, formerly there were named village centers marked by the ritual house of the dominant clan. In many villages there is a tradition that each of the clans inhabiting it was assigned a specific section of the village. Most of the villages were high on the mountain slopes before the Dutch, around 1913, forced many to move down to the coast (Kennedy 1955b: 258-59). Villages range from about a hundred to five hundred inhabitants, although some have over a thousand. Houses for unmarried young men are reported in East Flores and on Adonara and may well be found on Solor and Lomblen as well. Houses for unmarried young women are reported west of Ili Mandiri in East Flores, and on Adonara. [Arndt 1940: 98; Vatter 1932: 169, 174, 177.] **Housing.** Hip or gable-shaped roofs, covered with bundles of grass or palm-leaf strips and supported by posts of palm wood. Walls are of bamboo, and the floor is raised off the ground and supported on posts. The house shape is rectangular. [Vatter 1932: 68-70.]

ECONOMY. Inland villagers depend mainly on swidden agriculture, although they also hunt and fish. Coast dwellers are dependent on fishing and trading and have no fields. [Van Lynden 1851: 321; Kluppel 1873: 385.] **Agriculture.** The most important crop is maize, followed by rice grown in dry fields. Other crops include millet, sorghum, yams, cassava, sweet potatoes, gourds and melons, beans, peanuts, sugarcane, bananas, breadfruit, mango, papaya, pineapple, limes, coconuts, tobacco, cotton, and indigo. [Vatter 1932: 18-20, 106-07; van Lynden 1851: 320-21.] Agricultural land is generally owned by the clan. One field is chosen each year to be worked communally by all the clans in a village and as the site of the rituals that serve for all the village land in cultivation. In the whole of the Archipelago, it is the rule to work a field two years and then let it lie fallow for six or seven years. Maize and rice and often also sorghum and millet are sowed in the same field. Other small food plants are grown in small gardens. Irrigation is not practiced. [Vatter 1932: 99-113.] **Fishing and hunting.** Coastal fishing techniques include the use of basketry traps, fish poison, nets, spears, harpoons, kites, and bows and arrows. Deer, wild pigs, monkeys and birds are hunted. The same weapons are used for hunting and for war: the bow and arrow, the lance, and the short sword. A blunt arrow is used for birds, which are hunted for their feathers. Snares are used for wild pigs (Vatter 1932: 63-64). **Gathering.** When the harvest fails, women gather herbs, roots, and wild fruit, as well as mussels, snails, and crabs. In addition to their lontar palm wine tapping, men collect the numerous materials used in building and the manufacture of tools (Vatter 1932: 62-63). **Domestic animals.** Dogs, goats, pigs, a few sheep, buffalo, and chickens. Little care is taken of them; only young pigs are fed (Vatter 1932: 20, 64). **Industrial arts.** Industrial arts include making baskets and the weaving and dyeing of cloth by women. Pottery is obtained by trade. A few ironsmiths and carpenters are found in the coastal villages. [Van Lynden 1851: 321, 323-24; Vatter 1932: 61-68, 217-26.] **Trade.** Mountain dwellers trade agricultural products, coconuts, and goats to coastal villages for fish and manufactured products. Spices, ivory tusks, and swords are brought by traders from Macassar, Buton, Endeh, and Timor. [Van Lynden 1851: 321, 324-25; Kluppel 1873: 387-88.] **Property.** Village land, usually owned by the major clan, is divided into individual fields, which are allotted each year by the *tuan tana*. Generally on Flores, hunting and fishing rights and the gathering of building materials are free to anyone. Only trees planted for a specific purpose are limited. The house and household goods belong to the family. [Arndt 1951: 140-50; 1940: 108-09, 235-36; Ouwehand 1950: 59-61, 65-67; 1951; Vatter 1932: passim.]

KIN GROUPS. **Descent and kin groups.** Most communities have a segmentary social order based on patrilineal clans and lineages. In some areas of Adonara, the division into clans seems to have disappeared or lost its meaning, and its place has been taken by the patripotestal family. Some clans are spread throughout several villages; most are represented in only one village. The number of clans in a village is quite various; as many as 16 have been reported for some villages. The number of people in a clan varies from one or two in those which are dying out to over two hundred. [Arndt 1940; Vatter 1932: passim; Ouwehand 1950, 1951.] **Terminology.** Arndt (1937: 17) gives the following kin terms:

Fa	*ama, bapa*
Mo	*ina, ema*
Br(w.s.)	*naa*
Si(m.s.)	*bine*
Hu	*lake*
Wi	*kowae*

To these may be added the following from Leemker (1893):

ElBr, ElSi	*kaka*
YoBr, YoSi	*arin*
Brother-in-law	*opu*
Child	*ana*
Children	*klotte*

Ouwehand's information from Leloba, Flores, provides some of the essential features of the terminology (Ouwehand 1950: 56n). Relations traceable through the mother's brother are termed (*opu*) *belake* and are considered the wife-giving group. Those traceable through the father's sister are called *opu* (*wain*) and are considered the wife-taking group. *Belake* means mother's brother and father-in-law. *Opu* means father's sister's husband and father's sister's son. Ouwehand gives another term, *opu bine*, for relations through father's sister; a married sister is understood to belong to this group as well.

MARRIAGE AND FAMILY. Asymmetric affinal alliance is practiced in Wailolong and Leloba and presumably in the neighboring villages on the slopes of the Ili Mandiri in East Flores (Barnes 1968: 79-89; Kennedy 1955b: 159-62, 406-08; Ouwehand 1950: 55-57; Arndt 1940: 75; Vatter 1932: 74-75). Information given by Arndt and Vatter suggests that the institution is, or was, widespread in the Archipelago. **Mode.** Payment of bridewealth or a period of service in the home of the bride's father. Where affinal alliance is practiced, marriage is the occasion of a series of exchanges forming part of the continuing obligations between the allied clans or lineages. Ivory tusks are the principal valuables exchanged, although the exchange of a sister for a bride is reported in some places. Marriage by abduction is said to have existed in all the islands until it was outlawed by the Dutch. [Arndt 1940: passim; Vatter 1932: passim; Seegeler 1931: 51.] **Form.** Generally monogamous; polygyny is permissible but limited to the rich (Vatter 1932: 80). **Marriage rules.** In East Flores (Larantuka), marriage is prescribed with the classificatory mother's brother's daughter, with an explicitly reported preference for the genealogical mother's brother's daughter (Kennedy 1955b: 194-95). The other "cousin" relationships are prohibited (Arndt 1940: 3; ten Kate 1894a: 243). **Residence.** If bridewealth is paid, the couple live in the home of the husband's parents. If not, the first years of marriage are spent in residence with the wife's family (Arndt 1940: passim; Vatter 1932: passim). **Domestic unit.** A household may include—in addition to the husband, wife, and children—lineage relatives of the man, including unmarried (sometimes even married) younger brothers or cousins. Children without parents may live in a home as house slaves. [Vatter 1932: 70; Arndt 1940: 97, 231.] **Inheritance.** Inheritance is patrilineal. Ten Kate (1894a: 242) mentions that in the Padzi regions of Flores, Adonara, and Solor, the oldest son alone inherits from the father. The account given in the *Adatrechtbundels* (1930: *33, 395*) suggests that the older brother is nevertheless required to assist his younger brothers and to aid them in providing bridewealth at marriage. In the Ili Mandiri district of Flores, all the sons inherit together, and they alternate in using the land (Vatter 1932: 84). On Solor, family-owned land is divided among all the sons, usually by the father before his death (Arndt 1940: 236). In the parts of Adonara where clans and lineages have disappeared, the oldest son inherits all lands, and the younger sons must lease from him (Vatter 1932: 175). **Divorce.** Divorce is easily arranged and marked by a simple ceremony, except among nobles, for whom the ceremony lasts several days (Vatter 1932: 80). **Secondary marriage.** A widow is usually expected to marry a brother of her dead husband or a member of his clan, if she wishes to marry at all. If bridewealth has been paid for her, she is considered the property of her husband's clan and may be disposed of as they choose. [Arndt 1940: 25-26; Seegeler 1931: 52.]

SOCIOPOLITICAL ORGANIZATION. **Political organization.** In most villages, the head of the original or landowning clan is responsible for determining the times of planting and harvesting and takes the lead in directing communal ceremonies. He is known by the Solorese term *tuan alat* (Malay, *tuan tana*). In some regions, he must be asked for permission to cultivate any new land (Arndt 1940: 107). Where there is more than one landowning clan in a village, there will be more than one *tuan tana*. In addition, there is the institution of four ritual leaders, found throughout East Flores and Solor. The four offices, shared among the landowning clans or clan segments, are: *koten, kelen, hurit* (*hurin, hurint*) and *marang*. Commonly the *kepala koten* is the most prominent of the four and as a rule assumes leadership over affairs within the village, while the *kepala* (or *kelake*) *kelen* concerns himself with external affairs. The other two positions have only advisory authority. The powers of these individuals are tempered by the influence of the other village elders (cf. Vatter 1932: 81; Arndt 1940: 101-04; Ouwehand 1950: 57-58). Under the Dutch, the Solorese area was divided into administrative territories held by the six radjas of Larantuka, Adonara, Trong, Lamahala, Lawajong, and Lamakera, and was later consolidated under the Radja of Larantuka, who then held the title of "Zelfbestuurder" for the entire region (van Dijk 1925-34: 34). **Social stratification.** Landowning clans are relatively wealthy and powerful, and the requirements of bridewealth influence marriage decisions. Otherwise, social distinctions based on wealth do not seem clearly marked. Slavery formerly was widespread. **Social control and justice.** Conflicts within a clan are adjudicated by an assembly of clan leaders and old men of the clan. Several forms of ordeal are also employed (Vatter 1932: 83-84). **Warfare.** War parties are led by the *ata maan*, red men, who are proven warriors. Usually one side withdraws after a few of its members have fallen (Vatter 1932: 83; Arndt 1940: 116-21, 238-45). Formerly heads were taken in battles between Padzi and Demon; a head was normally placed under the main post when building a ritual house (Arndt 1938, 1951).

RELIGION. **Religious systems.** Many communities are either Muslim or, especially on East Flores, Roman Catholic. Others still retain their indigenous religion, which is of a familiar Indonesian pattern. **Supernaturals.** The High God is Lera (Rera) Wulan (Sun/Moon), and his female complement is Tana Ekan. The latter compound has the general sense of the earth and designates the lower world in opposition to the upper world inhabited by Lera Wulan. Alternative names for the High God are Lahatala, Letala, Latala, or Lahatala Dunia. Lesser spirits include the *nitu*, who inhabit the tops of trees, large stones, springs, and holes in the ground; Ile Woka, the god of the mountains; and Hari Botan, the god

of the sea. **Practitioners.** *Menaka*, men possessed by malignant spirits called *eo*, are responsible for all sorts of human misfortunes. *Molang* are capable of detecting and counteracting *menaka*. They also possess healing powers. They may be anyone: a man, a woman or child, a prominent person, or a slave. [Arndt 1951: 34, 131-34, 184-92.] **Ceremonies.** Prominent among ceremonial occasions are those connected with the building of a new *korke*, the clan ritual house, and those relating to the agricultural cycle, which Kennedy (1955b: 270) says includes 13 rites. [Arndt 1951; Vatter 1932: passim.] **Soul, death, and afterlife.** It is most often said that men have two souls, the *tuber* and the *manger*. The former may leave the body, but the latter may not. (Sometimes the reverse is claimed.) When a person dies, the *tuber* goes to Lera Wulan or is eaten by a *menaka* or by the *nitu*. The *manger*, however, goes to the land of the *kewokot*, the souls of the dead ancestors (Arndt 1951: 30-31, 51, 171-73; Vatter 1932: 88). It is also said that the world is divided into several levels, and that when a man dies he is reborn on the level below. After several lives, he completes a cycle and begins again. Commonly when a person dies the body is buried in a normal grave on the same day or at least within a day or two afterward. Only important men are left unburied for any length of time, and they may remain above ground for as long as three months (Vatter 1932: passim).

BIBLIOGRAPHY. *Adatrechtbundels* 1930; Arndt 1937, 1938, 1940, 1951; Barnes 1968; van Dijk 1925-34; Esser 1938; ten Kate 1894a; Kennedy 1955b; Kluppel 1873; Leemker 1893; van Lynden 1851; Ouwehand 1950, 1951; Salzner 1960; Seegeler 1931; Symons 1935; Vatter 1932.

ALOR-PANTAR

Synonyms. *Aloreezen, Alorese*

ORIENTATION. **Location and identification.** The islands of Alor and Pantar, at approximately 8° S. by 124° E., lie some 50 miles north of Timor, where they constitute an eastward extension of the Solor Archipelago. The topography is markedly precipitous, with relatively narrow coastal lowlands. Torrential rains during the winter months are followed by a hot, dry season lasting through September. [DuBois 1944; Vatter 1932: 10-21.] The population is rather sharply divided between Muslim coastal peoples, mainly immigrants from Timor, Kisar, and Flores, and autochthonous mountain dwellers comprised of pagans and Christians. The latter, predominantly Oceanic Negroid in physical type (Brouwer 1935), appear to be divided into an extraordinarily large number of discrete ethnolinguistic groups, especially on Alor. Brouwer (1935: 5-8) and Bouman (1943: 483-85) arrived at a classification, chiefly on physical and linguistic grounds, of seven major groupings or categories for the area as a whole, but the exact nature of these is unclear. DuBois (1944) and Nicolspeyer (1940), both anthropologists, worked independently in the Atimelang Valley area of north-central Alor among an Abui-speaking population; neither, however, undertook survey fieldwork among other tribes on the island. **Linguistic affiliation.** Classified within an Ambon-Timor group of Malayo-Polynesian by Esser (1938). Vatter (1932: 275, map) lists seven major language groups on Alor (Kabola or Adang, Kawel, Abui, Kelong, Kamang, Kolana, and Kui-Kramang) and five on Pantar (Belagar, Nedebang, Dëing, Mauta, and Lemma). East Solorese languages are spoken in enclaves along the northwest coasts of both islands, and Papuan languages are probably also present, according to Esser. **Demography.** A total of about 90,000 for the Alor-Pantar area (*Volkstelling 1930*). **History and cultural relations.** Although little is known of the past history of the islands, it appears evident that indigenous political institutions never developed beyond the village level. Present day coastal "radjas" were installed by the Dutch subsequent to 1908, but aside from infrequent trade relations with these coastal principalities the interior peoples were relatively little affected by culture change from the outside. In the 1940s Protestant missions conducted schools in some mountain communities, but these had little effect on the lives of the people, and Malay, the language of instruction, was understood by relatively few adults. [DuBois 1944.]

SETTLEMENT PATTERN AND HOUSING. Villages, seldom exceeding 150 inhabitants, are traditionally situated on mountain spurs or crests, although the Dutch encouraged decentralized habitation and the movement of villages to more accessible locations. An Abui village typically contains several dance places (*masang*), on each of which is located a large, raised lineage house (*kadang*) with a high pyramidal thatched roof. The occupants of a *kadang* consist of a single branch of a patrilineage (DuBois 1944: 19); nearby, apparently, are smaller houses (*fala*) occupied by the families of brothers or male kin of men resident in the *kadang*. Thus the village would appear to consist ideally of localized patrilineages, each with its own dance place centered in its own quarter or ward; available data are, however, unclear on this point. In the center of each dance place is a stone pile, and around the periphery the flat gravestones of the prominent dead are located. [DuBois 1944: 19; Nicolspeyer 1940: 32-40.]

ECONOMY. Subsistence is overwhelmingly reliant on agriculture, with hunting seasonally important. A seemingly self-contained system of exchange, involving pigs, gongs, and metal kettledrums, is associated with a highly-developed wealth-prestige pattern central to Alorese culture. **Agriculture.** Maize, the staple, is grown on swiddens, with secondary crops of rice (the ceremonial food), millet, beans, and a wide variety of tubers. During the annual dry season, food intake may be limited largely to cassava (Nicolspeyer 1940: 7). **Hunting.** Mainly pig hunting with bow and arrow during the dry season (Nicolspeyer 1940: 6-7). **Domestic animals.** Pigs, chickens, and goats, the former important as a form of currency. **Industries.** Chiefly wood carving and basketry. Pottery making and weaving are absent, with knowledge of metal casting limited to the eastern Alorese. In general, according to DuBois (1944), material products appear crude, and little prestige is attached to craftsmanship. **Division of labor.** Clear division of activities by sex, with subsistence in the hands of the women and with the men concerned largely with exchange and finance (DuBois 1944). **Trade and exchange.** Trade with coastal settlements is infrequent, although there is considerable exchange of goods among neighboring mountain villages. Pigs (raised locally) and metal gongs and kettledrums (imported originally from Java by Macassarese traders) are central to an elaborate pattern of exchange, in which concepts of profit, interest, credit, and reciprocity are present. This system, associated with a highly-developed wealth-prestige pattern, occupies the energies of most Alorese males from puberty to old age. [DuBois 1944.] **Property.** Major categories of property are land, pigs, gongs, and kettledrums. Gardens are individually owned by men and women and are inherited by both sexes from either parent (DuBois 1944: 22).

KIN GROUPS. **Descent.** Patrilineal. **Kin groups.** Patrilineages, *hieta*, were apparently at one time localized within villages, although variable residence after marriage seems to have obscured this pattern; nowadays it appears to be the rule that one branch, at least, must reside in the large lineage house, *kadang*. Information on a second type of kin group is less clear: DuBois (1944: 21-22) mentions a "male house" (*neng fala*), apparently a kind of skewed personal kindred, encompassing six patrilineal descent lines, i.e. males related to Ego through three ascending generations of mothers' brothers, reckoned bilaterally. A male Ego may apparently expect help from male kinsmen within various of these six descent lines with respect to exchange obligations, particularly those having to do with death feasts. The functions of a so-called "female house" (*mayoa fala*) are less well-defined by the culture. Members of this category include all bilaterally reckoned kin not included in the patrilineage nor in the male house category, essentially descendants of fathers' sisters (DuBois 1944: 21-22). Nicolspeyer, who also worked in the Abui-speaking Atimelang Valley, supposes an original structure of four exogamous lineages divided into two exogamous moieties. He posits *nengfala* as originally the wife-giving group and *majoafala* as the wife-taking group (Nicolspeyer 1940: 65-66). **Kin terminology.** DuBois (1944: 20) characterizes the kinship system as of simple Hawaiian type. Nicolspeyer (1940: 55-56, 68-70) gives the following terms of reference for Atimelang:

Mo	*ia*
Fa	*mama*
MoBr, FaBr, and their male generation fellows	*mama*
MoSi, FaSi, and their female generation fellows	*ia*
Ego's generation fellows of same sex	*moknehi*
Ego's generation fellows of opposite sex	*ura*

For Pantar, Needham (1956) presents evidence for a terminological distinction between cross and parallel cousins and the equation of MoBrDa/FaSiDa with wife—factors which he discusses with respect to the possible occurrence on Pantar of symmetric connubium.

MARRIAGE AND FAMILY. **Mode.** Girls at about the age of puberty are tattooed, and the teeth of both sexes are filed and blackened, but these operations are not ritually elaborated. Premarital sex is permitted, and young people appear to have considerable choice in the selection of a marriage partner. Marriage initiates a series of exchanges between groups of kinsmen. Gongs, kettledrums, pigs, maize, and rice figure in both "bride-price" and "dowry," although in the latter case they tend to be in smaller amounts. [DuBois 1944: 84-104.] **Form.** Polygyny occurs frequently, with wives quartered in separate households (Nicolspeyer 1940: 59). **Marriage rules.** Marriage with any known kin is considered improper, but does occur with second cousins (DuBois 1944: 104-06). Needham (1956) presents evidence for the existence on Pantar of bilateral cross-cousin marriage within a system of symmetric connubium, i.e. a regular set of affinal alliances through the reciprocal exchange of women. Nicolspeyer (1940: 42-45) evidently feels that some form of affinal alliance was also present formerly on Alor. **Residence.** Following payment of the highest valued kettledrum within the agreed bride-price, the bride goes to live with her husband (Nicolspeyer 1940). According to DuBois (1944), the actual occurrence of patrilocality is less than the ideally stated norm. **Domestic unit.** The household, according to DuBois (1944: 20), normally consists of a biologic family supplemented by other kin bilaterally reckoned, with a range of from one to eight persons. **Divorce and secondary marriage.** For Atimelangers, an average of "two divorces apiece" (DuBois 1944: 96). Both the levirate and sororate occur on Alor, according to Nicolspeyer (1940: 59-60).

SOCIOPOLITICAL ORGANIZATION. **Political organization.** No indigenous political integration above the village level. An administrative hierarchy of coast-al "radjaships," districts, and village headmen is a recent development, created originally by the Dutch colonial government. **Social stratification.** Wealth is the sole avenue to prestige, although formerly a man could gain status through his reputation as a warrior. There are no formal grades or ranks among "rich men," nor are there any other institutionalized expressions of rank in Alorese society. Wealth is dependent on the successful manipulation of an indigenous credit system in association with obligatory payments on occasions such as marriage, death, and the building of a new lineage house. Metal kettledrums (*moko*) are the "coin of the realm," although pigs, gongs, and rice also figure in the complicated financial transactions that occupy the minds of most male Alorese. A man gains prestige through successful manipulation of the system and the amassing of wealth in pigs, gongs, and drums (much of it "on paper" in the form of outstanding debts). An essential aspect of the pattern is the public display and accounting of one's wealth, together with public arguments and disputes between debtors and creditors. Rarely, quarrels lead to potlatchlike behavior, with the competitive destruction of valued property. Men are motivated to join the system not only by desire for prestige but also because it affords the only avenue to raising the bride-price necessary for marriage. Furthermore, a man is obliged to contribute to the death feasts of kinsmen, lest their departed spirits make him ill. [DuBois 1944.] **Social control.** Verbal and (occasional) physical aggression is common in connection with disputes over financial transactions. "Fines through challenge" (DuBois 1944: 125) and public ordeals are traditional methods of settling such disputes between fellow villagers. The Dutch introduced a system of litigation, with fines levied through public debates (DuBois 1944: 124). **Warfare.** Warfare was rarely on a large scale and consisted chiefly of family feuds over exchange transactions. The kinsmen of a man slain in a feud were formerly obliged to seek a head—for reasons of revenge and also to provide a "spouse" for their slain kinsman—and until about 1920, heads were bought and sold and had an equivalent value in gongs and *mokos* (DuBois 1944: 181).

RELIGION. **Supernaturals.** Personal familiars are inherited bilaterally, and there are in addition village and lineage guardian spirits and a host of local spirits. A common representation of the supernatural is a carved crocodilelike figure or "Naga." A category of "Good Beings" inhabits a village in the sky, and the belief, fostered by "prophets," that these beings will return to earth leads to the periodic development of cargolike cults. These beings are not necessarily equated with ancestral spirits, however, and in fact concern with the dead, beyond the fulfillment of the necessary funerary obligations, seems to be minimal. [DuBois 1944: 165-75; Nicolspeyer 1940: 14-17, 29-33.]

Practitioners. Seers, *timang*, function in curing rites with the aid of tutelary spirits; they do not appear to be possessed by these spirits, however (DuBois 1944). The *je-adua*, glossed by Nicolspeyer (1940: 16-17) as "water lord," officiates at maize harvest festivals in a water-sprinkling rite. **Ceremonies.** Sacrifice and "feeding" the spirits constitute the chief forms of ritual behavior. Major ceremonies occur in connection with periodic death feasts and the annual maize harvest. **Soul, death, and afterlife.** The corpse is wrapped in a shroud and buried in the ground. One aspect of the deceased's soul remains in the vicinity and must be placated by mourning and feasting on the fourth and ninth days after death. The family incurs debts during this period that must be repaid through a series of memorial death feasts, which may extend over several years. At the last of these, a buffalo is sacrificed and the soul of the deceased is finally banished from the village, no longer a threat to the living. The soul travels to an afterworld on an uninhabited island, but the concept is extremely vague. The Alorese take little interest in the dead subsequent to the final obligatory death feast. [DuBois 1944: 152-65; Nicolspeyer 1940: 18-19, 21-22.]

BIBLIOGRAPHY. Bouman 1943; Brouwer 1935; DuBois 1944; Esser 1938; Needham 1956; Nicolspeyer 1940; Vatter 1932; *Volkstelling 1930*.

TIMOR-ROTI *

THE TIMOR ARCHIPELAGO, including Roti, is the largest of the Lesser Sunda island groups. Little of Timorese history before 1500 has been firmly established, and a clear (though still fragmented) picture of Timorese ethnography begins to emerge only in the nineteenth century. The islands appear formerly to have been divided into dozens of kingdoms, each consisting of a collection of *suku* princedoms contiguous with one another. According to one interpretation, the aboriginal inhabitants were the Atoni, who were subsequently displaced from their former habitat by invaders from Malacca, arriving via Macassar in the Celebes and Larantuka in eastern Flores. These newcomers were the Tetum (Belu), who are believed to have settled sometime during the fourteenth century on the Benain Plain in what is now the Waihale *kefettoran*, one of the most favorable regions on Timor for economic exploitation. From this area, the Tetum apparently expanded, push-

ing the Atoni westward. The people of Waihale (or Wehali, as this kingdom was popularly called) politically dominated the easterly kingdoms for several centuries, maintaining what may be termed an empire. Western Timor was almost coterminous with another empire, that of the Serviao, whose emperor was called the Sonbai. The first European visitors to reach Timor were Portuguese who came from Malacca at the turn of the sixteenth century, and they were eventually followed by the Dutch. After a protracted struggle for supremacy, the two European powers in 1851 divided the island politically, with the Portuguese in the east and Oe-Cussi, and the Dutch in the west. Despite proselytizing as early as the sixteenth century, it is only in the last 50 years that Christianity has begun making serious inroads into the traditional religion. ● A remarkable feature of Timorese ethnography is the extraordinarily large number of different languages spoken in the eastern region. The term Belu is an Atoni word referring to this complex of tribes and languages—generally the peoples across the border in Portuguese Timor. The term is of limited use as an ethnic designation, but it does reflect the fact that the dozen or so language groups of central and east Timor share certain dominant culture traits in common—as contrasted to the Atoni and related groups of western (Indonesian) Timor. No authoritative linguistic study has yet been published, but from the already existing information it appears that Timor contains at least 14 different languages, some of which were analyzed by the linguist Capell (1943-45), who classified them as either Malayo-Polynesian or "Papuan." Those comprising the former group include Atoni, Vaikeno, Tetum, Galoli, Mambai, Tokode, and Idate; while among the latter group are Makassai, Cairui, Buna', and (possibly) Dagada. Cunningham (1966: 63) puts the number of Atoni at about 300,000, and according to Ormeling (1956: 69), the number of Tetum residing in Indonesia in the early 1950s was about 100,000. About the same number probably exists in Portuguese Timor. Berthe (1961: 5) gives the Buna' population as 65,000. From personal investigations, I estimate the Makassai population as about 70,000 individuals. These, in addition to Rotinese-speaking immigrants, are the largest linguistic groups on Timor. Although most

---

* This summary was prepared by David Hicks.

villages rely economically upon such crops as corn, rice, and sweet potatoes, the importance of a certain species to a particular village varies. Thus for the upland Makassai rice dominates corn, whereas for the lowland Tetum the reverse is the case. The same applies with regard to livestock. Both buffalo (or cattle) and pigs are reared in most princedoms, but in some villages (such as those of the Makassai) buffalo (or cattle) are considerably more important than pigs; whereas in others (especially those inhabited by lowland Eastern Tetum) buffalo are of scant economic importance compared to pigs. Other animals include chickens, goats, and horses. • The cultural traditions characterizing the different linguistic groups and the irregular topography (which inhibits communications between even neighboring princedoms) have as one consequence the production of an astonishingly rich and varied range of social institutions. Some Timorese social organizations are ordered according to a matrilineal/ uxorilocal regime, others are patrilineal/patrilocal, while others fit somewhere between these classificatory poles. One instance, at least, of a system of symmetric prescriptive alliance (or two-section system), that of the Atoni, is present, and the Vaikeno people may well operate a second. That most contentious of alliance systems, the asymmetrically prescriptive (whose structural nature has been most convincingly isolated in a series of analyses by Needham), is also found on Timor, among the Makassai, but may exist among the Mambai, Nauhete, and Dagada, as well. Various forms of preferential alliance arrangements also occur, but as yet no instance of a bilineal descent system or an example of a cognatic native society has been reported, though some of the Eastern Tetum villages are beginning to incline toward cognation. A most important structural kingpin, often bringing the "elements of kinship" into relation in Timorese social organizations, is the institution of bridewealth. Thus bridewealth of dimensions that are regarded locally as impressive almost invariably accompanies a patrilineal/patrilocal regime; whereas in those organizations where it is either absent or meager, a matrilineal/uxorilocal regime typically occurs. In several Timorese societies, if the bridegroom provides bridewealth he resides patrilocally and his children belong to

his descent group, but should he fail to give bridewealth he must reside uxorilocally and his children belong to their mother's clan; in such a personal situation bridewealth may be regarded as a selector among institutional possibilities. The ethnography of the great majority of princedoms is still unknown, and even the barest and most conventional ethnographic information has never been obtained for princedoms inhabited by Cairui, Nauhete, Galoli, Vaikeno, and Idate speakers. The peoples about whom most is known are the Atoni (Cunningham 1967a), Western Tetum (Vroklage 1952), Buna' (Berthe 1961), and Makassai; but the Dagada and Kemak (Kema') have also received attention. Much of the ethnographic work carried out in Timor in the last five years or so has yet to be made publicly available.

BIBLIOGRAPHY. Berthe 1961; Capell 1943-45; Cunningham 1966, 1967a; Ormeling 1956; Vroklage 1952.

EASTERN TETUM*

Synonyms. *Belu, Teto, Tettum, Tetun*

ORIENTATION. **Location and identification.** The people of central Timor, on both sides of the Indonesian-Portuguese border, call themselves Tetum or Tetun. They do not, however, use the name "Belu" (which is the term by which they are known to the Atoni) or "Teto" (a word occasionally employed by Portuguese writers). Some confusion arises over names ascribed to various subgroups of Tetum speakers. Since scores of princedoms exist (each having its own interpretation of "Tetum culture"), any broad classification of this widespread linguistic group can be of only heuristic significance; the most useful of such typologies distinguishes among three categories: Eastern Tetum, Southern Tetum, and Northern Tetum. The latter two are adjacent to one another, and for expository convenience one may employ the term "Western Tetum" when these two groups are descriptively contrasted with those to the east. This does not, however, necessarily mean that the Northern and Southern groups resemble each other close-

* This entry, together with the introductory note on Timor as a whole, was contributed by David Hicks, a member of the Department of Anthropology, State University of New York at Stony Brook. The Tetum data are based on fieldwork in Portuguese Timor during 1965-67. The author wishes to acknowledge his indebtedness to the London Committee of the London-Cornell Project for South-East Asian Studies and in particular its chairman, Professor Maurice Freedman of the University of Oxford.

ly than either resembles the Eastern Tetum; indeed, with respect to descent, affinity, and residence regulations, many eastern villages are virtually identical in structure with those of the Southern Tetum. The racial affiliations of these groups are mixed, those to the north showing in general more Papuan or Melanesoid features than the Southern Tetum. **Linguistic affiliation.** Malayo-Polynesian (Capell 1943-45). The Tetum language is in widespread use throughout Portuguese Timor as a second official language. **Demography.** Approximately 200,000, divided almost equally between Indonesian and Portuguese Timor (Ormeling 1956).

SETTLEMENT PATTERN AND HOUSING. **Settlement pattern.** A typical Eastern Tetum village (*povoacao*) may be segmented or not, depending upon whether it is an aristocratic or commoner community; but whereas an aristocratic village is made up of two patrilineal clans (*ahi matan*), a community of commoners contains but a single clan. Several such villages form a princedom (*fukun* or *suku*), which invariably consists of two aristocratic communities and several commoner villages. The average village appears as a collection of a number of house clusters or compounds (*cnua*), each of which may consist of up to a dozen houses (*uma*); a large village, having perhaps 300 inhabitants, will occupy as many as 80 compounds, each separated from the rest by a stretch of jungle but linked by a system of paths. As a consequence of the rule of postmarital patrilocal residence for males, each clan, and hence each village, ideally corresponds to a localized group. In practice, however, compounds pertaining to neighboring communities often intermingle, with the result that on the ground the village seems to lack any contiguous unity. In fact, the compounds of a single community sometimes straggle over as much as two square miles, and although most compounds are more restricted in the area they cover than this, the Tetum settlement pattern is always of a dispersed character. Villages vary widely in population size: in the Posto Sede (Viqueque Concelho), for instance, which consists of ten princedoms, the smallest village houses 80 persons, in contrast to the largest, which has 511. Within a compound of the lineage that provides the princedom with its *dato uain* (one of two autochthonous governors) is located the princedom council house or court (*uma bo'o*). In each village there is also found a council house belonging to that community in its own right. **Housing.** The well-built compound house (*uma cnua*) is the chief residence of a household and is the house that is occupied for most of the year. The other house (*uma to'os*) is a more makeshift edifice sited in each garden and used when household members are working at agricultural activities. The compound house, averaging 40 feet long and 15 feet wide, is raised on piles about a yard high. The roof, made from the leaves of the gebang tree,

is ridged. There are no windows, although one entrance is found at the front of the house and a second at the rear. Each compound house is divided into three sections, the largest of which is the bedroom (the central part), where all household members sleep on mats thrown on the floor. The smallest (the front part) is the storage area, where the family altar and reliquary are located. At the rear is the kitchen, the feminine part of the house in contrast to the two frontal sections, which are considered the masculine area. The men of the household spend much of their time on a front veranda; another veranda, running the length of the house, may be occupied by persons of either sex. Furniture is totally absent.

ECONOMY. **Subsistence.** Eastern Tetum economy differs among princedoms according to location. Those of the hilly zones to the north rely for subsistence on the cultivation of rice, whereas the southern villages of the coastal plain center their economy on maize production. In the uplands, buffalo rearing is preferred to pig raising, whereas to the south the reverse preference exists. Agriculture is of the swidden variety, and most crops are cultivated in gardens, each of which is owned by a household. Fishing, hunting, and gathering are of comparatively little economic significance, but animal breeding is important. In the south, pig meat is regularly consumed, whereas buffalo are killed only on the most important of ritual occasions, and only then if the lineage chiefly concerned is a socially eminent one. Chicken supplements the main diet, which for the most part consists of stew made from greens, toasted corn on the cob, and eggs. Meat is usually eaten only on communal occasions and does not constitute an everyday element of diet. **Industrial arts.** Several factors create specialization in the manufacturing of utensils and art objects: sex, descent group prerogatives, marital status, and individual talent and inclination. The quite impressive range of indigenous material culture includes pottery, iron tools, textiles, ropework of various kinds, baskets, mats, and containers for the lime used in betel chewing. Tetum art finds expression in weaving, dyeing cloth, wood carving, buffalo horn carving, and engraving patterns on lime containers. **Trade.** Most goods change hands in the market, a formal weekly affair occurring in every post and an occasion for persons of the same princedom to get together. A market may have a catchment region of as much as 400 square miles, but most traders come from much nearer, i.e. within a radius of 12 miles. Regular buyers and sellers, however, usually reside in the princedom containing the market. **Property.** In general, tangibles are owned by individuals, whereas intangibles are the property of descent groups. Examples of important tangible property include gardens, coconut trees, areca trees, livestock, houses, clothing, artifacts, and ornaments; intangibles include social status, eligibility for political offices, and eligibility for ritual prerogatives. Apart from a few things of feminine use (which pass from mother to eldest daughter), property descends patrilineally. An eldest son is favored with the bulk of the inheritance.

KIN GROUPS. **Descent.** Most Tetum villages east of the River Luca are regulated according to the rule of patrilineal descent, but further west, matrilineal descent prevails. As a principle of order, however, patrilineal descent is modified by the factor of residence, so that if bridewealth is withheld from the father-in-law's lineage, the bridegroom must reside uxorilocally (in which case his children belong to their mother's descent group). **Kin groups.** Theoretically, the largest exogamous descent group is the clan, which, if of aristocratic status, is divided into phratries (*uma cain*), themselves split into lineages (*feto fuan, mane fuan*), which ideally (though rarely in practice) correspond to a compound group (*cnua*). In principle, the descent group is a localized entity, but in practice (chiefly because of quarrels), the clan, phratry, and lineage are dispersed. At the head of each of these three major descent group segments are both a secular governor and a ritual one, the former being responsible for maintaining order in the descent group he heads while the latter safeguards the ritual welfare of his segment. A further secular authority, that of the council or court, is composed of the elders (*catuas*) of a descent group segment. The council and secular governor cooperate in managing the affairs of the group, but the greater weight of authority rests with the elders, who, provided they win the backing of their agnates, have the power to depose the governor. Since the elders' own position and authority depend upon the support they receive from the ordinary members of the descent group they represent, basic authority rests ultimately with villagers. The clan leader is *catuas*, as is the phratry master; the lineage head is *bahen mahibu*, the compound ruler *bahen*, and the household head *uma ulun*. The ritual governor at each of these segmentary levels is known by the same term as his secular partner, except that in his case the term *lulik* (sacred) is added as a suffix. **Kin terminology.** The relationship terminology indicates the existence of a nonprescriptive lineal descent system, though the terminological correspondence is not exact. Some of the key terms are as follows:

Fa, FaBr	*tei*
Mo, MoSi, FaSi	*nai*
ElBr, FaElBrSo, MoElSiSo, FaElSiSo	*maun*
YoBr, YoSi, FaYoBrCh, MoYoSiCh, FaYoSiCh	*alin*
ElSi, FaElBrDa, MoElSiDa, FaElSiDa	*bi'in*
Ch, BrCh, SiCh, MoBrChCh	*oan*
MoBr, MoBrWi	*bo'un*
WiFa, WiMo	*banin*
MoBrCh	*sai oan*
Wi	*fe'en*
SiCh	*tua noan*

MARRIAGE AND FAMILY. **Mode.** The Eastern Tetum have four types of marriage. By far the most common is *hafoli*, in which the bridewealth is slight and the status difference between wife-givers and wife-takers hardly perceptible. No exclusive rights and duties separate the affinal groups, and such obligations as exist chiefly concern ritual acts performed on the occasion of mutual rites of passage. Even between households, the direct exchange of females is possible, and although the lineage remains the formal alliance group, the really effective affinal ties are those binding such affines as MoBr/SiSo, SiHu/WiBr, WiFa/DaHu. In return for bridewealth the bridegroom's lineage secures control over the domestic services of the wife, her sexual services, and the future offspring of the union; in addition, the bridegroom has the privilege of residing patrilocally. Marriages of this kind rarely involve descent groups of different social class and when contracted are usually made within the princedom. The most distinctive characteristics of the second type of marriage, the *habani*, are that the bridegroom resides uxorilocally and is obliged to render bride service to his father-in-law for a varying number of years, and that the children belong to their mother's clan. The third type, the *fetosa-umane*, though today almost extinct, still exists in some eastern princedoms. In content it differs little from the Makassai system, although a structural difference of considerable significance does exist, in that unlike the Makassai alliance system, that of the Tetum is nonprescriptive. Nevertheless, it is of an asymmetric nature in which the alliance group is again the lineage, but the direct exchange of females is of course prohibited. The wife-givers are termed *umane* and the wife-takers are known as the *feto-oan*. Unlike the *hafoli* marriage, wife-givers and wife-takers occupy mutually exclusive roles, and the former have a precisely defined set of rights/duties toward their wife-takers, who in their turn are bound to the wife-givers by complementary rights/duties of a quite different kind. Further differences are that these rights/duties extend beyond the requirements of rites of passage to include such things as help in legal disputes, economic assistance, a status difference between the two categories of affine such that the wife-givers are superior to their partners, and the fact that the statistical frequency of lineage exogamy is much higher than in the case of the *hafoli*. The fourth type of marriage (*hafen*) is little more than concubinage and results when a female absconds from her natal compound to reside with her paramour as his mistress. No affinal bonds of a formal character result from this personal union, which is nevertheless regarded by the Tetum as a form of marriage. **Form.** Polygyny, sometimes of the sororal variety, is practiced, but monogamy is more frequently the custom. **Incest.** Strictly speaking, clansfolk cannot marry among themselves, but in practice only marriage between persons who can trace a kinship connection to the sixth genealogical level is eschewed, and this is considered the depth of a lineage. Examples of marriage between persons of as close as the third degree do occur, however, but infrequently. Exogamy rules also prohibit unions between fellow compound mates, whatever their genealogical distance, and this proscription is rarely violated. Cross-cousin marriage (MoBrDa or FaSiDa) is possible, and the matrilateral relative is in fact regarded as an especially desirable potential spouse. **Residence.** For male Ego, the postmarital residence is ideally patrilocal. **Domestic unit.** The basic social and economic unit is the household (*ema uma laran*), which, while it may correspond to the nuclear family, need not necessarily do so and more usually includes the household head's unmarried sisters, widowed mother, otherwise unattached female cousins, and other less closely related persons. **Inheritance.** Most of the inheritance devolves upon the deceased man's eldest son, who also holds some prior claim on any political office the dead father may have occupied. The youngest son, however, is the candidate whose claims must initially be considered if his father was the incumbent of any ritual office, and he is the son who inherits the house. No distinction is made otherwise between the real and movable wealth of the deceased, and once the claims of the senior son have been met and the house entrusted to the youngest, the other brothers share the rest of the property more or less equally among themselves. **Divorce.** Divorces and separations are fairly common and are distinguished simply in terms of the period during which the couple remain estranged; the act of leaving a spouse establishes a separation, which, in the event of it continuing for six or more months, serves to break the marriage. Divorce is possible only after an *hafoli* or *habani* union has occurred and is specifically prohibited in the *fetosa-umane* marriage. Bridewealth is never returned, but if it was originally given the children remain with their father; if not, they belong to their mother's descent group and so reside with her. **Secondary marriage.** Although the levirate is not institutionalized, a widow often becomes the mistress of one of her late husband's brothers. The sororate, of which sororal polygyny is a popular modality, is possible, but does not appear to be as frequent among the Tetum as among certain of the other Timorese groups, e.g. the Makassai. **Adoption.** A couple lacking offspring after a few years of married life typically adopt one or more children (especially males) from a family possessing more than its resources can adequately cope with. The child of a clan agnate is preferred. Gifts are presented to the natural parents, but the child is not regarded as having thereby been "purchased." Adoption above the age of about six is rare.

SOCIOPOLITICAL ORGANIZATION. **Political organization.** The largest autochthonous unit of political

effectiveness still functioning in Eastern Timor is the princedom, which until well into the present century formed part of what was traditionally the largest political unit, the kingdom (*rai* or *reino*). This wider unit was governed by a king (*liurai*), to whom the two rulers of each princedom in his kingdom owed fealty. These two rulers or governors, who continue to function in the contemporary native polity, are known respectively as the *macair fukun* and *dato uain*. The ownership of each office pertains to two privileged clans in the princedom. Both clans must be aristocratic and reside in different villages. Under these two governors is the office of headman and the governors of the various descent groups. The *macair fukun/dato uain* jointly preside over meetings of the princedom council and are responsible for executing the decisions of this council, which in another capacity acts as a law court. Neither figure is, however, of a despotic nature, and in the council gatherings as well as informally the princedom elders (especially those holding governorships of aristocratic segments) exercise considerable influence, to the extent that it is they who in effect decide issues of princedom significance (since they have as their political base the ordinary members of the princedom, with whom ultimate authority rests). Within each princedom the village headmen are responsible to the Portuguese administration, represented by an Administrator or a *chefe de posto*, officials with whom contact is maintained through the office of chief (*chefe de suku*). Officially, this latter figure is the princedom governor, but in everyday matters the *macair fukun/dato uain* are the effective heads of this political unit. Like these figures, the *chefe de suku* is elected by the villagers of the princedom, but unlike them, his appointment is subject to administrative approval. His most conspicuous duties involve passing government decrees down to the headmen, ensuring that they are carried out, collecting the annual tax, and organizing the annual census. The chief therefore occupies a position intermediate between two cultural worlds and forms an essential link between them. **Social stratification.** There are three social classes: royalty (*dassi*), aristocrats (*dato*), and commoners (*ema reino* or *ema*). Until the earlier years of the present century a fourth existed, that of the slaves (*ata*). Recruitment is by patrilineal descent; interclass marriages are theoretically proscribed, but in recent years this prohibition has become increasingly lax. Tetum social organization is strongly influenced by the concept of status, and at the root of all social categorizing is the fundamental distinction between aristocrats and commoners upon which the social identity of the individual rests. Royalty is, of course, a more elevated status than that of aristocrats, but it is moribund and its membership is dwindling. Although formal age-grades or age-sets are absent, as a principle of order relative age is a regulatory power of influence, and just as the eldest brother is entitled to the premium share of a father's bequest as well as deference from his age juniors, so, provided other social and ritual matters are equal, elder persons receive privileges and respect from younger individuals. Thus we find that political relations of superordination/subordination between descent groups or individuals are invariably couched in the idiom of relative age. **Social control and justice.** Justice is administered by a council of elders under the chairmanship of the governor of a particular descent group segment. If the matter cannot be decided or if the defendant remains dissatisfied with the court's verdict, it may be taken from a lower to a higher segmentary level. If still unsettled, the affair may progress by segmentary steps to the highest judiciary level which is that of the *chefe de suku's* court. Disputes are nearly always between individuals rather than descent groups; typical delicts include theft, allowing one's domestic livestock to damage a neighbor's garden, insult, and assault. Murder cases are dealt with by the Portuguese administration. Fines are the punishment for all crimes except murder, and the sanctions supporting the payment of a fine are the immediate one of ostracism and the ultimate one of banishment. **Warfare.** Until about 1914 skirmishes between princedoms —caused by the desire to steal buffalo, pigs, and slaves, as well as collect enemy heads—were quite frequent. To facilitate conquest or defense, military alliances, at times cemented by marriages, were often made between princedoms. Cannibalism was unknown in Eastern Timor, unlike headhunting, which was a popular activity whose raison d'être was ritual and social prestige. When peace returned to the warring princedoms, the captured heads were surrendered to the princedom from which their owners had come.

RELIGION. **Religious systems.** Catholic missions have been markedly successful among the Tetum, and the aboriginal religion is decaying rapidly. Nevertheless, many traditional ritual elements survive. The clan, for instance, is regarded by all villagers, whatever their religion, as a totemic group whose totem may be animal or plant and whose members must observe specific food taboos. Myths of origin justify the assignation of the totem and the necessity of observing the taboos. Despite the former importance of animal sacrifices, they never functioned to relate the descent group to its totem, but were instead directed toward ancestral spirits and other spirits believed to inhabit woods, stones, and streams. These were considered powerful enough to influence social and natural events so that, for example, by propitiating the buffalo spirit (which is embodied in stones of a rounded appearance) it was believed that the buffalo herd would continue to maintain itself. **Supernaturals.** Four chief categories of spirits may be isolated: (a) patrilineal ancestor spirits (*nitu*); (b) localized spirits (*rai na'in*), which can house themselves in stones,

animals (especially snakes), and more vaguely defined areas of the natural world such as forests; (c) malevolent spirits (*buan*), which do not identify themselves with any particular object or tract of land but which often dwell in lonely jungle places appearing at night to eat the soul of the unwary traveler; and (d) the souls of evil persons (*swangi*), usually sorcerers, who have died a "bad" death and are racked by a craving to consume the souls of mortals. A descent group's totem, even when an animal, is never considered a spiritual being but a kind of cultural hero who, on one or possibly more specific occasions in human history, appeared to its human relatives but who has since vanished from the social world. **Practitioners.** The specialist who most frequently mediates between the empirical and spiritual worlds is the *matan do'ok* (*matan* = to see; *do'ok* = far), "the one who sees far, into everything," a ritual category which may be translated as "soothsayer" or "medicineman." As a soothsayer, the *matan do'ok* is considered to have the ability to predict events, and in his capacity as medicineman to cure sickness and counter the evil influence of sorcerers and malevolent spirits. Anyone of either sex who has demonstrated to his own and potential clients' satisfaction his skill as a clairvoyant and physician may be regarded as a *matan do'ok*. The *macair lulik* is the chief priest of a princedom. This office is a male preserve which corresponds at the ritual level to the two political governors (*macair fukun/dato uain*). The *macair lulik's* main duty is ensuring good relations between the villagers and important princedom spirits, and to this end he performs sacrifices on behalf of the villagers. These sacrifices are most frequently made on the occasions of planting and harvesting, although the office has no function in relation to allocation or management of agricultural land. **Ceremonies.** The inhabitants of a princedom enact certain rites at the beginning of both maize and rice planting and again before the commencement of the rice harvest. At the request of villagers, rainmaking rites are conducted at irregular intervals by the *macair lulik*. In traditional times a complex of rituals attended the waging of war between rival princedoms. Before, during, and after the warriors campaigned, for example, the *macair lulik* conducted rites whose purpose was to ensure their safety, enable them to collect many enemy heads, and steal a plentiful supply of livestock from the enemy's herds. During their warriors' absence, the rest of the community had to observe certain ritual practices and respect specified taboos such as abstaining from sexual intercourse and eschewing the meat of certain animals. **Soul, death, and afterlife.** Everyone is believed to possess a soul (*bian*), which after death eventually dwells in the land of souls located somewhere in the jungle. Such a dead soul (*mate bian*) inhabits a world which to most informants who have a view on the matter appears to be located underground.

Beliefs concerning life after death are, however, vaguely formulated and unclear and are topics about which the Tetum rarely speculate. Formerly the coffin containing the corpse was placed in a tree, and some years later—in any case rarely more than seven—the bones were washed and reburied in the ground. Today the Administration requires that all corpses be encoffined and buried permanently.

BIBLIOGRAPHY. Capell 1943-45; Correia 1935, 1943; Das Dores 1907; Duarte 1964; Fernandes 1937; Forbes 1884, 1885; Hicks 1967; Mendes 1935; Ormeling 1956; Sa 1961; R. da Silva n.d.; S. da Silva 1889.

ATONI

Synonyms. *Dawan, Orang Gunung, Rawan, Timoreesch, Timoreezen, Timorese*

ORIENTATION. **Location and identification.** Atoni ("people," "men," short for Atoin Pah Meto, "people of the dry land") are the predominant population of most of Indonesian Timor. They inhabit the interior hills and mountain slopes throughout the central and western portions of the island, exclusive of the Belu districts (mostly Tetum, Buna', and Kemak peoples) and Kupang town with the adjacent island of Semau (mostly Helong and Rotinese immigrants). When first contacted by Europeans, the Atoni were divided into numerous small princedoms or domains, each independent and at war with the others. Linguistically and culturally, however, they recognize themselves as one people. The Atoni are called Dawan (Rawan) by Tetum and Buna' speakers; Indonesian-speaking lowlanders call them *orang gunung* ("mountain people") or *orang* Timor (i.e. Timorese; Dutch, Timoreezen or Timoreesch). The physical type throughout Timor is mixed; the Papuan or Melanesoid element is, however, most noticeable in the western part of the island among the Atoni, according to Mendes Correa (1944). Ormeling (1956) regards the Atoni as representative of an autochthonous population forced into less desirable areas by incursions of Belunese (principally Tetum) and Rotinese peoples. [Cunningham 1967a.] **Geography.** The landscape is one of hills and mountains, with deeply-cut river valleys. At lower altitudes much of the primary rain forest has been reduced to savannas or grasslands. The climate is dominated by two seasons—one of torrential rains, the other of nearly complete drought. Soils in general are poor and thin. [Ormeling 1956.] **Linguistic affiliation.** A Malayo-Polynesian language (Capell 1943-45); included by Esser (1938) in his Ambon-Timor group. **Demography.** Approximately 300,000 (Cunningham 1967a: 63). **History and cultural relations.** The sandalwood and beeswax of Timor attracted traders from Java and Malaya long before European contact, and indigenous princedoms are mentioned in early Chinese accounts. The extent to which the Atoni may have been in contact with ancient Hindu-Javanese cultural centers is unknown; political and religious forms do, however, seem to reflect considerable Hindu influence. Myths collected by Middelkoop (1938) attribute Atoni knowledge of rice and maize to a Belu invasion and the subsequent establishment by Belu princes of the kingdom of Sonbai in western Timor (cited in Ormeling 1956). The Dutch won control of western Timor from the Portuguese in the seventeenth century but did not effectively penetrate the interior until about 1910. Christianity and mission schools have been present for some 50 years, although less than one half of the Atoni are church members—and relatively few received the schooling necessary to enter the civil service. The Dutch signed contracts with native princes and adopted a policy of indirect rule. The present Indonesian government has made few changes in the prewar political structure, although they have weakened the power of native rulers in conformity with a long-range policy of centralized government administration. [Cunningham 1965, 1967a.]

SETTLEMENT PATTERN AND HOUSING. **Settlement pattern.** Hamlets, i.e. discrete groups of houses, are found along ridges and slopes. These are grouped into named hamlet clusters, several of which in turn form an administrative "village" containing anywhere from 50 to 200 households. The hamlet cluster is, however, the basic social unit in indigenous Atoni society. A village may contain a church and/or a school. In addition, Ormeling (1956) mentions the *lopo*, a "combination reception room, store house and work place" used for village festivals, but it is unclear whether this is an indigenous institution. [Cunningham 1966: 13; 1967a.] **Housing.** The house (*ume*), inhabited by a nuclear family, is the basic residential, economic, and ritual unit. Houses are characteristically of beehive shape, with high conical roofs which extend downward almost to the ground. Cunningham (1964) discusses the symbolism of parts of the house and the arrangement of space within the house in terms of cosmological beliefs and the concept of complementary dualism.

ECONOMY. Traditionally a subsistence economy based on agriculture. A few products such as vegetables, cattle, baskets, and palm wine are sold in local markets for cash, buyers being principally Chinese and Savunese. **Agriculture.** Swiddening, with maize the staple crop, although dry rice is also important. Some irrigated rice has been grown in river valleys in recent years. Piper betel, areca nut, bananas, and coconut are grown in household gardens. [Cunningham 1967a; Ormeling 1956.] **Domestic animals.** Chickens, pigs, and cattle are used primarily for slaughter at feasts and for bridewealth. Cattle, recently introduced, have largely replaced water buffalo in economic and ritual importance. **Industries.** Weaving and basketry mainly. There is no stone or metal work, although silver and gold ornaments, made by Ndaonese, are highly valued. **Property.** Village headmen nowadays control to some extent the allotment of village agricultural lands, although land in the past appears to have been within the control of certain lineages. The autonomy of lineages with respect to land has been weakened, however, by successive claims of Atoni rulers. Orchards, cattle, and heirloom ritual wealth may fall within a class of inherited lineage property, the management of which is normally established by primogeniture within the male line. To diminish a lineage estate through alienation or poor management angers the ancestors, who may retaliate by diminishing the offspring of the group. [Cunningham 1967a.]

MARRIAGE AND FAMILY. **Mode.** Payment of bride-price (cattle, coral beads, silver, and money) by the husband's lineage and a reciprocal gift of cloth and rice by the wife's lineage. Variations in rules governing bride-price payments serve to define the lineage membership of offspring as well as the status of the wife vis-à-vis her natal lineage. [Cunningham 1967a.] **Marriage rules.** The patrilineage is exogamous, although not so with respect to "male" and "female" branches. Marriage with a MoBrDa (or any girl of equal generation in that lineage) is prescribed. Direct exchange between two lineages with established affinal ties is highly valued, and bride-price payments are considerably lower in such cases, e.g. marriage between "male" and "female" branches of the same lineage. Wife-givers are superordinate to wife-takers in a variety of ritual and everyday occasions. [Cunningham 1966, 1967a.] **Residence.** A few years' bride service and matrilocal residence followed by a return to the man's hamlet is the ideal, although exceptions do occur (Cunningham 1967a). **Domestic unit.** Nuclear family.

KIN GROUPS. **Descent.** Descent groups (lineages) are conceptually patrilineal, but recruitment is ambilineal (Cunningham 1967b: 10). Normally, a child's membership in the father's lineage is established upon payment of a specific part of the bride-price; the mother's patrilineal lineage may, however, claim an offspring of her marriage as part of the bridewealth (Cunningham 1967a: 76-77). **Kin groups.** Localized patrilineages three to four generations in depth are the basic corporate and ritual units, and the essential units in payment of bride-price. Maximal nonlocalized lineages carry the same names as minimal lineages, but kin ties are fictive or untraceable; such groups have few functions although they do recognize maximal lineage exogamy. Among most Atoni, a wife is accepted ritually into her husband's lineage but retains certain rights with respect to her natal lineage. Lineages may consist of "male" and "female" branches

(persons recruited to lineage membership through fathers or mothers, respectively); the branches may intermarry, although the lineage as a whole is exogamous. Affinal ties between pairs of lineages are highly valued, and the degree to which a lineage can invoke such ties on festive occasions reflects its wealth and brings it prestige. [Cunningham 1966, 1967a.] **Kin terminology.** The Atoni have a Dravidian-type kinship terminology (Cunningham 1967b: 1).

SOCIOPOLITICAL ORGANIZATION. **Political organization.** Modern Indonesian Timor is divided into four administrative districts, each under an Indonesian civil servant. Within these districts are ten "self-governing territories" (*swapradja*, the former indigenous princedoms), each headed by a prince (*radja*) from a traditional ruling house. Subterritories (*kefettoran*) are headed by fettors, also members of ruling clans. Headmen, *temukung*, are responsible for administrative "villages" made up of hamlet clusters—the basic indigenous social unit. Localized lineages are categorized as "hamlet masters," i.e. those whose ancestors first settled the area, and "marrying people," those whose ancestors subsequently married into the local group. The former, as "masters of the soil," hold major rights to land and trees, and recruitment to political office is mainly from these lineages (Cunningham 1966: 14). ● The sociopolitical structure of traditional Atoni princedoms was characterized by a "star" pattern with respect to geographical layout and distribution of authority, i.e. four secular units surrounding and opposed to a central sacral unit—a concept found in neighboring parts of Indonesia (cf. Schulte Nordholt 1966). According to Cunningham (1965) this is another expression of the principle of "complementary dualism" within Atoni culture and is presumably attributable to early Hindu influence. **Social stratification.** Lineages are classed as noble, commoner, and (formerly) slave. The former are those presently or formerly acknowledged as rulers within a princedom. Great deference is paid to members of ruling clans, and villagers still make fields for respected rulers. Although Atoni princes did not traditionally control land, they did receive tribute, in return for which they conducted certain rituals. Much of the wealth of rulers must, according to adat, be expended in the sponsorship of great ceremonies. [Cunningham 1967a.] **Social control and justice.** The village headman collects taxes, allots land, maintains order, and acts as local magistrate—duties which traditionally were handled by warrior leaders, tribute gatherers, priests, and other functionaries. Cases may be appealed to the fettor (subdistrict level) or, rarely, to the radja. Assisting the headman are two functionaries chosen with the consent of the people and representing a traditional division of authority with respect to "internal" and "external" affairs—a dualistic pattern repeated elsewhere in Atoni culture in concepts of "secular" and "sacred" or of radja and fettor (Cunningham 1967a: 87). **Warfare.** Warfare between princedoms was formerly endemic. Boys prepared as warriors with training contests and initiation rites, and there is still prestige in claiming descent from a warrior line (Cunningham 1967a). Van Wouden (1935: 125-34) concluded that paired princedoms or segments thereof may have practiced mutual head-hunting, and interpreted this as another aspect of a pervasive pattern of complementary dualism (cited in Downs 1955: 57).

RELIGION. Protestant and Catholic missions have been active in Indonesian Timor since about 1910, but fewer than 50 percent of Atoni are church members, and traditional beliefs and rituals are still practiced. Atoni religion was associated with a world view based in part on ancient Hindu cosmology, e.g. dualistic concepts expressed in sociopolitical structure and symbolized and supported in myth and ritual. Belief in a Lord of the Upper World, lesser spirits, and ancestor spirits (*nitu*) is expressed in sacrificial rites conducted by officials on behalf of a princedom. Diviners or medicinemen (*mnane, meo*) discover the cause of specific misfortunes and treat illnesses caused by sorcery or the displeasure of spirits. Ancestors are propitiated at life cycle ceremonies by householders according to the ritual (*nono*) prescribed within particular lineages. Individuals may also acquire specific food taboos or protective animal spirits through dreams. [Cunningham 1967a.]

BIBLIOGRAPHY. Capell 1943-45; Cunningham 1964, 1965, 1966, 1967a, 1967b; Downs 1955; Esser 1938; Grijzen 1904; Kruyt 1923a; Mendes Correa 1944; Middelkoop 1938; Ormeling 1956; Schulte Nordholt 1966; van Wouden 1935.

HELONG*

Synonyms. *Helonese, Kupangese, Orang Semau*

ORIENTATION. **Identification and location.** The Helong are the remnants of a cultural group generally regarded as having once inhabited the whole of southwestern Timor. In the early seventeenth century, the Helong controlled only a small coastal stretch at the western tip of Timor. Pressed by the expansion of the native Atoni states, a Helong ruler (the "prince" or "king" of Kupang) sought an alliance with the Dutch, who eventually, in 1653, took possession of Kupang. Despite this alliance, a majority of

Helong subsequently migrated to the offshore island of Semau. Dutch-supported migration of Rotinese to Kupang and later to Semau further affected the Helong, and at present they are confined to one village, near the port of Tenau, on Timor, and to several villages on Semau. **Demography.** A Dutch administrative memoir for 1949 is reported (Ormeling 1956: 69) to have estimated the Helong population at 5,000, but this may have considered the entire population of Semau as Helong. A more conservative estimate might set the figure somewhat lower. **Linguistic affiliation.** Capell (1943-45) classifies Helong as an Indonesian language of the West Timor group. Lexically and syntactically, it is most closely related to Rotinese and Timorese (Atoni).

ECONOMY. Subsistence is dependent on the dry-field (*klapa*) cultivation of rice (*ale*) and maize (*ngae*). Offshore fishing is of considerable importance. The extent of lontar tapping, under Rotinese influence, is unknown.

KINSHIP AND MARRIAGE. The Helong are divided among numerous, perhaps as many as 45, name or descent groups (*ngala:* "name," "kind," "descent group"), and traditional rule was complementarily distributed between a radja (*laih*) and a fettor. Since van Hogendorp's report of 1773, most commentators mention the close association of the Helong radja with the crocodile, to whom young girls were supposedly offered. Transformations of the myth on which this legend is based are found among the Rotinese, Atoni, and southern Belu (cf. Jonker 1905: 430-36; Schulte Nordholt 1966: 156-58). Kinship terminology distinguishes Fa and FaBr from MoBr. The latter is equated with FaSiHu, HuFa, and WiFa; Mo and MoSi are distinguished from FaSi, who is equated with MoBrWi, HuMo, and WiMo. Such equations and distinctions might suggest symmetrical exchange marriage, but according to one informant, direct exchange is not desired, and when it occurs is attributed to Rotinese influence. There is no prescribed marriage, but there does exist a preference for MoBrDa/FaSiSo marriage. Since parallel and cross cousins are apparently not distinguished from Br and Si, the terminology ought to be considered separately from these stated marriage preferences. Of more significance, perhaps, is the degree to which the categories of elder and younger are consistently applied among kin in Ego's generation and in the first ascending generation.

BIBLIOGRAPHY. Capell 1943-45; Fox n.d.; van Hogendorp 1781-84; Jonker 1904, 1905; Ormeling 1956; Schulte Nordholt 1966.

---

* This account, written by James J. Fox, is based on published references to the Helong and is supplemented by information gathered from Helong in Kupang (1966).

ROTINESE*

Synonyms. *Atahori Rote, Hataholi Lote*

ORIENTATION. **Identification.** The Rotinese have long taken their name from some version of their island's name and combined this with a dialect word for "man" (Atahori Rote, Hataholi Lote). The principal name for Roti in ritual language is "Lote do Kale," and the expression for "man," "Hataholi do Dae Hena." The Rotinese insist that Rote or Roti is a Portuguese imposition. [Fox 1969.] By ancient tradition, the population is divided into two territorial divisions, Lamak-anan for the eastern half of the island, which is also known simply as "Sunrise," and Henak-anan for the western half, also known as "Sunset." Whether formerly these had political or other significance is difficult to ascertain. This dual classification now serves to characterize customary, dialect, and topographic differences between the east and the west. Within these divisions, the island is subdivided into 18 autonomous states, each ruled by its own "Lord." These domains are the maximal native political units. Each domain cultivates its own distinctive variation of dress, speech, and customary law. The Rotinese tend to be of short stature, of light build, and of Malay appearance. They are characteristically identified by their broad, sombrero-like, leaf hats. **Location.** Roti, off the southwestern tip of Timor, is the southernmost island of the Indonesian archipelago. The Rotinese have migrated in large numbers to the northeastern plains of Timor, to Kupang, and to the island of Semau. There they work as rice growers, lontar tappers, retailers, and, in Kupang, as civil servants (Ormeling 1956: 142-51). Small populations of Rotinese are also found on Sumba and Flores. **Geography.** The island consists of level areas of cultivation, bare rolling hills, palm or acacia savannas, and occasional patches of secondary forest. The east monsoon (April to October) brings a dry season of gusty, hot winds. The west monsoon, which brings a sporadic rain, is irregular; it may begin between November and January and it continues until April. **Linguistic affiliation.** Rotinese, according to Jonker (1915: Intro. XII), shows closest affinities with the Belu (Tetum) languages, Galoli, Timorese (Atoni), and Kupangese; and more distant affinities with the languages of Kisar, Leti, Moa, and Roma. Each of Roti's 18 domains cultivates its own manner of speech, and Jonker (1908, 1913), following Manafe (1889), distinguishes nine mutually intelligible dialects. One, that of the central domain of Termanu, has gained some prominence as a lingua franca. The Rotinese in addition possess a form of ritual, poetic, or high language which crosscuts dialect boundaries. **Demography.** Census figures for 1961 record a population of just over 70,500. There are probably another 30,000 Rotinese on Timor and Semau. Chinese merchants and Indonesia government officials live in the town of Baä. Roti has traditionally assimilated the excess population from the tiny island of Ndao. **History and cultural relations.** The Rotinese claim to have migrated from the north in separate groups by way of Timor. They also possess a tradition of accepting client-strangers from other islands. Each domain has its own traditional narratives associated with its ruling dynasty (Fox 1970a). Portuguese Dominicans established a mission on the island (then known as Savu Pequeno) in the late sixteenth century, but by 1662, the Dutch East India Company had signed treaties of contract with 12 of the domains of present-day Roti (Fox 1970a). The domains were recognized as autonomous states until the twentieth century. Since Independence, the Republic of Indonesia has recognized the 18 domains within an administrative structure of 4 districts (*ketjamatan*). The existence of an extensive school system in the nineteenth century gave the population an educational advantage in eastern Indonesia; it also stimulated emigration, and Rotinese now participate at all levels of Indonesian national life.

SETTLEMENT PATTERN AND HOUSING. **Settlement pattern.** Traditions assert that before the formation of domains, each clan group (or ancestor) held its own territory in the vicinity of some defensible walled redoubt. After the formation of the domains, these clans were assigned positions in the defense of the walled fortifications of their lords. With the establishment of peace under the Dutch, settlement became scattered. For administrative purposes, the Dutch attempted to recognize villages or village areas (now identified by a church or local school), but houses nowadays are dispersed individually and in small clusters wherever there is sufficient fresh water for drinking and gardening. **Housing.** The house, center of Rotinese life, is a rectangular structure with gabled ends and a thatched roof which extends nearly to the ground. The house proper, divided into a male and female half, is raised on posts beneath the roof. The roof also envelops a ground floor area with resting platforms where guests are received. Cooking is most often done in an adjacent thatched structure.

ECONOMY. A large proportion of Rotinese subsistence is derived from tapping and cooking to a syrup the juice of the lontar palm (*Borassus flabellifer* Linn). This syrup, mixed with water, provides the normal daily sustenance of most Rotinese. Solid food stuffs, especially rice and millet, are eaten sparingly and usually saved for feasting, when they are con-

---

* This account, written by James J. Fox, is based on fieldwork done on the island of Roti in 1965 and 1966. This research was supported by the National Institute of Mental Health and was conducted in Indonesia under the auspices of the Lembaga Ilmu Pengatahuan Indonesia.

sumed in great quantities with boiled meat. Some syrup is processed into thin square cakes of crystallized sugar. Syrup is also fermented to make a dark beer, which may be distilled to a fine sweet gin. **Agriculture.** Rice is the prestige food, but maize, millet, sorghum, a variety of tubers, various kinds of peas, green grams and beans, peanuts, squash, sesame, onions, garlic, and several kinds of cucumber are grown in dry fields and also in household gardens fertilized with animal manures. The principal fruit trees are the banana, papaya, breadfruit, nangka, djeruk, mango, and coconut. The Rotinese also grow tobacco, cotton, betel (the fruit rather than the leaves of the plant are preferred for chewing), and areca palms. ● In a dry region with an irregular monsoon, the Rotinese are remarkably capable wet-rice cultivators, who divert rivers and streams and utilize natural springs to water their fields. Although rice plots are individually owned, planted, and harvested, wet-rice fields are organized into corporate complexes whose members maintain a common fence and who appoint individuals to apportion water. Within the past hundred years, wet rice and maize have predominated over, but not entirely replaced, dry rice, millet, and sorghum. Dry fields are usually cleared by burning in November. Wet-rice fields are worked by driving herds of water buffalo through them after rain has softened the earth; other fields are worked with steel digging sticks and hoes. **Fishing, hunting, and gathering.** Fishing is a common daily occupation in the dry season. Offshore stone weirs trap fish as the tide recedes, and rivers yield a variety of small shrimp and eel. Women fish with scoop nets; men with spears or cast nets. Basket traps, poison, and hook and line are used to a lesser extent. Hunting is confined to small birds, a few remaining deer, and an occasional domestic pig gone wild. Honey, mushrooms, seaweed, and agar-agar are gathered to supplement the diet. **Domestic animals.** The Rotinese have herds of horses, water buffalo, sheep, and goats and most households have dogs, cats, pigs, and chickens. **Industrial arts.** Weaving of tie and dye cloths and basketry are the major domestic arts. Pottery, made in only a few areas with suitable clay, is traded throughout the island. Wandering Ndaonese goldsmiths attach themselves briefly to wealthy households for whom they work gold and silver jewelry. **Trade.** Trading is done mainly with Chinese and Muslims resident on the island. Animals and foodstuffs are traded for broadcloth, cotton thread, kerosene, tobacco, and areca nuts. Apart from native pots, occasional flintlocks, and betel, the Rotinese trade little among themselves. Interisland trade with Kupang on Timor is important. **Property.** Clans "own" water and possess the right to appoint a ritual head over the corporation of individuals who hold plots of land irrigated by that water. Land, trees, and animals are the property of individual households.

Native cloths, gold and silver jewelry, ancient *muti-salah* beads, and old weapons are the chief forms of movable wealth.

KIN GROUPS. **Descent.** Descent is ideally "patrilineal" and is, in fact, based on a system of inherited, altering names. Since these "hard names," no matter from whom they are inherited, are associated with the masculine aspect of the person, descent groups are conceived of as symbolically "male." If bridewealth has been paid, the child of the marriage belongs to his father's group and takes a part of his "hard name" from that of his father. This is the statistically overwhelming form of lineage ascription and name inheritance on Roti. The child of a woman for whom no bridewealth has been paid belongs necessarily to his or her mother's group and acquires a part of the mother's "hard name." Although not exclusively "patrilineal," there is no personally "optative" element in Rotinese lineage ascription. **Kin groups.** Each domain is comprised of a number of named clans (*leo*) which constitute its political units. Clans are divided into named lineages (*teik*) and these in turn into smaller "birth groups" (*bobongik*), and finally individual households (*uma*). Neither clans nor lineages are localized, though "birth groups" tend to cluster in the same general village area. **Kin terminology.** The Rotinese kin terminology has several levels of articulation. Fa and FaBr are distinguished from MoBr; Mo and MoSi are distinguished from FaSi. Same sex siblings and parallel cousins are classified according to relative age; opposite sex cross cousins are distinguished from parallel cousins. There is a special relationship, marked in the terminology, between MoBr and SiCh.

MARRIAGE AND FAMILY. **Mode.** The Rotinese recognize three levels of marriage depending upon (1) the amount of bridewealth given for the girl (2) the reciprocal prestations on the part of the girl's family (3) the amount of ceremony and feasting accompanying the marriage, and formerly (4) the length of bride service performed by the groom. Bridewealth may be paid in gold, in old silver rupiah, in water buffalo, or in sheep and goats; there exists a fixed conversion rate among these different forms of wealth. **Form.** Polygyny is permitted and is the ideal of the rich and the noble. **Extension of incest taboos.** Rotinese clans are not exogamous, although lineages are. Marriage is prohibited between siblings and close parallel cousins; more distant parallel cousins are, however, potential marriage partners. Marriage is preferred but in no way prescribed between cross cousins, the stated preference being for marriage with the MoBrDa. In Thie and Loleh, there exists a moiety system which partially regulates marriage. **Residence.** The youngest son inherits the paternal house and brings his wife there to live. All elder sons must establish a new residence before or shortly after marriage, usually in the same village area but never too close to the paternal house. **Domestic unit.** Elder sons and all daughters leave at marriage, but the youngest son resides with his parents after marriage. **Inheritance.** The eldest son inherits the right to represent his father in affinal ceremonies and inherits all affinal prestations; the youngest son inherits the house. Other wealth is divided equally among all sons. A daughter (or daughters) may inherit only when the household lacks a male heir. **Divorce.** Divorce is relatively easy, but permission must be obtained from the Lord's court. **Secondary marriage and adoption.** Levirate, sororate, and adoption are extremely rare.

SOCIOPOLITICAL ORGANIZATION. Each domain is ruled by a "male" Lord (*manek*), a complementary and executant "female" Lord (fettor), and a number of court lords chosen, ideally, from each of the clans of the domain. In every domain, one court lord is Head of the Earth (*dae langak*). He is the acknowledged upholder of customary law and has the right, in certain instances, to abrogate the Lord's decision. His clan claims settlement priority and ritual rights over the land. Nobility is associated with the clans of the "male" and "female" Lords; all others in a domain are commoners. The wealthy are frequently described as forming a separate class, but it is theoretically and, in fact, practically impossible for a wealthy commoner to become a noble. A former slave class has been absorbed within the other social categories. **Social control and warfare.** Means of settling disputes exist within the lineage and the clan and at the Lord's court. There exists no traditional means of settling disputes between domains, and in the past such disputes led to warfare. Since approximately 1850, domain warfare has given way to a pattern of lesser feuding and some raiding across borders which persists to this day. Headhunting may have been ritually associated with agricultural fertility but, as an institution, it appears to have been eliminated or transformed, perhaps as early as the eighteenth century.

RELIGION. **Religious systems.** Christianity has been preached on Roti since 1600 and has long been associated with some knowledge of Malay. Into the twentieth century less than one fifth of the population were baptized Christians, but wholesale conversion followed a national literacy campaign and government certification of its success. **Supernaturals.** Traditional religious practice centers on ancestral spirits and their opposites, malevolent spirits associated with the bush. Lontar-leaf representations of the ancestors are hung within the house, which itself can be regarded as a shrine to the ancestors (Fox 1970b). **Practitioners.**

There is no class of priests, although there exist men who are regarded as chanters and who recite long ritual poems at major feasts. Any man may offer to the spirits. A mother's brother must perform all life-cycle rituals for his sister's children. **Ceremonies.** Major ceremonies are concerned with marriage, house building, and death. Minor ceremonies occur in the seventh month of the first pregnancy, at hair-cutting, baptism, naming, whenever human blood has been shed, at specific times during the agricultural and palm-tapping year, and at the time of illness and on the recovery from illness. An annual ritual, *hus*, marking the end of one year and the beginning of another, has been abandoned in all domains except Thie and Dengka. In the *hus* cycle each clan that possessed ceremonial rights performed its own rituals according to a prescribed sequence of celebration. These separate feasts were attended by members of the other clans. The cycle ran for several weeks in August, September, or October, depending upon the domain and the number of its participating clans. Each *hus* involved ancestral invocations and requests for animal and plant fertility. Rituals also included horse racing, dancing, mock battles, and animal sacrifices. In the cycle there was usually one clan that performed rain rituals on a hilltop. **Illness and medicine.** Native curers, who use a variety of (secret) native medicines, have diminished in number. Formerly, for serious illness, a small feast was held to make special offerings to the spirits. Now Christians gather at these feasts to pray for the sick. **Soul, death, and afterlife.** The souls of those who have died a violent death are separated from other ancestral souls and become malevolent spirits who wander the earth. Funeral practices are the most elaborate of the Rotinese rituals. The deceased's mother's brother and mother's mother's brother, or their direct descendants, prepare the coffin and dig the grave. Dog sacrifice may accompany the making of the coffin, called the ship of the dead. There exist numerous formal ritual chants in praise of the dead. Burial is usually on the third day after death; feasts are given on this day, the seventh, ninth, and fortieth day, and further commemorative feasts may be given a year or even three years later. There are no secondary burial rites involving the exhumation of the corpse. The mother's brother "cools" or purifies the close mourners on the day following burial and releases them from their expected fast.

BIBLIOGRAPHY. De Clercq 1874; Fox 1965, 1968, 1969, 1970a, 1971; Graafland 1889; Heijmering 1842-43; Jonker 1905, 1908, 1911, 1913, 1915; Kruyt 1921; Manafe 1889; Niks 1888a, 1891; Ormeling 1956; van de Wetering 1922, 1923a, 1923b, 1925; Wichmann 1892. [See also the comprehensive bibliography in Fox 1968: 378-89.]

NDAONESE*

Synonym. *Ndau Ndau*

ORIENTATION. Ndao is an island with a habitable area of 9 sq. km. at a distance of approximately 12 km. from the west coast of Roti. Between Ndao and Roti is an even smaller island, Nuse, which also has a small Ndaonese settlement. The people refer to themselves as Ndau Ndau, from Ndau (Savunese: Dou), the term for man, combined with the island name. In 1961, the island had a population of 2,156 persons, giving it an official population density of nearly 240 per sq. km. The soil is poor, and the land is bare and given over largely to coconut palms. Despite a considerable lexical borrowing from Western Rotinese, Ndaonese is syntactically closely related to Savunese. Jonker (1903) provisionally classified the language as a dialect of Savunese. In dress (the Ndaonese have adopted the distinctive Rotinese lontar hat), in song, and in the motifs of the native *ikats* (dyed cloths), Rotinese influence is marked. Many Ndaonese of both sexes speak Rotinese. Most Ndaonese men are, however, multilingual. Since a treaty with the Dutch East India Company in 1756, Ndao has been recognized as an autonomous domain of Roti with its own Lord and fettor. Traditionally, Roti has assimilated the surplus population of Ndao.

ECONOMY. The men of Ndao are gold- and silversmiths who travel throughout the Timor Archipelago. On Roti and elsewhere, in addition to jewelry, the Ndaonese may sell or exchange native *ikat* cloth or take orders for the preparation of this cloth by the following dry season; men also sell pandanus mats, a further product of female labor. The island supports only a limited amount of house garden agriculture; the chief domesticated animals are pigs, chickens, and dogs. By a decision of a former Lord and his council, the island was thickly planted with coconut palms, and copra and coconut oil have become major exports. When the Ndaonese settle on Roti, they tend to become lontar tappers like the majority of Rotinese.

KIN GROUPS AND MARRIAGE. Descent is said to be "patrilineal." All descent groups are divided between the moiety of the Lord, *loasana*, and that of the fettor, *apulugi*. A stated rule is that *loasana* must exchange women with *apulugi*. There is, however, a single descent group, *lodo*, which belongs outside the moieties and hence is free to exchange with either moiety. [As a model, this system is virtually identical to the moiety system found in the domains of the Thie and Loleh of south-central Roti.] Lexically, the Ndaonese terminology appears to be an amalgam of

terms recognizable as cognates of Rotinese and Savunese relationship terms. Fa and FaBr are distinguished from MoBr, who is equated with FaSiHu and also HuFa and WiFa; Mo and MoSi are distinguished from FaSi, who is equated with MoBrWi and also HuMo and WiMo. This would accord with a two-section system of exchange marriage. Yet there appears to be no terminological distinction between cross and parallel cousins. Marriage is effected by the payment of bridewealth, which, by tradition, should be in the form of gold. The descent groups of both moieties are divided into two classes (the greater class: *loasana a'i* and *apulugi a'i*; the lesser class: *loasana iki* and *apulugi iki*) according to the amount of bridewealth they may demand for their women.

BIBLIOGRAPHY. Jonker 1903; Ormeling 1956.

SOUTHERN MOLUCCAS

THAT PART of eastern Indonesia lying between Timor and New Guinea is herein, following Kennedy (1942: 26), treated separately under the heading Southern Moluccas. It includes, from west to east, the following island groups: Wetar, Kisar, Leti (including Moa and Lakor), Luang-Sermata, Roma, Damar, Teun-Nila-Serua, Babar (including Wetan, Masela, Dawera, and Dai), Tanimbar, Kei, and Aru. Most of these groups are in turn comprised of numerous small islands, e.g. 66 in the Tanimbar group. The total land area of some 10,000 square miles is mostly hilly to mountainous and in part of volcanic origin, although in a few cases, such as Aru, lowland swamps and marshlands cover major portions of the island's surface. The native population probably does not much exceed the 125,000 estimate by Kennedy (1942: 26). The inhabitants of Tanimbar, Kei, and Aru in each case number in the tens of thousands; but of the remaining islands only Kisar, Leti, and Babar have sizable populations—8,300, 6,000, and 5,900, respectively, according to the 1930 Dutch census. Racially, the South Moluccan islanders are of mixed proto-Malay and Papuan stock, with Papuan features more noticeable in the east near New Guinea, e.g. on Tanimbar and Aru, and becoming less evident farther west, e.g. on Kisar and Leti. The South Moluccan languages are all classed by Esser (1938) within his Ambon-Timor group of Malayo-Polynesian. The area was long noted for the fierce qualities of its native inhabitants, with frequent reports of hostility to

---

* This account, written by James J. Fox, is based upon information gathered from Ndaonese on Roti and Timor.

outsiders and a propensity for headhunting and (in some instances) cannibalism. This part of Indonesia is for the most part isolated from the main currents of contemporary social change, and a few of the islands are still almost completely pagan (although Christianity has made inroads, notably on Kisar, Leti, and Tanimbar). Coastal Islamic communities also exist on most of the islands. Virtually no intensive fieldwork has been done in this area, and the ethnographic literature for the most part remains spotty and unsystematized (cf. Nutz 1959). In this regard, the Southern Moluccas remain among the least known regions in all of Indonesia. • There are evident cultural and historical affinities with New Guinea to the east, the Central Moluccas to the north, and Timor to the west. In addition, Macassarese and Buginese traders were long active throughout the Moluccas, and the Dutch early penetrated the area in the interest of maintaining their monopoly of the spice trade. The Southern Moluccas area is thus racially and culturally mixed, and this fact, coupled with the scant ethnographic literature, render hazardous any attempt to classify the region within a wider cultural sphere. Likewise, attempts to classify into smaller cultural subunits are fraught with problems. The present volume has therefore not attempted the former procedure and has restricted subclassification to a minimum. The term "Southwestern Islands," as used herein, groups together all of the South Moluccan islands exclusive of Kei, Tanimbar, and Aru. The term has been used previously in this sense for some purposes, e.g. the designation of adat or native law areas (cf. ter Haar 1948: 9, end maps), although at other times (e.g. Kennedy 1955a) it has been restricted to mean Wetar, Kisar, Leti, Roma, and Damar as opposed to Babar, Nila, Teun, and Serua (the Southeastern Islands). In still another usage, Kei, Aru, and Tanimbar have been designated as "southeastern" and all the others as "southwestern" (cf. Kennedy 1937: 270). The classificatory utility of these finer distinctions, given the relatively little that is known about these islanders and their cultures, is doubtful at best.

BIBLIOGRAPHY. Esser 1938; ter Haar 1948; Kennedy 1937, 1942, 1955a; Nutz 1959.

SOUTHWESTERN ISLANDS

ORIENTATION. The Southwestern Islands, off the northeast coast of Timor, can be divided into two main archipelagoes, viz. a northern arch (Roma, Damar, Nila, Teun, and Serua), generally volcanic and densely wooded, and a southern arch (Wetar, Kisar, Leti, Luang-Sermata, and Babar), in general less fertile, with savannalike landscapes. The inclusion of these island groups under a single heading is in part a reflection of history and geography, i.e. their location southwest of Banda, formerly a center of the important Moluccan spice trade. A collective treatment is, however, additionally warranted on grounds of rather pronounced cultural similarities (Scholz 1962: 100) and the fact that the peoples of all these islands have traditions of a common cultural home on Luang, in approximately the geographic center of the area (Sneeuwjagt 1935: 35-39). To protect the lucrative spice trade centered on Banda, the Dutch occupied the Southwestern Islands as early as the seventeenth century, but since the late 1800s the islands have been oriented toward Ambon, the Protestant missionary and government administrative center for the entire Moluccan area (Holleman 1943: 382-83).

SETTLEMENT PATTERN AND HOUSING. Concentrated settlement in fortified hilltop villages divided into clan wards or sections. Frequently a communal ritual or council house, in front of which stands a large wooden image representing the ancestral village founder. Due to Dutch encouragement of dispersed settlement in more accessible locations, this pattern has disappeared in many areas, and with it the large, raised multifamily houses, replaced almost everywhere by single-family dwellings. [Sneeuwjagt 1935: 58-64.]

ECONOMY. Cultivation of the staple, maize, on swiddens, together with rice, sweet potatoes, cassava, cucurbits, and millet. Sago is used as food on some islands, notably Kisar, Babar, Roma, and Damar. Bananas, coconuts, and breadfruit are important in the Roma-Damar group. [Sneeuwjagt 1935: 73-98.] The importance of wild honey and of beeswax as items of exchange on Wetar is mentioned by de Josselin de Jong (1947: 30), who also thinks that on that island the traditional staples may have been tubers and sago, with rice and maize the ceremonial foods.

KIN GROUPS. Descent. Variable. Some islands are patrilineal, some matrilineal, and on some, clan membership "vacillates between the two" (de Josselin de Jong 1937: 12). According to the same author, this situation may result from the fact that the clan organizations have developed from former "double" systems, in which patrilineal and matrilineal clans were organically connected. [de Josselin de Jong 1937,

1947; Holleman 1943: 410; Sneeuwjagt 1935: 112-15.] **Kin groups.** Traditionally, the lineage (Malay, *mata-rumah*) formed part of a larger kin group (Malay, *soa*), members of which claimed common descent from a mythical or fictive ancestor (Scholz 1962: 101). Nowadays, there is less emphasis on genealogical groupings and more on the village as a territorial unit; members of the aristocracy continue to maintain the traditional genealogical distinctions, however (Holleman 1943: 390). The lineage, at least, is still strictly exogamous on both Kisar and Wetar (de Josselin de Jong 1937, 1947). **Kin terminology.** The following terms for cognatic kin on Kisar are taken from de Josselin de Jong (1937: 16-17):

Fa	*hawaini, ha*
FaBr	*ha lapana*
FaSi	*irimi*
Mo	*nawaini, na*
MoBr	*saisai*
MoSi	*na lapana*
ElBr(m.s.)	*kaka*
YoBr(m.s.)	*noonoo*
Br(w.s.)	*nami*
Si(m.s.)	*lerene*
Si(w.s.)	*noonoo*
Male first cousins(m.s.)	*kaka*
Female " " (m.s.)	*lerene*
Male " " (w.s.)	*nami*
Female " " (w.s.)	*noonoo*

The affinal terminology shows some evidence of the former existence of asymmetric connubium.

MARRIAGE AND FAMILY.

On Wetar, infant betrothal is the rule. As a child, the girl is taken by the future husband to his home following a preliminary exchange of goods. When the girl approaches puberty, the couple go to live with her parents, where the man performs bride service for two years. Following this, the marriage proper takes place, marked by the exchange of a pig, a gong, and spears (man's side) vs. a pig, cloth, and ear pendants (girl's side). Thereafter the couple are free to live where they will, although in the case of interlocal marriages they usually settle in the man's village. [de Josselin de Jong 1947: 9-10.] Elsewhere nowadays it is more often the rule that a bride-price in money is paid by the lineage of the groom to the lineage of the bride. Marriage, prohibited between members of different social classes and between parallel cousins, is virtually everywhere by preference with a cross-cousin. Monogamy is now the rule, although formerly polygyny was permitted. On Kisar and Wetar, de Josselin de Jong found no contemporary evidence of fixed connubial relations between clans, but examination of kin terms and other evidence leads him to suppose the former existence on these islands of asymmetric connubium. [de Josselin de Jong 1937, 1947; Holleman 1943: 400; Riedel 1886b: 349-50; Renes 1962: 21.]

SOCIOPOLITICAL ORGANIZATION. **Political organization.** The village is the largest indigenous political unit, the institution of radjaships having been introduced by the Dutch. The village is administered by a government-appointed headman (Malay, *orang kaya*), with traditional authority vested in an adat chief (Malay, *tuan tanah*, "lord of the land"), who is at the same time chief of the kin group that claims direct descent from the village founder (Sneeuwjagt 1935: 119-24). On Wetar, the *tuan tanah,* assisted by the genealogical heads of lineages in the role of village elders, functions as village priest and as ritual leader in respect to all activities performed in the gardens. It is probable that the juxtaposition, here and on other islands, of *orang kaya* and *tuan tanah* reflects an aboriginal pattern of "double chieftainship," expressive of a sacred-secular dichotomy widespread in East Indonesia (de Josselin de Jong 1947). **Social stratification.** A former rigid castelike system, consisting of aristocracy (*marna*), commoners (*pore, wuhru*), and a lower class (*stam, atan*), which nowadays includes members of a former category of slaves. These classes are theoretically endogamous and hereditary, but are everywhere, according to de Josselin de Jong (1937: 11-16), degenerating into mere status categories, with membership criteria highly variable. They figure prominently in myths and formerly played an important role in the sociopolitical organization. **Warfare.** Formerly notorious with respect to prevalence of warfare and headhunting.

RELIGION. Largely Christianized at present, although aspects of the traditional religion are still remembered. **Supernaturals.** A Supreme Being (It Matromma, Maromak), sometimes in association with a male sun god and a female earth goddess. Ancestor spirits, represented by images of wood, bone, and gold, are important; hero-ancestors, who in myths are associated with the founding of ur-villages, approach the status of named deities. Earth and house-post spirits, as well as spirits of rice and maize, stones, and bees, are venerated—some as personal familiars in association with cults inherited in male and female lines from hero-ancestors. [de Josselin de Jong 1947: 23; Scholz 1962: 107-24; Sneeuwjagt 1935: 46-52; Tersteege 1935.] **Practitioners.** Lineage and *soa* chiefs function as religious specialists on behalf of their respective kin groups; the *tuan tanah* officiates at villagewide ceremonies (Scholz 1962: 107). **Ceremonies.** A major renewal festival (*porka*), held every seven years, was an occasion for public sexual license and the taking of heads (Sneeuwjagt 1935: 49-50; Tersteege 1935: 473-74). **Death.** Methods of disposing of the corpse vary: on Babar it is placed in a boat-shaped coffin on a scaffolding near the sea; on Leti, Luang, and Sermata, the dead are buried in the ground in a sitting position. There is a general belief that the souls of the dead go to nearby uninhabited islets. [Riedel 1886b: 394-95; Tersteege 1935: 468-70.]

BIBLIOGRAPHY. Holleman 1943; de Josselin de Jong 1937, 1947; Renes 1962; Riedel 1886b; Scholz 1962; Sneeuwjagt 1935; Tersteege 1935.

TANIMBAR*

Synonyms. *Orang Tanembar, Orang Timor Laut, Tanimbarese*

ORIENTATION. **Identification and location.** The people of the Tanimbar islands are called collectively Tanimbarezen in the Dutch ethnographic literature and Orang Tanembar by other Indonesians. They themselves, however, distinguish a number of subgroups based mainly on linguistic differences. The inhabitants of the northern island of Fordate call themselves Tomatenembar. Those on the main island, Jamdena, are known as Tomata Jamdena. The people of the smaller islands to the north and west of the main island refer to themselves as Tomata Iaru. The Tanimbar islands are the southernmost group of the Moluccan Archipelago, situated between 6°30'-8°20' S. and 130°40'-132°10' E. The old name is Timor Laut. **Linguistic affiliation.** At least five mutually unintelligible languages. Jamden, spoken along the east coast of the main island and on the northern tip of Selaru, is related to Tetum in the Timor Archipelago. Fordat, spoken on the islands north and west of Jamdena, is more closely related to Moluccan languages; the northern dialects of Fordat are strongly mixed with Kei. [Drabbe 1926, 1932a, 1932b, 1932c, 1935; Dyen 1965.] **Demography.** Drabbe gives 1940 figures for speakers of each of five languages: Jamden, 14,329; Fordat, 9,765; Selaru, 3,979; Latdwalam, 855; and Makatian, 308 (Drabbe, 1940: 262). **History.** Macassarese and Buginese traders visited the islands frequently during the sixteenth century, exchanging rice for slaves. A Dutch trading station was established in 1645, but was soon abandoned. The Dutch renewed their interest during the nineteenth century, but it was not until 1912 that a Dutch military expedition was able to gain control over the islands.

SETTLEMENT PATTERN AND HOUSING. **Settlement pattern.** Settlements nowadays are situated along the coast, but were formerly on the tops of steep rock formations above the sea. A village (*pnuwe* in Jamden) is always a densely nucleated cluster of 50 to 80 pile-dwellings. A wide street bisects the settlement, in the middle of which is a large pile of stones in the shape of a circular platform called a *natar* ("ship" in Jamden). Some villages have an

elliptical *natar* with a high front and rear, thus imitating the basic form of a boat. In most villages the *natar* serves as a meeting place for elders or as a dance place for the community. The entire settlement, often consisting of over 1,000 people, is surrounded by a wall of large stones, entered through a wooden gate decorated with carvings. **Housing.** The dwelling house (*das* in Jamden) is a rectangular structure built on piles about one and a half meters high. Walls are very low, and the steep, thatched, gable roof dominates the whole structure. Decorations resembling buffalo horns are often placed at the ends of the ridge pole. Inside are small compartments along the four walls, containing sleeping platforms. A *das* houses an extended family of 15 to 20 people. The men usually eat separately in another building (*lingat* in Jamden), which is used also as a meeting place where men may discuss current events and where they formerly prepared for headhunting raids. Many villages also have special houses for youth, where boys and young men can gather, sleep, or have meals. Other buildings include storage houses for crops, pavilions where both sexes may perform daily tasks, and public kitchens or fireplaces.

ECONOMY. The subsistence economy depends mainly on slash-and-burn agriculture and fishing. There is some hunting during slack periods in the agricultural cycle. Sago is collected during periods of food shortage. **Agriculture.** Staples are maize and yams, cultivated along with taro and cassava on swiddens. Rice, also cultivated on swiddens, was traditionally grown under the supervision of a particular lineage. Agricultural rituals are usually directed by a special adat functionary called *mangfaturuk* in Jamden. **Fishing.** The Tanimbarese practice torch fishing at night from outrigger canoes, using harpoons, spears, and lines. Another collective method is poisoning the water at the mouths of small rivers. Most people also fish individually, using traps, hooks, spears, harpoons, and bows and arrows. **Domestic animals.** Animal husbandry is unimportant, and is restricted to pigs, dogs, and fowl. Dogs are used for hunting. **Food and stimulants.** The main dish is maize, supplemented by yams, taro, and cassava, and baked in a Polynesian oven. Rice is consumed only at feasts and celebrations. The alcoholic beverage is palm wine (*tuak* in Jamden), also an important element in ritual offerings. The presentation of betel and tobacco is important in Tanimbarese etiquette. **Industrial arts.** The important traditional handicrafts are plaiting and weaving, the latter a female activity. Ornamental designs on cloth, created by the ikat technique, have an extensive symbolic meaning. Blacksmiths make iron tools, knives, and weapons. Iron is imported, as are the gold and copper coins that are worked into ornaments. The Tanimbarese make their own pottery by coiling and modeling techniques. They also make their own dug-out canoes, with outriggers, and their

---

* The author of this entry, Koentjaraningrat, is Professor of Anthropology in the University of Indonesia.

own plank-boats. **Trade.** Trading has existed for centuries with Macassarese, Buginese, and other islanders of the Moluccan and Timor archipelagoes. Imports included rice, ivory, iron, copper or gold coins, and guns; slaves, sago and Tanimbarese textiles were exported. **Land tenure.** Rights of disposal over particular pieces of arable land, forests, hunting grounds, and reefs were originally in the hands of particular lineages. These were patrilineal descendants of the people who first occupied the area. The senior members of the lineage were the direct descendants of the original settler, and the head of this senior family bore the honorary title of "lord of the area" or *nuse-nduan* (Jamdena). Members of the lineage had the right of usufruct and could open a swidden on lineage land after consulting another lineage functionary called the "lord of the land," or *ambat-nduan*. This man was an adat specialist with extensive knowledge of the history of each tract of lineage land; he also directed agricultural fertility rites and ceremonies and settled land disputes among lineage members. Nowadays these hereditary lineage functionaries have become symbolic ceremonial figures only.

KIN GROUPS. **Descent.** The Tanimbarese reckon descent patrilineally. **Kinship terminology.** Most kinship terms extend collaterally, and thus conform to the generation pattern. The following is a list of Jamdenese kin terms.

Fa, FaBr, FaSiHu	*ame*
Mo, MoSi, FaBrWi	*ene*
Br (male ego), Si (female ego)	*wai*
Br (female ego), Si (male ego)	
FaBrDa, MoSiDa	*ure*
Wi, Hu	*sau*
So, Da	*anak*
WiFa, HuFa	*memi*
WiMo, HuMo	*abe*
DaHu	*langin*
SoWi	*ketim*
FaMo, FaFa, MoMo, MoFa, SoDa, SoSo, DaDa, DaSo	*embu*

Kin groups. The basic kin group is the nuclear family or *tambil dalam* ("people sharing a sleeping platform"). The people with whom one shares the same house, a virilocal extended family called *das dalam*, are, however, equally important. Contemporary patrilineal relatives or "brothers" (*merwan awai*) are differentiated according to "brothers of the house" (*awai-dasar*), i.e. close, and "underbrothers" (*awai-babar*), i.e. remote relatives. The general term for patrilineal relatives is *tnjame-matan*, i.e. the patrilineal maximal lineage. Within the maximal lineage are the senior lineages, *das kejain* (senior house), the members of which can trace direct descent from the lineage ancestor. Jamdena lineages are nonlocalized, although this is less true of the smaller islands. Those lineages concentrated in a particular area form

traditional named groupings or phratries (*suau*). The *suau* may bear the name of the senior member lineage, or it may be called by the name of a locality or an animal. The Tanimbarese also have a term for all the matrilineal relatives (mother's relatives), namely the honorific term *nduwe*, which actually means "lords." In contrast, one's own patrilineal relatives are referred to as *uranak*, which means "children" or "dependents."

MARRIAGE AND THE FAMILY. **Mode.** The preferred marriage is with the mother's brother's daughter, although it is seldom practiced today. Marriage between members of the same *tnjame-matan* is prohibited. The period of courting is in Jamden called the *ndondu* period. When the boy knows the girl's parents well enough, he starts moving into their house, and the boy's maternal relatives, his *nduwe*, start collecting the bride-price (*beli*). Today people marry in the church and have a party at the bride's house, after which the bride's parents present the female gift to the boy's maternal relatives. **Form.** Polygyny has always been rare. Today strict monogamy is enforced by Catholicism. **Residence.** Ultimately virilocal, preceded by a period of one week to several months in the bride's parental home. **Domestic unit.** Usually a virilocal extended family.

SOCIOPOLITICAL ORGANIZATION. Sociopolitical organization does not extend beyond the village level, despite the existence of extensive intervillage networks of kin relationships. One lineage in a village is considered to be made up of the direct patrilineal descendants of the first settler. The members of this lineage are called the "village owners" (*pnuwe-nduan*). In addition to the headman or the oldest male of the *pnuwe-nduan* lineage, who is often also *nuse-nduan* ("lord of the area"), a village also has several *ambat-nduan* ("lords of the land"), who are adat specialists of the various tracts of lineage land. Other adat functionaries in Jamdenese villages are the "announcer," or *mangafwajak*, the "offerer," or *mangsombe*, the "speaker," or *mangatanuk*, and the "navigator," or *sori luri*. All the offices are hereditary, and the holders have traditional seats on the village stone platform (*natar*) at village gatherings. The "announcer" is the intermediary between lineages within the village and between his own village and others. The "speaker" assists him and also settles disputes (excluding disputes concerning land) among villagers. The "offerer" and the "navigator" direct and perform villagewide ceremonies. **Social stratification.** Seniority is an important element of social status. Village functionaries are usually direct descendants of senior lineages. They, their families, and relatives belong to the village nobility, called *mele* in Jamden. People who do not belong to *mele* families are *famudi*. Although slavery did once exist, there has never been a hereditary class of slaves. Debt slaves or those captured in war become ordinary *famudi* when they marry. *Famudi* may freely marry slaves, but *mele* girls may not marry *famudi* or anyone of a lower status.

RELIGION. Although the population is today almost completely Roman Catholic, many elements of the indigenous religion persist. **Indigenous belief system and supernaturals.** The Tanimbarese believe in a Supreme Being, usually called Ratu (a Malay term for "King"). In prayers he is often referred to as Limnditi-Fenreu, meaning "Moon and Sun." The most important among the benevolent spirits are the spirits of the deceased ancestors (*nitu mangmwate*), who live on an island far across the sea and who can be called on by the family at life cycle ceremonies. The spirits of the land are called *nuse ndunir;* those of the village, or the protectors of the village, are *bnuwe ndunir.* Malevolent spirits can cause sickness and death if not cared for by ceremonies called *rfain,* which means "to feed." There is widespread belief in witchcraft (*keswange*), related to the concept of *suangi* common in the Moluccan Archipelago. A person becomes *suangi* by fate at birth and may himself be unaware of his condition. **Practitioners.** Persons believed to have the ability to communicate with spirits are called *manganitu.* They perform household ceremonies along the life cycle of the individual, and may also function as curers. Many are also skillful masseurs and specialists in herbs and native medicines. In treating an ill man believed to have lost his soul, the *manganitu* know the shamanistic practice of catching the soul. The status is not hereditary, and a boy or girl can learn the knowledge and skill required by assisting an established *manganitu.* **Soul, death, and afterlife.** Traditional and elaborate mortuary practices are described by Drabbe (1940: 251-61). The body is inhumated in a sitting position with the knees drawn close to the chin. People believe that after death the soul (*smangat*) is released from the body and becomes a spirit (*nitu*) which travels to the abode of the dead, a place southwest of Jamdena.

BIBLIOGRAPHY. Drabbe 1926, 1932a, 1932b, 1932c, 1935, 1940; Dyen 1965; Schuster 1946; van Wijk 1931.

K E I*

Synonyms. *Ewab-Eilanders, Ewaf-Eilanders, Kei-Eilanders, Keiese, Keij-Eilanders, Orang Kei*

ORIENTATION. **Identification and location.** Kei-Islanders have Papuan physical features, but are much mixed with immigrant groups from elsewhere

---

* The author of this entry, Koentjaraningrat, is Professor of Anthropology in the University of Indonesia.

in Indonesia, e.g. Buginese, Macassarese, Balinese, Malays, Bandanese, Ceramese, and Ambonese. Recent in-migration of Chinese has added to the variety. The Kei Islands are an archipelago in the Banda Sea, between 5°-6°5′ S. and 131°50′-135°15′ E. **Demography.** According to the *Encyclopedia of the Netherlands Indies,* the population was over 30,000 in 1915. **Language.** Kei belongs to the Fordatic group (closely related to Fordat on Tanimbar) of the Moluccan subfamily of Malayo-Polynesian (Dyen 1965). **History.** A large proportion of the population is of foreign origin. Islam was introduced by Buginese missionaries, and in 1887 a Dutch civil servant reported the existence of close to 6,000 Muslims (van Hoëvell 1890: 119). To counteract the spread of Islam, the Dutch encouraged Roman Catholic as well as Protestant missionary activity, which intensified at the turn of the century. The Dutch established an administrative center in 1882.

SETTLEMENT PATTERN AND HOUSING. Settlements, formerly built on the tops of high, steep rocks or hills for protection, consisted of dense clusters of 20 to 50 houses, surrounded by a stone wall. An established settlement with a sense of identity is called a *negari.* Nowadays the Kei-Islanders lack a distinctive style of architecture. One common feature is the fact that houses are built on piles.

ECONOMY. The Kei-Islanders cultivate taro, yams, maize, and rice on swiddens which are opened with slash-and-burn techniques. They also collect sago in the swamps. Fishing is a major means of subsistence; the village population goes out, usually at night, in skillfully made plank boats or in dug-out canoes with outriggers, to fish collectively with spears, harpoons, hooks, and traps. For export and cash, the people make boats and canoes, cut timber, collect trepang, and produce copra. **Land tenure.** According to an early description (Pleyte 1893: 578-79), the village community, or *negari,* has the right of disposal over primary forest land and hunting grounds (*ngangan ras*). Members of the *negari* have the right of usufruct. Secondary forest land (*tanat was*) is usually controlled by particular patrilineal kin groups called *fam.* Members of the *fam* have the right of usufruct to such land and to fruit trees planted thereon.

KINSHIP. **Descent.** The Kei-Islanders reckon descent patrilineally. **Kin groups.** The most important kin group is the *fam,* a patrilineal lineage. There are small *fam,* whose members live concentrated in a few villages close together, but there are also very large *fam,* the members of which live in many villages spread over a large area. A village may thus contain members of a number of *fam.* One *fam,* or sometimes more than one, is senior, its members being the direct descendants of the people who first built the village. The *fam* as a whole are grouped into two phratries, the Ursiwa and the Urlima. The significance of this dual organization seems to have disappeared, however, in modern times.

MARRIAGE AND THE FAMILY. **Mode.** The bride-price, *harta*, consists of several parts, e.g. *wur-harta* and *wat-wilin,* and is reciprocated by a gift from the girl's relatives. To avoid a large bride-price, a young man may practice bride service (*nafdu*). The ideal marriage between a man and his mother's brother's daughter does not require a bride-price, since it is considered to re-establish an already existing relationship between a *fam* of bride-givers (*mang-ohoi*) and a *fam* of bride-receivers (*jan-ur*). Between the two *fam,* of which the bride-receivers are considered to be junior to the bride-givers, there exists a relationship of cooperation and mutual help in economic activities such as housebuilding.

POLITICAL ORGANIZATION. The village head is called the *rat* or *orang-kaja.* He is assisted by functionaries such as the *kapitan,* the *major,* and the *marinjo.* The latter is the hereditary village announcer. The lineage heads (*taen jan*) within a village are subordinate to the village head, while the senior lineage head often bears the title of "lord of the land" (*tuan tan*). The village religious functionary is the *metuduan,* while villages with a Muslim population have an imam. **Social stratification.** The traditional culture recognizes three social classes. The *mel-mel* are members of the ruling lineages of village heads, many of whom claim foreign descent. Many of the lineages of "lords of land" are not considered to belong to the *mel-mel,* however, but to the *ren-ren,* the class of ordinary people. In the old days there existed a class of slaves or *hiri-hiri.*

RELIGION. According to the *Encyclopedia of the Netherlands Indies,* there were in 1915 about 12,000 Muhammedans, 8,000 Catholics, 3,000 Protestants, and about 7,000 pagans. An important element in the indigenous religion was the belief in spirits of the dead (*nitu*). The mythology speaks also of Duan Lerwuan, believed to be the god of the sun, and of Duan Luteh, god of the moon. Other deities include Hejan Suwat, the god of the sea, and Lir Majoran, the god of agriculture. The spirits of those who died a violent death or of women who died in childbirth are especially feared. The Moluccan and East Indonesian belief in the witch (*suangi, swanggi*) also exists among the Kei-Islanders.

BIBLIOGRAPHY. Admiraal 1939; Dyen 1965; Geurtjens 1921a, 1921b, 1921c; van Hoëvell 1890; Klerks 1939; Pleyte 1893.

A R U*

Synonyms. *Aroe-Eilanders, Aroenezen*

ORIENTATION. **Identification and location.** Although the entire population of the Aru Islands has basically the same Papuan physical features, the people on the western coasts have been much mixed with Malayan groups from other parts of Indonesia. The west coast people generally look down upon the east coast people. The Aru-Island group is located in the Banda Sea between 5°18'-7°5' S. and 134°8'-134°56' E. **Demography.** The total population was about 13,000 in the middle of the nineteenth century (Bosscher 1853: 323-26). **History.** To protect their monopoly of the spice trade in the southern part of the Moluccas, the Dutch built a fortress at Wokam in 1659. In the second half of the eighteenth century, Dutch power in the Moluccas declined, with the result that Buginese and Macassarese merchants dominated trade with the Aru Islands. A century later, the Dutch renewed their interest and established an administrative center at Dobo in 1882, but only after 1904 did they succeed in gaining control over the islands.

SETTLEMENT PATTERN AND HOUSING. In the old days, Aru settlements (*negari*) were usually compact clusters of small dwellings on piles. The houses were occupied by extended families. A village communal house (*tempat pamali*) contained sacred objects such as gongs, drums, and Chinese ceramics.

ECONOMY. The subsistence economy consists of sago gathering, fishing, and some slash-and-burn agriculture. People of the west coast hunt pigs for meat. Bird of paradise feathers are exported, as are pearls and trepang. Trade is mainly in the hands of Macassarese and Buginese. **Land tenure.** The village has the right of disposal over certain lands surrounding the village, but lineages within the village also have rights to these lands.

POLITICAL ORGANIZATION. The village head, *orang kaja,* is assisted by several *kepala soa,* traditional heads of lineages with respect to control of land. Descendants of the oldest lineage of the village are the *tuan negeri.*

RELIGION. According to Baron van Hoëvell, there were over 400 Muslims and almost 600 Christians in 1890. Belief in spirits and in deities of nature is important in the traditional religion, as is belief in a village deity, *waer kota.* The general Moluccan belief in *suanggi* (witches) is also present on Aru.

BIBLIOGRAPHY. Bosscher 1853; van Hoëvell 1890.

---

* The author of this entry, Koentjaraningrat, is Professor of Anthropology in the University of Indonesia.

CENTRAL MOLUCCAS

F. L. COOLEY refers to what he calls an "Ambonese culture type" characteristic of Ambon, the adjacent regions of West Ceram (Seran) and intervening small islands. It is also in this restricted sense that he uses Central Moluccas (Muluku) as a quasi-cultural term (cf. Cooley 1962b). Actually it is evident that elements of a common culture type extend westward at least to Buru (van Wouden 1968: 78) and south to Banda, the Ceram Laut-Watubela Archipelago, and beyond (Nutz 1959; Deacon 1925). It is in this larger sense that the term Central Moluccas is used in the present volume. The reasons for these rather widespread cultural similarities have occasioned much speculation and debate among historically-minded anthropologists (cf. Rivers 1914, Haddon 1920, Speiser 1924, Perry 1918, Deacon 1925) as well as among those prone to structuralist interpretation (cf. de Josselin de Jong 1935, van Wouden 1968). As early as the fourteenth century, these islands became involved, as producers, in the famous East Indian spice trade, resulting in contact with Java, Goa, and other centers of acculturation to the west. The intermediary in this trade was the powerful Ternate sultanate, which by the mid-fifteenth century had abolished headhunting, introduced territorial government, and propagated Islam throughout much of the Central Moluccan area. Later, Christianity was introduced, first by the Portuguese and then by the Dutch, the latter making Amboina the center of administrative and missionary endeavor for the entire area. These many acculturative influences, persisting over some 400 years, have produced a highly composite culture, aptly termed "creole Moluccan" by H. Geertz (1963: 93). This cultural amalgam is most evident in coastal villages and centers of population concentration such as Ambon and Ternate. The interior "tribes" (e.g. Alune, Bonfia, Manusela, Seti, and Wemale on Ceram)—generally called Alfur or Alfuru by coastal peoples—have been absorbed in varying degrees into the prevailing "creole" stratum, and purely pagan communities are nowadays rare or nonexistent. It is thus virtually impossible to reconstruct pre-fifteenth century institutions to any extent, although certain presumably early patterns (e.g. a division into "five" and "nine") are evident throughout the Central Moluccan area. The often conflicting older literature on this subject is summarized by van Wouden (1968), while Kennedy's field surveys on Ambon and Ceram, undertaken in 1949-50, attempted to clarify inconsistencies in earlier reports; the results, however, remain inconclusive in many important respects (Kennedy 1955c). Van Wouden (1968) calls attention to structural similarities throughout eastern Indonesia, including the Central Moluccas, and Deacon (1925) summarizes various theories to account for similarities in myth and ritual as between the Central Moluccas and Melanesia. Although theories purporting to account for these wider cultural affiliations remain speculative, there is little doubt that the cultures of the Central Moluccan area cannot be understood without reference to Ternate and the lands to the west on the one hand, and to New Guinea and Melanesia on the other.

BIBLIOGRAPHY. Cooley 1962b; Deacon 1925; H. Geertz 1963; Haddon 1920; J. P. B. de Josselin de Jong 1935; Kennedy 1955c; Nutz 1959; Perry 1918; Rivers 1914; Speiser 1924; van Wouden 1968.

AMBONESE

Synonyms. *Amboinese, Uliassers*

ORIENTATION. **Location and identification.** The people of Ambon and the immediately adjacent small islands (Haruku, Nusa Laut, and Saparua, called collectively the Uliassers) in the Central Moluccas of eastern Indonesia. Most Ambonese clans derive their origin from the large island of Ceram immediately to the north, and it is evident that the culture of the Ambonese is a variant of the culture of Ceram, in particular of West Ceram. Kennedy (1955c) carried out survey fieldwork on both Ceram and Ambon, and his data, in combination with those from older sources such as Duyvendak (1926), Tauern (1918), Tichelman (1925), de Vries (1927), Vroklage (1936), and Jansen (1939), amply demonstrate a common cultural base, although in the case of Ambon this has been obscured by widespread conversion to Islam and Christianity. The physical type is mixed and somewhat variable, with a considerable addition of Papuan or "Melanesian" features. Coastal populations tend to be lighter in skin and more "Malay" in appearance, whereas inland the people are darker skinned on the whole. Throughout the Central Moluccas, including Ambon, villages are said to be either Patasiwa or Patalima (Ulisiwa or Ulilima), glossed by Cooley as "Nine Division" vs. "Five Division." Those villages classed together in either one of these categories seem to have certain similarities in adat, or to feel that they have. On Ambon there is some feeling that the terms refer to former groupings of villages (*uli*) ruled by radjas. Cooley, reasoning in part from information gathered by Kennedy, suggests that the terms may have their origin in the fifteenth-century expansion of the Ternate sultanate and the imposition of quasi-political confederations in areas such as Ceram (Cooley 1962b: 13ff.). **Linguistic affiliation.** Classed by Esser (1938) in his Ambon-Timor group of Malayo-Polynesian languages. Dyen (1965) places Ambonese, along with certain languages of Ceram, in an Ambic cluster of his Moluccan linkage, a classification essentially similar to that of Esser. According to Kennedy, Malay is the lingua franca; as of 1950 most inhabitants of Amboina (Kota Ambon) spoke a mixture of Dutch and Malay (Kennedy 1955c). **Demography.** The 1959 census of Ambon Island, excluding the municipality of Kota Ambon, listed 26 Christian villages with a total of 37,600 persons and 16 Muslim villages with a total population of 31,000; 5 villages, totaling 11,500 persons, were listed as "mixed." [Cooley 1967: 130.] **History and cultural relations.** A long history (some 400 years) of acculturation and exploitation, chiefly reflecting attempts by foreign powers to gain control of the lucrative spice trade. Intensive schooling and missionary activity under the Dutch resulted in large numbers of Ambonese entering the civil and military services prior to World War II. Many Christian Ambonese migrated to Ceram, New Guinea, and elsewhere as missionaries and pastors; others, working as sailors on Dutch vessels, migrated to Britain and the United States (Kennedy 1955c). Although according to Cooley (1967) the Ambonese nowadays classify themselves as wholly Christian or Muslim (51 and 49 percent, respectively), Kennedy found memories of indigenous pagan customs still very much alive in the minds of older informants.

SETTLEMENT PATTERN AND HOUSING. Villages are located near the coast, with the average size, for Christian communities, being 1,450 persons (Cooley 1967). According to Kennedy, many villages remember a *negri lama* in the hills where ancestral memorial stones are located. In addition to a church (or mosque) and a school, modern villages contain a combination meeting house and ceremonial (adat) structure, *baileu*. The Ambonese house is built on a low stone foundation with a dirt floor; the framework is of hewn beams, and the walls of plaited sago palm leaves, which also serve as thatching for the roof (Cooley 1967).

ECONOMY. Agriculture, mainly of the swidden variety, is limited by poor soils. According to Kennedy, the main foods in rural districts are sago, tubers, and vegetables, eaten with fish. Some rice is grown, but supplies must be supplemented by imports, and rice is considered a luxury food. The production of spices, chiefly cloves and nutmegs, has always been important to the cash economy. **Land tenure.** Village-owned land is largely uncultivated. Parcels of agricultural land (*dusun dati*) are owned or controlled by clans and subclans through associations of clan members (*anak dati*), each with a chief, *kepala dati*. Membership is restricted to male and unmarried female descendants of "original" or founding clans within a village area. [Cooley 1962a, 1962b.]

MARRIAGE AND FAMILY. **Mode.** The payment of a bride-price, consisting of cloth, brandy, plates, and (in some cases) money, is considered an important aspect of marriage. It is a common belief among Ambonese, however, that their ancestors on Ceram lacked this institution and that the taking of a head was a necessary precondition to marriage. Elopement, which is common nowadays, nevertheless requires payment of bride-price. An alternative, in cases where the payment cannot be met or where the girl's family lacks male heirs, is for the boy to marry matrilocally —in which case the children belong to the maternal clan. [Cooley 1962b: 20ff.; 1967.] **Marriage rules.** In principle, marriage is forbidden with any member of the bilateral personal kindred (*familie*), reckoned vertically to great-grandparents and laterally to two degrees of cousinship (Cooley 1962b). Van Wouden (1968: 21), citing Tauern (1918) and Schadee (1915), reports the existence on western Ceram of exclusive cross-cousin marriage, which he takes as evidence of a former unilateral marriage system of some kind. Kennedy's information on this subject is inconclusive (Kennedy 1955c: 230, 242-43). **Residence.** Strongly patrilocal in the past. Many couples still live patrilocally for a year or two after marriage, although neolocal tendencies are increasingly in evidence (Cooley 1962b). **Household.** Households tend to contain more than one nuclear family, due to temporary patrilocal residence of married sons.

KIN GROUPS. **Descent.** Patrilineal, although Cooley (1962b), following to some extent the conclusions of Kennedy (1955c), postulates a shift from matriliny (seemingly characteristic of western Ceram) to patriliny—possibly due to Islamic or Christian influences. **Kin groups.** The *rumah tau* (Malay, *mata rumah*) is a named, exogamous, patrilineal kin group, identified by Cooley (1962a) as a patriclan in Murdock's sense of the term. In-marrying women become members of their husbands' *rumah tau*, while localization, although not as strict nowadays, was formerly confined to wards or sections within the village. Clan membership regulates marriage and, through a system of titles (*gelaran*), access to land rights, social status, and political office. Associated with each clan is a "clan house," reputedly built by the clan founder and housing weapons, cloth, and other heirlooms identified with the clan ancestors. Stewardship over this house and its contents is hereditary, through eldest sons, within a particular family line. The clan house is (or was) associated with the clan ancestors and their ritual propitiation, including the upkeep of sacred memorial stones. Villages nowadays also contain *fam* (presumably of Dutch derivation), which in most cases are identical with *mata rumah* (Cooley 1962b: 105).

SOCIOPOLITICAL ORGANIZATION. Political organization.

The original migrants from Ceram came to Ambon in groups of interrelated lineages called *soa*. These *soa* communities were each headed by an *upu*, a descendant of an original *soa* leader, assisted by a military leader (*malessi*) and a religious leader (*mauweng*). Even prior to European contact these early settlements had coalesced into federations (*uli*) ruled by radjas, each containing an "original" settlement (*negri lama*) associated with the *mata rumah radja* (the ruling or "original" lineage), together with the *mata rumah tuan tanah*. Ruling lineages nowadays tend to claim descent from Java or southern Celebes, and it is likely that the federation process was imposed from these politically more sophisticated areas, either directly or indirectly through Ternate. [Cooley 1969: 142-43.] Under the Dutch, the authority of the *uli* federations was abolished in favor of politically independent village settlements governed by councils, *saniri*. The latter include the following officers, some of which are now nonfunctional: the ruler (radja), the *soa* chiefs, the *tuan tanah*, the adat chief, the *kapitan*, the *kewang*, and the *marinjo*. Political office tends to be hereditary within a village elite consisting of descendants of the founding ancestors, i.e. those who first cleared the land. The term *soa* may refer to an administrative subdivision within the village, but its basic connotation remains that of lineal descent—referring back to groupings of the interrelated lineages that migrated to Ambon from Ceram (Cooley 1969: 148). The authority of the old adat-based village councils has been weakened by the introduction of civil administration, together with the growing importance of both Christianity and Islam (Cooley 1969: 162-63). **Social differentiation.** Clans are socially differentiated into those descended from original founding ancestors (*asali*), those who have migrated in (*pendatang*), and those of foreign origin (*orang asing*). Higher political office and social status is hereditary within certain clans, mostly *asali*, and these constitute a ruling class (Cooley 1962b). Kennedy reported class consciousness to be marked, with the higher ranks among the ruling aristocracy tending to endogamous marriage. There is a recognized class of descendants of slaves, said to have been introduced by the Dutch (Kennedy 1955c). **Social control.** Socially approved behavior is equated with the will of the ancestors; violation of adat incurs the displeasure of ancestral spirits, visiting misfortune not only on the violator but on the entire community. Supervision of the adat and the apprehension and temporal punishment of offenders are in the hands of the village council, the successors to the ancestors (Cooley 1969).

RELIGION. Contact with the West brought Christianity, education, and partial acculturation to a European style of life. Europeanization, combined with earlier Islamization, has virtually obliterated the indigenous religion on Ambon, although it managed to survive until recent decades on Ceram. An important socioreligious institution on the latter island was that of the *kakihan* societies, which Deacon (1925), drawing chiefly on data from Tauern (1918), Martin (1894), and van Schmidt (1843), associates with the "Melanesian" physical type predominant in interior western Ceram—and specifically with the Patasiwa Hitam (the "tattooed Patasiwa"), a branch of the Patasiwa ("Nine Division") faction on that island. The *kakihan* were village-oriented societies of adult males—exclusive in-groups, according to Deacon, guaranteeing survival after death in a kind of elite afterworld. Periodic initiation of pubescent boys involved a ritual "devouring" of the initiates by a crocodile-like figure, exclusion of women and their deception by the production of frightening noises said to be the voice of the spirit within the *kakihan* house, and the sacrificing of pigs on stone altars. The Patasiwa Hitam were notorious headhunters, and the taking of heads was evidently at one time an essential part of these ceremonies. Deacon calls attention to marked similarities between these secret societies on Ceram and those of certain New Guinea tribes and draws conclusions about the historical migrations of peoples in this area of the Pacific. Downs, on the other hand, drawing on data from Jensen (1948) and Duyvendak (1926), attempts to place Ceram headhunting in a wider context, as part of an ancient division of society into opposing moieties (e.g. Patasiwa/Patalima) for the enactment of the basic theme of rebirth through death, symbolized by human sacrifice and the later taking of heads (Downs 1955).

BIBLIOGRAPHY. Cooley 1962a, 1962b, 1967, 1969; Deacon 1925; Downs 1955; Duyvendak 1926; Dyen 1965; Esser 1938; Holleman 1923; Jansen 1939; Jensen 1948; Kennedy 1955c; Martin 1894; Röder 1948; Schadee 1915; van Schmidt 1843; Tauern 1918; Tichelman 1925; de Vries 1927; Vroklage 1936; van Wouden 1968.

HALMAHERA*

THE LARGE ISLAND of Halmahera (ancient Gilolo, Djailolo) lies in the northern Moluccas, midway between northern Celebes and the western tip of New Guinea. Together with outlying islands (Morotai, Ternate, Tidore, Moti, Makian, Batjan, and Obi), it covers approximately 6,500 square miles. The Sula Archipelago, which links Halmahera with the Banggai Island chain off the east coast of Celebes, has historic and linguistic ties with Ternate and Batjan, but little is known of its indigenous inhabitants. Although there are reportedly some 30 "tribes" or ethnic categories resident on Halmahera, much of it is uninhabited or sparsely populated. The landscape is one of high, densely forested mountains; rivers are few and for the most part unnavigable, and travel in the interior is exceedingly difficult. The interior pagan peoples (Alfurs, Alfuros) are very little known; some are (or were until recently) nomadic hunters and gatherers. Islam, and to a lesser extent Christianity, have made considerable headway, and a good portion of the total population of over 150,000 is nowadays nominally either Muslim or Christian. The peoples of the northern Halmaheras speak languages which are classified by linguists (cf. Esser 1938; Capell 1962) as non-Austronesian, i.e. as showing no immediate relationship to the great majority of languages throughout Indonesia and the Philippines. The NAN languages of Indonesia (those of North Halmahera, interior West Irian, and possibly parts of Portuguese Timor), together with those of the aboriginal Australians, Tasmanians, and Andaman Islanders, have been tentatively combined in a proposed Indo-Pacific language phylum by Greenberg (cited in Murdock 1964: 123). Speakers of North Halmahera languages include: Ternatans,

Tidorese, Loloda, Tobaru, Galelarese, Tobelorese (including the nomadic Togutil), Sahu (including Waioli), Pagu (or Isam, including Tololiku), and Modole. These northern groups, comprising the bulk of the population, have been most subject to outside influence, and they have been the most mobile, expanding generally to the south at the expense of the South Halmahera groups. The latter, principally Buli, Maba, Patani, Weda, Sawai, and Gane on the mainland, plus Makianese and Batjanese on off-lying islands, speak Austronesian languages apparently related to those of coastal western New Guinea (cf. Esser 1938). The interior tribes of North Halmahera are generally of Mongoloid (Malay or "Indonesian") physical type, whereas those of the south tend to be more "Papuan" or "Melanesoid" in appearance. Coastal populations are markedly mixed, both physically and culturally, the result of contact over several centuries with traders, missionaries, and adventurers of Portuguese, Gujarat, Arab, Malay, and Dutch extraction. As part of the Republic of Indonesia, Halmahera is divided into two administrative regions, one belonging to the regional government of Ternate, the other to that of Tidore. Both are part of the province of Muluku, headed by a governor on Ambon. The area under Ternatan jurisdiction includes the island of Morotai and, on Halmahera itself, the whole of the northern peninsula and part of the southern peninsula below about 1°58' N. The region of Tidore includes the central portion of Halmahera together with the whole of the northeastern and southeastern peninsulas. This rather curious division reflects more or less accurately the territorial possessions of the former sultanates of Ternate and Tidore, once celebrated throughout the East for their power and regal magnificence—a result of their monopoly of the rich spice trade.

BIBLIOGRAPHY. Capell 1962; Esser 1938; Murdock 1964.

---

* This introductory section on Halmahera, together with the following six entries on specific Halmaheran peoples, were written by E. K. M. Masinambaw, a linguistic anthropologist associated with the Institute for Cultural Studies, Djakarta. Some demographic data and additional reference materials have been added by the editor.

TERNATANS

Synonyms. *Orang Ternate, Suku Ternate*

ORIENTATION. The term Orang Ternate can refer to those persons resident on the island of Ternate; to those who have emigrated elsewhere but who claim descent from the original inhabitants of the island; or to residents of other areas who, for a variety of reasons, identify with the island or its former sultanate. Thus the 1930 census listed over 42,000 "Ternatans," of whom only about 10,000 actually resided on Ternate, the rest being on Batjan, Obi, and along the west coast of Halmahera (*Volkstelling 1930: 5,* 39, 175ff.). The difficulty in defining ethnic Ternatans arises from the long history of physical and cultural assimilation to outside influences, in turn a result of competition among foreign powers for the riches of the Moluccan spice trade. The composite culture that is characteristic of former centers of the spice trade such as Ternate, Tidore, Batjan, and Ambon has been aptly termed "Creole Moluccan" by H. Geertz (1963: 93). The Ternate sultanate was for centuries an important influence throughout the Moluccan area; Islam was introduced by Javanese merchants in 1430 (de Clercq 1890), and by the end of the seventeenth century the sultanate extended from Celebes in the west to Ceram in the east. Rivalry with the sultanate of Tidore resulted in frequent warfare and consequent territorial conquest on the island of Halmahera, and it was not until 1814 that peace between the two sultanates was established. Portuguese traders and missionaries arrived in 1506 and the Dutch in 1599. Ternate was the seat of Dutch influence in the East prior to the establishment of Batavia in 1619. [De Clercq 1890; Baretta 1917.]

SETTLEMENT PATTERN AND HOUSING. Villages are located along the coast, near the mouths of rivers. There are very few settlements inland. Houses are generally arranged along streets, parallel with the coastline. Each larger village contains a square, around which are arranged the district head's office and residence, the school, the mosque, etc. [Baretta 1917.] Structures within the town of Ternate exhibit the style of the various settlers from outside Halmahera (Chinese, Arabs, Dutch). Rural houses are of thatch construction, built directly on the ground, although temporary field houses may be raised on piles.

ECONOMY. Sago, bananas, and cassava, grown on swiddens, are the staple crops on Ternate as throughout practically the whole of Halmahera. Supplementary crops include rice, maize, vegetables, and sugarcane. There are no large rice fields, and rice is consumed only on special occasions. Coconut (copra), cacao, coffee, and nutmegs are important cash crops. Fishing is an additional source of income.

SOCIOPOLITICAL ORGANIZATION. The traditional political organization consisted of a number of districts (*negeri*, headed by a *sangadji*) each comprising a number of villages (headed by *kimelahas*), and in each district there was a representative (*utusan*) of the Sultan. The modern administration is organized along roughly the same lines, with the jurisdiction of the regional governor on Ternate extending over approximately the same territory as the former sultanate.

RELIGION. Islam.

BIBLIOGRAPHY. Baretta 1917; de Clercq 1890; H. Geertz 1963; *Volkstelling 1930.*

TIDORESE

Synonyms. *Orang Tidore, Suku Tidore*

ORIENTATION. The homeland of the Tidorese is the island of Tidore, south of Ternate. Emigrés have settled along the west coast of Halmahera, from the village of Oba south to about Lifofa, and many Tidorese are also found in the Batjan and Obi islands. The total in 1930 was 26,000, of whom some 15,000 were resident on Tidore (*Volkstelling 1930: 5,* 39, 175). The first sultan was appointed in 1495, some half century after the introduction of Islam, and at one time the Tidore sultanate claimed a territory which included not only parts of Halmahera but also a number of islands off the coast of western New Guinea (Wilken 1893: 431ff.). Cultural influences on Tidore have in general been similar to those on Ternate, and, like Ternate, the culture is composite or "creole" in character.

SETTLEMENT PATTERN AND HOUSING. Settlement pattern is similar to that on Ternate. The walls of Tidorese houses consist of two layers of intertwined bamboo splints, the space between being filled with coral stones and sand. A thick coat of lime is added to the outer side of each bamboo layer, thus forming a solid wall, which from a distance appears to be of stone construction.

ECONOMY. The Tidorese are best known for their fishing activities, which extend as far as Batjan and Obi; much of the catch is dried and salted for export to Manado and Banda.

SOCIAL ORGANIZATION. Descent is traced through the male line. First cousins are permissible marriage partners, although no preference is given to any particular type of cousin marriage.

POLITICAL ORGANIZATION. The *sangadji* was the traditional district head and representative of the

Sultan, transmitting the latter's orders to subordinate heads, *kimelaha* and *hukum*.

RELIGION. Islam.

BIBLIOGRAPHY. *Volkstelling 1930;* Wilken 1893.

TOBELORESE

Synonyms. *Orang Tobelo, Suku Tobelo*

ORIENTATION. The Tobelorese homeland is the northern peninsula of Halmahera, approximately 1°29'-1°45' N. by 127°32'-128°1' E. Settlements of these people are found on the northern half of the island of Morotai and on Halmahera around the Kau Bay (Tobelo Boeng), near the town of Weda, and in Maba and Gane. Tobelorese are also found on Batjan, and they were the first settlers in the Obi islands (Coolhaas 1926). They are known in history as daring and much feared pirates, whose exploits extended far beyond the islands of Halmahera. Tobelorese, Galelarese, and Tobaru are all closely related languages, and together they constitute a separate grouping within the North Halmaheran languages. Galela is located on the northern peninsula, north of Tobelo, but Galelarese are also found on Morotai and on Batjan and Obi. The nomadic Togutil, primarily in the jungle areas of the northeastern peninsula, are closely related to the Tobelorese. Local sources estimate their number at about 200. The Modole and the Isam, or Pagu, are small groups living inland in the Kau area, while the Loloda (Loda), Tobaru, and Sahu are found on the western half of the northern peninsula. [Hueting 1921-22; Riedel 1885b.]

ECONOMY. The indigenous economy depended primarily on hunting, but modern Tobelorese are for the most part settled agriculturists. Rice and maize are planted on swiddens, together with cassava, bananas, sugarcane, and vegetables. Fishing—in deep water offshore, near coral reefs, and in the mouths of rivers—is done with hook and line, spears, and nets. Deer and wild pigs are hunted with spears and spring traps; dogs are used to track game. According to Hueting (1921-22), there was intensive trade with Tidore, Maba, and Patani—these latter areas supplying knives, hooks, basketry, and earthenware to Tobelo in exchange for rice. Tobelorese settlers on Batjan and Obi gather coconuts, nutmegs, damar, and rotan and also engage in fishing and pearl diving.

SOCIOPOLITICAL ORGANIZATION. The Tobelorese were formerly organized into four tribal villages headed by a *kimelaha*. According to Baretta (1917: 40), migrations have weakened these bonds to the extent that they have now disappeared altogether. Descent is patrilineal, with residence after marriage either patrilocal or neolocal. [On the other hand, Murdock (1967: 204), basing his information on Hueting (1921-22), infers bilateral descent from the absence of reported unilineal kin groups.] The parents of a boy conduct the preliminaries to engagement and marriage. A bride-price must be paid, and in addition there are a number of payments which the family of the groom must make, e.g. to "eliminate" the existence of a blood relationship between the prospective bride and groom; the closer the relationship the higher the payment. The woman, after payment of the bride-price, remains entitled to a share in the agricultural plots of her kinsmen. The basic kin terms are as follows:

Fa	*baba*
Mo	*ayo*
So, Da	*ngohaka*
Si	*firanga*
Br	*riyaka*
FaBr	*yea*
MoBr	*pepe*
FaSi, MoSi	*owa*
FaFa, MoFa	*ete*
FaMo, MoMo	*tofora*

RELIGION. Practically all Tobelorese adhere to the Christian (Protestant) religion, which was first introduced into the area in 1866 (Baretta 1917: 62). **Supernaturals and practitioners.** The ancient Tobelorese believed the air to be inhabited by a host of good and evil spirits, to which constant supplication should be directed to acquire favors as well as avoid disasters. There were benevolent and malevolent spirits of ancestors, evil spirits of the earth and air, and spirits of murdered people. Belief in a supreme spirit (*djou ma duhutu, gikimoi*) was vague, and little attention was paid to this being. Shamans (*gomahate*) originated from a school of pupils established by a wise man (*gosuong*), who was sent to earth by the *gikimoi*. Shamans were charged with maintaining belief in a supreme spirit and predicting future happenings while in a trance state; the office was acquired through training rather than birth (Baretta 1917). **Illness and medicine.** Illness was caused by the theft of a person's soul-substance (*gurumi*) on the part of an evil spirit. Curative rites were conducted by the shaman, who brought himself to a trance state during which his soul, assisted by a good spirit, traveled to the lord of the sky to recover the stolen soul-substance (Baretta 1917). **Soul, death, and afterlife.** Death rendered the deceased's soul (*goma*) vulnerable to attack by evil spirits. The soul was protected or liberated from this condition by the shaman, who, while in a trance state, conducted it to a secluded spot (a cave or an island across the sea) where it remained until cleansed of all impurities. It was then accepted into the community of ancestral spirits. This transitional event was signaled by the illness of one of the deceased's living relatives—a sign that the liberated *goma* of the departed was demanding offerings in honor of its new status. These demands were met by means of an elaborate death ceremony. [Baretta 1917.] According to Hueting (1921-22), the Tobelorese originally disposed of the corpse by placing it on a platform at some distance from the village. As of 1920, however, interment was also being practiced—in either case with the body wrapped in mats within a lidless coffin. Hueting recorded a periodic (five-year) ceremony for the dead (*hukara*), when the corpses of those who had died since the last *hukara* were unwrapped and the bones counted and gathered. The bones were washed and wrapped in pieces of cloth ornamented with elaborate paintings and placed in newly-made coffins. These were then carried into a village ritual structure (*halu*), where they were feasted and honored before being placed on raised, decorated platforms. [Hueting 1921-22: 174-78.]

BIBLIOGRAPHY. Baretta 1917; Coolhaas 1926; Hueting 1921-22; Murdock 1967; Riedel 1885b.

MAKIANESE

Synonyms. *Makiang, Orang Makian, Suku Makian*

ORIENTATION. The homeland of these people is the island of Makian, off the southwest coast of Halmahera. They have been migrating to Halmahera in increasing numbers and are also found in the Batjan islands, where they work as agriculturists, fishermen, and coconut gatherers.

ECONOMY. The soil of Makian is ill suited to rice cultivation, and the chief crops are maize and bananas. Most of the Makianese on Halmahera are engaged in the cultivation of coconut trees and in the processing of the nuts into copra. Fishing is done by means of rods, lines, and dragnets, or with giant fishtraps made from finely split bamboo (de Clercq 1890).

BIBLIOGRAPHY. De Clercq 1890.

BATJANESE

Synonyms. *Orang Batjan, Suku Batjan*

ORIENTATION. The homeland of this group is the Batjan Archipelago, off the southwest coast of Halma-

hera, consisting of over 80 islands. According to Coolhaas (1926), the total population of the Batjan Archipelago amounted to 10,767 in 1920, including Galelarese (the majority), Makianese, Tobelorese, Waiolis, and Tobarus. Of this total, some 1,500 were descendants of the indigenous population, concentrated within the single village of Labuha-Amasing. **History.** Batjan was formerly a sultanate whose rulers resided in eastern Makian. With the arrival of the Portuguese, they moved to Amasing on Great Batjan. The islands were at that time inhabited by various "tribes" (*soanang*) with delimited territories of their own, headed by chiefs whose indigenous names (*ambasaja, datu*) were later replaced by Ternatan ones (*sangadji, kimelaha*). Nearby Obi and Sula were once part of the Batjan sultanate; no trace remains now, however, of the indigenous Obi population.

RELIGION. Mixed Muslim and Christian.

BIBLIOGRAPHY. Coolhaas 1926.

SAWAI

Synonyms. *Orang Sawai, Sawaai, Suku Sawai*

ORIENTATION. Opinions differ with respect to the ethnic connotation of the term Sawai. According to one view, it includes the peoples of Buli, Maba, Patani, Weda, and Gane, as well as the Sawai proper. Alternatively, it is used to refer only to non-Muslim Sawai. Linguistically, these six groups are very closely related, probably variants of a single dialect. The Orang Buli are found along the east coast of Halmahera's northeastern peninsula. The Orang Maba inhabit practically the whole northern coast of the southeastern peninsula, while the Patani area covers the entire narrow tip of this peninsula to about the town of Spo. The whole southern coast of the peninsula and the eastern coast of the southern peninsula are occupied by Orang Sawai and by Orang Weda (Were). Maan (1951) made the following estimates with regard to the population of these groups: Buli, 1,000; Maba, 1,800; Patani (including Gebe), 2,700; Sawai, 800; Weda, 900; Gane, 1,500.

BIBLIOGRAPHY. Maan 1951.

WEST NEW GUINEA

MODERN ANTHROPOLOGICAL FIELDWORK in West New Guinea (formerly Netherlands New Guinea; now, as part of the Republic of Indonesia, West Irian) got under way only in the 1950s (for summary statements see Pouwer 1961; van Baal et al. 1961; de Bruijn 1958-59). Relatively little of this work has been published, and knowledge of West New Guinea languages and cultures is still somewhat fragmentary. The inhabitants—dark-skinned, woolly-haired, heavily bearded, with facial features often reminiscent of Australoid types—are known generally as Papuans, implying a relationship to the peoples of Papua across the border in what was formerly British New Guinea. They tend to live in small communities, separated by difficult terrain. The result is a seeming linguistic and cultural diversity that has as yet defied meaningful classification. There is, however, a significant linguistic division which can be applied throughout New Guinea. The peoples of the northern coast—including the extreme western tip of New Guinea (the Vogelkop, or Bird's Head) and the off-lying islands—in general speak Austronesian (AN) languages, genetically related to those of Indonesia and the Philippines; the rest of the island can be said to be inhabited by speakers of non-Austronesian (NAN) languages, generally referred to as Papuan (Capell 1969). The NAN languages of New Guinea have so far not been shown to be related individually or as families to any other known languages, although Greenberg has recently proposed such a relationship with those of Australia and Tasmania (cited in Murdock 1964: 123). • The present work concerns itself only with those portions of West New Guinea that are inhabited by speakers of Austronesian (AN) languages. The recording and classification of these languages have not progressed to the point where much can be said about them or the nature of their relationship to languages outside the area (Capell 1969). Dyen's lexico-statistical study included some 20 West New Guinea AN isolects; a few of these appear to be

related to Moluccan languages, but the remainder are ungrouped with any other Indonesian language family except at the phylum level (Dyen 1965). Findings of this nature indicate a historical relationship, probably fairly remote in time. Known trade and slaving contacts date from the present millennium, largely mediated through Ceram and Ternate in the eastern Moluccas, but also from the opposite direction, e.g. from Biak (Schouten Islands), off New Guinea's northern coast. The recent discovery of Dongson-type bronze drum fragments in the Ayamaru area of the Vogelkop indicates that trade relationships with Java, and ultimately with mainland Southeast Asia, may be of considerable antiquity (Elmberg 1959). Islam was introduced, along with the Malay language, probably from Ternate in the seventeenth century, and coastal settlements of Malay-speaking Muslims are common in the Vogelkop and in the southwest, e.g. the Arguni Bay area (van Baal et al. 1961). More recently, Christian Ambonese have moved out from the Central Moluccas as missionaries and pastors, with the result that Ambonese words are common in the vocabularies of a number of north coast languages (cf. Koentjaraningrat 1966). In general, the areas of greatest Indonesian influence include: the northern lowlands between Hollandia and Sarmi (Nimboran, Wakde, Bgu, coastal Sarmi); Geelvink Bay (Waropen, Napan, Wandaman, Numfor, Biak, Japen); the Vogelkop and off-lying islands (Amberbaken coast, Sarong, the area southwest of Lake Ayamaru, Waigeo, Salawati); McCluer Gulf-Bintuni Bay (Manikion, Babo, Fakfak); and the Arguni Bay area of the southwest coast. [Cf. van Baal et al. 1961.] The cultures of these areas are relatively little known, modern anthropological fieldwork being limited to groups such as Nimboran (Kouwenhoven 1956), Bgu (Koentjaraningrat 1966), Waropen (Held 1958), Biak-Numfor (Kamma 1954), Mejbrat (Elmberg 1968), Manikion (Pouwer 1960a), and the Arguni Bay tribes (van Logchem 1963). [For a recent comprehensive bibliography, see Australian National University 1968.] • Although located in widely differing ecological zones and thus varying markedly in specific content, the cultures of the West New Guinea peoples, both AN and NAN, are nevertheless similar in many respects to those of Indonesia —in particular to those of the Flores-Banda region of eastern Indonesia, the region characterized by the presence of a so-called Papuan or Melanesoid physical type. Similarities at the generalized pattern level would appear to include bilineal ("double unilateral") types of social organization; elaboration of the marriage relationship through institutionalized exchange of women and goods; the symbolic expression of complementary dualism in such things as house construction, myth, and ritual; headhunting, associated with bird (e.g. hornbill) symbolism; men's houses and secret societies; preoccupation with ancestral spirits and the preservation of the skulls and bones of the dead; the accumulation of wealth in such things as pigs, cloth fabrics, shells, and gongs; together with the elaboration of exchange relationships for purposes of individual status and prestige or within a context of magico-religious feasts aimed at the welfare of the entire community. [See van der Leeden 1960: 127ff.; Pouwer 1960b; Elmberg 1965; van Baal 1953-54; de Bruijn 1958-59.] The task of interpreting the meaning of such similarities, in culture-historical terms, lies beyond the scope of this volume. The prehistoric movements of peoples and ideas throughout this area, involving not only New Guinea and the Indonesian Archipelago but also, judging from a variety of evidence, the regions of Australia and Tasmania as well, can at present only be guessed at. Cultural parallels of the kind just mentioned may be the result of an ancient, widespread "Melanesoid" or "Australoid" stratum; they may reflect a movement or movements of AN speakers out of mainland Southeast Asia; or they may be the result of a reverse movement of peoples out of Melanesia back into Indonesia. The role of early trade in diffusing cultural forms and ideas should certainly not be overlooked because of preoccupation with hypothetical migrations and movements of peoples. Certainly there has been extensive transmigration within West New Guinea in relatively recent times—generally from east to west—resulting in a mixture of linguistic, cultural, and physical features that makes ethnological classification extremely difficult and further complicates the task of reconstructing cultural history in a wider areal sense (cf. Oosterwal 1966; de Bruijn 1958-59).

BIBLIOGRAPHY. Australian National University 1968; van Baal 1953-54; van Baal et al. 1961; de Bruijn 1958-59; Capell 1969; Dyen 1965; Elmberg 1959, 1965, 1968; Held 1958; Kamma 1954; Koentjaraningrat 1966; Kouwenhoven 1956; van der Leeden 1960; van Logchem 1963; Murdock 1964; Oosterwal 1966; Pouwer 1960a, 1960b, 1961.

CELEBES

The oddly shaped island of Celebes (Indonesian, Sulawesi) is extremely mountainous, with few navigable rivers and limited internal communication. The population, estimated at 3.5 million by Kennedy (1935: 484), reaches a density of over 100 per square mile only in the extreme north and south, where fertile volcanic soils make possible the growing of irrigated rice on a large scale. These two regions, Minahasa in the north and Macassar in the south, have been the areas of greatest Europeanization and economic development. The remainder of the island, except for intermittent enclaves of coastal Pasisir culture, has been inhabited right up until the twentieth century by swidden agriculturists, isolated on interior plateaus or in river valleys and around lakes remote from the outside world. Much of the island, in particular its southeastern portion, is sparsely populated. Three great gulfs, Bone, Tolo, and Tomini, divide the island into its characteristic spiderlike shape, with narrow, mountainous peninsulas stretching out to the north, east, southeast, and south. The northern peninsula, together with the Sangihe-Talaud archipelagoes, forms a natural bridge to the Philippines and, like the Sulu Archipelago extension of northern Borneo, has undoubtedly provided a natural causeway for the movement of men and ideas back and forth between the Indonesian and Philippine worlds. This fact is evident, for example, in the presence of Philippine-related languages throughout the northern portion of Celebes. The indigenous cultures of the interior seem originally not to have been organized beyond the level of the local valley or watershed—so-called "tribal territories" made up of politically independent villages related by affinal or cognatic kin ties and constituting what might best be thought of as endogamous ritual areas organized intermittently for common defense and headhunting. This pattern appears to be characteristic also of interior Borneo and Sabah, continuing north into the Philippines and beyond to aboriginal Formosa. In Celebes and Borneo, at least, the picture is modified continually by what appear to be intrusive ideas of rigid social stratification, a supernaturally sanctioned, chiefly aristocracy with a monopoly on various kinds of ritual wealth (buffalo, jars, brassware, cloth), and incipient territorial domains tributary to coastal Muslim sultanates. It would appear that these intrusive elements are traceable ultimately to the spread of Hindu-Javanese high culture throughout Indonesia subsequent to about the twelfth century A.D., mediated by the outward migrations of Malay, Javanese, and Buginese traders and adventurers and by the founding along coastal estuaries of small Muslim principalities or sultanates. Initiation of trade relations with interior tribes and subsequent political domination through indirect tributary arrangements which granted titles to tribal chieftains presumably led over time to the development of chiefly aristocracies among formerly politically unorganized hill tribes. The classification of Celebes ethnic groups in the present volume follows closely that of Kennedy (1935), who in turn relied heavily on the cultural and linguistic data of A. C. Kruyt and N. Adriani. Certain modifications to this scheme have been made in accordance with re-

cent linguistic research by J. Noorduyn (1968). The order of entries is a geographical one, beginning in the north with Minahasa. The peoples of the Sangihe and Talaud islands, north of the Minahasa, are, however, included in Volume 2, together with the Samal-speaking peoples of the Sulu Archipelago and Mindanao. The Bajau, or boat peoples of the northern and eastern coasts of Celebes, are included elsewhere in the present volume under "Sea Nomads."

BIBLIOGRAPHY. Kennedy 1935; Noorduyn 1968.

MINAHASA

KENNEDY (1935) included all the peoples of the northern peninsula of Celebes within a Minahasa Group, named for the numerically and culturally dominant Minahasans, in and around the port town of Manado. Other major "tribal" complexes include Bolaang Mongondow, Gorontalo, and Tomini, the latter, in the mountains at the neck of the peninsula, being mixed with the Toradja of central Celebes. The recorded history of this area is one of the rise and fall of petty kingdoms and their occasional confederation into larger entities for defense or conquest. It seems likely that the region was inhabited originally by peoples essentially of Toradja stock, the institution of territorial rulers, court life, and the sacred regalia of kingship having been introduced at a later date from Islamized Ternate or Mindanao. The Minahasa districts were almost totally Christianized under the Dutch; by virtue of education in mission schools, Minahasans and Manadenese were widely employed in the civil service prior to Independence in 1949.

BIBLIOGRAPHY. Kennedy 1935.

MINAHASANS

Synonym. *Minahasser*

ORIENTATION. **Identification.** The term Minahasa refers to the confederacy of tribes formed against the neighboring Bolaang Mongondow (Graafland 1898) and includes the following groups: Tontemboan or Tompakewa, Toulour, Tondano, Tombalu, Tonsea, Tonsawang or Tonsini, Bentenan or Ratahan, Ponosokan, Belang, and Bantik (Kennedy 1935; Watuseke

1962: 15). **Location.** Extreme northeastern section of Celebes' northern peninsula, in extremely mountainous terrain. **Linguistic affiliation.** There appear to be two dialect subgroups, both cognate to languages of the Philippines (Adriani 1925). **Demography.** In 1955, the provincial population (Minahasa together with the municipality of Manado) totaled 525,000. Fertile volcanic soils of interior valleys and plateaus support a relatively dense population (Watuseke 1961). **History and cultural relations.** The origin myth centers on Liminu'ut, who was born from a stone and who then married her son To'ar. Their children are the ancestors of the Minahasans. Settlement was in waves from Central Celebes, a main wave from the north (probably Philippines) and from the east. The northern peninsula of Celebes has a long history of intertribal feuding and warfare. Politics in this area was further complicated by interference from Ternate and by Spanish intrigue emanating from the Philippines. The Minahasa confederacy in 1679 sought aid from the Dutch in its struggles with Spain; the Dutch, however, did not succeed in integrating the area politically until the beginning of the twentieth century. Dutch influence in the Minahasa districts has, however, been profound, resulting in virtually complete Christianization, the growth of a sizable Eurasian population, and the disappearance of indigenous cultures. [Kennedy 1935; Godée Molsbergen 1928; Watuseke 1962.]

SETTLEMENT PATTERN AND HOUSING. Indigenous settlements were fortified, with houses raised high on stilts. Nowadays villages are open, arranged in rows of houses, each with a hedged yard. **Housing.** Formerly large pile dwellings, with apartments for from four to twelve families. Today single family houses on low piles, with plank walls and thatch roofs, are the rule. The veranda is open, storage is underneath, the kitchen is separate, and rice granaries are near the rice fields. [Adam 1925: 428-35; Graafland 1898: 1, 266-70.]

ECONOMY. **Agriculture.** Wet and dry rice are the staples, backed by maize and sago. Tobacco and coffee (introduced by the Dutch in 1822), coconuts, and cloves are grown commercially (Graafland 1898: 1, 147-56, 182-89). **Fishing and hunting.** Some fishing, plus hunting of wild pigs, snakes, and rats. **Domestic animals.** Horse, buffalo (used to draw a simple plow), goats, pigs, chickens, and dogs (the latter are occasionally eaten) (Kennedy 1935: 640-41). **Industrial arts.** Formerly hemp cloth (*koffo*) was woven. Bark cloth, basketry and mats, pottery, blacksmithing, and gold working, the latter two being specialized. Boatbuilding includes dugout canoes and plank-board, sea going boats, with sails and double outriggers (Graafland 1898: 1, 336-54, 404-08; Kennedy 1935: 648). **Trade.** Principally copra, cloves, and gold. **Division of labor.** Men do the heavier work in the fields, build houses, and take part in smithing and carpentry. Women work domestically; mind animals; make pottery, textiles, mats, and baskets; and do the lighter fieldwork. Cooperative groups (*mapalus*) work each member's land, assist in housebuilding, and sometimes loan money. Each *mapalus* is organized by a committee and may continue for many years (Adam 1925: 495-99; Kennedy 1935: 641; Taulu 1952: 82-89). **Land tenure.** Villages own the land in common (*kalakeran*), and fields are distributed annually by the chief according to household need. Fields may also be owned by families, but these revert to the common pool when no longer in use (Adam 1925: 488-95; Kennedy 1935: 651). Private land ownership is increasing, however (Taulu 1952: 13).

KIN GROUPS. **Descent.** Originally bilateral, according to Kennedy (1935: 649). **Kin groups.** The Tondano, Tombalu, Tonsea, and Tontemboan were divided into localized genealogical units (*walak*), each with its own territory and customs. Chieftainship was hereditary within certain noble families, usually within the male line. The present system of administrative districts has developed out of this ancient genealogical system (Kennedy 1935: 650; Taulu 1952: 76-77; Watuseke 1962). **Kinship terminology.** Kennedy (1935: 654) gives the following terms:

Grandparent	*apo*
Father, uncle	*ama, amang*
Mother	*ina, inang*
Aunt	*ra'a*
Sibling	*po'ou*
Elder sibling	*kaka*
Younger sibling	*rari*
Child	*anak, ana', saru, toya'ang*
Nephew, niece	*ito, ra'a*
Grandchild	*poyo*

MARRIAGE AND FAMILY. **Mode.** Though boys and girls choose each other, formal arrangements for marriage are made by a go-between, who negotiates with each family, except in the Ratahan and Tonsawang tribes (Adam 1925: 442). The boy moves to the girl's family, the ceremony includes payment of brideprice and a joint meal. A second feast (*fosso*) is held at the boy's family village (Adam 1925: 438-56; Graafland 1898: 1, 464-69). Today marriage is Christian. **Form.** Monogamous. **Extension of incest taboos.** Neither clan exogamy nor endogamy was evident. Marriage of "uncles/aunts" with "nephews/nieces" and between cousins was forbidden (Adam 1925: 451). **Residence.** Customarily matrilocal for one year, then neolocal (Adam 1925: 456; Kennedy 1935: 653). **Domestic unit.** Formerly the extended bilateral family, but now limited to the nuclear family. **Inheritance.** All those who contributed to the expenses of the funeral shared the inheritance. A widow received one third, a widower two thirds of their common property. According to Taulu (1952: 17), inheritance is equally divided among all children. [Adam 1925:

486-88.] **Divorce.** Adultery, childlessness, and quarrelsomeness are the commonest reasons for divorce, and a man may simply repudiate his wife (Adam 1925: 457-59). Children choose which parent to accompany if they are old enough; if not, they go with the mother. **Adoption.** Frequently occurs to compensate for childlessness, old age, lack of help, etc. Adoption is carried out in public and confirmed by a sacrifice and feast. The adopted child retains his ties with his own parents, but may inherit from his stepparents (Adam 1925: 469-77; Taulu 1952: 39-47).

SOCIOPOLITICAL ORGANIZATION. Traditional structure. The genealogical unit (*walak*) was headed by a chief (*tua'n teranak*), the eldest male of the senior generation, although Kennedy (1935: 650) states that the chiefship was hereditary from father to son and gives the following titles: *kapala in balak, pahendon'tua, pamatua*. Village administration was by chief, priests, war leader, and judge. The chief was elected by the elders (Domsdorff 1937: 354). **Contemporary structure.** Based on districts, subdivided into subdistricts and villages. These are headed by *hukum besar, hukum kedua,* and *hukum tua,* each being assisted by lesser officials (Kennedy 1935; Watuseke 1962: 72). **Social stratification.** Nobles, freemen, and slaves, although class distinctions were of relatively little importance. Nobles wore brass or gold arm and leg bands (Kennedy 1935). **Warfare.** Formerly endemic between *walak,* and particularly between Minahasa and Bolaang Mongondow. Warfare was probably centered on headhunting expeditions, which took place at the death of a chief. Warriors, wearing hornbill headdresses, were led by a priest-general (*teterusan*). [Graafland 1898: *1*, 407-13; Kennedy 1935: 656.]

RELIGION. The Minahasans are predominantly Christian, except for the Muslim Ponosakan (Watuseke 1961: 101). **Indigenous religion.** Luminu'ut is the earth goddess, To'ar the sun god. *Empung* are the influential ancestor spirits who dwell in trees and mountains. They are propitiated at household altars and keep the evil spirits (*sakit*) at bay (Graafland 1898: *1*, 206-17; Kennedy 1935: 660). **Practitioners.** *Walian,* or priest shamans, can be male or female. *Talengas* read omens expressed in bird calls, *tonaas* officiate at agricultural rites, *teterusan* are the warrior priests, and the influential elders are called *potu-osan* (Graafland 1898: *1*, 241-45). **Ceremonies.** The sacrificial feast (*fosso*) dominates religious life. There are family and village *fosso,* and all are aimed at honoring, propitiating, and seeking the assistance of the ancestors (*empung*). A great *fosso* is held every two years. *Fosso,* being expensive, are feasts for accumulating prestige (Graafland 1898: *1*, 218-41). **Illness and medicine.** Illness is attributed to spirits (*sakit*), breaking of taboos, and angry ancestors. Curing is by shamans, spirit possession, and a few herbal remedies (Adam 1925: 477-80; Graafland 1898: *1*, 473-77). **Soul, death, and afterlife.** Some tribes bury in a stone urn with a roof-shaped lid (*waruga, tiwukar*), and poor people are buried in hollowed-out logs. Tonsawang bury in the earth and erect a painted hut over the grave. All others erect a simple hut. Coffins are used today. The funeral is conducted by the *walian* (Kennedy 1935: 658 gives a special priestly title of *mawasal*), and the corpse is safely speeded to the world of the ancestors (Bertling 1931-32; Wylick 1941: 17-30).

BIBLIOGRAPHY. Adam 1925; Adriani 1925; Allard 1955; Bertling 1931-32; Domsdorff 1937; Godée Molsbergen 1928; Graafland 1898; Kennedy 1935; Tauchmann 1968; Taulu 1952; Watuseke 1961, 1962; Wylick 1941.

BOLAANG MONGONDOW

ORIENTATION. Identification and location. Of partly Minahasan, particularly Tonsea, origin. Located in the northern peninsula of Celebes, between the Minahasans and the Gorontalo, in largely mountainous country. Subgroups include: Buluan, Binangunan, Polian, Lombagin, and Dumoga. [Kennedy 1935; Dunnebier 1949; Wilken and Schwarz 1867b: 312-13.] **Linguistic affiliation.** Specified by Esser (1938) as Philippine. **Demography.** *Volkstelling 1930* gives a total of 63,000. Berzina and Bruk (1963: 81) give a more recent figure of 100,000. **History and cultural relations.** The Bolaang are coastal people who have merged with the inland and earlier settled Mongondow. They were ruled until 1950 as a principality under the Paduka Radja, who was elected by district chiefs (penghulu) from members of a royal family (Dunnebier 1949; Kennedy 1935; Taulu and Sepang 1961).

SETTLEMENT PATTERN AND HOUSING. Settlement pattern. Villages are strung out along roads, mostly on the upland plateaus. **Housing.** Formerly longhouses, resting on stilts and similar in style to those of the Minahasans.

ECONOMY. Primarily agricultural, supplemented by fishing, the collection of damar and rattan, and (formerly) gold mining. Staple is irrigated rice, with sago, maize, yams, and cassava variously given as costaples (Kennedy 1935: 640). Coconuts, coffee, and rice are also cash crops (Taulu and Sepang 1961: 49-50). Cooperative work groups (*momosad*) are reported (Notosoesanto 1933: 430), but these may be recent. **Domestic animals.** Pigs, cattle, buffalo, goats, and chickens. **Land tenure.** Village-owned land, with rights of usufruct going to individual villagers. Notosoesanto (1933: 422-29) reports sale, rent, mortgaging, and sharecropping of fields.

KIN GROUPS. **Descent.** Reported as bilateral by Notosoesanto (1933: 411). Kinship terminology from Kennedy (1935: 655):

FaFa, MoFa	*laki*
FaMo, MoMo	*baai*
Fa	*ama*
FaBr, MoBr	*pakuama'an*
Mo	*ina*
MoSi, FaSi	*pakunia'an*
Elder sibling	*guya-guyang*
Younger sibling	*ai-ai*
Sibling	*utat*
Child	*adi*
Grandchild	*ompu*

Kin groups. Notosoesanto (1933: 406-07) mentions bilateral kin groups, called *kaoem*.

MARRIAGE AND FAMILY. Spouses choose each other, but marriage negotiations, centering on bride-price, are conducted between the families. Bride-price varies with the girl's rank. The main ceremony is a joint meal of the two families at the bride's home (Dunnebier 1931; Notosoesanto 1933: 413-17). **Form.** Generally monogamy, but polygyny is frequent. **Extension of incest taboos.** Follows the rules of Islam. **Residence.** Kennedy mentions temporary matrilocality (1935: 653), and Notosoesanto (1933: 417) suggests temporary patrilocality. Both agree to subsequent neolocal residence. **Domestic unit.** Nuclear family. **Inheritance.** Equally divided among the children, but Dunnebier (1949: 271) mentions that in former times the ruler received part of every inheritance. **Divorce.** Frequent, and initiated by either spouse. If the wife is at fault, the bride-price is repaid (Notosoesanto 1933: 418-19).

SOCIOPOLITICAL ORGANIZATION. **Political organization.** Traditionally, the ruler was assisted by a council of advisors. Village headmen were appointed by the ruler until 1950, assisted by the elders of the kin groups (*kaoem*) (Notosoesanto 1933: 406-08). **Social stratification.** Basically nobles, commoners, and slaves, each with many subdivisions (Kennedy 1935: 652). Dunnebier (1949: 264) says that a child belonged to the class of his mother, but Kennedy says it was the class of the father in interclass marriages (1935: 649). **Social control and justice.** Exercised by village elders. **Warfare.** Intervillage feuding was common. Traditional enemies were the Minahasans, and headhunting in honor of dead chiefs was practiced.

RELIGION. The indigenous religion was apparently an ancestor cult. Islam dates to 1830, and Protestant missionaries have made inroads. **Supernaturals.** Ancestor and nature spirits (Wilken and Schwarz 1867a: 256-57). **Practitioners.** Traditionally, according to Wilken and Schwarz (1867a: 257-58), there were: *wolian*, who officiated at ceremonies; *tonawat*, who presided over agricultural rites; *talengo*, or diviners; and sorcerers. **Ceremonies.** Annual *monibi* ritual, combating evil spirits, and lesser, but more frequent, village-level *fosso* offerings (Dunnebier 1938: 32-36; Wilken and Schwarz 1867a: 258-75). **Illness and medicine.** Attributed entirely to ancestral and evil spirits, who are "divined" by *talengo* and "cured" by the *wolian* (Wilken and Schwarz 1867a: 259-75). **Soul, death, and afterlife.** The corpse was encoffined, kept in the house until the feast, then buried. Nowadays Islamic rites are followed.

BIBLIOGRAPHY. Berzina and Bruk 1963; Dunnebier 1931, 1938, 1949; Esser 1938; Kennedy 1935; Notosoesanto 1933; Taulu and Sepang 1961; *Volkstelling 1930;* Wilken and Schwarz 1867a, 1867b.

GORONTALO

Synonym. *Holontalo*

ORIENTATION. **Identification.** The term refers to a grouping of: Gorontalo proper, Buol, Boalemo, Kwandang, Bone, Limboto, Soewawa, and Attingola (Kennedy 1935, Korn 1939). **Location.** Northern peninsula between the Bolaang Mongondow and the Toli-toli, mostly on the Gorontalo plain. **Linguistic affiliation.** Four dialects, which in the west are closer to Toradja and elsewhere distinctly Philippine (Esser 1938). **Demography.** Approximately 350,000 (Berzina and Bruk 1963: 81). **History and cultural relations.** Warfare between Gorontalo and Limboto ceased with their confederation in 1673. Later they were joined by three other principalities to form the League of Five Brothers (Lima Pahala), which broke up in 1889 and came under rule of the Dutch (Bastiaans 1938; Haga 1931; Korn 1939).

SETTLEMENT PATTERN AND HOUSING. Formerly mountain dwellers, but now living in scattered villages on the plain or on the coast.

ECONOMY. Swidden rice, maize, and sago are staples of equal importance. Only the Buol prefer sago. Yams and millet are secondary crops, and coconut is grown commercially (Korn 1939). **Fishing and gathering.** Nets, traps, and harpoons are used for fishing on Lake Limboto. Rattan and damar are gathered for sale (Korn 1939). **Domestic animals.** Cattle are kept for draft purposes, horses for pack and riding. **Industrial arts.** The Buol make outstanding dyed cloth, with silk inlays, and sew fine clothes (Kennedy 1935: 643, 649). **Property.** Each spouse owns property separately, and only that obtained after marriage is held jointly (Samin Radjik Nur 1965).

KIN GROUPS. **Descent.** The actual form of descent is doubtful, but is given as formerly bilateral (Haga 1931: 214) and now, following Islam, patrilineal. **Kin** groups. Territorially based, genealogically identified groups, known in former times as *linula* or *kaom,* are now defunct.

MARRIAGE AND FAMILY. **Mode.** Follows Muslim pattern, arranged by a go-between, who also negotiates the bride-price—the amount of which depends on the girl's rank. **Form.** Polygyny is permitted. **Extension of incest taboos.** Islamic restrictions are observed. Cross-cousin marriage is preferred, though parallel-cousin marriage also occurs (Samin Radjik Nur 1965: 22-23). **Residence.** Initially matrilocal, then neolocal (Haga 1931). **Divorce.** Easily obtained. Children remain with the mother (Samin Radjik Nur 1965: 44). **Secondary marriage.** Sororate, and occasionally levirate. **Adoption.** Favored in cases of childless marriages.

SOCIOPOLITICAL ORGANIZATION. Originally, all principalities were governed from the Ternate Sultanate. Each tribe was headed by an hereditary chief (*olongia, marsaoleh*) and his assistants (*walaapulu*), who also formed a council for assisting the ruler in governing the confederacy (Haga 1931; Bastiaans 1939; Kennedy 1935). Bastiaans (1939) discusses the dualistic nature of the political structure of old Gorontalo, as expressed in the institution of dual or complementary rulers, and van Wouden (1941) points out the interrelation of myth and social structure in the kingdom of Buol. **Social stratification.** Haga (1931: 215) mentions four classes: the royal lineage, the nobility, commoners, and former slaves.

RELIGION. **Indigenous religion.** A supreme god (La) and influential evil spirits (*latilo oloto*) were served and propitiated by priests and priestesses (*ponggo*), who apparently used spirit possession (Kennedy 1935: 661). Today all Gorontalo are Muslims.

BIBLIOGRAPHY. Bastiaans 1938, 1939; Berzina and Bruk 1963; Esser 1938; Haga 1931; Kennedy 1935; Korn 1939; Samin Radjik Nur 1965; van Wouden 1941.

TOMINI

Synonyms. *Toli-toli, Tominiers*

ORIENTATION. **Identification and location.** Toradja in origin, there are numerous subgroups, including: Mautong or Mouton, Dondo, Boano, Umalasa, Balaesan, Tinombo, Petapa, Dampelasa, Kasimbar, Tolitoli, and the Tomini proper (Kennedy 1935: 507). The Tomini are located on the northern peninsula between the Gorontalo and the Western Toradja, with whom they have mixed. The country is mountainous, but there are also coastal groups intermixed with Gorontalo, Mandar, and Bugis immigrants. The influence of the latter is marked (Anonymous 1912: 35-37).

Demography. In 1930, the Tomini were estimated at 29,000 (*Volkstelling 1930*) and in 1961, at about 50,000 (Berzina and Bruk 1963: 81).

SETTLEMENT PATTERN AND HOUSING. Small villages on the coast, comprised of houses on stilts (Anonymous 1912: 47; *ENI*: 7, 422). The mountain-dwelling Dondo have in recent years mostly moved down to the coast.

ECONOMY. **Agriculture.** Maize and sago are staples, but wet rice was introduced in the early 1900s. Copra is raised commercially. Rattan and damar are collected (*ENI*: 7, 423-25; Anonymous 1912: 51-55).

KIN GROUPS. **Descent.** According to Nieboer (1929: 82), Mautong children "belong alternately to the father and the mother," indicative of some kind of ambilineal or nonunilineal pattern.

MARRIAGE AND FAMILY. **Mode.** Infant betrothal sometimes occurs. Bride-price depends on the girl's rank, and the ceremony follows Islam (Anonymous 1912: 49-50). **Inheritance.** Children inherit equally (Nieboer 1929: 82; Anonymous 1912: 51). **Divorce.** Frequent, with children choosing the parent with whom they will stay (Nieboer 1929: 82).

SOCIOPOLITICAL ORGANIZATION. A sultan or radja, assisted by a council, governs separate "tribes" or "principalities." Foreign settlements have their own headmen (*olongian*) (Anonymous 1912: 41-43). **Social stratification.** The Toli-toli recognize three classes: nobility, wealthy commoners, and lesser commoners. The Dondo stratify into chiefs and commoners (*ENI*: 7, 424). **Social control and justice.** Fines were levied, and a form of debt slavery existed (Anonymous 1912: 44-45).

RELIGION. Nothing is known of the indigenous religion, and all Tomini are now Muslim, though there is some evidence of ancestor worship (Anonymous 1912: 38-40, 50-51).

BIBLIOGRAPHY. Anonymous 1912; Berzina and Bruk 1963; *ENI* 1917-39; van Hoëvell 1892; Kennedy 1935; Nieboer 1929; *Volkstelling 1930*.

TORADJA

THE NAME TORADJA is derived from a term meaning "men of the mountains," applied by lowlanders to indigenous inhabitants of the high mountain ranges and interior valleys of central Celebes. Relative isolation within a rugged landscape has produced innumerable named groups or "tribes," which, despite local differences, conform to a similar culture type (Kennedy 1935: 562), extending from the limits of Buginese territory in the southwest to the beginning of the Gorontalo districts on the northern peninsula and bordered on the east by Loinang and Mori peoples. Within this rather extensive area, the physical type is generally Proto-Malay or Paleo-Mongoloid ("Indonesian"), with evidence here and there of a Veddoid substratum. In areas near the coast there is intermixture with the more Mongoloid Bugis. The languages, although influenced in the south by Buginese and in the north by intrusive Philippine dialects, appear to belong basically to a single language group or at least to closely related groups (Esser classified Sa'dan within a South Celebes group, separate from his Toradja group). It has been customary to consider the peoples of central Celebes within a three-fold division, Western, Eastern, and Southern Toradja (cf. Kruyt 1931a). For convenience of presentation, this convention is followed in the present volume; it reflects, as much as anything, differing degrees of exposure to cultural influences stemming from the old Hindu-Javanese states of southwestern Celebes (Luwu, Goa, Boni) and nearby Borneo. Nor do the divisions imply any kind of transcendent political organization; the indigenous Toradja seem not to have been organized politically beyond the level of the local village or congeries of neighboring villages. Kennedy (1935) estimated a total Toradja population (including the Southern Toradja or Sa'dan) of around 600,000, a figure approximately similar to a more recent estimate by Berzina and Bruk (1963: 82). Until recently these peoples were known primarily through the works of A. C. and J. Kruyt and Adriani, based on observations dating back to the 1890s. Their colorful cultures, especially the more striking aspects, such as headhunting, elaborate sacrificial and postmortuary rites, cave burial, and the presence of ancient carved stone monoliths and great glazed burial jars have occasioned much secondary analysis and historical reconstruction of a speculative nature (cf. Kruyt 1932h; Kaudern 1925-44). Many of the crucial questions concerning social organization, particularly with reference to contemporary interest in cognatic social structures in the adjacent Borneo-Philippine area, remain unanswered in the available data. A. C. Kruyt, to whose zeal can be attributed the bulk of the relatively extensive ethnographic record bearing on the peoples of Celebes, was a missionary and not an anthropologist (cf. Downs 1956 for a critique of his data on East Toradja). Modern anthropological fieldwork, such as the recent studies by C. H. M. Nooy-Palm among the Sa'dan Toradja, may fill the more important gaps in our knowledge of the interior mountain tribes of Celebes, certainly among the most interesting of all the peoples of Indonesia.

BIBLIOGRAPHY. Berzina and Bruk 1963; Downs 1956; Esser 1938; Kaudern 1925-44; Kennedy 1935; Kruyt 1931a, 1932h.

WESTERN TORADJA

Synonyms. *Koro Toradja, Palu Toradja, Parigi-Kaili Toradja, Sigi Toradja, Toradja Barat*

ORIENTATION. **Location and identification.** The northwestern portion of central Celebes, extending up the northern peninsula as far as Tomini territory. Mountainous except for the area around Palu Bay. Kennedy (1935: 506) divides the Western Toradja lands into (1) an eastern portion inhabited by so-called Mountain Toradjas, including Tawaelia, Napu, Besoa, Bada, Leboni, Rampi, and Rato (2) a western portion, chiefly the valley of the Koro-Lariang River, inhabited by so-called Pipikoro Toradjas, including Banasu, Kantewu, Koro, Baku, Winatu, Tole, Mohapi, Peana, and Gimpu (3) a northwestern portion around Lake Lindu and the valley of the Palu, including Kulawi, Pakuli, Lindu, Sigi, Toro, Sidondo, Pakawa, and Palu, and (4) a northern portion, including Parigi, Sausu, Kaili, Balinggi, Banawa, Ganti, Dolago, and Donggala. There is less homogeneity among these Western Toradja "tribes" than among the groups of Eastern Toradja. **Linguistic affiliation.** Considerable dialect diversity, especially as compared to the Eastern Toradja. Sometimes referred to collectively as *ria* (*ara*) languages, from the word for "to be." The Palu dialect serves as a lingua franca throughout most of the West Toradja area. **Demography.** A 1961 estimate of 180,000 by Berzina and Bruk (1963: 81).

SETTLEMENT PATTERN AND HOUSING. Villages were formerly fortified. Today there are small, nucleated hilltop villages, and scattered plains villages. Mountain villages have temples and smithies. There has been some government relocation into large, centralized communities. **Housing.** Housing types vary according to basic substructure of either horizontal or vertical beams, with roof running to the ground or to walls. Usually a single room, occupied by a small extended family (Kaudern 1925-44: *1*, 55-96; Kennedy 1935: 518-21; Kruyt 1938: *2*, 4).

ECONOMY. **Agriculture.** Wet and dry rice, with maize and sago providing secondary staples. Millet, taro, vegetables, fruit, sugarcane, and tobacco are grown. Irrigation and the plow are recent; formerly wet fields were prepared by driving cattle around in them. Rice is stored in granaries or bark cylinders. Wet-rice agriculture has a ritual leader (Kruyt 1938: *2*, chap. 15; Woensdregt 1928: 131-32). **Fishing and hunting.** Sea and lake fishing with traps and baskets, and eel fishing a specialty of the mountains. Toradja are passionate hunters of deer, pigs, marsupials, and apes. They use dogs, spears, snares, and blowguns (Kruyt 1938: *2*, 1-62). **Domestic animals.** Most groups raise water buffalo, but with little tending. Dogs, chickens, goats, sheep, and horses are also raised (Kruyt 1938: *2*, 33-54). **Industrial arts.** Ironworking is of relatively little importance. Gold is mined, but not worked locally. An exceptionally fine bark cloth is beaten by women, who in some groups also make pottery. [Kennedy 1935: 529-30; Kruyt 1938: *2*, chap. 18.] **Property.** The extended family owns common property in fields, buffalo, and (formerly) slaves. The nuclear household owns, and passes on to its children (especially daughters) such property as it acquires, e.g. fowl, pigs, and rice (Kruyt 1938: *3*, 154-55).

KIN GROUPS. **Descent.** Kruyt (1938: *3*, 27) suggests bilateral descent. Woensdregt (1929: 263) says children belong alternately to each parent, the first child to the father. **Kinship terminology.** This stresses generation:

GrFa	*ngkai*
GrMo	*tu'a*
Fa	*tama*
Mo	*ine* or *nene*
ElBr	*tukaka*
ElSi	*tua'i*
Sib	*mopotu*
Ch	*ana*
GrCh	*makumpu*

"Own" brother or sister may be indicated by a specific term: *kasangkompo* (belonging to one belly). [Kennedy 1935: 540-41.]

MARRIAGE AND FAMILY. **Mode.** Sexual relations are free, but marriages are arranged by a go-between. A bride-price (buffalo, brassware, cloth) is paid, but in some cases not until after the woman becomes pregnant (Kennedy 1935: 537). **Form.** Polygyny does occur among chiefs, but subject to the first wife's approval. **Divorce.** Children choose which parent they follow; infants remain with the mother. **Extension of incest taboos.** Intergenerational marriage is infrequent. Parallel-cousin marriage is taboo, but cross-cousin marriage allowed. Brother-sister exchange

is preferred and endogamy favored, though small groups make this difficult. Taboos can be ritually "washed away" (Kruyt 1938: *3*, 27; Kennedy 1935: 537). **Residence.** Matrilocal (Kruyt 1938: *3*, 27). **Domestic unit.** The extended family is apparently split into nuclear family households, all within a compound (Kaudern 1925-44: *1*, 37). **Inheritance.** A man's ancestral property is administered by female relatives, and daughters receive most of the inheritance from each parent. Private, or individually owned, property is confined to fruit trees, weapons, and clothes (Kennedy 1935: 537; Kruyt 1938: *3*, 64). **Divorce.** Divorce is common, adjudicated by village council if not mutual, and the delinquent pays a fine. Property obtained during marriage is distributed equally (Kruyt 1938: *2*, 55-58). **Secondary marriage.** Levirate, and infrequently the sororate, is reported for the To Bada by Woensdregt (1929: 289). **Adoption.** Usually of a sibling's child in case of childlessness (Kruyt 1938: *2*, 29).

SOCIOPOLITICAL ORGANIZATION. **Political organization.** The Bugis exercised a weak overlordship of the Toradja, who paid tribute. In some instances there were village confederacies (Kennedy 1935: 537), or villages were governed by a council of household heads who elected a chief (*kabosenya*). The To Bada village was based on a matrilineal unit (*hampaka*), centering on a temple and headed by an honorary chief (*mokole*) (Kennedy 1935: 535). In many tribal groups a noble class ruled (Kruyt 1938: *1*, 505-06). **Social stratification.** In most instances there were three classes: nobility, commoners, and slaves. Nobility and slaves were not found in all tribes. Slaves were also divided into hereditary (who belonged to the family) and war captives (Kruyt 1938: *1*, 512; Kennedy 1935: 539). **Social control and justice.** Offenses were punished by carefully graded fines, arbitrated by village elders. Important decisions could be arbitrated by a nobleman. Ordeals were usual, relying on sinking a spear into the ground (Kruyt 1938: *3*, 14-28). **Warfare.** War was the principal way of uniting the tribe. It was led by special war priests (*tadulako*), whose functions were split between a noble and commoner priest. Headhunting, for heads or scalps, was a usual accompaniment to warfare. Weapons included spears, swords, shields, and fiber helmets (Kruyt 1938: *2*, 147; Kennedy 1935: 543).

RELIGION. **Religious systems.** Traditional religion centered on ancestor spirits and belief in a life force. Islam and Protestantism have become dominant (Kruyt 1938: *2*, 456). **Supernaturals.** High gods include a creator, whose envoys are birds, and a god of fertility associated with the sun (Kruyt 1938: *2*, 442). A class of benevolent spirits manifest themselves as familiars of male and female shamans, and there are as well a host of nature spirits. The spirits of departed ancestors are invoked in a variety of rituals. **Practitioners.**

Shamans, male and female, become so by virtue of a dream or illness and subsequent apprenticeship to an established shaman. They function to strengthen or recover the life force of individuals and on a variety of occasions such as pregnancies and funerals. They are accompanied by assistants who translate the language of the guardian spirit speaking through the shaman. Some engage in transvestite behavior. Other specialists include war leader-priests, family heads, and occasionally members of the nobility. [Kruyt 1938: 2, 440ff.] **Ceremonies.** Include those concerned with rice cultivation, the blessing of buffalo, headhunting, and general welfare. Village temples may be differentiated into those dedicated to agriculture and the curing of illness vs. those concerned with warfare and headhunting. **Illness and medicine.** Illness usually attributed to witchcraft or sorcery. Shamans cure by recovering or strengthening life force of patient, utilizing divination, dog sacrifice, and extraction of foreign objects from patient's body. [Kruyt 1938.] **Soul, death, and afterlife.** The life-spirit or soul can leave the body at will, through the scalp or by way of the joints. Only after the postfunerary rites does the soul become a ghost or spirit, *rate*. The corpse is encoffined and buried, formerly beneath the house. There is a postfunerary rite at the grave nine days after burial, but such rites are not as elaborate as among the Eastern Toradja. Among the Bada a surviving spouse is trussed up knees to chest, covered with a bark cloth hood, and cared for by relatives during a nine-day mourning period. The burial of a person of rank had formerly to be preceded by the taking of a head. [Kruyt 1938; Woensdregt 1930.]

BIBLIOGRAPHY. Berzina and Bruk 1963; Kaudern 1925-44; Kennedy 1935; Kruyt 1938; Woensdregt 1928, 1929, 1930.

EASTERN TORADJA

Synonyms. *Bare'e, Poso-Todjo, To Lage, Toradja Timur*

ORIENTATION. **Location and identification.** Eastern central Celebes, mainly around Lake Poso and the valleys of the Poso, Laa, and Kalaena rivers. Bounded on the west by the Western Toradja, on the east by Mori and Loinang tribes, on the north by the Gulf of Tomini, and on the south by the (Buginese) kingdom of Luwu. Kennedy (1935: 506) divides the Eastern Toradja into: (1) the Poso-Todjo tribes along the Gulf of Tomini and the neck of the eastern peninsula, including Lalaeo, Ra'u, Bau, Todjo, and Poso (2) the Poso Lake tribes, including Pebato, Lage, Kadombuku, Onda'e, Payapi, Lamusa, Longkea, Buyu, Pu'u mBoto, Wotu, and Bantjea (3) those of the upper

valley of the Laa, east of Lake Poso, including Palende, Kalae, Tanandoa, Pakambia, Pada, and Pu'u mBana, and (4) the tribes of the upper Kalaena, south of Lake Poso, including Lampu, Tawi, Laiwonu, and Lembo. All these groups, or "tribes," are relatively homogeneous with respect to language and culture. Two other groups, the (To) Wana and (To) Ampana to the east of Lake Poso, were included by Kruyt (1930a) in his East Toradja category, although they might best be considered separately because of certain physical characteristics and "backward" culture traits (cf. Kennedy 1935: 506; Downs 1956: 1-2). **Linguistic affiliation.** All groups speak dialects of a single language, Bare'e, after the word for "no" (Adriani and Kruyt 1912-14: 3, 11-14). **Demography.** The 1961 estimate of 100,000 by Berzina and Bruk (1963: 81) compares with an estimate by Kennedy (1935) of around 60,000 and the 1930 census figure of 30,000 (*Volkstelling 1930*). These estimates, if at all accurate, indicate a steady rise in population.

SETTLEMENT PATTERN AND HOUSING. Similar to those of the Western Toradja, except that the rectangular, raised, gable-roofed houses are larger, generally containing anywhere from four to six nuclear families (although houses with up to sixteen families do occur) (Adriani and Kruyt 1950-51: 1, 169-92).

ECONOMY. Generally similar to the Western Toradja. H. Geertz (1963: 71ff.) assumes original shifting agriculture, a factor which, together with chronic headhunting, limited the size of settlements. Wet rice was introduced by the Dutch subsequent to 1905. Prior to acculturative changes under the Dutch, land was apparently village owned (sanctioned by belief in the spirits of ancestral village founders) and worked by individual families. Extended family property, including sago trees, buffalo herds, and slaves, appears to have been used primarily for ritual and bride-price, under the direction of a family head or chief.

KIN GROUPS. **Descent.** Bilateral (Adriani and Kruyt 1950-51: 2, 429). **Kin groups.** H. Geertz (1963) stresses the primacy of the village as a localized corporate kin group, with all members related by blood or marriage. Membership in a village is (or was) utrolateral, i.e. one could affiliate with either his mother's, his father's, or his spouse's village. This principle applies also to what were apparently extended families, corporate kin groups headed by a chief or headman who looked after family property. The extended family functioned as a ceremonial unit and also with respect to payment of bride-price, although the latter also involved the members of nonlocalized personal kindreds (H. Geertz 1963: 72-73). **Kin terminology.** Of Hawaiian type. Although minor variations occur, the major terms of reference, according to Adriani and Kruyt (1950-51: 1, chap. 13), are:

Fa	papa
Mo	ine
FaBr, MoBr	tama
FaSiHu, MoSiHu	tama
FaSi, MoSi	tete
FaBrWi, MoBrWi	tete
Siblings	kasangkompo
Cousins	kasangkompo

MARRIAGE AND FAMILY. Premarital sex is permitted. Marriage is usually village-endogamous or at least with someone from a neighboring village. A bride-price is paid to the girl's relatives and may not exceed the amount paid for her mother. Until the bride-price has been paid, any children belong to their mother (Adriani and Kruyt 1950-51: 2). Monogamy was formerly the rule, but polygyny is now permitted among groups influenced by the Buginese. First-cousin marriage, once forbidden, is now common, especially when accompanied by a ritual offering. Postmarital residence is stated by Adriani and Kruyt (1950-51: 2, 318) to be predominantly matrilocal, but according to H. Geertz (1963), couples could live ultimately in the village of either the bride or groom. The domestic unit is (or was) the extended family, consisting of from four to six nuclear families (Adriani and Kruyt 1950-51: 1, 170).

SOCIOPOLITICAL ORGANIZATION. **Political organization.** H. Geertz (1963), analyzing the data of Adriani and Kruyt, stresses the autonomy of the village; only occasionally, apparently, did kinship, ceremonial, or other ties minimize the endemic hostility among villages, even those in the same river valley or watershed. Chieftainship of the village was not hereditary, but rather chiefs were selected, usually from among extended family heads, on the basis of personal characteristics and wealth in buffalo. Their power was negligible. In those areas closest to centers of Buginese influence (the sultanates of Luwu and Mori) there did, however, develop the rudiments of supravillage chieftainship—village heads endowed by coastal sultans with tax-collecting powers, who used their positions to engage in trade and thus increase their own wealth. An integral part of this pattern was the fact that the coastal rulers, or datus, were thought to be endowed with supernatural powers. On the other hand R. E. Downs, also analyzing the data of Adriani and Kruyt, includes the concept of "tribe" as apparently something indigenous to the Eastern Toradja. The members of a "tribe" were conscious of being related to one another and of having a common "mother village," for which the tribe might be named. The villages comprising a "tribe," located within drum-signaling distance of one another, occasionally joined together for mutual defense and attended one another's death feasts—otherwise they were independent entities, and there were no tribal chiefs (Downs 1956: 3). It appears that these loosely defined "ritual areas" also differed linguistically, i.e. with respect to dialects of a common Bare'e language. **Social stratification.** Traditionally there were two classes, freemen and slaves, the latter hereditary in groups closest to lowland Buginese influence. War captives and debtors also became slaves, although the latter could buy their freedom; the former could be killed as sacrifice or as compensation to settle a blood feud. On the whole, however, slaves were not treated badly; the institution, along with headhunting, was abolished by the Dutch subsequent to 1905. [Adriani and Kruyt 1950-51; H. Geertz 1963.] **Social control and justice.** Similar to the Western Toradja. **Warfare.** Associated with headhunting and endemic in former times. Heads (scalps) were essential to the general welfare and were required at the death of a chief or the erection of a new village temple.

RELIGION. Cosmology, supernatural beliefs, practitioners, and ceremonies generally similar to those of the Western Toradja. Funerary customs differ somewhat, in that the Eastern Toradja engaged in secondary death rites, at which the bones were cleaned and rededicated before burial in caves. These rites were expensive, requiring the accumulation of much food and other wealth, including sacrificial buffalo. Consequently they were held at infrequent intervals. Secondary burial rites were prohibited by the Dutch on sanitary grounds, and since that time both Islam and Christianity have made inroads; the old religious beliefs are therefore fragmented at present. [Downs 1956: 77-91.]

BIBLIOGRAPHY. Adriani and Kruyt 1912-14, 1950-51; Berzina and Bruk 1963; Downs 1956; H. Geertz 1963; Kaudern 1925-44; Kennedy 1935; Kruyt 1918-20, 1930a, 1933a, 1938; *Volkstelling 1930.*

SOUTHERN TORADJA*

Synonyms. *Sa'dan Toradja, Sadang, Tae' Toradja*

ORIENTATION. **Location and identification.** The term Toradja refers to a number of ethnic groups of Paleo-Mongoloid stock inhabiting the regions of southwestern and central Celebes. Of these groups the Sa'dan or Tae' Toradja live in the northern part of southwestern Celebes, in the valleys of the upper Sa'dan River and its tributaries. Their major concentration is in the modern administrative unit called Tana Toradja, roughly between 2°40' and 3°25' S. and 119°30' and 120°25' W. **Geography.** Mountainous limestone country, through which the Sa'dan River cuts a canyonlike valley. Much of the country is

---

* The author of this entry, C. H. M. Nooy-Palm, did fieldwork among the Sa'dan Toradja in 1949 and 1966. She is at present a member of the Department of Anthropology, Koninklijk Instituut voor de Tropen, Amsterdam. A few data on religion from Kennedy (1935) have been added by the editor.

eroded due to deforestation. **Linguistic affiliation.** The Sa'dan Toradja speak an Austronesian language (Tae'), related to the language of the Rongkong, the Mangki, and the Buginese (van der Veen 1929). **Demography.** A 1966 census gives a total of 302,000. **History and origins.** According to tradition, the ancestors came in eight *lembang* (canoes), from the mythical island Pongko'. Tradition points to the southwest. As the genealogical records count approximately 25 forefathers, the Sa'dan may have been dwelling in their country for about 500 years. **Cultural relations.** Some cultural affinities with the Bare'e Toradja do exist, but the Sa'dan are more closely related to the Buginese and to the Toradja of Rongkong, Mamasa, and Mangki, immediately to the north and west (van der Veen 1929: 58-96 and map). The Duri, an Islamic people south of the Toradja, are also related to the Sa'dan. The Mamasa Toradja may be considered a branch of the Sa'dan Toradja, as their genealogies refer to Sa'dan ancestry. Sa'dan genealogies partly refer to Buginese forefathers, especially those of *puang* families, feudal lords in the southeastern part of Toradja country. Buginese formerly invaded the Sa'dan lands, but even then intermarriage took place between Sa'dan and Buginese nobility. With Dutch occupation in 1905, a period of considerable cultural change set in, and by 1966 some 35 percent of the population was Christian. Missionary schools became popular even before World War II, and at present there are Toradja with university degrees; many of them are officials.

SETTLEMENT PATTERN AND HOUSING. **Settlement pattern.** Villages formerly on summits of hills. (Hill tops were considered sacred, as the first ancestors descended there.) Villages sometimes surrounded by fortified walls, the settlement itself reached by tunnels (Grubauer 1913: 59). Under the Dutch, the Sa'dan were ordered to build their villages on the plains. The modern Toradja village is permanent, more or less hidden by gardens of bamboo, sugar palms, coconuts, and bananas. The village complex, consisting of separate farmsteads, is surrounded by rice fields. The place for the *bua'* ceremony, the place where the rites for the dead are held (*rante*), and the cemetery in the nearby rocky cliffs all belong to the village area. A village (*tondok*) is divided into two parts, *donalu* (*do,* high) and *diongnalu* (*diong,* low). Each of these forms a ceremonial unit, a *bua'* circle. In each division several *tongkonan* (houses founded by an ancestor) are situated. **Housing.** *Tongkonan* houses are raised on piles, with the roof rising at each end, like the bow and the stern of a ship. (In fact, houses are compared with *proa's*, for instance in ritual chants.) High gables project in front; poles support the gable peak. The walls consist of panels, decorated with painted engravings of a geometrical design, of which the stylized buffalo head is the most striking. A bird's head on a long neck and a realistic

buffalo head decorate the front part of the house. To the front pole, which supports the gable, buffalo horns are attached. One or more rice barns face the house. The *tongkonan* are a representation of the cosmos: the roof represents the sky, the northern part is the most sacred, etc.

ECONOMY. **Agriculture.** Staples are rice and maize. Rice is grown on terraced, irrigated rice fields and is of sacred origin. Plow and harrow are mostly drawn by men, as the buffalo is not considered a draft animal. Other crops are cassava, coconuts, bananas, and vegetables. Coffee is the most important cash crop. **Fishing and hunting.** Hunting is of little importance. Fishing is done in small ponds in the rice fields. **Domestic animals.** Buffalo represent a status symbol, used chiefly for ceremonial purposes. Buffalo milk is drunk—it is considered a medicine—and the meat is eaten at ceremonies (mostly funerals). Pigs and chickens are slaughtered at many rituals, the pigs mostly at funerals and at the consecration of a new *tongkonan*. Dogs are eaten in some parts of Tana Toradja, occasionally as sacrificial offerings. **Industrial arts.** Metalworking, wood carving, the making of pottery, and weaving and basketry are the main industrial arts. Some villages are known for their wood carving; other regions for the plaiting of bags. The products are sold at the local markets. Among specialists, the goldsmiths, the blacksmiths, the carpenters and the wood-carvers are the most prominent. **Trade.** There are several market rings, with a cycle of six market days, the markets being held at different places. **Property.** The major types of landed property are irrigated rice fields and coffee lands. In some parts of the country there were rich landowners, and a kind of feudal system existed. Share cropping is practiced nowadays.

KIN GROUPS. **Descent.** Descent is ambilineal. One must, however, follow the death ritual of one's mother's ramage. The titleholders in the ramage are chosen (by their kin and by the village council) in accordance with their ability and capacities. **Kin groups.** The largest kin group is the ramage, i.e. an ancestor-oriented, ambilineal group. These *pa'rapuan* trace their descent to an ancestor who may have descended from heaven onto a mountain some twenty generations ago. The ancestor or his son founded a *tongkonan*, a house, in which the important ritual belongings of the family are stored and to which a title may be attached. As time went on, new *tongkonan* were founded. Because of the ramage system, the *tongkonan* are ordered hierarchically, and a person's status is fixed by the *tongkonan* to which he belongs (he belongs to several *tongkonan*: his father's mother, his mother's father, etc., but there is one *tongkonan* to which he feels himself attached the most, e.g. the family house situated in the village where he lives).

The ramage system implies that one is allowed to marry in one's own ramage; one is also allowed to marry somebody belonging to another ramage. A person inherits his father's and his mother's property; he may be chosen as a titleholder of his father's or his mother's *tongkonan;* he may attend an important ritual of his father's or his mother's *tongkonan* or of his FaMo, or his MoFa, etc. At these large feasts, of which an important *tongkonan* is the center, the descendants of the whole *pa'rapuan* are assembled. The *sangrapu* is a division of the *pa'rapuan,* which encompasses from three to five generations. Relations with the relatives-in-law (*rampean*) are important, especially during feasts. **Kin terminology.** The principal terms of reference are given below:

Fa	*ambe'*
Mo	*indo'*
MoBr, FaBr	*pa'amberan*
MoSi, FaSi	*pa'indoran*
GrParents	*nene'*
Son	*anak muane*
Daughter	*anak baine*
Youngest child	*bongsu*

When ego is a male he refers to his brother as *sangmuane,*
to his sister as *anak dara*
his FaBrSo as his *sangmuane*
his FaBrDa as his *anak dara*
his FaSiSo as his *sangmuane*
his MoBrSo as his *sangmuane*
his MoBrDa as his *anak dara*
his MoSiSo as his *sangmuane*
his MoSiDa as his *anak dara*

MARRIAGE AND FAMILY. **Mode.** Premarital sex is common; among young people of low rank it is customary to choose their partners, but among people of rank marriage is arranged by the parents and relatives. The proposal is made by the groom's family. In most regions of Tana Toradja the bride-price is not paid unless the girl marries against the wishes of her parents. Among the Mamasa Toradja the bride-price is customary. **Form.** Polygyny is allowed, but occurs only among the wealthy. **Extension of incest taboos.** In a few districts marriages between first cousins are prohibited. In some of the districts ruled by *puang,* marriages between first cousins are allowed among *puang* families if four buffalo are killed. Among the Mamasa Toradja a marriage between FaSiSo and MoBrDa is preferred. **Residence.** Residence is predominately matrilocal. **Domestic unit.** The nuclear family household is the normal pattern. In the case of a polygynous marriage, each wife has her own household. **Inheritance.** Sons and daughters have an equal chance to inherit their parents' property, but their share depends on the number of buffalo they slaughter at the funeral feast. **Divorce.** Divorce is easy for either sex. **Secondary marriage.** The levirate does not occur. **Adoption.** Illegitimate children are adopted by the man, who afterward marries the mother.

SOCIOPOLITICAL ORGANIZATION. **Political organization. Traditional structure.** Political organization varies from simple structures at the village level to miniature states under a *puang.* In the former district of Kesu' several villages formed a federation, which probably had its origin in the defense against Buginese invaders. The federation is divided into three subfederations, each with a set of titles. Kesu' village organization is rather complicated. Each division of the village (*donalu* and *diongnalu,* "upper" and "lower") forms a circle to celebrate the large *bua'-kasalle'* feast. In each division are several prominent *tongkonan* (houses) with a title. As the *tongkonan* are ordered hierarchically, so are the titleholders. Thus in *donalu* the *sokkong baju* or *datu muane* (the Male Lord) is the most important title, in *diongnalu* the *datu baine* (Female Lord). As a rule both titleholders are men, though a woman of noble birth may also carry a title. Though the status of the *sokkong baju* is considered higher, the two titles are complementary. Other titles are the same in each division of the village, and the *tongkonan* of these titleholders are of lower status than those of the *datu muane* and the *datu baine.* Titleholders are called *to parengnge'.* The *to parengnge'* (noblemen) and *to makaka* (freemen) form the village council. Women of *to parengnge'* and *to makaka* families may also have a voice in this council, but *kaunan* (slaves) are not permitted to attend. ● During the Dutch colonial regime the three *puang*-states Sangalla', Ma'kale, and Mengkendek were called *tallu lembangna* (-the three proa's). The status of the *puang* of Sangalla' is the highest. His *tongkonan,* Kaero, is the center of the state; four *bua'*-federations (composed of several villages and their *tongkonan*) and three *lili* (tributaries) form part of it. The incorporation of the *lili* is the result of wars. The council of the state is called To A'pa, the Four (members), referring to these four "governors." Each of the *to a'pa'* has a title and a special function. **Social stratification.** In the three former *puang*-districts the following ranks can be distinguished: *puang* and *puang matasak* (the Ruler and his family); *anak disese* (a rank between the *puang* and the *to makaka*); *to makaka* (freemen); and *kaunan* (slaves). In Kesu', the society is stratified into: *to parengnge'* (noblemen); *anak patalo* (noblemen, but not of the same high status as the *to parengnge'*); *to makaka* (freemen); and *to kaunan* (slaves or serfs). Wealth is counted by the possession of land (rice fields) and buffalo. As a rule the *kaunan* have no land. Class distinctions are well defined, but nevertheless both upward and downward social mobility occurs. Slavery was abolished by the Dutch. **Social control and justice.** Control was in the hands of noblemen. Prior to the arrival of the Dutch, the worst crime was incest, punished by death. The same punishment applied to marriage between a man of *kaunan*-status and a woman of high rank. The death penalty was carried out by drowning, burning, spearing, or beheading (Kennedy 1953: 174). Cockfights and divination with a kind of reed played a part in ordeals. **Warfare.** Intervillage feuds and feuds between persons of noble status. Wars were waged against the Buginese and also against the Dutch. Headhunting was practiced until about 50 years ago, but never to a great extent.

RELIGION. **Religious systems.** Can be characterized as henotheistic religion, in which ancestor cult plays a prominent part. If the rituals are held, the ancestors bestow their benevolence on their living offspring. The cosmos is divided into an Upper World, a World of Men, and an Underworld. Another important division is that of the Abode of the South West, the realm of the *matua* or forefathers, and the Abode of the North East, the glorified ancestors or *deata*. The World of Men is between these two spheres. By carrying out an elaborate set of rituals, and by taking care not to transgress taboos set by the ancestors, equilibrium will be maintained. **Supernaturals.** Each of the three worlds has its god: Pong Tulakpadang is Lord of the World under the Earth; Pong Banggairante is Lord of the World of Men; Gauntikembong is the Lord of the Upper World. Though all three, particularly Pong Tulakpadang, may be regarded as otiose creators, man is created by Gauntikembong's grandson, Puang Matua, the Old God, the most prominent of all the gods. He is associated with the Sun, as Pong Tulakpadang is with the dark of night. The spouses of the deities sprang from rocks. Very important, and also called *deata* (gods), are the first ancestors who descended from heaven upon a mountain or rock. They are called *to manurun*. Their spouses emerged from the rivers. The *to manurun* are often called by their names at invocations; the other ancestors are mostly mentioned as a group, though their proper names are carefully known and are recited in genealogies. The ancestors are distinguished as follows: the *to matua*, who ordained the *aluk* (adat), the whole order, which man has to follow—their residence is the southwest (the land of origin of the Sa'dan Toradja); and the *deata*, the glorified ancestors who ascend to heaven after the proper death rites have been held for them. **Practitioners.** (1) The *to burake* are the most important practitioners. There are two kinds: (a) the *burake tattiku'*, or priestesses; and (b) the *burake tambolang*, transvestite priests who are supposed to be hermaphrodites. The bisexuality implies power to keep the cosmic order in balance, the synthesis of Under and Upper World, night and day, west and east, female and male. Both *burake* officiate at the *bua' kasalle*-feast. (2) The *to mebalun* or the *burake bombo* is the priest of the dead. He has to carry out the death ritual, which is considered unclean. Often he is a slave; his status is low and despised. (3) The *to ma'dampi* cures illness at the *maro* ritual. (4) The

to indo' padang officiates in most rites concerning the rice cult. None of the priests falls into trance. **Ceremonies.** The rituals form a cycle. The *merok*-feast is held after an elaborate form of death ritual is finished (van der Veen 1965). In this sense it is a thank offering. The *merok* can also be a feast of merit, given by a man who has become prosperous. At the same time it promotes the welfare of the ramage, being a feast in which all the members of the ramage take part. After this feast (often after a considerable time) the *bua' kasalle*-ritual is organized to promote the welfare of men, animals, and food crops (particularly rice) within a territory or *bua'*-circle. As in the case of *merok*, the *tongkonan* is the center of the feast. The *to burake* and the *to parengnge'* play important roles in the ritual. Only for a person who has organized the *bua' kasalle* during his lifetime can the most elaborate form of death ritual, the *dirapa'i*, be carried out. At this ritual many buffalo are killed, as is the case with other important death feasts, such as *dipalimung-* and *dipapitung-bongi*. **Soul, death, and afterlife.** When a man dies, he is first referred to as "a sick man"; the corpse is then taken to the most southern chamber of the house. After certain rites are held, he is called "a dead person"; then he is transported to the central chamber of the house. The soul of the dead can only go to Puja (the After World, the Realm of the Dead) when the entire death ritual has been carried out. The soul is supposed to ascend to heaven from Mount Bamba Puang (in Duri). The spirits of people of high rank become constellations between the Great Bear and the Pleiades. These constellations are considered to be seasonal indicators for agriculture, hence the importance of the ancestors for the rice (van der Veen 1966: 10). The corpse of a person of rank is wrapped or encoffined for a period during which the body fluids are collected. At the final death feast, which may not occur for some months or years, buffalo are tied to stone memorial posts and sacrificed, after which the deceased's remains are placed in a boat-shaped coffin within a hollowed-out cave high in the face of a cliff. [Kennedy 1935: 576ff.]

BIBLIOGRAPHY. Grubauer 1913; Kennedy 1935, 1953; A. C. Kruyt 1923c; J. Kruyt 1921; Nobele 1926; Nooy-Palm 1969; van der Veen 1929, 1940, 1965, 1966.

LOINANG

KENNEDY'S LOINANG GROUP includes the peoples of the eastern peninsula of Celebes (Loinang proper, Saluan, Balantak), together with the inhabitants of the off-lying Togian and Banggai islands (Bobongko and Banggai). Like the Minahasans and their neighbors, the Loinang appear to have been originally of Toradja stock, with later cultural influences emanating from Ternate. Although the physical type varies, the languages are closely interrelated, with marked similarities to those of the southern Philippines.

LOINANG

Synonyms. *Loinan, Loinanezen, To Loinang*

ORIENTATION. **Identification and location.** The term Loinang is used by coastal peoples to refer to mountain dwellers in the interior of the eastern peninsula of Celebes. The term is a pejorative one, and the various subgroups of Loinang prefer to designate themselves by the names of their headmen (Kruyt 1930b: 328). According to Kennedy (1935: 612ff.), the To Loinang are divided into those of Baloa and those of Linketing origin, the former probably originating in central Celebes, the latter most likely a mixture of indigenous elements with immigrants from Ternate. The two differ physically, the Baloa being more Veddoid in appearance. Warfare was formerly endemic between the two divisions (Kruyt 1930b: 337-54). **Linguistic affiliation.** Madi (from the word for "no"), or Loinan proper, belongs to the Loinan language group, which includes Balantak and Banggai. The Loinan languages are related to those of Gorontalo and ultimately the Philippines (Adriani and Kruyt 1912-14: 3, 275; *ENI: 5*, 31). **Demography.** About 14,500, according to *Volkstelling 1930: 5*, 31). **History and cultural relations.** Legends tell of coming from the kingdom of Boalemo and mixing with resident Saluan peoples (Dormeier 1947: 23-25; Kruyt 1930b: 340). Buginese have also infiltrated. Formerly under the sovereignty of the Sultan of Banggai, the Loinang came under Dutch rule in the early 1900s. At this time Islam and Christianity gained a hold (Dormeier 1947: 46-49, 183).

SETTLEMENT PATTERN AND HOUSING. Permanent villages ranging from 50 to about 700 people, forming a religious and social entity based on nuclear or extended family households (Dormeier 1947: 13; Kruyt 1930b: 534). **Housing.** Rectangular wood and bamboo houses raised on stilts. Verandalike areas contain hearths and sleeping quarters for unmarried males. The interior is divided into separate sleeping and reception areas. These traditional houses, strongly made and decorated with wooden sculpture, have been largely replaced by smaller dwellings modeled on those of the Minahasans (Kruyt 1930b: 365-76).

ECONOMY. **Agriculture.** Swiddens are universal, on which are grown rice, maize, sago, and millet. Clearing by cooperative groups begins with the fields of the group chief, who acts as an agricultural religious specialist (*tanaas*) with respect to members of his group (Kruyt 1930b: 412-31). **Hunting.** Pigs and birds are hunted with traps, snares, blowpipes with poison darts, and spears. Wild cattle are captured for use as sacrificial animals (Kruyt 1930b: 383-89). **Domestic animals.** Chickens, dogs, cats, and, recently, goats are kept. Dogs may be eaten, though taboo to women and priests. **Industrial arts.** Women make bark cloth and some pottery. **Land tenure.** Nuclear families own their fields.

KIN GROUPS. **Descent.** Bilateral (Kennedy 1935: 620). **Kin groups.** According to Dormeier (1947: chap. 3), closely related families are grouped together into wards (*langka-langkai*) within the village. The inhabitants of a village territory (*tombuk*) consider themselves kinsmen and function as a common ritual unit. Villages are grouped within larger "subtribal" units (*bosanjo*), whose members inhabit a common territory and claim descent from common ancestors. The chief (*bosanjo*) of a "subtribe" is selected from a family line claiming direct descent from a founding ancestor of the *bosanjo* territory.

MARRIAGE AND THE FAMILY. **Mode.** Spouses choose each other, but arrangements are negotiated between families. The bride-price is in two parts: *koe* (bride-price proper) and *patakon* (gifts to the girl's relatives as compensation for her loss). To marry a high-class girl, a man pays a larger bride-price to acquire standing. The bride-price traditionally consisted of slaves, spears, brass plates, and cloth (Kruyt 1930b: 448-55). **Form.** Monogamy and (recently among the chiefly aristocracy) polygyny. **Extension of incest taboos.** Subtribes aim for endogamy. Second degree cross-cousin and parallel-cousin marriage is preferred (Kruyt 1930b: 446-47) and intergenerational marriage avoided. **Residence.** Initially in some groups matrilocal, in others patrilocal, but in all eventually neolocal (Kruyt 1930b: 455-56). **Domestic unit.** Nuclear family, although patrilocal stem families occur. **Inheritance.** Among the Linketing, boys inherit twice as much as girls, and this general preference seems common (Dormeier 1947; Kruyt 1930b). **Divorce.** Kennedy (1935: 622) says it is easy, but Dormeier (1947: 227) claims it is discouraged by the chiefs. In case of a wife's adultery, the bride-price is repaid. **Adoption.** Fostering occurs, but not adoption (Kruyt 1930b: 471).

SOCIOPOLITICAL ORGANIZATION. **Political organization.** Village-based kin groupings are headed by a chief (*tonggol*), and these are grouped into ten *bosanjo* (subtribes), whose chiefs are sworn in by the Sultan of Banggai. Villagers pay to *bosanjo* chiefs tribute consisting of beeswax and rice and receive in return pottery and *motombing*, a kind of cloth money (Kruyt 1930b: 354-60). **Social stratification.** The chiefs form a local nobility. **Social control and justice.**

Exercised by the *tonggol*, with the assistance of divination and water ordeals (Dormeier 1947: 146-60; Kruyt 1930b: 360-65). **Warfare.** In former times war arose mainly over boundary disputes. War chiefs were called *talenga*, and weapons included swords, spears, and shields. Headhunting occurred on the death of a chief (Dormeier 1947; Kruyt 1930b).

RELIGION. **Supernaturals.** *Setan* are malevolent spirits, and *boehake* and *djin* are benevolent sea and land spirits. These are propitiated in the house. The main category of spirits is the *pilogot*, or ancestral spirits, which are associated with each social grouping, e.g. household, village, subtribe (Kruyt 1930b: 400-06). **Practitioners.** *Sando* are priests who deal with epidemics and the *bolia* deal with individual illnesses—they may be male or female, usually becoming possessed (Kruyt 1930b). **Ceremonies.** Dead chiefs are propitiated in the *mompasok* rites (Kennedy 1935: 625). The *monsale* harvest festival propitiates and thanks the *pilogot* and is conducted (in Linketing villages) by the chiefs (Kruyt 1930b: 403-06). **Illness and medicine.** When illness is caused by evil spirits, the *bolia* cure by recapturing the life force. This is done by enlisting the aid of good spirits, by sacrifice and through divination. Sickness caused by sorcery is treated by the *sando*, or healer (Kruyt 1930b: 395-97). **Soul, death, and afterlife.** Immediate burial in a three-sided coffin (boat-shaped among some groups). The grave is marked by a small hut, whose size varies with rank. Postfuneral rites are held on the third, seventh, and fourteenth days, but there is no evidence of elaborate secondary mortuary rites (Kruyt 1930b: 479-94).

BIBLIOGRAPHY. Adriani and Kruyt 1912-14; Dormeier 1947; *ENI* 1917-39; Kennedy 1935; Kruyt 1930b; *Volkstelling 1930*.

BALANTAK

Synonym. *Mian Balantak*

ORIENTATION. **Identification and location.** The extreme eastern end of the eastern peninsula, north of the Banggai Archipelago. The people, who call themselves Mian Balantak, are divided into two groups or factions, the Tanotoeran and the Dale-Dale, claiming descent from an ancestral pair (male and female, respectively) created on a mountain top by a creator god, Pilogot Mola. The two groups have religious and ceremonial significance, which may have included ritual or actual warfare. [Kruyt 1932h: 328-41; Dormeier 1947: 35.] **Linguistic affiliation.** The language is referred to as Sian, from the word for "no," and belongs to the Loinan language group (Adriani and Kruyt 1912-14: 3, 275). **Demography.** An estimated 11,000 in 1930, over one half of whom were Christian.

History and cultural relations. Originally subordinate to the kingdom of Boalemo, on the north coast of the peninsula. During the latter half of the nineteenth century, Boalemo, along with Balantak, became subject to Banggai, itself a tributary to the Ternate Sultanate. Dutch administration became effective after 1908, together with the spread of both Islam and Christianity. [Kruyt 1932h.]

SETTLEMENT PATTERN AND HOUSING. **Settlement pattern.** In accordance with a former pattern of shifting agriculture, houses were scattered among the fields, with small clusters around the local chief. The Dutch resettled them in villages (Kruyt 1932h: 341-43). **Housing.** Rectangular houses on stilts, with gable roofs made of bamboo and sago palm thatch. Interior layout somewhat similar to those of Loinang (Kruyt 1932h: 343-48).

ECONOMY. **Agriculture.** Swidden rice, yams, taro, and millet, with recently introduced wet-rice cultivation. Coconuts are important. Fields may be fenced (Kruyt 1934). **Fishing and hunting.** Pigs, marsupials, birds, and rodents are hunted with dogs, traps, spears, and blowpipes. Wild cattle (*anoa*) are captured for sacrificial feasts. Fishing is important only on the coast (Kruyt 1932h: 354-63). **Domestic animals.** Dogs, fowl, and goats. **Industrial arts.** Ironworking and barkcloth manufacture are mentioned by Kruyt (1932h: 353). **Land tenure.** The *bense* is the traditional landholding group (Kruyt 1934: 124-25).

KIN GROUPS. **Descent.** Bilateral. **Kin groups.** Basically similar to those of the Loinang. The *bosano* ("subtribe") occupies a well-defined territory, the members of which consider themselves kinsmen, descended from a common ancestor. The Balantak are divided into two *bosano*, the Tanotoeran and the Dale-Dale. Each *bosano* is composed of localized endogamous kin groups (*bense*), which also function as the basic landowning units. Within the *bense* are hamletlike groupings (*gensing*), consisting of related nuclear families. Chieftainship at the *bense* and *bosano* levels is restricted to members of the high-ranking family lines that claim direct descent from the ancestor who first cleared or founded a territory or locality. According to Kruyt (1932h: 340), the Balantak chiefly aristocracy is of foreign (Ternate?) origin. [Dormeier 1947.]

MARRIAGE. **Mode.** Sexual relations are free, and the girl is consulted before marriage, which is arranged by the boy's parents. A bride-price is paid at a joint feast of the two families in the bride's village (Kruyt 1933b: 61). **Form.** Polygyny is allowed, but a man cannot marry two sisters at the same time (Kruyt 1933b: 57). **Extension of incest taboos.** First-cousin marriage is allowed, but intergenerational marriages are forbidden (Kruyt 1933b: 57-58). **Resi-**

dence. Initially matrilocal; after three years the couple reside neolocally (Kruyt 1933b: 63). **Inheritance.** Children share equally, and in the case of a childless couple, one half goes to the remaining spouse and the other to the family of the deceased (Kruyt 1933b: 65). **Divorce.** By mutual consent, or, if only one party desires divorce, he or she pays compensation (Kruyt 1933b: 64-65). **Adoption.** Not allowed (Kruyt 1933b: 75).

SOCIOPOLITICAL ORGANIZATION. **Political organization.** The *bosano* chiefs were subject to the ruler of Banggai, to whom tribute of rice and beeswax was paid. This was collected by the *bense* chiefs, called *tonggol.* Dutch rule emphasized the village (Dormeier 1947; Kruyt 1932h: 339-43). **Social stratification.** *Bosano* chiefs are a local nobility, and formerly there were foreign-born slaves (Kruyt 1932h: 341). **Social control and justice.** Ritual justice (e.g. in case of the breaking of incest taboos) is administered by the *tonggol* (Kruyt 1932h: 348-52).

RELIGION. **Religious systems.** Traditional beliefs centered on ancestor worship. Since 1900, Islam and Christianity have been prominent. **Supernaturals.** Pilogot Mola is the creator sun god, who sends to each individual a spirit (*pololo*), contained in the placenta. Kere is the female earth goddess. *Pololo* in general are the house spirits who govern daily life (Kruyt 1932h: 373). There are also nature spirits, and mountain tops are considered sacred and miracle working (*berkat*) (Kruyt 1932h). **Practitioners.** Male or female priests (*bolian*) are shamans who speak in tongues as the medium of the *pololo* (Kruyt 1932h: 375-84; Kennedy 1935). **Ceremonies.** The *soemawi* is carried out every five or ten years on behalf of the community of kinsmen. There is also a harvest ritual, performed by each household with the aid of a priest, which is followed by the communal floating of a rice-filled boat out to sea (Kruyt 1932h: 384-90; 1934: 126-39). Regular propitiatory offerings are made to the spirits (*mangawauwau*) (Kennedy 1935: 629). **Illness and medicine.** Illness is caused by spirits and is cured by *bolian* with the aid of divination. Black magic is another cause of illness, which is cured by the sacrifice of dogs (Kruyt 1932g). **Soul, death, and afterlife.** Coffins are buried in the ground, although formerly they were sometimes suspended from an upright pole. Stillborn children are wrapped and left in the open. Sacrifices are made at the time of burial and on the seventh day thereafter. A year later, the main feast (*batangan*) is held, the grave cleaned, and a stone heap erected over it (Kruyt 1933b: 83-95).

BIBLIOGRAPHY. Adriani and Kruyt 1912-14; Dormeier 1947; Kennedy 1935; Kruyt 1932g, 1932h, 1933b, 1934.

BANGGAI

Synonyms. *Mian Banggai, Mian Sea-Sea*

ORIENTATION. **Identification and location.** The Banggai Archipelago, off the tip of the eastern peninsula of Celebes. The inhabitants are divided into two groups or factions: Mian Sea-Sea and Mian Banggai. The former, most populous on Peleng Island, are said by Kaudern (1937: 136) to be racially mixed, but with a noticeable Veddoid or Australoid element. Presumably they represent an autochtonous population long resident on Peleng, where ancient creation myths were enacted. The latter are mostly on Banggai Island, where traditional history and sacred places are concentrated around the royal dynasty, which is of foreign (Java, Ternate) origin. The Mian Sea-Sea were originally mountain dwellers, although since the Dutch period the population has gradually been resettled nearer the coast. [Kruyt 1932a: 69-71.] **Linguistic affiliation.** Mian Banggai and Mian Sea-Sea speak slightly different dialects of a single language, termed Aki, after the word for "no." Aki is a member of the Loinan language group, according to Adriani and Kruyt (1912-14: 3, 275). Coolhaas (1926: 418) sees affinities between Aki and the language of Sula Islanders to the east. **Demography.** In 1930 the figure given was 49,836, of whom 40,000 were on the island of Peleng. **History and cultural relations.** Made up of diverse groups, Banggai had a royal dynasty of Javanese origin, was at one time a dependency of Ternate, and then in 1908 became self-governing under the Dutch. The Mian Banggai have been more exposed to Islam than the Mian Sea-Sea, while Christianity has also made inroads (Dormeier 1947: 9; Kruyt 1931b).

SETTLEMENT PATTERN AND HOUSING. Originally houses were scattered among the fields. Under Dutch administration, villages became the norm (Kruyt 1932a: 71). **Housing.** Bamboo or wooden rectangular houses on piles with gable roof are the basic pattern. Those of the Mian Sea-Sea tend to be larger, possibly housing an extended bilateral kin group of some kind (Kruyt 1932a: 71-78).

ECONOMY. **Agriculture.** Swidden cultivation of yams and taro provides the staples (Kruyt 1932a). Wet rice is recent on the coast. Maize, vegetables, sago, bananas, and tobacco are supplementary, and coconuts are exported. Yam culture is ritually elaborated (Kruyt 1932e). **Fishing and hunting.** Fishing with hook and line, nets, spears, poison, and traps is basic to subsistence. Pigs, marsupials, and birds are hunted with spears, blowguns, and traps (Kruyt 1932a: 259-71). **Gathering.** Beeswax is traded, and was paid as tribute. **Industrial arts.** Boat building (particularly dugout canoes), cotton weaving, and brass founding by cire perdu are common among the Mian Sea-Sea. Ironworking was confined to Peleng and was of ritual significance (Kruyt 1932a: 78-87). **Trade.** Copra is the major export item, and trade is conducted by Chinese. Village markets are held every five days (Dormeier 1947: 260; van den Bergh 1948: 206-07). **Property.** Land is owned by the *basalo,* and rights of usufruct are assigned to the constituent *bense* groups (Dormeier 1947: 240). Husband and wife own separate property.

KIN GROUPS. **Descent.** Bilateral (Dormeier 1947: 189). **Kin groups.** The *basalo* is a bilateral kin group with common territory, ancestors, and rituals. This group is divided into smaller endogamous *bense* groups, one of which is the senior from which the chief is elected. *Bensilo* appears to refer to some kind of bilateral residential kin group (Dormeier 1947: chap. 3). **Kinship terminology.** Kruyt (1932d: 32) gives the following terms of reference:

Father	*tama*
Mother	*tina*
MoBr, FaBr	*pipi*
MoSi, FaSi	*kaka*
Sibling	*utu*
Nephew/niece	*pinanak*
Grandchild	*tumbu*

MARRIAGE AND FAMILY. **Mode.** Premarital sex forbidden, and marriages arranged through a go-between, who negotiates the bride-price. This varies with the rank of the groom, and is divided into four parts (one each for the bride's father, mother, family, and as a contribution to the ceremony) (Kruyt 1932d: 13-31; van den Bergh 1948: 197-200; Dormeier 1947: chap. 8). **Form.** Polygyny is permitted, but is rare. **Extension of incest taboos.** Intergenerational marriages are prohibited, but cousin marriages are preferred, and a lower bride-price is paid (Kruyt 1932d: 14-18; Kennedy 1935: 622). **Residence.** Among the Sea-Sea, residence is ambilocal, but for the Banggai it is initially matrilocal, then neolocal (Kruyt 1932a: 18-20). **Property.** Children inherit equally from parents, but not until both are dead (Dormeier 1947). **Divorce.** When by mutual consent, property is divided two-to-one in favor of the husband. Either spouse may initiate divorce. **Adoption.** This occurs in case of childlessness. The Banggai allow step-siblings to marry, but the Sea-Sea do not (Kruyt 1932d: 59-60).

SOCIOPOLITICAL ORGANIZATION. **Political organization.** The Banggai principality, including the eastern peninsula of Celebes, is ruled by the I Toeoetoe (of Javanese origin), who was formerly appointed by the Sultan of Ternate and who is assisted by a hierarchy of advisors drawn from the senior families of the various *basalo*. The ruler is invested with supernatural power and has little actual contact with the people (Dormeier 1947: 115; Kruyt 1931b). Under the Dutch, villages and village headmen were introduced. **Social stratification.** The nobility includes

the ruling family, and commoners are subdivided into the principal *basalo* families, commoners, and slaves or their descendants (Dormeier 1947: chap. 4). **Social control and justice.** Witches, poisoners, and debtors were killed by those who considered themselves wronged (Kruyt 1932a: 249), and the chief's authority seems to have been limited. Headhunters were hired to wreak vengeance (Kennedy 1935: 625).

RELIGION. **Religious systems.** Traditional beliefs in ancestral spirits (*pilogot*) are retained alongside Islam and Christianity. **Supernaturals.** A Supreme Being (*Temeneno*) and his four sons look after yam culture, hunting, fishing, and bees. There are four categories of *pilogot*, which represent (1) accumulated life force of the living and dead kin, *batanaas* (2) the accumulated strength of all placentas, *pali* (3) life force of the amniotic fluid, *mboli*, and (4) menstrual power, which protects against black magic, *balani* (Kennedy 1935: 631). *Balakat* are sacred places and objects (mountain tops, stones, etc., associated with ancestral creation myths) to which powers are attributed (Kruyt 1932b). **Practitioners.** The *talapoe* is a shamanlike priest who counters black magic (Kruyt 1932b: 129; Kennedy 1935: 631). **Ceremony.** The *batong* is a promissory ceremony carried out in cases of illness or misfortune. **Illness and medicine.** Illness is caused by spirits or black magic, and cure is by divination, sacrifices, and counter magic (Kruyt 1932f: 141-50). **Soul, death, and afterlife.** After death, the soul joins the *pilogot* who reside in the center pole of the house. Coffins are buried in a marked grave, and mortuary sacrifices are performed every seven days till the forty-ninth day (Kruyt 1932f: 150-72).

BIBLIOGRAPHY. Adriani and Kruyt 1912-14; van den Bergh 1948, 1953; Coolhaas 1926; Dormeier 1947; Kaudern 1937; Kennedy 1935; Kruyt 1931b, 1932a, 1932b, 1932c, 1932d, 1932e, 1932f.

BUNGKU-LAKI

UNDER THE RUBRIC, Mori-Laki Group, Kennedy included all the peoples of southeastern Celebes, together with the off-lying islands of Wowoni, Butung, Tukangbesi, Muna, and Kabaena—recognizing, however, that his classification was based on inadequate knowledge and subject to revision. On linguistic grounds, Esser (1938) and recently Noorduyn (1968) placed mainlanders (Mori, Laki, Bungku) in a language group (Bungku-Laki) separate from islanders; the latter (Muna, Butonese, Laiolo) they class in a separate Muna-Butung group. This division is followed in the present volume. The Toradja physical type is predominant throughout the Mori-Laki area; like the Sa'dan Toradjas, the peoples of this southeastern region have experienced the impact of nearby Buginese culture, in particular the development of a sharply segregated ruling class.

BIBLIOGRAPHY. Esser 1938; Noorduyn 1968.

MORI

Synonyms. *Moriërs, To Mori*

ORIENTATION. **Location and identification.** Central Celebes, at the neck of the southeastern peninsula. A region of lofty wooded mountains and deep valleys, bordered on the north by the lands of the Eastern Toradja. J. Kruyt (1924) divides the population into (1) Upper Mori in the vicinity of the La River, including Molio'a, Molong Kuni, and Ulu Uwoi (2) Lower Mori south of the La, including Watu and Moiki (3) Malili Mori around Lake Matana, including Matano, Tambe'e, Padoe, and Karunsi'e. The physical type is in general similar to that of the Toradja. There has been considerable Buginese influence, e.g. patterns of social stratification, and the ruling aristocracy among the Mori tribes appears to be of foreign origin (Kennedy 1935: 586ff.). Otherwise, Mori customs resemble most closely those of the Eastern Toradja. **Linguistic affiliation.** Classed by Esser (1927: 2) in the Bungku-Laki group. Kennedy (1935: 571) calls attention to Philippine connections. **Demography.** About 12,000 (*Volkstelling 1930: 5, 32*). **History and cultural relations.** Subject to Bungku, then Ternate, and finally the Dutch in 1906.

SETTLEMENT PATTERN AND HOUSING. Villages range on an east-west axis, with a central village temple (*lobo*), in which captured heads were kept. Each house, on stilts, has a reception room and several sleeping rooms (Adriani and Kruyt 1900: 197-98).

ECONOMY. **Agriculture.** Formerly swidden-rice cultivation, which has partially given way to wet rice. Secondary crops include maize, taro, and tobacco. Coffee is a cash crop grown by the Upper Mori (*ENI*: 7, 99-100; J. Kruyt 1924: chap. 5). **Industrial arts.** Pottery, blacksmithing (especially swordmaking), brass founding by cire perdu. Markets (*olus*) and trade are controlled by Bugis. Double outrigger canoes are built and sailed.

KIN GROUPS. **Descent.** Descent is bilateral. According to Kennedy (1935: 598), the social organization is basically similar to that of the Eastern Toradja except for the presence of an aristocratic ruling class of Bugis origin. **Kin terminology** (based on J. Kruyt 1924: 29-33 and Kennedy 1935: 602):

Grandparent	*oeë* or *ue*
Fa	*ana* or *ama*
FaBr, MoBr	*na'ana*
Mo	*ine* or *ina*
FaSi, MoSi	*na'ina*
Older sibling	*aka*
Younger sibling	*uai*
Siblings of same mother	*mepaekompo*
Cousin	*mepoteha*
Child	*ana*
Nephew/niece	*laki-ana*
Grandchild	*ana oeë* or *ana ue*

MARRIAGE AND FAMILY. **Mode.** Families negotiate through go-betweens over bride-price, which depends on rank and wealth (J. Kruyt 1924: 34-38). **Form.** Polygyny is the rule among the nobility (J. Kruyt 1924: 41). **Extension of incest taboos.** First-cousin marriage forbidden except among nobility. Marriage between children and parents' siblings forbidden, although the taboo may be removed by the *montoto eko* ritual (J. Kruyt 1924: 33; Kennedy 1935: 600). **Residence.** Initially matrilocal, then neolocal. **Domestic unit.** The nuclear family. **Inheritance.** Property is inherited equally by all children (J. Kruyt 1924: 42). **Divorce.** Occurs by mutual consent or as a result of adultery by the woman or ill-treatment of the wife (J. Kruyt 1924: 39-40). **Adoption.** Only siblings' children may be adopted, and adoption is rare (J. Kruyt 1924: 44).

SOCIOPOLITICAL ORGANIZATION. **Political organization.** Ruling aristocracy is intrusive (Buginese). Local kin groups are headed by elders, who elect a member as chief (J. Kruyt 1924: 16-24). **Social stratification.** *Mokole* are the foreign-born aristocracy, believed to be of divine descent, at whose top is the *datu ri tana*. *Bonto* are prestigious (wealthy), but common born. Commoners are *palili*. Descendants of slaves are known as *atas* (J. Kruyt 1924: 16-24; Kennedy 1935: 599). **Warfare.** Commonly against hereditary enemies; headhunting expeditions on the death of kin group chief (J. Kruyt 1924: 54-58, 80-82). Headhunting rites similar to those of the Eastern Toradja (Kennedy 1935: 603).

RELIGION. Traditionally, beliefs centered on ancestral and nature spirits. Islam now predominates. **Supernaturals.** The most important are: Ue Ue Wulaa, the god of smallpox; Ue Alemba, the rice goddess; Anambulaa, god of fate; Ue Rini, god of air and omen birds—the latter being augured by *tondanos*, particularly to diagnose illness. Good and evil spirits are known as *onitu*. [Kennedy 1935: 609; J. Kruyt 1924.] **Practitioners.** *Wuraka,* or priestesses, with spirit familiars; *sando,* a lesser category of priest; and *tondanos,* or augurers. **Ceremonies.** The most important is the rewrapping and interment of bones (*woke*), carried out every three to five years in honor of deceased ancestors (J. Kruyt 1924: 132-39). An annual ceremony associated with ironworking occurs, and dogs are sacrificed in cases of illness, headhunting, and death (A. C. Kruyt 1931a: 33-35, 46-47). **Soul, death, and afterlife.** Funerals vary according to class, with members of the upper class being buried in graves, others exposed on scaffolds. At a death feast, *tewusu*, the bones are cleaned and encoffined in caves. Secondary death rites for aristocrats may be highly elaborate (cf. Kennedy 1935: 605). Islam now predominates, especially among the Lower Mori (J. Kruyt 1924: 77; van Wylick 1941: 152-61).

BIBLIOGRAPHY. Adriani and Kruyt 1900; *ENI*; Esser 1927; A. C. Kruyt 1900, 1931a; J. Kruyt 1924; Kennedy 1935; *Volkstelling 1930*; van Wylick 1941.

LAKI

Synonyms. *Lalaki, Tokeas, To Laki*

ORIENTATION. **Identification and location.** The name Laki means "big men" and may refer to their headhunting prowess. They comprise a number of smaller groups: Wiwirano, Labeau, Aserawanua, Mowewe, Mekongga, and Tamboki. Located in the southern portion of the southeastern peninsula south of the Mori, to whom they are related linguistically and culturally (Kruyt and Kruyt 1921: 691-720; Kennedy 1935; Treffers 1914: 198). The region is mountainous jungle, subject to monsoons. **Linguistic affiliation.** Esser (1938) assigns them to a Bungku-Laki group. **Demography.** A 1930 estimate of about 100,000 (*Volkstelling 1930*: 5, 32). **History and cultural relations.** The Laki were recently detached from the To Mori and moved from their original habitat at Lake Towuti (Kruyt 1922: 428). Since they were always tributary to the states of Luwu and Bone, and have long been in close contact with Buginese, Islamic influence is strong.

SETTLEMENT PATTERN AND HOUSING. **Settlement pattern.** Treffers (1914: 195) reports a scattered settlement pattern, which, since Dutch administration, has become centralized in villages. **Housing.** Houses, on stilts, are divided into a number of rooms separated by cotton or bark curtains. Rice granaries are separate (Treffers 1914: 215-17). Kennedy (1935: 593) says that the houses are single roomed.

ECONOMY. **Agriculture.** Dry-rice swiddens, now supplemented by wet-rice cultivation. Sago is equally staple. **Hunting.** Deer are hunted with dogs and blowguns. **Industrial arts.** Some ironworking, especially of broadswords (formerly) and spears (Kennedy 1935: 596). Dugout canoes are made, and there is some basket weaving.

KIN GROUPS. Similar to the Eastern Toradja with respect to both descent and kin groups (Kennedy 1935: 587). **Kin terminology.** Kruyt gives the following terms (1922: 429, 432-33):

FaSi, MoSi	*naina*
FaBr, MoBr	*ma'ama*
WiBr	*ela*
HuSi	*bea*

MARRIAGE AND FAMILY. **Mode.** Bride-price depends on rank and is greater for the eldest daughter (Kruyt 1922: 441-47). Among the To Laki proper, the boy serves a probationary period at his in-laws' home (Treffers 1914: 209-11). **Form.** Polygyny is an indication of wealth. **Extension of incest taboos.** The To Mowewe prohibit first-cousin marriage, brother-sister exchange, and intergenerational marriage. Taboo infractions can be removed by the *mosewe* ritual (Kruyt 1922: 429-34; Kennedy 1935: 600). **Residence.** Initially matrilocal and afterward neolocal (Kruyt 1922: 445). Among the To Mekongga it is matrilocal for the first year, patrilocal for the second year, and finally neolocal (Elbert 1912: 274). **Inheritance.** Daughters are favored above sons, and the eldest daughter inherits more (Kruyt 1922: 467-68).

SOCIOPOLITICAL ORGANIZATION. Chiefs of traditional kin groups (*anakia*) were elected, but had little power. **Social stratification.** Nobles (*anakia*) and commoners (*maradika*). Formerly there were slaves (Treffers 1914: 201-02). **Headhunting.** Took place at illness and death and was led by a specialist (*tadu*), usually against the To Maronene and To Muna (Schuurmans 1934). Successful headhunters had the title *tamalaki*, and the blood and brains of the victim were consumed (Kennedy 1935: 603).

RELIGION. **Religious systems.** The indigenous system was based on worship of ancestors and nature spirits, each of whom had their own priests. Today most are Muslim (van den Klift 1922: 68-70; Treffers 1914: 203-06). **Ceremonies.** *Monahoe ndao* opens the agricultural cycle and is the major ceremony of the year (Kruyt 1922: 434-38; van den Klift 1922). **Soul, death, and afterlife.** Corpses were formerly exposed on a scaffold for from two to five years. At secondary mortuary rites, the bones were collected and placed in caves, with those of the nobles contained in jars. Islamic rites prevail today (Gouweloos 1937; van Wylick 1941: 165-76). Kennedy reports elaborate grave mounds for nobles (1935: 608).

BIBLIOGRAPHY. Elbert 1912; Esser 1938; Gouweloos 1937; Kennedy 1935; van den Klift 1922; Kruyt 1922; A. C. Kruyt and J. Kruyt 1921; Schuurmans 1934; Treffers 1914; *Volkstelling 1930*; van Wylick 1941.

BUNGKU

Synonyms. *Boenkoenezen, To Bungku*

ORIENTATION. **Identification and location.** Eastern Celebes, along the Gulf of Tolo and on the island of Wowoni. Inland, the Bungku groups are bounded by lands of the Eastern Toradja and To Mori. Included are the following subgroups: Lambatu, Epe, Rete, Ro'uta, and Wowoni (Kennedy 1935). **Linguistic affiliation.** According to Esser (1938), Bungku belongs to a Bungku-Laki group, related to Philippine languages. **Demography.** (*Volkstelling 1930: 5, 32*) gives a figure of 14,140.

SETTLEMENT PATTERN. Formerly they lived in the mountains, but now along the shore in multiroom houses (*ENI: 7, 99*; Kennedy 1935: 593).

ECONOMY. Dry-rice swiddens, with secondary crops of maize, sago (among the Lambatu), sweet potato, and coconut (Goedhart 1908: 518-21).

MARRIAGE AND FAMILY. A bride-price is paid, and rites follow Islam (Kruyt 1900: 216-17).

SOCIOPOLITICAL ORGANIZATION. Formerly a principality, subject to Ternate. A supreme chief or ruler, assisted by four district chiefs and a varying number of village chiefs. Chieftainship is hereditary within certain families, but subject to ability. Stratification tends to be in classes of chiefs (i.e. nobles), commoners, and, formerly, slaves (Goedhart 1908: 489-506, 517-18).

RELIGION. Largely Islam, with remnant beliefs in spirits. **Illness and medicine.** Illness caused by spirits, who remove breath. Healing by priestesses (*sando*), who are possibly shamans (Kruyt 1900: 221-22, 224-25). **Soul, death, and afterlife.** Formerly the corpse was exposed on a scaffold until the funeral feast (*umato*), at which time the bones were collected and interred in a cave. Today Islamic rites are followed.

BIBLIOGRAPHY. *ENI*; Esser 1938; Goedhart 1908; Kennedy 1935; Kruyt 1900; *Volkstelling 1930*.

MARONENE

Synonyms. *Kabaenas, Moronene*

ORIENTATION. **Identification and location.** The Maronene are often considered a subgroup of the To Laki. They live in extreme southeastern Celebes, from where they have migrated to the nearby island of Kabaena. **Linguistic affiliation.** Noorduyn (1968) assigns them to a separate category within the Bungku-Laki language group.

SETTLEMENT PATTERN AND HOUSING. They live in widely scattered houses, raised on piles (Elbert 1912: *1*, 238).

ECONOMY. **Agriculture.** Dry-rice swiddens, but sago is apparently the staple. **Hunting.** Deer and buffalo are hunted; beeswax and dammar are collected and traded (Elbert 1912: *1*, 240). Mats and baskets are woven (Elbert 1912: *2*, 31-42).

MARRIAGE AND FAMILY. Go-betweens arrange marriages. The boy serves a one- to three-year probationary period with his future parents-in-law, during which sexual relations between the couple are forbidden (Elbert 1912: *1*, 272-73). **Residence.** Neolocal.

RELIGION. Ancestor spirits and nature spirits are traditional, and Islam is now prevalent (Elbert 1912: *1*, 271-72). **Soul, death, and afterlife.** The corpse may be preserved unburied for up to one year. Graves are marked by mounds or decorated posts (Elbert 1912: *1*, 270-71; Kennedy 1935: 608). Headhunting was once common.

BIBLIOGRAPHY. Elbert 1912; Kennedy 1935; Noorduyn 1968.

MACASSARESE–BUGINESE

THE MACASSARESE (population around two million) and Buginese, or Bugis (some three million) are the dominant peoples of the southern peninsula of Celebes, the former concentrated in the extreme southern tip, focusing on the port town of Macassar, the latter somewhat to the north, extending all the way to the head of the Gulf of Bone and adjoining the lands of the Sa'dan Toradja. This fertile, volcanic area, devoted to irrigated-rice agriculture, supports the highest population density in all of Celebes. The two peoples are similar culturally, and according to Kennedy (1935: 664) were probably of Toradja stock originally, although altered radically by foreign contact, chiefly from Malay and Javanese sources. They differ mainly with respect to language, although both are members of a single language group, which, according to Esser (1938), includes Luwu, Sa'dan, Pitu-Uluna-Salu, Mandar, and Seko. The Macassarese and Buginese have long had a script (of probable Malay origin) incised on lontar palm leaves. The southern peninsula was in pre-Dutch times fragmented into a number of warring kingdoms, with Goa or Gowa (Macassarese) and Bone or Boni (Buginese) dominant. The Dutch captured Macassar in 1675 and thereafter supported the Goa ruling family. Macassarese and Buginese (the latter in particular) were for centuries active in trading and piracy, and their colonizing propensities are evident in the histories of small coastal principalities throughout much of Indonesia. Goa, through the strategic port town of Macassar, controlled the lucrative Moluccan spice trade until its capture by the Dutch. Islam became the dominant religion in the seventeenth century and remains so today. Under the Dutch the former kin-based political structure was gradually incorporated within a governmental administrative hierarchy, and members of royal families transferred to civil service positions, a process that has continued since Independence in 1949.

BIBLIOGRAPHY. Chabot 1967; Esser 1938; H. Geertz 1963; Kennedy 1935, 1953.

MACASSARESE

Synonyms. *Goanese, Makassarese*

SETTLEMENT PATTERN AND HOUSING. Villages near Macassar may contain from 100 to 200 or more houses, although those in rural locations are considerably smaller. The house is raised on piles, rectangular in shape, and with a gable roof. The interior is divided by bamboo partitions or mats into sleeping quarters for from six to ten persons, although Kennedy (1935) reports up to 20 inhabitants in a single house. Villages nowadays tend to consist of endogamous, localized segments of larger nonunilineal kin groups (Chabot 1967). Village leaders are likely to be members of the dominant kin group in the village, with the headman elected from among candidates put forward by the various kin groups. Chabot suggests that formerly a village was normally inhabited by members of a single kin group.

SOCIOPOLITICAL ORGANIZATION. Myths emphasize the divine origin of ruling families by virtue of direct descent from heavenly beings. Kennedy (1953) reported a ruling aristocracy, commoners, and (formerly) slaves. Actually, as reported by Chabot (1950) and analyzed by H. Geertz (1963), the Macassarese see everyone ranged on a continuous scale of prestige, with considerable upward and downward mobility. A man's status is determined in part by that of his parents, but most importantly by the amount of the bride-price paid for his sisters and daughters. Thus much of the dynamic of Macassarese life is provided by the financial and political manipulations relevant to payment of bride-price. An individual is aided in these status-oriented manipulations by membership in localized nonunilineal corporate descent groups (ramages, according to Murdock 1967: 202), through either his father or mother. Thus there are several such groups potentially open to an individual at birth, and ultimate membership is by choice. A

localized kin group constitutes a ritual unit for the worship of its founding ancestors, represented by sacred objects such as swords, parasols, metal plates, plows, and the like. A local prince or ruler is the head of a kin group, which by advantageous marriages and other means has gained wealth and prestige—partly through the reputation of its sacred objects as being particularly powerful. A ruler's domain consists of followers who are held to him partly by kin ties but also by his personal charisma, as being of divine descent and in possession of sacred objects of particular power. Thus the history of the Macassarese is one of the constant rise and fall of petty kingdoms consequent on the vagaries of marital alliances and the shifting allegiance of followers.

RELIGION. Islam, but with vestiges of old animistic beliefs. Rituals involving the propitiation of ancestral spirits, represented by a kin group's sacred objects, are carried out by non-Islamic specialists, *bissu* or *pinati*. These individuals formerly exercised priestly functions with respect to agricultural and death rites as well. Funerary rites nowadays follow Islamic custom, but Kennedy (1935: 683; 1953) cites evidence of former buffalo sacrifice, bone washing, and cave burial, all conforming to the general Toradja pattern.

BIBLIOGRAPHY. Chabot 1950, 1967; Friedericy 1933; H. Geertz 1963; Kennedy 1935, 1953; Murdock 1967.

MUNA-BUTUNG

THE PEOPLES OF THE ISLANDS off southeastern Celebes—Wowoni, Butung, Tukangbesi, Muna, and Kabaena—speak closely related languages and form a single cultural unit (Kennedy 1935; Esser 1938). Their closest affinities are with the Mori-Laki peoples on the adjacent mainland, although this entire region has been subject to marked acculturative change due first to Buginese domination and later to economic exploitation under the Dutch. For convenience of presentation, the inhabitants of Salajar Island off the Macassar coast are included in the present section, although they are culturally almost identical with the Macassarese—Buginese.

BIBLIOGRAPHY. Esser 1938; Kennedy 1935.

MUNA

Synonyms. *Moenanezen, To Muna*

ORIENTATION. **Identification and location.** Inhabitants of the sandy coral island of Muna, south of the southeastern peninsula. Closely related to the Butonese and, like them, part of the Sultanate of Butung prior to Dutch intervention in 1910. **Linguistic affiliation.** Esser (1938) assigns them to a Muna-Butung cluster. **Demography.** About 16,000 in 1930 (*Volkstelling 1930*). **History and cultural relations.** They believe themselves to be part Bugis and part Toradja (Couvreur 1935).

SETTLEMENT PATTERN AND HOUSING. Houses formerly scattered among swiddens (Couvreur 1935), with one large settlement—Kota Muna. **Housing.** Houses on piles, made of plaited grasses, with high roofs (Elbert 1912: *1*, 156-57).

ECONOMY. **Agriculture.** Swidden-grown maize the staple, backed by sweet potato, sugarcane, vegetables, tobacco, and coffee. Kapok is grown and traded (Elbert 1912: *1*, 151-52). **Industrial arts.** Kapok and cotton weaving (Elbert 1912: *1*, 152). **Land tenure.** The island is divided into village territories; village councils distribute usufruct rights to villagers. Ultimate ownership is vested in the Sjarat (Council) Muna (Couvreur 1935: chap. 21).

MARRIAGE AND FAMILY. **Mode.** Payments are made to the girl's family on engagement and at marriage, the amount depending on the rank of the boy. The boy serves a probationary period with his prospective parents-in-law, which gives rise to a high frequency of elopement. Slaves and their descendants may not marry each other, though they may cohabit. Noble women may not marry non-noble men (Couvreur 1935: 82-109). **Form.** Polygyny is frequent among people of high rank. **Extension of incest taboos.** Marriage is forbidden between stepchildren and first cousins (Couvreur 1935: 95). **Inheritance.** Sons and daughters inherit equally. **Divorce.** Infrequent.

SOCIOPOLITICAL ORGANIZATION. **Political organization.** The Lakina Muna was elected by the Council (Sjarat Muna) and represented the Sultan of Butung. He technically ruled through a hierarchy of advisors and officials, one of whom, the Bonto Belano, was actually the de facto ruler. Local level chiefs (*mino* and *kino*) lived in the capital (Kota Muna) and were selected from the families of their predecessors. The Dutch ruled from 1910 to 1949 (Couvreur 1935; Elbert 1912: *1*, 182-85). **Social stratification.** Social strata are still quite distinct. *Kaoem* are the higher nobility, *wakale* the lower nobility, *mardeka* are commoners who in turn are subdivided into three classes, and finally there is a class of slaves and their descendants. Each class is entitled to certain prerogatives, ornaments, clothing, and songs. Men may marry down, but not women (Couvreur 1935: chap. 5).

RELIGION. Islam.

BIBLIOGRAPHY. Couvreur 1935; Elbert 1912; Esser 1938; *Volkstelling 1930*.

BUTONESE

Synonym. *Boetoneezen*

ORIENTATION. **Location and identification.** The people of Butung Island, off the southern tip of the southeastern peninsula of Celebes. Closely related linguistically and culturally to the peoples of the neighboring islands of Muna and Tukangbesi. Basically of Toradja physical type, but with a noticeable Veddoid substratum. The Sultanate of Wolio, in the southwestern part of the island, is the result of cultural influences stemming from the nearby Buginese. [Elbert 1912: *1*, 227-32; Kennedy 1935: 590.] **Linguistic affiliation.** Esser (1938) assigns them to a Muna Butung group. The nobility speak an official dialect, Wolio, and there is a written literature (Anceaux 1952: 1-2). **Demography.** In 1930 they numbered about 300,000 (*Volkstelling 1930*). **History and cultural relations.** The Butonese are noted sailors and traders and have emigrated widely, especially to the Moluccas. The islands of Butung, Muna, Tukangbesi, Kabaena, and Wowoni, together with the adjacent mainland, formerly constituted the Sultanate of Butung, which came under direct Dutch rule in 1908 (Ligtvoet 1878: 31-112).

SETTLEMENT PATTERN AND HOUSING. Before 1910, houses were scattered, with only Baubau, the seat of the Sultan of Wolio, fortified. **Housing.** Houses were built of wood, on piles (Elbert 1912: *1*, 138-39).

ECONOMY. **Agriculture.** Maize is the staple, with some dry rice. Millet and sweet potato are secondary: cotton and coconut are important crops. **Industrial arts.** Boatbuilding, brass founding, mat and basket weaving. **Trade.** The region was formerly a center of piracy and slave trade. Trade is still important in maize, kapok, and bitumen, mined on Butung (Elbert 1912: *1*, 206-18).

KIN GROUPS. **Descent.** Patrilineal, according to van den Berg (1940: 531) and Elbert (1912: *1*, 205).

MARRIAGE AND FAMILY. **Mode.** Follows Islam; bride-price is negotiated by a village elder acting as go-between (Elbert 1912: *1*, 203-04). **Form.** Polygyny is allowed. **Extension of incest taboos.** All cousin marriage is prohibited, as is brother-sister exchange (van den Berg 1940: 531). **Residence.** Initially matrilocal, then neolocal (Elbert 1912: *1*, 203).

SOCIOPOLITICAL ORGANIZATION. **Political organization.** The Sultan is elected by a council of nobles. The Sultanate is divided into districts headed by a *bonto* or *bobato,* and these are divided in turn into villages headed by chiefs and their councils (van den Berg 1939, 1940: 532-34; Elbert 1912: *1,* 175-87). **Social stratification.** Strongly marked class distinctions are still evident between *kaomoe,* aristocracy; *walaka,* nobility; and *maradika,* or commoners, who are in turn subdivided.

RELIGION. The indigenous system was characterized by an ancestor cult (Elbert 1912: *1,* 198), but now the Butonese are completely Muslim. **Supernaturals.** Belief in natural spirits has replaced belief in ancestor spirits (Elbert 1912: *1,* 139, 199-203). **Practitioners.** As well as the Muslim officials, each village has a *bisa,* who officiates in all non-Islamic rituals (van den Berg 1940: 535-37). **Ceremonies.** Van den Berg (1940: 537-43) describes a communal "first rice" ceremony. **Soul, death, and afterlife.** Generally Islamic, with graves marked by coral piles (Elbert 1912: *1,* 196-99).

BIBLIOGRAPHY. Anceaux 1952; Elbert 1912; Esser 1938; Kennedy 1935; Ligtvoet 1878; van den Berg 1939, 1940; *Volkstelling 1930.*

SALAJAR

Synonyms. *Salayar, Saleier, Saleierezen, Saleyrees*

ORIENTATION. **Identification and location.** Inhabitants of the island of Salajar and adjacent islands (e.g. Bonerate) southeast of the southwestern peninsula. So close to Bugis that some authorities, cf. Berzina and Bruk (1963), do not differentiate them. **Language affiliation.** According to Esser (1938), Salajar is a dialect of Macassarese. Laiolo, spoken in southern Salajar, is a dialect of Butonese. **Demography.** *Volkstelling 1930* gives their number as 67,510. **History and cultural relations.** Immigrants from Java settled in the twelfth and thirteenth centuries. Salajar has been subject to Goa and Macassar (Engelhard 1884: 398-489).

SETTLEMENT PATTERN AND HOUSING. **Settlement pattern.** Houses are scattered over the fields, but there are a few villages (Kriebel 1920: 206; Nooteboom 1937b). **Housing.** Plank-walled, thatch-roof houses, on piles. Each house has a kitchen, veranda, and bedrooms (Engelhard 1884: 303-06).

ECONOMY. Formerly trading, slaving, and piracy were the base of the economy. **Agriculture.** Maize is the staple, backed by cassava, millet, and dry rice. Coconuts and lemons are cash crops (Nooteboom 1937b: 14-22). There is some evidence of cooperative associations (Nooteboom 1938: 564). **Fishing.** This is the main occupation of the coastal people; sea cucumber, turtle, and shellfish are also important (Engelhard 1884: 336-47; Kriebel 1920: 213-15; Noote-

boom 1937b: 26-27). **Gathering.** Forest products, such as beeswax and dammar, are important on the smaller islands (Engelhard 1884: 336). **Domestic animals.** Buffalo, horses, and goats (Nooteboom 1937b: 22-26). **Industrial arts.** Boatbuilding, weaving, and coconut oil (Nooteboom 1937b: 27-29). **Trade.** Copra, lemons, and dried fish are exchanged for rice and tobacco (Nooteboom 1937b: 29-31). A special credit system (*modala*) also operated (Engelhard 1884: 319-20), and rotating loan associations are reported (Nooteboom 1938).

MARRIAGE AND FAMILY. **Mode.** Identical with Macassarese. Bride-price according to girl's rank, and given to the girl (Engelhard 1884: 359-60; Kriebel 1920: 209). **Extension of incest taboos.** Cousin marriage is preferred (Kriebel 1919: 1107). **Divorce.** Rare. **Secondary marriage.** Levirate is common (Kriebel 1919: 1107).

SOCIOPOLITICAL ORGANIZATION. **Political organization.** The island is divided into regencies, and the ruler may be a woman. Regalia are sacred. Villages are grouped into districts headed by *gelarang* (Kriebel 1920: 217-19). **Social stratification.** Nooteboom (1937b: 4-5) lists the following sharply defined classes: descendants of rulers, nobility, commoners, and descendants of slaves.

RELIGION. Islam has been dominant since the seventeenth century, but traditional beliefs are still important, especially in malevolent spirits (Nooteboom 1937b: 6; Engelhard 1884: 347-59, 368-70). **Soul, death, and afterlife.** Formerly coffins were placed in caves. Now, bodies after shrouding are buried in cemeteries, and postfuneral rites are held up to 100 days after death. Graves are marked by stone mounds (Engelhard 1884: 366-67, 371-98).

BIBLIOGRAPHY. Berzina and Bruk 1963; Engelhard 1884; Esser 1938; Kriebel 1919, 1920; Nooteboom 1937a, 1937b, 1938; *Volkstelling 1930.*

TOALA

Synonyms. *Telu Limpoe, To Ale*

ORIENTATION. **Identification.** The name means "forest people," and they are probably the aboriginal inhabitants (Sarasin 1905-06: *2,* 50). They live in the mountains of southwestern Celebes in a single village named Samudae (Kennedy 1935: 494), having been moved from caves under the influence of the Buginese. When first studied in 1902, Veddoid characteristics were marked, linking these people with a population substratum noticeable among Loinang, Laki, Muna, and other groups of eastern Celebes. **Demography.** Sarasin and Sarasin (1905) give their number as about 100.

ECONOMY. Formerly hunting and gathering, they carried on silent trade with neighboring tribes. They learned agriculture, mainly the cultivation of rice, maize, and vegetables, from the Bugis.

KIN GROUPS. Probably nuclear family.

MARRIAGE. Monogamous, with patrilocal residence. Marriage forbidden within the immediate family (Kennedy 1935: 501).

SOCIOPOLITICAL ORGANIZATION. Three sub-tribes: Tete, Urupae, and Telangkere. Formerly ruled by an hereditary chief (*balisao*), they changed to an elected chieftainship (*matoa*) after Buginese conquest.

RELIGION. Converted to Islam by Bugis, though still (in 1913) largely pagan (Kennedy 1935: 502).

BIBLIOGRAPHY. Kennedy 1935; Sarasin 1905-06; Sarasin and Sarasin 1905.

BORNEO

THE RELATIVELY great antiquity of man on Borneo and the role of that island as a cultural crossroads in prehistoric and early historic times are just beginning to be appreciated (cf. Harrisson 1958b; Harrisson and Harnett 1969; Harrisson and O'Connor 1970; Cheng Te-K'un 1969; Coedès 1968; Wang Gungwu 1958). Outside influences have clearly been many and varied, but the extent of their role, versus that of indigenous development, in shaping the cultures of Borneo remains to be worked out. Certain it is that the island remains one of the more interesting areas of the world, ethnologically speaking; despite increasing coastal Muslim and Christian missionary influence since World War II, an impressive proportion of Borneo's Dayak population—numbering approximately two million, according to Kennedy (1935: 325)—retain viable, integrated cultures, reflecting an infectious exuberance and enthusiasm for life that is rare in the civilized world. There is as yet no satisfactory ethnic classification of these peoples despite a wealth of ethnographic data, much of it published in the *Sarawak Museum Journal* in recent decades. Previous classifications, e.g. Hose and McDougall (1912) and Kennedy (1935), have agreed with respect to delimitation of certain relatively well-defined groups, e.g. the Iban, but have disagreed with respect to categories such as Murut, Melanau, Bisaya, and Kadayan. Recourse was had to a kind of residual pigeonhole, Klamantan or Kelamantan, for groups that seemed not to fit conveniently elsewhere. Leach's (1950) objections to these attempts are well taken; however,

his suggestion of a "Para-Malay" category as a way around the difficulty, although perhaps useful for government censuses, fails to reflect basic ethnohistoric relationships. Difficulties of classification can be attributed to several factors. There is abundant evidence that Borneo has been a crossroads of racial and cultural influences stemming from a variety of directions—from Sumatra and the mainland to the west, from Java to the south, from the Sulu and Bisayan Philippines to the northeast, and probably from Formosa and southeast China as well. As a result, the racial, cultural, and linguistic picture is one of considerable complexity. The confusion of ethnic names resulting from the bisection of the island in colonial times by an international border—the one side British, the other Dutch—has added to the problem. Finally, the major portion of the available ethnographic data is highly specific, both to locality and subject matter. Although in historical depth and fullness of description these data are virtually unmatched elsewhere in Southeast Asia, there have as yet been few attempts to synthesize them. A major obstacle to such attempts is the virtual absence of modern linguistic field surveys. The recent work of Hudson (1967a, 1970), Prentice (1970), and others is just now beginning to fill this gap, but until work is completed for major portions of the island, any classification of the Borneo peoples must remain tentative. For these reasons, the ordering of entries in the present work does not pretend to the status of a definitive classification. Where possible, the assigning of ethnic names and groupings has attempted to reflect recent linguistic fieldwork, but in general the ordering is a simple geographic one, starting with the Dusunic peoples in the north and ending with the Barito River Dayaks in the south. The Malays of the coastal fringe are dealt with elsewhere in this volume under the entry for Coastal Malays; the Chinese under the entry by that title. Two groups, the Ilanon and Bajau of Sabah, are entered in Volume II, since they are more properly considered under Mindanao and Sulu (Samal-speaking) peoples, respectively.

BIBLIOGRAPHY. Cheng Te-K'un 1969; Coedès 1968; Harrisson 1958b; Harrisson and Harnett 1969; Harrisson and O'Connor 1970; Hose and McDougall 1912; Hudson 1967a, 1970; Kennedy 1935; Leach 1950; Prentice 1970; Wang Gungwu 1958.

DUSUN*

Synonyms. *Idaan, Kadazan*

ORIENTATION. **Identification and location.** Orang Dusun is a coastal Malay term carrying the connotation of "backwoods" or "country," a euphemism for aborigines, specifically those midway between coast and highland interior. [The term occurs with this meaning, e.g. in Brunei for groups of Bisaya speakers and in Kalimantan Tengah for certain groups in the middle Barito area.] It is commonly used in northern Borneo to refer to a congeries of separate, named groups located within Sabah's West Coast and Interior Residencies, speaking closely related languages, but nowadays differing considerably with respect to social and cultural usages (Appell and Harrison 1969). The term Kadazan, originally restricted to the Dusun of Penampang and Papar, is rapidly achieving the status of a generic term for all Dusun speakers. Islamized Dusun, in particular those on the east coast of Sabah, are generally called Idahan (Ida'an); this term sometimes appears in the older literature as Idaan, meaning Dusun in general. The Dusunic peoples are commonly referred to in the literature as comprising some twelve or so groups or categories, named in most cases for a stream or river system. Those on the western coastal

plains, primarily irrigated-rice agriculturists, include Putatan, Papar, Tuaran, Penampang, Tempasuk (Kadamaian), and Marudu. Those in interior foothill or upland areas include Rungus, Kiau, Tegas (Tagas, Tahgas), Ranau, and Tambunan. Some interior groups, e.g. Rungus, are primarily swidden agriculturists, whereas the Ranau and Tambunan grow irrigated rice on extensive upland plains just behind the Crocker Range. Hose and McDougall's (1912) ethnological classification of Borneo peoples grouped Dusun with Murut, including those of both Sabah and Sarawak. Kennedy (1935) included Dusun and Murut, together with certain other peoples in Sarawak and Brunei, in a Klamantan category, which he felt represented an indigenous "Indonesian" culture stratum in Borneo. The importance of an alleged Chinese influence on Dusun culture has frequently been mentioned, but it would seem that more basic ethnolinguistic affiliations may lie to the north, in the direction of the Batan–Botel Tobago area and, ultimately, aboriginal Formosa. [Rutter 1929; Evans 1923, 1953; Prentice 1970; Appell and Harrison 1969.] **Linguistic affiliation.** Prentice (1970) postulates two linguistic subfamilies, Dusunic (Dusun and Bisaya) and Murutic (Sabah Murut and Tidong), within an Idahan family of languages, which in turn forms part of the Northern Indonesian branch (Dyen's Philippine hesion) of Austronesian. Dusun dialects are closely related but not necessarily mutually intelligible. Malay is the traditional lingua franca in coastal areas. Kadazan, a coastal dialect adopted by missionary educators, has gained semiofficial status and is now the medium of a newspaper intended for Dusun readers (Prentice 1970). **Demography.** A total of 145,229, according to the 1960 census, although the problems of defining ethnicity for census purposes make this figure only approximate (cf. Appell 1968a). **History.** It is the view of Glyn-Jones (1953: 12-13) that the Dusun were originally an interior hill people and that their occupation of the coastal plains is a relatively recent phenomenon. Those on the west coast, particularly in the Penampang area, have long been influenced by government economic schemes and Christian schools. Among educated Dusuns (Kadazan is now the preferred term), there is an emerging ethnic awareness and the beginnings of a nationalist movement. Contact with Bajau traders and Chinese merchants has been extensive, as has intermarriage with Chinese.

SETTLEMENT PATTERN AND HOUSING. Although there is nowadays considerable variation in settlement and housing patterns, the Dusun appear to have been originally a longhouse people. In the Tempasuk River area, villages containing single-family dwellings are scattered over the coastal plain and along the river's course inland for some 30 miles. Inland, the landscape changes to lalang-covered foot-

---

*Most of the published data on Dusunic peoples are based on groups that practice wet-rice agriculture, and the present summary of Dusunic culture reflects this fact. By way of contrast, the entry that follows, by George Appell, describes the Rungus of Kudat District, a people whose subsistence is based on the growing of hill rice in swiddens and who in some other respects, also, may be atypical of the general Dusunic culture pattern.

hills; here villages composed of several raised, plank-walled longhouses with up to eight doors are located on hilltops along either side of the river and its tributary streams (Evans 1923, 1953). On the inter-montane rice plains behind the Crocker Range, e.g. among the Tambunan, single-family dwellings grouped in hamletlike clusters are the rule, but in the surrounding hills, villages consist of three or so longhouses, averaging 10 to 30 doors each (Williams 1965).

ECONOMY. Appell and Harrison (1969) estimate that Dusun peoples on the average derive some 70 percent of their total subsistence from agriculture, principally rice, with secondary crops of maize and cassava. Coastal groups generally rely on irrigated wet rice (using plow and buffalo), supplemented by swid-dening where feasible. Irrigated wet rice is likewise the principal crop on the interior upland plains, among both Tambunan and Ranau Dusun, supplemented by swiddening on the surrounding hillsides. Williams (1965) thinks that wet rice is a relatively recent development in these areas. It appears that few Dusun nowadays rely wholly or principally on slash-and-burn agriculture, although this is still the case among the Rungus in the hilly interior of the Kudat Peninsula. Hunting is generally unimportant as a source of food, as is fishing (except for groups who have access to the coast). Domestic animals (pigs, chickens, cattle, buffalo) are important as food and ritual sacrifice. Traditional items of wealth include gongs, beads, brass canon, knives and spears, and Chinese jars. The more ancient of these are regarded as animate; they figure in ritual, marriage negotiations, and social differentiation. Brassware armlets, anklets, and collars were valued by coastal Kadamaian, among whom women wore corsets of rattan coils threaded with small brass rings (Evans 1923). In modern times, cattle and buffalo have acquired standard conversion values in terms of older forms of wealth.

SOCIAL ORGANIZATION. The data on Dusunic social organization are at present incomplete and, on several points, conflicting or unclear. A widespread origin legend (recorded independently by Glyn-Jones, Evans, Rutter, and Williams) includes variations on the theme of a flood and later dispersal from an original homeland in the highland interior. Such myths appear to have been associated in the past with localized groupings, bongkawan, based in part on an ideology of descent from ancestral founders of ur-villages, identified in some cases with elements of wood, clay, or stone. Membership in a bongkawan appears also to have been associated with use of a common headhouse (cf. Glyn-Jones 1953: 89-90). For contemporary Tambunan (Sensuron) Dusun, Williams (1965: 48-49) has reported corporate ambilineal descent groups, senAkAgun. Conversely, Appell and Harrison (1969) report an absence of cognatic kin

groups among both Rungus and Ranau Dusun, although they leave open the possibility that descent constructs may be used e.g. to validate property rights. Williams reports for Tambunan an exogamous personal kindred reckoned vertically to include great-grandparents and laterally to include third cousins, and encompassing both agnatic and affinal kin. Appell and Harrison (1969), however, report kindreds absent among both Rungus and Ranau. Marriage with a first cousin is everywhere incestuous, but frequently can be accomplished by payment of a fine to "cool" the union. Regulation of marriage beyond this degree varies considerably. Glyn-Jones (1953: 88-89) reports that wealthy families regularly violate incest taboos in order to keep irrigated rice land within the family. Bride-price, expressed in terms of traditional items of wealth such as gongs and jars, is everywhere important. Residence after marriage is not jurally prescribed, and there is considerable variation in this regard. Independent nuclear families, with occasional polygyny, are the rule, although stem families do occur (Appell and Harrison 1969). Evans (1953: 200ff.) provides evidence of a former pattern of social ranks or classes, including an endogamous aristocracy based on ownership of traditional wealth. There would seem to be considerable similarity between Evans' description and the interpretation by Leach (1950) of Sabah Murut (Tagal) longhouse social structure.

RELIGION. Evans (1953) describes for the Tempasuk Dusun a pantheon of named deities as well as a host of lesser spirits including ghouls, spirits of disease, fertility, etc. A rice soul concept and bird omenology appear common to most if not all Dusunic peoples; ancestor cults appear weakly developed or absent altogether. Practitioners include female priestesses or spirit mediums who function in communal and household ceremonies with reference to curing sickness and recalling lost souls as well as in divinatory and renewal ceremonies. These latter may include long invocations in a spirit language during which a spirit familiar speaks through the priestess. Evans (1953: 534ff.) and Glyn-Jones (1953: 96) describe a type of village renewal ceremony held at infrequent intervals and involving major expenditures of wealth and effort. Ritual on these occasions includes the ceremonial preparation of rice beer, the invocation of jar spirits by priestesses, buffalo sacrifice, and offerings to village guardian stones. Certain of Evans' remarks indicate that such ritual/festival occasions were in the past sponsored by members of an aristocratic "house-owning" group on behalf of the entire longhouse. At death the soul travels, by a hazardous route, to Mt. Kinabalu. Jar burial was apparently widespread formerly, although nowadays many coastal groups bury in coffins in village graveyards. Headhunting was apparently also widespread—among some groups skulls were kept in a small raised structure or head-house; among others, on the gallery area of the long-house. The headhunting complex included the erection of memorial stones and the tattooing of warriors following a successful raid (Evans 1953: 294ff.).

BIBLIOGRAPHY. Appell 1968a; Appell and Harrison 1969; Evans 1923, 1953; Glyn-Jones 1953; Hose and McDougall 1912; Kennedy 1935; Leach 1950; Prentice 1970; Rutter 1929; Staal 1923-25; Williams 1960, 1965.

RUNGUS DUSUN*

ORIENTATION. **Identification and location.** Between 6°36'-6°53' N. and 116°37'-117°14' E., in a variety of elevations on the southern two thirds of the Kudat Peninsula and in the middle region of the Melabong (Bengkoka) Peninsula of the Kudat District, Sabah. The Rungus are a group of Dusun speakers who distinguish themselves from other Dusun speakers in the area by various cultural markers, including the autonym of Rungus and a self-conscious dialect, or isoglot (Appell 1968b). The Kudat Peninsula is considered to be their original homeland; those occupying the Melabong Peninsula across Marudu Bay first moved there sometime in the not-too-distant past but before the arrival of the British, and movement of individuals and families back and forth continues. About one third of the total Rungus population lives on the Melabong Peninsula. **Geography.** The Brooke Range that forms the spine of the Kudat Peninsula peters out into low, rolling hills at the most northerly end of the Rungus distribution. The drainage pattern is immature, with numerous streams and small rivers. Valleys are narrow and separated by low, steep-sided hills ranging from about 2,000 feet down to 150 feet at the northern end. Vegetation is primarily secondary forest in various stages of regeneration, with occasional patches of lalang. **Linguistic affiliation.** Dusunic subfamily within the Idahan family of languages, part of the Northern Indonesian branch of Austronesian (Prentice 1970). **Demography.** Appell (1965), using head-tax rolls and other information, estimated that for the 1960-62 period there were approximately 6,229 Rungus living in unmixed villages; the population of villages of Rungus mixed with other Dusunic groups was estimated at 4,617 people. **History.** Prior to the arrival of the British in 1881, the Rungus were under the influence of the Sultanate of Brunei, and Muslims along the Kudat coast gave titles to Rungus headmen. Slave raids and plundering by southern Philippine peoples were greatly feared, but headhunting by Dusunic groups in the Kudat area ceased prior to the

*The author of this entry, George N. Appell, carried out research among the Rungus in 1959-60 and 1961-63. He is at present Research Associate in Anthropology at Brandeis University.

arrival of the British, probably as a result of coastal Muslim influence. Beginning in the early 1900s, the Chinese assumed a variety of agricultural pursuits, including the planting of rubber and coconuts, with the result that sections of traditional Rungus lands have fallen into Chinese hands. European missionaries entered Sabah following the organization of government by the British, and a Basel Mission was established in Rungus territory in 1961. The British administration and the missionaries attempted to change economies based on swidden agriculture to ones based on irrigated rice or cash crops of rubber and coconut, although these changes have as yet had relatively little effect on the Rungus, and they remain one of the least acculturated of any of the Dusun groups.

SETTLEMENT PATTERN AND HOUSING. **Settlement pattern.** The territory of a village encompasses the drainage area of a stream or river. Each village consists of one or more hamlets, and each hamlet may be composed of one or more longhouses. In the past, the ideal village settlement model was one longhouse per village. A hamlet may be occupied from one to ten or fifteen years, although membership is constantly changing as individual families move in or out. The reasons for domestic family moves and the desertion of hamlets include illness or fear of illness, death, conflict among fellow longhouse members, and, when the nearby swidden areas have been temporarily exhausted, a desire to be nearer more productive agricultural areas. Return to a former site occurs when the forest has regenerated sufficiently for use, which may take from six to fifteen years. The mean village size on the Kudat Peninsula is 137.7 persons, with a range of from 42 to 395. Rungus villages lack any kind of community structure, such as a headhouse, which is reported to be characteristic of some other Dusunic groups. **Housing.** The raised longhouse appears to be much more unitary in structure and social organization than it actually is. As the longhouse comes into existence through the lateral accretion of individual domestic family apartments, there are no common structural elements (with the exception of the two entry ladders at either end). There are two main sections of each apartment: the enclosed private section and the gallery section. The former consists of a hearth, a general working area beyond the hearth, and a raised sleeping area. It is separated from adjoining sections by bark walls. The gallery section includes an aisleway by the compartment wall, a section for storing rice-pounding blocks or mortars, and a general working and lounging area. The series of individually-owned, adjoining gallery sections produces a long aisleway and lounging area running the entire length of the longhouse.

ECONOMY. **Agriculture.** The major crop is hill rice grown in swiddens, supplemented by maize and cassava. Agricultural tools include a parang for clearing brush and a weeding knife. The dibble stick is used to plant rice and maize seeds and also in some cases to plant rice seedlings in the irrigated fields. **Fishing and hunting.** Fishing is done primarily with basketry traps and scoops. However, poisoning is known, and some fishing by line and hook is done. Hunting is done primarily by throwing spears, although a few shotguns are owned. **Gathering.** The major products gathered include a wide variety of wild fruits, as well as fruit from owned and tended trees. Wild plant roots are sometimes dug and used for food when agricultural products are scarce. Honey is also collected. **Domestic animals.** Pigs and chickens are raised by all families and are used primarily for ritual sacrifice to spirits. Water buffalo are kept by some families as beasts of burden, for riding, and occasionally for sacrifice at death ceremonials of important and wealthy individuals. **Industrial arts.** Basketry containers are made by men, and one or two men in each village know how to use the Malayan forge to make knives and other cutting implements from iron purchased from shops. Generally speaking, craftsmen have no higher status than other people, with the exception of females who know how to weave ritual clothing and who because of their skill command a higher bride-price. Skirts, as well as a variety of other clothing with ritually significant patterns, are woven on a belt loom. **Trade.** Weekly markets are held at the high point of navigation along the rivers. Here coastal Muslims and Chinese exchange fish and manufactured goods for the agricultural products of the Rungus. A great deal of internal trade occurs within the Rungus territory, in which rice is exchanged for brassware, gongs, jars, and other scarce goods. **Property.** The accumulation of property, specifically *dapu*, is a major focus of Rungus society. *Dapu* includes gongs, brassware, antique plates and bowls, and jars, purchased both from agricultural surpluses and profits from the buying and selling of such property. Thus the accumulation of *dapu* demonstrates both the skills and abilities of the male founder of the domestic family in the swidden activities and also his shrewdness and skill in the lengthy bargaining that occurs in any purchase or sale. The bride-price consists almost entirely of *dapu*; the latter also functions as a means of creating family savings, which at times of crop failure can be converted into rice and other consumables. Other important items of property include female and male ritual clothing, old beads, and brass wire coils that are worn on arms, legs, neck, and waist. Incorporeal property includes the invocations, chants, and prayers of religious specialists. Traditionally, the village holds residual rights to the land within its territory, within which resident domestic families have the right to cultivate swiddens. No permanent rights are established by domestic families through clearing of village land. Modern items of property include coconut plantations and wet-rice fields, the residual ownership of which lies with individuals and not the village. Such cases are as yet relatively rare among the Rungus of Kudat Peninsula.

KIN GROUPS. **Descent.** Bilateral, with sex-linked inheritance of certain items. **Kin groups.** No kin groups in the usual sense of the term exist among the Rungus or related Dusunic groups in the Kudat District. The establishment of a kin tie is not necessary for longhouse or village membership, although few individuals desire to join local groupings in which there are no kin. Rights to fruit trees, however, if not previously divided up among the planter's children, may be claimed from both parents. These rights are not held by a social grouping, and the descendants never interact as such. Instead, the descendants of the original planter may be considered a collectivity (Appell 1967a) in which the rights to access of fruit trees are held by the members in severalty. The same situation appears to hold among the Dusunic peoples of Tuaran for the much more important heirloom jars. The kindred as a self-conscious collectivity, whose members hold in severalty identical obligations to a propositus and share a similar body of norms, does not exist among the Rungus (see Appell 1967a). Rungus kin terms of reference are as follows:

GrFa	*aki'*
GrMo	*odu'*
Fa	*tama'*
Mo	*tidi'*
FaBr, MoBr	*kamaman*
FaSi, MoSi	*kominan*
Child	*anak*
Br, Si	*opinai*
GrCh (m.s.)	*muaki'*
GrCh (w.s.)	*muodu'*
First cousin	*pinsan haring*
Second cousin	*pinsan kin duvo'*

MARRIAGE AND FAMILY. **Mode.** Bride-price is paid by the groom's domestic family. The amount paid in each case is determined by extended negotiation, based in part on the relative wealth of the families concerned. **Form.** Marriage is generally monogamous. Polygynous marriages involving two wives, rarely three, occur in cases of wealthy men and when an adulterous relationship arises with the wife's unmarried sister, usually as a result of residing with her sister and brother-in-law. In cases of polygynous marriage, separate longhouse apartments for each wife are preferred. **Extension of incest taboos.** First-cousin marriages may take place only after payment of a ritual fine and special items in the bride-price to "cool" the marriage. Second-cousin marriage has some preference, in that it consolidates the wealth of grandparents. Illicit sexual relations of any type form a major concern of Rungus society. Such relations are considered to anger the spirits that hold up the world so that they become hot. This heat is then visited on the couple themselves, and unless the spirits are appeased by the sacrifice of a pig, it spreads from them to their domestic families, swiddens, longhouse, domestic animals, to the village, and eventually to the world at large. This results in illness and death, drought and disease in the swiddens, and infertility in people, animals, and crops. **Residence.** Postnuptial residence for one year in bride's domestic family. Following this, the first longhouse apartment is built in bride's village. Postnuptial residence in groom's village in intervillage marriage may occur in those cases where the groom is the youngest child and is expected to care for aged parents. **Domestic unit.** A domestic family is founded when a couple establishes a separate longhouse apartment and swidden. In addition to the children produced by the founders, this unit may include one parent (rarely two) of one of the founders. It is expected that an aged parent or widow will reside with the youngest child, and this occurs in all cases except where the surviving parent is the father and the youngest child is a daughter, in which instance the father prefers to reside with a son. **Inheritance.** There is a tendency for sex-linked inheritance, in which gongs and jars go to sons, while female clothing, jewelry, and those types of brass containers that are kept in the compartment go to daughters. The eldest son and the eldest daughter are expected to receive the heirloom property of father and mother respectively, but if there is ample property, this qualification, as well as the previous one of sex-linked inheritance, are not necessarily followed. Furthermore, in dividing their inherited property, parents must consider the fact that it is owned corporately by the whole family. Property is thus divided among the children on the basis of a complex series of values that take into consideration the degree of participation of the child in the economic and moral order of the family as well as the desire to provide a complete outfit of gongs, jars, and brassware for each child as he sets up his separate household. **Divorce.** Equally available to males and females. On divorce, the accumulated earnings of the domestic family are divided between husband and wife, with a slightly larger share going to the husband (if no fault lies on his side), due to his greater efforts in the swidden. **Secondary marriage.** After death of a spouse, the survivor must obtain the permission of his in-laws before he or she may marry again. This involves a ritual gift, and permission is rarely refused. If an unmarried sibling of one's dead spouse is available, it is expected that some consideration of this person be given as a potential spouse. **Adoption.** No formal adoption exists. Cross-sex twins are separated, with one being raised by another family due to fear of incest.

SOCIOPOLITICAL ORGANIZATION. **Political organization.** Traditional community leaders were those who had little fear in dealing with outsiders, who had become wealthy through their skill in trading agricultural products for heirloom property, and who displayed skill in resolving disputes. Such individuals were often given titles by coastal Muslims to solidify their informal leadership. No formal sanctions lay in the hands of these leaders, but those skilled in adat and adjudication frequently developed influence in a particular region. The status of leader often remained within a family line, passing to a brother, or a son-in-law, and then to a grandchild. With the arrival of the British formal headmen for each village were appointed. **Social stratification.** In the past, slaves—primarily debt slaves—existed. Stratification was and is on the basis of wealth, but this is informal. **Social control and justice.** Complaints and delicts are argued before an informal village meeting composed of all male founders of domestic families who wish to attend. Decisions are by consensus and are based on decisions made in previous cases. No social controls are available except ostracism. Delicts unresolved reappear in bride-price negotiations in an oblique manner and result in a request for additional *dapu* from the groom's family to mollify the injured party. In the past, trials by ordeal and by oath occurred. **Warfare.** The Rungus formerly engaged in warfare for heads and booty, and raids between distant Dusunic groups took place. Active participants were warriors who had received guardian spirits through ordeals. Cannibalism occurred ritually at a sacrifice for cleansing the community, in which a non-Dusunic individual, purchased from coastal Muslims, was used.

RELIGION. **Supernaturals.** A supreme being, Minamangon, resides in the uppermost of the seven layers of heaven. A rice spirit exists for each family member and is called back each year to the swiddens and then sent home at the end of the agricultural year. All old property has spirits that are sacrificed to and treated generously to encourage other spirits to join the domestic family and thereby increase wealth. The most important category of spirits are the *rogon*, irascible, malevolent spirits who cause illness by stealing and abusing souls or by putting their "domestic animals," i.e. worms, water buffalo, and the like, into the body. **Practitioners.** The major religious practitioners and the focus of the female status hierarchy are the female spirit mediums. The ideal female is one who has memorized the extended epic hymns used at ceremonies to cure illness, who has a variety of reliable spirit familiars and guardian spirits so that she can go into and out of trance easily, and who knows all the ritual patterns in weaving cloth. The spirit familiar does not enter the body of the spirit medium nor does her trance state end in a loss of consciousness. Males who know the long epic chants for the rice spirits and prayers for property do not have spirit familiars, nor do they go into trances. **Ceremonies.** Village renewal and cleansing ceremonies take place about every decade. For the most important of these, a human sacrifice was formerly needed. Renewal ceremonies occur for most families every several years to satisfy a debt made to a *rogon* for health, to appease the *rogon* of the longhouse apartment, and/or to ensure the future health and well-being of the family. The ceremonial aspects of the agricultural year begin when the rice is planted and the rice spirits are summoned to the family's swidden. As the rice grows, particularly if it does not appear healthy, various sacrifices may be made to the rice spirits and to those spirits controlling agricultural pests. These involve extended epic prayers and the sacrifice of chickens. At the end of threshing, additional chickens are sacrificed to the rice spirits, and rice wine is made. And finally at the conclusion of the agricultural year, weddings, memorial ceremonies for the deceased, family renewal ceremonies, and sacrifices to the spirits of property are held. **Illness and medicine.** Illness is a major concern, and fear of the disease-causing *rogon* and their appeasement form a major focus. Any harm befalling any of an individual's seven souls will cause illness. These souls can wander from the body during dreams and become lost or be captured by a *rogon* and tortured. Sacrifices to *rogon* appease them and return the errant souls to the body of the sick person. **Soul, death, and afterlife.** Each individual has six souls located in the various joints of the body and a seventh soul that inhabits the whole body. On death, the seventh soul goes to Nabalu (Mt. Kinabalu), where it dwells with the souls of its family as on earth. The six other souls may become *rogons* and ghosts. In addition, each individual has a spirit that goes to one of the seven layers of heaven, and it is these spirits that become the spirit familiars consulted by the spirit mediums. On death, the body is dressed and viewed by friends and relatives for a day and then buried in a wooden box in the cemetery nearest to the longhouse where the death occurred. The grave is outlined by stones, and sometimes a roof is built over it. Extremely wealthy individuals may occasionally be buried in a jar. On the first year after death in which there is a sufficient harvest, a memorial ceremony is held, in which all relatives and friends are called to partake of food and drink and send the soul finally to Nabalu.

BIBLIOGRAPHY. Appell 1964, 1965, 1966, 1967a, 1967b, 1968a, 1968b, 1968c, 1968d; Appell and Harrison 1969; Prentice 1970.

MURUT

MURUT, A TERM of lowland origin meaning simply "hill people," is commonly applied to peoples inhabiting the mountainous interior of Borneo in an area extending generally from 5°20′ to 3°20′ N. (from Keningau in Sabah south to the headwaters of the Baram and Bahau on opposite sides of the Sarawak-Kalimantan border). The fact that the area is intersected by the political boundaries of former British North Borneo, Dutch Borneo, and Sarawak has contributed to a confusion of names and ethnic identities, and lack of precise linguistic and cultural information has, until relatively recently, precluded any definitive classification of these peoples. Recent work by the linguist Prentice (1970) has established the position of "Sabah" or "Northern" Murut within a language family (Idahan) related to the North Indonesian (Philippine) branch of Austronesian; whereas "Sarawak" or "Southern" Murut languages have been classified as belonging to the West Indonesian branch of Austronesian (cf. Dyen 1965). The suggestion by Prentice that this linguistic distinction be recognized terminologically has been adopted in the present volume with the designation of the "Northern" Muruts of Sabah as *Idahan Muruts* (see entry below, under this title). Prentice also recommends the eventual adoption of a similarly suitable term for the "Southern" Muruts of Sarawak-Kalimantan. Pending final determination of linguistic relationships in this latter area, the present volume has adopted the expedient of naming these people *Kelabitic Muruts*, after the best-described culture type within the area (see entry below, under this title). Despite the evident linguistic difference, Idahan and Kelabitic Muruts share a number of distinctive cultural characteristics. The extent of cultural similarities and differences, and their meaning for the interpretation of culture history in this part of Borneo, are as yet unclear. Similarities are evident in respect to several aspects of warfare, religion, and burial practice. If Leach's data from Kemabong (Leach 1947, 1950: 73-75) are representative of indigenous Idahan Murut, then there would appear to be a common social structural pattern as well. Irrigated wet rice, grown on upland intermontane plains, occurs sporadically throughout the area; although it is commonly assumed that upland wet-rice culture is a recent introduction, there is some evidence that this type of agriculture in the Bornean interior may be of some antiquity (cf. LeBar n.d.). It may be the case that there is (or was) a basically similar culture type throughout the Murut area and that the major differences have to do with the elaboration among the Kelabits of the ritual importance and social distinctiveness of an aristocratic elite based on the accumulation of traditional wealth and its redistribution at elaborate mortuary feasts—a difference which would seem to reflect the greater influence on Kelabitic Muruts of the neighboring Kayan-Kenyah culture.

BIBLIOGRAPHY. Dyen 1965; Leach 1947, 1950; LeBar n.d.; Prentice 1970.

IDAHAN MURUT*

Synonyms. *Northern Murut, Sabah Murut, Tagal, Taggal, Tagol, Tagul*

ORIENTATION. **Identification.** The term Murut ("hill-people") is applied in Borneo to two completely dissimilar sets of ethnic groups, neither of which uses the term itself. In Sabah it refers to the groups inhabiting the Interior Residency south of Keningau (who are known in Sarawak as Tagal); while in Sarawak it refers to the groups living in the Lawas and Trusan areas of the 5th Division (known in Sabah as Lun Daye). Both types extend for an unknown distance southeastward into Kalimantan, where they are indiscriminately referred to as Murut or simply as Dayak. Linguistically, the two Murut sections have little in common. Although the languages of both are Austronesian, in no case does the percentage of shared cognates between a "Sarawak Murut" and a "Sabah Murut" language exceed 38 percent. Terms such as "Sarawak Murut" and "Sabah Murut" are unsatisfactory, since "Sabah Muruts" are also found in Sarawak and vice versa, and since there are far more "Sarawak Muruts" in Kalimantan than there are in Sarawak. Moreover, like the alternative terms "Southern Murut" and "Northern Murut," they imply that the groups concerned are merely geographically separated subdivisions of a single ethnolinguistic entity. The solution suggested here is to use the name of the appropriate language-family as a distinguishing prefix, thus "Idahan Murut" in place of "Sabah Murut." The creation of a suitable alternative for "Sarawak Murut," however, is attendant upon the delimitation and naming of the linguistic family concerned. **Classifica**

*The author of this entry, D. J. Prentice, is a member of the Indonesian Department, Australian National University. His data on Murut culture refer, unless otherwise indicated, to the Timugon village of Mandalom, where he resided for 18 months in 1965-66 and 1967-68.

tion and location. On linguistic and cultural grounds, the Idahan Muruts can be divided into two main sections: Lowland and Highland. This division corresponds closely with that proposed by Rutter (1922: 63-73; 1929: 34-36).

A. *Lowland Murut*:

1. *Timugon* (Poros, Sandewar, Sandiwar, Temogun, Tenom Murut, Timogon, Timogun, Timugan, Timugun). Divided into four subgroups: (a) *Bukow* on the Bukau River (coastal side of the Crocker Range); (b) *Bintaq* (the letter "q" signifies a glottal stop) on the lower Padas around Beaufort and upstream to Mile 65; (c) *Kapagalan* on the right bank of the Pegalan around Melalap; and (d) *Poros* on both banks of the Pegalan and Padas rivers, extending for about 7 miles north and south of Tenom. Each uses the term "Timugon" exclusively of itself, and has other names for the other groups.

2. *Nabay* (Dabai, Keningau Dusun, Keningau Murut, Nabai, Rabai). Along the Pegalan Valley and its right-bank tributaries in the neighborhood of Keningau.

3. *Baukan* (Baokan, Bokan, Boken, Bokon, Bokun, Bukan, Bukun, Ulunno-Bokon). In the upper reaches of the Sook River and its tributaries, including the villages of Tulid, Pau, Tiong and Kindasan.

B. *Highland Murut* (in Sabah, frequently referred to as "Pensiangan Murut" or "Tagal"):

1. *Paluan* (Makeealiga, Makialiga, Peluan). Three subgroups can be recognized: (a) *Paluan* proper, in the hills east of the Tenom Plain (i.e. the headwaters of the Punti, Dalit, and Keramatoi), in the Padas Valley between Kemabong and Sogo, and in the Crocker Range along the Pangi River; (b) *Dalit* (Sook Muruts), on the lower reaches of the Dalit, Sook, and Keramatoi and on the surrounding plain; and (c) *Sapulut* (Sepulot, Sepulut, Sipulote Murut), on the Talankai and its tributaries north of Agis. The members of the last subgroup have no name for themselves as a whole, and use a village- or river-name as identification. They are here called "Sapulut" after the river and government station of the same name, around which most of them are concentrated.

2. *Sumambuq* (Bol Murut, Pensiangan Murut, Pentjangan, Rundum Murut, Semambu, Tagal, Taggal, Tagol, Tagul). Extending over a wide area, embracing (a) the valley of the Mengalong upstream from Sindumin,

together with neighboring areas of Sarawak; (b) the Padas and its tributaries, from Kemabong southward to the confluence of the Padas and Saprian; and (c) the Tagal and its tributaries. Like the Sapulut of Paluan, this group has no autonym above the village level. Evidence suggests that a different variety of the Sumambuq dialect is spoken along each major river, and that there are parallel cultural differences. More research is needed for an adequate definition of these subgroups. It is considered preferable to reserve the term "Tagal" for the subgroup located on the river of the same name, and to use the term "Sumambuq" (an exonym of uncertain origin) for the whole group.

3. *Alumbis* (Loembis Murut, Lumbis Murut). On the river of the same name in Indonesian Kalimantan, and extending northward into the Pensiangan district of Sabah.

Geography. The Lowland Muruts are mainly plains-dwellers, inhabiting the coastal plain of the Klias Peninsula and the intermontane plains of Tenom, Keningau, and Sook. These locations have made them more accessible to external influences. The Timugon, in particular, have a comparatively long history of contact with non-Murut groups. The area of the Highland Muruts, on the other hand, is mostly very rugged country, intersected by innumerable steep-sided mountain ranges. The whole region enjoys a tropical climate, with little or no seasonal variation in either temperature or rainfall. The intermontane plains, however, being in the rainshadow of the Crocker Range, have a relatively low rainfall (60-70 inches per annum). [Lee 1965.] **Linguistic affiliation.** The Idahan Murut languages are very closely related to each other and have a shared cognate count averaging 70 percent. Together with Dusun, Tidong, and Bisaya, they form part of the Idahan language family. This family, in which are included all the indigenous languages of Sabah—as well as some speech forms found in adjoining areas of Brunei, Sarawak, and Kalimantan—is in turn part of the North Indonesian (or Philippines) branch of the extensive Austronesian family. Except in remoter areas, nearly all Murut men and most of the women have some knowledge of Sabah Malay, which is basically Bazaar Malay, with strong Brunei dialect influence. [Prentice 1969a: 1-2.] **Demography.** According to Jones (1966: 69), a total of 22,138 "Muruts" were enumerated in the 1960 Sabah census. However, this figure certainly includes an unknown number of "Sarawak Muruts" (perhaps about 2,000), and it probably excludes speakers of Idahan Murut languages living in the Beaufort and Keningau areas, who often class themselves as "Bisaya" and "Dusun" respectively. Allowing for all

these factors, and for natural increase in the population since the census, the number of Idahan Muruts can be roughly estimated at 35,000. Until the 1960 census, the so-called "decline of the Muruts" caused much concern in official circles, and at least nine investigators worked on this problem between 1931 and 1960. As pointed out by Appell (1968a: 27-42), however, their conclusions are of little value, since they are "based on the fallacious assumption of the social and cultural homogeneity of the Murut populations." It seems certain that depopulation affected different ethnic groups at different times, and that there never was a "Murut decline" as such. **History and cultural relations.** As stated by Woolley (1962), the Timugon have no knowledge of any migration to their present location. However, all the Lowland Muruts, in common with the Dusun groups, believe that after death their souls migrate to a place called Nabalu (i.e. Mt. Kinabalu, some 80 miles to the north). The Highland Muruts, on the other hand, locate their souls' resting place on Mulundayoh, Antulai, or Lumaku, all mountains in the Highland Murut area. [Rutter 1929: 220, 223-25.] The Timugon creation myth recounts the story of a great flood and of the repopulation of the world from elements of clay and bamboo (Prentice 1969b). The traditional enemies of the Timugons were the Paluans, who surround them on three sides, and continual head-hunting feuds persisted until the early twentieth century (Daly 1888: 14, 16, 19-21). Until the coming of the Europeans, the Timugons' only contact with the outside world was with traders from the coast or tax collectors from the Sultan of Brunei, to whom for some time they were nominally subject. The first European contact seems to have occurred in 1872; the next 20 years witnessed profound changes in the Timugon environment. The establishment of Chartered Company administration, the growth of Tenom as a trading center, the foundation of the great rubber estates on Timugon territory at Sapong and Melalap, and the arrival of the railway connecting Tenom with Kota Kinabalu (then Jesselton), all contributed to the social revolution which continues today. Christianity did not obtain a foothold among the Idahan Muruts until after the Second World War. Most conversions have taken place in the Sumambuq areas, where the Borneo Evangelical Mission is active. [Landgraf 1956: 8-9; Leach 1947: 13.]

SETTLEMENT PATTERN AND HOUSING. **Settlement pattern.** In all the Murut groups, the traditional settlement consisted of a raised longhouse, situated on the tongue of land between a river and its tributary and taking its name from the tributary. Except in the remoter parts of the Highland Murut area, this pattern has been replaced by non-nucleated villages strung out along the tributary (Leach 1947). In 1885, Daly saw Timugon longhouses measuring 100 x 50 feet

(1888: 13-14), yet by 1921 only two or three small longhouses remained (Woolley 1962). In February 1968, however, one Timugon longhouse of seven "doors" (family compartments) was still in use at the village of Tuan, five miles north of Tenom. **Housing.** The Lowland Murut and Paluan longhouse consists of a central passageway, with individual family compartments on one side and a common veranda on the other. The longhouse of the Highland Murut (except the Paluan), on the other hand, has compartments on both sides of the passageway, which opens out into a square common area in the center of the house. The middle of this central common area is occupied by one of the most interesting phenomena of Highland Murut culture: the *papan* (or *lansaran*). This is a section of plank flooring about six feet square, which is sunk one foot lower than the normal floor level. It rests on springy saplings lashed to the underside of the house, so that it springs up and down like a trampoline. The *papan* is used both for religious singing and dancing and for jumping competitions, in which young men try to leap high enough to grasp some object suspended from the ceiling. [Clarke 1952: 17-18; Rutter 1922: 330; 1929: 64, 85, 116.]

ECONOMY. The traditional subsistence economy has been replaced by a cash economy in virtually all Lowland Murut communities and in many highland communities. **Agriculture.** All Idahan Murut groups, even the semi-urbanized Timugons, cultivate hill rice by the slash-and-burn method, although in some areas cassava and sago have equal importance as staple foods. Agricultural ritual, however, is exclusively concerned with the rice crop. Irrigated-rice cultivation is found only among the three lowland groups, where it appears to be of relatively recent origin. Other crops grown include maize, bananas, yams, sweet potatoes, sugarcane, tobacco, and (in some areas) coffee. Fruit crops include langsat, durian, breadfruit, citrus fruits, papaya, and soursop. [Headly 1947; Landgraf 1956: 4-6; Rutter 1929: 86-99.] **Fishing and hunting.** Fishing methods include the use of tuba poison (usually a communal affair), castnets, fixed nets, rod-and-line, and a variety of traps. The traditional hunting method involves the use of the blowpipe, spear, and dogs. Among the Timugon, the complicated art of blowpipe-making has been lost, and the blowpipe is being superseded by the shotgun. Still in use, however, is a great variety of bird- and animal-traps, using pits, nets, lassos, and spears. Animals hunted for food are (in order of importance) wild pigs, three species of deer, squirrels, monkeys, flying foxes, and birds. [Woolley 1936; 1962: chap. 12.] **Gathering.** The gathering of jungle produce still plays a considerable part in supplying food and other necessities. The Timugons gather ferntips, bamboo-shoots, herbs, various wild or semi-wild fruits, timber, bamboo, rattan, beeswax, latex, and a variety of resins. **Domestic animals.** The chief domestic animals are poultry, pigs, dogs, and cats. Poultry is kept mainly for use as food on ceremonial occasions, though some fighting-cocks are reared (especially in Highland Murut areas). Pigs represent a form of wealth and are used in sacrifices and in the payment of bride-prices and fines. Dogs are employed for hunting and as watch-dogs; while cats are kept solely to keep down rats and mice. Water buffalo and oxen are bred by wealthier individuals for the same purposes as pigs. They are never used as beasts of burden, although those groups who practice irrigated-rice cultivation employ them for harrowing and plowing. It is significant that Daly makes no mention of the presence of cattle in the Timugon area in 1885. **Food and stimulants.** Rice, sago, and cassava are the staple foods. Fish, meat, and vegetables are regarded as being of secondary importance and may or may not be present at a meal. The only stimulants in everyday use are tobacco and betel nut, the latter used only by older women. The most important stimulant, however, is *tapai*, a beer made of rice or cassava. The consumption of *tapai* plays a very important role in Murut culture, being an essential accompaniment to funerals, weddings, religious ceremonies, planting, harvesting, housebuilding, departures and homecomings, the arrival of guests, and the settlement of personal disputes. Except in the first instance, it is accompanied by singing, dancing, and the playing of gongs and other musical instruments, which arts are not practiced at any other time. A very large part of the material and spiritual culture is therefore lost when tapai-drinking is abandoned, as is happening among various Highland groups under the influence of fundamentalist Christianity. **Industrial arts.** As far as can be ascertained, none of the Idahan Murut groups ever practiced the manufacture of metal, pottery, or cloth, which were obtained by trading with neighboring groups who possessed the necessary skills. Barkcloth garments are still sometimes worn on ceremonial occasions. The two most decorative arts are basketwork and carving. Using basketwork techniques (diagonal weaving and plaiting), the Muruts make mats, hats, baskets, and various decorative coverings from a variety of bamboos, rattans, and grasses. Several dyes are used to produce intricate patterns. Over 100 different named patterns are known, the names and distribution of which vary from group to group. The art of woodcarving had a highly religious significance, intricately carved and painted panels and figures being used to decorate graves and (in Highland areas) the dancing platform, or *papan*. [Alman and Alman 1963: 32-65; Rutter 1929: 120-21; Woolley 1929, 1932.] **Trade.** Continual warfare among the Murut groups probably inhibited trade until recent times. The most important articles of trade were salt, gongs, jars, knives, cloth, and (later) shotguns, which were obtained by barter from neighboring peoples or from itinerant traders from the coast. The *tamu* system of regular markets held on neutral ground, which existed among the Dusun groups, did not develop in the Murut areas, although it was introduced later by the Chartered Company. [Landgraf 1956: 10-11.]

KINSHIP. **Kin groups.** The main kin group is the nuclear family. The extended family and village play secondary and undefined roles in the kinship structure. The village appears to constitute an exogamous unit, and this probably applies to the longhouse also. Descent appears to be bilateral, with a patrilineal bias. **Kinship terminology.** The following terms of reference are used by the Timugon:

Mo	*inaq*
Fa	*amaq*
ElSb	*akaq*
YoSb	*aliq*
Cousin	*pantukir*
Ch	*anak*
SbCh	*akon*
PaBr	*kamaman*
PaSi	*kaminan*
PaFa	*aki*
PaMo	*aruq*
ChCh	*akupu*

MARRIAGE AND FAMILY. **Mode.** Prenatal betrothal and infant betrothal were occasionally practiced by the Timugon, but were not regarded as binding. Normally, a father arranges his son's betrothal and marriage and negotiates the terms with the girl's father. The betrothal fee may be in cash or in kind (a blowpipe, a *parang*, some cloth, or some jewelry). The *mulo*, or bride-price, consists of two parts: the *pulut* (bride-price proper) and the *balanjaq dapur* (expenses for the feast). A cash ceiling has been applied to the *pulut* by the administration, while the *balanjaq dapur* usually consists of one buffalo plus cash. Various courses are open in the event of the boy's family being unable to meet the bride-price; these include elopement, legalized cohabitation, payment by instalments, and loans from relatives. In all cases, the *pulut* at least must eventually be paid in some form or another. The only exception occurs when a man has no sons. In this case, he may allow one of his daughters (usually the youngest) to marry without payment of *mulo*, on condition that she and her husband remain in his house to care for him in his old age. [Rutter 1922: 306-10; 1929: 145-54, 211-13; Woolley 1962: chaps. 3-5.] **Form.** Monogamy is the norm, though polygyny is not infrequent. The first wife takes the place of the husband's parents in arranging the wedding and negotiating the bride-price. [Rutter 1929: 154-56; Woolley 1962: chap. 2.] **Extension of incest taboos.** Sexual relations and marriage are technically forbidden between: (a) full or half brother and sister; (b) father and daughter; (c) uncle and niece; and (d) first cousins or descendants of first cousins to the fifth generation. People breaking these taboos were formerly speared to death. Unions between first cousins are still regarded as grave offenses and threats to the well-being of the whole community, but they are allowed on payment of *sagit*. [Rutter 1929: 141-43; Woolley 1962: chap. 2.] **Residence.** Residence is patrilocal—at least until the first child is born, when the couple may set up a house of their own. **Inheritance.** Woolley (1953: 1-2, 15) divides inheritable property into "*pesaka*" (lineage property) and "*pencharian*" (acquired property). These terms are Malay, however, and as no vernacular equivalents are known, it is doubtful whether this is a relevant distinction in Timugon society (Landgraf 1956: 11-12). Males seem to have precedence over females as heirs, although females may own and inherit all types of property in their own right. [Rutter 1929: 166-69; Woolley 1953; 1962: chap. 4.] **Divorce.** If a husband divorces his wife, he forfeits the whole *mulo*; if a wife divorces her husband, the *pulut* must be returned. Widows and divorcées may remarry (in the case of widows, after the statutory period of mourning has elapsed). [Rutter 1929: 156-64; Woolley 1962: chap. 2.]

SOCIOPOLITICAL ORGANIZATION. **Political organization.** Traditional Murut political institutions are obscure. Most commentators (Tregonning 1965: 107; Woolley 1962: chap. 1) agree that there was no concept of a paramount chieftainship. However, Headly (1947: 4, 6-7) and Leach (1947: 4, 5-6) maintain that, among the Highland Muruts at least, each tribe had a hereditary chief known as the "Ullun Antong." In Timugon, *antung* means simply "rich, powerful man." Landgraf (1956: 22-23) thinks it likely that neighboring villages gave allegiance to a single *ulun antung* and that the domains of such men were the equivalent of what today are identified as subtribes. Leach (1950) adds that river valley alliances of this kind were probably largely kin based, i.e. interlonghouse affinal ties. Under the contemporary system, which is based on that created by the Chartered Company, each district has a number of Native Chiefs or "Orang Kaya-Kaya," who are responsible to the District Officer and preside over the native courts in settling disputes concerned with the *kaadatan* (body of customary law). [Headly 1947: 4-7; Landgraf 1956: 14-16; Leach 1947: 2-6; Rutter 1929: 68-69; Tregonning 1965: 102-28; Woolley 1962: chap. 1.] **Social stratification.** There appear to be no formal class divisions in Timugon society, except for the now obsolete division into slaves and freemen. Some families are, however, much wealthier than others, and their wealth (traditionally, heirloom jars, gongs, beads, and swords) tends to perpetuate itself through inheritance and higher bride-prices. Leach (1947: 6), on the other hand, posits three formal, named, social classes for the Sumambuq Muruts of the Pensiangan district, namely *"maiyu," "kamaiyu,"* and *"babarok."* Since these three terms are merely the normal words for "big," "not big," and "small" (*maayo, kaa maayo,* and *boborok*) respectively, and since Leach did not visit the Pensiangan district during his one week's stay in the Murut area and does not state the source of his information, his suggestion must be viewed with some caution. Until the early twentieth century, there were three classes of slaves in Timugon society. The lowest were prisoners-of-war, *rakop*. A *rakop* eventually could be accepted as a member of the tribe, and become an *ulipon*. If he married another *ulipon*, he and his wife and children would remain *ulipon* and would have to live with his master. If, however, he married a free woman, he would become a debt-slave or *ulun-ulun* (except in the very unlikely event of his being able to afford the bride-price), and would have to live with his father-in-law. Any free man who was thus indebted to another likewise became an *ulun-ulun*. [Headly 1947: 4-7; Leach 1947: 2-6.] **Warfare.** This took the form of organized headhunting raids on the longhouses of other tribes. Captured heads were regarded with utmost veneration and were honored by a special ceremony after the raid and at intervals later on. The usual fighting weapons were the sword, spear, and blowpipe. (For Rundum, Rutter mentions in addition wooden shields, quilted jackets overlaid with shell, and rattan caps with hornbill feathers.) Headhunting feuds were sometimes settled by making a tally of the people killed by each side. The winning side would hand over enough persons to make the number even. The people thus surrendered were treated as *rakop*, slaves; they might be killed or used as ritual sacrifices by their captors. [Headly 1947: 5-6; Rutter 1922: 331-39; 1929: 181-209; Woolley 1962: chap. 13; Daly 1888: 19-21.]

RELIGION. **Supernaturals.** The most important supernaturals are the *masundu*. They are essentially human in character, living in the sky, and consisting of the Creator "Grandfather Kapuunoq" (from *puun,* "origin") and his kindred. They are neither benevolent nor malevolent. A larger class includes the *riwato,* nonhuman and mostly dangerous to human beings. The *muayaq,* who were originally human beings, live on earth but are invisible. They are not considered harmful. [Rutter 1929: 227.] **Practitioners and ceremonies.** Among the Highland Murut tribes, any woman who has a knowledge of the ceremonies and procedures involved may act as a spirit-medium, or *babalian*. It is among the Lowland Muruts, however, that the institution has reached its highest degree of development. In the Timugon areas, its membership is restricted to specialists arranged in three ranks or orders, who hand down their art to young girls of the same tribe, preferably to their own daughters. Major rituals, such as *rawak* (exorcising of persons or houses), which lasts for three days and nights and

involves communication with a spirit familiar during a self-induced trance, can only be performed by *babalian* of the highest order. Ceremonies are accompanied by incantations, couched in part in an archaic idiom known as *tabalian*. The functions of the *babalian* are restricted to exorcising spirits and curing illness. Other religious or semireligious ceremonies, such as tooth filing and harvest ceremonies, are conducted by the head of the household. [Woolley 1962: chap. 8.] **Soul, death, and afterlife.** Men, domestic animals, and rice plants all have souls known as *ambiluo*. During harvest ceremonies, the rice souls (*ambiluo ru bilor*) are addressed as *aruq kaw,* "you grandmothers." A man's *ambiluo* migrates to Nabalu after death and does not interfere with the living. Before a dead person's *ambiluo* can reach Nabalu, it has to be ferried over a large river by a *masundu* known as "Grandfather Mangangob" (i.e. "doorkeeper"). Human beings are unique in possessing a second soul (*saliguor*), which remains on earth and is likely to molest the living if, for example, the death rites were not properly carried out or if its owner died a "sharp" death (i.e. one not resulting from old age or sickness). The most common form of interment is primary jar burial, which takes place some seven days after death. Burial is in a village cemetery, and a grave-house is constructed over the grave. There is evidence to suggest that at one time burial did not take place until after the following harvest. In the meantime, the jar was placed near the door of the house, covered with a pyramid of hard-packed earth, and surrounded by a low fence. Reflections of this custom may survive in the burial practices of other Idahan Murut groups. Among the Baukan, for example, the jar is not buried but merely placed on the ground and covered with earth. In Sumambuq areas near Pensiangan, the jar is placed in a grave-house built on piles, where it remains until the following harvest. The contents are then removed, placed in a second jar, and buried in the ground. [Rutter 1922: 290-93, 302-05; 1929: 214-15, 220-26; Woolley 1962: chap. 9.]

BIBLIOGRAPHY. Alman and Alman 1963; Appell 1968a, 1968b; Clarke 1952; Daly 1888; Forrest 1779; Genderen Stort 1916; Headly 1947; Hose and Mc-Dougall 1912; Jones 1966; Landgraf 1956; Leach 1947, 1950; Lee 1965; Lees 1966; Prentice 1969a, 1969b, 1970; Roth 1896; Rutter 1922, 1929; Tregonning 1965; Woolley 1929, 1932, 1936, 1953, 1962.

KELABITIC MURUT

Synonyms. *Kelabit, Lun Bawang, Lun Daya, Lun Daye, Southern Murut, Sarawak Murut, Kemaloh-Kelabit*

ORIENTATION. **Identification.** Kelabitic Murut is here used in a generic sense for a scattered population in north-central Borneo—generally the border area dividing Sarawak, Brunei, Sabah, and Kalimantan—but extending westward as far as the Brunei Bay littoral. Terms such as "Southern Murut" or "Sarawak Murut" have in the past been used to distinguish these peoples from the "Northern Muruts" of Sabah, who reportedly differ from them both culturally and linguistically. The extent and classificatory significance of such differences is not entirely clear. Murut is a coastal (Muslim) exonym meaning simply "hillman" and is not recognized by the people so designated. Rather, they refer to themselves by longhouse or river valley, *pa*, e.g. Pa Tabun, "people of the Tabun River." There is a considerable (but as yet undetermined) degree of linguistic homogeneity among the Kelabitic peoples. [Southwell 1949; Bolang and Harrisson 1949.] The Kelabits (from Pa Labid, "people of Labid River") and closely related peoples of the Kelabit-Kerayan highland are the best known of all Kelabitic Muruts. Here, in interior upland intermontane basins, are people growing irrigated rice, keeping large herds of cattle, and practicing a death cult with associated megalithic content. This Kelabit culture type, which shows evidence of contact and borrowing from Kenyah-Kayan, extends into Kalimantan and the upper tributary system of the Sesayap. [Harrisson 1959a.] Muruts outside the Kelabit-Kerayan highland, e.g. those along the middle Limbang, Trusan, and Lawas river valleys of Sarawak, lack wet-rice agriculture. They grow rice on swiddens and differ in some respects from the Kelabit type, as do the Potok, Milau, Saban, and Tabun, named populations associated with river valleys on the northeastern, eastern, southeastern, and northwestern margins, respectively, of Kelabit country (Harrisson 1954, 1959a). Kelabitic Muruts are most numerous in northwestern Kalimantan, and it is this area that is generally considered by these people as their traditional homeland (Southwell 1949; see also Harrisson 1967, Appendix A, for origin legend supporting this view). **Location.** Kelabit-Kerayan highland of north-central Borneo, roughly 4°15′-3°20′ N. by 115°20′-116°0′ E. Extending southeast in Kalimantan to the headwaters of the Bahau, east to the upper Mentarang, and northeast in the Kemaloh, Raya, and other river valleys of northwest Kalimantan. In Sarawak, the upper Baram and Tutoh, the middle Limbang, the entire Trusan valley, and the Brunei Bay littoral, including Lawas area. A few Kelabitic Muruts have moved recently into the Ulu Padas area of Sabah, where they are known locally as Lun Daya. [Harrisson 1959b; Bolang and Harrisson 1949.] **Geography.** The Kerayan-Kelabit highland, at about 3,000 feet altitude, is an area of wide alluvial valleys marked by extensive complexes of irrigated-rice fields. Foothills around the valley bottoms have been extensively deforested. Hills and mountain ranges are covered with dense jungle vegetation, much of it secondary growth. Rain falls throughout the year, and

temperatures are relatively cool, with reports of occasional hailstorms. Fauna include deer, pigs, monkeys, and squirrels. Rhinoceroses were formerly numerous. There are many varieties of birds, including seasonal (migrating) varieties. [Schneeberger 1945.] **Linguistic affiliation.** Kelabitic Muruts speak at least six dialects of what is reportedly a single language grouping, called variously "Kemaloh," "Kelabitic," or "Murut-Kelabit." Pa Kemaloh, the dialect of the middle Sesayap, Ulu Padas, and Ulu Trusan, is becoming the standard for the entire area as a result of the translating and missionary efforts of the Borneo Evangelical Mission. [Southwell 1949; Bolang and Harrisson 1949.] Kemaloh-Kelabit dialects are reported to differ significantly from those of the Idahan Muruts of Sabah (Prentice 1970). Dyen (1965) tentatively includes Kelabit with Kenyah and Kayan in a "Kelabitic cluster" within Western Indonesian. **Demography.** Murut-Kelabit in Sarawak and Brunei were enumerated in the 1940 census at 6,000. The 1947 census of Sarawak and Brunei returned a total of 5,198. There are known to be proportionately more of these people on the Kalimantan side of the border. **History and cultural relations.** Harrisson believes that the Murut-Kelabit were once more widespread, not only within the highlands but right down to Brunei Bay, including the lower reaches of the Limbang and Trusan. There is some evidence that the first known Sultan of Brunei to accept Islam was probably of part "Kelabit" and part "Bisaya" stock (Harrisson 1959a: 57ff.). The pre-Brooke Muruts of the middle Lawas and Trusan were once numerous and powerful and are said to have levied tribute on produce traded upstream from the coast (Pollard 1933: 140-41). Kelabitic Muruts may formerly have been more widespread to the east in Kalimantan, perhaps down to the coast at Tarakan. It does appear, however, that the subcoastal areas inland from Tarakan and right up to the headwaters of the Sembakung and Sebiku on the Sabah border are at present inhabited by Tidong and related peoples, a largely Islamized population speaking languages related to those of the Idahan Muruts of Sabah rather than the Kelabitic languages of Sarawak. ● According to Harrisson, the Kelabits had probably pioneered the interior highland from the southeast and were in process of expanding south and west when they were checked by the vigorous incursions of Kayan-Kenyah peoples in the eighteenth and nineteenth centuries. Although megalithic remains are widespread in the Kelabit highlands, many in now uninhabited valleys, it is unlikely that this part of Borneo was permanently occupied much before the early centuries of the Christian era (Harrisson 1959a: 8-11). Kelabits have had considerable contact with both Kenyah and Kayan—riverine peoples to the south, east, and west. The Kelabit highland has traditionally been virtually self-sufficient in rice and salt. The latter, produced from local wells, has long been a trade item with surrounding peoples and a source of wealth to the Kelabits (Harrisson 1959a: 70-71). Until World War II, the Kelabit-Kerayan highlands were relatively little known to the Western world. More recently, Christian missionaries have made converts among Muruts of both Sarawak and Kalimantan. Throughout the area the consumption of rice beer at feasts of merit, secondary burial rites and customs surrounding the cult of the dead are fast disappearing (Harrisson 1954: 115-19).

SETTLEMENT PATTERN AND HOUSING. **Settlement pattern.** Kelabits inhabit wide alluvial valley plains in the highlands. The pattern is one of dispersed longhouses on low ridges or elevations close to the valley floor, each house located near a stream and overlooking irrigated-rice fields and grasslands grazed by cattle. The Bah, one such plain in the headwaters of the Baram, extends north-south for some 30 miles; within this plain are nine longhouses, i.e. villages, averaging about 100 people each. Each longhouse identifies with a stretch of a particular stream; each has a more or less accepted territory which it exploits for agricultural purposes. [Harrisson 1959a: 1-15.] **Housing.** Kelabit longhouses, up to 250 feet in length, average about 100 persons (200 maximum). The house is on piles and is divided by a single longitudinal wall into veranda on one side and living area on the other. Kelabits do not divide the living area by walls into separate compartments; rather, each family's living space is marked by a hearth set in the floor. Each nuclear family is responsible for building and maintaining its part of a longhouse, but access throughout the structure is open to all. Each family's heirloom jars are kept in its own living area. Traditionally, adolescent girls sleep on platforms above the living-working area, under the thatched gable roof; boys on a part of the veranda reserved to them. Livestock are kept beneath the house at night. Rice granaries, small huts on piles, are dotted about the plain at some little distance from the house. [Harrisson 1959a: 23-25; 1959b: 56-60.] Murut swidden farmers of the Trusan-Lawas districts, farther west toward the coast, build smaller longhouses, averaging about ten families. These are usually built on a hill or spur overlooking a stream. Surrounding hillsides are planted to swidden rice. The house is divided longitudinally into veranda and living area; the latter in turn is walled off into individual family compartments—and in this respect differs from Kelabit custom. Granaries are at some distance from the house. [Pollard 1933: 144ff.]

ECONOMY. Subsistence is everywhere based chiefly on agriculture, with rice the staple. Hunting and fishing are seasonal or part-time occupations, but nevertheless an important source of protein. The flesh of domestic animals is eaten only on ritual occasions. Much of the rice crop is consumed in the form of fermented rice beer. Alluvial plains on the headwaters of the Baram, Trusan, and Kerayan support a surplus economy based on irrigated rice, cattle, and salt. The latter, produced from local wells, is an important item of trade with surrounding groups. Kelabit-type cultures in economically favored areas are characterized by patterns of wealth accumulation and economic exchange, and their expression in the social and ceremonial life of the people—particularly within aristocratic family lines. Elements of this culture type are present outside the Kelabit-Kerayan highland. **Agriculture.** Kelabits grow rice in irrigated padi fields. Low dykes divide an acre into as many as 300 subdivisions. Elaborate systems of walkways, windmills, and lines frighten birds and other pests from the fields. Irrigation, pest control, and harvesting are highly cooperative. Seedlings, started in special plots, are transplanted to flooded fields, but no use is made of either plow or draft animal in connection with rice agriculture (Harrisson 1954: 106). A planting calendar is based on the annual flights of migratory birds. Some Kelabits supplement rice with maize, manioc, and/or sago, but most are self-sufficient in rice. Sweet potato, keladi, cucumbers, and tobacco are grown in kitchen gardens. [Harrisson 1959a: 39, 84-90; 1959b: 62-64; Pollard 1933: 148-49.] **Fishing, hunting, and gathering.** Hunting, mainly after the rice harvest, provides meat of deer, monkey, and wild pig. Men make occasional long hunting trips with dogs. The blowpipe is the traditional weapon. Fishing is done in the larger streams by men, using stone and basketry traps. Women take smaller fish and shrimps from streams and padi fields. Honey is collected occasionally. [Harrisson 1959a: 84ff.] **Domestic animals.** Kelabits keep cattle, buffalo, goats, and pigs. The meat of these animals is consumed only on ceremonial occasions (Harrisson 1959b: 62-64). **Industries.** Loincloths and skirts were formerly made from barkcloth. Pottery is shaped with a stone and a carved beater; no wheel is used. Weaving is done with pineapple fibers. The Kelabits do simple blacksmithing, but are not as skilled as the Kenyah. [Harrisson 1959a.] **Property and trade.** Among the wet-rice growing Kelabits, individual families have traditional ownership rights to land, based on generations of use. Highly valued heirloom property in the form of gongs, beads, and jars (some probably of Chinese T'ang dynasty manufacture) symbolizes the status of aristocratic families. These, plus buffaloes, rice beer, and packages of salt, figure in a complicated exchange system whereby aristocratic families maintain their status and memorialize their dead through elaborate feasts of merit and the erection of megalithic monuments. [Jars and brassware are valued by non-Kelabit Muruts downriver in the Trusan-Lawas districts, but the extent to which they figure in the social and ceremonial life of the people is unclear.] Some degree of specialization and trade occurs among Kelabit longhouses within the same or nearby valleys, e.g. mats, pots, and knife handles. Kelabits also carry on an active trade with surrounding Kenyah and Kayan peoples, largely locally produced salt in exchange for buffaloes, jars, gongs, beads, and fancifully worked knife blades. [Harrisson 1959a: 72, 26-29; 1954: 109.]

MARRIAGE AND FAMILY. **Mode.** Kelabits condone premarital sex, although ideally such experimentation should be limited to members of one's own class. The great death feasts, bringing together people from many longhouses, are major occasions for courting and forming alliances. In practice, the longhouse group tends to be exogamous—particularly with respect to the class-endogamous aristocrats. The ceremonial observance of a marriage is minimal; a marriage is not taken seriously until the wife becomes pregnant. Among Kelabits there is no marriage settlement of the *brian* type, at least among social equals. However, a boy of lower-class status must pay a substantial bride-price if he wishes to marry the daughter of an aristocrat. [Harrisson 1959a: 65, 121.] Non-Kelabit Muruts in both Sarawak and Kalimantan attach considerable importance to the payment of bride-price at marriage, regardless of class. Payment is usually in kind (buffaloes, jars, gongs) made to the bride's parents. Child betrothal is reported for Muruts in the Trusan-Lawas districts. [Pollard 1933: 151-54; Sandin and Balang Siran 1963: 88-93.] **Incest.** Kelabits are theoretically prohibited from marrying any relative closer than third cousin, but "people often do it" (Harrisson 1959a: 32). **Residence.** Considerable variation. Among Kelabits, the ideal appears to be initial matrilocal residence, but there are apparently numerous exceptions (Harrisson 1959a). Among Muruts in the Trusan-Lawas districts, it appears that residence may be variable, depending on which side sponsors the marriage feast, but with a tendency to patrilocality (Pollard 1933: 151-54). In the Beroewen-Kemaloh river area of northwestern Kalimantan, residence is apparently ambilocal until the arrival of the first child, after which time the couple is free to choose where they will live (Sandin and Balang Siran 1963: 88-93). **Domestic unit.** The nuclear family occupying a living space or compartment ("door") within a longhouse. **Inheritance.** Among Kelabits, traditional use rights to wet-rice lands are apparently inherited within family lines. Movable property is in part subject to sex-linked inheritance: jars in the male line, beads in female line, and gongs and buffaloes in both. An eldest son traditionally inherits his father's most valuable jar(s). However, other considerations may complicate these normative rules. The entire Kelabit area is characterized by a pattern of social competition and material exchange, centered on the inheritance priorities of those who pay for elaborate feasts and memorials to the deceased. Those heirs or in-laws who contribute or intrigue the most on these occa-

sions can lay claim to the largest share of the inheritance. It is this fact that adds much to the flavor and dynamic of social life.

KINSHIP. Descent is presumably reckoned ambilaterally. This method seems to be consistent with the kin terminology recorded by Needham "from a Sarawak Murut informant" (Needham 1955a: 221):

Fa	*tman*
Mo	*tinan*
Uncle	*taman pinakan*
Aunt	*tinan pinakan*
Sib	*kinanak*
ElSb	*kinanak lokraya*
YoSb	*kinanak loksoot*
Cousin	*kanid*
Child	*anak*
Nephew/niece	*anak menakan*

Marriage is theoretically prohibited with any relative closer than a third cousin. Within the Kelabit longhouse, the "leading aristocrat of the group" has his hearth in the center, and to the right and left are the families of his nearest relatives (Harrisson 1959b: 65-66). The headman (leading aristocrat) among Muruts of Kalimantan may reckon his descent and that of his longhouse group from a named male ancestor 17 generations removed; this ancestor figures, in turn, in a legend recounting the origin and spread of all Muruts from the union of a hero-ancestor pair, male and female (Harrisson 1967: Appendix B). Among Kelabits, residents of other longhouses are invited to a great death feast from a radius of about a day and a half walk. It is at these feasts that the youth from different longhouses may meet and form marriage alliances. An area this size can be regarded as a common ritual area and as the maximal area of relationships by marriage; and it may be supposed that the longhouses within this area will approximate a territorially-based kin group united by largely affinal ties. Judging from these bits of evidence, Kelabitic Murut kinship appears structured to some degree as outlined by Leach (1950: 73-75) for Muruts of the Kemabong area, Southwest Sabah, usually classed as Northern or Idahan Muruts. This structural type includes (1) the longhouse as a statistically exogamous kingroup (2) an exogamous, house-owning group related largely through paternal links, and (3) a loosely grouped cluster of longhouses related through largely affinal links and forming a quasi-political unit. Whether such similarities are indicative of an historic culture common to Muruts or simply part of a culture stratum once common to large areas of Borneo is at present unclear.

SOCIOPOLITICAL ORGANIZATION. **Social stratification.** Kelabits in practice tend to divide the membership of a longhouse into "good" (aristocratic) and "bad" (lower-class) categories. Aristocratic status depends above all on inherited wealth (jars, beads, gongs, porcelains, stoneware). Class differences are seldom expressed overtly in everyday life, but in times of crisis the leading aristocrat has the final word. No aristocrat has full authority, however, unless he possesses at least one old (Chinese) dragon jar. There is evidence that among Kalimantan Muruts, at least, the "house owning group" of aristocrats (Leach 1950) claims direct descent from a named male ancestor considered antecedent to the entire longhouse. Slaves, i.e. descendants of prisoners of war or strays from unrelated longhouses, are by definition those without kinship or affinity within the longhouse group. [Harrisson 1959b: 65-66; 1959a: 107.] In Kelabit thinking, aristocrats are supposed to lead, and it was aristocrats, mainly, who led headhunting parties, or who actually took heads, in former days. There appears to have been a connection between this taking of heads, the ownership or guardianship of jars, and legitimized political authority on the part of aristocrats within the longhouse context—associated with the continued well-being of the longhouse and the danger of ultimate petrifaction if the house should become spiritually "cold." Aristocratic marriages tend to be longhouse-exogamous and class-endogamous. Heirloom wealth should be kept in aristocratic hands. Much of the dynamic of Kelabit life is supplied by the negotiations and intrigues surrounding the accumulation of wealth, considerations of relative wealth at marriage, jockeying among heirs for preferential inheritance of wealth, and the use of wealth and its distribution at elaborate funeral rites for deceased aristocrats. [Harrisson 1959a.] Class differences are likewise in evidence among Muruts in downriver areas of Sarawak. Here there are people of "noble" or "high" birth as well as "poor people" and "slaves." Slaves, jars, and pigs were the "accepted currency" in former days in the Lawas-Trusan districts. [Pollard 1933: 151-54.] **Political organization.** Authority within a Kelabit longhouse is relatively diffuse. The leading aristocrat has the final word in settling crisis situations, and thus functions in effect as headman. There is occasional mention in the literature of "paramount chiefs" with apparent authority over more than one longhouse. Banks' (1937: 427) mention of Kelabit chiefs in this connection seems to refer to longhouses that "claim kin." **Headhunting.** Intervillage feuding was common in pre-Brooke times in Sarawak, and although headhunting was reportedly not as widespread or as passionately pursued by Muruts as by Kayans and Ibans, it was nonetheless practiced in former times and was revived to some extent at the close of World War II. Among Kelabits the causes of headhunting seem to have been (1) renewal of vitality of longhouse and land (2) intervillage feuds, and (3) acts of individual protest. Headhunting was associated with aristocracy, and the skulls of enemies were hung on the longhouse veranda in front of the living area of the leading aristocrat. The greatest insult, and a cause of intervillage feuds, was to take the head of an aristocrat. Successful headhunters were welcomed with feasting and dancing, and offerings were made to a new head for a time, after which it was added to the existing collection of skulls. Apparently the Kelabits made no use of special head houses or skull shelves. Feuds were on occasion concluded by payment of compensation—jars, brassware, or slaves. The latter, among the Kelabits, were ceremonially speared to death by the side being compensated. [Harrisson 1959a: 90-107; Pollard 1933: 145.]

RELIGION. The indigenous religion was designed to maintain the well-being of the longhouse and its inhabitants. Well-being was associated with ideas about "hot" and "cold" and the ultimate sanction for nonobservance of taboos and rituals—"cooling" and eventual petrifaction of the longhouse. Aristocratic status, headhunting, megaliths, and heirloom jars appear to have been intimately associated with this belief system. Since shortly before World War II, the indigenous religion has been disintegrating under the impact of Christianity. **Supernaturals.** Among the Kelabit, a vaguely defined creator, a pantheon of deities, and a variety of lesser spirits are propitiated or consulted in times of crisis. In general, however, major reliance is placed on rituals at death, in particular the death of aristocrats; if these are properly performed the powerful spirits will leave the living alone. [Harrisson 1959a: 29.] **Practitioners.** The Kelabit have occasional recourse to old men who function as mediums. These call on their guardian spirits for aid and are consulted about such things as the start of rice planting (Harrisson 1959a: 40). **Death.** Kelabit ideas about death are associated with beliefs about "hot" and "cold." Sudden deaths or other catastrophes are signs that a longhouse is becoming "cold," i.e. in spiritual imbalance. Spiritual balance is maintained in part through the presence of leading aristocrats and, most importantly, through elaborate rituals at their death. The details of funerary practices vary considerably. Among Kelabits, primary burial of an aristocrat is generally in a boat-shaped wooden coffin, although the corpse is occasionally placed in a stoneware jar in a crouched position (Harrisson 1962a: 10-11). The coffin, fitted with a bamboo drain, may be kept on the longhouse veranda for a year or more, after which the bones are removed and placed in a jar or stone vat for secondary burial. The latter may be in a family-reserved area or simply in an isolated spot in the jungle. [Harrisson 1959a: 108ff.] Muruts of the Lawas-Trusan districts (Sarawak) place the body of an aristocrat in a jar sealed with dammar, fitted with a bamboo drain, and kept within the longhouse for a varying period of up to several years. The bones are then transferred to another jar for secondary burial. Poor people may simply be buried in a wooden coffin.

162

[Pollard 1933: 154; 1935: 226.] Secondary burial is the occasion for an elaborate feast, which ends the mourning period for near relatives. Among Kelabits the expense of a death feast, *irau*, prohibits its occurrence more often than once every four or five years—usually coinciding with the demise of a famous aristocrat. The occasion memorializes at the same time other deaths, particularly those of poorer people, that have occurred within the longhouse in the period since the last *irau*. These are occasions for several days of feasting, drinking rice beer, dancing, and courting. The *irau* culminates in the sacrifice of a buffalo tied to a post and ceremonially speared to death. The deceased is permanently memorialized by the erection of an incised stone, dolmen, or monolith, and by the excavation of ditches and/or the cutting of openings through the vegetation on the crests of hills. The considerable expense of the feast and labor involved in a large *irau* is borne by the relatives of the deceased, utilizing family wealth in the form of salt, buffaloes, rice beer, gongs, and beads. In addition, the family may incur debts in the form of labor and/or material goods, which it is obliged to repay with interest at a later date. Aristocratic families vie with one another with respect to the elaborateness of these "feasts of merit" for deceased members. A deceased aristocrat is remembered for the size and expense of his *irau*, and the relative status of aristocratic families is in part determined by remembered headhunting prowess and expensive death feasts of former members. The Kelabit highlands contain a large number of megalithic remains, memorials of former death feasts, including stone bridges, seats, burial vats, burial grottoes, and avenues of monoliths. [Harrisson 1954, 1959a, 1959b; Banks 1937.]

BIBLIOGRAPHY. Banks 1937; Bolang and Harrisson 1949; Dyen 1965; Harrisson 1954, 1959a, 1959b, 1962a, 1967; Leach 1950; Needham 1955a; Pollard 1933, 1935; Prentice 1970; Sandin and Balang Siran 1963; Schneeberger 1945; Southwell 1949.

BISAYA*

Synonyms. *Bisayah, Besaya, Jilama Bawang, Jilama Sungai*

ORIENTATION. **Identification.** The peoples called Bisaya (alternatively, Bisayah, or more rarely, Besaya) generally inhabit the lower or middle reaches of those rivers in Northern Sarawak and Western Sabah that flow into Brunei Bay. In Brunei, the term is often applied to closely related groups (Orang Bukit, Dusun,

*This entry by Roger D. Peranio is based chiefly on 14 months of anthropological fieldwork among the Limbang River Bisaya of Sarawak, supplemented by brief trips to the Brunei Bisaya (Tutong River) in 1958.

Tutong Dusun) on the Tutong river (Bewsher 1959; Harrisson 1962b). On Labuan Island in Brunei Bay, some members of the formerly larger Bisaya population say that their ancestors there go back many generations; they claim a relationship to Limbang and Klias River Bisaya (Harrisson 1956: 43). The term is sometimes used by Limbang Bisaya to apply to small groups (otherwise called Orang Bukit) living on two tributaries of the Baram River (the Linai and the Tutoh), and the upper reaches of the Belait River. On the mainland of Sabah, the name Bisaya is principally applied today to those Muslim wet-rice agriculturalists (interspersed among other groups) who live in the lower reaches of the area watered by the Padas and Klias rivers (Headly 1950; Harrisson 1962b) and also near Bundu and Kuala Penyu (Rutter 1922: map, 52, 79; Jones 1962b). In Sarawak, most of the Bisaya are pagan, with a scattering of Christian converts and even fewer Muslims. • Bisaya culture represents an adaptation to a special set of circumstances, involving among other things the behavior patterns of a riverine people who are neither "coastal," "upriver," nor "hill." As the Bisaya put it, they are a "people of the middle" (*tangah-tangah*) as well as a "people of the river" (*jilama bawang, jilama sungai*), meaning that they inhabit the middle reaches of the Limbang River. Despite their sense of identity as a special group with unique customs, the Bisaya at the same time stress the cosmopolitan nature of their culture by pointing to borrowed customs. But such customs, they say, are given their own unique spirit when performed by a Bisaya. • Present-day Limbang Bisaya have no explanation as to the derivation or meaning of their name; none of the proposed explanations is entirely adequate, as Carroll (1960) recognizes. A related problem concerns the nature of the historical relationships, if any, existing between groups in northwestern Borneo and those groups inhabiting the Bisayan Islands of the central Philippines (cf. Araneta and Bernad 1960; Harrisson 1962b). • Leach classifies the Bisaya as Para-Malay. Thus, the Muslim Melanau and Kedayan rate as Malays, as do "about half of the Bisaya-Bukit group in Sarawak" (Leach 1950: 33). Presumably, the Sabah Bisaya (who are largely Muslim) would also be classed as Malays. However, Leach would include the Sarawak (and Brunei) pagan Bisaya, the Orang Bukit, and the pagan Melanau under the Para-Malay heading. It should be emphasized, however, that the Limbang Bisaya fiercely resist attempts at conversion to Islam, even though they have borrowed (or assimilated) many important cultural usages from the Malays. In view of the similarities in language (Appell 1968b) and culture, the Bisaya should probably be placed with the Sabah Dusun and related groups in Sarawak and Brunei in a culture-area labeled Bisaya-Dusun. **Linguistic affiliation.** Prentice (1970) groups Bisaya with the indigenous languages of Sabah (Dusun, Murut) as members of an Idahan language family, in turn part of the North Indonesian branch (Dyen's Philippine hesion) of Austronesian (Dyen 1965). **Demography.** The 1960 census (Jones 1962a) gives a figure of 2,803 Bisaya for all of Sarawak. Harrisson (1964: 177) estimates that in 1960 there was a total of approximately 7,000 Bisaya in Brunei, and the 1960 Sabah census lists 10,053. **History and cultural relations.** Contemporary Bisaya preserve a creation myth according to which the first man, Asik, descended from the union of two semi-human creatures, brother and sister, inhabitants of a legendary Mt. Kiyangan. With supernatural help, he learned to grow rice and developed the sacred Bisaya adat. In addition to the effects of recent borrowing from Malays, the Bisaya hold to a theory of common descent, a key figure in this shared ancestry being the culture hero, Alak Batata. In the decades preceding the annexation in 1890 of the Limbang District by the Brooke government, tribal groups were considered subjects of the Brunei Sultan, under the direct control of hereditary lords (*pangeran*) with quasi-feudal rights over specific districts. Local Malays are important to the Bisaya, mainly as suppliers of buffalo, boats, and seafood. Some Bisaya consider it prestigeful to employ Malays as ritual slaughterers of buffalo at major feasts, and in addition there are always Bisaya willing to pay handsome sums for Malay medicines. A few Chinese have married Bisaya women and live in Bisaya villages, but most live apart in the bazaar centers along the rivers.

SETTLEMENT PATTERN AND HOUSING. **Settlement pattern.** Bisaya villages are nucleated and built in ribbonlike fashion along the banks of rivers. The scattered inland settlements rarely qualify as villages because of their impermanence. Every person, wherever he lives, has a landing stage, *pangkalan*, in one of the permanent riverine villages, where, after death, his mortuary lamp must be set afloat. Every village has a number of rice granaries. There are no public buildings or men's houses. Village populations vary between a minimum of 30 and a maximum of 200 persons, the average being about 93. True villages, in the Bisaya sense, consist of permanent settlements having two or more houses, one of which usually, but not invariably, is a "longhouse," defined as a structure with four or more apartments (*lobok*). Nowadays, houses seldom exceed seven apartments, although formerly they were said to be somewhat larger. **Housing.** Longhouses are rectangular, up to 200 feet long, and built on piles 10-15 feet above the ground. They are divided longitudinally into two parts, a closed veranda and inner living quarters, and may be entered from either end by means of notched ladders, owned by housefounders. The veranda is the place where guests are received and where major ceremonies are performed. The inner apartments are not partitioned.

ECONOMY. **Agriculture.** The staple is rice, both dry and wet varieties. Catch crops grown in the rice swiddens include chilies, maize, cucumbers, bottle gourds, pumpkins, yams, cassava, eggplant, green beans, melons, and spinach. Fruit trees include bananas, breadfruit, coconut, and jackfruit. Swidden land is generally used for one year and fallowed for seven to ten years. Wet-rice land is rarely used for more than two successive years, due to factionalism, poor harvests, and inauspicious omens. The Bisaya have shown no inclination to adopt the plow. The traditional wooden dibble continues to be used by all. Water buffaloes are used to trample wet-rice fields. **Fishing and hunting.** Rod and net fishing are minor activities. Slightly more important is communal fishing, wherein the fish are stupified with tuba root poison. Hunting for forest swine, wild buffalo, deer, and pheasant is of greater importance than fishing. The important implements are guns, spears, and blowpipes. **Gathering.** A great variety of plants are collected, mainly by women. Food plants include ferns, amaranths, and wild fruit. Other products of importance are medicinal plants, honey, camphor, dammar resin, and gutta percha. **Domestic animals.** The main domesticated animals are buffaloes, pigs, and chickens. Dogs and cats are kept, but never as pets. The major pets are fighting cocks, monkeys, and birds. **Food and stimulants.** The staple is rice, supplemented by chilies, ferns, or fish. Sago gruel is eaten rarely and for very brief periods. Buffalo meat is served at feasts, along with rice liquor (*pengasi*), served in large jars fitted with long "straws." **Industrial arts.** The Bisaya never had knowledge of the arts of forging and smelting metals, they lacked the loom, and apparently had no knowledge of pottery-making. Originally clothing was made of bark. Carpentry and woodcarving are well developed. **Trade.** The Bisaya formerly traded extensively with the Malays, providing sago, rice, and jungle products in exchange for such things as cloth, earthenware, glazed ceramics, brassware, silver objects, and metal tools. Nowadays such trade is almost exclusively in the hands of the Chinese. Trade with upriver groups is on a small scale; occasionally, Bisaya provide such products as camphor, dammar resin, and rice (to the Muruts, Kelabits, and, more recently, the Iban) in exchange for large "war boats" and salt. **Property.** All property is classed into: (1) heirloom or ancestral property (2) personal property, excluding land (3) joint property of husband and wife, and (4) shared house group property, restricted to cannons, jars, model houses and boats, magical necklets, and musical instruments. Shared house group property is "held" by a housefounder, who has primary rights; whoever occupies his apartment after his death continues to have primary rights. All others have rights of use only. Generally speaking, shared property does not pass out of the village where the original holder was born.

Riparian land is used for building houses and cultivating fruit trees. Although villagers may build houses wherever there is unused land, certain village sites tend to be associated with the names of prominent families; as houses are demolished, new houses are built by the descendants of previous housefounders on these traditional sites. However, the rights to particular sites are usufructuary in the sense that if family lines become extinct, or rights are not continually exercised, the land becomes available to all villagers. Each village has overrights to certain inland tracts of land, usufructuary rights to which are established by clearing and subsequent cultivation. Such rights are inherited ambilineally. Through the use of known descent lines (*raian*), individuals may activate rights to several parcels of land simultaneously.

KINSHIP. **Descent.** The Bisaya descent system is cognatic and ambilineal (Peranio 1959), utilizing cognatic descent categories without accompanying corporate descent groups. These descent categories, then, are in no sense ambilineal ramages (Firth 1957), since the latter are corporate. The simplest is the descent line or single-line genealogy (*raian*), used to validate and/or re-establish land rights, as arguing points in marriage negotiations and other transactions, and to pay homage to renowned individuals, especially at funeral feasts. An individual may affiliate with one or several descent lines, manipulating them as best he can to enhance his status. A larger category, with slightly less clearly defined characteristics, is the cognatic descent cluster (*nasap somok*), consisting of a prominent localized "axial line of descent" and related accessory lines. Accessory descent lines provide important sources of cooperative labor, contribute to competitive feasts, and provide support in major disputes. The most amorphous grouping, having the broadest range, is the dispersed (nonlocalized) cognatic descent cluster (*nasap gaiyoh*), consisting of axial and accessory descent lines and those cognates living in villages at varying distances from the core. The mutual obligations of peripheral and core relatives in the dispersed cluster are not precisely defined. Cognates living in neighboring villages are often a much-needed source of wives or husbands, especially where proper mates cannot be found nearer at hand. **Kin groups.** The major kin groups are the apartment family (*sanan lobok*) and the house family (*sanan alai*). Only the apartment family is fully corporate, sharing a common larder, pooling resources, and having a common hearth, common rituals, and common prayers for crops. The house family shares certain ceremonial objects, observes common taboos, cooperates in house repair, and shares major rituals, but does not act otherwise as a fully corporate group. The rule of exogamy applies to persons reared in the same apartment, regardless of whether they are members of the same nuclear (or stem) family. There is no specific prohibition on intermarriage between members of different apartment families of the same house, but it is considered potentially dangerous for those closer than second cousins. Although not a kin group in the strict sense, the personal kindred as an ego-centered category has several referents in Bisaya society. In general, all those consanguineal kinsmen who are of some social importance to an individual and are known to him by name are called *rumostari*. Close kindred are expected to aid one another in emergencies, attend and contribute to one another's major rituals, exchange gifts, and support one another in disputes. The obligations of distant kindred are less precise, but include provision of wives where preferred mates are in short supply. **Kin terminology.** The Bisaya have: (1) Eskimo cousin terminology (terms of reference only) (2) lineal aunt/uncle, niece/nephew terms (terms of reference), and (3) bilateral symmetry, with none of the of the skewing typical of lineage systems.

Lineal terms of reference are as follows:

GrFa	*yaki*
GrMo	*yadu*
Fa	*yama*
Mo	*indu, ina*
PaElSib	*yuwa*
PaYoSib	*yunchu*
Sib	*stari*
ElSib	*kako*
Cousin	*anak inchan*
Ch	*anak*
SibCh	(*anak*) *nakon*
GrCh	*anak aki*

MARRIAGE AND FAMILY. **Mode.** Parents take the initiative in arranging first marriages, especially if their children are young. Some families follow a procedure known as "pairing," an informal matching of a boy and a girl, starting when they are about eight or nine years old. Great concern is shown by parents over premarital chastity. For women of childbearing age, a minimum bride-price of one buffalo and $50.00 is paid to the parents of the bride. The marriage is not considered to be truly "settled" (*tatap*) until there is physical consummation, at a time determined by one of the mothers-in-law (depending on where the couple plan to reside). **Form.** Monogamy is the prevalent form of marriage. Limited polygyny is a prerogative of the wealthy. A man may marry a deceased wife's sister if she is agreeable, but there is no marked preference for this form of marriage. Sororal polygyny is expressly forbidden. **Extension of incest taboos.** The Bisaya express a definite preference for second- and third-cousin (both cross and parallel) marriage, followed in preference by marriage with first cousins. Where near kin cannot be found, then fourth or fifth cousins are considered almost as suitable. With the exception of husband and wife, it is improper for members of the nuclear family to have sexual relations with one another. Other relations prohibited are uncle/niece, aunt/nephew, grandmother/grandson, grandfather/granddaughter, brother-in-law/sister-in-law, father-in-law/daughter-in-law. Prohibitions are extended to close collateral relatives of most of the above, but one may marry the second or third cousins of all by paying a fine. **Residence.** Residence is ambilocal, either in the same apartment as the parents or in the apartment of close kin in the same house. A couple may live in an independent apartment only after the birth of children. **Domestic unit.** The genealogical composition of the apartment family, *sanan lobok*, may vary, although the average size is around 5.6 members. Nuclear and stem families, which succeed one another in a developmental cycle, are commonest; next most frequent is the cognatic composite family, in which cross-sex siblings are joined by their spouses and children to form a common domestic unit. **Inheritance.** Inheritance is ambilateral; there is equal inheritance for sons and daughters. However, certain objects tend to be sex-typed, e.g. ritual spears and cannon. **Divorce.** Easily obtained by both sexes. If the divorced pair have children, these are usually asked to choose which parents they wish to "follow." If no children have been born, the bride-wealth is returned to the husband and his family, except in cases where adultery on the man's part has been proven. In two villages studied, over 40 percent of the males and 36 percent of the females had terminated their first marriages in divorce. **Adoption.** Adoption is common and includes temporary fosterage as well as "true" adoption, in which the adoptive family incorporates the child as a full member, with full rights of inheritance.

SOCIOPOLITICAL ORGANIZATION. **Political organization.** Little is known of the traditional political organization of the Limbang Bisaya. Before Brooke rule, there were said to be informal meetings at which Tuahs (prominent elders, including titled men such as Orang Kaya) met to discuss village affairs. There were no village headmen. Government-appointed headmen were introduced about 1930. **Social stratification.** Bisaya society is essentially based on kinship. There is no true system of social classes. The major determinants of status are based on wealth (in the form of buffaloes and brassware), feast-giving abilities (ultimately dependent on wealth), and age. Titled families do tend to have more wealth, but they must use a good deal of it in feastgiving, acting as redistributors in a kinship network. **Social control.** The major forms of social control are gossip, ridicule, and supernatural sanctions in the form of oaths. Before Brooke rule, feuding seems to have been endemic and is hardly less so today. Minor disputes are heard before village headmen. In special instances, a kind of ordeal procedure is used, involving a necklet of animal teeth believed to have special powers (Peranio 1959). **Warfare.** The Bisaya have tended to engage in defensive rather than offensive warfare; there is no tradition of headhunting.

RELIGION. **Religious systems.** Although the Bisaya have been exposed to Islam for some centuries, they seem to have been little influenced by it. Their religion is basically animistic, involving shamanism (with divination) and spirit mediumship (with trance phenomena). The Bisaya lack a true ancestor cult, but do honor the names of prominent village ancestors at certain large-scale feasts by reciting genealogies and recounting tales of their major exploits. **Supernaturals.** Spirits of the dead include (1) *biruau* (or *birau*), who appear during public curing ceremonies and are usually benign if not beneficent. They include the ancestral hero "Tuan Langit," who is also the familiar of all spirit mediums (2) *lamatai*, spirits of the recent dead, but also including the *mundau* (mythical tiger spirit) and *sampar* (a river spirit). These spirits are usually malevolent, but most will change into harmless *lingu awan* (minor sky spirits) if proper mourning procedure is followed. Spirits of the living include: (1) *lingu iyau*, the separable souls of living humans, animals, and plants (2) *genau*, spirits contributing to personal style, bearing, gait, temperament, and basic attitudes toward life, and (3) *libong*, a trance spirit. **Practitioners.** Practitioners include the *dukun*, or herbalist-curer, who has no public functions as such. *Dukun* are usually linked in a type of hereditary relationship with certain families. The spirit medium (*penomboi* or *belian*) cures sick people at public ceremonies. Both *dukun* and *penomboi* may be of either sex. **Ceremonies.** The major agricultural ceremony is the harvest or "crocodile" *temarok*, to which the wealthy are expected to contribute large amounts of food. The *makan selamat* is basically a health feast, which the Bisaya claim they share with the Malays. It is given as a preventative measure or as a thanksgiving feast after illness. The major funerary ceremony, *makan salong*, is given 30 days after burial. Both *makan salong* and *makan selamat* bring great prestige to the sponsors. **Soul, death, and afterlife.** Disease is believed caused by soul loss, and the aim of a spirit medium performance is to retrieve the soul. The Bisaya believe that souls of the dead go to one of seven villages "in the land behind the sun."

BIBLIOGRAPHY. Appell 1968b; Araneta and Bernad 1960; Bewsher 1959; Carroll 1960; Dyen 1965; Firth 1957; Haddon 1901, 1925; Harrisson 1949, 1956, 1962b, 1964; Headly 1950; Jones 1962a, 1962b; Kennedy 1935, 1955d; Leach 1950; Peranio 1959; Prentice 1970; Rutter 1922.

TIDONG*

Synonyms. *Tedong, Tiroon, Tirones, Camucones*

ORIENTATION. **Identification and location.** The term Tidong means "hill" or "hill people" in the Tarakan dialect of Tidong (Beech 1908: 86fn.). It is used in the literature to refer to an Islamized population found principally along the Sembakung and Sibuku rivers of eastern Kalimantan, from their headwaters to the delta area north of the island of Tarakan, southward from Tarakan along the eastern coast of Borneo to the mouth of the Bolongan River, and northward to Tawau and around the adjacent coastline of Sabah, encircling Cowie Harbour. An additional settlement is located in Sabah on the Labuk River opposite the town of Klagan. It is doubtful whether all, or even most, of these people identify themselves as Tidong. They appear instead to comprise a heterogeneous collection of local populations, many of differing ethnic origins, who have adopted similar patterns of coastal or riverine settlement and a common set of religious institutions derived from Islam, and who have been identified by neighboring groups as constituting a separate category, distinct from both the non-Islamic interior people who surround them and the other Muslim groups living in close proximity along the coast. [Beech 1908; Rutter 1922.] **Linguistic affiliation.** The Tidong as a whole are without any apparent linguistic unity. According to Beech, whose brief study (1908) is virtually the only source of information available, the "Tidong language" represents a fusion of Malay and Kayan. Cense and Uhlenbeck (1958: 29-30) reject this view and call attention instead to the lack of similarity between the two varieties of "Tidong" recorded by Beech—Tarakan and Bolongan—and to the affinities that exist between the former and the Sabahan dialects of Murut. More recently, Prentice (1970) established the existence of a Tidong language group within the Murutic subfamily of Idahan languages. The Idahan language family, which includes Dusunic and Sabahan Murut languages, is in turn part of the Northern Indonesian branch of Austronesian. However, the persons who speak Tidong languages are only partially the same as those who are ordinarily classified in the ethnographic literature as Tidong. Beech identifies four "dialects" of Tidong: Tarakan, Bolongan, Nonukan, and Sembakong; while Genderen Stort (1916) mentions five: Tarakan, Sembakong, Penchangan, Sedalir, and Tidong proper (spoken on the upper reaches of the Sembakong River). ● Prentice includes only three languages in his Tidong group: Tarakan, spoken along the eastern coast of Borneo from Tarakan Island to Cowie Harbour; Tinggalan (Sembakong), along the middle reaches of the Sembakong River and its tributaries; and Tangara', at the headwaters of the Kinabatangan and Kuamut rivers in Sabah. The speakers of Tangara' (Tengara) are generally classified as "Murut" (cf. Rutter 1929: 35) and are culturally much more similar to neighboring Murut-speaking peoples than they are to either of the other Tidong-speaking groups. Saralir (Sedalir), which is described as "Tidong" by Genderen Stort, is placed in the Murut language group by Prentice. Not enough data presently exist to allow for the classification of Tidong proper, while Bolongan, regarded by Beech as the second major variety of "Tidong," is found by Prentice to be not only a non-Tidong language but a completely non-Idahan one as well. Its linguistic affinities are still uncertain, although Prentice has suggested (personal communication) that its closest ties are probably with the Ngadju-Dayak language group of Kalimantan. In addition, Prentice notes that it is likely that the languages spoken on the Sibuku River of Kalimantan and "Tawau Murut" spoken on the Kalabakan and Serudong rivers of Sabah will ultimately be shown to belong to the Tidong group as well. Like the Tangara', the speakers of Tawau Murut are identified in government censuses and in the ethnographic literature as "Murut." [Aernout 1885; Beech 1908; Cense and Uhlenbeck 1958; Genderen Stort 1916; Prentice 1970.] **Demography.** There are no population figures available for Kalimantan, but according to the 1960 census, the Tidong numbered 4,417 in Sabah (Jones 1962b: 51). **History and cultural relations.** The Tidong are a heterogeneous people, who, either by moving from the interior into a coastal and estuarine environment or by having been present there aboriginally, were brought into contact with marine-oriented groups (such as the Tausug and Bugis) from whom they borrowed heavily, becoming in the process Islamized and culturally differentiated from other, linguistically allied, Murutic-speaking peoples. Spanish records report that the "Camucones" or Tidong were involved with the Tausug and other southern Philippine people in carrying out coastal raids and depredations against Spanish-controlled settlements and shipping as early as the beginning of the seventeenth century and that they continued to engage in such activity throughout the next two centuries. During the eighteenth and nineteenth centuries, the Tidong provided sago, cowries, tortoise shell, and other items for the markets of Sulu, and according to Forrest (1779: 335, 375), part of the Tidong population was then under the political control of the Tausug Sultanate at Jolo. The Tausug reportedly enforced a trade monopoly on the group, which prevented them from selling their goods except through Tausug agents. Aernout (1885) reports that according to Tidong traditions, the group once formed an autonomous political unit. Its center of

*The author of this entry, Clifford Sather, engaged in fieldwork in Semporna District of Sabah in 1964-65. He is a member of the Department of Anthropology and Sociology, Vassar College.

power was reportedly a fortified stronghold on the island of Sibatik, called Belaian Djawa. This was later destroyed by the Tausug, and part of its population brought under the suzerainty of the Jolo Sultanate, while the remainder sought refuge under the protection of the Sultan of Kutai. Aernout reports that at the time he visited the region, in the late nineteenth century, most of the Tidong area in what is now northeastern Kalimantan was then administered by political leaders allied with the Sultan of Bolongan.

SETTLEMENT PATTERN AND HOUSING. Pile dwellings, arranged in an irregular, linear pattern, along the banks of rivers or streams, frequently just above the tidal level. [Beech 1908.]

ECONOMY. Fields along river banks are planted to rice (some of which is reportedly irrigated), manioc, yams, sugarcane, coconuts, sago, and bananas (Beech 1908). The Tidong are reportedly skilled boatmen and are described by Beech as making boats up to 12 feet in length, with dugout keels and sideboards made of planks fastened together with rattan cords. Domestic animals are apparently of little importance; chickens are kept, but are eaten only on ceremonial occasions.

KIN GROUPS. Descent. Although there are no descriptions of the system, kinship appears to be bilateral. Kin terminology. Beech lists the following kin terms, which differ somewhat, but not substantially, from those given by Aernout for the Tarakan Tidong:

Fa	iama'
Mo	ina
FaBr, MoBr	pansulud-iama'
FaSi, MoSi	ina-lumat
ElBr, ElSi	iaka
YoBr, YoSi	iadi
Ch	anak
GrPa	iadu'
GrCh	anak-iadu'
Cousin	tili Beech gives tiliganda and tilidua for "first" and "second cousin," respectively

RELIGION. The Tidong as a whole have only recently been Islamized, and it is likely that some Murutic-speaking groups are currently in the process of becoming Muslim and thus identified as "Tidong." Forrest, writing in 1779, reports that the Tidong were then still "pagan" and for this reason were looked down upon by neighboring coastal groups (1779: 375). According to Beech (1908), every Tidong village had a mosque and an imam responsible for conducting weddings, circumcisions, and funerals. In addition, Beech describes divination and trance sessions, during which spirits (setan) are consulted or exorcised from persons suffering from illness or psychological disturbance. Both male and female mediums are men-

tioned, some of whom claim to be possessed by as many as ten familiars. According to Beech, these are believed to be only partially controllable and may cause the death or sickness of another person against the wishes of those whom they have possessed.

BIBLIOGRAPHY. Aernout 1885; Cense and Uhlenbeck 1958; Beech 1908; Forrest 1779; Genderen Stort 1916; Jones 1962b; Prentice 1970; Rutter 1922, 1929.

KENYAH-KAYAN-KAJANG

Synonym. *Bahau*

ORIENTATION. Identification. Following Leach (1950), the term Kenyah-Kayan-Kajang is here used to denote a culture complex which includes in addition to the well-known Kenyah and Kayan peoples a great many smaller riverine "tribes" and longhouse units in both Sarawak and Kalimantan, which were largely subsumed by Kennedy (1935), following Nieuwenhuis, under the generalized category Bahau. Included here are "tribes" such as Sekapan, Kajaman, Lahanan, Punan Bah, and Sipeng on the upper Rejang, as well as numerous longhouse groups on the Tinjar and Tutoh rivers (Sebop, Berawan, Long Kiput, Long Suku, Batu Blah, etc.), all in Sarawak (Leach 1950: 50-51; Pollard and Banks 1937). Similar groups in Kalimantan include Long Glat, Pnihing, Uma Suling, Uma Pagong, and Saputan on the upper Mahakam; Long Wai and Tring on the middle Mahakam; Segai on the upper Berau; Kindjin on the middle Kayan; Pnihing on the upper Kapuas; and Uma Suling and Uma Pagong on the Mendalem (Kennedy 1935: 352). These lesser groups, some of which have been identified by the generic term Kajang by Leach, all appear to be undergoing varying degrees of assimilation to either Kayan or Kenyah. Some appear to be remnant or offshoot groups of Kenyah, or to be representative of an earlier widespread culture stratum (Harrisson 1964). The overall similarity of custom and social structure among all these peoples justifies the reference to a Kenyah-Kayan-Kajang culture type. Adequate linguistic and cultural data on many of these groups are lacking, however, and any such categorization must therefore be regarded as subject to revision. Kayans occupy principally the middle reaches of the major rivers of central Borneo—the Kayan, Mahakam, Kapuas, Rejang, and Baram. The "real" Kenyahs are nowadays concentrated in the Apo Kayan watershed, although they are found in widely scattered villages throughout the Kayan area. According to Kennedy (1935: 347), the lofty rolling plateau country of the Apo (upper) Kayan Batang in the heart of Borneo is the center of diffusion of the "most highly civilized tribes of the island," noted for their elaboration of class and status differences, the ceremonial etiquette of their aristocratic chiefs, their fine craftsmanship and decorative art, and the spectacular, richly ornamented, raised tombs, the final resting places of their great chiefs. Sentiments of common ethnic identity are especially strong among Kayans. Both Kayans and Kenyahs are divided into numerous named local communities, all more or less independent. Each Kayan subgroup has a tradition and genealogy which relates it to the traditional homeland in the Apo Kayan (Kennedy 1935: 353). **Location.** A fairly continuous area comprising practically all of central Borneo from about 1°–3° N. and from around 113°–116°30′ E. **Demography.** It is probable that the total of all Kayan and Kenyah in Borneo does not exceed 100,000. Harrisson (1964), citing figures from the 1960 census, gives 16,000 Kayan and Kenyah in Sarawak. Kennedy, citing Nieuwenhuis (1904-07) and Lumholtz (1920), gives the following figures for Kalimantan: Kenyah—25,000 in Apo Kayan; Kayan—1,200 in Apo Kayan and upper Mahakam (Kennedy 1935: 358). **Linguistic affiliation.** Kayan and Kenyah seem to be closely related languages, although the latter is considerably more differentiated than the former (Kennedy 1935: 359). Dyen (1965) tentatively classifies both within a "Kayic cluster," which, together with Kelabit, forms a Kelabitic cluster within his Hesperonesian linkage. Basic affiliations seem to be with western Indonesia rather than the Philippines. **History and cultural relations.** Both Kayan and Kenyah claim the Apo Kayan—the highlands in Kalimantan around Long Nawang where the Kayan River has its source—as their traditional homeland in Borneo. The Kenyahs appear to have been in the central Bornean highlands (until recently in relatively remote areas) for a considerable time, and there are cultural similarities between these people and the Kelabitic Muruts somewhat farther to the north. In contrast to the Kayans, who everywhere speak closely related dialects, the various Kenyah subgroups appear relatively diverse as regards both language and custom. The Kayans, by all accounts, are a migratory and conquering people, relatively late arrivals to the central highlands, having come into the area from the south and east. During the eighteenth and nineteenth centuries, Kayans headhunted and pillaged throughout the upper Rejang and Baram watersheds and as far as the Totoh and Limbang (Brunei). They gradually displaced, assimilated, or enslaved Murut and other populations throughout these regions. Under the Brooke regime, strong repressive measures were instituted, and the Kayans (and headhunting Kenyahs as well) were gradually brought within the confines of peaceful government. Headhunting ceased for the most part in the early 1900s. Christianity first became effective among the Kenyahs of Dutch Borneo about 1935 and, since World War II, has spread rapidly among Kenyahs and Kayans of Sarawak. In parts of the area, it has assumed the form of Bungan, a nativistic cult origi-

nating in the Long Nawang district of the upper Kayan in Kalimantan. [Hose and McDougall 1912: 2, 257ff.; Southwell 1959; Prattis 1963.]

SETTLEMENT PATTERN AND HOUSING. **Settlement.** Generally among Kenyahs, longhouse equals village. Among Kayans, it is more usual that a cluster of houses forms a village. Leach emphasizes that the component houses of such a village quite often consist of several distinct "tribal" or "dialect" groups. It appears that complex village settlements of this type may have been more common formerly. Each village or longhouse community exploits an area along a river or stream. Houses are moved (usually downstream) periodically, due to soil exhaustion or inauspicious omens; a household may return to a former site after 12-15 years. A Kayan longhouse may be up to 1,000 feet long, with 100 or more "doors," i.e. with 500-plus inhabitants. The average is about 40 "doors," i.e. 200-300 people. Kenyah houses average somewhat smaller. Houses are built parallel to a river and within 50 yards or less of its banks. **Housing.** Kayan longhouses are famous for their massive size and durability of construction, largely of ironwood planks. Each house, raised on massive ironwood piles, is divided lengthwise into a public "street" or working area (veranda), and a private living area (family compartments). The latter, each containing a clay hearth, are separated by plank walls, and each has access to the veranda through its own door. Each door (family) group owns the planks and beams comprising its part of the house. Main beams and doors are carved and end walls decorated with wooden representations of animal horns. Older boys and bachelors sleep in reserved portions of the veranda; unmarried girls and female slaves in their respective family compartments. Separate rice barns, raised on piles, are located near the house. The doors of the "house-owning group"—the house chief and his immediate relatives—are located in the central part of the structure and constitute a focal point of social and religious activity. In Kayan longhouses, the ritual skulls are hung opposite these doors; the ritual stones of the Kenyah and Kajang peoples are located on the ground outside the longhouse, opposite the house chief's door. The members of a longhouse are largely related by ties of kinship and form a common ritual unit. [Kennedy 1935: 360-63; Hose and McDougall 1912: 1, 56 and 2, 16; Leach 1950: 63-64.]

ECONOMY. Subsistence is primarily by swidden agriculture. The Kenyah-Kayan-Kajang are distinctly riverine peoples, and fishing contributes relatively more to the diet than does hunting. Rice is the staple, much of it consumed in the form of fermented rice beer. **Agriculture.** Shifting cultivation of hill rice on swiddens. Some maize, yams, pumpkins, cucumbers, and tobacco. Wild sago as a famine food. Wild honey is collected. A two-year fallow cycle exhausts available land in about 12-15 years, forcing a move to a new location. Among some Kenyah groups, women appear to be in charge of most activities concerning rice, including selection of seed and performance of ritual concerned with growth. [Kennedy 1935: 359-60.] **Hunting and fishing.** Hunting with dogs, mainly for wild pig. The blowpipe (made chiefly by Kenyahs) is the traditional weapon. Fishing is done with bamboo traps and weirs, throw nets, and hook and line, but the chief method is by stupifying with tuba root poison. **Domestic animals.** Pigs, goats, dogs, and chickens. Pigs and chickens are kept mainly for animal sacrifice. **Industrial arts.** Both Kayan and Kenyah are known for skilled ironworking, blowpipery, basketry, woodworking, and canoemaking. Their swords and knife blades, chased and inlaid, are coveted throughout central Borneo and constitute an item of trade. Decorative wood carving, sculpture, and painting on wood are highly developed, as are techniques of decorative lashing. Tattooing is a highly developed art among these peoples. Other crafts include the making of bark cloth, weaving, and (formerly) pottery-making. Skilled craftsmen and artisans come mainly from the middle or commoner class. [Kennedy 1935; Southwell 1959.] **Property.** Brass gongs and old Chinese jars are valued heirlooms, although they do not, apparently, function as ritual objects. Ancient glass, porcelain, and faience beads are the most coveted of all forms of wealth and serve as a medium of exchange and as ceremonial objects (Kennedy 1935: 354).

MARRIAGE AND FAMILY. Kayan-Kenyah marriage is generally class-endogamous, and is particularly so for aristocratic (chiefly) families. Commoners tend to marry within the longhouse or subtribal community, although in such cases marriage with first cousins is prohibited. Aristocrats form marriage alliances outside the longhouse, and in their case considerations of class-endogamy outweigh any scruples against first-cousin marriage. Bride-price among commoners is largely optional. In longhouse-endogamous marriages, the couple lives with the parents of either partner until a new house is built, after which they are entitled to a compartment of their own. In such cases, service for the bride's parents replaces payment of a bride-price. In cases of longhouse-exogamous marriages, a bride-price is paid if residence is immediately patrilocal; if matrilocal, no payment is made (Kennedy 1935: 371-74; Leach 1950: 78). According to Hose and McDougall (1912: *1*, 76), Kayan aristocratic marriages are usually matrilocal for two or three years, and then patrilocal. **Polygyny.** After contracting an "official" upper-class marriage, an aristocrat may marry the girl of his choice, often a lower-class member of the same local community. The offspring of such marriages tend to form an intermediate group of indefinite status, upward or downwardly mobile according to

personal characteristics (Leach 1950: 76; Kennedy 1935: 374). **Domestic unit.** The nuclear family resident in a walled compartment within the longhouse. Includes unmarried girls and female slaves. **Inheritance.** Property is inherited equally by all heirs. Gongs, weapons, and canoes tend to go to sons; beads to daughters (Kennedy 1935: 373). **Divorce.** Reported to be rare among Kayans. Sterility the usual cause. **Adoption.** Fairly common.

KINSHIP. **Descent.** Bilateral or ambilateral (Kennedy 1935; Leach 1950). **Kin groups.** Localized communities generally bear the name of a river basin, prefixed in the case of Kayans by *uma* ("house" or "village," e.g. Uma Pliau). The Kenyah prefix is more generally *lepo* or *leppu* ("tribal group"). These appear to be localized segments of larger groupings, the so-called "subtribes" of much of the ethnographic literature. Each *uma* has its traditional history of migrations and chiefly genealogies, in many cases its particular dialect, and in all probability its own set of ritual customs. Kayans divide themselves into at least 15 such "subtribes." Kenyahs and related peoples evidence less cohesiveness of a tribal nature than do Kayans, although the "real Kenyahs" of the Apo Kayan do identify themselves as such, and here the various divisions recognize the superiority of chiefs of the Lepo Tau. Localized segments of a Kayan subtribe generally occupy village clusters along the banks of a common stream. Among the various Kajang groups, as well as among Kenyahs and occasionally among Kayans, a "subtribe" may consist nowadays of a single village or longhouse. Multilonghouse villages seem to have been more the norm in former times. Leach (1950: 63) calls attention to the fact that the component houses of such a village often consist of several distinct "tribal" or "dialect" groups. [Hose and McDougall 1912: *1*, 63ff.; Kennedy 1935: 371-73.] The families of a longhouse or village cluster tend to be interrelated, through both consanguineal and affinal ties. This is true particularly of commoners (slaves are descendants of outsiders and thus by definition nonkinsmen). Personal kindreds, reckoned bilaterally, tend to overlap, particularly in smaller longhouse communities, to approximate localized ramages (Leach 1950: 68). Aristocratic chiefly families form marriage alliances outside the local community, frequently with members of other tribal or linguistic groups. In former times, these were the basis of political alliances as well. As a result, the aristocracy of the entire Kenyah-Kayan-Kajang complex constitutes a closely affiliated kin group that overrides tribal affiliations and reinforces social stratification throughout the area (Leach 1950: 76). **Kin terminology.** Kin terminology reflects an emphasis on generation levels and an almost completely bilateral method of reckoning descent. Eskimo-type cousin terminology is characteristic. [Leach 1950: 60A; Kennedy 1935: 375.] A complicated naming

170

system involves the use of nominal prefixes to indicate the status of an individual vis-à-vis the birth of a child or the death of this or subsequent children. Name titles, which can change throughout life, reflect the death of a variety of relatives other than children (Kennedy 1935: 376; Pollard and Banks 1937).

SOCIOPOLITICAL ORGANIZATION. **Social stratification.** Class differences are relatively strong throughout the Kenyah-Kayan-Kajang area. In Sarawak, aristocrats (largely members of chiefly families) are called *ipun uma* ("ancestors of the house"), corresponding to Leach's "house-owning group." Middle-class commoners (skilled artisans and farmers) are called *panyun*, and slaves (descendants of prisoners of war), *lupau*. Aristocrats, by virtue of strictly class-endogamous marriage alliances across tribal and linguistic boundaries, constitute an interrelated and politically dominant stratum throughout the area. Aristocratic chiefly families are wealthy in gongs, beads, and jars; they own rights to the exploitation of birds' nest caves; and by virtue of controlling the labor of slaves, they can grow relatively more rice than commoners. These differences are most marked among Kenyahs. [Kennedy 1935: 371-74; Hose and McDougall 1912: *1*, 69-70; Leach 1950: 76-77.] **Political organization.** Each longhouse has a headman or chief, an aristocrat, who, with his near relatives, occupies the compartments in the center of the structure. Multilonghouse Kayan villages have in addition a village chief, *primus inter pares* among the several house chiefs. Normally there is no formal political structure above the village level, although Kayans in the eighteenth and nineteenth centuries mounted large organized military expeditions under paramount chiefs. House (village) chiefs are expected to take the lead in warfare, the administration of justice, and in the supervision of omens and religious ritual. The position is elective, but ordinarily an able son succeeds his father as chief. Aristocrat-chiefs command considerable respect and prestige, particularly among Kenyahs, where they are in charge of the labor of slaves and of longhouse heirloom property. Kenyah chiefs are trained from youth in the command of oratory, which, with the ceremonial drinking of rice beer, figures in all formal occasions. Much attention is paid to proper etiquette and behavior on these occasions. Kenyah chiefs may claim descent from named (ancestral) deities and can recite genealogies of up to 19 generations. [Kennedy 1935: 371-73; Hose and McDougall 1912: *1*, 69-70 and *2*, 12; Southwell 1959.] **Social control and justice.** Aristocrat-chiefs wield much authority, although this is tempered by an informal council of elders. The chiefs judge offenses and impose fines consisting of gongs, swords, and spears (Hose and McDougall 1912: *1*, 65). **Warfare.** Both Kenyahs and Kayans engaged in headhunting in the past, and the former are reported to

have been the most notorious headhunters in Borneo except for Ibans (Kennedy 1935: 369-71). Kayans, apparently, were less addicted to this activity. The Kayans did, however, conduct expeditions of 1,000 or more men, organized under paramount chiefs, for the purpose of conquest—especially the capture of slaves—or for revenge (Hose and McDougall 1912: *1*, 158ff.; Kennedy 1935: 369-71). Among Kenyahs, headhunting was necessary in connection with *mamat*, head feasts, which terminated mourning periods and accompanied initiation into a graded system of statuses, *suhan*, for warriors. Successful headhunters were entitled to wear a panther tooth in the ear, a hornbill feather headdress, and a tattoo of special design (Kennedy 1935: 385). Headhunting raids were conducted by small parties of 10 to 20 men, operating by stealth and surprise. Much attention was paid to omens, especially birds. Following their use in *mamat* ceremonies, the heads were hung on the longhouse veranda, opposite the living quarters of the house chief. Since the abolition of headhunting early in this century, use has been made of old heads or of various substitutes; the spread of Christianity since World War II has meant the abridgement or abolishment altogether of head feasts in much of the area.

RELIGION. **Supernaturals.** Both Kayans and Kenyahs possess a pantheon of named anthropomorphic deities, including a Supreme Being and consort. There are numerous patron deities of activities such as war, agriculture, weaving, and the like, as well as a host of spirits both good and evil. The spirit realm, also the afterworld of spirits of the dead, is conceived of in vivid and explicit terms. Altar posts outside the longhouse serve as receptacles for food offerings to patron gods. Kenyah posts include representations of human figures carved in the round, and it is thought by Hose and McDougall that these represent deified ancestors. Ritual stones outside Kenyah and Kajang longhouses are the homes of household guardian spirits. Bird omens—particularly those involving the hawk—and (pig) liver divination are important in everyday life. Through these means, the will of the gods is made manifest to man. The many wild animals that figure in Kayan-Kenyah omenology are regarded in this sense as messengers of the gods, and man's behavior toward them is surrounded with a variety of prohibitions and taboos. [Kennedy 1935: 380; Hose and McDougall 1912: *2*, 12.] **Practitioners.** Mediums or shamans, *dayong*, may be male or female; they achieve their status through apprenticeship, with payment of a fee, to another *dayong*. Kenyah *dayong* on occasion dress in fanciful head masks and leaf cloaks. Techniques include induced trance states, during which the *dayong* may speak in an esoteric "spirit language." On these occasions the *dayong* may project his own soul, sometimes accompanied by a spirit familiar, to find the lost souls of those who are ill or to conduct the souls of those who have died to the spirit world. *Dayong* apparently figure also in agricultural ceremonies and may invoke spirits of male courage at a head feast. Kayans rely more on rituals conducted by *dayong* than do Kenyahs. [Kennedy 1935: 381.] **Ceremonies.** Agricultural rituals figure largely in the life of both Kayans and Kenyahs. The planting ritual of the Kayans includes the appearance of masked men representing benevolent spirits; by dancing, they exorcise the evil spirits that might harm the rice. The ritual concludes with competitive spinning of tops. Kenyahs perform somewhat similar rituals, apparently borrowed from Kayans, when the rice grains are mature. [Kennedy 1935: 383-84.] **Head feasts.** Periodic head feasts, *mamat*, appear to be central to the whole way of life of the Kayan-Kenyah-Kajang peoples, although with the spread of Christianity and other acculturative influences, they are fast disappearing. New heads seem to have been required for a variety of purificatory ceremonies, e.g. the termination of the mourning period for a deceased relative or the completion of a new longhouse. *Mamat*-type rituals also seem to have been associated with the initiation of warriors into a graded system of statuses, *suhan*. Kennedy has described the *mamat* (head feast) ceremony of the Kenyahs, among whom it was most highly developed, basing his account on that of Elshout (1926), who lived for some years at Long Nawang in the Apo Kayan. The feast, which lasts for nine days and nights, begins when a captured head is brought into the longhouse. The head, arranged at the top of a pole decorated with leaves and surrounded by warriors smeared with the blood of sacrificed chickens, is offered to the spirits of male courage, *bali akang*. Boat races are held on the second day. At night shamanesses invoke the *bali akang* spirits; warriors dance constantly and may in a frenzy bite the slain head. On the third day, the longhouse ritual stones are brought to the veranda in front of the house chief's door. The stones, with warriors in attendance, are covered with leaves, and the blood of sacrificed chickens, brought singly by girls of noble rank, is allowed to spill over them. Each girl in turn also smears blood on the arms of the assembled warriors. This is followed by the ritual rolling of the stones on the veranda floor by warriors, the balancing of stones by the house chief, the arrangement of the stones in a pile to support a pole with the captured head attached, and vying among men and boys of the village to touch the head. In the 1920s, the period to which this account refers, old heads or wooden substitutes were being used in the Apo Kayan. [Kennedy 1935: 384-89.] Additional data on the *mamat* feasts, also from the Kenyah of Long Nawang in the Apo Kayan, have been published by Harrisson (1966). These feasts were apparently part of a system (*suhan*, or *suan*) of initiation into a "brotherhood of warriors," whereby men throughout their lifetimes progressed through a complicated sequence of grades, each symbolized by an object such as sword, hornbill, bark cloth, leopard's tooth, etc. Feasts were organized periodically by men wishing to *suhan*, i.e. rise in grade, and the timing depended on the ability of the participants (or that of their longhouses) to marshall the large quantities of rice beer and livestock required. The rites were conducted by elders of the aristocracy; there were no women participants, according to Harrisson's informants. Fresh heads were required for these festivals, which were also the occasion for admitting young men into the "brotherhood." Members of the higher grades were entitled to wear fine bark-cloth cloaks and elaborate hornbill feather headdresses. The very highest grades appear to have involved their occupants in something like a taboo status vis-à-vis men of lower grade. Writing boards were kept by participants as mnemonic records of grades taken. [Harrisson 1966.] Harrisson likens the *mamat* festivals to the great multipurpose feasts of other Borneo pagans, e.g. the *irau* death feasts of Kelabits and the Iban's Gawai Antu. According to Galvin (1966), there is a likelihood that the *mamat* feasts, with accompanying *suhan* rites, were at one time part of a ritual complex surrounding secondary burial. **Soul, death, and afterlife.** Man is possessed of two souls. At death one may become an evil spirit and haunt the living; the other goes to a land of the dead in the spirit world. It must be led thither by the (projected) soul of a medium chanting while in a trance state. The journey is a complicated one with many pitfalls, including the crossing of a ghostly river. Kenyah and Kayan groups for the most part practice primary disposal of the corpse in a wooden coffin; secondary burial, at least within the past century, is rare or absent, and Kennedy recorded only one remote Kenyah group practicing secondary jar burial. Some of the so-called Kajang peoples do, apparently, perform secondary burial rites, often disposing of the bones in a jar or similar receptacle (cf. Hose and McDougall 1912). The coffin is made from a hollowed log, carved and painted, and often boat-shaped. Disposal of the corpse is arranged as soon after death as possible, allowing for construction of a coffin and for gathering of friends and relatives. For a great chief, an assemblage of several thousand persons was apparently not unusual. The coffin is carried to the graveyard, either up or downstream, in a ceremonial procession of canoes. It is exposed on a high platform, usually containing a replica of a house. The size of the burial platform and the richness and elaboration of carving and decoration reach spectacular proportions in the case of famed chiefs of high rank and great wealth. Alternative procedures among some Kenyahs include placing the coffin in a niche at the top of a massive upright post; the Pnihing, Uma Suling, and Peng place their coffins, arranged in tiers in some instances, in rock shelters. The mourning period following burial varies in length with the rank of the deceased. During this period relatives are subject to a variety of taboos and prescribed behaviors, including the wearing of bark cloth. Mourning was traditionally ended by the taking of a head for a *mamat* festival. Galvin (1966) thinks these *mamat* head feasts were at one time part of a ritual complex surrounding secondary burial. According to Kennedy, most tribes of the Bahau complex formerly speared a slave to death at the death of a great chief. [Kennedy 1935: 379-80.]

BIBLIOGRAPHY. Dyen 1965; Elshout 1926; Galvin 1966; Harrisson 1964, 1966; Hose and McDougall 1912; Kennedy 1935; Leach 1950; Lumholtz 1920; Nieuwenhuis 1904-07; Pollard and Banks 1937; Prattis 1963; Southwell 1959.

MELANAU

Synonyms. *A Liko, Liko, Liko Melanu, Melanu, Milano*

ORIENTATION. **Identification and location.** Melanau is a Malay term for the indigenous population of Sarawak's central west coast, between the mouths of the Rejang and Baram and extending inland for about 20 miles. A mainly swampy, tidal environment, intersected by rivers such as the Oya, Muka, and Bintulu (see Leach 1950: map facing p. 46; Morris 1953: map facing p. 3). The usual ethnonym is *a liko*, "people of the river," with a specific referent such as *a liko oya*, "people of the Oya River." The area was long dominated by a Brunei Malay Muslim aristocracy, with the result that a majority of Melanau have adopted Islam and *masok Melayu*, "become Malay." The term *liko Melanu* is sometimes used to distinguish pagan Melanau from their Muslim or Christian congeners (cf. Aikman 1959: 94). Local groups identify with a particular river or stream and have no sense of overall ethnic identity. Broad similarities in language and custom do make it possible, however, to distinguish a Melanau culture type. Modern Melanau can best be characterized as the Malayized representatives of an old West Borneo culture stratum, allied historically to inland pagans, e.g. Kajaman on the upper Rejang, classified in the present volume as part of a Kenyah-Kajang culture complex. [Morris 1953.] **Linguistic affiliation.** An Austronesian language, most likely more closely related to the languages of western Indonesia than to those of Northern Indonesia and the Philippines. Within Borneo, the most closely related languages appear to be those of the Kenyah-Kayan-Kajang complex. Melanau dialects include Oya, Mukah, Matu, Sibu, and Balingian—all mutually intelligible. Bintulu and Kanowit, although not mutually intelligible, appear closely related to Melanau proper. [Cense and Uhlenbeck 1958: 18-19.] **Demography.** According to the 1947 census 35,000, of whom

26,000 were Muslim, 800 Christian, and the remainder pagan. Aikman (1959: 88), speaking of the 1930s, reports an Oya River population of around 4,000 Muslims, 4,000 pagans, and 5,000 Christians. The 1960 census gives 44,661 Melanau, but includes in this category groups such as Kajaman, Lahanan, Sekapan, and Sipeng, which elsewhere in this volume, following Leach (1950), are included in a Kenyah-Kajang category. **History and cultural relations.** The Melanau area was ceded by Brunei to the government of Rajah Brooke in 1860. Prior to this time, it had been controlled by Brunei aristocrats, or *pangeran*. Islamization has continued from Brunei days to the present. The Brooke regime encouraged the commercial production of sago, and nowadays the economy of many villages is based wholly on the production of sago as a cash crop. Local Chinese are the middlemen in this trade.

SETTLEMENT PATTERN AND HOUSING. The local community was formerly a single, large, fortresslike longhouse, located for strategic purposes at the juncture of two streams. Nowadays the typical village consists of small, Malay-style houses, arranged in a ribbon pattern along the bank of a stream and containing from 100 to 1,000 inhabitants. Villages tend to be divided into named segments, which occupy the sites of former longhouses. Dwellings in predominantly Muslim villages tend to be occupied by single nuclear families; those in pagan villages may house from three to four nuclear families, i.e. an extended or joint family. Although most people in a village are likely to be related, the village is not regarded as a kinship unit, nor does it function as a land-owning unit. [Morris 1953, 1967.]

ECONOMY. Subsistence presumably based originally on rice, sago, and other jungle foods and, on the coast, on fishing. Nowadays the interior economy, especially, is based on sago—and, more recently, rubber—as commercial crops. Fishing continues as an important source of food, particularly along the coast. Stock raising is relatively unimportant, although pigs and chickens are eaten (the former in pagan villages only). The family is the basic economic unit, although rights to sago land are individually owned. Rights to rice land were probably at one time held jointly by descendants of the man or men who first worked the land. Traditional wealth consists of gold ornaments, old brass cannon and other brassware, Chinese porcelain plates, old beads, ancient ground stone axeheads, and pigs' tusks (Morris 1953: 20). In addition, Noakes (1949) records the extraordinary value placed on old bowls, plates, and jars of imported Chinese and Siamese celadonware.

KINSHIP. Cognatic (ambilateral). The personal kindred is reckoned vertically to include great-grandparents and laterally to include third cousins. A person's kindred has no economic or corporate functions, but it does function as a virtually endogamous unit with respect to marriage. Genealogical connections, for purposes of establishing rank, are traced bilaterally as far back as great-great-grandparents. A descent line is identified with a particular rank, i.e. the rank of the ancestor from which it stems, and an individual invokes one or another of the potential lines available to him, depending on the circumstances. Ideally, one chooses a line through the father's side, but it is possible to claim a maternal line if this seems more advantageous, e.g. in manipulating marriages to gain prestige. [Morris 1953, 1967.] **Kin terminology.** The following terms of reference are taken from Morris (1953: 109ff.):

GrPa	*tipou*
Fa	*tama*
Mo	*tina*
PaSib (o. than Pa)	*tua lai*
PaSib (y. than Pa)	*tua merou*
ElBr	*janak lai*
ElSi	*janak merou*
Cousin	*jipou*
Ch	*anak*
Nephew/niece	*nakan*
GrCh	*sou*

MARRIAGE AND FAMILY. **Mode.** Bride-price is important and is graded according to the rank claimed for the girl by her father. The grades are designated according to items of traditional wealth, particularly brassware, although payment nowadays is more often in money or land. The larger portion of the payment goes to the bride, the remainder to members of her immediate family. **Form.** Monogamy. Polygyny is legally possible but virtually unknown (Morris 1953: 75). **Marriage rules.** Sex and marriage are prohibited within the nuclear family and between close relatives of different generations. Sex or marriage with a first cousin is ritually improper, but does occur, subject to payment of a fine. The ideal marriage is that between second cousins of the same social rank (Morris 1953, 1967). **Residence.** There is a general tendency to matrilocal residence, both initially and permanently (Morris 1953: 58, 102). **Domestic unit.** The nuclear family household is apparently the rule among most Melanau, although in the pagan village studied by Morris, 40 percent of the households were occupied by joint families (Morris 1953: 102). The household is an independent unit, responsible for growing its own food, maintaining its own food taboos, and performing its own ritual (Morris 1967). **Inheritance.** Property, including land, is inherited in equal shares by children of both sexes. Adopted children commonly do not share in such inheritance rights.

SOCIOPOLITICAL ORGANIZATION. **Political organization.** Formerly the politically independent long-house communities along a stretch of river or stream tended to identify together, e.g. as "we, the people of Oya." Interstream, and even intercommunity enmity and raiding, were common (Morris 1953, 1967). Aikman (1959: 87-88) mentions legends of former Melanau chiefs, one of whom challenged the Brunei Sultanate, but the exact nature of an earlier supravillage political organization, if any, remains uncertain. The Brunei-appointed *pangeran* tended to control single river systems, or portions thereof, and modern government districts conform largely to this old pattern. Each village now has a headman, a purely administrative post sanctioned by government. He is chosen from among a group of elderly men of rank and property, *a-nyat*, the titular leaders of the village. The *a-nyat* are adat experts, particularly with respect to matters of bridewealth and marriage; they sanction all marriages within the village and can thus regulate attempts by lower-rank men to gain prestige by manipulating the marriage system. It was this core of aristocratic elders that formerly provided leaders in various pursuits, e.g. warfare. [Morris 1953, 1967.] **Social stratification.** Cognatic descent lines are identified with a system of five or so social ranks, *bangsa*, each line taking the rank of the particular ancestor from whom it stems. In theory, a child takes the rank of its father; in practice, individuals invoke either patrilateral or matrilateral lines, depending on the advantage to be gained in a particular circumstance. Ranks may be categorized roughly into upper (aristocracy), middle, and lower (including slaves), and are identified with a graded system of traditional items of bridewealth consisting of swords, spears, cloth, and brassware, as well as a hierarchy of titles. In former times, ranks may have conformed to endogamic classes with economic and political functions; wealth and political power within the longhouse were apparently restricted to an aristocratic core group, descendants of the founders of the longhouse, who occupied rooms in the center of the structure. The development of a cash economy and the abandonment of longhouses have tended to alter these patterns. Although proper etiquette between ranks is still observed, the traditional bride-price is rarely paid in full, and marriages are not always rank endogamous. In practice, men use the system to raise their own prestige; a lower-rank man of wealth gains prestige by claiming the prerogatives of a high-rank wedding for his daughter (including the stated traditional bride-price, regardless of whether it is actually paid). This he does by invoking a high-rank descent line for her, one that may be different from his own and higher than that of his own father. As expressed by Morris, the system nowadays is best characterized as a graded system of social honors, used for the expression of prestige. [Morris 1953, 1967.] **Slavery.** Prisoners of war were formerly enslaved, and persons in debt could voluntarily enter slavery. Slaves might in theory buy their freedom, but were subject to rigid marriage restrictions, i.e. they were virtually an endogamous caste. Although slavery is prohibited nowadays, people are still stigmatized by virtue of slave descent.

RELIGION. A vaguely remembered cosmology includes the idea of layered upper, middle, and underworlds. The inhabitants of these worlds coexist within a preordained order; man is endangered whenever this order is disrupted. Order and equilibrium can be maintained or restored by proper observance of adat—the body of prescribed custom given to man by the gods. The latter communicate their advice and wishes to man through the behavior of animals—particularly birds—interpreted through the medium of augurs. Curing and death rites are nowadays the focus of Melanau ceremonial; belief in a variety of spirits appears to be strongly developed, especially among pagan Melanau, but there is little evidence of a cult of ancestral spirits. [Morris 1967.] **Supernaturals.** Anthropomorphic deities include a creator, Alatala. Biliong, associated with the moon, punishes humans who disturb the natural order by mocking animals; this he does by visitations of thunder and hail and the threat of petrifaction. Spirits, *tou*, generally do not interfere with humans unless angered by neglect or infraction of adat; if not ritually fed at prescribed intervals they may become angry and cause illness. [Morris 1967.] **Practitioners.** Appear to be associated mainly with diagnosis and treatment of illness. Recourse is had first to an herbalist/magician, *dukun*, and usually also to a carver of spirit images, called *bilum*. Other specialists function as shamans and/or spirit mediums. Shamans, *bayoh*, are mostly women, since men resist assuming a role reportedly once associated with transvestism. (For reference to transvestite behavior at Mukah in 1910, see Newington 1961.) Shamans are "chosen" by spirits associated with certain descent lines; the person chosen becomes ill and will die unless the spirit's overtures are accepted (Morris 1953: 143ff.). Shamanistic curing ceremonies are graded, depending on the seriousness of the illness. The ultimate is *aiyum*, lasting up to nine nights and involving several shamans. Techniques include drum beating and chanting to call up the spirit familiar. Magic stones are made to enter the patient's body in order to drive out the offending spirit, a process aided by blowing on the body or stroking it with long leaves. Swinging is utilized as a technique to induce good spirits to enter the body of the swinger. [Morris 1967.] **Ceremonies.** There was formerly a rice cult, but its importance relative to curing and death ceremonies is unclear. An annual village cleansing and purification ceremony, *kaul*, includes an invitation to the spirits to join a procession of boats to the village, where they are fed and their blessing invoked (Morris 1953: 95ff.,

145). **Soul, death, and afterlife.** All living things are composed of (1) a body (2) emotions (3) a soul, and (4) a life principle. The soul can leave the body during illness, and at death it journeys by canoe to the Land of the Dead (Morris 1953: 143). Death was formerly a major occasion for the public display of wealth and for validation of rank and prestige. Nowadays the corpse is disposed of soon after death. It may be carried to the grave on an elaborately carved bier, with various accouterments, including a model boat fitted with carved spirit images. The body is buried in the ground in a canoe-shaped coffin, and (for the well-to-do) a wooden grave house is constructed over the grave. The journey of the soul to the Land of the Dead is long and hazardous. To aid the soul, lengthy death chants, enacting the details of the journey, were in former times a necessary part of funerary ritual. Mourning relatives remain under strict taboos for varying periods up to five days. Postmortuary rites include cockfighting and the journey, by spirit canoe, of a spirit medium to visit the soul of the deceased in the Land of the Dead. ● According to Morris (1953: 146-49), famed aristocrats were formerly interred in massive ironwood burial posts, accompanied by the ritual sacrifice of a slave; most bodies were, however, buried in the ground accompanied by utensils, clothing, gold, and beads, appropriate to the rank of the deceased. According to information obtained by Jumuh (1949), the burial posts, up to 30 feet above the ground, were erected by individuals during their lifetime; a considerable labor force and expenditure of time and wealth was necessary to transport and erect a memorial this size. The ceremony of erecting the post was accompanied by bird omenology and, under some circumstances, by the sacrifice of a slave. Primary and secondary treatment of the corpse, in particular that of an aristocrat, seems to have varied considerably. Jumuh (1949) mentions placement of the corpse within the hollowed-out burial post, in a squatting position, with arms around knees. Alternatively the body, on a bier, was left in a fork at the top of the post. As a further alternative, the body was sometimes encoffined within a small, roofed hut, raised on piles, the coffin fitted with a drain which allowed the fluids of decomposition to flow to the ground. Various of these procedures might be accompanied by the sacrifice of a slave and by elaborate feasts. Kennedy (1935) and Newington (1961) report in addition the secondary burial of the bones, following decomposition, in a jar placed at the top of the memorial burial post. The jar, when it became filled with the bones of deceased relatives of the founder, was placed in a hollowed-out cavity within the post.

BIBLIOGRAPHY. Aikman 1959; Cense and Uhlenbeck 1958; Jumuh 1949; Kennedy 1935; Leach 1950; Morris 1953, 1967; Newington 1961; Noakes 1949.

KEDAYAN

Synonyms. *Kadayan, Karayan, Kerayan*

ORIENTATION. Malay-speaking, wet-rice agriculturists, living along the coasts of northern Sarawak and Brunei. Although it is popularly believed that these people are relatively late arrivals in Borneo—perhaps immigrants from Java—little is known of their customs and ethnic affiliations (Harrisson 1959c). Leach (1950: 78) thinks that they, like the Bisaya, may be simply Malayized, i.e. Islamized, representatives of an earlier widespread culture stratum of the Murut-Kelabit type. Kedayans, along with Bisayas and Melanaus, were classed together by Hose in his Klemantan group, which he thought was representative of a very early culture stratum in Borneo.

BIBLIOGRAPHY. Harrisson 1959c; Leach 1950.

PUNAN-PENAN

NOMADIC forest dwellers still roam the mountains of interior Borneo, where the great river systems of Sarawak and Kalimantan have their source. The most general term for these people is Punan, a word common to many inland dialects and meaning "up river" or "headwaters" (Harrisson 1949). Local groups or aggregates, however, are usually known by, and themselves use, a local name, hence the great number of Punan "tribes" reported in the literature, e.g. Aput, Bah, Basap, Bukat, Gang, Lusong, Magoh, Milau, Penyabong, Piku, Saputan. The terms Bukit and Bukitan, meaning "hill people" or "mountain people," appear to have been originally generic exonyms on the order of Punan. In modern Kalimantan Tengah (the province of Central Kalimantan) the usual generic term is Ot, "upstream" or "upper region" (cf. Avé's sections on the Kalimantan Dayaks and the Ot Danum Dayaks, elsewhere in this volume). Terms such as Punan, Bukit, and Ot are in practice used by village-dwelling riverine peoples (Dayaks) for those peoples farther inland who do not live in villages or along rivers, i.e. forest nomads. The problem of ethnic classification is complicated by the fact that some of the forest peoples are fully nomadic, some partially so, and some fully settled and partly or virtually wholly acculturated to neighboring riverine Dayaks, e.g. Saputan and Penyabong in the Barito-Mahakam watershed; Bukitan and Ukit in Sarawak. This is a continuing process, apparently accelerated in recent decades, with the result that names and locations of groups may change frequently. In the Baram River area of Sarawak, inhabited largely by Kenyah-speaking peoples, forest dwellers are known as Penan, which Urquhart (1951) derives from the Kenyah Sebup term *mennan*, "to live temporarily in the jungle." In this area, the term refers to two tribes or aggregates of nomads or former nomads, and in addition serves as a common ethnonym among the people so designated. As made clear by R. Needham in the entry following, these people are undergoing an accelerating process of acculturation, many having settled down in longhouses after the manner of their riverine neighbors. • By all accounts those Punan-Penan who are still nomadic are characterized by a relatively meager cultural inventory and extreme informality of social relationships. They subsist chiefly on game and wild sago, relying on trade with patron village tribes for necessities such as salt and tobacco. Their total numbers are unknown; those in Sarawak were estimated in the 1947 census to number somewhat over 1,600, although Needham (below) was able to account for over 1,700 nomadic Penan, alone, in 1952. The linguistic affiliations of the Punan-Penan languages are likewise unknown. Penan dialects appear to be most closely related to those of Kenyah speakers, but whether this is true of nomads in other parts of Borneo is unclear. Kennedy (1935: 346) suggests that the various Kenyah peoples may have been culturally similar to contemporary Punan before their adoption of complex socioreligious ideas from an intrusive Kayan culture.

BIBLIOGRAPHY. Harrisson 1949; Kennedy 1935; Urquhart 1951, 1959.

*PENAN**

Synonyms. *Pennan, Punan, Poonan* (Dutch *Poenan,* French *Pounan*)

ORIENTATION. **Identification.** The Penan are an indigenous population of forest-dwellers in the interior of Borneo. There has long been confusion in the

---

*The author of this entry, Rodney Needham, is University Lecturer in Social Anthropology, Oxford. He carried out field research in Borneo in 1951-52 and again in 1958.

ethnographic literature about their identification. For the most part they have been referred to as "Punan" and have thus been aggregated with a number of other peoples, mostly forest nomads, in widely separated parts of the island. As late as 1947 the existence of any distinct Punan people was called into question by an authority who had sought them in vain in central Borneo (Cole 1947). Later investigation confirmed the published indications that there are a number of nomadic peoples in Borneo, mostly known as Punan, of whom the Penan are one. The Penan refer to themselves as such (pən△n), and distinguish themselves by language and institutions from the various nomadic Punan groups and from the long-house Punan Ba (Needham 1954b; 1955). They compose two tribes, Eastern and Western, separated in the main by the Baram River. Although the tribes recognize each other as true Penan, i.e. as culturally similar forest nomads, there are marked differences between them. These linguistic and social disparities are sufficient to justify the ethnographical separation of the Eastern and the Western Penan into two distinct societies. There are also characteristic physical features which make a further general difference between the tribes, but the Penan population as a whole is not racially distinct from the other peoples of the interior of Borneo. They exhibit no Negrito or Veddoid traits. Culturally, they belong to the middle Borneo grouping of peoples, distinguished from the Lun Daye (including Muruts) to the northeast and from the Iban to the southwest. Their cultural affinities are with the congeries of related peoples known as Kenyah. **Location.** Approximately 2°45′–4°15′ N., 113°25′–115°50′ E. They are mostly in Sarawak; some are in Kalimantan (Indonesian Borneo), and a few in Brunei. There is no Penan territory, but the groups are interspersed between the settlements of other peoples. The Penan have tended to move toward the coast of the China Sea; one Eastern group and sixteen Western groups have settled in the Baram and Tinjar valleys and in the lowlands between the Kemena and Bakong rivers. A few Eastern groups have in recent years moved west of the Baram, into the region south of the Kalulong massif. **Geography.** Primary rain forest, cut by numerous streams and rivers. Stands of wild sago grow at lower levels and in pockets of soil in the mountains. Fruits include durian, rambutan, and mangosteen. The chief wild animals of importance are pigs, monkeys, deer, shrews, snakes, and anteaters. Rhinoceros have become practically extinct within the lifetime of older men. Fish are plentiful, and there are many species of birds, including the hornbill. **Linguistic affiliation.** Two fairly contrasted dialects, Eastern and Western, which are not always mutually intelligible. Eastern Penan is the more homogeneous. The Western Penan dialect is practically identical with Sebup. Both dialects belong to the Kenyah family of languages, although both tribes

tend to adopt words from the settled peoples with whom they come into contact, e.g. Kayan, Kelabit, Kenyah, Iban, Malays. There is no indigenous form of writing, nor can any Penan leading the traditional life either read or write in any medium. Fronded sticks (*saang*) with appendages of leaves, cane, or firewood are thrust into the ground in order to convey messages about travel, food, numbers, health, and so on (Arnold 1958). **Demography.** There is no exact census of the Penan, but in 1952 they were numbered at 2,626, divided as follows: Eastern Penan, 906; Western Penan, 852; settled groups, 868. The total population is probably rather less than 3,000, divided into about 70 groups (Needham 1953). There are indications that the Penan have been constantly increasing in numbers and that they continue to do so. **History.** Culturally the Penan form part of the general movement of peoples from the upper Kayan River, over the central chain of mountains, and down the Baram and Tinjar valleys toward the coast. The Western Penan have a tradition that they originated from Bateu Kéng Sian (Turtle-shell Rock) in the upper reaches of the Lua River, a tributary of the Peliran, in the headwaters of the Rejang. Genealogies extend back to about 1810, and the subsequent moves and fission of groups between the Balui to the west and the Ivan, Pejungan, and Luda rivers to the east, can be plotted by reference to these. The Eastern Penan do not share this tradition, and their genealogies are far shallower. They have much less knowledge of their past, but they appear to have come from the Pejungan and through the Lio Matu area, at the headwaters of the Baram, and thence northwestward through the mountains that form the right watershed of this river. They have expanded in that direction as far as the Medalam, a major tributary of the Limbang River, and into the interior of Brunei State. Politically, the bulk of the Penan fall under the government of Sarawak. There has long been a trend to abandon nomadism and to practice agriculture in fixed settlements. This has latterly been intensified at the urging of colonial administrators. The oldest Penan settlements in Sarawak—those on the Niah, Suai, and Buk rivers—date probably from the first two decades of the nineteenth century. There are indications that assimilation to the settled peoples is taking place at an increasingly rapid rate, and it is probable that the Penan will eventually vanish as a distinct people. **Cultural relations.** Penan of both tribes, but the Western more than the Eastern, are influenced by the longhouse peoples in language, dress, tattooing, and in many of their ideas. Each nomadic group is under the dominance of the headman of a longhouse, and individual families are in turn subject to upper-class members of these settled tribes. The latter express great contempt for the Penan, refer to them as animals, and claim them as their property. The Penan are timid and abashed in their presence. They need to trade with the settled peoples, however, in order to remain nomads, and the goods they bring in are a source of much profit to their patrons. Before firm government was established, the Penan were under the protection, secured by blood pact, of the patrons, who jealously guarded their own economic rights in Penan trade against headhunting or intrusion on the part of other longhouse groups (Pauwels 1935: 351-52). The only reported form of incursion into Penan society is when an Iban battens on a group, sometimes taking one of the women, in order to acquire very cheaply a store of bezoar stones and mats. Individual Kenyah sometimes journey into the forest to trade with Penan, outside the regular meetings and free of the government price levels maintained at them, but they do not stay.

SETTLEMENT PATTERN AND HOUSING. **Settlement pattern.** Local groups range in size from 15 to 75 persons, with a mean of about 32. They are named after the rivers with which they are associated historically or currently, e.g. Penan Akah, Penan Silat. The Eastern Penan build a main camp in the territory that they exploit, and then move as a group from one temporary camp to another, using the main camp as a base and for the storage of forest products until it is time to move to another area or to go to a trading meeting. The Western Penan live in a main camp for up to two years and exploit the area in smaller groups of a family or two, while the old and sick and certain others stay behind. In each tribe, the main camp consists of dwellings; there is no temple or bachelors' house. The disposition of the huts follows no special or symbolic form, but there are distinctions between Eastern and Western main camps. The Eastern Penan build in a close cluster, high on a ridge, but within ready reach of water. The Western Penan build on level ground near a river, often in a line, and sometimes with the huts placed end to end in the form of a longhouse. **Housing.** The huts are made of saplings, with roofs consisting of matlike stretches of dried fan-palm leaves sewn together; these are sometimes supplemented by green leaves of the same kind, and the sides may be partly closed against rain and wind with leaves or bark. The Eastern hut is built some feet off the ground on piles; among the Western Penan it is based directly on the ground, with only a few inches between the sapling floor and the soil. There is no completely standard arrangement of the interior in either; e.g. the hearth (made of earth, with stones to support the pan) can be at any point. Generally there are no partitions inside a hut, and when among the Western Penan a number of huts are built in line, they afford a clear view right through. There are no movable furnishings.

ECONOMY. Traditionally, and still for the most part in fact, the Penan are hunters and gatherers. A few groups grow small and precarious supplementary crops of cassava. The settled groups plant dry rice. The staple food for the forest dwellers is the wild sago palm, exploited throughout the year. The most prized game animal is the wild pig; the most common prey is monkey—primarily gibbons and macaques—but practically any creature (with the exception of omen animals and leeches) may be hunted and eaten. All food, from sago flour to the smallest bird, is shared with scrupulous equality among all members of the group. Game is hunted with blowpipe and spear; the darts are poisoned, but not the spear. In recent years, an increasing number of individuals have acquired shotguns; ammunition is obtained at the trading meetings. Among the Western Penan, fish are caught by hook and line or by dam and derris root. Fruits are abundant in season, and animals are fatter at this time. The only domestic animal is the hunting dog, often acquired from the settled tribes. The Western Penan make blowpipes with an iron bit, and they are skilled smiths. Today the iron comes in foundry-produced bars through trade, but these Penan claim that they have always known, like the Kenyah (Arnold 1959: 124), how to smelt local ore and how to work it with stone hammers and anvils (cf. Pfeffer 1963: 129). They also carve excellent sheathes and hilts. The Eastern Penan do not have these skills, and protest that they are unable to acquire them, so that they rely more directly on trade. Both tribes weave cane mats, which fetch good prices (for the middlemen) in the lowland markets. Baskets, mats, roofing, bamboo containers, and domestic utensils are all made by the Penan from local materials. There is no distinct status of artist or craftsman.

TRADE. Trading meetings are held about three times a year with Kenyah and other overlords at their longhouses on the rivers. In recent decades, they have for the most part been conducted under government supervision, which checks the more extreme forms of cheating. The Penan bring in cane mats and unworked forest products such as damar, wild rubber, bezoars, hornbill feathers, anteater scales, and, formerly, rhinoceros horns. These they exchange, on disadvantageous terms, for spearheads, cutting implements, cooking pans, beads, earrings, bracelets, loincloths, skirts, matches, etc. There are no Penan markets, nor is there any other form of regular internal trade among Penan groups. There is much gift exchange, but goods earned by trade are not subject to the rule of equal sharing. **Property.** There are no rights in land or in its resources, except that bezoar stones, hornbill feathers, etc. belong to the hunter and that damar and wild rubber belong to those who collected or worked it. The return on these forest products, in the form of what Penan call "hard" goods acquired by trade, is individually owned. There are stated punishments for theft, but no actual cases are known. Huts are built by the families who sleep in them, but they are not negotiable property. The group has no bounded territory of its own, and for another group to hunt in the neighborhood would not be a trespass.

KIN GROUPS. **Descent.** Kinship is reckoned cognatically, with a patrilineal emphasis; an individual takes the father's name, and in a genealogy masculine connections tend to be remembered more readily than feminine. **Kin groups.** There are no discrete groups defined by descent. The local group usually consists of close relatives. All Penan are regarded as kin, whether or not genealogical connections can be established. **Kin terminology.** The terminology is nonlineal and is applied in a widely classificatory fashion. There are slight differences between the Eastern and Western terminologies:

EASTERN	WESTERN	
tepun	*tepun*	grandparent
tamen	*tamen*	father
tinen	*tinen*	mother
vé	*vi*	uncle, aunt
padé	*padi*	sibling
[*padé*] *tuken*	[*padi*] *tuken*	elder sibling
[*padé*] *tadin*	[*padi*] *tadin*	younger sibling
padé pata	*padi pesak*	cousin
anak	*anak*	child
ahong	*aong*	nephew, niece
ayam	*ayam*	grandchild
kivan	*kivan*	parent-in-law, child-in-law
banen	*banen*	husband
do	*redu*	wife
sabai	*sabai*	brother-in-law
lango	*langu*	sister-in-law
ruai	*ruai*	spouse of sibling-in-law
lieng	*bieng*	sibling-in-law after death of connecting spouse

Teknonyms are employed, and also a system of "death-names," which are prefixed to the personal names of those who have lost relatives by death (Needham 1954f, 1954g, 1959, 1965).

MARRIAGE AND FAMILY. **Mode.** Ideally there is a bridewealth, higher among the Western Penan than among the Eastern, consisting of swords, blowpipes, cloth, etc., but in practice little if anything is ever given when the marriage takes place within the group. There is no ceremony, nor is any official or group consent required. **Form.** Preponderantly monogamous, but not obligatorily so. There is no preference for sororal polygyny or for polygyny itself. Polyandry has been alleged (Hose and McDougall 1912: 2, 183), but is said by the Penan to be impossible. **Marriage prohibitions.** Penan of either tribe may in general marry a person of any category, other than *tamen, tinen,* and current *kivan,* provided the relationship is at the second degree. An exception, and a difference

between the two tribes, affects the cousin. The Eastern Penan may marry the first cousin and frequently do so; the Western may not. There is no prescribed or preferred category. Marriage often takes place between genealogical levels, e.g. between *vé* and *ahong*; usually it takes place between individuals of roughly the same age, and this factor overrides category. Marriage between individuals of disparate ages is much disapproved and does not occur. [Needham 1966.] **Residence.** Marriage usually and by preference takes place within the group. When the parties belong to different groups, the man should remain with his wife's group for a year or so, or until a child has been born, but the decision depends in each case on the particular circumstances and it may not be practicable to fulfill this expectation. **Domestic unit.** Nuclear family—rarely, a polygynous family—with the addition of dependents such as widowed parent, visitor, etc. **Inheritance.** There are no fixed rules, and there is little property to inherit that an individual will not already possess. Siblings and children have first claims, which they adjust among themselves according to need. **Divorce.** By mutual consent, or at the instance of either party, without ceremony or any authorization. Causes include adultery, idleness, and bad temper, but not barrenness. **Secondary marriage.** There is no widow-inheritance, levirate, or sororate. **Adoption.** Possible but not common. There are no prescribed categories. An orphan may be adopted by either a brother or a sister of the deceased parent. A childless woman may beg a baby from another woman who already has a large family; the promise can be made before the child in question is born.

SOCIOPOLITICAL ORGANIZATION. **Political organization.** The group is usually headed by a recognized elder, but he has no real power. The office is not in principle hereditary, but is frequently transmitted from father to son. There is no council or any other formal organization of the group, nor are there any institutions transcending the level of the local community. **Social stratification.** There are no social classes, though certain Western groups speak in terms (copied apparently from longhouse tribes) of aristocrats, *maren,* and commoners, *panyin,* in describing the difference between elders and others. There are not, and never have been, any slaves (*ulun*) among the Penan. Relative age is the most general and the most important social differential, but there are no age sets or recognized age-grades. There is no formal training and no initiation into manhood. Among the Western Penan, and perhaps less commonly among the Eastern Penan, a youth will assume the penis pin when he begins to lead an active sexual life; this involves perforating the glans penis and is done either by the youth himself or with the help of a friend. The shaft of the pin is thrust through this hole when it is healed, and the apparatus is worn in intercourse to increase the stimulation of the girl. Tattooing is not a general practice. Western Penan sometimes adopt simple designs on the shoulders and the throat, such as are worn by the Iban; the Eastern Penan do not usually tattoo at all. The lobes of the ears are punctured for earrings, and a hunter who has killed a clouded leopard wears the fangs in holes bored in the helices of the ears, but these are not signs of stages in initiation. None of these tokens of maturity involves ritual or any kind of collective participation. **Social control and justice.** There is no formal control of a Penan group, nor is any individual who has an alternative obliged to remain with it. In matters of communal concern, the general will of the mature men, backed by the opinions of the women, prevails. Forms of ordeal, divination, oaths, and conditional curses are referred to in connection with the resolution of disputes, but they are practically never put into effect. **Warfare.** The Penan claim that they have never initiated attacks on others, and not even their longhouse neighbors report it of them. They themselves have until recently been prime targets for headhunters, of whom they are still in dread. There is no cannibalism. Contemporary Penan, especially the Eastern tribe, are remarkable for their pacific character and their abhorrence of physical violence.

RELIGION. Christianity has spread among the Penan since the end of the Second World War, evangelical Protestantism among the Eastern Penan and Roman Catholicism among the Western, but a large proportion of the groups, both nomadic and settled, remain pagan. The longest settled groups in the coastal lowlands are Muslim. The major characteristics of the indigenous religion of the Penan are in general, and in a somewhat impoverished form, those of the Kenyah religion as described by Elshout (1923, 1926). There is neither totemism nor an ancestor cult. Shamanism, in a form common in central Borneo, is practiced. Omen creatures (deer, snakes, and a number of birds) are recognized, as among the Kenyah. **Supernaturals.** There is a supreme creator-divinity, Peselong, sometimes credited with a wife, Bungan. He has little concern for human affairs, and these are most influenced by innumerable spirits (*baléi*); some of these are malevolent, but most of them animate the environment and account for noteworthy things and events. **Practitioners.** Shamans (*dayung*) cure illness by summoning their spirit familiars and by chanting against the spirits who are responsible. There are no priests. **Ceremonies.** There are no major religious ceremonies, and there is no religious calendar. Blood taken from the petitioner's foot is sacrificed to a thunder god, Baléi Liwen, to avert storms brought on by mockery of animals (Needham 1964). Chicken feathers offered in cleft fronded sticks serve as surrogates for real victims in expiation of wrongdoing, such

as adultery. Human hair is also offered in this way after a funeral. **Illness and medicine.** Disease is caused by specific classes of spirits, bringing fever, bellyache, etc. These are mollified by the shaman. Headaches, as well as the unease consequent upon bad dreams, can be relieved by making a fronded stick with a rudimentary human face (*butun*); the pain, or the inauspiciousness, is transferred to this stick, which is left in the forest, sometimes near a stream which will carry the influence away. There are very few indigenous medicines. Certain leaves may be chewed or macerated and placed over a cut, but in general wounds and boils are allowed to suppurate. The usual remedy for sickness is to sit by the fire. Penan of both tribes readily accept Western medicines. **Soul, death, and afterlife.** Among the Eastern Penan, the individual possesses three souls (*sahé*), associated with the pupils of the eyes, the hair of the head, and the trunk of the body. The Western Penan speak of only one soul (*beruwen*). After death, souls go to the land of the spirits above the sky, where they lead a life like that on earth only with easeful abundance and no pain or illness. The body is buried, either under the hut in which the death occurred or in the forest; in either case the camp is abandoned and the group moves a few miles away and does not return for some months.

BIBLIOGRAPHY. Arnold 1958, 1959; Banks 1949; Cole 1947; Coomans de Ruiter 1932; Elshout 1923, 1926; Hose and McDougall 1912; Needham 1953, 1954f, 1954g, 1959, 1964, 1965, 1966; Pauwels 1935; Pfeffer 1963; Urquhart 1951.

IBAN

Synonym. *Sea Dayak*

ORIENTATION. **Identification.** A Proto-Malay riverine people, practicing shifting agriculture in the low hills behind the coast of Sarawak in western Borneo. One of the best described and most populous of any of the pagan peoples of Borneo. When first contacted by Europeans in the 1840s, some groups, in league with Malays, were engaged in coastal piracy; this pursuit, atypical of most Iban, led Europeans to call them "Sea Dayaks." The term Iban, originally a linguistic borrowing from Kayan, was later adopted by government and is now in general use among all tribes in interior Sarawak (Freeman 1960: 160). The Iban are further differentiated by the names of river systems or political districts, e.g. Saribas, Skrang, Undup, Ulu Ai, Lemanak, Balau. The Sebuyau appear to be a para-Malay people derived from Iban; the Millikin of the Sadong River area seem intermediate between Sea and Land Dayak (Leach 1950: 54). All Iban, however, have in common a homogeneous language and a complex of religious belief and ritual that make them essentially one people. They differ from other Bornean pagans with respect to both social structure (Leach 1950: 54) and language (Kennedy 1935: 456). The prime source on Iban is Freeman, whose fieldwork was in the heavily forested upper Baleh, Second Division, among pioneering rice farmers who were presumably more representative of aboriginal conditions than the settled, rubber-holding groups nearer the coast. **Location.** Predominantly in Sarawak. Also some in the upper Kapuas River area in Kalimantan (e.g. the Maloh and other named subgroups). In Sarawak, along the rivers intersecting low foothills inland from the coast, extending from Kuching right up almost to Brunei (Leach 1950: map facing p. 46). In addition, Iban young men, journeying in search of wealth and prestige, are met with throughout Borneo and adjacent islands. **Linguistic affiliation.** Classed by Cense and Uhlenbeck (1958: 7ff.) as a Malay dialect. Linguistic differences within Iban are minimal. Kennedy (1935: 456) cites Hose to the effect that Iban resembles the old Malay spoken in Sumatra before the spread of Islam, and adds that it is widely divergent from other Bornean (Dayak) languages. **Demography.** In Sarawak approximately 238,000, according to the 1960 census. Reliable figures on the Iban population of Kalimantan are lacking. **History and cultural relations.** Iban tradition tells of early migrations into Sarawak from the headwaters of the Kapuas across the border in Indonesian Borneo (cf. Sandin 1967). Kennedy (1935), summarizing earlier reports by Hose and McDougall (1912), Gomes (1911), and Low (1848), calls attention to theories of Sumatran origin, based in part on inferences from linguistic data. The Iban have in historic times spread throughout subcoastal Sarawak in an unending search for agricultural land, much of this being aggressive expansion with warfare, headhunting, and enslavement of women and children. Headhunting and marauding were gradually stopped by the Brooke government; headhunting ceased about 1920, except for a brief resurgence at the end of World War II. In recent years, Iban have become increasingly involved in government-sponsored education, rubber planting schemes, etc., and the Christianized and sophisticated Iban of Saribas show little resemblance to their up-country congeners. [Jensen 1966; Kennedy 1935.]

SETTLEMENT PATTERN AND HOUSING. **Settlement pattern.** Along the tributaries of the upper Rejang, an area of pioneer settlement, a single longhouse, usually named for a founder, constitutes an autonomous local community. These were formerly linked together in diffuse territorial groupings, or "tribes." A longhouse contains on the average 14 doors, i.e. apartment (*bilek*) families, totaling some 85 individuals. The range is from 4 to 50 *bilek*. Although most families in a longhouse are related cognatically, the local community is not a corporate (landowning) group. However, all families are jointly responsible for the ritual state, i.e. the spiritual well-being, of the longhouse community. The prime responsibility in this regard is in the hands of the *tuai burong*, the specialist in augury (principally bird omenology). **Housing.** The raised longhouse along the banks of a stream is characteristic of the Iban under aboriginal conditions. Longhouses may extend up to 1,000 feet, although most are considerably smaller. Individual apartments are walled, and open through a door onto a longitudinal roofed gallery, beyond which is an open platform running the length of the structure. The gallery serves as a village hall and meeting place on ceremonial occasions. Rice is stored in bark bins in an overhead loft. Iban longhouses are not as well built as those of the Kayan. The field house, *dampa*, is a smaller replica of the longhouse. [Freeman 1960: 69; 1970.]

ECONOMY. Subsistence is based primarily on the growing of hill rice, but rubber as a supplementary cash crop is becoming increasingly important. The Iban socioeconomic-religious system depends for its fullest expression on the unlimited availability of virgin rain forest, hence the insatiable appetite for new land and the inexorable expansion over much of Sarawak (Freeman 1970: 276ff.). Within the framework of a mainly subsistence economy, a *bilek* family, as custodian of a corporate estate, attempts to accumulate traditional wealth, e.g. gongs, by producing a surplus of rice for sale or trade or by the custom of young men going off on journeys, *bejalai*, to work for wages. A good portion of any surplus production is expended on religious festivals, which bring both spiritual benefits and social prestige. **Agriculture.** The shifting cultivation of rice is regarded by the Iban as distinctive of their way of life. Rice agriculture is sanctified in myth and lore and is surrounded with ritual, e.g. bird augury. Stellar lore figures prominently in the timing of agriculture pursuits, and there is a strongly developed concept of rice soul, with accompanying ritual and taboos (Jensen 1966). Each *bilek* family constitutes an economic unit, farming its own fields and cooperating with closely related families only during clearing and harvest. Each family maintains its own, named, sacred strain of padi seed and its own sacred whetstone. The latter figures in rites, formerly including human sacrifice, at the start of the annual farming cycle (Freeman 1970: 51). Fields are used for two seasons and then fallowed for 10 to 20 years. Seed rice, the care and selection of which is in the hands of women, is dropped into holes made with a dibble. Cucumbers, pumpkins, and gourds are planted with the rice as catch crops; cassava and maize are grown around the edges of the fields. Glutinous rice, grown in lesser quantities, is used mainly in the production of rice beer, a necessary part of any ritual. With the gradual exhaustion of the land around a longhouse, farms may in time be strung out over several miles of river and distant five or so hours. At this point several closely related *bilek* families customarily join in building a field house, *dampa*, in order to exploit a distant valley. A *dampa* is occupied usually for five to six years, after which the group moves to a new valley. Dispersed farming by individual *dampa* groups continues in this fashion until the land nearer the main longhouse has completed a fallow of 10 to 20 years. The cycle is then begun again, with all families working directly out of the main longhouse. The agricultural year lasts for nine to ten months, so that a family is out in its *dampa* for a good part of the year, returning to the longhouse for two to three months after harvest and intermittently during the rest of the year. [Freeman 1970.] **Fishing and hunting.** Occasional hunting, mainly of wild pigs and deer, using dogs, nets, and traps. Fishing is an important source of food, using traps, nets, and hook and line. Communal tuba fishing is popular. [Kennedy 1935: 458.] **Domestic animals.** Dogs are used in hunting and pigs and chickens for sacrifice. Chickens and chicken eggs figure prominently in religious symbolism and ritual, as do fighting cocks. **Industrial arts.** The Iban are skilled iron workers and weavers and Kennedy (1935) mentions the making of large war canoes. For festive occasions, women wear corsets of rattan hoops strung with small brass beads. The teeth of both sexes may be filed and blackened, and the men prize their extensive body tattoos, although these apparently have little ritual significance (Kennedy 1935: 461). **Property.** Movable property is chiefly in the form of traditional wealth, e.g. gold, bronze gongs, old Chinese jars, weapons, smoked heads, fabrics, beads, and brass cannon. Individual *bilek* families establish ownership of land by clearing virgin jungle. Such land, including that in secondary growth, continues as part of the corporate estate of a family, ceasing to be so only if the family moves out of the longhouse. All forms of movable property are likewise bound up in the corporate estates of individual families. [Freeman 1970: 130ff.]

KINSHIP. Filiation, i.e. membership by birth in a corporate *bilek* family, is utrolateral (ambilateral) in that there is an equal chance that it is the *bilek* of the father or that of the mother but never both at the same time (Freeman 1960: 68). Murdock (1960: 5) prefers to label this situation bilateral. The personal kindred includes an individual's cognatic kin, reckoned vertically to include grandparents and laterally to include second cousins. Most marriages are kindred-endogamous, and there is a strong tendency toward marriage within the longhouse community. Work groups are composed largely of kinsmen drawn from the leader's kindred, although such groups commonly contain affinal relatives as well (Freeman 1960: 73). Leach (1950: 70-71) points out that a core or house-

owning group may maintain an elaborate genealogy which, because of the overlapping of personal kindreds within a longhouse, is common to most of the inhabitants. The genealogy preserved by the core group of leading families thus provides a set of coordinates from which kinship separation is reckoned. Leach calls attention to the Polynesian parallels in this and other features of Iban social structure. **Kin terminology.** The following terms of reference are drawn from Freeman (1960):

GrFa	*aki*
GrMo	*ini*
Fa	*apai*
Mo	*indai*
PaBr	*aya*
PaSi	*ibo*
Sib	*menyadi*
Cousin	*petunggal*
Ch	*anak*
SibSo	*akan*
SibDa	*endo*
GrCh	*ucho*

Cousin terminology is in Murdock's usage Eskimo for terms of reference but Hawaiian for terms of address (Freeman 1960: 162, note 27).

MARRIAGE AND FAMILY. **Mode.** Relatively few restrictions on premarital sex or on choice of a marriage partner. No substantial bride-price or dowry, according to Freeman (1960), although Leach (1950) reports an initial period of bride service and matrilocal residence among some Iban. **Form.** Monogamy, according to Freeman (1970). Kennedy (1935: 464) reports polygyny absolutely forbidden, while according to Leach (1950: 70), it is restricted to men of exceptional wealth. **Marriage rules.** Marriage forbidden between siblings and between close cognatic kin of different generations. Cousin marriage, including that with first cousins, is preferred, and no distinction is made in this respect between cross and parallel cousins. [Freeman 1960.] **Residence.** Ambilocal (Freeman's term is utrolocal). **Domestic unit.** The *bilek* family is customarily a stem family of three generations, averaging six members. As a corporate unit it has ownership rights to its longhouse apartment, *bilek*, as well as to land and heirloom property. As a ritual unit it maintains its own sacred charms, sacred rice strain, ritual formulas and taboos. The perpetuity of its corporate character is ensured by a son or daughter remaining in the ancestral apartment after marriage and succeeding to the *bilek* estate. An inmarrying spouse receives full rights to family membership and participates in the family estate—at the same time relinquishing all such rights in his or her natal family. [Freeman 1960, 1970.] **Inheritance.** Children have equal rights of inheritance so long as they remain members of their natal *bilek* family. Outmarrying siblings receive a minor share of the family estate and thereafter relinquish all further claims. They in turn, however, acquire full inheritance rights to the estate of the family into which they marry. [Freeman 1960: 68-69; 1970: 28ff.] **Divorce and secondary marriage.** Divorce is relatively easy—by mutual consent or, if unilateral, by the payment of a small fine. Divorce beyond the age of 35 is, however, unusual. This is the age at which a man normally comes into control of a *bilek* estate; thereafter a stable marriage, with children, is essential to successful estate management (Freeman 1970). Secondary marriage is rare, especially if the surviving spouse is of middle age (Freeman 1960: 39). **Adoption.** A childless couple customarily adopts the child of a close cognate in order to ensure continuity of the *bilek* as a corporate entity (Freeman 1960: 160).

SOCIOPOLITICAL ORGANIZATION. **Political organization.**

Longhouse communities are independent, autonomous entities, each with a headman, *tuai rumah*, responsible for safeguarding and administering the adat and also nowadays with limited jural powers conferred by government. The position is not rigidly hereditary, in that any male cognate may succeed. Each constituent family within a longhouse is also an independent unit, free to join other longhouses where there are cognatic kin. Within a longhouse, a core group of *bilek* families linked by close cognatic kin ties and descended from ancestral founders [Leach's (1950) house-owning group] occupies adjacent apartments in the center of the structure. The longhouse communities along a major stretch of river were formerly joined by cognatic kin ties into diffuse territorial groupings or "tribes," characterized by endogamy, mutual prohibitions on taking of heads, and mutual settlement of disputes by peaceful means. These "clusters of kindreds" were the Skrang, Lemanak, Ulu Ai, etc. Dayaks of nineteenth-century accounts. There is still an awareness of old tribal divisions and intertribal enmities, particularly in pioneer areas such as the upper Rejang, where availability of virgin forest makes wide dispersal of cognatic kin possible. These tribal groupings were politically unorganized, although influential men, *orang kaya*, have always played quasi-political roles. Nowadays, the Iban live within administrative districts, each in charge of a government-appointed *penghulu*, many of whom are former *orang kaya*. [Freeman 1960: 70ff.; 1970.] **Social control and justice.** Disputes and infractions of adat within the longhouse community come before the headman, *tuai rumah*, who, in company with a panel of elders, judges the affair and imposes fines or other punishments. Major ritual offenses may be punished by expulsion from the community or, in former times, by capital punishment accompanied by the sacrifice of a slave to cleanse the community of ritual pollution (Freeman 1970: 70-71, 109ff.). Kennedy (1935: 464) mentions trial by ordeal (immersion under water by diving experts representing the litigants) and

"liar's heaps" of stones erected to perpetuate a particularly infamous infraction of adat. **Social stratification.** Kennedy (1935: 466) remarks on the relatively undifferentiated society of Ibans as compared with, e.g., Kayans. Nevertheless, attainment of personal and social prestige is a valued goal, symbolized by ownership of heirloom wealth and ability to sponsor major religious festivals. A man normally achieves this status by becoming senior male in a *bilek* household and by subsequent management and manipulation of a *bilek* corporate estate (Freeman 1960: 75ff.). Typically, a man in his younger years goes off seasonally on journeys, *bejalai*, earning personal prestige by virtue of the wealth he brings back to his family and the elaborate tattoos he displays on his body—attainable only while away on a journey. Only after a series of such journeys can a man begin the sponsorship of major festivals, which confers prestige in middle and old age (Freeman 1970: 222ff.). In this connection, Howell (1908-10) mentions that formerly it was necessary that a man participate in successful headhunting expeditions before he was allowed to sponsor the *kenyalang*, or Hornbill Festival, the great ceremony commemorating the capture of enemy heads. Prisoners of war, particularly women and children, formerly became the property of individual *bilek* families. Persons thus enslaved were treated well, though considered socially inferior. Nowadays there is reluctance to marry anyone known to be of slave descent (Freeman 1960: 74). **Warfare.** Formerly there were no mechanisms for settling intertribal disputes, and feuding and headtaking were endemic (Freeman 1970: 111). Weapons of war included iron-pointed spears, blowguns, shields, and war cloaks and helmets decorated with feathers. The Iban have the reputation of having been at one time the most ferocious headhunters in all of Borneo. Warriors were organized into large raiding parties, which often traveled by canoe. Heads were preserved by smoking. Headhunting seems formerly to have been an integral part of the Iban socioreligious system and is woven into the ideology and mythology. Whether it was original with the Iban or fostered by contact with Malays, as Kennedy (1935: 466ff.) implies, is a moot question.

RELIGION. The ritual cultivation of rice is, in Iban eyes, central to their way of life. It is what makes them distinctively Iban. Creation myths recount the sacred origin of the Iban way of life, and lengthy genealogies establish Iban pedigrees, i.e. descent from the god, Sengalang Burong. The spirit world and the world of mortals are intimately linked in delicate equilibrium, and man's duty is to follow the adat, given to man by the gods, in order that this equilibrium may be maintained. The gods take an active interest in the affairs of men; augury, divination, and omenology—the media whereby the counsel and desires of the gods are revealed to mortals—play large roles in the everyday life of Ibans. [Jensen 1966.] **Supernaturals.** The Iban trace their descent to the god, Sengalang Burong, from whom much of the Iban adat is derived. He is manifested to men in the form of the Brahmany kite (a kind of hawk) and is mainly concerned with warfare and headhunting. There is a pantheonlike concept of lesser deities, related to Sengalang Burong, as well as a host of spirits, demons, and culture heroes—all of which figure in myths and stories. Animals and birds are not deified, but are identified with the gods in that the latter express themselves through the behavior and calls of animals and (particularly) omen birds, as well as through dreams. The interaction of man with the supernatural is constant—in dreams, augury, and sacrifices—but culminates in the great religious festivals, e.g. at death or harvest time (Jensen 1966). Central to these festivals are lengthy incantations by ritual experts descriptive of a journey to the territory of the gods and an invitation to them to join the festivities. On these occasions the ritual expert may use as a mnemonic aid a kind of writing board, *papan turai* (cf. Harrisson and Sandin 1966). **Practitioners.** The functions of curer and ritual expert may be combined in one person, who may also be augur and/or headman, although this is rare. The status of *manang*, i.e. curer or shaman, usually held by a male, is divided into various grades marked by apprenticeship and initiation. The highest usually involves transvestite behavior. Curing rites may involve chanting in a special language and dancing to a trance state, during which the *manang* is in communication with his spirit familiar. In this condition, his soul may travel forth in search of the lost soul of the patient (Kennedy 1935). The status of *lemambang*, i.e. ritual expert or priest, may be filled by members of either sex, although males predominate. Ritual experts specialize in learning the lengthy chants and invocations performed at religious festivals, *gawai*. On these occasions the functions of the *lemambang* resemble those of a priest. The augur, *tuai burong*, specializes in bird omenology and is responsible for the ritual status and spiritual well-being of the longhouse. [Jensen 1966; Freeman 1970.] **Ceremonies.** Religious festivals, *gawai*, include (1) incidental small-scale ceremonies usually having to do with illness (2) agricultural ceremonies, the chief of which is *gawai batu*, the Whetstone Festival (3) those ceremonies originally related to headhunting and warfare, the chief of which is *gawai kenyalang*, the Hornbill Festival, and (4) the Festival of the Dead, *gawai antu*. Most festivals are a combination of feasting, drinking, and merrymaking, together with religious ritual. The latter generally includes sacrificial offerings, long chants and invocations, the arrival of invited spirits to participate in the festivities, the ritual drinking of rice beer, the ritual use of old glazed jars, cock fighting, and the ritual sprinkling of the blood of sacrificed chickens. Among the greatest of festivals in former times was the *gawai kenyalang*, the so-called Head Feast, at which captured heads were feted and ritually fed. As part of this ceremony a tall pole was erected at the top of which was placed the carved figure of a Hornbill (*Buceros Rhinoceros*), pointing in the direction of the enemy. [Jensen 1966; Kennedy 1935; Howell 1908-10.] Major religious festivals are commonly cosponsored by several *bilek* families. Planning usually begins two years or so in advance, in order that the necessary rice and other goods can be accumulated. The average Iban family is able to participate in this fashion only once in every eight to ten years, and in fact many poorer families never succeed in accumulating the necessary capital (Freeman 1970: 262). **Soul, death, and afterlife.** According to Freeman (1970: 21), the Iban conceive of a soul, *semengat* (which may at times leave its abode within the mortal body), and also a kind of secondary soul, *ayu*, in the form of a plant growing in company with other *ayu* on a mythical mountain; the health of these plant-souls determines the health of the living. After death, according to Jensen (1966), the soul goes to an abode of the dead, an exact replica of the land of the living. After an indefinite time the soul dissolves into dew, which is taken up in growing rice ears, which eventually are eaten by men, who in turn die, etc. Burial is in a wooden coffin within a community (longhouse) cemetery, accompanied by all the material trappings of the deceased's earthly status; jars and gongs may be broken and left on the surface of the grave. The members of the *bilek* family to which a man belonged at the time of his death are obligated to arrange for proper burial rites, observe the necessary mourning restrictions, and provide for postfunerary rites, including the Festival of the Dead, *gawai antu* (Freeman 1970). Kennedy (1935) reports alternative methods of disposing of the corpse, including occasional platform burial, the placing of shamans in coffins hung in trees, and the occasional burial of children in jars. **Gawai antu.** The Feast of the Dead, an obligatory postfunerary ceremony, may be held a year or more after death at a time when several bereaved families can join together as cosponsors. The *gawai antu* is essentially a communion feast, joining the living with the souls of the dead. The latter are called by the ritual expert and arrive in a spiritual boat (Kennedy 1935). The ritual includes the preparation of a carved wooden hut, *sungkup*, which is placed over the grave (Sandin 1961). The greatest elaboration of *gawai antu* ritual is found among the Saribas River Iban (Jensen 1966).

BIBLIOGRAPHY. Cense and Uhlenbeck 1958; Freeman 1960, 1970; Gomes 1911; Harrisson and Sandin 1966; Hose and McDougall 1912; Howell 1908-10; Jensen 1966; Kennedy 1935; Leach 1950; Low 1848; Murdock 1960; Sandin 1961, 1962, 1967.

KALIMANTAN DAYAKS*

Synonyms. *Dajak, Daya*

THE FORMER Dutch residencies of South Borneo and West Borneo comprise the modern Indonesian provinces of Central Kalimantan (Kalimantan Tengah, abbr. Kalteng) and West Kalimantan (Kalimantan Barat, abbr. Kalbar). The peoples of this southern part of Borneo can be grouped into four categories: (1) *Malays.* A designation for diverse peoples who have only the Islamic religion in common. Included are: (a) Orang Bandjar, i.e. Bandjarese centering in the town of Bandjarmasin and surroundings (b) Malay-speaking coast populations, a mixture of several Dayak groups with Malays from Sumatra, Bugis from Sulawesi (Celebes), Javanese, Arabs, and others. They do not identify as a single group but call themselves after the region where they have settled, e.g. Orang Kotawaringin, Orang Sampit (c) members of small Dayak tribes who have adopted Islam, forming separate communities after their conversion. (2) *Migrants.* Those from other Indonesian islands who have settled in the coastal regions but have not yet mixed with the local population: seafaring Bugis from southern Celebes, active in fishing and trade; Madurese from the island of Madura, agriculturists and traders; Javanese, wet-rice farmers and small traders; Chinese, mostly engaged in trade. (3) *Dayaks.* A collective name for a great many predominantly non-Muslim ethnic and linguistic groups—e.g. Ngadju, Maanyan, Lawangan—who live along the banks of the larger river systems, growing rice on swiddens and collecting forest produce such as rattan, ironwood, rubber, resin, and skins. Settlement is relatively permanent. Dayaks who convert to Islam usually retain their Dayak tongue for some time but refer to themselves as Orang Melayu. Ngadju Dayaks who have taken to Islam, however, call themselves Dayak Islam. The Dutch employed the terms Dayak (Dajak) and Biadju in a generic sense beginning in the mideighteenth century. Dayaks

now accept the designation, except in some parts of West Kalimantan, where Daya is preferred. (4) *Ot.* Ot (Punan) is a generic term for non-Muslim nomads living in the foothills and mountains to the north of Dayak country. Unlike the riverine Dayaks, they live on land in the interior, where they subsist primarily on wild sago and tubers supplemented among some groups by semipermanent dwellings where a part of the tribe grows rice and vegetables. In the forest-clad, hilly regions of the upper Barito, and in the center of Kalimantan, where the big rivers have their source, live an unknown number of Ot (the term more often used in Kalteng) and Punan (the usual word in Kalbar): Ot Balui, Ot Usu, Ot Maruwei, Ot Siau, Punan Kareho, Punan Bungan-Bulit, Melatung, Panjawung, and others. Ot (Punan) peoples do not appear to differ fundamentally in physical appearance from Dayaks; and in regions rich in game, fruit, and sago trees they appear in better physical condition than many Dayaks. • The largest Dayak group in Central Kalimantan province is that of the Ngadju, whose villages lie along the big rivers, from the Barito in the east to the Sampit in the west. They are known by other Dayak groups as "*oloh* ('people') Kahayan." The Kahayan dialect of Ngadju has become the lingua franca throughout the province and is understood even in parts of South Kalimantan and the Melawi region of West Kalimantan. This Kahayan dialect [Hudson's (1967a) Kapuas isolect of Southwest Barito] is locally called Bara-dia, following the Ngadju system of designating dialect differences according to the word for "no" or "not," thus *bara* ("to have") and *dia* ("no"). Other Ngadju dialects with large numbers of speakers include Bara-bare in the Sampit drainage (Hudson's Ba'amang isolect of Southwest Barito) and Bara-djida in the Barito River area (probably Hudson's Bakumpai). The Bakumpai, although they are a Ngadju-speaking people, are usually considered as a distinct ethnic group; they appear to be descended from Ngadju Dayaks who adopted Islam and later intermarried with Bandjarese and other Islamized Dayaks in the Barito River area. The Oloh Bakumpai (as traders, rubber planters, and farmers), together with the Oloh Kahayan (as traders, farmers, teachers, and administrative personnel), have the widest distribution within

*The contributor of this section, J. B. Avé, is Keeper of the Indonesian Department, Rijksmuseum voor Volkenkunde, Leiden. His data are largely from three field trips to southern Kalimantan, 1960-64, during which he undertook anthropological surveys on the Kahayan, Melawi, and Saruyan river systems. Some comparative data on classificatory terminology have been added by the editor.

Kalteng of any Dayak group. The situation on the upper Mentaya River, an area of mixed ethnicity, has been documented by Miles (1965, 1970, 1971). ● The second largest Dayak group in Kalteng is that of the Ot Danum, from *ot* ("upper region," "upstream") and *danum* ("water," "river"), thus "people who live in the upper regions along rivers," i.e. along the headwaters. The term is a generic one, covering a number of named, culturally related subgroups sharing a common origin myth and speaking closely related dialects of a common language (Hudson's Northwest Barito). Ot Danum dialects are mutually intelligible, whereas Ot Danum and Ngadju, although related linguistically, are not. All Ot Danum men and many women, however, can speak Bara-dia Ngadju. Ot Danum speakers are found along the headwaters of the large rivers of Kalteng, from the Murung in the east to the Saruyan in the west; a smaller number live in the upper Melawi region of West Kalimantan. According to tradition, the Ot Danum were originally four subgroups: Dohoi, Pananjoi, Tabahoi, and Siang. The Pananjoi apparently no longer exist as such; the Tabahoi are found nowadays in a few villages on the affluents of the upper Melawi; the Siang, on the upper Barito, are the largest Dayak tribe in that area. They occupy a distinct position within the Ot Danum group by virtue of their atypical origin as recounted in the creation myth and the fact that they speak a relatively aberrant dialect of Ot Danum. The Dahoi, numerically the largest of all Ot Danum subgroups, are also the most widely dispersed; they are scattered throughout all the Ot Danum areas—e.g. mixed with Tabahoi on the upper Melawi—and also living in ethnically mixed communities with other Dayaks, e.g. on the upper Mentaya. Smaller groups of Ot Danum speakers, e.g. Sahije, Sabaung, and Ela, have most likely split off in the past from one or another of the four major subgroups. The Ot Danum are regarded by the Ngadju as their cultural forebears; Ngadju *damangs* commonly defer to Ot Danum *damangs* in matters of cultural origins. ● Other Dayak groups in Kalteng include the relatively well-known Maanyan and Lawangan in the middle Barito region. The little-known Tundjung, living along the eastern affluents of the upper Barito between the Barito and Mahakam river drainages,

are probably to be classed linguistically with groups from the lower and middle Mahakam basin —from whence the Kalteng Tundjung came and where the majority of these people still live. The terms Dusun and Murung, sometimes used in the literature as names of specific ethnic (Dayak) groups in the Barito drainage, are simply geographical designations referring to peoples of the *dusun* (middle and lower) or *murung* (upper) regions. Farther west, in the middle Sampit (Mentaya) area and beyond to the Lamandau and Arut rivers in the Kotawaringin area, are numerous lesser-known groups, e.g. Tamuan, Lamandau, Arut, Delang. Some of these, e.g. Tamuan, appear to be basically Dayak but speak strongly Malayanized languages—probably a reflection of the historically pervasive Malay influence characteristic of much of West Kalimantan. It is not clear whether the Mamah Darat mentioned by H. Mallinckrodt (1924: 128) is a collective name for Dayaks of Kotawaringin Barat or the name of a specific group. ● The ethnic picture in the province of West Kalimantan differs considerably from that in Central Kalimantan as described above. This is a result largely of differing historical influences having to do with the opening up of the interior to trade under the Dutch and of the relatively greater role of Malays as traders and colonizers in Kalimantan Barat. Malays and Chinese are found today far in the interior, usually in the role of traders, and often living in ethnically mixed communities with Dayaks. The latter, with the exception of the Ot Danum in the upper Melawi and the Iban in the Lake Region and the Embaluh and Palin river basins, exist nowadays as small, scattered communities—ill-defined ethnically and with confused and fragmented historical traditions. They are known in much of the literature under the generic term Klamantan or Land Dayak. Many Dayak groups have partially or wholly converted to Islam; some, e.g. the Kebahan of the lower and middle Melawi, exist as distinct groups not reckoned among Malays. Dayak languages in this province tend to be heavily Malayanized and the lingua franca is Malay, which, mixed with Dayak words, is called "Malayu Ulu" (Upriver Malay). Hudson (1970) questions the assumption of a "Land Dayak" language and culture type for all or most of West Kalimantan.

In a recently-completed linguistic survey of Borneo, he found groups of non-Muslim, partly longhouse-dwelling, swidden agriculturists—inhabiting an area from Pontianak south to the Java Sea—speaking languages closely similar to Malay, but exhibiting none of the features characteristic of classic Malay culture. Furthermore, these groups do not appear particularly close to Land Dayaks either linguistically or culturally. Hudson proposes the term "Malayic Dayak" for these languages, and suggests that Malayic Dayak speakers, together with Ibans, represent a category similar to that of "aboriginal Malays" on the Malay Peninsula—people whose Malay-speaking ancestors arrived on Borneo prior to the spread of Islam in Southeast Asia. Thus the commonly-held view of the Malay element in the languages of West Kalimantan as due to (relatively recent) "Malayanization" of essentially Dayak, e.g. Land Dayak, type languages will apparently have to be revised.

BIBLIOGRAPHY. Hudson 1967a, 1970; H. Mallinckrodt 1924; Miles 1965, 1970, 1971.

NGADJU

Synonyms. *Biadju, Oloh Kahayan*

ORIENTATION. Kennedy (1935) provisionally classified a great many of the riverine non-Muslim Dayak peoples of southern Kalimantan within one cultural complex, which he called Ngadju. The complex as defined by Kennedy extends from east of the Barito drainage westward all the way to Kotawaringin, and from the limit of the southern (Bandjarese) coastal lands north to the Mahakam Valley and the Melawi—an area roughly between 111°30′–115°30′ E. and 0°30′–3°30′ S. Within his Ngadju complex, Kennedy distinguished the following tribal and subtribal categories: (1) Ngadju, including Biadju, Kahayan, Katingan, Tamoan, Saruyan, and Kotawaringin (2) Maanyan, including Siong and Patai (3) Lawangan, including Lawangan proper, Dusun, Tabuyan, and Bukit, and (4) Ot Danum, including Ot Danum proper, Murung, Siang, and Taman. The four "tribal groups," Ngadju, Maanyan, Lawangan, and Ot Danum, were also recognized by J. Mallinckrodt (1928); like Kennedy, he sensed an essential similarity in language and culture among these peoples and classed them together as a single complex. Kennedy's Ngadju complex is approximately equivalent to Hudson's Barito language family with respect to both ethnic composition and geographic extent. (Hudson would limit the westward extension of Barito languages to the Sampit, whereas both Kennedy and Mallinckrodt would place them farther to the west—into a transitional area with Land Dayak languages and cultures.) Hudson (1967a) classifies his Barito isolects into four major subgroups (Northwest, Northeast, Southwest, and Southeast) largely equivalent, respectively, to the Ot Danum, Lawangan, Ngadju, and Maanyan of Kennedy and Mallinckrodt. Schärer's great work (1963) on the Ngadju Dayak restricts the use of this term to people living on the lower and middle reaches of the Barito, Kapuas, Kahayan, and Katingan, although the traditional Ngadju tribal area is the Kahayan River, from whence they have spread out to become the most numerous and the economically, politically, and culturally dominant people in southern Kalimantan. Since Ngadju appears in the literature in both a generic and a specific sense, it seems best, following Hudson, to adopt the term Barito complex for the various peoples Kennedy designated under the term Ngadju, reserving the latter for speakers of Bahasa Ngadju (Hudson's Southwest Barito). The Barito tribal complex extends northward to the Mahakam and upper Kapuas river systems, where lies a transitional area between the Barito culture type and peoples of the Kenyah-Kayan-Kajang complex. This mountainous area (the Schwaner-Müller ranges of central Borneo) is one of great ethnic and linguistic complexity, containing a mosaic of Ot Danum languages and Kayan-related languages (Uma Suling, Pnihing, Long Glat, etc.), as well as forest nomads (Ot, Punan) who speak dialects evidently related to Kenyah but heavily influenced by neighboring contact languages (Kennedy 1935: 391ff.; Cense and Uhlenbeck: 1958). Westward, the Barito culture type extends to the Saruyan River system and somewhat beyond; Ot Danum speakers along the upper tributaries of the Saruyan, Mentaya, and Melawi, on both sides of the Schwaner Range, mark its farthest northwest extension. This is the boundary area between Central Kalimantan and the province of West Kalimantan, the latter inhabited primarily by Malays and Malays mixed with so-called Land Dayak tribes. Kennedy noted that his Ngadju seem culturally more similar to Land Dayaks than to Kenyahs and Kayans. Kennedy (1935) presented a summary of generalized culture traits for his Ngadju complex, drawing chiefly on the observations of Grabowsky (1884, 1889a, 1889b, 1907, 1908), J. Mallinckrodt (1924-25, 1925a, 1925b, 1925c, 1926, 1927, 1928) and Lumholtz (1920).

SETTLEMENT AND HOUSING. Two- or three-family dwellings on piles common. Longhouses generally rare or absent, except among the Ot Danum. Villages in the Barito Valley area characterized by a central community house, used for meetings and ceremonial festivals.

ECONOMY. Main reliance on cultivation of dry rice and a few vegetables in swiddens. Degree of permanency variable. Shifting cultivators likely to have permanent residential centers, to which they return periodically for ritual purposes. Fishing relatively important, hunting less so; the latter with dogs and lances for wild pigs; blowpipe the traditional weapon for small game. Industrial arts include plaiting and basketry (important as trade items); iron working; pottery; weaving (Ot Danum, like Kenyah, have separate structures where women weave); canoe making (esp. Maanyan); tattooing; wood carving and decorative arts relatively highly developed.

SOCIAL ORGANIZATION. Descent and inheritance bilateral, with preference for initial matrilocal residence. Marriage usually with member of same social unit and permitted with all but close relatives. The "tribe" divided into (1) subtribes, *tampara, paong, utus* (2) smaller bilateral, nonexogamous units, *umang, sawirit, saderah, tambak, pandam, humputan, ungkup,* inhabiting a single village or section of a village (3) extended families, *bubuhan, panakan,* generally including fourth-generation descendants of a common great-grandfather (4) biological family, *kabali.* Marriage usually endogamous within (1) and (2) and exogamous with respect to (3) and (4).

POLITICAL ORGANIZATION. Maximum political integration at the level of the subtribe, in many instances not extending beyond the village level. Only among the Lawangan and Kotawaringin has there been a development of paramount chiefs. Generally a distinction between freemen and slaves, but only the Ot Danum have a developed social hierarchy, probably due to Kayan-Kenyah influence. Headhunting, except among the Ot Danum, apparently never developed to the extent that it did among Kayans and Kenyahs. The recent custom of killing slaves at death rites for chiefs may be associated with former headhunting practices. Sword blades and wooden shields generally of Kayan-Kenyah pattern; warriors formerly wore protective, poncholike cloaks of bark cloth padded with kapok or covered with overlapping bone plates.

RELIGION. Generally a supreme god of the upper world (male) and one of the under world (female). Numerous spirits, good and bad, acknowledge their own radjas or lords. Priests and/or priestesses speak in esoteric spirit language while possessed by spirits; they function at funerary rites and specialize in long death chants leading the soul of the deceased to the spirit world. Their ritual behavior on these occasions may include a strongly sexual content. Omenology, so important among the Kayan-Kenyah peoples, is less in evidence among Ngadjus. Head cults and the use of masks in religious ritual, likewise important among Kayans and Kenyahs, are either unimportant or altogether absent among some Ngadju groups. Ancient glazed jars of probable Chinese origin considered as sacred property and as possessing a spiritual power.

DEATH. Primary burial in wooden coffin, kept either above or below ground for periods ranging up to several years. Secondary burial rites include removal of remains from coffin and deposition within a raised tomb or on a platform. Some groups cremate remains before final disposition. Secondary mortuary rites tend to be long and elaborate, involving rituals conducted in a community meeting house, animal sacrifice and smearing of participants with blood, lengthy chants by priests and priestesses, and erection of large wooden memorial images. Details of rituals vary greatly among groups, but overall pattern is similar. Tattooing and tooth filing for both sexes among most groups, although latter may be optional. The penis bar, *palang,* is found only among the Katingan, who also (along with Ot Danum) practice male supercision.

BIBLIOGRAPHY. Cense and Uhlenbeck 1958; Grabowsky 1884, 1889a, 1889b, 1907, 1908; Hudson 1967a; Kennedy 1935; Lumholtz 1920; J. Mallinckrodt 1924-25, 1925a, 1925b, 1925c, 1926, 1927, 1928; Schärer 1963.

*MAANYAN DAYAKS**

ORIENTATION. Maanyan Dayaks are located in a fairly restricted area centering in the drainage of the Patai River, a tributary of the Barito some 90 miles north of Bandjarmasin. From here emigré villages have spread northward into Lawangan territory. According to legend, the Maanyan people emerged as a distinct ethnic group some centuries ago; their legendary homeland was in the Ulu Sungai district of what is now South Kalimantan. Here they inhabited a single village and followed a single adat, which included mass lustration (burning) of the bones of the dead. Outside incursions forced the breakup of traditional society into four subgroups, which eventually migrated to their present location. Each subgroup now consists of a number of villages occupying a specific territory along a stream or within a drainage area. Each is named, e.g. Padju Epat ("Four Villages"), and each constitutes a traditional, self-conscious adat area. The subgroups differ among themselves chiefly with regard to treatment of the remains of the dead; Padju Epat death rites culminate in cremation of the bones, whereas those of the other subgroups do not. The Maanyan total about 35,000. As a whole they share a common language, a common historical tradition, and a common adat. There is no indication that

*This summary has been compiled by the editor from the publications of A. B. Hudson, chiefly (1966) and (1967b).

188

indigenous political structure extended beyond the village level; ritual and kinship ties do, however, link the villages within the territory of the subgroup.

SETTLEMENT AND HOUSING. **Settlement: the residential nucleus.** The true village, *tumpak*, is a residential nucleus consisting of a number of houses laid out along a street parallel to a river. Padju Epat *tumpak* range between 35 and 600 or so inhabitants, with an average of about 200. Each has its traditional land area (from 17-38 square miles), as well as its own headman, adat head, and adjudicating elders. Each is a politically independent unit. Specialized village structures include a raised, open-sided, shingle-roofed, meeting hall, *balai*, used for litigation and death rites. Just outside the main entrance to the village are tall wooden posts surmounted by carved human figures—the homes of village guardian spirits. Outside the village is a cemetery for primary burials; a cremation site, *papuian*, consisting of a pile-supported scaffolding on a mound of earth; and a "*tambak* graveyard" for secondary burial of cremated bones of the dead. These secondary burial sites contain from one to eight or more *tambak*, lidded ironwood caskets raised on posts and in some cases decorated with carved buffalo heads; each is named and is associated with a particular bilineal descent group. **Settlement: extra-village settlement.** Each nuclear (or stem) family within the village has its own swidden plot(s) and field house, *dangau*. Families tend to spend more time in *dangau* residence on swiddens, coming into the home village mainly for special and ritual occasions. Those villagers who farm at a distance from the village tend to cluster in swidden hamlets, *bantai*. These may resemble ephemeral villages, with substantially built *dangau* and ceremonial structures; however, they lack the guardian spirits, the carved wooden guardian images, and the ancestral spirit houses that characterize the true *tumpak* village. *Bantai* do not normally continue in existence for more than a few years, although it is possible for a *bantai* to achieve *tumpak* status through the medium of a costly ceremony. **Housing.** True longhouses are absent and were probably never characteristic of the Barito area except in the north among Siang and Murung (Ot Danum) peoples. Permanent houses in the nuclear *tumpak* villages are called *lewu*. These are of substantial construction, raised on piles, with plank walls and floors. *Lewu* houses nowadays accommodate from one to several related nuclear families; evidently these households were larger in former times (up to 25 or so people) and the houses themselves were larger and raised high (up to 20 feet) on massive ironwood posts.

ECONOMY. Subsistence is mainly based on agriculture, supplemented by seasonal fishing in rivers. Hunting, traditionally done with dogs and blowpipes, is unimportant nowadays. Cash crops include fruit, rubber, and lumber, and fruit constitutes an important part of the diet. Market centers link Maanyan villages with one another and with larger centers on the Barito. The Maanyan are noted for production of dugout canoes, which are traded downriver to Bandjarmasin. **Agriculture.** Rice is grown on swiddens, which may be located up to ten miles from the village. Swiddens are planted to rice the first season or so, then to cassava, sugarcane, bananas, peppers, eggplant, squash, etc. Rubber and fruit trees may be planted in swiddens and allowed to grow during fallowing; they are not felled when the land is cleared again for agricultural use. Field houses may be substantial, designed for extended occupation. **Wealth.** Currency is now in form of Dutch and Indonesian coinage; Chinese porcelain plates formerly served as a medium of exchange, e.g. in the payment of ritual fines. Gongs of varying sizes and age formerly figured in the economic exchange system and heirloom gongs are important descent group property, thought to have purifying and protective properties. Old gongs, jars, plates, and weapons must be present for the proper performance of most religious rituals. **Property.** The *dangau* family may hold heirloom property in trust for larger descent groups, and each also owns and perpetuates a strain of sacred padi, the abode of the rice spirit. Ambilineal descent groups, *bumah*, perpetuate usufructory rights in village-owned land.

MARRIAGE. **Mode.** Sex is considered dangerous unless a couple has received proper ritual protection—which can be obtained only through the marriage ceremony. Marriages are usually arranged by parents, although elopement is more frequent now than formerly. There is a formal betrothal ceremony, attended by the full *lewu* family descent groups of both partners. The actual marriage ceremony is usually accompanied by payment of a bride-price, consisting of money, gongs, and other heirloom goods. There is a high degree of village and regional endogamy. As a result, everyone in a village is likely to be related by affinal or consanguineal kin ties. **Residence.** Traditionally, marriage commences with a five-year period of uxorilocal residence, though this period of "bride service" can be shortened by payment of a graduated series of fines. Ultimate postmarital residence is ambilocal. Choice of ultimate residence is important, because it establishes for both partners primary membership with a particular *lewu* family as well as the *tambak* group of that family, and with all other descent groups of which that family is a segment. Descent group affiliations, in turn, determine access to primary land use and heirloom property rights. **Extension of incest taboos.** The maximal kindred includes bilaterally-related relatives within the range of fourth ascending and fourth descending generations, as well as cousins reckoned to the third degree. In practice, the activation of kin ties includes affines, and the active kindreds of household members tend to overlap. Kindred come together on the occasion of life cycle ceremonies of members and also for cooperative work projects. There are relatively few kin-based restrictions on marriage. Intergenerational marriage is generally proscribed, but can occur with the payment of a fine. Cousin marriage is usually preferred. Almost a third of Padju Epat marriages are kindred-endogamous. Descent groups, i.e. *lewu*, *bumah*, and *tambak*, are all agamous with respect to marriage. **Household.** The permanent village house, *lewu*, is inhabited by an extended family unit consisting of several related nuclear families, each economically independent of the others and each owning a *dangau* field house. *Lewu* households average about 8 members nowadays, but were formerly larger, averaging around 25 members. The *dangau* family, with a median of 4 members, is the primary production and consumption unit. Neighboring *dangau* families engage in cooperative work sessions on swiddens. Families also sponsor life cycle ceremonies for members, usually held in the village house, *lewu*, of the sponsoring *dangau* family. **Polygyny.** Limited to about 4 percent in Padju Epat. Tends to be virilocal, with either separate or joint residence for wives. **Divorce.** Fairly easy and relatively common, occurring in 25 percent of Padju Epat marriages. Most frequent cause is incompatibility.

KIN GROUPS. **Descent.** Bilineal (bilateral). **Kin groups.** (1) The *bumah* is an agamous, bilineal (ambilineal), descent group, consisting of members of a given line of descent from one or another of eight pairs of great-great-grandparents. The total of these lines equals an individual's total kindred. Individuals choose to activate one or another of these lines according to circumstances. The latter are chiefly concerned with differential inheritance rights to descent group estates, consisting of land-use rights, trees, houses, and heirloom property. In each succeeding generation, one member functions as custodian of this estate. This status is passed on within *lewu* households, so that in time these form a distinct descent line, *tutur*, within the larger *bumah*. Heirloom property (old gongs, jars, weapons, etc.) are a most important factor in status differentiation among various *bumah*; some have achieved a name, along with associated wealth and fame; others have not. The importance of descent groups in controlling property is, however, lessening as a result of new economic pressures and the decline of indigenous religious ritual. (2) The *tambak* group consists of the bilineal descendants of a founder of a *tambak* (ash receptacle, last resting place for ashes of the dead). Before marriage an individual belongs to the *tambak* group of his natal *dangau* family. After marriage, depending on residence, he may affiliate with that of his spouse or retain his natal *tambak* membership. Padju Epat had 22 such groups in 1963.

Each group is associated with a particular home village and permanent residential house, *lewu*, although members may actually live in several villages. The home village household serves as the locus of the descent line, *tutur*, of the successive custodians of *tambak* heirloom property. There is evidence that *tambak* groups were formerly associated with a stratified class system. (3) The *lewu* household descent group includes those bilineal descendants of the founder of a village house, *lewu*, who maintain affiliation with their natal household after marriage, plus their in-marrying spouses. A residential household unit contains one or more constituent *dangau* nuclear families who are economically independent but co-owners of the village house and of heirloom property, and who observe common food taboos and on occasion act as a ritual unit. Every *lewu* household is a member of the *tambak* group of its founder. An individual's ultimate kin group affiliation and access to property rights are determined at marriage, whereby an in-marrying spouse acquires membership in the *lewu* household descent group of his partner. Segmentation of a household descent group can occur through splitting off of component *dangau* families. However, daughter households continue to come together at annual postharvest feeding of the ancestral spirits resident in the rafters of the home village *lewu*. **Kin terminology.** Kin terms of reference approximate, in Murdock's terms, a lineal-Eskimo system, terms of address a generational-Hawaiian system. Following are terms of reference for Padju Epat:

PaFa	*kakah*
PaMo	*nini*
Fa	*amah*
Mo	*ineh*
PaBr	*mama*
PaSi	*tutu*
ElSib	*tata*
YoSib	*ani*
Cousin	*tuwari* (also sp. term for sib. and 1st cousin and for second and third cousin)
Ch, SibCh	*ia*
SibCh	*aken*
ChCh	*umpu*

Teknonymy is practiced with reference to the parents of a first child, and to their status later as grandparents of a child of a first child.

SOCIOPOLITICAL ORGANIZATION. **Political.** Nowadays village functionaries include a headman, his assistant, a secretary, swidden manager, adat head, etc., mostly created by the Dutch. Traditionally, each village had a single head, *patis* or *damang*, who combined the functions of adat judge and village chief. These positions were elective, with a tendency to be confined within certain family lines in patrilineal succession. Such families had to be of "good" or "noble" stock. **Social differentiation.** There is some evidence for the existence in former times of four classes: "nobles," *bangsawan*; "warriors," *panglima*; "common people," *panganak rama*; and "slaves" or "clients," *walah*. Each *tambak* (ossuary) is said to have been associated with one of these; and the *tambaks* in a "graveyard" are arranged in rank order, with those of higher class upstream, lower class downstream. Hudson concludes that formerly there was probably a "free class," i.e. nobles and warriors, on the one hand and a slave class on the other. Positions of political authority were within noble family lines, although not all nobles were leaders and not all *panglima* were actual warriors. The "commoner" sector was most likely made up of those members of noble and warrior *tambak* groups genealogically removed from the family line of the founder of the group. "Slaves" were debtors and prisoners of war and their descendants—as clients or dependents of free class patron families. Slaves were given secondary funerary rites, but their ashes could not be interred in free class *tambak*; rather, they were put in large earthen jars. Nowadays class distinctions are still present beneath the surface although rapidly disappearing. **Social control and justice.** The traditional adat specifies graded series of fines for transgressions of property rights and violations of custom. These were formerly paid in Chinese porcelain plates (nowadays in money), accompanied by the slaughter of one or more animals. The payment of ritual fines and the ritual sprinkling of blood restores the social and spiritual imbalance of the community caused by breaking of adat. Adjudicating elders, *mantir*, with a head, *pangulu*, hear arguments on both sides and arrive at a decision. There is now in addition a district adat head, *damang*, to whom cases can be appealed. An ultimate threat is social excommunication from the adat community. **Warfare.** There is some evidence in the religious ritual of former headhunting, but this practice, along with warfare, evidently ceased early in the nineteenth century. It is difficult to say how important or how widespread either was in pre-Dutch times.

RELIGION. Padju Epat Maanyan are 78 percent Kaharingan (native animist), 18 percent Christian, and 3 percent Muslim. Kaharingan is an animistic belief system with associated rituals designed to maintain harmonious relations with ancestral spirits and with spirits of trees, plants, animals, etc. Rituals include spirit propitiation and village welfare ceremonies, agricultural ceremonies, curing rites, and life cycle ceremonies, the most important of which is a nine-day death ritual, culminating in *idjambe*. **Practitioners.** Shamans (*wadian*, corresponding to the more general term, *balian*) are of seven types, six female and one male. Each type has its characteristic spirits and specialized ritual. Shamans must be susceptible to spirit possession and trance states, must be expert dancers, and must be capable of memorizing countless chants. They function as healers, as priests at funerary rites, and also as specialists in the recitation of creation myths, traditional histories, and genealogies of great families. They are a source of entertainment as dancers but do not function as prostitutes. **Concept of the soul.** The body is inhabited by a life-giving spirit which can depart during sickness. Shamans conduct curing rites, during which they attempt to recover the wandering spirit. The spirit of a deceased person remains in the vicinity until it is guided to the afterworld during secondary burial rites, *idjambe*. Some spirits of the dead return from the afterworld as *nanju*. A *nanju* returns to its former earthly abode, i.e. the village house, *lewu*, where it lives in the rafters and protects the members of its former household. These ancestral spirits must be fed during annual postharvest ceremonies. An out-marrying member of a household feeds the spirits of the family into which he marries.

DEATH. **Primary burial.** Among the Padju Epat Maanyan, primary burial occurs as soon after death as possible, usually as soon as a suitable coffin can be made. The latter is constructed of a hollowed-out log, boat-shaped and fitted with a lid. The coffin, with the corpse inside, is sealed with resin and buried in the village graveyard; it is placed either in a simple grave with a framework of sticks over it or in a box grave surmounted with a more elaborate houselike structure. The latter procedure, reserved nowadays for persons of high socioeconomic status, involves fitting a jar to a hole in the bottom of a box in such a way that the jar can later be released without disturbing the grave. The box, with attached jar, is lowered into the grave with the jar hanging suspended over a pit in the bottom of the grave. The coffin, with a hole in its bottom, is then lowered inside the box and positioned in such a way that the bottom opening rests over the neck of the jar—thus allowing the body fluids to drain into the jar during decomposition and dessication. This arrangement appears to be a modern adaptation of an earlier custom outlawed by the Dutch for health reasons. Formerly a deceased member of the noble or aristocratic class was sealed within a coffin fitted with a bamboo drain and jar. The coffin, thus equipped for the collection of body fluids, was kept within the house until the secondary mortuary rite, *idjambe*— often for a period of a year or more. **Postburial rites.** The necessity of collecting the body fluids of the decomposing corpse appears to be associated with *ngiler*, a postburial ceremony held 49 days after death. In the case of aristocrats of the noble class, this ceremony assumes large proportions, with as many as 300 or more guests and the preparation of much rice beer and the assembling of many animals for ritual slaughter and for food. The two- or three-day ceremony includes ritualized drinking of rice beer and formal speeches by specialists in clever and humorous oratory—with male and female speakers alternating in lauding and deprecating the deceased. Food and personal goods for the deceased are deposited on the grave, and the jar, with fluids of bodily decomposition, is released so that it falls to the bottom of the pit beneath the coffin. [Formerly, the contents of this jar were inspected by a village elder. See Roth (1896: *1*, 163) for translation of an 1877 account of this custom by Tromp, who said that if inspection revealed "too much matter in the jar, a punishment is imposed, as the relatives have not done their duty." This reference to "duty" may be to prescribed behavior of near relatives during the mourning period and its importance for community welfare.] **Mourning.** Near-relatives are expected to go into mourning for a period of 49 days following death. They must all observe a variety of food restrictions, and one of them, usually an old person, goes into voluntary seclusion for the seven days following death. These first seven days, especially, constitute a period of ritual danger for the entire village, and various behavioral and food taboos apply to some or all villagers during the mourning period. [It appears that the postburial rite, *ngiler*, held 49 days after death, may mark the end of the mourning period and the observation of prescribed behaviors by relatives on behalf of the village. If the relatives have not "done their duty" vis-à-vis the community, i.e. if they have neglected proper observance of food taboos, etc., a "punishment" is imposed on them on behalf of the community.] **Secondary death rites.** Among the Padju Epat subgroup of Maanyan, the final rites for the dead include a cremation ceremony, *idjambe*. This is held by a village in cooperation with its daughter emigré villages when accumulated burials (i.e. corpses, *mayat*) reach an optimum number of around 200. To conduct a ceremony with anything less than this number imposes too great an economic burden on the sponsors, i.e. those families having corpses for *idjambe*. Emigré villages bring their accumulated dead back to the home village for cremation. The main stages in this nine-day ceremony are: (1) Assembling the *idaran*, a structure made of carved and painted (writing?) boards resembling a barge, on which are stacked newly-made, boat-shaped coffins containing the exhumed and cleaned bones of corpses to be cremated. Each coffin holds the remains of those corpses belonging to a single *tambak* group. If the oldest and highest ranking corpse in a coffin is male, a carved *naga* (serpent head) is attached to it; if female, a *garuda* (bird head). The *idaran* is constructed within the village meeting house, *balai*, on a specially prepared floor made by lashing together thin poles laid side by side. With the completion of the *idaran*, the souls of the dead are ready to begin their final journey to the afterworld. (2) Sacrifice of a water buffalo (formerly one for each *tambak* group involved). The animal is tied to a post outside the *balai* and is cere-

monially killed by men with repeated thrusts of their spears. Evidence for the relation of this custom to former human sacrifice is conflicting. (3) Cremation is carried out on the *papuian*, a ceremonial structure some distance from the village, consisting of a platform and scaffolding of ironwood especially fireproofed for the occasion. A platform, *lansaran*, is constructed adjoining the *papuian*, to hold the coffins. These are placed a few at a time on the *papuian*, ends up, and burned. The members of *tambak* groups burn the coffins of their own dead, collect the ashes and bones, and transport them in large gongs to their respective *tambaks*. These are ossuaries located in a special area outside the village and made in the form of lidded ironwood boxes raised on posts. They are decorated and carved with buffalo heads and other designs and opened only on the occasion of *idjambe*. The ritual pattern during the nine-day *idjambe* ceremony includes: advance brewing of large quantities of rice beer and assembling of scores of pigs and chickens for blood sacrifice; ritual (competitive) rice beer drinking and ritual (paired) oratory; beating of large gongs; ritual cockfights, with each bird representing a particular *tambak* group; participation of *wadian* (female shamans) in preparation of special food for souls of the dead, in animal sacrifice, and in chanting—the latter lasting through most nights of the ceremony; and the seven-stepped ladder as a symbol of entry and exit of souls of the dead. **Postcremation ceremonies.** Seven days after *idjambe*, the sponsoring *tambak* groups hold a ceremony severing the last ties with their dead. This act is symbolized by cutting and destroying with knives various parts of the *papuian* and *balai*, including the seven-stepped ladder. The ceremony includes the ritual use of a piece of human skull and a war shield, as well as traditional war dances and songs. Associated with this ceremony is a mock battle between "attackers" and "defenders" of the *balai*. There is some evidence that in former times each *tambak* group was expected to furnish a fresh head for this ceremony.

BIBLIOGRAPHY. Hudson 1966, 1967b; Roth 1896.

OT DANUM DAYAKS*

ORIENTATION. Ot Danum, from *ot* ("upper region") and *danum* ("river"), thus "people who live in the upper regions along rivers," is a generic term, covering a number of named culturally related subgroups sharing a common origin myth and speaking closely related dialects of a common language. Four major

---

*The contributor of this section, J. B. Avé, is Keeper of the Indonesian Department, Rijksmuseum voor Volkenkunde, Leiden. His data are from anthropological surveys on the Kahayan, Melawi, and Saruyan rivers in 1960-64.

(traditional) subgroups, Dohoi, Tabahoi, Pananjoi, and Siang, occupy an uninterrupted 180-mile-long belt, stretching from the upper Melawi in the modern Indonesian province of West Kalimantan through the upper Barito in Central Kalimantan, at roughly 0°–1° S. The Ot Danum total about 30,000, of whom some 8,000 live in West Kalimantan. A common origin myth tells the story of two brothers and two sisters who descended from the skies on a golden *palangka* (altar). The brothers came down in the headwaters of the Kahayan, the sisters in the upper Barito region. While hunting, the brothers saw tracks of human beings. They traced these over the entire upriver region of what is now Central Kalimantan and finally met the sisters on the upper Barito. Here they married. The younger brother married the younger sister and stayed in the Barito basin, this couple becoming the forebears of the Siang. The elder couple went to live in the headwaters of the Kahayan, where they became the ancestors of the Dohoi, Tabahoi, and Pananjoi. Ngadju Dayaks regard the Ot Danum as their cultural forebears, and the Ot Danum themselves remember the migration of their ancestors, who, coming from the upper Ambalau (Ot Danum: Mambaru), crossed the mountains and settled along the upper Kahayan, later descending to its mouth. This would confirm Ngadju tales and genealogies of culture heroes coming from the Kahayan river basin. Genetic relationship is also evident in the languages, although Ngadju and Ot Danum are mutually unintelligible.

SETTLEMENT PATTERN AND HOUSING.

Villages average 100 to 400 inhabitants. The traditional house is a rectangular longhouse, *betang*, raised 6 to 15 feet above the ground on ironwood posts. A gallery runs the entire length of the front of the building (facing the river), with the entrance in the middle. Rooms for families and unmarried youths are situated on the inner side of the gallery. Longhouses are seldom erected nowadays; in Central Kalimantan, especially, they are being replaced by dwellings designed for from one to six families. The *repau umo* —the house on the swiddens where the nuclear family spends a large part of the year—is a less elaborate structure. Granaries are rarely seen; in general, each house has large bark containers in which rice is stored.

ECONOMY.

Swidden agriculture is the primary means of subsistence, with rice the staple crop. Cassava, taro, maize, sweet potatoes, and vegetables are also grown. Fishing and hunting are pursued throughout the year, and fishing, especially, is an important source of food. Gathering of forest products for sale is an important activity between agricultural cycles. Whole families participate in panning for gold. **Domestic animals.** Dogs, pigs, and chickens. In a few villages, cows are kept for consumption at major celebrations. Water buffalo are herded in distant hamlets, because they easily turn wild and would be dangerous to villagers. **Industrial arts.** Agricultural and hunting implements are forged locally, using the double piston bellows. In earlier times, native iron ore was extracted in some localities. The Ot Danum are known throughout Central Kalimantan for the quality of their plaited rattan hats, baskets, and mats. Clothing was formerly woven from native fibers or made from bark. **Trade.** Items traded to the outside include rattan artifacts, canoes, and forest products. Itinerant traders visit the villages periodically; goods may also be taken to market centers located on major rivers just below the lowest rapids. **Property.** Land around a village within a radius of two miles is the property of the village. Each villager has the right of disposal over his share, which he may sell to a fellow villager but not to an outsider. Land that has lain fallow (for anywhere from 5 to 15 years, depending on the scarcity of land locally) may be claimed by anyone.

KINSHIP.

Descent. Bilateral. **Kin terminology.** For certain family relationships there are two terms, a general term used by others and a term of address used for the relative in question by his closest kin:

GrPa	*tatu*
Fa	*amai*
Mo	*inai*
FaBr, MoBr	*mama*
FaSi, MoSi	*mina*
ElBr, ElSi	*oka*
YoBr, YoSi	*ari*
Cousin	*akon*
Ch	*anak*
GrCh	*osu*

MARRIAGE AND FAMILY.

Mode. When agreement has been reached between the couple's parents, the man's group makes a symbolic gift, followed by another gift when the intended marriage is announced. When the marriage takes place another gift, the bride-price, is given. The costs of the wedding feast are borne by the family of the bride. **Form.** Monogamy, with limited polygyny. **Extension of incest taboos.** Cousins are preferred, but marriages between patri-parallel first cousins and between different generations are prohibited. **Residence.** At present, couples make an effort to have their own houses after marriage, but circumstances often force them to live with the family of the husband or wife. According to the older people, uxorilocality was formerly customary. **Domestic unit.** The monogamous nuclear family is the ideal nowadays, but stem families are not uncommon. **Inheritance.** At the death of the parents, all children are supposed to inherit equally. Often, however, the oldest child (whether son or daughter) receives somewhat more than his or her siblings. **Divorce and secondary marriage.** A second wife may only be taken with the consent of the first. If a wife dies, the widower can marry one of her younger sisters, but this is not a rigid rule.

SOCIOPOLITICAL ORGANIZATION. **Political organization.** The village head is nowadays a government official. There are still adat chiefs, called *demang*, but they no longer have district responsibilities as they did under the Dutch. In general, they are well informed about the history and customs of their people, and some enjoy great prestige. **Social stratification.** There is little evidence of an institutionalized class system, although in the past Ot Danum society did know slavery. Every village has individuals with more property and better houses than the rest, but these differences can vary as the result of a bad harvest or good luck in panning gold. **Warfare.** In former times, the Ot Danum were greatly feared by other Dayaks and by Malays. They, in turn, had a healthy respect for the Ot and Punan in the source regions of the great rivers. Continual conflicts among Dayaks came to an end as the result of a ceremonial agreement among representatives of almost all the Dayak groups in the upper Melawi and South Borneo, known as the Peace of Tumbang Anoi (Damai Tumbang Anoi), which occurred in 1894 and is still a live subject among Dayaks.

RELIGION. **Death.** Souls of the dead stay at first in the vicinity of their former homes and then make the journey to the land of the spirits, *lowu liau*. The journey is made possible by a ceremony in which close relatives contribute necessary supplies for the trip. After a long time in *lowu liau*, the soul "dies"; in order to be reborn it dissolves itself in fruits or plants that will be eaten by people. When this occurs, the soul can then be reborn as the soul of a child. The dead are buried in the ground. After a three- to seven-day *pali* (taboo) period, a *njorat* is held, which may be characterized as a provisional feast of the dead. Only after some time is a *daro* held, usually by several families together. The bones are not removed from the ground, however; the grave is only cleaned and a new roof built for it. The *daro*, for which at least a water buffalo must be killed, lasts only one day and is a much simpler affair than the *tiwah* of the Ngadju. Figures called *hampotong* are carved in wood to commemorate the deceased, and long poles, called *toras*, are erected, 30 feet high for men and shorter for women. [Epple 1927; J. Mallinckrodt 1924-25.] The Ot Danum have a practitioner who cures the sick, fulfills various religious functions, and recites myths and legends to the accompaniment of music. There are several hundred Christian Ot Danum, mainly Protestant in Central Kalimantan and Catholic in West Kalimantan.

BIBLIOGRAPHY. Epple 1927; J. Mallinckrodt 1924-25.

LAND DAYAKS

Synonym. *Bidayuh*

ORIENTATION. **Identification.** The term Land Dayak has its origins in attempts by Europeans to distinguish between Ibans (so-called Sea Dayaks) and other pagans dwelling inland from Kuching. The term has since been applied more widely to a poorly-defined category of peoples in present-day southern Sarawak and western Kalimantan. Kennedy (1935: 419ff.) felt justified in referring to a Land Dayak culture type, transitional between his Ngadju and Klamantan types, with its center of distribution the western "horn" of Borneo—the region inland from Pontianak. In this view, Sarawak is culturally marginal. Within the category Land Dayak there are customarily subsumed a great many so-called "tribes," for the most part local communities of a single village or cluster of villages named for some feature of the landscape. Western observers have also referred to these Dayaks by the name of the administrative district in which they are located. The Manyukei, Ayou, Desa, Sidin, and Mualang are among the best-known groups in what is now Indonesian West Borneo: they are located for the most part in the old Malay states of Landak, Tayan, Sambas, and Sekadau. Tribal names and designations mentioned in the literature on Sarawak (e.g. Roth 1896: *1*) include the following: Aup, Bukar, Brang, Engrat (Mingrat), Engkroh, Grogo, Jagoi, Kuap, Kadup, Lundu, Lara, Samarahan, Sarambau, Sau, Sedumak, Selakan, Sentah, Sennah, Singgie, Sibungo, Simpoke, Sigu, and Taup. **Location.** The majority of Land Dayaks would appear to be located in (Indonesian) West Kalimantan, where Dayak villages are found along tributary streams throughout the inland area behind Pontianak and Sambas. The Land Dayaks of Sarawak are concentrated along the upper tributaries of the Lundu, Sarawak, Samarahan, and Sadong rivers, all in the administrative First Division. **Geography.** Land Dayak country in Sarawak is characterized by an undulating landscape averaging a few hundred feet above sea level, largely covered with secondary growth, and occasionally interrupted by forested limestone peaks. Rainfall averages 150 inches, with a monsoon season from October to March. Average maximum temperatures range from a daytime 85° to 75° at night. **Linguistic affiliation.** Dyen (1965) classifies Sentah (a Sarawak Land Dayak language) within his Hesperonesian linkage. Although Dyen leaves open the question of the specific subgrouping of Sentah within Hesperonesian, its closest ties would appear to be with other languages of the West Indonesian branch of Malayo-Polynesian. Hudson (1970) has recently questioned the assumption of a "Land Dayak" language type for all or most of West Kalimantan, proposing rather to distinguish between Land Dayak and

Malayic Dayak languages. **Demography.** According to the 1960 census, Land Dayaks in Sarawak numbered 57,619. Kennedy (1942) estimated the total of all Land Dayaks in Borneo at 200,000. **History and cultural relations.** Western Borneo has for centuries been exposed to the acculturative influence of Chinese, Javanese, and Malays. The ancient Hindu-Javanese empire of Madjapahit reportedly established colonies in the districts of Kapuas, Sambas, and Landak. Coastal (Islamic) Malay principalities exploited inland Dayak populations prior to European intervention, and in Sarawak the Land Dayaks lost much land as a result of harassment and headhunting raids of Ibans. The Dutch supported expansion of Malay rule in the interior, and at the end of the nineteenth century virtually the whole of the Kapuas river system was brought under joint Dutch-Malay rule. Land Dayaks nowadays are reputed to have a "slave complex" as a result of this long history of exploitation. Christian missions have been active for well over a hundred years, and in Sarawak a minority of educated Christian Dayaks now hold positions as clerks and schoolteachers.

SETTLEMENT PATTERN AND HOUSING. **Settlement pattern.** Sarawak Land Dayak villages are relatively large, a population of 600 or more being not uncommon (Leach 1950: 66ff.). Nowadays, villages are located near streams, although in former times fortified settlements on hills seem to have been more common. Usually there is more than one longhouse in a village; these may be interconnected by raised walkways. There is a tendency to form village aggregates or clusters through a process of community fission (Geddes 1954). A common feature of Land Dayak villages is the so-called "headhouse," better described as a combination men's house, community council house, and ceremonial center. This structure consists of a large circular (sometimes octagonal, occasionally square) room or hall with a high conical roof, the whole raised on piles up to 30 feet in height and entered through a trapdoor in the floor. Captured human heads (skulls) are stored here, and a large drum is suspended above the floor (cf. Low 1848: 280; Kennedy 1935). Geddes (1954) found no evidence of association with particular religious cults or age-grades, and the exact nature of the former ceremonial functions of these structures remains unclear. **Housing.** Longhouses, usually more than one to a village, are the rule, although single-family dwellings are not unknown. In the Sadong area, the largest longhouses contain about 30 doors. The basic floor plan appears similar in Sarawak and Indonesian Borneo—a single gallery, along one side of which doors open to individual family compartments. [Geddes 1954; Kennedy 1935; Leach 1950.]

ECONOMY. Subsistence is based primarily on rice agriculture, supplemented by fishing and some hunting. Many households, even in the interior, grow rubber and coffee as cash crops. The food supply is supplemented by the use of wild sago in off years. **Agriculture.** Rice, often mixed with cucurbits, beans, and maize, is grown by shifting cultivation on hillside swiddens. Job's tears, *inyok*, is planted around the periphery of the swiddens. In addition to their swidden rice, Sadong Dayaks always grow some irrigated rice by damming streams in naturally swampy areas (Geddes 1954: 64ff.). **Industrial arts.** Iron working is well developed. Brass and rattan coils are worn by women around the waist, arms, or lower legs, the exact style varying considerably from one watershed area to the next. **Trade.** The need for salt has long been a factor in furthering the contact of interior tribesmen with coastal peoples. In Indonesian Borneo, Malays and other middlemen in this trade live far inland along the major rivers. **Property.** Among Dayaks on the upper Sadong in Sarawak, villagers may freely clear unused land within the village territory. Use rights to existing agricultural lands are determined by membership in bilineal descent lines from the ancestors who first cleared the land (Geddes 1954: 59ff.).

KINSHIP. **Descent.** Geddes (1954) stresses the polygenetic character of Sadong Dayak villages and their capacity to incorporate migrant groups or even groups with no known genealogical connection. Common residence, rather than genealogical relatedness, is the prime consideration in determining village membership; marriage ties compensate for the lack of systematic genealogical relationships between founders of households in creating bonds of kinship and community. Within this system, the household emerges as the basic kingroup and as the effective ritual and economic unit, and the village or village cluster as the maximum ritual unit, held together by common residence and affinal ties, and observing common taboos and common omens. Descent does, however, figure in the determination of land use. Rights to existing agricultural land are inherited bilineally, reckoning back usually two generations. Those living descendants who share use rights in land cleared by a common ancestor are called by the collective term *turun*. In practice, individuals choose to invoke one or another descent line according to their personal needs and preferences. **Kin terminology.** Geddes (1954: 15) gives the following terms of reference for the Sadong Dayaks, Sarawak. (Leach [1950] also gives terminologies for various Sarawak Land Dayak groups.)

GrFa	*babuk*
GrMo	*taiyung*
Fa	*amang*
Mo	*ayang*
PaElSib	*amba*
PaYoSib	*bujuh*
ElSib	*umbu*
YoSib	*adi*

First cousins	*adi tungar*
Second, etc.	
cousins	*adi kawan*
Ch	*anak*
GrCh	*sungku*

Teknonyms (Fa of so-and-so, GrFa of so-and-so) may be extended to refer to any kinsman or even nonkinsman on a suitable generation level.

MARRIAGE. Mode.
Bride-price is negligible or absent. The Sadong Dayak groom presents betel and lime to the girl's father, and there is a ceremony, attended by the personal kindreds of the couple, featuring speeches by village elders. **Incest.** The personal kindred, including grandparents and first cousins together with their spouses, is exogamous, but there are few restrictions on marriage other than this. There is a tendency to village endogamy, with the result that most villagers are related through either consanguinal or affinal kin ties (Geddes 1954). **Residence.** Kennedy (1935: 426ff.), drawing largely on the observations of Schadee (1910) in the Landak and Tayan districts of the middle Kapuas, Indonesian Borneo, reports a decided matrifocal preference with respect to residence and inheritance. Kennedy's later fieldwork in the Sanggau area failed, however, to confirm this (Kennedy 1955d). Postmarital residence among Sadong Dayaks in Sarawak is, according to Geddes (1954), ambilocal, with the choice being made primarily as a result of economic factors. **Household.** The mature household consists most often of a stem family containing on the average about eight persons. The household is the basic economic unit (Geddes 1954).

SOCIOPOLITICAL ORGANIZATION.
The village cluster appears to be the maximum sociopolitical unit. Hierarchies of chiefs, all with Malay titles, are found nowadays, but to what extent these are purely imposed offices is not known. A headman, *orang kaya*, usually selects a relative to succeed him, but his choice must be passed on by the village men sitting in council. The authority of a headman is considerably tempered by the weight of public opinion, although if a headman also happens to be a powerful priest his influence and prestige may be considerable (Geddes 1954). Kennedy (1935: 426), citing data from Indonesian Borneo, confirms the selection of chiefs within family lines and adds that chiefly lineages tend therefore to form an endogamous quasi-aristocracy. According to Geddes (1954), there is little evidence of differences in rank or prestige among Sadong River Dayaks. Families do, however, attempt to amass items of traditional or ritual wealth, such as old jars, beads, necklaces, silver belts, and brass cannons and gongs (Geddes 1961: 43). **Social control.** Village chiefs impose fines, formerly paid in the form of jars (St. John 1862: *1*, 165ff.). According to Geddes (1954), the concept of *panum*, whereby supernatural punishment is visited on the offended party should the offender fail to compensate for his offense, acts as a powerful incentive toward conventional settlement of disputes. **Warfare.** Land Dayaks have apparently never been noted as a warlike people. They did, however, engage in sporadic headhunting, although never on the scale of the Ibans.

RELIGION. Religious systems.
Kennedy, drawing largely on data from Indonesian Borneo, reports belief in a supreme being—variously Duwata, Tapa, Batara Guru—overshadowed by the cult of the (ancestral) spirits, offerings and invocations to fetish stones and other objects (*guna*) and homage paid the war god, Kamang Trio. Priests (*borik*) and priestesses (Malay, *balian*) function as curers, chiefly in recovering lost souls. Shamanistic practices such as spirit possession are probably borrowed from Malays, while recovery of souls by projection of the therapist's own soul is more typically Bornean (Kennedy 1935). It is probable that political authority was formerly associated with inherited religious status, although any such pattern has been largely obliterated by a long history of subordination to coastal powers (cf. Leach 1950). **Supernaturals.** Geddes (1954, 1961) classifies Sadong Dayak supernaturals into (1) remote deities, including a vaguely defined supreme deity or originator, *tampa raiyuh* (2) numerous earth-dwelling spirits or demons, *antu*, generally harmful and the cause of most illness, and (3) ancestral spirits, who, as protective agents, constitute the most important force in the affairs of men. **Practitioners.** In Sadong Dayak villages, old men function as priests of the ancestor cult. Chief reliance is on technically precise recitation of lengthy chants and invocations, learned during apprenticeship to an existing practitioner. Female priestesses mainly invoke deities of a women's cult, but also engage, as spirit mediums, in recovering lost souls. A class of male shamans or spirit mediums, *manang*, in addition to entering trance states induced while swinging, engage in more spectacular feats, such as walking on upturned knife blades. [Geddes 1954, 1961.] **Ceremonies.** The protection of ancestral spirits is sought through periodic communal ceremonies combining festivity with religious ritual, the greatest and most pleasing to the spirits being the festival for a newly-taken head. Agricultural rites, conducted mainly by priests of the ancestor cult, include ritual eating of glutinous rice, drinking of Job's tears wine, chewing of betel, and smearing of the bodies of participants with turmeric (sometimes mixed with blood). Myths detailing the doings of culture heroes validate these ritual behaviors (Geddes 1954, 1961). Specific food and activity taboos (Malay, *pantang*) observed among certain villages and families are inherited matrilineally, according to Kennedy (1935: 434). A common way of obtaining the favor of the spirits is by closing off a

household or village to all contact for a period of days, during which its members fast. This period of self-abnegation (*porik*; Malay, *pemali*) ends with a feast and food sacrifices (cf. St. John 1862: *1*, 169-70). **Head feasts.** According to Geddes, the taking of a new head among the Sadong Dayaks was the occasion for a five-day festival to which the ancestral spirits were invited. Ritual food offerings, dancing, and invocations were held on the longhouse veranda, after which the skull was hung in the headhouse, little attention being paid to it thereafter (Geddes 1954: 21). Schadee's data on the Manyukei of Lower Landak District, former Dutch Borneo, indicate that head feasts were held on a variety of occasions, including the death of a noted chief or warrior. Headhunting, which ceased in this area about 1924, was associated with the cult of the war god, Kamang Trio. The cult, confined to men, included food offerings of dogs smeared with blood. Bits of the brain and other portions of a newly-taken head might on occasion be mixed with rice wine and consumed by victorious warriors. A tall pole, surmounted by a wooden image of a bird and pointing in the direction of the enemy village, was erected as part of the ritual associated with these head feasts (Schadee 1931, cited in Kennedy 1935). **Death and afterlife.** Sadong Dayaks bury their dead in a village cemetery the day after death. The body is laid out at home with a display of family heirloom wealth and later buried in a wooden coffin in a niche grave. Only professional village undertakers may enter the cemetery (Geddes 1954). According to St. John (1862: *1*, 163-65), cremation was formerly universal among wealthy families in western Sarawak, but virtually absent farther east in the Sadong area. Some Indonesian Borneo groups formerly placed the ashes of cremated bodies in glazed jars, which were then buried. Others encoffined their dead, who were then placed in carved wooden tombs, *sandong*. At the death of a warrior chief among the Landak District Dayak, his soul is thought to pass into a wooden image fashioned in his likeness. This is set up in a grove outside the village, sacred to the war god, Kamang Trio, and containing images of former chiefs. Dedication of the new image formerly required the taking of a fresh human head, whereafter the soul of the chief was free to proceed to the land of the spirits (Kennedy 1935, citing Schadee 1931).

BIBLIOGRAPHY. Cense and Uhlenbeck 1958; Dyen 1965; Elam 1937; Geddes 1954, 1961; Harrisson and O'Connor 1970; Hudson 1970; Kennedy 1935, 1942, 1955d; Leach 1950; Low 1848; Roberts 1949; Roth 1896; St. John 1862; Schadee 1910, 1931; Scott 1908; Voegelin and Voegelin 1965.

BIBLIOGRAPHY

ABBREVIATIONS

AA	*American Anthropologist*, various places.
Ab.	*Adatrechtbundels*, The Hague, 1910-49.
Bijd.	*Bijdragen tot de Taal-, Land- en Volkenkunde van Nederlandsch-Indië*, Den Haag.
BSN	*Behavior Science Notes*, New Haven.
BSRBG	*Bulletin de la Société Royale Belge de Géographie*, Bruxelles.
ENI	*Encyclopaedie van Nederlandsch-Indië*, 8 vols., The Hague, 1917-39.
GTNI	*Geneeskundig Tijdschrift voor Nederlandsch-Indië*, Jakarta.
IAE	*International Archives of Ethnography*, Leiden.
IG	*De Indische Gids*, Amsterdam.
JAI	See *JRAI*.
JRAI	*Journal of the Royal Anthropological Institute of Great Britain and Ireland* (*Journal of the Anthropological Institute of Great Britain and Ireland*–before 1898), London.
JRASMB	*Journal of the Royal Asiatic Society, Malayan Branch*, Singapore.
KS	*Koloniale Studiën*, Weltevreden.
KT	*Koloniaal Tijdschrift*, Den Haag.
M	*Het Missiewerk*, s'Hertogenbosch, 's-Gravenhage.
MEB	*Mededelingen van het Bureau voor de Bestuurszaken der Buitenbezettingen bewerkt door het Encyclopaedisch Bureau*, Weltevreden.
MNZ	*Mededeelingen van wege het Nederlandsch Zendelinggenootschap*, Rotterdam.
NION	*Nederlandsch-Indië, Oud en Nieuw*, Amsterdam.
SMJ	*Sarawak Museum Journal*, Kuching.
SWJA	*Southwestern Journal of Anthropology*, Albuquerque.
Tijd.	*Tijdschrift voor Indische Taal-, Land- en Volkenkunde*, Batavia.
Tijd. BB	*Tijdschrift voor het Binnenlandsch Bestuur*, Batavia.
TNAG	*Tijdschrift van het Koninklijk Nederlandsch Aardrijkskundig Genootschap*, Amsterdam, Utrecht, Leiden.
TNI	*Tijdschrift voor Nederlandsch Indië*, Zalt-Bommel, Nijmegen, Bussum, Den Haag, Amsterdam.
VKAW	*Verhandelingen der Koninklijke Nederlandse Akademie van Wetenschappen, Afdeling Letterkunde*, Amsterdam.
VBGKW	*Verhandelingen van het Bataviaasch Genootschap van Kunsten en Wetenschappen*, Batavia.
VKIT	*Verhandelingen van het Koninklijk Instituut voor Taal-, Land- en Volkenkunde*, Den Haag.

Abdullah, Taufik
    1966   "Adat and Islam: an examination of conflict in Minangkabau," *Indonesia 2*: 1-24. Bibliography contains references to other relevant sources.
    1970   "Some notes on the Kaba Tjindua Mato: an example of Minangkabau traditional literature," *Indonesia 9*: 1-22. Bibliography contains references to other relevant sources.

Adam, Leonard
    1925   "Zeden en gewoonten en het daarmede samenhangend adatrecht van het Minahassische volk [Manners and customs and related adat law of the Minahasa]," *Bijd. 81*: 424-99.

Adams, Marie Jeanne
    1969   "System and meaning in East Sumba textile design: a study in traditional Indonesian art," New Haven, *Yale University, Southeast Asia Studies, Cultural Report Series 16*.
    1970   "Myths and self-image among the Kapunduk people of Sumba," *Indonesia 10*: 81-106.

Adiwidjaja, R. I.
    1954   *Kesusastran Sunda* [*Sundanese literature*], Djakarta.

Admiraal, J. W.
    1939   "Adatverband op de Kei-eilanden [Adat relationship on the Kei-Islands]," *MEB 55*: 19-33.

Adriani, N.
    1925   "De Minahasische talen [The languages of the Minahasa]," *Bijd. 81*: 134-64.
    1928   "Spraakkunstige schets van de bewoners der Mentawei-eilanden [Linguistic sketch of the inhabitants of the Mentawei Islands]," *Bijd. 84*: 117.

Adriani, N., and Alb. C. Kruyt
    1900   "Van Posso naar Mori [From Posso to Mori]," *MNZ 44*: 135-214.
    1912-14   *De Bare'e sprekende Toradja's van Midden Celebes* [*The Bare'e-speaking Toradja of Central Celebes*], 3 vols., Batavia, Landsdrukkerij.
    1950-51   *De Bare'e sprekende Toradja's van Midden Celebes* [*The Bare'e-speaking Toradja of Central Celebes*], 2d ed., revised, 3 vols. *VKAW 54-56*.

Aernout, W.
    1885   "Een woordenlijstje der Tidoengsche taal [A Tidong word list]," *IG 7*: 536-50.

Aikman, R. G.
    1959   "The Melanaus," in *The Peoples of Sarawak*, Tom Harrisson, ed. Kuching: 85-94.

Aken, A. P. van
    1915   "Nota betreffende de afdeeling Koerintji [Notes concerning the district of Korintji]," *MEB 8*, 1-86.

Allard, E.
    1955   "Laporan sementara tentang bagian kedua penjelidikan dilapangan atas susunan kemasjarakatan orang-orang Indo-Eropah di Indonesia," [Provisional report on the second part of fieldwork research on the social structure of the Indo-Europeans in Indonesia], *Bahasa dan Budaja* (Djakarta) *3, no. 5*: 27-40.

Alman, Elizabeth, and John Alman
    1963   *Handcraft in North Borneo*, Jesselton.

Anceaux, J. C.
    1952   "The Wolio language: outline of grammatical description and texts," *VKIT 11*.

Ancona, H. G. J. d'
    1935   "Adathoofden te Enggano [Adat-chiefs on Enggano]," *KT 24*: 489-96.

Anonymous
    1912   "Nota betreffende het landschap Toli-Toli [Memorandum on the region of Toli-Toli]," *Tijd. 54*: 27-57.

Appell, George N.
    1964   "The long-house apartment of the Rungus Dusun," *SMJ 11*: 570-73.

1965 "The nature of social groupings among the Rungus Dusun of Sabah, Malaysia," unpublished Ph.D. dissertation, Australian National University.

1966 "Residence and ties of kinship in a cognatic society: the Rungus Dusun of Sabah, Malaysia," *SWJA 22:* 280-301.

1967a "Observational procedures for identifying kindreds: social isolates among the Rungus of Borneo," *SWJA 23:* 192-207.

1967b "Ethnography of Northern Borneo: critical review of some recent publications," *Oceania 37:* 178-85.

1968a "A survey of the social and medical anthropology of Sabah: retrospect and prospect," *BSN 3:* 1-54.

1968b "The Dusun languages of Northern Borneo: Rungus Dusun and related problems," *Oceanic Linguistics 7:* 1-15.

1968c "Ethnographic profiles of the Dusun-speaking peoples of Sabah, Malaysia," *JRASMB 41:* 131-47.

1968d "Social groupings among the Rungus, a cognatic society of Sabah, Malaysia," *JRASMB 41:* 193-202.

Appell, George N., and Robert Harrison
1969 "Ethnographic classification of the Dusun-speaking peoples of Northern Borneo," *Ethnology 8:* 212-27.

Araneta, F., and M. A. Bernad
1960 "'Bisayans' of Borneo and the 'Tagalogs' and 'Visayans' of the Philippines," *SMJ 9:* 542-64.

Arndt, Paul
1929-30 "De Ngada's en hun geestenwereld," *De Katholieke Missien 90-93, 122-24, 151-52.*

1929-31 "Die Religion der Nad'a (West-Flores, Kleine Sunda-Inseln)," *Anthropos 24:* 817-61; *26:* 353-405, 695-739.

1931 *Grammatik der Sika-Sprache,* Ende, Flores.

1932a "Die Megalithenkultur der Nad'a (Flores)," *Anthropos 27:* 11-63.

1932b *Mythologie, Religion und Magie im Sikagebiet (östl. Mittelflores),* Ende, Flores.

1933a "Grammatik der Ngad'a-Sprache," *VBGKW 72:* 3.

1933b *Gesellschaftliche Verhältnisse im Sikagebiet (östl. Mittelflores),* Ende, Flores.

1936-37 "Déva, das Höchste Wesen der Ngadha," *Anthropos 31:* 894-909; *32:* 195-209, 347-77.

1937 *Grammatik der Solor-Sprache,* Ende, Flores; Arnoldus-Drukkerij.

1938 "Demon und Padzi, die feindlichen Brüder des Solor-Archipels," *Anthropos 33:* 1-58.

1940 "Soziale Verhältnisse auf Ost-Flores, Adonare und Solor," *Anthropos: Internationale Sammlung Ethnologischer Monographien Bd. 4, Ht. 2,* Münster, Aschendorf.

1951 "Religion auf Ostflores, Adonare und Solor," *Studia Instituti Anthropos, vol. 1,* Wien-Mödling, Verlag und Druck der Missionsdruckerei St. Gabriel.

1952 "Zur Religion der Dongo auf Sumbawa," *Anthropos 47:* 483-500.

1954 "Gesellschaftliche Verhältnisse der Ngadha," *Studia Instituti Anthropos 8,* Wien-Mödling, Verlag der Missionsdruckerei St. Gabriel.

1955 "Die Rangschichten in der Gesellschaft der Ngadha," *Ethnologica 2:* 272-77.

1956 "Krankheit und Krankheitsursachen bei den Ngadha (Mittel-Flores)," *Anthropos 51:* 417-46.

1958 "Hinduismus der Ngadha," *Folklore Studies* (Tokyo) *17:* 99-136.

1959a "Totenfeiern und Bräuche der Ngadha," *Anthropos 54:* 68-98.

1959b "Tod und Jenseitvorstellungen bei den Ngadha auf Flores," *Anthropos 54:* 370-79.

1960a "Opfer und Opferfeiern der Ngadha," *Folklore Studies* (Tokyo) *19:* 175-250.

1960b "Mythen der Ngadha," *Annali Lateranensi 24:* 9-137.

1961 "Wörterbuch der Ngadhasprache," *Studia Instituti Anthropos 15,* Posieux, Freibourg, Suisse.

1963 "Die wirtschaftliche Verhältnisse der Ngadha," *Annali Lateranensi 27:* 13-189.

Arnold, Guy
1958 "Nomadic Penan of the upper Rejang (Plieran), Sarawak," *JRASMB 31:* 40-82 (published in 1964).

1959 *Longhouse and jungle: an expedition to Sarawak,* London, Chatto & Windus.

Atmadja, M. P., and J. T. J. Uijfferbroek
1891 "Huwelijksgebruiken op het Eiland Bawean [Marriage customs on Bawean Island]," *Tijd. 34:* 533-38.

Australian National University, Department of Anthropology and Sociology
1968 *An ethnographic bibliography of New Guinea,* 3 vols., Canberra, Australian National University Press.

Avé, J. B.
1970 "Suggestions for a more practical classification of the ethnic groups in the Republic of Indonesia," in *Anniversary Contributions to Anthropology: Twelve Essays Published on the Occasion of the 40th Anniversary of the Leiden Ethnological Society,* Leiden, E. J. Brill: 95-123.

Baal, J. van
1941 "Het Alip-Feest te Bajan," *Djawa 21:* 313-54.

1947 *Over wegen en drijfveren der religie [On ways and motivation of religion],* Amsterdam.

1953-54 "Völken," in *Nieuw-Guinea,* W. C. Klein, ed. 3 vols., 's-Gravenhage, Staatsdrukkerij: *2,* 438-70.

Baal, J. van, et al.
1961 "Urgent research in New Guinea," *International Committee on Urgent Anthropological and Ethnological Research, Bulletin 4:* 13-16 (Vienna).

Bachtiar, Harsja W.
1967 "Negeri Taram: a Minangkabau village community," in *Villages in Indonesia,* Koentjaraningrat, ed., Ithaca, Cornell University Press: 348-85.

Bachtiar Rifai
1958 *Bentuk Milik Tanah dan Tingkat Kemakmuran; Penjelidikan Pedesaan didaerah Pati, Djawa Tengah (Land tenure and the prosperity level; a village study in Pati, Central Java),* unpublished Ph.D. thesis, Bogor, University of Indonesia.

Bader, Hermann
1953 "Die Reifefeiern bei den Ngada (Mittelflores, Indonesien)," *St.-Gabrieler Studien 12,* Mödling bei Wien, St.-Gabriel-Verlag.

1960 *Bali, Studies in life, thought and ritual,* by Dutch Scholars of the Twentieth Century; Vol. 5 of the series, *Studies in Indonesia,* The Hague, W. Van Hoeve, for the Koninklijk Instituut voor de Tropen.

Banks, E.
1937 "Some megalithic remains from the Kelabit country in Sarawak, with notes on the Kelabits themselves," *SMJ 4:* 411-37.

1940 "The natives of Sarawak," *JRASMB 18:* 49-54.

1949 *Bornean mammals,* Kuching, Kuching Press.

Baretta, J. M.
1917 "Halmahera en Morotai," *MEB 13*.

Baring-Gould, Sabine, and C. A. Bampfylde
1909 *A history of Sarawak under its two white rajahs*, London, H. Sotheran.

Barnes, R. H.
1968 An ethnographic survey of Lomblen and neighbouring islands, eastern Indonesia, unpublished B.Litt. thesis, Oxford, University of Oxford.

Bastiaans, J.
1938 "Het verband tusschen Limbotto en Gorontalo [The relation between Limbotto and Gorontalo]," *Tijd. 78*: 215-47.
1939 "Batato's in het oude Gorontalo, in verband met den Gorontaleesche staatsbouw [Batato in old Gorontalo, in connection with the structure of the Gorontalo state]," *Tijd. 79*: 23-72.

Bastin, J.
1965 *The British in West Sumatra (1685-1925)*, Kuala Lumpur, University of Malaya Press.

Bateson, Gregory
1937 "An Old Temple and a New Myth," *Djawa 17*: 219-307.
1963 "Bali: The Value System of a Steady State," in M. Fortes, ed., *Social Structure: Studies Presented to Radcliffe-Brown*, New York, Russell and Russell: 35-53.

Bateson, Gregory, and Margaret Mead
1942 "Balinese character: a photographic analysis," *New York Academy of Sciences, Transactions*.

Batuah, Ahmad, and A. Madjoindo
1963 *Tambo Minangkabau [Minangkabau traditions]*, Djakarta, Dinas Penerbitan Balai Pustaka.

Beckering, J. D. H.
1911 *Beschrijving der eilanden Adonara en Lomblem, behoorende tot de Solor-Groep [Description of the islands of Adonara and Lomblen, belonging to the Solor Archipelago]*, TNAG 28: 167-202.

Beech, M. W. H.
1908 *The Tidong dialects of Borneo*, London, Oxford University Press.

Beets, K. Th.
1933 *Memorie van overgave van de afdeeling Gajo-en Alaslanden [Transfer memorandum of the district Gayo-and Alasland]*, Amsterdam, Royal Institute for the Tropics (manuscript).

Bekkum, P. W. van
1946a "De Machtsverschuivingen in Manggarai, West Flores [Shifts of power in Manggarai, West Flores]," *Cultureel Indië 8*: 122-30.
1946b "Geschiedenis van Manggarai, West Flores [History of Manggarai, West Flores]," *Cultureel Indië 8*: 65-75.

Belo, Jane
1935 "The Balinese temper," *Character and Personality 4*: 120-46.
1936 "A study of a Balinese family," *AA n.s. 38*: 12-31.
1940 "Bali: rangda and barong," *Monographs of the American Ethnological Society 16*.
1953 "Bali: temple festival," *Monographs of the American Ethnological Society 23*.
1960 *Trance in Bali*, New York, Columbia University Press.

Belo, Jane, ed.
1970 *Traditional Balinese culture*, New York, Columbia University Press.

Berg, C. C.
1938 "Javaansche Geschiedschrijving" [Javanese historical writing], in *Geschiedenis van Nederlandsch Indië*, 6 vols., W. F. Stapel, ed., Amsterdam.

Berg, E. J. van den
1939 "Adatgebruiken in verband met de Sultans installatie in Boeton [Adat customs in connection with the Sultan's installation at Butung]," *Tijd. 79*: 469-528.
1940 "Een rijstfeest in Lawele [A rice-ceremony in Lawele]," *Tijd. 80*: 530-43.

Bergh, J. D. van den
1948 "Banggaise ethnologica," *M 27*: 147-56, 193-207.
1953 *Spraakkunst van het Banggais [Banggai grammar]*, Den Haag, M. Nijhoff.

Berthe, Louis
1961 "Le mariage par achat et captation des gendres dans une société semi-féodale: les Buna' de Timor central," *L'Homme 1*: 5-31.

Bertling, C. T.
1931-32 "De Minahasische 'Waroega' en Hockerbestattung [The Minahasa 'Waroega' and prehistoric burial]," *NION 16*: 33-51, 75-94, 111-16; *17*: 97-104.

Berzina, M. A., and S. I. Bruk
1963 *The population of Indonesia, Malaya and the Philippines* (Translation of *Naselenie Indonezii, Malaii i Filippin*, Akademiia Nauk SSSR, 1962. JPRS Translation No. 19, 799, Washington, D.C., 21 June, 1963).

Beukering, J. A. van
1947 *Bijdrage tot de anthropologie der Mentaweiers*, Utrecht, unpublished Ph.D. dissertation.

Bewsher, R.
1956 "Bisayan accounts of early Bornean settlements in the Philippines recorded by Father Santaren," *SMJ 7*: 48-53.
1959 "The Bisaya group," in *The Peoples of Sarawak*, Tom Harrisson, ed., Kuching: 95-102.

Bijlmer, H. J. T.
1929 "Outline of the anthropology of the Timor-archipelago," *Indisch Comité voor Wetenschappelijke Ondersoekingen 3*, Weltevreden (Batavia).

Boland, B. J.
1950 "De Zending in de Ontmoeting van Oost en West [Missionary activity in the meeting of East and West]," *Sticusa Jaarboek 1950*: 61-74.

Bolang, A., and Tom Harrisson
1949 "Murut and related vocabularies, with special reference to North Borneo terminology," *SMJ 5*: 116-24.

Bonington, M. C. C.
1935 Extracts from the census report on the Andaman and Nicobar Islands, 1931, in *Census of India, 1931, vol. 1* (India), Part 3 (Ethnographical), 172-87, J. H. Hutton, ed., Simla, Government of India Press.

Börger, F.
1932a "Wie ein Punen bei den Mentaweiern verläuft," *Berichte der Rheinischen Missionsgesellschaft 44-54*.
1932b "Von Punen der Mentaweier," *Berichte der Rheinischen Missionsgesellschaft 17-29*.

Bose, Saradindu
1964 "Economy of the Onge of Little Andaman," *Man in India 44*: 298-310.

Bosscher, C.
1853 "Statistische Aanteekeningen Omtrent de Aroe-Eilanden (Statistical Notes on the Aru-Islands)," *Tijd. 1*: 323-26.

Bouman, M. A.
1925 "Toeharlanti. De Bimaneesche Sultansverheffing [Toeharlanti. The elevation of the Bima Sultan]," *KT 14*: 710-17.

1943 "De Aloreesche dansplaats [The Alorese dancing place]," *Bijd. 102:* 481-500.

Bousquet, Georges Henri
1939 "Recherches sur les deux sectes musulmanes 'waktou telous' et 'waktou lima' de Lombok," *Revue des Études Islamiques 13:* 149-77.

Brabander, A. de
1949 "Het oude adat-huwelijk in het Maumeregebied [Old adat-marriage in Maumere District]," *M 28:* 225-36.

Brandes, J. L. A.
1884 *Bijdrage tot de vergelijkende klankleer der Westersche afdeeling van de Maleisch-Polynesische taalfamilie* [Contribution to the comparative phonetics of the Western branch of the Malayo-Polynesian family of languages], Utrecht.

Brink, S. van den
1923 "The Ragi and their use by Sasak of Central Lombok," *Tijd. 63:* 201-03.

Brouwer, D.
1935 *Bijdrage tot de anthropologie der Aloreilanden* [*Contribution to the anthropology of the Alor Islands*], Amsterdam, Uitgeversmaatschappij Holland.

Bruijn, J. V. de
1958-59 "Anthropological research in Netherlands New Guinea since 1950," *Oceania 29:* 132-63.

Bruner, Edward M.
1961 "Urbanization and ethnic identity in North Sumatra," *AA 63:* 508-21.

Bühler, A.
1949 "Sammelreise Bühler-Sutter" (unpublished manuscript).

Bühler, A., and E. Sutter
1951 "Sumba-Expedition des Museums für Volkerkunde und Naturhistorischen Museums in Basel," *Verhandlungen der Naturforschenden Gesellschaft von Basel 52:* 181-217, 267-302.

Calon, L. F.
1890-91 "Woordenlijstje van het dialekt van Sikka," *Tijd. 33:* 501-30; *34:* 283-363.
1893 "Eenige opmerkingen over het dialekt van Sikka," *Tijd. 35:* 129-99.
1895 "Bijdrage tot de kennis van het dialekt van Sikka," *VBGKW, vol. L.*

Capell, Adrian
1943-45 "Peoples and languages of Timor," *Oceania 14:* 191-219, 311-37; *15:* 19-48.
1962 "Oceanic linguistics today," *Current Anthropology 3:* 371-428.
1969 *A survey of New Guinea languages,* Sydney, Sydney University Press.

Carreon, M. L.
1957 "Maragtas: the Datus from Borneo," *SMJ 8:* 51-99.

Carroll, John
1960 "The word Bisaya in the Philippines and Borneo," *SMJ 9:* 499-541.

Castles, Lance
1967 "The ethnic profile of Djakarta," *Indonesia 1:* 153-204.

Cense, A. A., and E. M. Uhlenbeck
1958 "Critical survey of studies on the languages of Borneo," *Koninklijk Instituut voor Taal-, Land- en Volkenkunde, Bibliographic Series 2,* 's-Gravenhage, Martinus Nijhoff.

Chabot, H. Th.
1950 *Verwantschap, Stand en Sexe in Zuid-Celebes* [*Kinship, Class and Sex in South Celebes*], Groningen and Djakarta, J. B. Wolters.

Chang, Kwang-chih
1967 "Bontoramba: A village of Goa, South Sulawesi," in *Villages in Indonesia,* Koentjaraningrat, ed., Ithaca, Cornell University Press: 189-209.

Chang, Kwang-chih
1969 "Fengpitou, Tapenkeng, and the prehistory of Taiwan," *Yale University Publications in Anthropology 73.*

Chatelin, L. N. H. A.
1881 "Godsdienst en bijgeloof der Niassers (Religion and superstition of the Niasans)," *Bijd. 26:* 109-67.

Cheng, Te-k'un
1969 *Archaeology in Sarawak,* Toronto, Toronto University Press.

Cipriani, Lidio
1953 "Report on a survey of the Little Andaman during 1951-53," *Bulletin of the Department of Anthropology, Government of India 2:* 61-82, published by the Manager of Publications, Delhi, 1956.
1954 "A survey of Little Andaman during 1954," *Bulletin of the Department of Anthropology, Government of India 3:* 66-94, published by the Manager of Publications, Delhi, 1959.
1955 "On the origin of the Andamanese," Appendix E in *Census of India, 1951, vol. 17, Andaman and Nicobar Islands:* 66-71.
1966 *The Andaman Islanders,* edited and translated by D. Taylor Cox, London, Weidenfeld and Nicolson.

Clarke, M. C.
1952 "The Murut home," *Man 52:* 17-18, 34-36.

Clercq, F. S. A. de
1874 "Allerlei over het eiland Roti," *Bijd. 21:* 291-312.
1890 *Bijdrage tot de Kennis der Residentie Ternate,* Leiden.

Coedès, Georges
1968 *The Indianized states of Southeast Asia,* Honolulu, East-West Center Press (translated from the 1964 French edition).

Cole, Fay-Cooper
1947 "Concerning the Punans of Borneo," *AA n.s. 49:* 340.

Cool, Wouter
1897 *With the Dutch in the East: an outline of the military operations in Lombok, 1894,* translated from the Dutch by E. J. Taylor, London, Amsterdam; Luzac.

Cooley, Frank L.
1962a "Ambonese adat: a general description," New Haven, *Yale University, Southeast Asia Studies, Cultural Report Series 10.*
1962b "Ambonese kin groups," *Ethnology 1:* 102-12.
1967 "Allang: a village on Ambon Island," in *Villages in Indonesia,* Koentjaraningrat, ed., Ithaca, Cornell University Press: 129-56.
1969 "Village government in the Central Moluccas," *Indonesia 7:* 139-64.

Coolhaas, W. Ph.
1926 "Medelingen betreffende de onderafdeling Batjan [Information on the subdistrict of Batjan]," *Bijd. 82:* 403-84.
1942 "Bijdrage tot de Kennis van het Manggaraische Volk; West Flores [Contribution to the knowledge of the Manggarai people; West Flores]," *TNAG 59:* 148-77, 328-60.

Coomans de Ruiter, L.
1932 *Uit Borneo's Wonderwereld: schetsen over dieren en planten [From Borneo's magic world: sketches of animals and plants],* Batavia, Visser.

Correia, Armindo Pinto
1935 *Gentio de Timor,* Lisboa.
1943 *Timor de lés a lés,* Lisboa.
Cortesão, Armando
1944 *The Suma Oriental of Tomé Pires,* 2 vols., Hakluyt Society, London.
Couvreur, A.
1917 "Aanteekeningen nopens de samenstelling van het zelfbestuur van Bima [Notes concerning the composition of Bima's self-government]," *Tijd. BB 52*: 1-18.
1924 *Het Inlandsch Gemeentewezen in de onderafdeeling Bima* [*Native municipal life in the subdivision Bima*], The Hague, Archives Department of Internal Affairs (unpublished manuscript).
Couvreur, J.
1935 "Ethnografisch overzicht van Moena [Ethnographical survey of Muna]," Leiden, Koninklijk Instituut voor Taal- Land- en Volkenkunde (mimeographed).
Covarrubias, Miguel
1956 *Island of Bali,* New York, Alfred A. Knopf.
Crisp, J.
1799 "An account of the inhabitants of the Poggy or Nassau Islands," *Asiatick Researches 6*: 77-91.
Cuisinier, Jeanne
1956 "Un Calendrier de Savu," *Journal Asiatique 244*: 111-19.
Cunningham, Clark E.
1958 "The postwar migration of the Toba-Bataks of East Sumatra," New Haven, *Yale University, Southeast Asia Studies, Cultural Report Series.*
1964 "Order in the Atoni house," *Bijd. 120*: 34-68.
1965 "Order and change in an Atoni Diarchy," *SWJA 21*: 359-82.
1966 "Categories of descent groups in a Timor village," *Oceania 37*: 13-21.
1967a "Soba: an Atoni village of west Timor," in *Villages in Indonesia,* Koentjaraningrat, ed., Ithaca, Cornell University Press: 63-89.
1967b "Recruitment to Atoni descent groups," *Anthropological Quarterly 40*: 1-12.

Dahl, Otto
1951 *Malagache et Maanjan: une comparaison linguistique,* Oslo, Arne Gimnes Forlag.
Daly, D. D.
1888 "Explorations in British North Borneo, 1883-87." *Proceedings of the Royal Geographical Society 10, no. 1*: 1-24.
Dam, H. ten
1950 *Nita dan Sekitarnja,* Bogor (Java).
Damste, H. T.
1923 "Heilige Welfsels op Lombok [Sacred vaults on Lombok]," *Tijd. 63*: 176-82.
Das Dores, Raphael
1907 *Diccionario Teto-Português,* Lisboa.
Datta-Majumder, N.
1955 "Supernatural world of the Tarik of Car Nicobar," *Bulletin of the Department of Anthropology, Government of India 4*: 1-6 (published in 1959).
Deacon, A. B.
1925 "The Kakihan society of Ceram and New Guinea initiation cults," *Folk-Lore 36*: 332-61.
Deschamps, H. J.
1936 *Les Antaisaka,* Tananarive (Madagascar).
Dewey, Alice C.
1962 "Trade and social contract in Java," *JRAI 92*: 117-90.

1963 *Peasant marketing in Java,* New York, Free Press of Glencoe.
Dijk, L. J. van
1925-34 "De zelfbesturende landschappen in de Residentie Timor en onderhoorigheden [Autonomous subdivisions in the Residency of Timor and its dependencies]," *IG 47*: 528-40, 618-23; *56*: 708-12.
Djajadiningrat, P. A. H.
1913 *Critische Beschouwing van de Sadjarah Banten* [*A critical appraisal of the Sadjarah Banten*], Haarlem.
Djojodigoeno, M. M. M., and R. Tirtawinata
1940 *Het Adatprivaatrecht van Middel-Java* [*Adat Private Law of Central Java*], Bandung.
Dobby, E. H. G.
1950 *Southeast Asia,* New York, John Wiley.
Domsdorff, A. M.
1937 "De Minahasische dorpsgemeenschap in haar genetisch verband (1928) [The Minahasa village-society in its genetic connection, 1928]," *Ab. 39*: 344-59.
Dongen, G. J. van
1910 "De Koeboes in de Onderafdeeling Koeboestreken der Residentie Palembang [The Kubu in the Kubu district of Palembang]," *Bijd. 63*: 181-336.
Donselaar, W. M.
1872 "Aanteekeningen over het eiland Savoe [Notes on Savu Island]," *MNZ 16*: 281-332; Naschrift: 332-40.
Dormeier, J. J.
1947 "Banggaisch adatrecht [Banggai adat law]," *VKIT 6.*
Downs, Robert E.
1955 "Head-hunting in Indonesia," *Bijd. 111*: 40-70.
1956 *The religion of the Bare'e-speaking Toradja of Central Celebes,* dissertation, 's-Gravenhage, University of Leiden.
Drabbe, M. S. C.
1926 *Spraakkunst der Fordaatsche Taal. Spraakkunst der Jamdeneensche Taal* [*Grammar of the Fordat language. Grammar of the Jamden language*], Batavia, Verhandelingen voor Indische Taal-, Land- en Volkenkunde, 68.
1932a *Beknopte Spraakkunst en Korte Woordenlijst der Slaroësche Taal* [*Short grammar and word list of the Slaru language*], Batavia, Verhandelingen voor Indische Taal-, Land- en Volkenkunde, 71.
1932b *Woordenboek der Jamdeensche Taal. Jamdeensch-Nederlandsch* [*Dictionary of the Jamden language. Jamden-Dutch*], Batavia, Verhandelingen voor Indische Taal-, Land- en Volkenkunde, 71.
1932c *Woordenboek der Fordaatsche Taal. Fordaatsch-Nederlandsch* [*Dictionary of the Fordat language. Fordat-Dutch*], Batavia, Verhandelingen voor Indische Taal-, Land- en Volkenkunde, 71.
1935 "Aanvulling van de Spraakkunst der Jamdeensche Taal [Supplement to the grammar of the Jamden language]," *Tijd. 75*: 623-33.
1940 *Het Leven van den Tanimbarees. Ethnografische Studie over het Taminbaresche Volk* [*The life of the Tanimbarese. Ethnographic study of the Tanimbarese people*], Leiden, E. J. Brill.
Drewes, G. W. J., and P. Voorhoeve, eds.
1958 "Adat Atieh," *VKIT 24.*
Duarte, Jorge
1964 "Barlaque," *Seara* (Dili, Timor) *n.s. 2*: 92-119.
DuBois, Cora
1944 *The people of Alor,* Cambridge, Harvard University Press.

Dubois, H. M.
1938 "Monographie des Betsileo," Paris, Université, Institut d'Ethnologie, *Travaux et Mémoires 34.*

Dunnebier, W.
1931 "Verloven en trouwen in Bolaäng Mongondou [Betrothal and marriage in Bolaang Mongondow]," *Tijd. 71:* 530-622.

1938 "De plechtigheid 'waterscheppen' in Bolaang Mongondow [The ceremony of 'water scooping' in Bolaang Mongondow]," *Tijd. 78:* 1-56.

1949 "Over de vorsten van Bolaang Mongondow [On the rulers of Bolaang Mongondow]," *Bijd. 105:* 219-74.

Dutch East Indies
1933-36 Department van Economische Zaken. Tijdelijk Kantoor voor de Volkstelling [Department of Economic Affairs. Interim Office of the Census], *Volkstelling 1930,* 8 vols., Batavia, Landsdrukkerij.

Duyvendak, J. P.
1926 *Het Kakean-genootschap van Seran [The Kakean-Society of Ceram],* Almelo, Hilarius.

Dyen, Isidore
1965 "A lexicostatistical classification of the Austronesian languages," *Indiana University Publications in Anthropology and Linguistics, Memoir 19, International Journal of American Linguistics.*

Elam, E. H.
1937 "Land Dayaks of the Sadong District, Sarawak," *SMJ 4:* 373-94.

Elbert, J.
1912 *Die Sunda-Expedition des Vereins für Geographie und Statistik zur Frankfurt a.M.,* 2 vols., Frankfurt am Main, H. Minjon.

Elmberg, John-Erik
1959 "Further notes on the northern Mejbrats (Vogelkop, western New Guinea)," *Ethnos 24:* 70-80.

1965 "The Popot feast cycle," *Ethnos 30* (supplement): 1-172.

1968 "Balance and circulation; aspects of tradition and change among the Mejbrat of Irian Barat," *Ethnographical Museum of Stockholm, Monograph Series, 12.*

Elshout, J. M.
1923 *Over de Geneeskunde der Kěnja-Dajaks in Centraal-Borneo in verband met hunnen Godsdienst [On the medical practices of the Kenyah Dayaks of Central Borneo in relation to their religion],* Amsterdam, Müller.

1926 *De Kěnja-Dajaks uit het Apo-Kajangebied: bijdrage tot de kennis van Centraal-Borneo [The Kenyah Dayaks of the Apo Kayan region: a contribution to the knowledge of Central Borneo],* The Hague, Nijhoff.

Engbers, J. H. D.
1898 "Troonopvolging in het rijk van Sika [Succession in the kingdom of Sika]," *Berichten uit Nederlandsch Oost-Indië 10,* no. 4: 54-63.

Engelhard, H. E. D.
1884 "Mededeelingen over het eiland Saleyer [Information on the island of Salajar]," *Bijd. 33:* 263-516.

Enthoven, J. J. K.
1903 *Bijdragen tot de Geographie van Borneo's Westerafdeeling [Contributions to the geography of Borneo's western division],* 2 vols., Leiden, E. J. Brill.

Epple, K. D.
1927 "Heidnische Vorstellungen vom Jenseits und christliches Sterben in Borneo," *Evangelisches Missions-Magazin* (Basel) *71:* 227-71.

Ermen, C.
1913 "Tribal names on the Limbang River," *SMJ 1:* 149-50.

Esser, S. J.
1927 "Klank- en vormleer van het Morisch [Phonetics and morphology of Mori]," *VBGKW 67:* pts. 3, 4.

1938 "Talen [Languages]," in *Atlas van Tropisch Nederland. Het Koninklijk Aardrijkskundig Genootschap in Samenwerking met den Topografischen Dienst in Nederlandsch-Indies,* 's-Gravenhage, M. Nijhoff.

Evans, I. H. N.
1923 *Studies in religion, folklore and custom in British North Borneo and the Malay Peninsula,* Cambridge, Cambridge University Press.

1953 *The religion of the Tempasuk Dusuns of North Borneo,* Cambridge, Cambridge University Press.

Feith, Herbert
1957 "The Indonesian elections of 1955," Ithaca, *Cornell University, Interim Reports Series, Modern Indonesia Project, Southeast Asia Program.*

Fernandes, Abilio José
1937 *Método prático para aprender o Tetum,* Macau.

Firth, Raymond
1957 "A note on descent groups in Polynesia," *Man 57:* 4-8.

Fischer, H. Th.
1957 "Some notes on kinship systems and relationship terms of Sumba, Manggarai and South Timor," *Internationales Archiv für Ethnographie 48:* 1-31.

1966 "Toba Batak kinship terms," *Oceania 36:* 253-63.

Forbes, Henry Ogg
1884 "On some of the tribes of the island of Timor," *JAI 13:* 402-29.

1885 *A naturalist's wanderings in the Eastern Archipelago,* London.

Forrest, Th.
1779 *A voyage to New Guinea and the Moluccas from Balambangan,* London, G. Scott.

Fortier, David H.
1964 *Culture change among Chinese agricultural settlers in British North Borneo,* unpublished Ph.D. thesis, Columbia University [UM 65-7353].

Fox, James J.
n.d. "Some Helong tales" (unpublished manuscript).

1965 *Roti and Savu: A literary analysis of two island societies in eastern Indonesia,* unpublished B. Litt. thesis, Oxford.

1968 *The Rotinese. A study of the social organization of an eastern Indonesian people,* unpublished D. Phil. thesis, Oxford.

1969 "A note on the name of the island Roti/Rote," *Man 4,* no. 4.

1970a "On bad death and the left hand," in *Handbook on Right and Left,* Rodney Needham, ed., in press.

1970b Personal communication.

1971 "A Rotinese dynastic genealogy: structure and event," in *The Translation of Culture: Essays to E. E. Evans-Pritchard,* Tom O. Beidelman, ed., London, Tavistock.

Fox, Robert B.
1967 "Excavations in the Tabon Caves and some problems in Philippine chronology," in *Studies in Philippine Anthropology,* Mario D. Zamora, ed., Manila, Alemar's: 88-116.

Franken, H. J.
1960 "The festival of Jayaprana at Kalianget," in

Bali, Studies in Life, Thought and Ritual, The Hague, W. van Hoeve.

Freeman, Derek
1960   "The Iban of Western Borneo," in *Social Structure in Southeast Asia,* George P. Murdock, ed., *Viking Fund Publications in Anthropology No. 29:* 65-87.
1970   "Report on the Iban," *London School of Economics, Monographs on Social Anthropology No. 41* (first issued in 1955).

Friedericy, H. J.
1933   "De standen bij de Boegineezen en Makassaren [Class structure of the Buginese and Macassarese]," *Bijd.* 90: 447-602.

Funke, F. W.
1953   "Das Problem der Orang Abung: Ein Beitrag zur Bevolkerungsstruktur von Südsumatra," *Zeitschrift für Ethnologie* 78 (1).
1955   "Herkunft und Wanderung der Nicht-Abung-Völker in Lampung," *Zeitschrift für Ethnologie* 80: 259-97.
1958-61 *Orang Abung: Volkstum Süd-Sumatras im Wandel,* 2 vols., Leiden, E. J. Brill.

Galis, K. W.
1949a   "Een en ander over de sociale structuur in Kaur," *Tijd.* 83: 27-58.
1949b   "Een en ander over de religieuze structuur in Kaur," *Tijd.* 83: 247-85.

Galvin, A. D.
1966   " 'Mamat' (Leppo Tau—Long Moh)," *SMJ* 13: 296-304.

Ganguly, P.
1961   "Religious beliefs of the Negritos of Little Andaman," *Eastern Anthropologist* 14: 243-48.

Geddes, William R.
1954   "The Land Dayaks of Sarawak; a report on a social economic survey of the Land Dayaks of Sarawak presented to the Colonial Social Science Research Council," *Colonial Research Studies, no. 14,* London, H.M. Stationery Office.
1961   *Nine Dayak nights,* London, Oxford University Press (reprinted from the 1957 edition).

Geertz, Clifford
1956a   *The development of the Javanese economy. A socio-cultural approach,* Cambridge, MIT Press.
1956b   "Religious behavior in a central Javanese town, some preliminary considerations," *Economic Development and Culture Change* 4: 134-58.
1957   "Ritual and social change: A Javanese example," *AA* 59: 32-54.
1959   "Form and variation in Balinese village structure," *AA* 61: 991-1012.
1960a   "The Javanese Kijaji: The changing role of a culture broker," *Comparative Studies in Society and History* 2: 228-49.
1960b   *The religion of Java,* Glencoe, Ill., Free Press.
1963a   *Agricultural involution. The process of ecological change in Indonesia,* Berkeley, University of California Press.
1963b   *Peddlers and princes, social development and economic change in two Indonesian towns,* Chicago, University of Chicago Press.
1964a   "Internal conversion in contemporary Bali," in *Malayan and Indonesian Studies,* J. Bastin and R. Roolvink, eds., Oxford, Clarendon Press.
1964b   "Tihingan: A Balinese village," *Bijd.* 120: 1-33.
1965   *The social history of an Indonesian town,* Cambridge, MIT Press.
1966   "Person, time and conduct in Bali: An essay in cultural analysis," New Haven, *Yale University,*

Southeast Asia Studies, Cultural Report Series, No. 14.
1967   "Politics past, politics present: Some notes on the contribution of anthropology to the study of the new states," *Archives Européennes de Sociologie, Vol. 8.*

Geertz, Hildred
1959   "The Balinese village," in *Local, Ethnic and National Loyalties in Village Indonesia; A Symposium,* G. William Skinner, ed., New Haven, *Yale University, Southeast Asia Studies, Cultural Report Series.*
1961   *The Javanese family: A study in kinship and socialization,* New York, Free Press of Glencoe.
1963   "Indonesian cultures and communities," in *Indonesia,* Ruth T. McVey, ed., New Haven, HRAF Press, 24-96.

Geertz, Hildred, and Clifford Geertz
1964   "Teknonymy in Bali: Parenthood, age-grading and genealogical amnesia," *JRAI* 94: 94-108.

Geise, N. J. C.
1952   "Bedujs en Moslims in Lebak Paráhijang, Zuid-Banten," *Annali Lateranensi* 16: 319-444.

Genderen Stort, P. van
1916   "Nederlandsch - Tidoengsch-Tinggálàn - Dájàksche woordenlijst," *VBGKW* 61 (5): i-iv, 1-100.

Gennep, J. L. van
1921   "De Madoerezen," in *De Volken van Nederlandsch Indië,* 2 vols., J. C. van Eerde, ed., Amsterdam, Elsevier: 2, 183-96.

Geurtjens, H.
1921a   *Spraakleer der Keieesche Taal [Grammar of the Kei language],* VBGKW 63.
1921b   *Woordenlijst der Keieesche Taal [Vocabulary of the Kei language],* VBGKW 63.
1921c   *Uit een Vreemde Wereld, of het Leven en Streven der Inlanders op de Kei-eilanden [Out of a strange world, or the life and works of the natives of the Kei-Islands],* 'sHertogenbosch.

Glyn-Jones, Monica
1953   *The Dusun of the Penampang Plains in North Borneo,* London, Colonial Social Science Research Council (mimeographed).

Godée Molsbergen, E. C.
1928   *Geschiedenis van de Minahassa tot 1829 [History of the Minahasa until 1829],* Weltevreden (Batavia), Landsdrukkerij.

Goedhart, O. M.
1908   "Drie landschappen in Celebes [Three districts in Celebes]," *Tijd.* 50: 442-548.

Goethals, Peter R.
1959   "The Sumbawan village," in *Local, Ethnic and National Loyalties in Village Indonesia,* G. William Skinner, ed., New Haven, *Yale University, Southeast Asia Studies, Cultural Report Series:* 11-23.
1960   "Task groups and marriage in Western Sumbawa," *Proceedings of the 1959 Annual Spring Meeting of the American Ethnological Society,* Seattle, University of Washington Press: 45-59.
1961a   "Aspects of local government in a Sumbawan village," Ithaca, *Monograph Series, Modern Indonesia Project, Cornell University.*
1961b   *Kinship and marriage in West Sumbawa,* unpublished Ph.D. dissertation, Yale University.
1967   "Rarak: A swidden village of West Sumbawa," in *Villages in Indonesia,* Koentjaraningrat, ed., Ithaca, Cornell University Press: 30-62.

Gomes, Edwin H.
1911   *Seventeen years among the Sea Dyaks of Borneo,* London, Seeley.

Goris, R.
1960a "The religious character of the village community," in *Bali, Studies in Life, Thought and Ritual*, The Hague, W. van Hoeve.
1960b "Holidays and holy days," in *Bali, Studies in Life, Thought and Ritual*, The Hague, W. van Hoeve.
1960c "The temple system," in *Bali, Studies in Life, Thought and Ritual*, The Hague, W. van Hoeve.
1966 "Aanteekeningen over Oost Lombok [Notes on East Lombok]," *Tijd. 76:* 196-248.

Goris, R., and P. L. Dronkers
n.d. *Bali, cults and customs*, Republic of Indonesia, Ministry of Education and Culture, Djakarta.

Gould, J. W.
1956 "Sumatra–America's pepperpot, 1784-1873," *Essex Institute Historical Collections 92:* 83-152, 203-51, 295-348.

Gouweloos, M. J.
1937 "Het doodenritual bij de To Wiaoe [Funeral rites among the To Wiau]," *MNZ 81:* 19-46.

Graaf, H. J. de
1941 "Lombok in the seventeenth century," *Djawa 21:* 357-60.

Graafland, N.
1889 "Het eiland Rote," *MNZ 33:* 239-77.
1898 *De Minahassa*, 2 vols., Haarlem, F. Bohn.

Grabowsky, F.
1884 "Der District Dussun Timor in Süd-Ost Borneo und seiner Bewohnor," *Ausland 57:* 444-49, 469-75.
1889a "Der Tod, das Begräbnis, das Tiwah oder Todtenfest bei den Dajaken," *IAE 2:* 177-204.
1889b "Familie, Verwandtschaft, und Freundschaft bei den Olo Ngadju in Südost-Borneo," *Bijd. 38:* 463-66.
1907 "Der Häuserbau, die Dörfer und ihre Befestigungen bei den Dajaken Südost-Borneos," *Globus 92:* 69-75.
1908 "Der Reisbau bei den Dajaks Südost-Borneos," *Globus 93:* 101-05.

Grader, C. J.
1960 "The irrigation system in the region of Jembrana," in *Bali, Studies in Life, Thought and Ritual*, The Hague, W. van Hoeve.

Grandidier, A., and G. Grandidier
1908-28 *Ethnographie de Madagascar*, 4 vols., Paris, Imprimerie Nationale.

Greenberg, Joseph H.
1953 "Historical linguistics and unwritten languages," in *Anthropology Today*, A. L. Kroeber, ed., Chicago, University of Chicago Press: 265-86.

Grijzen, H. J.
1904 "Mededelingen omtrent beloe of Midden-Timor [Notes on the Belu of Central Timor]," *VBGKW 54.*

Grubauer, Albert
1913 *Unter Kopfjägern Zentral-Celebes*, Leipzig.

Gullick, J. M.
1958 "Indigenous political systems of western Malaya," *London School of Economics, Monographs on Social Anthropology No. 17.*

Gupta, A. K.
1955 "The Andaman and Nicobar Islands," Appendix A in *Census of India, 1951, vol. 17, Andaman and Nicobar Islands:* 41-60.

Guritno, Pandam
1958 *Masjarakat Marangan [The Marangan community]*, Jogjakarta, Panitia Sosial Research, Universitas Gadjah Mada (mimeographed).

Haar, B. ter
1948 *Adat law in Indonesia*, New York, Institute of Pacific Relations.

Haddon, Alfred Cort
1901 "A sketch of the ethnography of Sarawak," *Archivio per l'Anthropologia e Etnologia 31:* 327-55.
1920 "Migrations of culture in British New Guinea," *JRAI 50:* 20-31.
1925 *The races of man*, Cambridge, Cambridge University Press.

Haga, B. J.
1931 "De Lima-Pahalaä (Gorontalo): volksordening, adatrecht en bestuurspolitiek [The Lima Pahalaä (Gorontalo): social structure, adat law and administrative politics]," *Tijd. 71:* 186-314.

Hagen, B.
1908a *Die Orang Kubu auf Sumatra*, Frankfurt am Main, Joseph Baer.
1908b "Beitrag zur Kenntnis der Orang Sekka (Sakai) oder Orang Laut, sowie der Orang Lom oder Mapor, zweier nicht-muhamedanischer Volksstämme auf der Insel Banka," *Abhandlungen zur Anthropologie, Ethnologie, und Urgeschichte, Festschrift*, 37-46, Frankfurt am Main.

Hamka
1950a *Ajahku: Riwajat Hidup Dr. Abd. Karim Ambullah dan Perdjuangan Kaum Agama*, Djakarta.
1950b *Sedjarah Islam di Sumatera*, Pustaka Nasional, Medan.
1963 *Adat Minangkabau Menghadapi Revolusi*, Firma Tekad, Djakarta.

Harimurti Kridoleksono
1964 "Perhitungan Leksikostatistik atas Delapan Bahasa Nusantara Barat serta Penentuan Pusat Penjebaran Bahasa² itu Berdasarkan Teori Migrasi [Lexicostatistical analysis of eight West Indonesian languages, based on migration theory]," *Madjalah Ilmu² Sastra Indonesia, 2:* 319-52.

Harrisson, Tom
1949 "Notes on some nomadic Punans," *SMJ 5:* 130-46.
1954 "Outside influences on the upland culture of Kelabits of North Central Borneo," *SMJ 6:* 104-25.
1956 "'Bisaya': Borneo-Philippine impacts of Islam," *SMJ 7:* 43-47.
1958a "Some origins and attitudes of Brunei Tutong-Belait-Dusun, North Borneo 'Dusun' and Sarawak 'Bisayan', Meting and other peoples," *SMJ 8:* 293-321.
1958b "The Caves of Niah: a history of prehistory," *SMJ 8:* 549-96.
1959a *World within: A Borneo story*, London, Cresset.
1959b "The Kelabits and Muruts," in *The Peoples of Sarawak*, T. Harrisson, ed., Kuching: 57-71.
1959c "Some tasks of research in Borneo," *Bulletin, International Committee on Urgent Anthropological and Ethnological Research, No. 2:* 76-77.
1962a "Borneo death," *Bijd. 118:* 1-41.
1962b "'Bisaya' in North Borneo and elsewhere," *Journal of the Sabah Society 2:* 1-8.
1964 "The peoples of North and West Borneo," in *Malaysia: A Survey*, Wang Gungwu, ed., London and New York, Pall Mall Press and Praeger: 163-78.
1966 "A Kalimantan writing board and the Mamat festival," *SMJ 13:* 287-95.
1967 "Ethnological notes on the Muruts of the Sapulut River, Sabah," *JRASMB 40:* 111-29.
1970 *The Malays of south-west Sarawak before Malaysia: a socio-ecological survey*, London, Macmillan.

Harrisson, Tom, and Stanley J. O'Connor
1970 "Gold and megalithic activity in prehistoric and

recent West Borneo," Ithaca, *Cornell University, Southeast Asia Program, Data Paper 77.*

Harrisson, Tom, and Thomas Harnett
1969   "Excavations of the prehistoric iron industry in West Borneo," Ithaca, *Cornell University, Southeast Asia Program, Data Paper 72.*

Harrisson, Tom, and Benedict Sandin
1966   "Borneo writing boards," *SMJ 13:* 32-286.

Hawkins, Everett D.
1967   "Indonesia's population problems" in *Asia's Population Problems,* S. Chandrasekhar, ed., New York, Frederick A. Praeger: 119-45.

Hazairin
1936   *De Redjang: de volksordening, het verwantschaps-, huwelijks- en erfrecht [The Redjang: regulation of people, laws of blood relationship and inheritance],* Bandung, A. C. Nix.

Headly, D.
1947   *A report on the Muruts living in the Labuan and Interior Residency* (Jesselton, mimeographed).
1950   "Some Bisaya folklore," *SMJ 5:* 187-92.

Hederer, G., and W. Lehmann
1950   *Die Inland-Malaien von Lombok und Sumbawa,* Göttingen.

Heerkens, P.
1930   *Flores, de Manggarai,* Uden.

Heijmering, G.
1842-43   "Zeden en gewoonten op het eiland Rottie [Manners and customs on the island of Roti]," *TNI 5:* 531-49, 623-39; *6:* 81-98, 353-67.

Heiligers, N.
1920   "Memorie van Overgave van de Onderafdeeling Savoe [Transfer memorandum on the subdistrict of Savu]," Seba, Savu (unpublished manuscript).

Heine-Geldern, Robert
1928   "Die Megalithen Südostasiens und ihre Bedeutung für die Klärung der Megalithenfrage in Europa und Polynesien," *Anthropos 23:* 276-315.
1935   "The archaeology and art of Sumatra," in *Sumatra, Its History and People,* Edwin Loeb, Wien, Verlag des Instituts für Völkerkunde: 305-35.
1942   "Conceptions of state and kingship in South East Asia," *Far Eastern Quarterly 2:* 15-30.
1947   "The drum named Makalamau," *India Antiqua, A Volume of Oriental Studies Presented to J. P. Vogel,* Leiden: 167-79.

Helbig, K.
1933   "Bei den Orang Loeboe in Zentral-Sumatra," *Baessler Archiv 16:* 164-87.

Held, G. J.
1958   "The Papuas of Waropen," *Koninklijk Instituut voor Taal-, Land- en Volkenkunde, Translation Series 2,* The Hague, M. Nijhoff.

Helfrich, O. L.
1888   "De eilandengroep Engano [The archipelago of Enggano]," *TNAG 5 (pt. 2):* 272-314, 565.

Hicks, David
1967   *Eastern timorese society* (unpublished typescript of a field report for the London-Cornell Project for East and South-East Asian Studies).

Hidding, K. A. H.
1929   *Nji Pohatji Sangjang Sri,* Ph.D. thesis, University of Leiden, Dubbeldeman.
1935   *Gebruiken en Godsdienst der Soendanezen [Custom and religion of the Sundanese],* Batavia.

Hinlopen, P. A. M., and P. Severijn
1855   "Verslag naar een onderzoek der Poggi-eilanden [Report of an investigation of the Poggy Islands]," *Tijd. 3:* 319-37.

Hissink, J. H.
1904   "Het papadonwezen en zijne attribution [The *papadon* rite and its regalia]," *Tijd. 47:* 69-167.

Hoessein, Mohammad
1932   "Sedjarah Keradjaan Redjang Empat Petulai [A history of the kingdom of the four Redjang Brothers]," Muara Aman (unpublished manuscript).

Hoëvell, G. W. W. C. van
1890   "De Kei-eilanden," *Tijd. 33:* 102-09.
1892   "Een bezweringsfeest (*mapasaoe*) te Mooeton [An exorcism ceremony (*mapasaoe*) at Mautong]," *IAE 5:* 69-71.

Hogendorp, W. van
1781-84   "Beschrijving van het eiland Timor [Description of the island of Timor]," *VBGKW 1:* 192-214; *2:* 405-18.

Holleman, F. D.
1923   *Het adatgrondenrecht van Ambon en de Oeliasers [Adat law concerning landholding on Ambon and the Uliassers],* Delft, Molukken Instituut.
1943   "Adatrechtelijke gegevens, voornamelijk van het eilandje Nila, alsmede van de eilandjes Seroea en Teoen [Notes on adat law, mainly of the island Nila, as well as of the islets Serua and Teun]," *Ab. 42:* 380-487.

Holt, Claire
1967   *Art in Indonesia: continuities and change,* Ithaca, Cornell University Press.

Hoop, A. N. J. van der
1932   *Megalithic remains in South Sumatra,* Zutphen, W. J. Thieme.

Hooykaas, C.
1964   "Agama Tirtha, Five studies in Hindu-Balinese religion," *VKAW 70.*
1966   "Surya-Sevana, The way to God of a Balinese Siva priest," *VKAW 72.*

Hooykaas-van Leeuwen Boomkamp, J. H.
1961   "Ritual purification of a Balinese temple," *VKAW 68.*

Hose, Charles
1893   "A journey up the Baram River," *Geographical Journal 1:* 193-207.
1926   *Natural man: a record from Borneo,* London, Macmillan.

Hose, Charles, and William McDougall
1912   *The pagan tribes of Borneo,* 2 vols., London, Macmillan (reprinted in 1966).

Hoven, W.
1927   *De Pasemah en haar verwantschaps-, huwelijks- en erfrecht [Pasemah laws concerning blood-relationship, marriage and inheritance],* Wageningen.
1930a   *Verslag nopens een dienstreis naar Sumba en Sumbawa [Report on a tour of duty on Sumba and Sumbawa],* Koninklijk Instituut voor de Tropen, Amsterdam (unpublished manuscript).
1930b   *Militaire Memorie over de Afdeeling Sumbawa* (with vocabularies), Koninklijk Instituut voor de Tropen, Amsterdam (unpublished manuscript).

Howell, William
1908-10   [A collection of articles on the Sea Dayak], *Sarawak Gazette vols. 38-40* (HRAF, OC6 Iban File, Source No. 2).

Hudson, Alfred B.
1966   "Death ceremonies of the Ma'anyan Dayaks," *SMJ 13:* 341-417.
1967a   "The Barito isolects of Borneo," Ithaca, *Cornell University, Southeast Asia Program, Data Paper 68.*

1967b *Padju Epat: The ethnography and social struc-ture of a Ma'anjan Dajak group in Southeastern Borneo,* Ph.D. thesis, Cornell University (UM 68-3507).

1970 "A note on Selako: Malayic Dayak and Land Dayak languages in Western Borneo," *SMJ 18:* 301-18.

Hueting, A.
1921-22 "De Tobelorezen in hun Denken en Doen [The Tobelorese in their thinking and actions]," *Bijd.* 77: 217-358; 78: 137-342.

Hughes-Hallett, H.
1938 "An account of a Berhantu ceremony," *JRASMB* 16: 102-08.

Ijsseldijk, A.
1898 "Een huwelijksplechtigheid te Kotting [A mar-riage ceremony at Kotting]," *Berichten uit Ned-erlandsch Oost-Indië 10:* 40-44.

Indonesia, Biro Pusat Statistik
1960 *Statistical pocketbook of Indonesia,* Djakarta.

Indonesia, Kementerian Penerangan (Ministry of Information)
1954 "Suku Bangsa Kubu (Kubu tribes)," in *Su-matera Selatan 9,* Djakarta.

Jacobs, Julius
1894 *Het familie- en kampongleven op Groot-Atjeh [Family and kampong life in Great Atjeh],* Lei-den, E. J. Brill.

Jacobs, Julius, and J. J. Meijer
1891 *De Badoej's,* Den Haag.

Jansen, H. J.
1939 "Ethnographische bijzonderheden van enkele Am-bonsche negorijen, 1938 [Ethnographic particu-lars from a few Ambonese negeri, 1938]," *Bijd.* 98: 325-68.

Jaspan, Mervyn A.
1959 "A provisional list of Indonesian ethnic groups," *Sosiografi Indonesia 1:* 75-90 (Panitia Social Research, Gadjah Mada University, Jogjakarta).

1964a *Folk literature of South Sumatra: Redjang Ka-Ga-Nga texts,* Canberra, Australian National Uni-versity Press.

1964b *From patriliny to matriliny: Structural change among the Redjang of Southwest Sumatra,* Can-berra, Australian National University, Ph.D. thesis (offset edition).

1964c "A note on Enggano," *Man 64:* 109-13.

1968 "Symbols at work: Aspects of kinetic and mne-monic representation in Redjang ritual," *Bijd.* 123: 476-516.

1969 *Traditional medical theory in South-East Asia,* Hull, University of Hull Publications.

Jasper, J. E.
1906 "Het Eiland Bawean en Zijn Bewoners [The Is-land of Bawean and its inhabitants]," *Tijd. BB* 31: 231-80.

1908 "Het eiland Soembawa en zijn bevolking. Naam-lijst (Maleisch, Soembawasch, Bimaneesch, Ja-vaansch, Madoereesch)," *Tijd. BB 34:* 60-147.

1928 *Tengger en de Tenggereezen [Tengger and the Tenggerese],* Weltevreden, G. Kolff.

Jay, Robert R.
1963 *Javanese villagers: Society and politics in rural Modjokuto,* New York, Free Press of Glencoe.

Jensen, A. E.
1948 *Die drei Ströme: Züge aus dem geistigen und religiösen Leben der Wemale, einem Primitiv-Volk in den Molukken,* Ergebnisse der Frobenius-Expedition 1937-1938 in die Molukken und nach Holländisch Neu-Guinea, Vol. 2, Leipzig, Har-rassowitz.

Jensen, Erik
1966 "The Iban world," *SMJ 13:* 1-31.

Johns, Anthony H.
1958 "Rantjak Dilabueh: A Minangkabau Kaba," Ithaca, *Cornell University, Southeast Asia Pro-gram, Data Paper 32.*

Jones, L. W.
1962a *Sarawak: Report of the Census of Population taken on 15 June 1960,* Kuching.

1962b *North Borneo: Report on the Census of Popula-tion taken on 10 August 1960,* Kuching.

1962c *Brunei: Report on the Census of Population taken on 10 August 1960,* Kuching.

1966 *The population of Borneo: A study of the peo-ples of Sarawak, Sabah and Brunei,* London.

Jonker, J. C. G.
1893-96 Bimaneesch-Hollandsch woordenboek, Bima-neesche Teksten, Bimaneesche spraakkunst [Bi-manese-Dutch dictionary, Bimanese texts, Bi-manese grammar], *VBGKW 47 (1, 2).*

1903 "Iets over de taal van Dao [Notes on the lan-guage of Ndao]," in *Album-Kern (Opstellen geschreven ter eere van Dr. H. Kern),* Leiden, E. J. Brill: 85-89.

1904 "Eenige verhalen in talen gesproken op Soem-bawa, Timor en omliggende eilanden [Some tales in the languages spoken on Sumbawa, Timor and neighboring islands]," *Bijd.* 56: 245-89.

1905 "Rottineesche Verhalen [Rotinese tales]," *Bijd.* 58: 369-464.

1908 *Rottineesch-Hollandsch woordenboek [Rotinese-Dutch Dictionary],* Leiden.

1911 *Rottineesche teksten en vertaling [Rotinese texts and translations],* Leiden.

1913 "Bijdrage tot de kennis der Rottineesche tong-vallen [Toward an understanding of Rotinese dialects]," *Bijd.* 68: 521-622.

1915 *Rottineesche Spraakkunst [Rotinese grammar],* Leiden.

1934 "Soembaneesche teksten [Sumbanese texts]," *Bijd.* 90: 211-334.

Josselin de Jong, J. P. B. de
1935 *De Malaische Archipel als Ethnologisch Studie-veld [The Malay Archipelago as an ethnological field of study],* Leiden, J. Ginsberg.

1937 "Studies in Indonesian culture I. Oirata, a Ti-morese settlement on Kisar," *VKAW 39:* 1-289.

1947 "Studies in Indonesian culture II. The communi-ty of Erai (Wetar)," *VKAW 50:* 1-152.

Josselin de Jong, P. E.
1951 *Minangkabau and Negri Sembilan: Socio-political structure in Indonesia,* Leiden (reprinted in Djakarta, 1960).

Joustra, M.
1924 *Overzicht der Litteratuur Betrefende Minang-kabau,* Amsterdam, Minangkabau Instituut.

1926 *Batakspiegel,* 2d ed., Leiden.

1936 *Overzicht der Litteratuur Betrefende Minangka-bau 1929-1936,* Amsterdam, Minangkabau In-stituut.

Jumuh, George
1949 "Jerunei," *SMJ 5:* 62-68.

Junus, Mahmud
1958 *Turutlah Hukum Warisan dalam Islam,* Pustaka Mahmudiah, Djakarta.

1960 *Pendidikan Islam di Indonesia [Islamic education in Indonesia],* Pustaka Mahmudiah, Djakarta.

BIBLIOGRAPHY

Junus, Umar
1964   "Some remarks on Minangkabau social structure," *Bijd.* 120: 293-326.
1966   "The Payment of Zakat Al-Fitrah in a Minangkabau Community," *Bijd.* 122: 447-54.

Kähler, Hans
n.d.   *Beiträge zur Ethnologie der Insel Simalur* (*Simeuloeë*), Batavia, Lux.
1942-45 "Über Mischsprachen in Indonesien," *Anthropos* 37-40: 889-90.
1952   "Sprach und Kulturschichten auf der Insel Simalur an der Westküste von Sumatra," *Actes du IVe Congres International des Sciences Anthropologiques et Ethnologiques* 2: 254-60.
1960   "Ethnographische und linguistische Studien über die Orang Darat, Orang Akit, Orang Laut und Orang Utan im Riau-Archipel und auf den Inseln an der Ostküste von Sumatra, *Veröffentlichungen des Seminars für Indonesische und Südseesprachen der Universität Hamburg, Band 2*, Berlin, Dietrich Reimer.
1965   "Dialect and language," *Lingua 15*: 497-514.

Kamma, F. C.
1954   *De messiaanse koréri-bewegingen in het Biaks-Noemfoorse cultuurgebied* [*The messianic Koréri movement in the Biak-Numfor culture area*], 's-Gravenhage (Leiden thesis).

Kana, N. L.
1966   *A preliminary study of the East Sumbanese social organization and religion*, unpublished M.A. thesis, Cornell University.

Kate, H. F. C. ten
1894a   "Verslag eener reis in de Timorgroep en Polynesië [Report of a journey to the Timor Archipelago and Polynesia]," *TNAG 11*: 195-246.
1894b   "Een en ander over anthropologische problemen in Insulinde en Polynesië [Concerning anthropological problems in the Malay Archipelago and Polynesia]," *Feestbundel opdragen op Dr. P. J. Veth*, Leiden: 209-14.

Kaudern, Walter
1925-44 *Ethnographical studies in Celebes*, 6 vols., Göteborg, Etnografska Museet.
1937   "Anthropological notes from Celebes," *Ethnologiska Studier 4*: 84-126.

Keereweer, H. H.
1940   "De Koeboes in de onderafdeeling Moesi Ilir en Koeboestreken (The Kubu in the Musi Ilir and Kubu districts)," *Bijd.* 99: 357-96.

Keers, W.
1941   "Anthropologische beschouwingen over de bewoners van Zuid-West en Zuid-Midden Celebes [Anthropological speculations on the peoples of Southwest and Southcentral Celebes]," *GTNI* 81: 1783-1836.
1948   "An anthropological survey of the eastern Little Sunda Islands, the Negritos of the eastern Little Sunda Islands, the Proto-Malay of the Netherlands East-Indies," *Koninklijk Vereeniging Indisch Instituut, Mededelingen 74, 26*.

Kemal, Iskandar
1964   *Sekitar Pemerintahan Nagari Minangkabau dan Perkembangannja, Tindjavan tentang Kerapatan Adat*, Padang, Pertjetakan Daerah Sumatera Barat.

Kennedy, Raymond
1935   "The ethnology of the Greater Sunda Islands," unpublished Ph.D. thesis, Yale University (UM 67-4797).
1937   "A survey of Indonesian civilization," in *Studies in the Science of Society*, George P. Murdock, ed., New Haven, Yale University Press: 267-97.
1942   *The Ageless Indies*, New York, John Day.
1943   "Islands and peoples of the Indies," Washington, D.C., *Smithsonian Institution War Background Studies 14*.
1953   "Fieldnotes on Indonesia: South Celebes 1949-50," Harold C. Conklin, ed., New Haven, Human Relations Area Files.
1955a   *Bibliography of Indonesian peoples and cultures*, rev. ed., 2 vols. Thomas W. Maretzki and H. Th. Fischer, eds., New Haven, Southeast Asia Studies, Yale University, by arrangement with the Human Relations Area Files.
1955b   "Fieldnotes on Indonesia: Flores, 1949-50," Harold C. Conklin, ed., New Haven, Human Relations Area Files (Source No. 5 in OBI Indonesia File).
1955c   "Fieldnotes on Indonesia: Ambon and Ceram, 1949-50," Harold C. Conklin, ed., New Haven, Human Relations Area Files (Source No. 4 in OBI Indonesia File).
1955d   "Fieldnotes on Indonesia: West Borneo 1949-50," Harold C. Conklin, ed., New Haven, Human Relations Area Files (Source No. 6 in OBI Indonesia File).
1962   *Bibliography of Indonesian peoples and cultures*, 2d rev. ed., Thomas W. Maretzki and H. Th. Fischer, eds., New Haven, Southeast Asia Studies, Yale University, by arrangement with the Human Relations Area Files.

Kent, R. K.
1970   *Early kingdoms in Madagascar 1500-1700*, New York, Holt, Rinehart and Winston.

Kern, H.
1892   "Savuneesche bijdragen. Grammatische inleiding [Savunese contributions: grammatical introduction]," *Bijd. 41*: 157-96, 513-53.

Keuning, J.
1953-54 "Toba-Bataks en Mandailing-Bataks," *Indonesië* 7: 156-73.
1955   "Enggano, de geschiedenis van een verdwenen cultuur [Enggano, the history of a disappearing culture]," *Indonesië 8*: 177-213.
1958   "The Toba-Batak, formerly and now," Ithaca, *Cornell University Southeast Asia Program, Modern Indonesia Project, Translation Series*.

Kiliaan, H. J.
1897   *Madoereesch Spraakkunst* [*Madurese grammar*], 2 vols., Batavia.
1898   *Nederlandsch-Madoereesch Woordenboek* [*Dutch-Madurese dictionary*], Batavia.
1904-05 *Madoereesch-Nederlandsch Woordenboek* [*Madurese-Dutch dictionary*], 2 vols., Leiden.

Kleiweg de Zwaan, J. P.
1913-15 *Die Insel Nias bei Sumatra*, 3 vols., Den Haag, M. Nijhoff.
1925   *De rassen van den Indischen Archipel* [*The races of the Malay Archipelago*], Amsterdam, J. M. Meulenhoff.
1929   "Bijdrage tot de anthropologie van Celebes [Contribution to the anthropology of Celebes]," *TNAG* 46: 782-91.

Klerks, J.
1939   "Gegevens over Keieesche Huwelijksadat [Data on Keiese marriage adat]," *Bijd. 98*: 285-323.

Klift, H. van den
1922   "Het monahoe ndao [The monahoe ndao]," *MNZ* 66: 68-77.

Kluppel, J. M.
1873   "De Solor-Eilanden," *Tijd. 20:* 378-98.

Koentjaraningrat
1956   "A preliminary description of the Javanese kinship system," New Haven, *Yale University, Southeast Asia Studies, Cultural Report Series.*

1961   "Some Anthropological Observations of Gotong Rojong Practices in Two Villages of South Central Java," Ithaca, *Cornell University, Modern Indonesia Project Series.*

1966   "Bride-price and adoption in the kinship relations of the Bgu of West Irian," *Ethnology 5:* 233-44.

1968   "Javanese data on the unresolved problems of the kindred," *Ethnology 7:* 53-58.

Korn, B.
1939   *Nota over de onderafdeelingen Gorontalo en Boalemo* [Memorandum on the subdistricts of Gorontalo and Boalemo], Amsterdam, Royal Institute for the Tropics (manuscript).

Korn, V. E.
1936   *Het Adatrecht van Bali* [Adat law of Bali], 's-Gravenhage.

1953   "Batakse offerande [Batak sacrifice]," *Bijd. 109:* 32-51, 97-127.

1960   "The village republic of Renganan Pergeringsingan," in *Bali, Studies in Life, Thought and Ritual,* The Hague, W. Van Hoeve.

Kouwenhoven, W. J. H.
1956   *Nimboran: a study of social change and social-economic development in a New Guinea society,* Den Haag, J. N. Voorhoeve.

Kreemer, J.
1910   "De Loeboes in Mandailing," *Bijd. 66:* 303-36.
1922-23 *Atjeh,* 2 vols., Leiden, E. J. Brill.

Kriebel, D. J. C.
1919   "Grond- en waterrechten in de onderafdeeling Saleier [Land- and water rights in the subdistrict of Salajar]," *KT 8:* 1086-1109.

1920   "Het eiland Bonerate [The island of Bonerate]," *Bijd. 76:* 203-21.

Krulfeld, Ruth
1966   "Fatalism in Indonesia: a comparison of socioreligious types on Lombok," *Anthropological Quarterly 39:* 180-90.

Kruyt, Alb. C.
1900   "Eenige ethnografische aanteekeningen omtrent de Toboengkoe en de Tomori [Some ethnographical notes on the To Bungku and To Mori]," *MNZ 44:* 215-48.

1918-20 "Measa, eene bijdrage tot het dynanisme der Bare'e-sprekende Toradja's en enkele omwonende volken [Measa, a contribution to the dynanism of the Bare'e-speaking Toradja and some neighboring peoples]," *Bijd. 74:* 233-60; 75: 36-133; 76: 1-116.

1921   "De Roteneezen," *Tijd. 60:* 266-344.

1922   "Een en ander over de To Laki van Mekongga [Observations on the To Laki of Mekongga]," *Tijd. 61:* 427-70.

1923a   "De Timoreezen," *Bijd. 79:* 347-490.
1923b   "De Mentawaiers," *Tijd. 62:* 1-188.
1923c   "De Toradja's van de Sa'dan, Masoepoe- en Mamasa-rivieren [The Toradjas of the Sa'dan, Masupu and Mamasa rivers]," *Tijd. 63:* 81-176, 259-402.

1924   "Een bezoek aan de Mentawei-eilanden [A visit to the Mentawei Islands]," *TNAG 41:* 19-49.

1930a   "De To Wana op Oost-Celebes [The To Wana on East-Celebes]," *Tijd. 70:* 397-627.

1930b   "De To Loinang van den Oostarm van Celebes [The To Loinang on the eastern peninsula of Celebes]," *Bijd. 86:* 327-536.

1931a   "Het hondenoffer in Midden-Celebes [The sacrifice of dogs in central Celebes]," *Tijd. 71:* 439-529 and map.

1931b   "De vorsten van Banggai [The rulers of Banggai]," *KT 20:* 505-28, 605-23.

1932a   "De bewoners van den Banggai-Archipel [The population of the Banggai Archipelago]," *TNAG 49:* 66-89, 249-72.

1932b   "De pilogot der Banggaiers en hun priesters [The pilogot of the Banggai and their priests]," *Mensch en Maatschappij 8:* 114-35.

1932c   "De zwarte kunst in den Banggai Archipel en in Balantak [Black magic in the Banggai Archipelago and in Balantak]," *Tijd. 72:* 727-41.

1932d   "Banggaische studiën [Studies on Banggai]," *Tijd. 72:* 13-102.

1932e   "De landbouw in den Banggai Archipel [Agriculture in the Banggai Archipelago]," *KT 21:* 473-92.

1932f   "Ziekte en dood bij de Banggaiers [Illness and death among the Banggai]," *Bijd. 89:* 141-71.

1932g   "Balantaksche Studiën [Studies on Balantak]," *Tijd. 72:* 328-90.

1932h   "L'immigration prehistorique dans les pays des Toradjas occidentaux," *Hommage du Service Archaeologique des Indes Neerlandaises su Premier Congrès des Préhistoriens d'Extrême-Orient à Hanoi, 25-31 Janvier, 1932,* Batavia.

1933a   "De oorsprong van de priestertaal in Posso [The origin ot the priest-language in Poso]," *Verslagen en mededeelingen der Koninklijke Akademie van Wetenschappen 76, serie B, no. 7.*

1933b   "Van leven en sterven in Balantak [Life and death in Balantak]," *Tijd. 73:* 57-95.

1934   "De rijstbouw in Balantak [Rice growing in Balantak]," *Tijd. 74:* 123-40.

1938   "De West-Toradjas op Midden Celebes [The West-Toradja in Central Celebes]," 5 vols., *VKAW 40.*

Kruyt, A. C., and J. Kruyt
1921   "Reis naar Kolaka [Voyage to Kolaka]," *TNAG 38:* 689-704.

Kruyt, J.
1921   "De Boea' en eenige andere feesten der Toradja van Makala en Rantepao [The Bua' and some other ceremonies among the Makala and Rantepao Toradja]," *Tijd. 11:* 45-78, 161-87.

1924   "De Moriërs van Tinompo [The Mori of Tinompo]," *Bijd. 80:* 33-217.

Kuperus, G.
1937a   *Het cultuurlandschap van West-Soembawa* [The cultural landscape on West Sumbawa], Groningen, Batavia.

1937b   "Tot welken adatrechtskring dient West-Soembawa gerekend te worden? [To what adat area should West Sumbawa belong?]," *KT 26:* 605-11.

1938   "Beschouwing over de ontwikkeling en den huidigen vormenrijkdom van het cultuurlandschap in de onderafdeeling Bima (Oost-Soembawa) [On the development and present wealth of farms in the subdivision Bima (Eastern Sumbawa)]," *TNAG 55:* 207-39.

1941   "Veranderingen in het grondgebruik in West-Flores [Changes in land use in West Flores]," *Tijdschrift voor Economische Geographie 32:* 86-96.

1942a   "De Madjapahitsche onderhoorigheid Seran [Ceram as a Madjapahit dependency]," *TNAG 59:* 771-74.

1942b   "De 'oerwoudsteppe' van N.O. Soemba als element van het cultuurlandschap beschouwd [The grass plains of Northeastern Sumba seen as an element of the cultural landscape]," *Sociaal Geografische Mededeelingen*: 124-65.

Landgraf, John L.
1956   *Interim report to the Government of the Colony of British North Borneo on field work done under the supervision of the Department of Medical Services, 1954-1955,* Jesselton, Government Printing Office.

Last, J.
1955   *Bali in de Kentering (Bali in transition),* Amsterdam, De Bezige Bij.

Leach, Edmund R.
1947   *Report on a visit to Kemabong, Labuan and Interior Residency, British North Borneo, 1-8th November, 1947,* Beaufort (mimeographed).
1950   "Social science research in Sarawak," *Colonial Research Studies 1,* London, H.M. Stationery Office.

LeBar, Frank M.
n.d.   "Legend, culture history, and geomorphology in the Kelabit-Kerayan Highland of North Central Borneo," *JRASMB* (in press).

LeBar, Frank M., Gerald C. Hickey, and John K. Musgrave
1964   *Ethnic Groups of Mainland Southeast Asia,* New Haven, HRAF Press.

Lee, Yong-leng
1965   *North Borneo (Sabah): a study in settlement geography,* Singapore, Eastern University Press.

Leeden, A. C. van der
1960   "Social structure in New Guinea," *Bijd. 116:* 119-49.

Leemker, H. H. O.
1893   "Woordenlijstje van de Soloreesche Taal [A brief dictionary of Solorese]," *Tijd. 36:* 421-61.

Lees, Shirley P.
1966   "Murut orthography," *Sabah Society Journal 3:* 90-98.

Leigh, Michael
1964   "The Chinese community of Sarawak: a study of communal relations," *University of Singapore, Singapore Studies on Malaysia 6.*

Lekkerkerker, C.
1916   *Land en Volk van Sumatra,* Leiden, E. J. Brill.
1933   "Enkele nieuwe gegevens over Soembawa [Some new data on Sumbawa]," *TNAG 50:* 73-81.
1935   "Sapoedi en Bawean. Overbevolking en Ontvolking [Sapoedi and Bawean. Overpopulation and depopulation]," *KT 24:* 457-74.

Letterboer, J. H.
1902   "Jaarverslag betreffende de zending op Savoe [Annual report concerning missions on Savu]," *MNZ 46:* 82-95.
1904   "Verslag over de zending op Savoe in 1903 [Report on the missions on Savu]," *MNZ 48:* 350-60.

Liddle, William
1967   "Suku Simalungun: an ethnic group in search of representation," *Indonesia 3:* 1-30.

Ligtvoet, A.
1876   "Aanteekeningen betreffende den economischen toestand en de ethnographie van het rijk van Sumbawa [Notes on the economic condition and ethnography of the kingdom of Sumbawa]," *Tijd. 23:* 555-92.
1878   "Beschrijving en geschiedenis van Boeton [Description and history of Butung]," *Bijd. 26:* 1-112.

Linton, Ralph
1928   "Culture areas in Madagascar," *AA, n.s. 30:* 363-90.

Loeb, Edwin M.
1928   "Mentawei social organization," *AA, n.s. 30:* 408-33.
1929a   "Mentawei religious cult," *University of California, Publications in American Archaeology and Ethnology 25 (no. 2):* 185-247.
1929b   "Mentawei myths," *Bijd. 85:* 66-245.
1929c   "Shaman and seer," *AA, n.s. 31:* 60-85.
1935   *Sumatra, its history and people,* Vienna, Institut für Völkerkunde.

Logchem, J. Th. van
1963   *De Argoeniërs: Een Papoea Volk in West Nieuw-Guinea,* Utrecht, thesis.

Low, Hugh
1848·   *Sarawak: its inhabitants and productions,* London, Bentley.

Lumholtz, Carl S.
1920   *Through central Borneo: an account of two years' travel in the land of the head-hunters between the years 1913 and 1917,* 2 vols., New York, Charles Scribner's Sons.

Lynden, D. W. C. Baron van
1851   "Bijdrage tot de kennis van Solor, Allor, Rotti, Savoe en omliggende eilanden, getrokken uit een verslag van de Residentie Timor [Contribution to the knowledge of Solor, Alor, Roti, Savu and surrounding islands, extracted from a report from the Residency of Timor]," *Natuurkundig Tijdschrift voor Nederlandsch-Indië 2:* 317-36, 388-414.

Maan, G.
1951   *Proeve van een Bulisch Spraakkunst [A provisional grammar of Bulish],* 's-Gravenhage.

Maasland, J. H.
1940   "De bloedgroepen der Loeboes en Oeloes in Tapanoeli [The bloodgroups of the Lubu and Ulu in Tapanuli]," *GTNI 80:* 1341-48.

Mallinckrodt, H.
1924   "De adat gemeenschappen in Zuid-Borneo [Adat communities in South Borneo]," *KS 8:* 127-56.

Mallinckrodt, J.
1924-25   "Ethnografische mededeelingen over de Dajaks in de Afdeeling Koealakapoeas [Ethnographic communication on the Dayaks of Kuala Kapuas District]," *Bijd. 80:* 397-446, 521-600; *81:* 62-115, 165-310.
1925a   "De hoofdenrechtspraak in de onderafdeeling Boentok [Administration of justice in Buntok District]," *KS 9:* 149-76.
1925b   "Het priesterwezen bij de Dajaks van Kota Waringin [Priesthood among the Dayaks of Kotawaringin]," *IG 47:* 588-602, 708-22.
1925c   "De Njoeli-beweging onder de Lawangan-Dajaks van de Zuider-en Oosterafdeeling van Borneo [The Njuli movement among the Lawangan Dayaks of South and East Borneo]," *KS 9:* 396-424.
1926   "Het huwelijksrecht bij de Dajaks in de Onderafdeeling Boentok [Marriage laws among the Dayaks of Buntok District]," *Tijd. 66:* 553-603.
1927   "De stamindeeling van de Maanjan-Sioeng-Dajaks [Tribal divisions among the Maanyan-Siong Dayaks]," *Bijd. 83:* 552-92.
1928   *Het Adatrecht van Borneo,* 2 vols., Leiden.

Man, Edward Horace
1882-83   "On the aboriginal inhabitants of the Andaman Islands," *JAI 12:* 69-175, 327-435.

1886 "A brief account of the Nicobar Islanders, with special reference to the inland tribe of Great Nicobar," *JAI* 15: 428-50.

1889 "The Nicobar Islanders," *JAI* 18: 354-94.

1933 *The Nicobar Islands*, London, Billings & Sons (compiled posthumously).

Manafe, D. P.
1889 "Akan Bahasa Rotti [Concerning the language of Roti]," *Bijd.* 38: 634-48.

Mansoer, Jasin et al.
1954 *Propinsi Sumatera Tengah [The province of Central Sumatra]*, Padang, Djawatan Penerangan.

Manurung, P. K., S. P. L. Tobing, and W. R. Situmeang
1954 *Propinsi Sumatera Selatan [The Province of Southern Sumatra]*, Palembang, Djawatan Penerangan.

Marsden, William
1783 *The history of Sumatra*, 1st ed., London, Thomas Payne.

1811 *The history of Sumatra*, 3d ed., London, Longman, Hurst, Rees, Orme, and Brown.

1830 *Memoirs of a Malayan family*, London, Oriental Translation Fund.

1966 *The history of Sumatra*, London, Oxford University Press (reprint of 3d ed., 1811).

Martin, K.
1894 *Reisen in den Molukken, in Ambon, den Uliassern, Seran und Buru*, Leiden.

McNicoll, Geoffrey
1968 "Internal migration in Indonesia: descriptive notes," *Indonesia* 5: 29-92.

Meerburg, J. W.
1891 "Proeve Eener Beschrijving van Land en Volk van Midden Manggarai (West Flores), Afdeeling Bima, Gouvernement Celebes en Onderhorigheden [A sample description of the area and population of Central Manggarai (West Flores), Division Bima, Province of Celebes and subordinate regions]," *Tijd.* 26: 434-84.

Mendes, Patrício Manuel
1935 *Dicionário Tetum-Português*, Dili (Timor).

Mendes Correa, A. A.
1944 *Timor Portugues, Republica Portuguesa, Ministerio das Colonias, Memorias: Serie Antropologica e Etnologica 1*, Lisboa, Imprensa Nacional de Lisboa.

Mennes, H. M. M.
1931 "Eenige Aanteekeningen over de Onderafdeeling Manggarai op het Eiland Flores [Some notes on the sub-division Manggarai of the Island of Flores]," *KT* 16: 242-66, 371-90.

Meye, F.
1964 *Sikaneesch-Hollandsch Woordenboek*, Ruteng (Flores) (unpublished typescript).

Middelkoop, P.
1938 "Iets over Sonba'i, het bekende vorstengeslacht op Timor [Something about Sonba'i, the well-known royal house on Timor]," *Tijd.* 78: 392-509.

Miles, Douglas
1965 "Consumption and local mobility on the Upper Mentaya," *Oceania* 36: 121-31.

1970 "The Ngadju Dayaks of Central Kalimantan, with special reference to the Upper Mentaya," *BSN* 5: 291-319.

1971 "Kinship and social change on the Upper Mentaya," in *Festschrift in Honor of Ian Hogbin*, L. Hiatt and C. Jayawardena, eds., Sydney, Angus and Robertson.

Militaire Memorie over de Afdeeling Sumbawa

1930 (with vocabularies), Amsterdam, Koninklijk Instituut voor de Tropen (unpublished manuscript).

Milone, Pauline Dublin
1966 "Urban areas in Indonesia: administrative and census concepts," Berkeley, *University of California, Research Series, No. 10, Institute of International Studies*.

Minderop, C., and G. Vriens
1950 "De Missie in Indonesië [Missionary activity in Indonesia]," *Sticusa Jaarboek 1950*: 75-88.

Mitchell, Istutiah Gunawan
1969 "The socio-cultural environment and mental disturbance: three Minangkabau case histories," *Indonesia* 7: 123-63.

Modigliani, E.
1894 *L'isola delle donne. Viaggio ad Engano*, Milano, Ulrico Hoepli.

Moertono, Soemarsaid
1968 "State and statecraft in old Java: a study of the later Mataram period, 16th to 19th century," Ithaca, *Cornell University, Monograph Series, Modern Indonesia Project*.

Moestapa, H. H.
1946 *Over de Gewoonten en Gebruiken der Soendanezen [On the customs of the Sundanese]*, translated by M. Sastrahadiprawira and others, Den Haag.

Morison, H. H.
1936 *De Mendapo Hiang in het District Korintji*, Batavia, de Unie.

Morris, H. S.
1953 "Report on a Melanau sago producing community in Sarawak, *Colonial Research Studies No. 9*, London, H.M. Stationery Office.

1967 "Shamanism among the Oya Melanau," in *Social Organization: Essays Presented to Raymond Firth*, Maurice Freedman, ed., London, Cass: 189-216.

Moszkowski, M.
1908 "Uber zwei nicht-malayische Stämme von Ost-Sumatra," *Zeitschrift für Ethnologie* 40: 229-39, 635-55.

1909 *Auf neuen Wegen durch Sumatra*, Berlin, Reimer.

Müller, T.
1931 *Die "grosse reue" auf Nias. Geschichte und Gestalt einer Erweckung auf dem Missionsfelde*, Gütersloh, C. Bertelsmann.

Munnik, F. J.
1926 "Een Korte Mededeeling Omtrent de Madoereesche Stierenrennen [A short account of Madurese bull-racing]," *Djawa* 6: 276-78.

Murdock, George Peter
1959 *Africa: its peoples and their culture history*, New York, McGraw-Hill.

1964 "Genetic classification of the Austronesian languages: A key to oceanic culture history," *Ethnology* 3: 117-26.

1967 "Ethnographic atlas: a summary," *Ethnology* 6: 109-236.

Murdock, George Peter, ed.
1960 "Social structure in Southeast Asia," *Viking Fund Publications in Anthropology* 29.

Naerssen, F. H. van
1938 "Hindoejavaansche overblijfselen op Soembawa [Hindu-Javanese remains on Sumbawa]," *TNAG* 55: 90-100.

Nag, Moni
1967 "The people of Great Nicobar," *Indian Museum Bulletin* 2: 29-35.

Naim, Mochtar
1968 *Menggali Hukum Tanah dan Hukum Waris Mi-*

nangkabau [*Collected land and inheritance laws of Minangkabau*], Padang, Center for Minangkabau Studies Press.

Nasroen, M.
1957 *Dasar Falsafat Adat Minangkabau [Philosophical background of Minangkabau adat]*, Djakarta.

Needham, Rodney
1953 *The social organisation of the Penan*, unpublished D.Phil. thesis, University of Oxford.
1954a "A note on the blood pact in Borneo," *Man 54:* 90-91.
1954b "Penan and Punan," *JRASMB 27:* 73-83.
1954c "A note on some nomadic Punan," *Indonesië 7:* 520-23.
1954d "Reference to the dead among the Penan," *Man 54:* 10.
1954e "Siriono and Penan: a test of some hypotheses," *SWJA 10:* 228-32.
1954f "A Penan mourning-usage," *Bijd. 110:* 263-67.
1954g "The system of teknonyms and death-names of the Penan," *SWJA 10:* 416-31.
1955a "A note on some Murut kinship terms," *JRASMB 28:* 159-61.
1955b "Punan Ba," *JRASMB 28:* 24-36.
1956 "A note on kinship and marriage on Pantara," *Bijd. 112:* 285-91.
1957 "Circulating connubium in Eastern Sumba; a literary analysis," *Bijd. 113:* 168-78.
1959 "Mourning-terms," *Bijd. 115:* 58-89.
1964 "Blood, thunder, and mockery of animals," *Sociologus, n.F. 14:* 136-49.
1965 "Death-names and solidarity in Penan society," *Bijd. 121:* 58-76.
1966 "Age, category, and descent," *Bijd. 122:* 6-10, 15-19.
1968 "Endeh: terminology, alliance and analysis," *Bijd. 124:* 305-35.
1970 "Endeh, II: test and confirmation," *Bijd. 126:* 246-58.
1971 "Penan friendship-names," in *The Translation of Culture; Essays to E. E. Evans-Pritchard*, Tom O. Beidelman, ed., London, Tavistock: 203-30.

Neumann, J. B.
n.d. *Halima. Hartstocht en ijdelheid in de Lampongsche Wereld [Passion and vanity in the Lampong world]*, Amsterdam [before 1917].

Newington, P. C. B.
1914 "Customs observed at death among the Bisayas of Sarawak," *SMJ 2:* 188-90.
1961 "Melanau memories," *SMJ 10:* 103-07.

Nicolspeyer, M. M.
1940 *De sociale structuur van een Aloreesche bevolkingsgroep [The social structure of an Alorese people]*, Rijswijk, V. A. Kramers (Leiden thesis).

Nieboer, F. J.
1929 "Gegevens over Parigi [Information about Parigi]," *Ab. 31:* 80-84.

Nieuwenhuis, A. A. J.
1948 *Een Anthropologische Studie van Tengger en Slamet Javanen*, Leiden, Eduard Ydo.

Nieuwenhuis, Anton Willem
1904-07 *Quer durch Borneo*, 2 vols. Leiden, E. J. Brill.

Nieuwenhuyzen, T.
1932 *Sasaksch Adatrecht [Sasak adat law]*, Leiden, E. J. Brill.

Nigam, R. C.
1960 "Little known tribes of Andaman Islands—their problems and prospects," *Vanyajati 8:* 90-97.
1962a "The Onge of Little Andaman—their settlements and population," *Vanyajati 10:* 44-53.

1962b "The Onge of Little Andaman—their settlements and population," *Vanyajati 10:* 84-92.
1963 "The Onge of Little Andaman—their maintenance institution," *Vanyajati 11:* 147-56.

Niks, J. F.
1888a "De Rottineesche nederzettingen op Timor [Rotinese settlements on Timor]," *MNZ 32:* 95-97.
1888b "Berichten omtrent Savoe [Information about Savu]," *MNZ 32:* 81-94.
1891 "Het eiland Rotti (Rote)," *Nederlandsch Zendingstijdschrift 3:* 321-43.
1893 "Eene verzameling strafbepalingen, die in het Regentschap Seba worden toegepast, met eenige opmerkingen van J. F. Niks [A collection of penal regulations as applied in the Regency of Seba, with a few remarks by J. F. Niks]," *Nederlandsch Zendingstijdschrift 5:* 339-57.

Nimmo, H. Arlo
1968 "Reflections on Bajau history," *Philippine Studies 16:* 32-59.

Noakes, J. L.
1949 "Celadons of the Sarawak coast," *SMJ 5:* 25-37.

Nobele, E. A. J.
1926 "Memorie van overgave betreffende de onderafdeeling Makale [Transfer memorandum concerning the subdistrict of Makale]," *Tijd. 16:* 1-143.

Noer, Deliar
1963 *The rise and development of the modernist Muslim movement in Indonesia during the Dutch Colonial period (1900-1942)*, Ithaca, Ph.D. dissertation, Cornell University. (Bibliography contains references to other relevant sources.)

Noorduyn, J.
1968 A list of the languages of Celebes (personal communication).

Nooteboom, Charles
1937a "Een besnijdenisfeest op Saleier [A circumcision ceremony on the island of Salajar]," *Tijd. 77:* 636-41.
1937b *Memorie van overgave van de Onderafdeling Salajar [Transfer memorandum on the subdistrict of Salajar]*, Amsterdam, Royal Institute for the Tropics (manuscript).
1938 "Een merkwaardig economisch spel op Saleier [A remarkable economic performance on the island of Salajar]," *KT 27:* 562-65.
1939 "Versieringen van Manggaraische Huizen [Ornaments of Manggarai houses]," *Tijd. 79:* 221-38.
1940 "Oost-Soemba; een volkenkundige studie [East Sumba; an ethnographic study]," *VKIT 3.*
1950 "Enkele Feiten uit de Geschiedenis van Manggarai, West Flores [Some facts on the history of Manggarai, West Flores]," in *Bingkisan Budi. Een Bundel Opstellen aan Dr. Philippus Samuel van Ronkel*, Leiden, A. W. Sijthoff.

Nooy-Palm, C. H. M.
1968 "The culture of the Pagai Islands and Sipora, Mentawei," *Tropical Man 1:* 152-241.
1969 "Dress and adornment of the Sa'dan Toradja," *Tropical Man 2:* 162-94.

Notosoesanto, R. P.
1933 "Bolaäng Mongondouw," *KS 17:* 401-33.

Nutz, Walter
1959 "Eine Kulturanalyse von Kei; Beiträge zur vergleichende Völkerkunde Ost-indonesiens," *Ethnologica, Beiheft 2*, Düsseldorf, Michael Triltsch Verlag.

Obdeyn, V.
1929 "De Langkah Lama der Orang Mamak van Indragiri," *Tijd. 69:* 353-435.

Onvlee, L.
1930 "Opmerkingen over verwantschapsbetrekkingen bij de Soembaneezen [Remarks on blood relationships among the Sumbanese]," *Tijd. 70:* 343-47.
1949 "Naar aanleiding van de stuwdam in Mangili (Opmerkingen over de sociale structuur van Oost-Soemba) [On the subject of the dam in Mangili (Remarks on the social structure of East Sumba)]," *Bijd. 105:* 445-59.
1970 Personal communication.

Oosterwal, G.
1966 "West Irian: population patterns and problems," *Asian Studies 4:* 291-302.

Ormeling, F. J.
1956 *The Timor problem: a geographical interpretation of an undeveloped island,* Groningen and Djakarta, J. B. Wolters.

Oudemans, A. C.
1889 "Engano," *TNAG 6, pt. 2:* 109-64.

Ouwehand, C.
1950 "Aantekeningen over volksordening en grondenrecht op Oost-Flores [Notes on population and land laws of East Flores]," *Indonesië 4:* 54-71.
1951 "De Gemohin, een maatschap op Adonara [The Gemohin, a society on Adonara]," *Bijd. 107:* 379-91.

Overbeck, H.
1926 "Karapan (Bull-racing)," *Djawa 6:* 271-75.

Pa' Kamar
1926 "Geschiedenis van Madoera [History of Madura]," *Djawa 6:* 231-50.

Palmer van den Broek, W. F.
1936 *Aanvullende memorie betreffende de onderafdeeling Gajo Loeös [Supplementary memorandum on the subdistrict Gayo Loeös],* Amsterdam, Royal Institute for the Tropics (manuscript).

Palmier, Leslie H.
1960 "Social status and power in Java," *London School of Economics, Monographs on Social Anthropology 20,* Athlone Press.

Parlindungan, Mangaradja Onggang
1964 *Pongkinangolngolan Sinambela gelar Tuanku Rao,* Penerbit Tandjung Pengharapan.

Parnell, E.
1911 "The tribute paid in former days to the Sultan of Brunei," *SMJ 1:* 125-30.

Pauwels, P. C.
1935 "Poenan's in de Onderafdeeling Boeloengan [Punans in the subdistrict of Bulungan]," *KT 24:* 342-53.

Pelzer, Karl J.
1963 "Physical and human resource patterns," in *Indonesia,* Ruth T. McVey, ed., New Haven, HRAF Press: 1-23.

Peranio, Roger D.
1959 "Animal teeth and oathtaking among the Bisaya," *SMJ 9:* 6-13.

Perry, William James
1918 *The Megalithic culture of Indonesia,* London and New York, Longmans Green.

Pfeffer, Pierre
1963 *Bivouacs à Bornéo,* Paris, Flammarion.

Pleyte, C. M.
1893 "Ethnographische Beschrijving der Kei-eilanden [Ethnographic Description of the Kei-Islands]," *TNAG 10:* 561-86, 797-840.
1909 "Artja Domas [Domas image]," *Tijd. 51:* 494.
1912 "Badoejsche Geesteskinderen [Spiritual children of Badui]," *Tijd. 54:* 215-426.

Pollard, F. H.
1933 "The Muruts of Sarawak," *SMJ 4:* 139-55.
1935 "Some comparative notes on Muruts and Kelabits," *SMJ 4:* 223-27.

Pollard, F. H., and E. Banks
1937 "Teknonymy and other customs among the Kayans, Kenyahs, Kelamantans and others," *SMJ 4:* 395-409.

Portman, M. V.
n.d. *Notes on the languages of the South Andaman group of tribes,* Calcutta, Government Press.
1899 *A history of our relations with the Andamanese,* 2 vols., Calcutta, Office of the Superintendent of Government Printing.

Postma, P. A.
1961 *Tengger Selajang Pandang (A survey of the Tengger area),* Djakarta (unpublished paper).

Pouwer, J.
1960a "Bestaansmiddelen en sociale structuur in de oostelijke Vogelkop [Subsistence and social structure in the eastern Vogelkop]," *Nieuw-Guinea Studiën 4:* 214-34, 309-27.
1960b "'Loosely Structured' Societies in Netherlands New Guinea," *Bijd. 116:* 109-18.
1961 "New Guinea as a field for ethnological study," *Bijd. 117:* 1-24.

Prajudi Atmosoedirdjo
1952 *Vergelijkende Adatrechtelijke Studie van Oostjavase Madoerezen en Oesingers [Comparative study on the adat law of the East Javanese and Usingese],* Amsterdam.

Prattis, Ian
1963 "The Kayan-Kenyah 'Bungan Cult' in Sarawak," *SMJ 11:* 64-87.

Prentice, D. J.
1969a "Papers in Borneo linguistics, No. 1," *Pacific Linguistics, Series A, No. 20.*
1969b *The Murut languages of Sabah,* Canberra, Ph.D. thesis, Australian National University.
1970 "The linguistic situation in northern Borneo," in *Pacific Linguistic Studies,* S. A. Wurm and D. C. Laycock, eds., *Pacific Linguistics, Series C, No. 13.*

Radcliffe-Brown, A. R.
1922 *The Andaman Islanders,* Cambridge University Press (reprinted by the Free Press of Glencoe in 1948).

Radjab, Muhammad
1950 *Semasa Ketjil Dikampung,* Djakarta, Balai Pustaka.
1964 *Perang Paderi Di Sumatera Barat (1803-1838),* Djakarta, Balai Pustaka.
1969 *Sistem Kekerabatan di Minangkabau,* Padang, Center for Minangkabau Studies Press.

Raffles, Lady
1830 *Memoir of the life and public services of Sir Thomas Stamford Raffles,* London, John Murray.

Raja Ram, M. G.
1960 "My contact with the Shom-Pens of Dogmar River—Great Nicobar (February 1960)," *Bulletin of the Anthropological Survey of India, Government of India 9:* 74-80.

Ray, S.
1913 "The languages of Borneo," *SMJ 4:* 1-196.

Renes, P. B.
1962 "Circulerend connubium in de Leti-archipel [Circulating connubium in the Leti Archipelago]," *Kula 3:* 20-25 (Leiden).

Riedel, J. G. F.
1885a "The Savu or Haawu group, with a sketch map," *Revue Coloniale Internationale 1:* 303-10.

1885b "Galela und Tobeloresen," *Zeitschrift für Ethnologie 17:* 58-89.

1886a "The island of Flores or Pulau Bunga: the tribes between Sika and Mangaroai," *Revue Coloniale Internationale 2:* 66-71.

1886b *De sluik- en kroesharige rassen tusschen Selebes en Papua* [*The lank- and crisp-haired races between Celebes and Papua*], Den Haag, M. Nijhoff.

Rivers, W. H. R.
1914 *The history of Melanesian society*, 2 vols., Cambridge, Cambridge University Press.

Robequain, Charles
1954 *Malaya, Indonesia, Borneo and the Philippines*, London, Longmans Green.

Roberts, Gordon
1949 "Descent of the Sadong Bidayuh," *SMJ 5:* 88-94.

Röder, J.
1948 *Alahatala: Die Religion der Inlandstämme Mittelcerams*, Bamberg, Meisenbach.

Roos, S.
1872 "Bijdrage tot de kennis van taal-, land- en volk op het eiland Soemba [Toward an understanding of the language, land and people of the island of Sumba]," *VBGKW 36:* 1-125.

Rosalim, M.
1966 *Monografi Pasemah*, Lahat, Kantor Pemerintah Daerah Tingkat II (unpublished manuscript).

Rosidi, Ajip
1966 *Kesusastran Sunda Dewasa Ini* [*Sundanese literature today*], Bandung, Penerbit Tjupumanik.

Roth, Henry Ling
1896 *The natives of Sarawak and British North Borneo*, 2 vols., London, Truslove and Hansen (reprinted in 1968).

Rouffaer, G. P.
1923-24 "Chronologie der Dominikaner-Missie op Solor en Flores, vooral Poeloe Ende, ca 1556-1638 [Chronology of the Dominican mission on Solor and Flores, especially Pulau Ende, 1556-1638]," *Nederlandsch-Indië Oud en Nieuw 8:* 204-22, 256-60.

Royen, J. W. van
1927 *De Palembangsche Marga en haar Grond- en Waterrechten* [*Land and water rights in Palembang margas*], Leiden, van den Berg.

1928 "De staatkundige zijde van het Papadonwezen [The political aspect of the Papadon institution]," *KS 12, no. 6.*

1930 "Nota over Lampongsche Mergas," *Mededelingen van de Afdeeling Bestuurszaken der Buitengewesten van het Department van Binnenlandsch Bestuur, Series B, No. 7.*

Rutter, Owen
1922 *British North Borneo: an account of its history, resources and native tribes*, London, Constable.

1929 *The pagans of North Borneo*, London, Hutchinson.

Ryan, E. J.
1961 *The value system of a Chinese community in Java*, Cambridge, unpublished Ph.D. thesis, Harvard University.

Sá, Artur Basílio de
1961 *Textos em Teto da Literatura Oral Timorense*, vol. 1, Lisboa.

St. John, Spenser
1862 *Life in the forests of the Far East*, 2 vols., London, Smith, Elder.

Salim, E., S. Samsudin, I. Suwarni, and R. Astuti
1959 *Kehidupan Desa di Indonesia. Suatu Case Study daripada 23 Desa di Djawa* [*Village life in Indonesia, case studies of 23 villages on Java*], Djakarta, Lembaga Penjelidikan Ekonomi dan Masjarakat, Fakultas Ekonomi Universitas Indonesia.

Salzner, Richard
1960 *Sprachenatlas des Indopazifischen Raumes*, Wiesbaden, Harrossowitz.

Samin Radjik Nur, S. H.
1965 *Perkawinan adat Gorontalo* [*Customary marriage in Gorontalo*], Makassar, Universitas Hasanuddin (dissertation).

Samson, A. L.
1936 "Ontleend aan een nota van den assistent-resident A. L. Samson van ongeveer 1926 over de staatkundige organisatie van de *ori* (dorpsbond) *Moro'o* op Nias [Concerning the political organization of *ori* (village association) *Moro'o* on Nias, derived from a memorandum by the Assistant Resident, A. L. Samson, *of about 1926*]," *Ab. 38:* 439-52.

Sandin, Benedict
1961 "Gawai Antu: Sea Dayak feast of the departed Spirits," *SMJ 10:* 170-90.

1962 "Gawai Batu: The Iban Whetstone Feast," *SMJ 11:* 392-408.

1967 *The Sea Dayaks of Borneo before White Rajah rule*, London, Macmillan.

Sandin, Benedict, and Balang Siran
1963 "A Murut wedding in Kalimantan," *SMJ 11:* 88-93.

Sarasin, Fritz
1905-06 *Versuch einer Anthropologie der Insel Celebes*, 2 vols., Wiesbaden, C. W. Kreidel's Verlag.

Sarasin, Paul, and Fritz Sarasin
1905 *Reisen in Celebes*, 2 vols., Wiesbaden, C. W. Kreidel's Verlag.

Sarkar, S. S.
1953 "The origin and migration of the Negritos in the Andaman Islands," *Man in India 33:* 266-74.

Sartono Kartodirdjo
1966 *The Peasants' Revolt of Banten in 1888. Its conditions course and sequel. A case study of social movements in Indonesia*, 's-Gravenhage, H. L. Smits (Ph.D. thesis, University of Amsterdam).

Schadee, M. C.
1910 "Het familieleven en familierecht der Dajaks van Landak en Tajan [Family life and law of the Landak and Tajan Dayaks]," *Bijd. 63:* 390-489.

1915 "Heirats- und andere Gebräuch bei den Mansela und Nusawela Alfuren in der Unterabteilung Wahaai der Insel Seram," *IAE 22:* 129-38.

1931 "La Coutume de la chasse aux têtes et la sacrifice chez les Dyaks de Landak et Tayan," *BSRBG 55:* 3-30.

Schärer, Hans
1963 "Ngaju religion: the conception of God among a South Borneo people," *Koninklijk Instituut voor Taal-, Land- en Volkenkunde Translation Series 6*, The Hague, M. Nijhoff.

Schmidt, van
1843 "Aanteekeningen nopens de zeden, gewoonten en gebruiken, benevens de vooroordeelen en bijgelovigheden der bevolking van de eilanden Saparoea, Haroekoe, Noessa Laut, en van een gedeelte van de zuidkust van Ceram, in vroegeren en lateren tijd [Notes concerning the customs, habits, and usages as well as the prejudices and superstitions of the population of the islands Saparoea, Haroekoe, Noessa Laut, and of a part

of the south coast of Ceram, in more remote and more recent times]," *TNI* 5: 491-530, 583-622.

Schmidt, Wilhelm
1906   *Die Mon-Khmer Völker: ein bindeglied Zwischen Völkern Zentralasiens und Austronesiens*, Braunschweig, F. Vieweg.

Schneeberger, Werner
1945   "The Kerayan-Kelabit Highland of Central Northeast Borneo," *Geographical Review* 35: 544-62.

Schneider, A.
1941   "Sekola wa'awosa. Die Selbstständigen-bewegung auf Nias," *Evangelische Missions Zeitschrift* 2: 301-11.

Schneider, G.
1958   "Die Orang Mamma auf Sumatra," *Vierteljahrschrift der Naturforschenden Gesellschaft in Zürich 103*, no. 5.

Schnitger, F. M.
1937   *The archaeology of Hindoo Sumatra*, Leiden, E. J. Brill.
1964   *Forgotten kingdoms in Sumatra*, Leiden, E. J. Brill.

Scholz, F.
1962   *Der Herr des Bodens in Ostindonesien*, thesis, University of Cologne.

Schrieke, B.
1920   "Bijdrage tot de Bibliografie van de huidige godsdienstige beweging ter Sumatra's Westkust [Contribution to the bibliography of modern religious development on Sumatra's West Coast]," *Tijd.* 59: 249-325.
1955   "The causes and effects of Communism on the west coast of Sumatra," *Indonesian Sociological Studies: Selected Writings, Part I*, The Hague, van Hoeve.
1960   "The Communist uprisings of 1926-1927 in Indonesia: key documents," edited and with an introduction by Harry J. Benda and Ruth T. McVey, Ithaca, *Cornell University, Translation Series, Modern Indonesia Project*: 97-177.

Schröder, E. E. W. G.
1917   *Nias, ethnographische, geographische en historische aanteekeningen en studien [Nias, ethnographical, geographical and historical notes and studies]*, 2 vols., Leiden, E. J. Brill (vol. 2: plates and maps).

Schüller, C. W.
1936   "Megalithische Oudheden in de Palembangsche Bovenlanden en Overheidszorg [Megalithic antiquities in the Palembang Highlands and governmental care]," *Tijd.* 76: 391-97.

Schulte Nordholt, H. G.
1966   *Het politieke systeem van de Atoni van Timor* (Academisch Proefschrift, Vrije Universiteit te Amsterdam), Driebergen, Van Manen.

Schuster, Carl
1946   "Some artistic parallels between Tanimbar, the Solomon Islands and Easter Island," *Cultureel Indië* 8: 1-8.

Schuurmans, J.
1934   "Het koppensnellen der To Laki [Headhunting among the To Laki]," *MNZ* 78: 207-18.

Scott, J. B.
1908   "Harvest festivals of the Land Dyaks," *Journal, American Oriental Society* 29: 236-80.

Seegeler, C. J.
1931   *Nota van Toelichting betreffende het zelfbesturende landschap Larantoeka . . . , 29 Augustus 1931 [Memorandum of elucidation concerning the autonomous subdivision of Larantuka . . . , Au-*

gust 29, 1931], Amsterdam, Royal Tropical Institute (unpublished manuscript).

Selosoemardjan
1962   *Social changes in Jogjakarta*, Ithaca, Cornell University Press.

Sevink, J.
1914   "Een tocht om den Dobo [A journey around the Dobo]," *Berichten uit Nederlandsch Oost-Indië* 26: 3-23.

Sharma, S. K.
1964   *Census of India, 1961, vol. 17, Andaman and Nicobar Islands*, Parts II and III, Tables, Delhi, Government of India.
1966   *Census of India, 1961, vol. 17, Andaman and Nicobar Islands*, Part I, General Report, Delhi, Government of India.

Shyamchaudhury, N. K.
1955   "Territorial arrangement, traditions and village organisation in Car Nicobar Island," *Bulletin of the Department of Anthropology, Government of India 4*: 1-12.

Sibree, James
1880   *The great African island: chapters on Madagascar*, London, Trübner.

Siegel, C. H.
1901   "Rapport over een Reis naar het Eiland Bawean [An account of a trip to Bawean Island]," *Tijd. BB* 20: 370-78.

Siegel, James T.
1966   *Religion, trade, and family life in Atjeh*, doctoral dissertation, University of California, Berkeley (Ann Arbor, University Microfilms, 67-8652).
1969   *The rope of god*, Berkeley and Los Angeles, University of California Press.

Silva, Ramos da
n.d.   *Dicionário Tétum-Português*, Macau.

Silva, Sebastião Manuel Aparício da
1889   *Dicionário Português-Tetum*, Macau.

Singarimbun, M.
1967   "Kutagamber: a village of the Karo," in *Villages in Indonesia*, Koentjaraningrat, ed., Ithaca, Cornell University Press: 115-28.

Skinner, G. William
1963   "The Chinese minority," in *Indonesia*, Ruth T. McVey, ed., New Haven, HRAF Press: 97-117.

Skinner, G. William, ed.
1959   "Local, ethnic, and national loyalties in village Indonesia," New Haven, *Yale University, Southeast Asia Studies, Cultural Report Series*.

Sneeuwjagt, R. J. C.
1935   *Memorie van overgave van de onderafdeling Zuid-Wester Eilanden [Transfer memorandum of the sub-district Southwestern Islands]*, Amsterdam, Royal Tropical Institute (manuscript).

Snouck Hurgronje, Christiaan
1893   *De Atjehers*, 2 vols., Batavia, Landsdrukkerij; Leiden, E. J. Brill.
1903   *Het Gajoland en zijne bewoners [Gayoland and its inhabitants]*, Batavia, Landsdrukkerij.
1906   *The Achehnese* (translated by A. W. S. O'Sullivan), 2 vols., Leiden, E. J. Brill.

Soebijakto
1965   *Beberapa Unsur Kehidupan Masjarakat Penduduk Tengger [Several elements of Tenggerese community life]*, Djakarta (unpublished paper).

Soedjito Sosrodihardjo
1957   *Kedudukan Pemimpin dalam Masjarakat Desa [The position of the head in a village community]*, Jogjakarta (unpublished thesis, Gadjah Mada University).
1959   *A sectarian group in Java with reference to a*

midland village. A study in the sociology of religion, London (unpublished M.A. thesis, London School of Economics).

Soepomo Poedjosoedarmo
1968 "Javanese speech levels," *Indonesia 6:* 54-81.

Soepomo, R.
1931 "Verslag omtrent het Onderzoek naar het Adatgrondenerfrecht in het Gewest Jogjakarta Buiten de Hoofdplaats [Report on an investigation on adat land tenure in Jogjakarta, outside the capital]," *Indisch Tijdschrift van het Recht 133:* 1-118.

Solheim, Wilhelm G.
1969 "Reworking Southeast Asian prehistory," *Paideuma 15:* 125-39.

Sopher, David E.
1965 "The Sea Nomads: a study based on the literature of the Maritime boat people of Southeast Asia," *Memoirs of the National Museum 5,* Singapore.

Sosrodanoekoesoemo, R.
1927 "Literatuur en Kunst in Madoera [Literature and arts in Madoera]," *Djawa 7:* 162.

Southall, Aidan
1971 "Ideology and group composition in Madagascar," *AA 73:* 144-64.

Southwell, C. Hudson
1949 "Structure of the Murut language," *SMJ 5:* 104-15.
1959 "The Kayans and Kenyahs," in *The Peoples of Sarawak,* Tom Harrisson, ed., Kuching: 39-56.

Speiser, F.
1924 *Südsee Urwald, Kannibalen. Reisen in den Neuen Hebriden und Santa-Cruz-Inseln,* Stuttgart, Strecker and Schröder.

Staal, J.
1923-25 "The Dusuns of Borneo," *Anthropos 18-19:* 958-77; *20:* 929-51.

Staveren, J. A. van
1916 "De Rokka's van Midden-Flores," *Tijd. 57:* 117-75.

Stevenson, G.
1935 "Religion of the Car Nicobar," in *Census of India, 1931, vol. 1 (India),* Part III (Ethnographical), Delhi, Manager of Publications, Government of India: 187-91.

Suchtelen, B. C. M. M. van
1921 "Endeh (Flores)," *MEB 26.*

Sungkawa
1957 "Naha Aja Aksara Sunda? [Does a Sundanese script exist?]," *Kiwari 1.*

Sutaarga, Amir M.
1966 *Prabu Siliwangi [King Siliwangi],* Bandung.

Suzuki, Peter
1958 "Critical survey of studies on the anthropology of Nias, Mentawei and Enggano," *Koninklijk Instituut voor Taal-, Land- en Volkenkunde, Bibliographical Series 3,* Den Haag, M. Nijhoff.
1959 *The religious system and culture of Nias, Indonesia,* Den Haag, Excelsior (Ph.D. thesis, Leiden).

Swellengrebel, J. L.
1960 "Introduction" to *Bali, Studies in Life, Thought and Ritual,* The Hague, W. van Hoeve.

Symons, J. J. M. F.
1935 *Memorie van overgave van de onderafdeling Oost Flores en Solor Eilanden en Maomere [Transfer memorandum on the subdistricts of East Flores, Solor and Maumere],* Amsterdam, Royal Tropical Institute (unpublished manuscript).

Tanner, Nancy
1966 "Speech repertoires and social correlates in Minangkabau," paper delivered at the Annual Meetings of the American Anthropological Association, Pittsburgh.
1969 "Disputing and dispute settlement among the Minangkabau of Indonesia," *Indonesia 8:* 21-67.

Tauchmann, Kurt
1968 *Die Religion der Minahasa Stämme (Nordost-Sulawesi),* München, Klaus Renner (dissertation).

Tauern, O. D.
1918 *Patasiwa und Patalima,* Leipzig, R. Voigtländer's Verlag.

Taulu, H. M.
1952 *Adat dan hukum adat Minahasa [Tradition and adat law of the Minahasa],* Tomohon (Celebes), Membangun.

Taulu, H. M., and A. U. Sepang
1961 *Sedjarah Bolaang Mongondow [History of Bolaang Mongondow],* Manado (Celebes), Raume.

Teeuw, A.
1958 *Lombok, een dialect-geografische studie,* 's-Gravenhage, Maritinus Nijhoff.

Teffer, M.
1875 "De Savoe-eilanden," *MNZ 19:* 205-33.

Tersteege, B. H.
1935 "Het animisme op de Zuid-Wester Eilanden [Animism on the Southwestern Islands]," *KT 24:* 462-78.

Tichelman, G. L.
1925 "De onderafdeeling Amahei, Seran [The subdistrict Amahei, Ceram]," *TNAG 42:* 653-724.

Tideman, J.
1922 *Simeloengoen,* Leiden.
1935 "Land en volk van Bengkalis," *TNAG 52:* 788-816.

T'ien, Ju-k'ang
1953 "The Chinese of Sarawak: a study of social structure," *London School of Economics, Monographs on Social Anthropology 12.*

Tobing, Philip O. L.
1963 *The structure of the Toba-Batak belief in the high god,* Macassar, South and Southeast Celebes Institute for Culture.

Treacher, W.
1889 "British Borneo: sketches of Brunei, Sarawak, Labuan, and North Borneo," *Journal of the Royal Asiatic Society, Straits Branch 20-21:* 13-74, 19-122.

Treffers, F.
1914 "Het landschap Laiwoei in z. o. Celebes en zijne bevolking [The district of Laiwoei in southeastern Celebes and its inhabitants]," *TNAG 31:* 188-221.

Tregonning, Kennedy Gordon
1965 *A history of modern Sabah (North Borneo 1881-1963),* 2d ed. [Kuala Lumpur], for the University of Singapore by the University of Malaya Press.

Tricht, B. van
1928 "Levende Antiquiteiten in West-Java [Living antiquities in West Java]," *Djawa 8:* 399-412.

Urquhart, I. A. N.
1951 "Some notes on jungle Punans in Kapit District," *SMJ 5:* 495-533.
1959 "Nomadic Punans and Pennans," in *The Peoples of Sarawak,* Tom Harrisson, ed., Kuching: 73-84.

217

Van Niel, Robert
1960   *The emergence of the modern Indonesian elite,* The Hague and Bandung, W. van Hoeve.
Vatter, Ernst
1931   "Die Ngada, ein Megalith-Volk auf Flores," *Der Erdball 5:* 347-51.
1932   *Ata Kiwan, unbekannte Bergvölker im Tropischen Holland,* Leipzig, Bibliographisches Institut A. G.
Veen, H. van der
1929   "Nota betreffende de grenzen van de Sa'dansche taalgroep en het haar aanverwante taalgebied [Memorandum concerning the boundaries of the Sa'dan language group and related language areas]," *Tijd.* 69: 58-97.
1940   *Tae' (Zuid-Toradjasch) - Nederlandsch Woordenboek,* 's-Gravenhage.
1965   "The Merok Feast of the Sa'dan Toradja," *VKIT 45.*
1966   "The Sa'dan Toradja chant for the deceased," *VKIT 49.*
Vergouwen, J. C.
1933   *Het Rechtsleven der Toba-Bataks,* 's-Gravenhage.
1964   "The social organization and customary law of the Toba-Batak of Northern Sumatra," The Hague, M. Nijhoff, *Koninklijk Instituut voor Taal-, Land- en Volkenkunde, Translation Series 7* (translation of "Het Rechtsleven der Toba-Bataks").
Verheijen, J. A. J.
1951   *Het Hoogste Wezen bij de Manggaraiers [The High God among the Manggarai],* Wien-Mödling, Uitgeverij van het Missiehuis St. Gabriel.
Verloop, G. N.
1905   "Het Eiland Bawean [The Island of Bawean]," *Tijdschrift voor Nijverheid en Landbouw 70.*
Verschuer, F. H. van
1883   "De Badjo's," *TNAG 7:* 1-7.
Veth, P. J.
1873   *Atchin,* Leiden, G. Kolff.
Veth, P. J., et al.
1881-92 *Midden-Sumatra,* 4 vols., Leiden, E. J. Brill.
Vlekke, Bernhard H. M.
1959   *Nusantara, a history of Indonesia,* The Hague and Bandung, W. van Hoeve.
Voegelin, Carl F., and Florence M. Voegelin
1964   "Languages of the world: Indo-Pacific fascicle one," *Anthropological Linguistics 6,* Bloomington, Indiana University, Anthropology Department, Archives of Languages of the World.
1965   "Languages of the world: Indo-Pacific fascicle four," *Anthropological Linguistics 7,* Bloomington, Indiana University, Anthropology Department, Archives of Languages of the World.
1966   "Languages of the world: Indo-Pacific fascicle eight," *Anthropological Linguistics 8,* Bloom.ngton, Indiana University, Anthropology Department, Archives of Languages of the World.
Vogelesang, A. W. L.
1922   "Eenige Aanteekeningen Betreffende De Sasaks op Lombok [Some notes on the Sasaks of Lombok]," *KT 2:* 260-306.
Volkstelling 1930. See Dutch East Indies.
Vollenhoven, C. van
1918-33 *Het Adatrecht van Nederlandsch-Indië [The adat law of the Netherlands Indies],* 3 vols., Leiden.
Voorhoeve, P.
1948   "Voorschriften voor de Sembahjang in het Soembawanees [Rules for divine service in Sumbawanese]," *Tijd.* 82: 380-400.
1955   "Critical survey of studies on the languages of

Sumatera," *Koninklijk Instituut voor Taal-, Land- en Volkenkunde, Bibliographical Series 1,* 's-Gravenhage, M. Nijhoff.
Vosmaer, J. N.
1862   "Kort berigt omtrent Geliting (noordkust van Flores) [Brief report on Geliting (north coast of Flores)]," *Tijd.* 11: 147-54.
Vredenbregt, J.
1964   "Bawean migration," *Bijd.* 120: 109-37.
Vries, G. de
1927   *Bij de Berg-Alfoeren op West-Seran [Among the mountain Alfurs of West Ceram],* Zutphen, W. J. Thieme.
Vroklage, B. A. G.
1936   "Die sozialen Verhältnisse Indonesiens: eine Kulturgeschichtliche Untersuchung, Vol. 1, Borneo, Celebes und Molukken," *Anthropos-Bibliothek 4, Part 1,* Münster.
1952   *Ethnographie der Belu in Zentral-Timor,* 3 vols., Leiden, E. J. Brill.

Wallace, A. F. C.
1951   "Mentaweian social organization," *AA 53:* 370-75.
Wang, Gung-wu
1958   "The Nanhai trade: a study of the early history of Chinese trade in the South China Sea," *JRASMB 31:* 3-135.
Warneck, F.
1909   *Die Religion der Batak,* Leipzig.
Watuseke, F. S.
1961   "Demografi tentang Minahasa [Demography of Minahasa]," *Medan Ilmu Pengetahuan* (Djakarta) 2: 93-103.
1962   *Sedjarah Minahasa [History of Minahasa],* Manado, Pertjetakan Negara.
Weber, Max
1902   "Iets over walvischvangst in den Indischen Archipel [On whaling in the Indian Archipelago]," in *Rumphius Gedenkboek,* Haarlem, Uitgegeven door het Koloniaal Museum te Haarlem: 89-93.
Wellan, J. W. J.
1932   *Zuid-Sumatra,* Wageningen, Veenman & Zonen.
Wellan, J. W. J., and O. L. Helfrich
1923   *Zuid-Sumatra: Overzicht van het literatuur der gewesten Bengkoelen, Djambi, de Lampongsche Districten en Palembang,* The Hague, Het Zuid-Sumatra Instituut.
Westenenk, L. C.
1922   "Rentjong-schrift, II. Beschreven hoorns in het landschap Krintji [Redjang script, II. Inscribed horns in the Kerintji district]," *Tijd.* 61: 95-110.
Wetering, F. H. van de
1922   "De afkomst der Roteneezen van het eiland Rote [The origin of the Rotinese on the island of Roti]," *MNZ 66:* 312-26.
1923a   "De naamgeving op Rote [Name giving on Roti]," *Tijd.* 63: 402-19.
1923b   "Het Roteneesche huis [The Rotinese house]," *Tijd.* 63: 452-95.
1925   "Het huwelijk op Rote [Marriage on Roti]," *Tijd.* 65: 1-36, 589-667.
1926   "De Savoeneezen," *Bijd.* 82: 485-575.
Wheatley, Paul
1964   *Impressions of the Malay Peninsula in ancient times,* Singapore, Donald Moore.
Whitehead, George
1924   *In the Nicobar Islands,* London, Seeley, Service.
Wibisono, Singgih
1956   "Tengger," *Bahasa dan Budaja 4.*

Wichmann, A.
1891 "Bericht über eine . . . Reise nach dem Indischen Archipel: Flores," *TNAG 8:* 187-293.
1892 "Die Insel Roti," *Petermanns Geographische Mitteilungen 38:* 97-103.

Widjojo Nitisastro
1959 "The government, economy and taxes of a central Javanese village," Ithaca, *Cornell University, Monograph Series, Modern Indonesia Project.*

Wijk, N. A. van
1931 "Het Stervend Heidendom op de Tanimbar Eilanden [Dying heathenship on the Tanimbar Islands]," *KT 16:* 359-70.

Wijngaarden, J. K.
1890a "Het eiland Randjoewa [Randjoewa Island]," *MNZ 34:* 332-34.
1890b "Eerste Verslag [First report]," *MNZ 34:* 366-83.
1892 "Savoeneesche tijdrekening [Savunese reckoning of time]," *MNZ 36:* 16-33.
1894 "Savoeneesche straffen [Savunese penalties]," *MNZ 38:* 207-26.
1896 *Sawuneesche woordenlijst,* Den Haag.

Wilcox Palmer, A.
1967 "Situradja: a village in highland Priangan," in *Villages in Indonesia,* Koentjaraningrat, ed., Ithaca, Cornell University Press: 299-325.

Wilken, G. A.
1893 *Handleiding voor de vergelijkende volkenkunde van Nederlandsch-Indië* [*Manual for the comparative ethnology of the Netherlands East Indies*], Leiden, E. J. Brill (Human Relations Area Files, Source No. 2, OBI Indonesia File).

Wilken, N. P., and J. A. Schwarz
1867a "Het heidendom en de Islam in Bolaäng Mongondou [Paganism and Islam in Bolaang Mongondow]," *MNZ 11:* 255-83.
1867b "Allerlei over het land en volk van Bolaäng Mongondou [Miscellanea concerning the country and people of Bolaang Mongondow]," *MNZ 11:* 285-400.

Williams, Lea
1960 *Overseas Chinese nationalism: the genesis of the pan-Chinese movement in Indonesia, 1900-1916,* Glencoe, Ill., Free Press.

Williams, Thomas Rhys
1960 "A Tambunan Dusun origin myth," *JRASMB 33:* 95-103.
1965 "The Dusun: a North Borneo society," *Case Studies in Anthropology,* New York, Holt, Rinehart and Winston.

Willmott, Donald E.
1960 *The Chinese of Semarang: a changing minority community in Indonesia,* Ithaca, Cornell University Press.
1961 "The national status of the Chinese in Indonesia, 1900-1958," rev. ed., Ithaca, *Cornell University, Southeast Asia Program, Modern Indonesia Project Monograph Series.*

Wilson, Peter J.
1971 "An ethnographic survey of the Tsimihety of Madagascar," *BSN 6:* 33-60.

Winkler, J.
1925 *Die Toba-Batak auf Sumatra,* Stuttgart.

Wirjo Asmoro
1926 "Iets over de 'Adat' der Madoereezen [Notes on the 'adat' of the Madurese]," *Djawa 6:* 251-61.

Woensdregt, J.
1928 "De landbouw bij de To Bada' in Midden Celebes [Agriculture among the To Bada in Central Celebes]," *Tijd. 68:* 125-255.
1929 "Verloving en huwelijk bij de To Bada' in Midden Celebes [Engagement and marriage among the To Bada in Central Celebes]," *Bijd. 85:* 245-90.
1930 "Lijkbezorging bij de To Bada' in Midden Celebes [Disposal of the dead among the To Bada in Central Celebes]," *Bijd. 86:* 572-611.

Wongsosewojo, R. Ahmad
1926a "Gebruiken bij Bouw en Tewaterlating van een Prauw in het Sampangsche [Customs concerning the construction and launching of a canoe in the Sampang area]," *Djawa 6:* 262-63.
1926b "De Visvangst op Madoera [Fishing on Madura]," *Djawa 6:* 263-70.

Wooley, G. C.
1929 "Some notes on Murut basketwork and patterns," *JRASMB 7:* 291-315.
1932 "Murut basketwork," *JRASMB 10:* 23-28.
1936 "Some Murut hunting customs," *JRASMB 14:* 307-13.
1953 "Murut adat: customs regulating inheritance amongst the Nabai tribe of Keningau and the Timogun tribe of Tenom," *Native Affairs Bulletin 3,* Jesselton (reprinted).
1962 "The Timoguns: a Murut tribe of the interior, North Borneo," *Native Affairs Bulletin 1,* Jesselton (reprinted).

Wouden, F. A. E. van
1935 *Sociale Structuurtypen in de Groote Oost,* Leiden, Ginsberg.
1941 "Mythen en maatschappij in Boeol [Myth and society in Buol]," *Tijd. 81:* 333-410.
1956 "Locale Groepen en Dubbele Afstamming in Kodi, West Sumba [Local groups and double descent in Kodi, West Sumba]," *Bijd. 112:* 204-46.
1968 "Types of social structure in Eastern Indonesia" (trans. of "Sociale Structuurtypen in de Groote Oost" by Rodney Needham), *Koninklijk Instituut voor Taal-, Land- en Volkenkunde, Translation Series 11,* The Hague, M. Nijhoff.

Wylick, Carla van
1941 *Bestattungsbrauch und Jenseitsglaube auf Celebes,* Den Haag.

Ypes, W. K. H.
1932 *Bijdrag tot de kennis van de stamverwantschap, de inheemsche rechtsgemeenschappen en het grondenrecht der Toba en Dairi-Bataks* [*Contribution to the knowledge of tribal blood relationships, native legal communities and the land-holding laws of the Toba and Dairi Bataks*], 's-Gravenhage, M. Nijhoff.

Zollinger, H.
1850 "Verslag van eene reis naar Bima en Soembawa en naar enige plaatsen op Celebes, Saleier en Flores [Report of a journey to Bima and Sumbawa and to a few places on Celebes, Saleier and Flores]," *VBGKW 23:* 1-224.

INDEX OF ETHNIC NAMES

Ethnonyms in the Indonesian area very often incorporate prefixed elements meaning "man," "people," "village," "house," "river," or the like, e.g. *a, ata, cata (hata), djang, dou, lepo, long, lun, mian, oloh, orang, ot, to, ulu (oeloe), uma, urang, wong.* Where such names occur in the literature, the primary entry in the index is to the prefixed element, the second element appearing as a cross-reference to the primary entry.

Abeus. See *Djang Abeus*
Abui—ALOR-PANTAR, 95
ABUNG, 35
Achehnese—ATJEHNESE, 15
Achinese—ATJEHNESE, 15
Adang—ALOR-PANTAR, 95
Ai. See *Ulu Ai*
Aka-Bo—ANDAMANESE, 5
Aka-Cari—ANDAMANESE, 5
Akah—PENAN, 178
Aka-Jeru—ANDAMANESE, 5
Aka-Kede—ANDAMANESE, 5
Aka-Kol—ANDAMANESE, 5
Aka-Kora—ANDAMANESE, 5
Aka-Bea—ANDAMANESE, 5
Akar-Bale—ANDAMANESE, 5
Aket—KUBU, 46
Aki—BANGGAI, 139
Akik—KUBU, 46
Akit—KUBU, 46
Alas—GAYO, 19
Ale. See *To Ale*
Alfur—CENTRAL MOLUCCAS, 116
Alfuros—HALMAHERA, 119
A Liko—MELANAU, 173
Aloreezen—ALOR-PANTAR, 94
Alorese—ALOR-PANTAR, 94
ALOR-PANTAR, 94
Alumbis—IDAHAN MURUT, 155
Alune—CENTRAL MOLUCCAS, 116
Amboinese—AMBONESE, 116
AMBONESE, 116
Ampana—EASTERN TORADJA, 132
Ampat Lawang—PASEMAH, 34
Anak Soongey—PEKAL, 30
Anak Sungei—PEKAL, 30
ANDAMANESE, 4
Angkola—BATAK, 20
Antandroy—MALAGASY, 2
Antankarana—MALAGASY, 2
Antanosy—MALAGASY, 2
Anteifasy—MALAGASY, 2
Anteimoro—MALAGASY, 2
A-Pucikwar—ANDAMANESE, 5
Aput—PUNAN-PENAN, 176
Arguni Bay tribes—WEST NEW GUINEA, 123
Aroe-Eilanders—ARU, 115
Aroenezen—ARU, 115
ARU, 115
Arut—KALIMANTAN DAYAKS, 186
Aserawanua—LAKI, 142
Ata Biang—SIKANESE, 88
Atahori Rote—ROTINESE, 106
Ata Kiwan—SOLORESE, 91
Ata Krowe—SIKANESE, 88

Ata Manggarai—MANGGARAI, 81
Ata Sika—SIKANESE, 88
Atchinese—ATJEHNESE, 15
Atimelangers—ALOR-PANTAR, 96
ATJEHNESE, 15
ATONI, 103
Attingola—GORONTALO, 128
Aup—LAND DAYAKS, 194
Awak. See *Urang Awak*
Aweus. See *Djang Aweus*
Ayou—LAND DAYAKS, 194

Babar Islanders—SOUTHWESTERN ISLANDS, 110
Babian. See *Orang Babian*
Babo—WEST NEW GUINEA, 123
Bada—WESTERN TORADJA, 130
Badjavanese—NGADA, 83
Badjaw—SEA NOMADS, 13
Badoei—BADUI, 57
BADUI, 57. See also *Orang Badui*
Baduj—BADUI, 57
Bah—PUNAN-PENAN, 176
Bahau—KENYAH-KAYAN-KAJANG, 168
Bajau Laut—BORNEO, 148; SEA NOMADS, 13
Baku—WESTERN TORADJA, 130
Bakumpai—KALIMANTAN DAYAKS, 185
Balaesan—TOMINI, 129
BALANTAK, 138. See also *Mian Balantak*
Balau—IBAN, 180
Bali-Aga—BALINESE, 60
BALI-LOMBOK-SUMBAWA, 60
BALINESE, 60
Balinggi—WESTERN TORADJA, 130
Balingian—MELANAU, 173
Balui. See *Ot Balui*
mBana—EASTERN TORADJA, 132
Banasu—WESTERN TORADJA, 130
Banawa—WESTERN TORADJA, 130
BANDA. See FLORES-BANDA
Bandjarese—KALIMANTAN DAYAKS, 185
BANGGAI, 139. See also *Mian Banggai*
Bang Hadji—REDJANG, 31
Banjakkers—SIMALUR-BANYAK, 38
Bantamese—BADUI, 58
Banten—SUNDANESE, 54
Bantik—MINAHASANS, 125
Bantjea—EASTERN TORADJA, 132
BANYAK. See SIMALUR-BANYAK
Baokan—IDAHAN MURUT, 154
Bara—MALAGASY, 2
Bare'e—EASTERN TORADJA, 132

Barito Complex—NGADJU, 187
Barok—SEA NOMADS, 13
Basap—PUNAN-PENAN, 176
BATAK, 20
Bathin. See *Orang Bathin*
BATIN, 30. See also *Orang Batin*
BATJANESE, 122
Batta—BATAK, 20
Battak—BATAK, 20
Batu Islanders—NIASANS, 39
Batu Blah—KENYAH-KAYAN-KAJANG, 168
Bau—EASTERN TORADJA, 132
Baukan—IDAHAN MURUT, 154
Bawang. See *Lun Bawang*
Bawean. See *Orang Bawean*
Baweanese. See BAWEAN ISLANDERS
BAWEAN ISLANDERS, 59
Bedoej—BADUI, 57
Bekulau. See *Djang Bekulau*
Belang—MINAHASANS, 125
Belagar—ALOR-PANTAR, 95
Bele Tebo. See *Djang Bele Tebo*
Belu—EASTERN TETUM, 98
Benkulen Malays—COASTAL MALAYS, 13
Bentenan—MINAHASANS, 125
Benua—KUBU, 46
Berawan—KENYAH-KAYAN-KAJANG, 168
Besaya—BISAYA, 163
Besemah—PASEMAH, 34
Besoa—WESTERN TORADJA, 130
Betsileo—MALAGASY, 2
Betsimisaraka—MALAGASY, 2
Bezanozano—MALAGASY, 2
Bgu—WEST NEW GUINEA, 123
Bhai. See *Cata Bhai, Hata Bhai*
Biadju—NGADJU, 187
Biak—WEST NEW GUINEA, 123
Biang. See *Ata Biang*
Bidayuh—LAND DAYAKS, 194
Bima. See *Doü Bima*
BIMANESE. See SUMBAWANESE-BIMANESE-DOMPU
Binangunan—BOLAANG MONGONDOW, 127
Bintaq—IDAHAN MURUT, 154
Bintulu—MELANAU, 173
BISAYA, 163
Bisayah—BISAYA, 163
Blah. See *Batu Blah*
Boalemo—GORONTALO, 128
Boano—TOMINI, 129
Bobongko—LOINANG, 136
Bodhas—SASAK, 65

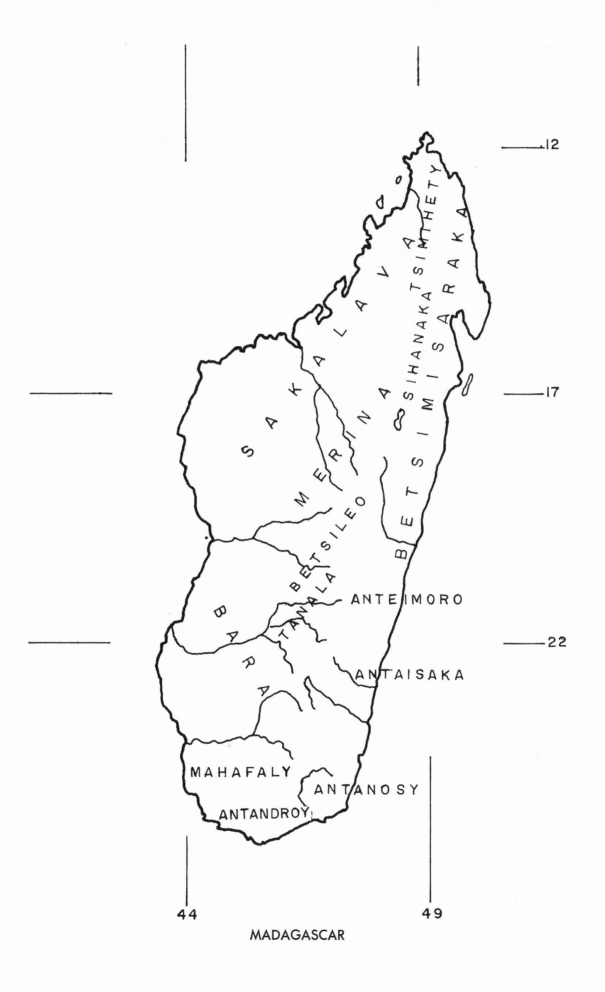

MADAGASCAR

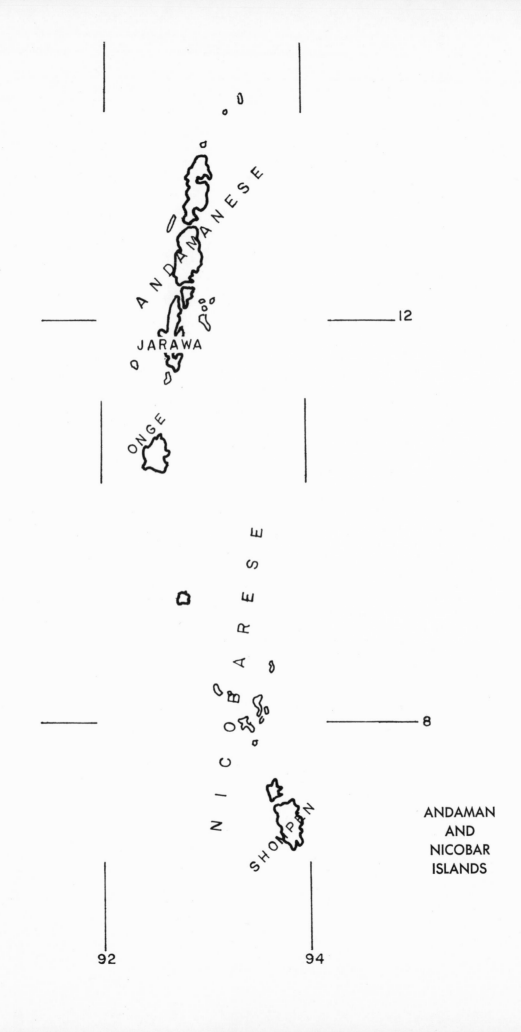

ANDAMAN
AND
NICOBAR
ISLANDS

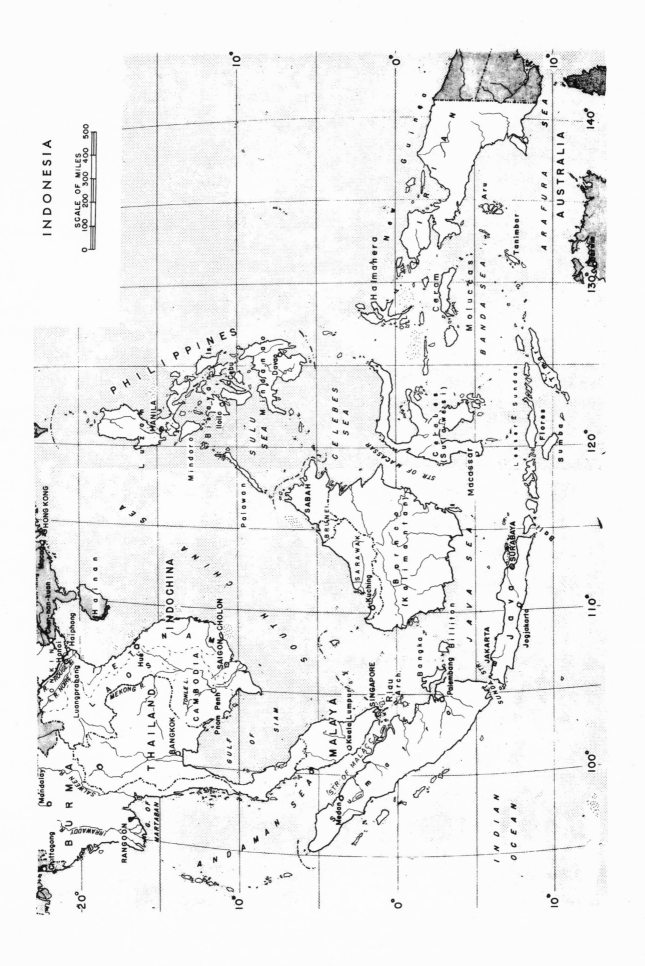

INDONESIA

SCALE OF MILES
0 100 200 300 400 500

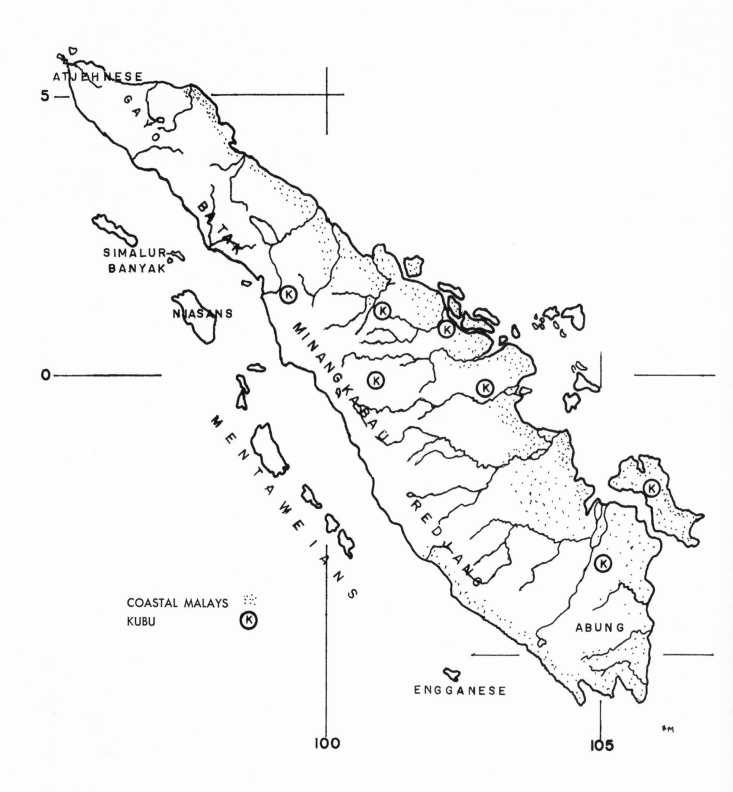

ATJEHNESE

5

GAYO

BATAK

SIMALUR-
BANYAK

NIASANS

MINANGKABAU

MENTAWEIANS

0

REDJANG

ⓀK

ⓀK

ⓀK

ⓀK

ⓀK

ⓀK

ⓀK

ⓀK

COASTAL MALAYS
KUBU   ⓀK

ABUNG

ENGGANESE

100   105

SUMATRA

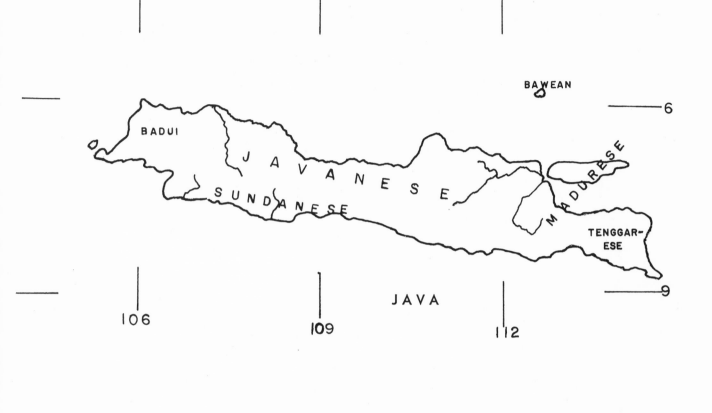

BAWEAN

BADUI

J A V A N E S E

S U N D A N E S E

MADURESE

TENGGAR-ESE

6

9

JAVA

106   109   112

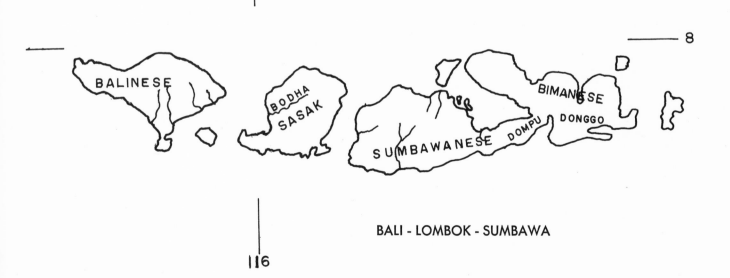

8

BALINESE

BODHA
SASAK

SUMBAWANESE   DOMPU

BIMANESE

DONGGO

116

BALI - LOMBOK - SUMBAWA

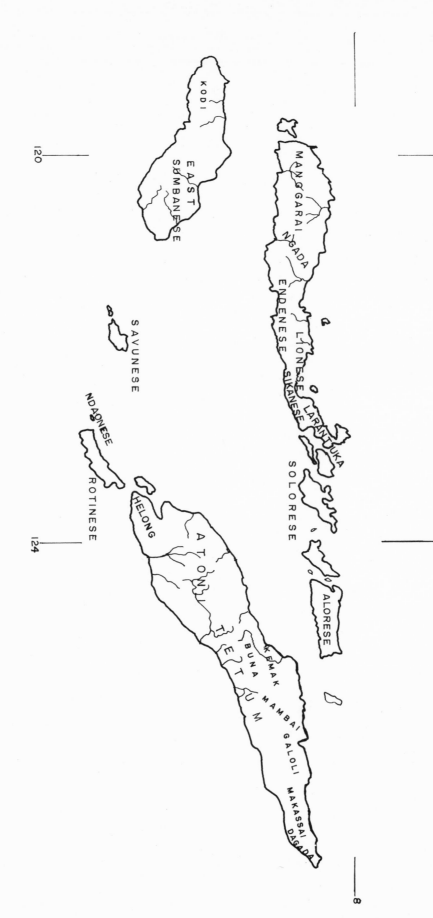

SUMBA - FLORES - TIMOR

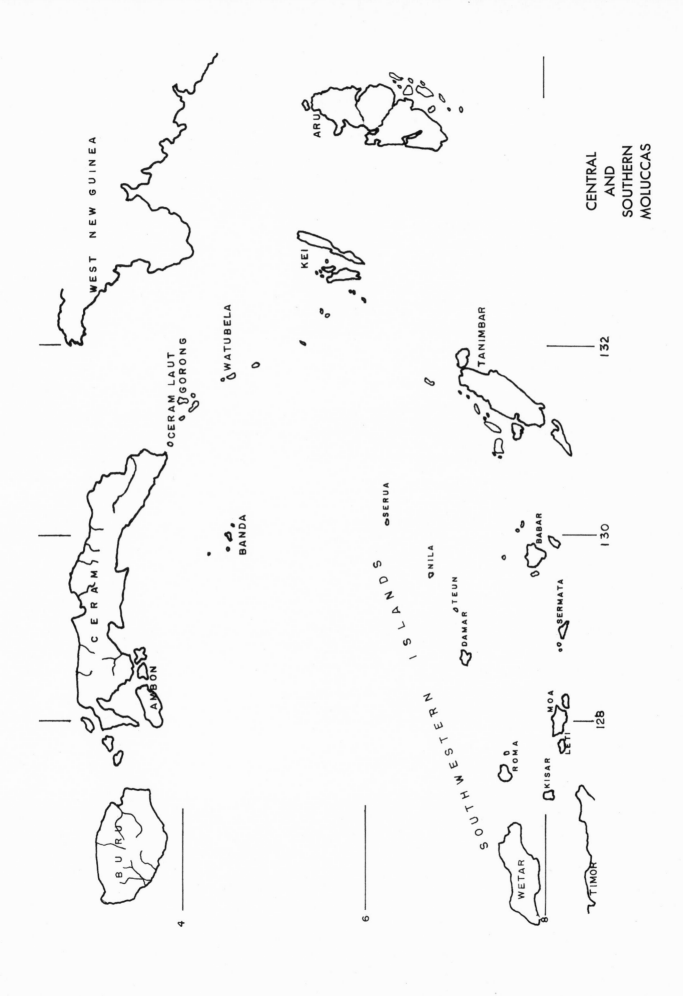

CENTRAL AND SOUTHERN MOLUCCAS

WEST NEW GUINEA

ARU

KEI

CERAM LAUT
GORONG
WATUBELA

CERAM

AMBON

BANDA

SERUA

TANIMBAR

132

NILA
DAMAR
TEUN

BABAR

130

SERMATA

BURU

S O U T H W E S T E R N   I S L A N D S

MOA

ROMA

KISAR
LETI

128

WETAR

TIMOR

4

6

8

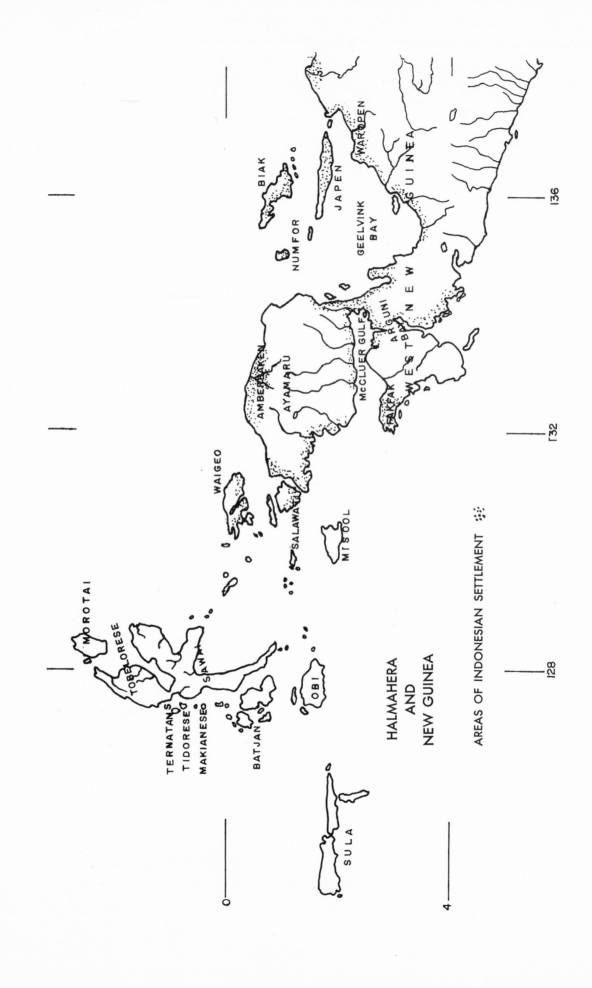

BIAK

NUMFOR

JAPEN

WARUPEN

GEELVINK
BAY

N E W   G U I N E A

AMBERBAKEN

AYAMARU

McCLUER GULF

ARGUNI

FAKFAK

W E S T B A K   N E W

WAIGEO

SALAWATI

MISOOL

MOROTAI

TOBELORESE

SAWAI

TERNATANS
TIDORESE
MAKIANESE

BATJAN

OBI

SULA

HALMAHERA
AND
NEW GUINEA

AREAS OF INDONESIAN SETTLEMENT

0

4

128

132

136

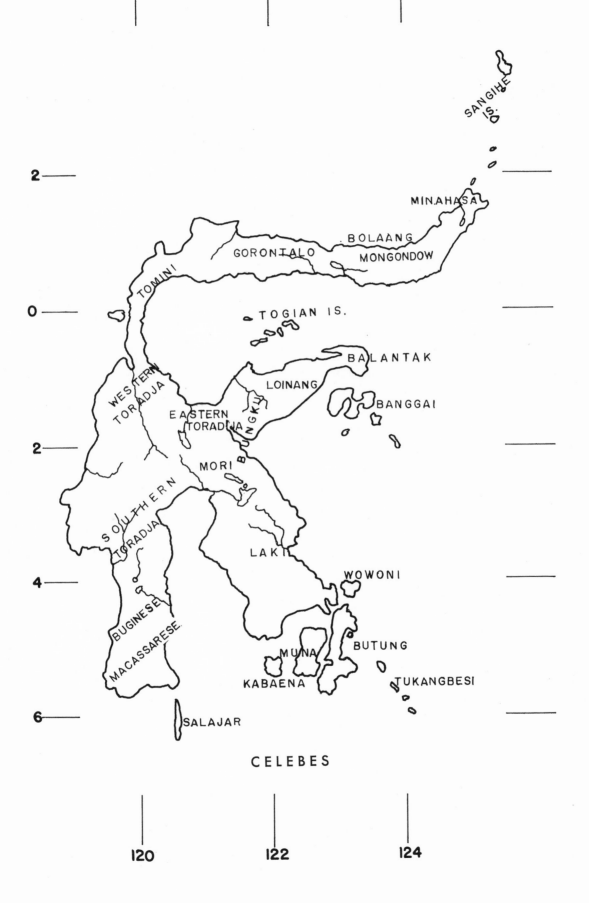

CELEBES

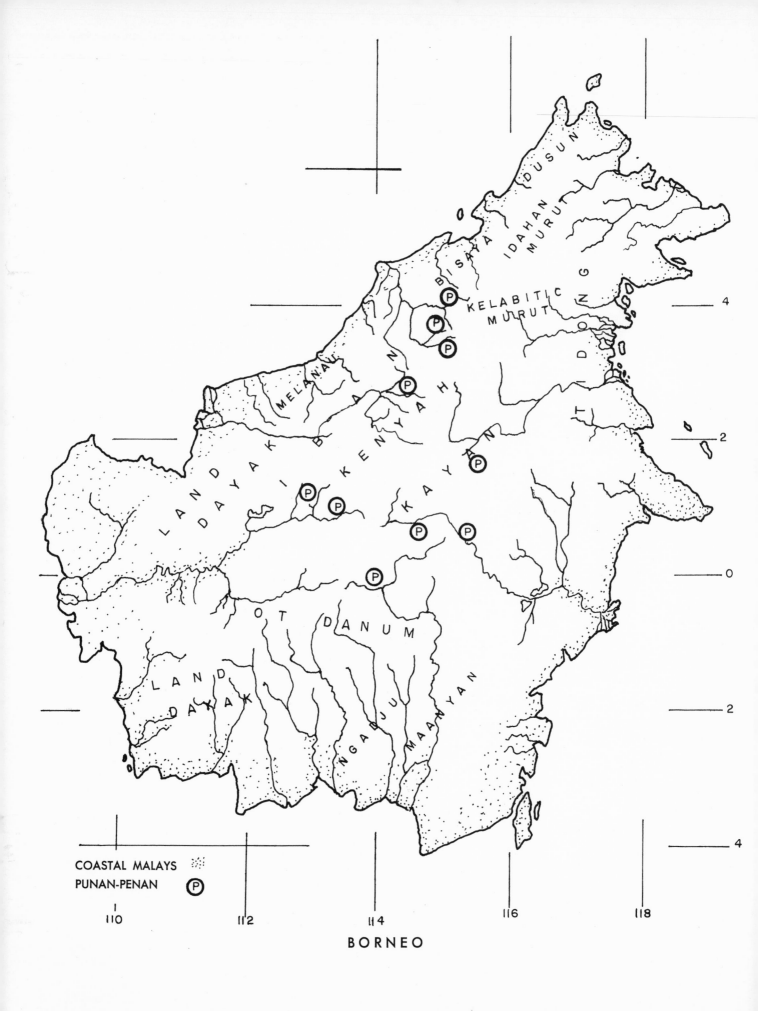

COASTAL MALAYS

PUNAN-PENAN   Ⓟ

BORNEO